THE EPIDEMIOLOGY OF AIDS

The Epidemiology of AIDS

Expression, Occurrence, and Control of Human Immunodeficiency Virus Type 1 Infection

Edited by

Richard A. Kaslow, M.D., M.P.H.
Chief, Epidemiology and Biometry Branch
National Institute of Allergy and Infectious Diseases
National Institutes of Health
Bethesda, Maryland

Donald P. Francis, M.D., D.Sc.
Centers for Disease Control
AIDS Adviser
California Department of Health Services
Berkeley, California

New York   Oxford
OXFORD UNIVERSITY PRESS
1989

Oxford University Press

Oxford   New York   Toronto
Delhi   Bombay   Calcutta   Madras   Karachi
Petaling Jaya   Singapore   Hong Kong   Tokyo
Nairobi   Dar es Salaam   Cape Town
Melbourne   Auckland

and associated companies in
Berlin   Ibadan

Published by Oxford University Press, Inc.
200 Madison Avenue, New York, New York 10016

Oxford is a registered trademark of Oxford University Press.

Library of Congress Cataloging-in-Publication Data

The Epidemiology of AIDS.

Includes bibliographies and index.
1. AIDS (Disease)—Epidemiology.   I. Kaslow,
Richard A.   II. Francis, Donald P.   [DNLM: 1. Acquired
Immunodeficiency Syndrome—epidemiology.   WD 308 E635]
RA644.A25E65   1989   362.1'969792   89-9318
ISBN 0-19-505058-4

9 8 7 6 5 4 3 2 1
Printed in the United States of America
on acid-free paper

To Leanne, Karen and the rest of our families, for their encouragement and patience, and to the countless afflicted who sacrificed their precious time and privacy in the hope of sparing those who follow them.

Preface

No other subject of medical or scientific inquiry has ever stimulated such a profusion of published information so rapidly as AIDS. By the latter half of 1988 the number of articles catalogued in the National Library of Medicine AIDS Bibliography reached nearly 500 per month. Fortunately, exponentially accumulating information has been an extremely effective weapon in the war against this infectious disease. As we considered preparing this volume, we sensed that the new knowledge had carried us at least to "the end of the beginning" of our victory over the human immunodeficiency virus. That seemed to be an appropriate time to assemble the available information on the epidemiology of the infection into a coherent framework, comprehensible by the largest possible number of professionals engaged in health sciences and health care and by interested persons outside the field of health. We viewed the book then—and still view it—simply as another opportunity to focus attention on the peril of AIDS and on the potential for enlightened human responses to it.

December 1988

R.A.K.
D.P.F.

Contents

Contributors

Michael S. Ascher, M.D., F.A.C.P.
Deputy Chief, Viral & Rickettsial
  Disease Laboratory
California Department of Health
Room 454
2151 Berkeley Way
Berkeley, CA 94704

James R. Allen, M.D., M.P.H.
AIDS Program
Center for Infectious Diseases
Centers for Disease Control
1600 Clifton Road, N.E.
Building 6, Room 288
Atlanta, Georgia 30333

Bruce Brew, M.D.
Department of Neurology, Room
  C799
Memorial Sloan-Kettering Cancer
  Center.
1275 York Avenue
New York, NY 10021

Thomas Coates, Ph.D.
Division of General Internal
  Medicine
Room A-405
University of California Medical Ctr.
Box 0320
400 Parnassus Avenue
San Francisco, CA 94143

Robert Edelman, M.D.
Clinical & Epidemiological Studies
  Branch

National Institute of Allergy &
  Infectious Diseases
National Institutes of Health
9000 Rockville Pike
Building 31, Room 7A-52
Bethesda, MD 20892

Donald P. Francis, M.D., D.Sc.
AIDS Adviser, Room 715
Department of Health Services
State of California
2151 Berkeley Way
Berkeley, CA 94704

Gerald H. Friedland, M.D.
Professor of Medicine
Centennial Building, 3rd Floor
Montefiore Medical Center
Albert Einstein College of Medicine
111 E. 210th Street
Bronx, NY 10467

Patricia N. Fultz, M.D.
Yerkes Regional Primate Research
  Center and Department of
  Pathology,
School of Medicine
Emory University
Atlanta, Georgia 30322

Harry W. Haverkos, M.D.
Chief, Clinical Medicine Branch
Division of Clinical Research
National Institute on Alcohol, Drug
  Abuse, and Mental Health
  Administration

Parklawn Building, Room 10A08
5600 Fishers Lane
Rockville, MD 20857

Harold W. Jaffe, M.D.
AIDS Program
Center for Infectious Diseases
Centers for Disease Control
1600 Clifton Road, N.E.
Room 271 G-22
Atlanta, Georgia, 30333

Warren D. Johnson, Jr., M.D.
Division of International Medicine
Cornell University
Medical College
A431 1300 York Avenue
New York, NY 10021

Richard A. Kaslow, M.D., M.P.H.
Chief, Epidemiology and Biometry
  Branch
National Institute of Allergy and
  Infectious Diseases
National Institutes of Health
Westwood Building, Room 739
Bethesda, MD 20892

Jeffrey S. Mandel, Ph.D.
AIDS Professional Education Project
Department of Psychiatry
University of California
P.O. Box 0984
San Francisco, CA 94143-0984

Jonathan M. Mann, M.D., M.P.H.
AIDS Program
Division of Communicable Diseases
World Health Organization
Avenue Appia
1211 Geneva 27, Switzerland

Henry Masur, M.D.
Deputy Chief,
Critical Care Medicine Department
Building 10, Room 10D48

National Institutes of Health
Bethesda, Maryland 20892

Alison C. Mawle
AIDS Program
Immunology Branch
Center for Infectious Diseases
Centers for Disease Control
Building 1, Room 1202 (A25)
Atlanta, Georgia 30333

J. Stephen McDougal, M.D.
AIDS Program
Center for Infectious Diseases
Centers for Disease Control
Building 1, Room 1202 (A25)
Atlanta, Georgia 30333

Thomas Merigan, Jr., M.D.
Division of Infectious Diseases
S156 Stanford University
School of Medicine
Stanford, CA 94305

John Mills, M.D.
Division of Infectious Diseases
Department of Medicine
San Francisco General Hospital
Building 80, Ward 84
995 Potrero Street
San Francisco, CA 94143

Michael Mills, J.D.
Partner in Law Firm of Mayer,
  Brown and Platt
529 Madison Avenue, 10th Floor
New York, New York 10022

Edward F. Morales, Ph.D.
Bayview Hunters Point Foundation
San Francisco and Center for AIDS
  Prevention Studies (CAPS)
MIRA
6025 3rd Street
San Francisco, CA 94124

Janet K. A. Nicholson
AIDS Program
Immunology Branch
Center for Infectious Diseases
Centers for Disease Control
Building 1, Room 1202 (A25)
Atlanta, Georgia 30333

Nancy Padian, Ph.D.
Epidemiology Program
102 Haviland Hall
University of California, Berkeley
Berkeley, CA 94720

Jean W. Pape, M.D.
Division of International Medicine
Cornell University
Medical College
A431 1300 York Avenue
New York, New York 10021

Anthony Pascal, Ph.D.
Senior Economist
Rand Corporation
1700 Main Street
Santa Monica, CA 90406-2138

Thomas Peterman, M.D.
Medical Officer
Division of Sexually Transmitted
   Diseases
Center for Prevention Services
Freeway Park
Centers for Disease Control
Atlanta, GA 30333

Michael A. Polis, M.D.
Epidemiology and Biometry Branch
National Institute of Allergy and
   Infectious Diseases
National Institutes of Health
Westwood Building, Room 739
Bethesda, MD 20892

Richard Price, M.D.
Department of Neurology, Room
   C799

Memorial Sloan-Kettering Cancer
   Center
1275 York Avenue
New York, NY 10021

Thomas C. Quinn, M.D.
Johns Hopkins Hospital
600 North Wolfe Street
Blalock 1111
Baltimore, MD 21205

Martha F. Rogers, M.D.
Chief of Pediatric and Family Studies
AIDS Program
Center for Infectious Diseases
Building 6, Room 285
Centers for Disease Control
Atlanta, GA 30333

Paul L. Rogers, M.D.
Assistant Professor of Anesthesiology
   and Critical Care Medicine
Presbyterian University Hospital
DeSoto at O'Hara Street, Room 1304
Pittsburgh, PA 15213

George Rutherford, M.D.
AIDS Office
Department of Public Health
Epidemiology and International
   Health
University of California
1111 Market Street
San Francisco, CA 94103

Alfred J. Saah, M.D., M.P.H.
Associate Professor of Epidemiology
Department of Epidemiology
Johns Hopkins University
School of Hygiene and Public Hlth.
550 North Broadway, Suite 701
Baltimore, Maryland 21205

John J. Sidtis, M.D.
Department of Neurology, Room
   C799

Memorial Sloan-Kettering Cancer
    Center
1275 York Avenue
New York, NY 10021

Gail Skowron, M.D.
Division of Infectious Diseases
Stanford University School of
    Medicine
300 Pasteur Drive
Room S156
Stanford, CA 94305

James L. Sorenson, Ph.D.
Substance Abuse Services

San Francisco General Hospital
Department of Psychiatry
1001 Potrero Avenue, Ward 92
San Francisco, CA 94110

Ron Stall, Ph.D.
1618 Castro, #507
San Francisco, CA 94114

Warren Winkelstein, Jr., M.D.
19 Warren Hall
University of California, Berkeley
School of Public Health
Berkeley, CA 94720

I
BIOLOGIC AND CLINICAL EXPRESSION

The Biology of Human Immunodeficiency Viruses

PATRICIA FULTZ

The causative agent of the acquired immunodeficiency syndrome (AIDS) has been shown unequivocally to be a retrovirus termed human immunodeficiency virus (HIV) (Barre-Sinoussi et al., 1983; Gallo et al., 1984; Levy et al., 1984). Since 1983, when the virus was identified, much has been learned about its molecular structure and biologic properties. The genomes of several isolates of HIV from different areas of the world have been sequenced, proteins encoded in the viral genome have been identified, and their individual functions have been studied. Epidemiologic data and clinical observations on immunologic abnormalities in AIDS patients helped to identify the primary target cells for HIV as CD4$^+$ lymphocytes and cells of monocytic origin, with the CD4 molecule itself serving as the virus receptor (Klatz-mann et al., 1984b; Dalgleish et al., 1984; McDougal et al., 1986). HIV has been shown to be cytopathic for some cells in which it replicates, particularly CD4$^+$ T cells. These findings led to a reasonable hypothesis to explain the severe immuno-deficiency in persons infected with HIV. This chapter summarizes virus–host inter-actions and biologic properties of HIV that may influence infection and play a role in disease progression.

THE RETROVIRUS FAMILY

The retrovirus family of human and animal viruses consists of subfamilies—Onco-virinae, Spumavirinae, and Lentivirinae—examples of which are listed in Table 1.1. The oncoviruses historically are classified by morphology, as seen by electron microscopy, into type A, B, C, or D. Spumaviruses have a distinctive morphology, which is similar but not identical to that of type C oncoviruses in its prominent surface projections. Although lentiviruses resemble type D oncoviruses morpho-logically, the two classes can be distinguished, because intracisternal A-type parti-cles are observed in type D- but not lentivirus-infected cells.

    The retrovirus subfamilies can also be categorized by the arrangement of spe-cific genes in their single-stranded RNA genomes. Although all retroviruses possess *gag, pol,* and *env* genes that code for core proteins, reverse transcriptase and pro-tease enzymes, and viral envelope proteins, respectively, the lentiviruses appear to

Table 1.1. The Retrovirus Family

Subfamily	Morphologic Type	Specific Viruses
Oncovirinae	A	Intracisternal immature particles (not infectious)
	B	Mouse mammary tumor virus (endogenous)
	C	Simian and Moloney sarcoma; gibbon ape, murine, feline, and bovine leukemia viruses; human and simian T-lymphotropic viruses types 1 and 2
	D	Mason-Pfizer monkey virus, SAIDS retroviruses types 1 and 2 (SRV-1, SRV-2)
Spumavirinae	—	Simian and human foamy viruses
Lentivirinae	—	Maedi/visna, caprine arthritis encephalitis, and equine infectious anemia viruses; simian, bovine and feline immunodeficiency viruses; human immunodeficiency viruses types 1 and 2

Classification is based on morphology, pathogenesis, restriction enzyme maps, gene sequences, and serology.

have a more complex genome organization than other retroviruses. The additional genes, some of which are regulatory, may play a role in the pathogenesis of lentiviruses, which are associated with slowly progressive diseases that often affect the central nervous system. The proviral forms of all retroviruses contain, at both ends of the genomic DNA, direct repeat sequences called long terminal repeats (LTRs), which encode regulatory elements that control virus expression.

The life cycle of retroviruses begins with the binding of the virus to its receptor on the cell surface, followed by internalization and uncoating to reveal the genomic RNA. After viral RNA is converted into linear double-stranded DNA by the reverse transcriptase enzyme, the DNA enters the nucleus, where it circularizes and either remains free (lentiviruses and some oncoviruses) or integrates at random into the host cell's chromosomal DNA (all retroviruses). From its position in the host DNA, the retrovirus proviral DNA can either remain latent or be transcribed and translated into viral messenger RNA and proteins. The *gag* proteins and newly synthesized genomic RNA form immature core particles that move to the cell membrane, where they associate with *env* gene products inserted in the membrane. This complex buds from the cell, the core condenses, and the mature virion is formed. The long latency periods between initiation of retroviral infections and development of disease may be a consequence of insertion of viral DNA into host cell chromosomes, where the virus can remain dormant for extended periods.

THE HIV FAMILY

The HIV family of retroviruses includes not only the isolates originally associated with AIDS (lymphadenopathy-associated virus [LAV], human T-lymphotropic virus type III [HTLV-III], and AIDS-associated retrovirus [ARV]), now termed HIV-1, but also more recently isolated viruses of human (LAV or HIV type 2 [LAV-2, HIV-2] and SBL-6669) (Clavel et al., 1986; Albert et al., 1987) and simian (SIV) (Daniel et al., 1985; Fultz et al., 1986a; Murphey-Corb et al., 1986) origin. Isolates of HIV-2 and SIV are approximately 75 percent homologous to each other

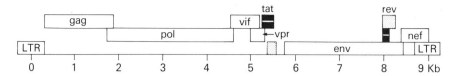

Figure 1.1. Genome organization of HIV-1 showing relative reading frames of individual genes. Both the *tat* and *rev* genes are encoded in two exons, in different reading frames, as indicated by identical shaded areas. The different genes and their functions are: *gag*, core proteins necessary for capsid formation; *pol*, enzymes required for virus replication; *env*, external glycoproteins; *vif* and *nef*, probably regulatory proteins; *tat* and *rev*, regulatory proteins essential for virus replication; *vpr*, unknown function. Kb, kilobases. (Source: Gallo et al., 1988.)

in nucleotide sequence, and both show only about 40 percent homology overall to HIV-1 (Guyader et al., 1987; Chakrabarti et al., 1987). The SIV$_{agm}$ strain appears to be equally divergent from HIV-1, HIV-2, and SIV (Fukasawa et al., 1988). However, both HIV-2 and SIV can clearly cause AIDS or an AIDS-like disease in humans and simians, respectively (Clavel et al., 1987; Letvin et al., 1985; Fultz et al., unpublished data). Although the following discussion is based on studies with HIV-1, in general, the concepts should also be applicable to HIV-2, unless otherwise stated.

Viruses in the HIV family are classified as lentiviruses based on morphology, genomic organization, percentage of nucleic acid identity to RNA (Gonda et al., 1985, 1986; Chiu et al., 1985), and cross-reactivity of antibodies to proteins (Montagnier et al., 1984a) of other lentiviruses. Mature lentivirus particles contain an eccentric, bar-shaped core that is formed after the virus buds from the cell membrane. The envelope glycoprotein of HIV has two properties in common with that of visna virus, the prototype lentivirus: its size, which is much larger than *env* gene products of type C oncoviruses, and a large number of potential glycosylation sites (Sonigo et al. 1985). These two viruses also have an open reading frame, *vif* (formerly designated *sor* or *Q* in HIV and *Q* in visna) between the *pol* and *env* genes (Wain-Hobson et al., 1985; Sonigo et al., 1985; Ratner et al., 1985) (see Fig. 1.1 and Gallo et al., 1988). HIV contains four additional genes not identified in other lentiviruses: *tat* (Arya et al., 1985; Sodroski et al., 1985), *rev* (formerly *trs/art*), (Sodroski et al., 1986b), *nef* (formerly 3'-*orf* or *F*) (Franchini et al., 1986), and *vpr* (formerly *R*) (Wong-Staal et al., 1987). An additional open reading frame, termed *vpx* (formerly *X*) and not seen in isolates of HIV-1, was identifed in SIV and HIV-2 (Chakrabarti et al., 1987; Franchini et al., 1987; Guyader et al., 1987). In addition, SIV$_{agm}$ has no *vpr* gene. The *tat* and *rev* genes code for proteins with regulatory functions that are essential for virus replication and probably act at both transcriptional and translational levels. The coding sequences for both of these genes are novel for retroviruses, because they are composed of multiple exons (Arya et al., 1985; Sodroski et al., 1985, 1986b). The functions of the *vif, nef,* and *vpr* gene products are not known, but the former two are thought to be regulatory. All of the proteins, including those with regulatory and those with unknown functions, are recognized by serum from some HIV-infected persons.

ROLE OF CELLULAR TROPISM IN PATHOGENESIS
AND TRANSMISSION OF HIV

It is well established that HIV preferentially infects and replicates in T lymphocytes bearing the cell surface molecule CD4 (Klatzmann et al., 1984a; Dalgleish et al., 1984). The process by which HIV-1 integrates, replicates and establishes latency in the cell is depicted in Figure 1.2 Infection by HIV is not limited to CD4$^+$ T lymphocytes; infection of cells of monocytic/macrophage origin (Gartner et al., 1986; Ho et al., 1986; Nicholson et al., 1986), some B cells (Montagnier et al., 1984b), and colorectal cells (Adachi et al., 1987) also has been demonstrated. The ability of HIV to infect cells other than T lymphocytes is apparently related to the presence of the CD4 molecule (Maddon et al., 1986), which serves as the receptor for the virus and also plays a role in the cytopathic effects of HIV on CD4$^+$ cells (Lifson et al., 1986). The major surface glycoprotein, gp120, encoded by the *env* gene of HIV, appears to bind directly to CD4 (McDougal et al., 1986). This interaction between gp120 and CD4 not only allows entry of the virus into the cell but also is responsible for syncytia formation (Lifson et al., 1986; Sodroski et al., 1986a) and at least some cell death. Certain strains of HIV-2, including one isolated from a patient with an AIDS-like illness, do not cause cell fusion or typical cytopathic effects on CD4$^+$ cells (Evans et al., 1988; Kong et al., 1988). Direct cell-to-cell transfer of virus via fusion is one mechanism by which the virus may escape immune elimination, particularly by neutralizing antibodies. There is no evidence that other proteins encoded in the HIV genome play a role in cytopathic effects. (See Chapter 2.)

Figure 1.2. Replication and establishment of latency of HIV-1 infection. (Adapted from De Clerq, 1986.)

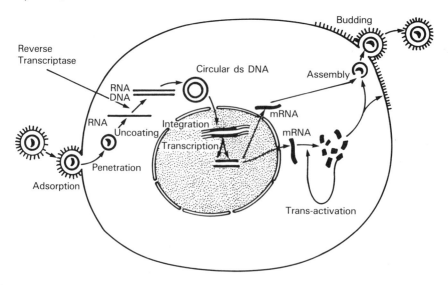

PATHOGENESIS OF HIV

The pathogenesis of HIV infection is characterized by a long latent period during which CD4[+] T-helper cells are gradually lost, resulting in severe immunodeficiency. Efforts to define more precisely the pathophysiology of HIV infections have focused on studies of the natural history of infection in defined high-risk populations and in animal models. The latter consist of HIV infection of chimpanzees (Alter et al., 1984; Fultz et al., 1986c) and, more recently, infection of macaque monkeys with the closely related simian immunodeficiency virus, SIV (Desrosiers and Letvin, 1987). These model systems may provide information on factors that influence progression to AIDS and on features of the immune response necessary for protection against infection and disease. They should also be valuable in the development of prophylactic and therapeutic drugs and vaccines.

To observe extensive replication and cell death in HIV-infected cultures of normal human lymphocytes, the cells must be activated (McDougal et al., 1985). Not all CD4[+] lymphocytes will be activated at one time; therefore, this may be one explanation for the gradual loss of CD4[+] cells in HIV-infected persons. The body probably fights to maintain a critical balance between loss of CD4[+] cells through cytopathicity of HIV or lysis by immune destruction and regeneration of CD4[+] cells. It may take multiple stimuli to activate different subsets and to destroy significant numbers of CD4[+] helper cells. It is also possible that latent infection by HIV of not only T cells but also monocytes impairs normal cellular function to such an extent that the cells cannot effectively respond to invading pathogens.

Several groups (e.g., Ho et al., 1986; Nicholson et al., 1986) have demonstrated that, in general, HIV is not cytopathic for monocytes/macrophages and replicates to low, often undetectable, levels in in vitro cultures. However, infected monocytes readily transmit infectious virus to susceptible CD4[+] cells. Thus, tropism for and cytopathic effect on CD4[+] lymphocytes and replication and sequestration in intracytoplasmic vacuoles in macrophages, which serve as reservoirs of infectious virus (Gendelman et al., 1988), are properties of HIV that could account for the progressive loss of helper T cells and resulting immunodeficiency.

Latent infection of monocytes/macrophages by HIV might also provide an ideal mechanism for spread of infection to the central nervous system. HIV has been isolated from brain tissue and cerebrospinal fluid of AIDS patients (Levy et al., 1985a; Ho et al., 1985b), suggesting that the virus is neurotropic. Maddon et al. (1986) demonstrated that CD4 is present on cells in the brain. Most HIV RNA- or antigen-positive cells in brain tissue from infected persons appear to be of monocytic origin (Koenig et al., 1986), but some data suggest that on occasion neurons or glial cells may be infected (Wiley et al., 1986).

Several groups (e.g., Gendelman et al., 1986; Rando et al., 1987; Mosca et al., 1987) have recently shown in vitro that herpesviruses can activate the expression of genes under control of the HIV LTR. These data imply that, in persons infected with both HIV and a herpesvirus, the herpesvirus could activate HIV in latently infected cells, resulting in increased virus production. However, there is no evidence that activation occurs in vivo or that increased virus production results in progression to AIDS. Furthermore, there is no epidemiologic evidence that herpesviruses are cofactors in the development of AIDS.

Another factor that may influence the pathogenesis of HIV infection is the particular strain(s) of HIV with which a person is infected. All isolates of HIV studied by direct sequencing or restriction enzyme mapping of genomic RNA are different (Benn et al., 1985; Wong-Staal et al., 1985; Alizon et al., 1986), with the most variability in the *env* gene (Starcich et al., 1986). Differences in isolates have been observed not only at the molecular level, but also in their biologic properties; i.e., some isolates replicate much better in macrophage-type cells than in T lymphocytes (Gartner et al., 1986), and some isolates are more cytopathic than others (Dahl et al., 1987; Anand et al., 1987). Isolates of HIV obtained at different times from the same individual show heterogeneity at the molecular level (Hahn et al., 1986)—a property of other lentiviruses—suggesting that the pathogenicity of HIV variants present in one person may also differ and evolve with time. Increased cytopathogenicity does seem to correlate with disease progression (Cheng-Mayer et al., 1988).

VIROLOGIC ASPECTS OF TRANSMISSION

Detection of HIV in T lymphocytes and macrophages led to the prediction that HIV infection would be found in any body fluid or tissue containing these cells. This prediction has been confirmed. HIV has been isolated not only from blood and blood products but also from semen (Ho et al., 1984; Zagury et al., 1984), female genital secretions (Vogt et al., 1986; Wofsy et al., 1986), saliva (Groopman et al., 1984; Levy et al., 1985b), tears (Fujikawa et al., 1985), breast milk (Thiry et al., 1985), cerebrospinal fluid (Levy et al., 1985a; Ho et al., 1985b), and urine (Levy et al., 1985b). Transmission by blood and blood components has been well documented (see Chapter 10). In contrast, persons living in households with AIDS patients are at extremely low risk for infection (if there is no sexual contact); this suggests that whether or not saliva, urine, and tears contain HIV, these fluids usually do not transmit infection (see Chapter 4). Some mucosal surfaces may be more conducive to HIV transmission than others. A chimpanzee became infected with HIV after only one exposure of cell-free virus to the vaginal mucosa, but not after exposure to oral mucosa (Fultz et al., 1986b).

Differences in efficiency of transmission by exposure to secretions or body fluids from HIV-infected persons could result from variation in (1) the amount of infectious virus in a particular specimen, (2) the route by which the uninfected person was exposed, (3) the health status of the infected person, or (4) the HIV isolate itself. Because HIV has been isolated from blood cells of a majority of infected persons, whether they were asymptomatic or ill (Gallo et al., 1984; Levy et al., 1984), most samples of their blood must contain HIV in an infectious form or in a latent form that is easily activated to produce infectious virus. In contrast, HIV has been isolated from a low proportion of samples of saliva, tears, or plasma (Ho et al., 1985a; Levy et al., 1985b), suggesting low titers of infectious virus in these fluids. Although it is known that either cell-free virus or HIV-infected lymphocytes are sufficient to establish infection, neither the minimum amount of virus nor the lowest number of infected cells required for human transmission is known. It has been determined (Arthur et al., 1987) that as few as four tissue culture infectious doses of the HTLV-IIIB strain of HIV inoculated intravenously are sufficient to establish infection in a chimpanzee.

The health status of the HIV-seropositive sexual partner may influence trans-missibility of HIV. Virus was isolated more frequently from peripheral blood mononuclear cells (PBMC) of patients with lymphadenopathy or other earlier man-ifestations (Gallo et al., 1984) than from AIDS patients or healthy carriers, sug-gesting that there may be more infected cells during early stages of disease than in late stages after diagnosis of AIDS. Also, Harper et al. (1986), using in situ hybrid-ization techniques, detected HIV-infected cells at a very low frequency in periph-eral blood from patients in later clinical stages of infection. However, there is no general agreement on the time at which an infected person is most likely to transmit the virus. In addition, no studies have actually quantified the numbers of infected cells in blood from persons at different stages of disease. The numbers of infected PBMC in chimpanzees are high early after inoculation and then decline 10^3- to 10^4-fold during subsequent months after infection (Fultz et al., 1986c). In HIV-infected persons, during the first 2 weeks following acute infection and in late stages of dis-ease, cell-free virus frequently can be isolated from and HIV core antigen can be detected in plasma (Gaines et al., 1987a,b; Falk et al., 1987). Whether fluids from a person with cell-free virus are more infectious than those containing primarily cell-associated virus, as in healthy carriers, is not known.

Finally, it is not uncommon for different isolates of viruses, including retro-viruses, to exhibit varying degrees of infectivity and pathogenicity. As discussed earlier, isolates of HIV exhibit molecular and biologic heterogeneity, with some isolates being more cytopathic than others in vitro. The virus and the exposed host may play separate but important roles in determining whether HIV is transmitted during any one encounter.

NATURAL HISTORY OF INFECTION

The natural history of HIV infection is a long-term, persistent process typical of lentiviruses. Early after infection, however, an acute mononucleosislike syndrome associated with seroconversion to HIV can develop (Cooper et al., 1985; Ho et al., 1985c). Acute neurologic disease coincident with seroconversion to HIV has also been described (Carne et al., 1985; Piette et al., 1986), suggesting that the virus gains entry into the central nervous system during or very soon after systemic spread of infection. HIV has been isolated from blood, plasma, and cerebrospinal fluid of patients during acute illness and prior to seroconversion (Ho et al., 1985c; Gaines et al., 1987a,b); HIV antigen has also been detected in sera (Goudsmit et al., 1986) and plasma (Gaines et al., 1987b) during acute illness and either preced-ing or at the time of antibodies' first appearance. In most documented cases, sero-conversion occurred either during acute illness (Ho et al., 1985c) or up to 10 weeks after onset of symptoms and was estimated to occur approximately 6 to 12 weeks after presumed exposure. Both transient IgM and persistent IgG antibodies were detected (Cooper et al., 1987), with antibodies to *env* gene products gp120 and gp41 generally appearing first or at the same time as antibodies to the major *gag* protein, p24. These were followed by the appearance of antibodies to *pol* gene products, p66/51 and p34 (Gaines et al., 1987b; Cooper et al., 1987). More recently, antibod-ies to the *nef* and *vif* gene products were detected in some serum samples prior to antibodies to other HIV gene products (L. Montagnier, personal communication).

A recent controversial report (Ranki et al., 1987) suggested that infection can occasionally occur up to 34 months before antibodies are detected by conventional EIA. In some persons studied, only antibodies to the putative regulatory proteins encoded by the *vif, nef* and *tat* genes were detected. These findings were critically dependent on a conventional EIA that could have lacked the degree of sensitivity now available. On the other hand, newer techniques have demonstrated the presence of virus months before a serologic response is detected (see Chapter 6).

Intervals between infection with HIV and seroconversion have been determined precisely in chimpanzees experimentally inoculated with various strains of HIV. In general, responses of chimpanzees are in agreement with estimated seroconversion times for persons infected with HIV. Chimpanzees seroconvert as early as 3 weeks after inoculation with the majority having detectable antibodies by 6 to 8 weeks (Fultz et al., 1986b,c; Goudsmit et al., 1987; Nara et al., 1987). Both transient IgM and persistent IgG HIV-specific antibodies were detected, with antibodies to *env* and *gag* gene products detectable at about the same time. As in HIV-infected persons, antibodies to *pol* gene products are detected somewhat later than antibodies to *env* and *gag* proteins. Chimpanzees also produce antibodies to p27, encoded by the *nef* gene, which can be detected at approximately the same time as antibodies to gp120 and p24 (L. Montagnier, personal communication).

In general, HIV has been isolated from PBMC of infected chimpanzees as early as 2 weeks after virus inoculation, although with some strains of HIV-1 (e.g., ARV-2), virus has not been isolated for up to 5 months after inoculation (Fultz et al., 1987). This apparent difference in pathogenicity in chimpanzees may apply to humans as well. Whereas HIV could be isolated from PBMC of chimpanzees at any time during more than 3 years of infection, cell-free virus was rarely isolated from plasma beyond the first month after inoculation (Fultz et al., 1986b,c, and unpublished data). Thus, chimpanzees and humans develop antibodies to HIV proteins in the same time course, and both also show the same early viremia, which disappears as HIV becomes primarily cell-associated. One factor of HIV infection of chimpanzees that detracts from the usefulness of this model for human infection is that, with the exception of prolonged substantial lymphadenopathy (Alter et al., 1984; Hu et al., 1987), neither AIDS nor other earlier clinical signs of immunodeficiency have developed in an HIV-infected chimpanzee. However, the duration of HIV infection in the majority of HIV-infected chimpanzees has been relatively short.

HIV-infected persons generally develop antibodies to all HIV-encoded proteins, including regulatory proteins. Evaluation of serum samples from different patients at every stage of disease and from the same people over extended periods of time indicates that an overall decrease in HIV-specific antibodies (Kaminsky et al., 1985) and specific loss of antibodies to the major core protein, p24, are predictive of disease progression (Weber et al., 1987; Allain et al., 1987; Lange et al., 1986). The decline in antibodies to p24 has been associated with the onset of antigenemia, which tended to persist and increase in concentration with time. Both the loss of antibodies to p24 and HIV antigenemia preceding onset of AIDS suggest that active replication of HIV contributes to development of AIDS. Laurence et al. (1987) also found an association between loss of IgG-mediated inhibitory activity to the HIV reverse transcriptase and progression of disease. Interestingly, the correlation between decreased antibody to p24, antigenemia, and severity of disease seen in European patients was not observed in at least one group of African patients (Baillou et al., 1987).

Although neutralizing antibodies can be detected in serum from HIV-infected persons, the titers of this activity are generally low (Clavel et al., 1985; Weiss et al., 1985) and may develop slowly after seroconversion (Weber et al., 1985; Groopman et al., 1987). In agreement with this, variation (ranging from 3 to 9 months) in the time from inoculation of chimpanzees with HIV to detection of neutralizing activity has been observed (Fultz, unpublished data). Although there is suggestive evidence (Robert-Guroff et al., 1987) that neutralizing antibodies may influence disease progression, in general, neutralizing activity in serum from persons in all stages of infection appeared to correlate poorly with clinical status (Weiss et al., 1985; Weber et al., 1987; Groopman et al., 1987).

Just as HIV isolates differ in their infectivity (see earlier), there is evidence that some strains of HIV may be more pathogenic than others and that the particular strain with which a person is infected may influence whether AIDS will develop. Piot et al. (1984) documented two clusters of five heterosexual persons who were related through sexual activity only, and all five persons in both groups died from AIDS. Although HIV-2 can clearly cause AIDS, there is some indication that HIV-2 may not be as pathogenic as HIV-1.

Differences in pathogenicity, as well as in other biologic properties of various isolates of HIV, are a reflection of the extreme heterogeneity observed at the nucleotide level in all HIV isolates so far sequenced. This heterogeneity results, in part, from an inherently high mutation rate indigenous to retroviruses. The high frequency of mutation provides the possibility that a more pathogenic variant may be generated over time in an individual. In addition, an accumulation of mutations might allow some variants to escape from immune surveillance—a phenomenon that occurs in other lentiretroviruses. Failure to be recognized by an ongoing immune response might allow a variant to replicate unchecked, with increased likelihood of disease induction.

Although nucleic acid sequence heterogeneity is greatest in the *env* gene, it is found throughout the genome in all genes, including those with regulatory or unknown functions. Guy et al. (1987) recently postulated that the *nef* gene product may play a role in establishment and maintenance of latent infections. This gene has been shown to vary up to 27 percent in nucleotide sequence between different HIV-1 isolates (Alizon et al., 1986). That observation could imply variability in the capacity of different HIV isolates to establish latent infection. Thus, the natural history of HIV infection in any one individual could differ from that in others, depending on the particular isolate with which a person is infected, whether a person is exposed to multiple isolates with varying pathogenicity, or whether a person is infected with other pathogens that could activate latent HIV. Superimposed on these variables is the competence of a person's immune system to control spread of the virus

SEROPOSITIVITY: WHAT DOES IT MEAN?

Because virus can be isolated fom asymptomatic healthy persons as well as ill patients, it must be assumed that any seropositive individual can transmit infection to others. In cases where no virus can be isolated from PBMC or serum of an HIV-seropositive person (i.e., virus is latent), it is still possible that transfer of a latently infected cell to a new host would activate expression of HIV and establish a new infection. At this time, therefore, persons who have seroconverted must be considered infectious for the remainder of their lives.

False-positive results following both EIA and immunoblot occur in less than 0.001 percent of persons tested properly (Burke et al., 1988). Whenever equivocal results are obtained on HIV testing, the test should be repeated on a new serum sample taken at least 3 to 6 months later. Equivocal results could result from nonspecific reactivity due to some unrelated intercurrent infection or immunologic abnormality (e.g., IgM hypergammaglobulinemia; Fultz, unpublished data) or HIV-specific antibodies at the borderline level of detectability. In the latter case, increased titers of HIV-specific antibodies and an unequivocal EIA result will develop with time if a true infection exists.

In addition to an indication of recent infection, weak reactivity of antibodies to viral antigens detected by immunoblot could indicate a poor immune response to a particular viral protein, or, if a person has been infected for an extended period, it could indicate loss of antibodies to a particular protein. As discussed previously, loss of antibodies to p24 appears to correlate with development of antigenemia and progression of disease. Gradual loss of antibodies to all HIV proteins could indicate that the virus is latent, and insufficient antigen is being expressed to stimulate continual antibody production. As indicated earlier, however, a latently infected person should still be considered potentially infectious to others.

False-negative antibody tests are an additional concern at the present time. As already discussed, persons acutely infected with HIV may not have generated sufficient amounts of antibodies to be detected, yet high titers of virus and virus-infected cells can be detected by culture and by assays specific for viral antigen. Because HIV antigen is primarily detected only early after infection or in late stages of disease, it is probably not efficient to screen persons for the presence of HIV antigen. However, the polymerase chain reaction technique (Ou et al., 1988) promises to improve detection of latently infected individuals and discriminate infection from passive antibody transfer in newborns. A second group that might show false-negative reactions is persons infected with variants of HIV, such as HIV-2, which do not always elicit cross-reactive antibodies (Clavel et al., 1986). Synthetic peptides have been generated that discriminate between HIV-1 and HIV-2; they appeared to have high sensitivity and specificity when incorporated into an EIA (Norrby et al., 1987). Although HIV-2-type viruses have rarely been detected in persons living in North America, they are present in Europe and Africa, and the development of EIA tests capable of detecting the two viruses simultaneously seems advisable. (See also Chapter 3.)

SUMMARY

HIV is a lentiretrovirus with a genetic complexity not seen previously among any class of retrovirus. Its insidious nature is severalfold: HIV is tropic and lytic for immunologically important CD4$^+$ T-helper cells; it integrates into host cell DNA, where it can remain dormant for extended periods; it latently infects cells of monocyte lineage that can migrate throughout the body; it is neurotropic; and its antigenic and biologic properties are heterogeneous. Although much has been learned about the HIV family of retroviruses, continued dissection of molecular and biologic properties of HIV is required in order to develop more successful intervention.

ACKNOWLEDGMENT

Supported by NIH grant RR-00165 to Yerkes Regional Primate Research Center.

REFERENCES

Adachi A, Koenig S, Gendelman HE, Daugherty D, Gattoni-Celli S, Fauci AS, Martin MA (1987): J Virol 61:209.

Albert J, Bredberg U, Chiodi F, Bottiger B, Fenyo EM, Norrby E, Biberfeld G (1987): AIDS Res Hum Retroviruses 3:3.

Alizon M, Wain-Hobson S, Montagnier L, Sonigo P (1986): Cell 46:63.

Allain J-P, Laurian Y, Paul DA, Verroust F, Leuther M, Gazengel C, Senn D, Larrieu M-J, Bosser C (1987): N Engl J Med 317:1114.

Alter HJ, Eichberg JW, Masur H, Saxinger WC, Gallo R, Macher AM, Lane HC, Fauci AS (1984): Science 226:549.

Anand R, Siegal F, Reed C, Cheung T, Forlenza S, Moore J (1987): Lancet 2:234.

Arthur LO, Robey WG, Pyle SW, Bess JW, Nara P, Kelliher J, Gilden RV, Fischinger PJ (1987): Presentation at Cold Spring Harbor Meeting on Modern Approaches to New Vaccines Including Prevention of AIDS, September.

Arya SK, Guo C, Josephs SF, Wong-Staal F (1985): Science 229:69.

Baillou A, Barin F, Allain J-P, Petat E, Kocheleff P, Kadende P, Goudeau A (1987): J Infect Dis 156:830.

Barre-Sinoussi F, Chermann JC, Rey F, Nugeyre MT, Chamaret S, Gruest J, Dauguet C, Axler-Blin C, Brun-Vezinet F, Rouzioux C, Rozenbaum W, Montagnier L (1983): Science 220:868.

Benn S, Rutledge R, Folks T, Gold J, Baker L, McCormick J, Feorino P, Piot P, Quinn T, Martin M (1985): Science 230:949.

Burke DS, Brundage JF, Redfield RR, Damato JJ, Schable CA, Putman PA, Visintine R, Kim HI (1988): N Engl J Med 319:961.

Carne CA, Tedder RS, Smith A, Sutherland S, Elkington SG, Daly HM, Preston FE, Craske J (1985): Lancet 2:1206.

Chakrabarti L, Guyader M, Alizon M, Daniel MD, Desrosiers RC, Tiollais P, Sonigo P (1987): Nature 328:543.

Cheng-Mayer C, Seto D, Tateno M, Levy JA (1988): Science 240:80.

Chiu I-M, Yaniv A, Dahlberg JE, Gazit A, Skuntz SF, Tronick SR, Aaronson SA (1985): Nature 317:366.

Clavel F, Klatzmann D, and Montagnier L (1985): Lancet 1:879.

Clavel F, Guetard D, Brun-Vezinet F, Chamaret S, Rey M-A, Santos-Ferreira MO, Laurent AG, Dauguet C, Katlama C, Rouzioux C, Klatzmann D, Champalimaud JL, Montagnier L (1986): Science 233:343.

Clavel F, Mansinho K, Chamaret S, Guetard D, Favier V, Nina J, Santos-Ferreira M-O, Champalimaud J-L, Montagnier L (1987): N Engl J Med 316:1180.

Cooper DA, Gold J, Maclean P, Donovan B, Finlayson R, Barnes TG, Michelmore HM, Brooke P, Penny R (1985): Lancet 1:537.

Cooper DA, Imrie AA, Penny R (1987): J Infect Dis 155:1113.

Dahl K, Martin K, Miller G (1987): J Virol 61:1602.

Dalgleish AG, Beverley PCL, Clapham PR, Crawford DH, Greaves MF, Weiss RA (1984): Nature 312:763.

Daniel MD, Letvin NL, King NW, Kannagi M, Sehgal PK, Hunt RD, Kanki PJ, Essex M, Desrosiers RC (1985): Science 228:1201.

Desrosiers RC, Letvin NL (1987): Rev Infect Dis 9:438.

Evans LA, Moreau J, Odehouri K, Legg H, Barboza A, Cheng-Mayer C, Levy JA (1988): Science 240:1522.

Falk LA, Paul D, Landay A, Kessler H (1987): Lancet 1:1547.

Franchini G, Robert-Guroff M, Wong-Staal F, Ghrayeb J, Kato I, Chang TW, Chang NT (1986): Proc Natl Acad Sci USA 83:5282.

Franchini G, Gurgo C, Guo H-G, Gallo RC, Collalti E, Fargnoli KA, Hall LF, Wong-Staal F, Reitz MS Jr (1987): Nature 328:539.

Fujikawa LS, Salahuddin SZ, Palestine AG, Masur H, Nussenblatt RB, Gallo RC (1985): Lancet 2:529.

Fukasawa M, Miura T, Hasegawa A, Morikawa S, Tsujimoto H, Miki K, Kitamura T, Hayami M (1988): Nature 333:457.

Fultz PN, McClure HM, Anderson DC, Swenson RB, Anand R, Srinivasan A (1986a): Proc Natl Acad Sci USA 83:5286.

Fultz PN, McClure HM, Daugharty H, Brodie A, McGrath CR, Swenson B, Francis DP (1986b): J Infect Dis 154:896.

Fultz PN, McClure HM, Swenson RB, McGrath CR, Brodie A, Getchell JP, Jensen FC, Anderson DC, Broderson JR, Francis DP (1986c): J Virol 58:116.

Fultz PN, Srinivasan A, Greene CR, Butler D, Swenson RB, McClure HM (1987): J Virol 61:4026.

Gaines H, Albert J, Von Sydow M, Sonnerborg A, Chiodi F, Ehrnst A, Strannegard O, Asjo B (1987a): Lancet 1:1317.

Gaines H, von Sydow M, Sonnerborg J, Albert J, Czajkowski J, Pehrson PO, Chiodi F, Moberg L, Fenyo EM, Asjo B, Forsgren M (1987b): Lancet 1:1249.

Gallo RC, Salahuddin SZ, Popovic M, Shearer GM, Kaplan M, Haynes BF, Palker TJ, Redfield R, Oleske J, Safai B, White G, Foster P, Markham PD (1984): Science 224:500.

Gallo RC, Wong-Staal F, Montagnier L, Haseltine W, Yoshida M (1988): Nature 333:504.

Gartner S, Markovits P, Markovitz DM, Kaplan MH, Gallo RC, Popovic M (1986): Science 233:215.

Gendelman HE, Phelps W, Feigenbaum L, Ostrove JM, Adachi A, Howley PM, Khoury G, Ginsberg HS, Martin MA (1986): Proc Natl Acad Sci 83:9759.

Gendelman HE, Orenstein JM, Martin MA, Ferrua C, Mitra R, Phipps T, Wahl LA, Lane HC, Fauci AS, Burke DS, Skillman D, Meltzer MS (1988): J Exp Med 167:1428.

Gonda MA, Wong-Staal F, Gallo RC, Clements JE, Narayan O, Gilden RV (1985): Science 227:173.

Gonda MA, Braun MJ, Clements JE, Pyper JM, Wong-Staal F, Gallo RC, Gilden RV (1986): Proc Natl Acad Sci USA 83:4007.

Goudsmit J, DeWolf F, Paul DA, Epstein LG, Lange JMA, Krone WJA, Speelman H, Wolters EC, Van der Noordaa J, Oleske JM, Van der Helm HJ, Coutinho RA (1986): Lancet 2:177.

Goudsmit J, Smit L, Krone WJA, Bakker M, Van der Noordaa J, Gibbs CJ, Epstein LG, Gajdusek DC (1987): J Infect Dis 155:327.

Groopman JE, Salahuddin SZ, Sarngadharan MG, Markham PD, Gonda M, Sliski A, Gallo RC (1984): Science 226:447.

Groopman JE, Benz PM, Ferriani R, Mayer K, Allan JD, Weymouth LA (1987): AIDS Res Hum Retroviruses 3:71.

Guy B, Kieny MP, Riviere Y, Le Peuch C, Dott K, Girard M, Montagnier L, Lecocq J-P (1987): Nature 330:266.

Guyader M, Emerman M, Sonigo P, Clavel F, Montagnier L, Alizon M (1987): Nature 326:662.

Hahn BH, Shaw GM, Taylor ME, Redfield RR, Markham PD, Salahuddin SZ, Wong-Staal F, Gallo RC, Parks ES, Parks WP (1986): Science 232:1548.

Harper ME, Marselle LM, Gallo RC, Wong-Staal F (1986): Proc Natl Acad Sci USA 83:772.

Ho DD, Schooley RT, Rota TR, Kaplan JC, Flynn T, Salahuddin SZ, Gonda MA, Hirsch MS (1984): Science 226:451.

Ho DD, Byington RE, Schooley RT, Flynn T, Rota TR, Hirsch MS (1985a): N Engl J Med 313:1606.

Ho DD, Rota TR, Schooley RT, Kaplan JC, Allan JD, Groopman JE, Resnick L, Felsenstein D, Andrews CA, Hirsch MS (1985b): N Engl J Med 313:1493.

Ho DD, Sarngadharan MG, Resnick L, Dimarzo-Veronese F, Rota TR, Hirsch MS (1985c): Ann Intern Med 103:880.

Ho DD, Rota TR, Hirsch MS (1986): J Clin Invest 77:1712.

Hu S-L, Fultz PN, McClure HM, Eichberg JW, Thomas EK, Zarling J, Singhal MC, Kosowski SG, Swenson RB, Anderson DC, Todaro G (1987): Nature 328:721.

Kaminsky LS, McHugh T, Stites D, Volberding P, Henle G, Henle W, Levy JA (1985): Proc Natl Acad Sci USA 82:5535.

Klatzmann D, Barre-Sinoussi F, Nugeyre MT, Dauguet C, Vilmer E, Griscelli C, Brun-Vezinet F, Rouzioux C, Gluckman JC, Chermann JC, Montagnier L (1984a): Science 225:59.

Klatzmann D, Champagne E, Chamaret S, Gruest J, Guetard D, Hercend T, Gluckman JC, Montagnier L (1984b): Nature 312:767.

Koenig S, Gendelman HE, Orenstein JM, DalCanto MC, Pezeshkpour GH, Yungbluth M, Janotta F, Aksamit A, Martin MA, Fauci AS (1986): Science 233:1089.

Kong L, Lee S-W, Kappes JC, Parkin JS, Decker D, Hoxie JA, Hahn BA, Shaw GM (1988): Science 240:1525.

Lange JMA, Paul DA, Huisman HG, DeWolf F, VandenBerg H, Coutinho RA, Danner SA, Van der Noordaa J, Goudsmit J (1986): Br Med J 293:1459.

Laurence J, Saunders A, Kulkosky J (1987): Science 235:1501.

Letvin NL, Daniel MD, Sehgal PK, Desrosiers RC, Hunt RD, Waldron LM, Mackey JJ, Schmidt DK, Chalifoux LV, King NW (1985): Science 230:71.

Levy JA, Hoffman AD, Kramer SM, Landis JA, Shimabukuro JM, Oshiro LS (1984): Science 225:840.

Levy JA, Hollander H, Shimabukuro J, Mills J, Kaminsky L (1985a): Lancet 2:586.

Levy JA, Kaminsky LS, Morrow WJW, Steimer K, Luciw P, Dina D, Hoxie J, Oshiro L (1985b): Ann Intern Med 103:694.

Lifson JD, Reyes GR, McGrath MS, Stein BS, Engleman EG (1986): Science 232:1123.

Maddon PJ, Dalgleish AG, McDougal JS, Clapham PR, Weiss RA, Axel R (1986): Cell 47:333.

McDougal JS, Mawle A, Cort SP, Nicholson JKA, Cross GD, Scheppler-Campbell JA, Hicks D, Sligh J (1985): J Immunol 135:3151.

McDougal JS, Kennedy MS, Sligh JM, Cort SP, Mawle A, Nicholson JKA (1986): Science 231:382.

Montagnier L, Chermann JC, Barre-Sinoussi F, Chamaret S, Gruest J, Nugeyre MT, Rey F, Dauguet C, Axler-Blin C, Vezinet-Brun F, Rouzioux C, Saimot G-A, Rozenbaum W, Gluckman JC, Klatzmann D, Vilmer E, Griscelli C, Foyer-Gazengel C, Brunet JB (1984a): Human T-Cell Leukemia/Lymphoma Virus. Cold Spring Harbor, NY: Cold Spring Harbor Laboratory.

Montagnier L, Gruest J, Chamaret S, Dauguet C, Axler C, Guetard D, Nugeyre MT, Barre-Sinoussi F, Chermann J-C, Brunet JB, Klatzmann D, Gluckman JC (1984b): Science 225:63.

Mosca JD, Bednarik DP, Raj NBK, Rosen CA, Sodroski JG, Haseltine WA, Pitha PM (1987): Nature 325:67.

Murphey-Corb M, Martin LN, Rangan SRS, Baskin GB, Gormus BJ, Wolf RH, Andes WA, West M, Montelaro RC (1986): Nature 321:435.

Nara PL, Robey WG, Arthur LO, Asher DM, Wolff AV, Gibbs CJ Jr, Gajdusek DC, Fischinger PJ (1987): J Virol 61:3173.

Nicholson JKA, Cross GD, Callaway CS, McDougal JS (1986): J Immunol 137:323.

Norrby E, Biberfeld G, Chiodi F, VonGegerfeldt A, Naucler A, Parks E, Lerner R (1987): Nature 329:248.

Ou C-Y, Kwok S, Mitchell SW, Mack DH, Sninsky JJ, Krebs JS, Feorino P, Warfield D, Schochetman G (1988): Science 239:295.

Piette AM, Tusseau F, Vignon D, Chapman A, Parrot G, Leibowitch J, Montagnier L (1986): Lancet 1:852.

Piot P, Quinn TC, Taelman H, Feinsod FM, Minlangu KB, Wobin O, Mbendi N, Mazebo P, Ndangi K, Stevens W, Kalambayi K, Mitchell S, Bridts C, McCormick JB (1984): Lancet 2:65.

Rando RF, Pellett PE, Luciw PA, Bohan CA, Srinivasan A (1987): Oncogene 1:13.

Ranki A, Valle S-L, Krohn M, Antonen J, Allain J-P, Leuther M, Franchini G, Krohn K (1987): Lancet 2:589.

Ratner L, Haseltine W, Patarca R, Livak KJ, Starcich B, Josephs SF, Doran ER, Rafalski JA, Whitehorn EA, Baumeister K, Ivanoff L, Petteway SR, Pearson ML, Lautenberger JA, Papas TS, Ghrayeb J, Chang NT, Gallo RC, and Wong-Staal F (1985): Nature 313:277.

Robert-Guroff M, Giardina PJ, Robey WG, Jennings AM, Naugle CJ, Akbar AN, Grady RW, Hilgartner MW (1987): J Immunol 138:3731.

Sodroski J, Patarca R, Rosen C, Wong-Staal F, Haseltine W (1985): Science 229:74.

Sodroski J, Goh WC, Rosen C, Campbell K, and Haseltine WA (1986a): Nature 322:470.

Sodroski J, Goh WC, Rosen C, Dayton A, Terwilliger E, Haseltine W (1986b): Nature 321:412.

Sonigo P, Alizon M, Staskus K, Klatzmann D, Cole S, Danos O, Retzel E, Tiollais P, Haase A, Wain-Hobson S (1985): Cell 42:369.

Starcich BR, Hahn BH, Shaw GM, McNeely PD, Modrow S, Wolf H, Parks ES, Parks WP, Josephs SF, Gallo RC, Wong-Staal F (1986): Cell 45:637.

Thiry L, Sprecher-Goldberger S, Jonckheer T, et al (1985): Lancet 2:891.

Vogt MW, Witt DJ, Craven DE, Byington R, Crawford DF, Schooley RT, Hirsch MS (1986): Lancet 1:525.

Wain-Hobson S, Sonigo P, Danus O, Cole S, Alizon M (1985): Cell 40:9.

Weber JN, Weiss RA, Roberts C, Weller I, Tedder RS, Clapham PR, Parker D, Duncan J, Carne C, Pinching AJ, Cheingsong-Popov R (1987): Lancet 1:119.

Table 2.2. Phenotypic Markers for Leucocytes

Marker—Generic Designation	Monoclonal Antibody Used for Detection	Distribution (Function)
CD1	Leu6, OKT6	Thymocytes, Langerhans' cells
CD2	Leu5, OKT11	T cells (E rosette receptor)
CD3	Leu4, OKT3	T cells (component of antigen receptor)
CD4	Leu3, OKT4	T helper/inducer cells, monocytes
CD8	Leu2, OKT8	T suppressor/cytotoxic cells
CD11	Leu15, OKM1	T suppressor cells, NK cells, monocytes, and granulocytes (CR3 receptor)
CD15	Leu-M1, My1	Monocytes, granulocytes
CD20	Leu16, B1	B cells
CD21	Anti-CR2, B2	Mature B cells
CD25	Anti-Tac, anti-IL2R	Activated T cells (IL2 receptor)
Anti-HLA class II	Anti-Ia, anti-HLA-DR	B cells, monocytes, activated T cells (HLA class II)

Well before the AIDS epidemic, clinical studies of acquired and congenital immunodeficiency syndromes had established that certain types of immunologic defects tend to be associated with certain types of infections or malignancies. For instance, viral, fungal, or protozoal infections tend to occur in patients with T-cell defects, whereas gram-positive (and gram-negative) bacterial infections are more of a problem in patients with B-cell, antibody, or complement deficiencies. Some infections, such as *Pneumocystis carinii* pneumonia and progressive multifocal leukoencephalopathy, are truly opportunistic in that they are virtually unheard of in subjects with intact immune systems. Other infections as well as certain malignancies occur in both normal and immunodeficient subjects. Here, the distinction is in the severity, dissemination, or life-threatening nature of the infection. These associations have been made through accumulated clinical observations and are not absolute. Nevertheless they have been clinically useful in diagnostic prediction and clinical management (e.g., when characteristic infections occur, one considers a certain type of defect, and, conversely, when certain types of defects are present, one can expect these characteristic infections).

CELLULAR TROPISM OF HIV

All mammalian cells tested will replicate HIV when HIV is introduced into the cells as cloned and integrated proviral DNA by transfection (Rosen et al., 1985; Fisher et al., 1985; Levy et al. 1986). Therefore, the apparent preferential infectivity of native HIV-1 for certain cell types must relate to events that occur before proviral transcription: penetration, uncoating, reverse transcription, or integration. Infection and replication have been most consistently demonstrated when exogenous HIV is added to activated T cells or CD4$^+$ T cell lines. In cultures of normal human lymphocytes (stimulated with phytohemagglutinin and cultured in the presence of IL2), cytoplasmic virus appears and then disappears in a proportion (1 to 10 percent) of cells (many of which form syncytia), followed by release of virus detected by assays for particulate reverse transcriptase (RT) activity, viral antigen, and infectivity. Virus infection is associated with loss of the CD4 molecule from the surface of infected cells (McDougal et al., 1985b; Hoxie et al., 1986) and, ultimately, loss of CD4$^+$ T cells from the culture (Klatzmann et al., 1984; Fauci et al., 1985; McDougal et al., 1985a,b). Residual non-CD4$^+$ cells are not susceptible to a second infection with HIV-1 (Klatzmann et al., 1984; McDougal et al., 1985b). Thus, the essential immunologic feature of AIDS can be reproduced in vitro during a relatively short period of culture (1 to 2 weeks) (Klatzmann et al., 1984; Fauci et al., 1985; McDougal et al., 1985b). A preferential tropism for CD4$^+$ cells has also been demonstrated when separated cell populations (Klatzmann et al., 1984, 1985; McDougal et al., 1985b) or continuous cell lines are examined (Popovic et al., 1984b; Gallo et al., 1984; Fauci et al., 1985; Dalgleish et al., 1985; Levy et al., 1985b), although infectivity for some non-T cells has been reported (see the following discussion).

The CD4 molecule has binding avidity for the gp110 envelope glycoprotein of HIV-1, and this appears to be a major determinant of cellular susceptibility to natural infection with HIV-1. Evidence that the CD4 molecule functions as a receptor for the virus is fourfold. First, certain monoclonal antibodies to CD4 will prevent or limit the infectivity and replication of HIV-1 in T cells (Popovic et al., 1984a; Dalgleish et al., 1985; Klatzmann et al., 1985; McDougal et al., 1985b). Second, virus preferentially binds to the surface of CD4$^+$ cells, with reciprocal inhibition of virus and CD4 mAb binding by each other (McDougal et al., 1985b). Similarly, virus-infected cells bind and fuse with uninfected CD4$^+$ cells (but not CD4$^-$ cells), resulting in syncytia formation that can be inhibited by α-CD4 mAbs (Dalgleish et al., 1985; Lifson et al., 1986; Sodroski et al., 1986c). Third, direct demonstration of a bimolecular complex of the CD4 molecule and viral gp110 has been obtained in radioimmunoprecipitation experiments (McDougal et al., 1986a; Hoxie et al., 1986). Fourth, when human cell lines that ordinarily do not express the CD4 molecule and that cannot be productively infected with native HIV-1 are rendered CD4-positive by transfection with the human CD4 gene, virus binds, and the cells are permissive for viral replication (Maddon et al., 1986).

Although evidence that the CD4 molecule acts as a receptor for HIV-1 is convincing, whether CD4 expression is both necessary and sufficient for infection and how other cellular or metabolic features modulate the process remain areas of active investigation and some controversy. In addressing these issues, it is helpful to view cellular infection with HIV-1 in three stages: infection (i.e., binding, penetration, and the intracellular processing such as reverse transcription and integration of proviral DNA required to render HIV replication-competent); replication (synthesis, assembly, and release of infectious progeny); and consequences for the infected cell (cell death, functional impairment, symbiosis). Experiments that measure events at one stage may not always be used to draw valid conclusions about another stage.

It has been suggested that HIV-1 preferentially infects a subset of CD4$^+$ cells based on observations made in infected people (Nicholson et al., 1984, 1985a; Fauci, 1984) or in vitro (Klatzmann et al., 1984; Dalgleish et al., 1985). However, virtually all CD4$^+$ T cells are *potentially* susceptible to HIV, because, under optimal conditions of HIV exposure, activation, and culture, nearly all (>99 percent)

CD4$^+$ cells are ultimately depleted. Nevertheless, there are clear differences in the amount of HIV-1 replication and the rate of cell death between so-called resting CD4$^+$ cells and CD4$^+$ cells that are proliferating or have been activated by mitogens or lymphokines. Although activated and nonactivated CD4$^+$ cells bind HIV-1 equivalently (McDougal et al., 1985b). HIV-1 penetration, replication, and cell death occur much more slowly and less efficiently in nonactivated CD4$^+$ cells (McDougal et al., 1985b; Zagury et al., 1986; Fouchard et al., 1986). This distinction may be clinically relevant. Activation/proliferation may not be an important determinant of susceptibility to infection, but it may influence the balance between destruction and regeneration of already infected CD4$^+$ cells and the pace at which cell depletion and immunodeficiency occur. This phenomenon may have implications in risk groups whose life-style or therapy results in repeated antigenic stimulation of T cells.

The mechanism by which HIV-1 infection causes CD4$^+$ cell death remains obscure. In comparison to transforming retroviruses, HIV infection results in more abundant viral RNA and nonintegrated DNA (Wong-Staal and Gallo, 1985; Sodroski et al., 1985; Rabson et al., 1985). Therefore, it seemed reasonable that unique genetic regions of the virus involved in transcriptional and translational control are responsible for the lytic potential of this virus. Studies of deletions, mutations, and transfection with functional HIV-1 genes have eliminated the *vif, nef, tat,* and *rev (art)* genes for such a role (Sodroski et al., 1986a–c; Fisher et al., 1986) (see Chapter 1).

Recently, two laboratories using quite different approaches have implicated the *env* gene. Fisher et al. (1986) derived HIV-1 clones with mutations in the 3′ end of the *env* gene that were infectious but not cytopathic. Sodroski et al. (1986c) found that cells transfected with the *env* gene form syncytia with uninfected CD4$^+$ cells, a phenomenon presumed tantamount to cell death. The CD4 molecule itself is also an essential component for cell death: syncytia formation requires the presence of CD4 (Dalgleish et al., 1985; Lifson et al., 1986; Sodroski et al., 1986c; Maddon et al., 1986); and introduction of HIV-1 into CD4$^-$ cells results in virus replication but not cell death (DeRossi et al., 1986). Sodroski et al. (1986c) argue that a mechanism by which infected cells sequester uninfected cells may explain how massive CD4$^+$ cell depletion can occur when so few cells with demonstrable intracellular HIV-1 are detected in vivo or in vitro. Furthermore, if cell–cell interaction is a major mechanism of cell death, it may explain why infectivity is so difficult to interrupt with fluid-phase reagents such as neutralizing antibody. Despite the attraction of this interpretation, it is clear that death of individually infected cells occurs quite efficiently, as demonstrated by Fouchard et al. (1986b) in single cell experiments.

The relative importance of syncytia formation and direct viral destruction of individually infected cells in explaining CD4$^+$ cell depletion in vivo remains to be determined. In either case, the focus on an interaction between *env* gene products and CD4 has been further extended by Hoxie et al. (1986), who demonstrated that intracellular complexes of envelope and CD4 proteins accumulate in HIV-1 infected cells. If such complexes are somehow toxic or disturb intracellular or membrane protein transport sufficiently to cause cell death, the envelope–CD4 interaction may be a critical determinant of cell death as well as infectivity.

Because most studies of cell tropism measure replication, phenotypic depletion, and release of virus, it has been difficult to distinguish whether virus exists in a low-level, replicative form or truly latent state (proviral DNA only without transcription products) in some cell types. Infection at low cell density or CD4$^-$ outgrowths from a predominantly lytic infection of CD4$^+$ cells has yielded cells that produce low levels of HIV-1 or can be induced to produce HIV with agents such as iododeoxyuridine or allogeneic stimulation (Hoxie et al., 1985; Folks et al., 1985, 1986a; Zagury et al., 1986; Fouchard et al., 1986a). These outgrowths often contain defective rather than wild-type virus (Folks et al., 1986b; Mawle et al., 1986). Virus replicates at low levels in some cell types such as nonactivated T cells or monocytes and results in negligible (or slow) cell death. These cells may be a more stable reservoir for virus, but their relevance to viral persistence in the human host remains to be determined.

Although the CD4 molecule is expressed at highest density in a subset of T cells, other cell types may express this molecule and are susceptible to infection. Particles compatible with HIV-1 have been observed in monocyte-derived cells such as macrophages, dendritic cells, and Langerhans' cells by electron microscopic examination of tissue specimens (Gyorkey et al., 1985; Armstrong and Horne, 1985; Kolata, 1986). Monocytes express low levels of CD4 (Wood et al., 1983) and will bind HIV-1, and binding is inhibited by α-CD4 mAb (Nicholson et al., 1986a). Monocytes and the monocytic cell line U-937 retain infectious HIV-1 for long periods in culture and will transmit productive viral infection to T cells (Levy et al., 1985a,b; Dalgleish et al., 1985; Ho et al., 1986; Gartner et al., 1986; Nicholson et al., 1986a).

Virus replicates at much lower levels in monocytes, which appear less susceptible to the cytopathic effect of the virus than T cells (Levy et al., 1985a; Ho et al., 1986a; Gartner et al., 1986; Nicholson et al., 1986a). Montagnier et al. (1984) first reported HIV-1 replication in B cell lines, which were later found to express CD4 (Dalgleish and Clapham, 1985). Neuropsychiatric symptoms may be prominent in HIV-1 infection, and HIV-1 has been identified in brain tissue by in situ hybridization and culture (Shaw et al., 1985; Ho et al., 1985a; Levy et al., 1985; Gartner et al., 1986; Stoler et al., 1986). The affected cell type appears to be monocytes or monocyte-derived microglial giant cells (Koenig et al., 1986; Gartner et al., 1986). Human brain tissue expresses a truncated form of the CD4 gene (Maddon et al., 1986), but whether the coded protein is expressed at the cell surface, whether it binds virus, and whether neural tissue expressing this truncated form of CD4 is susceptible to natural infection have not been determined.

Taken together, available evidence indicates that the CD4 molecule functions as a receptor for HIV-1, that the binding of CD4 to HIV-1 envelope is a major determinant of cell tropism and perhaps cell death as well, that all human CD4$^+$ cells are potentially susceptible to infection, and that the metabolic (activation) state of the cell is a major determinant of the extent and rate of virus replication. It remains unclear whether there are other rate-limiting steps involved in cell penetration, how penetration occurs, and whether there are additional intracellular and metabolic features unique to human cells that govern replication, persistence, and the cytopathic effect.

SIGNIFICANCE AND USE OF CD4$^+$ T CELL COUNT* AND CD4$^+$/CD8$^+$ RATIO

A depressed ratio of helper to suppressor/cytotoxic T cells has been a characteristic and consistent finding since the earliest reports of AIDS (Gottlieb et al., 1981; Masur et al., 1981; Siegal et al., 1981). Inverted ratios in AIDS are due to a marked decrease in the absolute number of helper/inducer T cells and a variable number (increased, normal, or decreased) of suppressor/cytotoxic T cells (Schroff et al., 1983; Ammann et al., 1983; Fahey et al., 1983; Fauci et al., 1984). The in vitro biology of the virus predicts that numerical depletion of CD4$^+$ cells would reflect the primary lesion more accurately than would the CD4$^+$/CD8$^+$ ratio. However, determinations of absolute T helper cell number and T helper/suppressor ratio both have their place in clinical evaluation of HIV-1-infected subjects.

In early infections and in asymptomatic infection, ratio is more sensitive to reciprocal changes in CD4$^+$ and CD8$^+$ cell counts that occur, whereas abnormally low CD4$^+$ cell counts are unusual. For instance, an infectious mononucleosislike syndrome has been described in association with acute exposure to HIV-1 and HIV-1 seroconversion. Immunologic profiles consist of normal or low-normal numbers of CD4$^+$ cells, a normal or elevated number of CD8$^+$ cells, and a low or low-normal CD4$^+$/CD8$^+$ ratio (Cooper et al., 1985). In studies of asymptomatic risk groups members where multiple immunologic tests were performed, HIV-1 exposure has been most highly associated with a depressed helper/suppressor ratio (reflecting a low normal count of CD4$^+$ and high-normal count of CD8$^+$ cells) (Melbye et al., 1984; Nicholson et al., 1985b; Eyster et al., 1985; Goedert et al., 1986), although a low number of CD4$^+$ cells rather than ratio was the best correlate in one study (Goedert et al., 1984).

Unexposed (seronegative) risk group members are either immunologically normal or, as a group, have milder abnormalities of borderline statistical significance (Melbye et al., 1984; Goedert et al., 1984; Tsoukas et al., 1984; Eyster et al., 1985; Nicholson et al., 1985b; Schwartz et al., 1985). Subjects with common but less severe clinical manifestations have abnormalities intermediate between those of AIDS patients and asymptomatic risk group members. Abnormally low CD4$^+$ cell counts are found in most AIDS patients at diagnosis (65 to 95 percent), and virtually all patients who survive long enough will eventually develop this abnormality. Abnormally low CD4$^+$ cell levels are unusual in asymptomatic infected subjects ($<$5 percent) and infrequent in AIDS-related syndromes ($<$20 percent). When a low level does occur in these clinical subgroups, it is a poor prognostic sign (see the following discussion).

In patients with AIDS, absolute numbers of CD4$^+$ cells or CD4$^+$/CD8$^+$ ratio abnormalities are independent of risk group but are related to disease manifestation and duration of AIDS diagnosis. Patients with Kaposi's sarcoma as the sole manifestation of disease have less severe abnormalities than those with opportunistic infections. Those who recover from opportunistic infections generally have

---

*It is generally accepted that both the number or count of T helper cells and the percentage of all lymphocytes represented by T helper cells measure the same biologic effect. Since most investigators have presented data in terms of the CD4$^+$ cell count or number, discussion of effects on T helper cells in this chapter and in others have likewise used those terms.

more CD4$^+$ T cells than those who do not, and, once the diagnosis of AIDS is made, progressive depletion of CD4$^+$ T cells with time is the rule (Mildvan et al., 1982; Ammann et al., 1983; Fahey et al., 1983; Schroff et al., 1983; Fauci et al., 1984; Lane et al., 1985a).

Clinically, a reasonable case can be made for the use of CD4$^+$ T cell determinants for monitoring HIV-1-infected patients, since these cells are the primary target of infection and their depletion reflects the severity of immunodeficiency better than any other test. An initial determination followed by periodic determinations about every 6 months could be helpful in confirming clinical impressions of stability or deterioration, and a very low level may prompt closer observation. While reasonable, commercially available phenotyping is quite expensive. Moreover, it is not yet clear that patients will benefit significantly from any management change, prophylaxis, or therapeutic intervention dictated by a change in CD4$^+$ cell levels per se. The majority of patients with low CD4$^+$ cell levels who are developing the complications of AIDS will have early clinical findings and the practical emphasis is on diagnosing and treating the complication rather than confirming a low CD4$^+$ cell level. Insofar as CD4$^+$ T-cell determinations may become part of staging systems for HIV-1 infection and represent a useful objective measure of response to therapy, CD4$^+$ cell levels may become part of entrance criteria for clinical drug trials, as is already the case for several trials of 3'-azido-3'-deoxythymidine (AZT) and other antiviral agents now under way.

CODETERMINANTS OF PROGRESSIVE IMMUNODEFICIENCY

Numerous retrospective and prospective studies have found that the onset of non-specific symptoms (fever, weight loss, asthenia, etc.) and abnormally low numbers of CD4$^+$ T cells are poor prognostic signs in HIV-1-infected subjects (Fahey et al., 1983; Metroka et al., 1983; Goedert et al., 1984; Abrams et al., 1984; Schwartz et al., 1985; Eyster et al., 1985; Lane et al., 1985a; Fishbein et al., 1985; Melbye et al., 1986; Polk et al., 1987). Although there are clinical and immunologic features that serve as markers for more severe disease, it has generally been difficult to identify clinical, immunologic, or virologic features that act additively or synergistically with HIV-1 exposure in predicting the degree of T-cell abnormalities and the likelihood of culmination with clinical AIDS (see Chapter 6). It should be noted for clarification that certain features of life-style or therapy have been shown to increase the likelihood of exposure to HIV-1; however, determinants of clinical or immunologic outcome once a person has become infected have been difficult to identify. Indeed, the only consistent factor shown to have a rough correlation with degree of T-cell abnormality and with increasing likelihood of developing AIDS is duration of infection with HIV-1 (Eyster et al., 1985; Jaffe et al., 1985; Schwartz et al., 1985; Goedert et al., 1986; Melbye et al., 1986). Although the duration of infection is related to the degree of T-cell abnormality, clearly there is great heterogeneity in the rate at which infected people develop progressive disease.

With a few exceptions, it has generally not been possible to identify cofactors (other than duration of infection) such as chronic antigenic stimulation, other infections, elements of life-style, or therapy that contribute to the pace of progressive immunodeficiency and the occurrence of opportunistic infections (Goedert et al., 1984, 1986; Eyster et al., 1985; Nicholson et al., 1986b, 1987; Melbye et al., 1986). Investigators who have observed features significantly associated with progressive disease have generally found it difficult to extricate the particular finding from the confounding influence of duration of infection (usually because these data are unknown or incomplete in the particular studies) or to show that the feature acts synergistically with or independently of CD4$^+$ cell levels (see Chapter 6). The following features have been associated with greater subsequent depletion of CD4$^+$ T cells and/or increased likelihood of developing AIDS: low CD4$^+$ cell levels, duration of infection, or nonspecific symptoms (all referenced earlier); higher antibody titers to cytomegalovirus (Polk et al., 1987); lower antibody levels to HIV-1 (Polk et al., 1987), especially titers to the envelope protein (McDougal et al., 1987); lower levels of antibody that inhibit reverse transcriptase activity (Laurence et al., 1987); continued illicit drug abuse in intravenous drug users (Friedman et al., 1986); and infection with more virulent strains of virus (Asjo et al., 1986). These associations and others have been found in studies of groups but may lack sufficient discriminatory power to be of great predictive value in an individual patient.

THE MAJOR COMPONENTS OF THE IMMUNE SYSTEM IN HIV-1 INFECTION

Heterogeneity of CD4$^+$ T Cells

The CD4$^+$ T cell population is functionally and phenotypically heterogeneous. A preferential loss of the CD4$^+$ subset identified with TQ1 or Leu8 monoclonal antibodies has been described in infected subjects studied before the onset of AIDS (Nicholson et al., 1984; Wood et al., 1986). This subset is the prime responder in antigen-induced T-cell proliferative assays and in the autologous mixed-lymphocyte reaction. These two responses are consistently depressed or even abrogated in HIV-1 infection and may be the earliest qualitative defects in the immune system in HIV-1 infection (Gupta and Safai, 1983; Smolen et al., 1985; Lane and Fauci, 1985).

Beyond the loss of responsiveness to pan-T-cell mitogens, which is depressed as a result of numerical depletion of T cells (Lane et al., 1983; Lane and Fauci, 1985, Fauci et al., 1985), there appears to be an intrinsic defect in the capacity of surviving T cells to recognize soluble antigen (Lane and Fauci, 1985). Antigen-specific proliferative responses are felt to be an in vitro correlate of delayed-type hypersensitivity (DTH). Skin test reactivity is impaired in HIV-1 infection with total anergy manifest in patients with more severe T-cell depletion (Gottlieb et al., 1981; Masur et al., 1981; Siegal et al., 1981; Mildvan et al., 1982; Lane and Fauci, 1985). The reason or basis for the apparent CD4$^+$ subset imbalance found early in infection is obscure. There is no preferential infectivity of HIV-1 for these subsets in vitro (McDougal et al., 1985b), and the perturbations described do not appear to have prognostic significance. As disease progresses, all CD4$^+$ subsets are depleted (Nicholson et al., 1985a) with dramatic depression in all T-cell functional assays.

Suppressor/Cytotoxic Cells

$CD8^+$ T cells may be normal, elevated, or depressed in number. Elevations are more frequent early in infection and in asymptomatic subjects, whereas in end-stage disease, $CD8^+$ T cells may decline in parallel with $CD4^+$ T cells, resulting in panlymphopenia (Stahl et al., 1982; Ammann et al., 1983; Fahey et al., 1983; Schroff et al., 1983; Lane and Fauci, 1985). There is no evidence that normal $CD8^+$ cells are susceptible to natural infection with HIV-1: although HIV-1 introduced into $CD8^+$ cells will replicate, it is not cytopathic (DeRossi et al., 1986). $CD8^+$ cells depend on $CD4^+$ T cells for induction of effector function and possibly for maintenance of precursor numbers as well. Thus, the changes in this population are most likely a secondary consequence of HIV-1 infection.

The extent to which these "reactive" changes reflect an immune response or a clinically relevant response to HIV-1 is unlikely to be answered by studies that rely on $CD8^+$ cell enumeration only. There are two reasons for this. First, changes in functional or phenotypic $CD8^+$ subsets might take place in different directions or at different rates and not be reflected with sufficient precision in total $CD8^+$ cell enumeration. Second, if $CD8^+$ cell count first increases then decreases during the course of infection, bidirectional correlations in cross-sectional studies cannot be obtained without some arbitrary division of the data, and data from patient groups studied serially are insufficient for meaningful conclusions. Most studies have failed to find a clinically useful relation between $CD8^+$ cells and course of infection or outcome (Fahey et al., 1983; Metroka et al., 1983; Goedert et al., 1984; Abrams et al., 1984; Schwartz et al., 1985; Eyster et al., 1985; Lane and Fauci, 1985; Fishbein et al., 1985; Melbye et al., 1986).

Phenotypic subsets of the $CD8^+$ population have been examined using two-color immunofluorescence analysis. Nicholson et al. (1986b) examined HIV-1-infected, asymptomatic homosexual men and found that $CD8^+$ elevations were due to increased numbers of $CD8^+$ cells that do not express the Leu15 marker, a phenotypic subset associated with cytotoxic function (Clement et al., 1984b). In HIV-1-infected men, but not in uninfected men, higher cytotoxic subset ($CD8^+$ Leu15$^-$) numbers were correlated with higher $CD4^+$ cell numbers, suggesting that the correlation was HIV-1-specific and possibly reflected control of infection. However, the cytotoxic subset elevation did not confer a lesser risk for the subsequent development of AIDS (Nicholson et al., 1987). Another marker, Leu7, subdivides $CD8^+$ cells as well as a portion of cells with NK cell function and may occur on all cytotoxic cells at some point in their differentiation. $CD8^+$ Leu7$^+$ cells are increased in asymptomatic HIV-1-infected homosexual men, in hemophiliacs, and in patients with AIDS, although no clear relation to $CD4^+$ cell levels or clinical outcome has been ascertained (Lewis et al., 1985; Prince et al., 1985a; Nicholson et al., 1986b; Stites et al., 1986). Elevated numbers of T cells bearing the T10 or Ia markers have been reported, and these occur within the $CD8^+$ population (Salazar-Gonzales et al., 1985; Nicholson et al., 1984; Schroff et al., 1983). These are considered markers for activation and/or immaturity, but it is curious that other markers more specific for immaturity (T6) or for activation/proliferation (Tac, 4F2, T9) are not elevated. An elevation in T10 cells is more common in patients with AIDS than in HIV-1-infected people without AIDS. In patients with AIDS, it is a poor prognostic sign with respect to survival but is not of value in predicting an AIDS outcome in asymptomatic HIV-1 infection (Fahey, 1986). Whether the increased number of CD8$^+$ cells identified phenotypically as cytotoxic cells or as activated/ immature cells reflects the existence of cells with specificity for HIV-1 has not been determined. In any event, these perturbations do not result in heightened or fully differentiated suppressor or cytotoxic function in systems using other (non-HIV-1) antigens or nonspecific stimuli (see later).

A poorly responsive immune system may result form a loss of helper induction or an excess of suppressor influences. Much early work focused on the possibility that an excess of abnormal suppressor phenomena occurs in AIDS patients. Purified CD8$^+$ cells have been titrated into a variety of in vitro functional assays, and no evidence for excessive or abnormal suppressor activity has been found (Lane et al., 1983; Benveniste et al., 1983; Nicholson et al., 1984; Smolen et al., 1985; Lane and Fauci, 1985). Although there is little evidence for excessive suppression by cells, suppressor factors have been detected in T-cell culture supernates (Laurence et al., 1983; Laurence and Mayer, 1984), in HIV-1 preparations (Pahwa et al., 1985; Siegel et al., 1984), and in sera (Cunningham-Rundles et al., 1983). The role, relationship, and relative contribution of suppressor influences in the pathogenesis of AIDS remain to be defined. On balance, however, the prominent features of functional and phenotypic immunodeficiency are quite adequately explained by CD4$^+$ T-cell depletion without the need to invoke excess suppression.

Functional studies of virus-specific, MHC-restricted cytotoxicity and alloreactive cytotoxicity have shown that they are severely impaired in patients with AIDS or AIDS-related symptoms and reasonably well preserved in asymptomatic, HIV-1-infected people, although subtle defects may occur in the latter group as well. Systems examined include responses to allogeneic cells (Gerstoft et al., 1985; Sharma and Gupta, 1985), influenza (Shearer et al., 1985), cytomegalovirus (CMV) (Rook et al., 1983, 1985b), and Epstein-Barr virus (EBV) (Mawle et al., 1985; Birx et al., 1986). In many cases, defective responses were restored or potentiated by pretreating responder cells with the lymphokine, IL2 (Rook et al., 1983; Gerstoft et al., 1985; Sharma and Gupta, 1985), suggesting that the defect is one of induction or differentiation rather than a lack of CD8$^+$ precursors.

HIV-1-specific cytotoxic cells (CTL) have recently been demonstrated in both humans and chimpanzees. Lymphocytes isolated from the lungs of seropositive patients suffering from lymphocytic alveolitis and lymphocytic interstitial pneumonia are able to kill HIV-1-infected alveolar macrophages in an HLA-restricted manner (Plata et al., 1987). These lymphocytes are CD8$^+$ and carry the marker D44, which is specific for the cytotoxic subset of CD8$^+$ cells. Fresh peripheral blood lymphocytes from seropositive individuals, patients with AIDS, or patients with related clinical features are able to kill autologous EBV-transformed lymphoblastoid cells infected with a vaccinia construct containing either the envelope protein or the gag protein of HIV-1 (Walker et al., 1987). Addition of α-CD3 to the assay inhibited killing, though the phenotype of the effector cells remains to be determined.

The clinical significance of these findings is not yet clear. Since virus-specific, HLA-restricted cytotoxicity appears to play a central role in the resolution of a number of viral diseases, it is encouraging that it can be demonstrated in infected individuals. However, further studies are necessary to determine whether the presence of cytotoxic effector cells has any bearing on clinical outcome.

Since all patients tested were presumably infected with different strains of HIV-1, the fact that CTL could be consistently detected using a single HIV-1 strain as target is promising for vaccine development. In chimpanzees immunized with a vaccinia construct containing the envelope glycoprotein, clones can be grown out that are specifically cytotoxic for lymphoblastoid cell lines expressing the envelope glycoprotein (Zarling et al., 1987). Thus a CTL response can be induced by vaccination and needs to be considered in the assessment of a potential vaccine.

Walker et al. (1986) discovered that CD8[+] cells from some HIV-1-infected subjects limit HIV-1 replication. Apparently, the mechanism does not involve cytotoxicity of infected cells, but it is restricted to inhibition of replication in autologous cells. Whether the phenomenon is HIV-1-specific, requires prior exposure to HIV, is restricted by the MHC, or has clinical relevance for disease outcome remain to be determined. Nevertheless, this system may offer promising insights for control of HIV-1 infection by the human host.

Cells that are cytotoxic for a wide range of tumor cell lines without the need for prior exposure to the target cell line are defined functionally as natural killer (NK) cells. They reside largley but not exclusively within a lymphocyte subpopulation known as large granular lymphocytes (LGL) and a proportion may express the CD8, Leu15, Leu7, or Leu11 markers which, when used alone or in combination, yield cells enriched for NK activity. However, precise morphologic–phenotypic–functional definition has been elusive (Lanier et al., 1984). Cells expressing NK-associated phenotypes and NK function tend to be well preserved in asymptomatic HIV-1-infected people but decline with advanced disease (Lopez et al., 1983; Creemers et al., 1985; Poli et al., 1985a; Jothy et al., 1985; Nicholson et al., 1986b; Siegal et al., 1986). When depressed, NK function can be potentiated by IL2 (Rook et al., 1983, 1985a; Reddy et al., 1984; Lifson et al., 1984). Again, this suggests that loss of function is not a result of active suppression and that effector-precursors are present, but signals required for the induction of effector function are absent.

LGL function and HIV-1 infection are of special interest for several reasons. First, cells infected with HIV-1 may be rendered susceptible to lysis by NK cells from normal, nonimmune people (Ruscetti et al., 1986) and by related cell types that mediate antibody-dependent cellular cytotoxicity (Rook et al., 1987). Second, a subpopulation of LGL (lacking NK activity) produces interferon alpha (IFNα), which potentiates NK function and depresses HIV replication in vitro (Gidlund et al., 1978; Fitzgerald et al., 1982; Ho et al., 1985b). Third, loss of IFNα production (concomitant with loss of NK function) may act synergistically with CD4[+] T-cell depletion and herald the onset of opportunistic infections (Lopez et al., 1983; Siegal et al., 1986). The extent to which IFNα and NK function limit infection in vivo and whether preservation of these functions would prevent progression are unknown.

B Cells, Immunoglobulins, and Antibody Response to Vaccination

Hypergammaglobulinemia, elevated levels of immune complexes, and polyclonal B-cell activation are common findings in HIV-1-infected people (Schroff et al., 1983; Gottlieb et al., 1983; Ammann et al., 1984; Lane et al., 1983; Fauci et al., 1984; Lightefoote et al., 1984; McDougal et al., 1985c). Although immunoglobulin levels are high, AIDS patients mount relatively poor antigen-specific antibody responses after vaccination. Primary responses are affected to a greater degree than secondary responses (Lane et al., 1983; Ammann et al., 1984; Bernstein et al., 1985).

Of special concern is the antibody response to vaccination in HIV-1-infected people who are not symptomatic. Concern is warranted for several reasons. First, these people are reasonable candidates for vaccinations that are reserved for groups at increased risk of certain vaccine-preventable diseases, and it is important to know whether they mount protective responses to vaccination and, if not, whether special immunization regimens would be required. Second, adverse consequences, particularly to live virus vaccines, is a recognized risk in immunosuppressed subjects. Therefore, it is important to know whether asymptomatic HIV-1-infected subjects have subtle defects that place them at increased risk of adverse reactions. Third, it is theoretically possible that immune stimulation following immunization might augment HIV-1 replication and hasten $CD4^+$ cell depletion. Fortunately, these concerns appear to be unwarranted, but data are somewhat limited. Huang et al. (1987) immunized asymptomatic HIV-1-infected people and people with persistent generalized lymphadenopathy with influenza and pneumococcal vaccines and found normal antibody responses, no adverse reactions, and no untoward effects on $CD4^+$ cell numbers.

In retrospective studies of children with AIDS or symptomatic HIV-1 infection who were immunized prior to diagnosis with measles–mumps–rubella vaccine, protective levels of measles antibody were found in 60% (Krasinski et al., 1986). Furthermore, no increased frequency of adverse reactions has been noted in children given live virus vaccines prior to diagnosis of HIV infection (CDC, 1986). Until more data accumulate, it has been prudently recommended that people with asymptomatic HIV-1 infection be immunized in accordance with recommendations for immunocompetent people, realizing that they are also considered candidates for vaccines that are reserved for patients at higher risk of contracting infectious diseases. People with symptomatic immunosuppression in association with HIV-1 infection should avoid live virus vaccines but receive inactivated vaccines according to recommendations for immunosuppressed patients (CDC, 1986).

For antibody responses to most antigens (T-dependent antigens), T helper cells are required. When tested as isolated T cells with normal B cells (in a pokeweed mitogen-driven assay for immunoglobulin production), T helper cell function is normal or depressed depending on the severity of T-cell depletion in the patients selected for study (Mildvan et al., 1982; Lane et al., 1983; Benveniste et al., 1983; Nicholson et al., 1984; Pahwa et al., 1984; Ammann et al., 1984; Lane and Fauci, 1985). However, purified B cells from patients are poorly responsive when mixed with normal T cells and are not stimulated by direct B-cell activators such as formalinized staphylococci or anti-IgM (Lane et al., 1983; Mildvan et al., 1982; Nicholson et al., 1984; Pahwa et al., 1985). They do respond to late-acting B-cell growth factors and exhibit a high rate of spontaneous proliferation, and a substantial number exist in peripheral blood as differentiated immunoglobulin-secreting cells, as detected in a reverse hemolytic plaque-forming cell assay (Lane et al., 1983; Pahwa et al., 1984; Martin et al., 1986). Thus, an abnormal amount of apparently spontaneous, polyclonal B-cell stimulation occurs, rendering the B cells poorly responsive to normal early-activation signals.

HIV-1 has been shown to be a polyclonal B-cell stimulator acting either directly (Schnittman et al., 1986; Pahwa et al., 1985) or indirectly through the action of T cells (Pahwa et al., 1986). As discussed, HIV-1 can infect some B cell lines that express the CD4 molecule, but it is not clear what proportion of normal B cells express CD4 or whether infection of B cells is required for polyclonal stimulation. Exposure of normal B cells to HIV-1 does not entirely reproduce all the features of B-cell stimulation found in AIDS patients, but exposure to Epstein-Barr virus (EBV) does (Lane and Fauci, 1986). This has led to the postulate that abnormalities of immunoregulatory T cells allow infection or reactivation of other viral infections such as EBV or CMV that, in turn, are B-cell activators. EBV and CMV exposure is a nearly universal finding in AIDS patients (Rogers et al., 1983; Quinnan et al., 1984), but it has been difficult to distinguish EBV or CMV exposure from active infection or reactivation much less obtain correlations with immunoglobulin or B-cell abnormalities (Crawford et al., 1984). Other postulated mechanisms (for which there is less experimental support) include the possibility that the phenotypic abnormalities described within the CD4$^+$ cell compartment (Nicholson et al., 1984) result in a CD4$^+$ subset imbalance that favors helper effects and diminishes the induction of suppressor effects resulting in unrestrained B cell activation and the proposal that HIV-1-infected T cells elaborate B-cell-stimulating factors. Lymphokine induction by cells transformed by HTLV-1 does occur but has not been found with the cytopathic HIV-1 (Salahuddin et al., 1984, Arya and Gallo 1985).

Monocytes/Macrophages

As mentioned, blood monocytes and their tissue counterparts, macrophages, express the CD4 molecule and can be infected with HIV-1. HIV-1-infected monocytes may contribute to viral persistence and neurologic infection and be an especially difficult problem in designing effective antiviral therapies (see Chapter 17). A number of defects in monocyte function have been reported in HIV-1-infected individuals. It has not been determined whether these defects result from direct infection with HIV-1 or are a consequence of immunoregulatory T-cell abnormalities or supervening infectious complications. For the most part, these defects are inconsistently found and most likely to be detected in patients with severe endstage disease. For instance, the number of circulating monocytes is generally normal throughout infection but may decline with progressive disease in association with CD4$^+$ T-cell depletion (Polk et al., 1987). Similarly, defects in chemotaxis, phagocytosis, intracellular killing, cytotoxicity, and class II MHC expression are most consistently found in patients with severe immunodeficiency and clinical complications (Pinching et al., 1983; Murray et al., 1984; Heagy et al., 1984; Smith et al., 1984; Washburn et al., 1984; Poli et al., 1985b). Antigen presentation by monocytes from HIV-1-infected subjects or by normal monocytes infected with HIV-1 has been incompletely studied. The poor proliferative response to soluble antigen is an early and consistent feature of HIV-1 infection (Lane and Fauci, 1985b), and a defect in antigen presentation by monocytes is conceivably a contributing factor (Prince et al., 1985b).

Lymphokines and Other Soluble Serum Substances

IL2 production in response to mitogens is depressed in HIV-1-infected people, and this deficiency is proportionate to the degree of T-cell depletion in the cell preparation tested (Ciobanu et al., 1983; Hauser et al., 1984; Prince et al., 1984; Murray et al., 1985; Alocer-Varela et al., 1985; Gluckman et al., 1985). On a per-cell basis, surviving T cells respond normally to the addition of exogenous IL2 (proliferation, IL2 receptor expression, enhancement of cytotoxic and NK activity) (Gluckman et al., 1985; Reddy et al., 1984; Murray et al., 1985; Hauser et al., 1984). Similarly, the apparent decreased production of immune or gamma interferon reflects a numerical depletion of T cells rather than a qualitative defect in production or responsiveness (Murray et al., 1984, 1985; Fauci et al., 1985).

An unusual form of IFNα that is acid-labile has been described in AIDS patients (Eyster et al., 1983). This form of interferon is apparently produced by B cells (Boumpas et al., 1984) and may result from polyclonal B-cell activation as a direct or indirect consequence of HIV-1 infection.

Anti-lymphocyte antibodies are detected in many HIV-1-infected subjects. The antibodies are heterogeneous with respect to specificity for CD4$^+$, CD8$^+$, or B cells, and no correlation with clinical or immunologic features of the disease has been found (Williams et al., 1984; Tomar et al., 1985). They too are probably a result of intense polyclonal B-cell stimulation.

Immune complexes are consistently found in AIDS patients and in a high proportion of people at risk for AIDS (Gottlieb et al., 1983; Lightefoote et al., 1984; Gupta and Licorish, 1984; McDougal et al., 1985c). Levels reflect the severity of T-cell depletion, hypergammaglobulinemia, and infectious complications (McDougal et al., 1985c) and are probably responsible for decreased Fc receptor-mediated clearance by the mononuclear phagocytic system (Bender et al., 1984). Immune complex diseases such as idiopathic thrombocytopenic purpura or renal complications may occur in the course of HIV-1 infection (Morris et al., 1982; Rao et al., 1984).

Immunoreactive alpha-1-thymosin, a thymic hormone, is elevated in AIDS patients (Biggar et al., 1983; Hersch et al., 1983). The elevation is somewhat surprising, since the thymic histology found at autopsy is similar to the involution found in T-cell congenital immunodeficiencies which are usually associated with low rather than high levels of hormone (Incefy et al., 1977; Elie et al., 1983; Joshi and Oleske, 1985). A serologic cross-reaction between alpha-1-thymosin and the HIV-1 core protein, p17, has been described, and it is possible that the competitive radioimmunoassay used to detect alpha-1-thymosin is affected by p17 antigen or antibody rather than detecting true hormone (Sarin et al., 1986).

Neopterin is a cellular purine metabolite, and beta-2-microglobulin is a small protein associated with class I MHC structures on the surface of all nucleated cells. Elevated serum and urine levels of these substances correlate with cell destruction or turnover in a number of diseases including AIDS (Grieco et al., 1984; Wachter et al., 1983).

IMMUNE RESPONSES TO HIV INFECTION

People infected with HIV-1 mount and sustain a vigorous antibody response to HIV-1 (Sarngadharan et al., 1984; Schupbach et al., 1985; Biggar et al., 1985; Kaminsky et al., 1985). With advanced immunodeficiency, as occurs in AIDS patients, antibody titers to most viral proteins diminish with the curious exception of antibody titers to the transmembrane protein, gp41 (Schupbach et al., 1985; Biggar et al., 1985; McDougal et al., 1987).

In established infection, it is not clear what role antibody plays in limiting infection, although it is clear that progression often occurs despite the presence of antibody. Lower levels of antibody to HIV-1 as measured by EIA (Polk et al., 1987) or Western blot (McDougal et al., 1987) have been shown to be a poor prognostic sign in HIV-1-infected homosexual men. In the latter study, the association with progression was particularly strong for lower antibody titers to the envelope protein, gp110 (McDougal et al., 1987). Neither study could determine whether low antibody to HIV-1 was related to duration of infection, but both studies found the association with progression to be independent of CD4$^+$ cell levels (which were also highly predictive of subsequent AIDS), suggesting that the relationship was not simply a consequence of severe immunodeficiency. Human anti-HIV-1 sera almost universally contain antibodies to the envelope protein, gp110 (Montagnier, 1985; Barin et al., 1985; Kitchen et al., 1986), that binds to the CD4 molecule, and these sera do inhibit virus binding to CD4$^+$ T cells in reasonably high titer (McDougal et al., 1986b). They also demonstrate a limited capacity to inhibit (neutralize) viral infectivity (McDougal et al., 1985a; Weiss et al., 1985; Robert-Guroff et al., 1985). Spread of infection in vitro (and possibly in vivo) may occur through cell–cell fusion (syncytia), a process dependent on virus–CD4 interaction but which may be more resistant to inhibition by fluid-phase antibody (Dalgleish et al., 1985; Lifson et al., 1986; Sodroski et al., 1986c). Antibody will also mediate antibody-dependent cellular cytotoxicity (ADCC) of virus-infected cells (Rook et al., 1987). Despite inferences from in vitro and clinical observations that antibody may be a determinant of the pace at which viral infection and CD4$^+$ cell depletion occur, it is clearly not effective in totally eliminating an established infection. However, it is still possible that appropriate vaccination may prevent infection from an initial exposure when virus load is likely to be substantially lower than in established infection.

For many viral diseases, antibody induced by vaccination or as a result of primary infection protects against infection upon subsequent exposure, but it is the cellular response that is primarily responsible for resolution of infection. HIV-1 is unique in that the very cells that initiate a cellular response to HIV-1 are the cells destroyed by HIV-1. The sustained antibody response to HIV-1, which most certainly requires antigen-specific T–B collaboration, suggests that HIV-1-specific T cells do exist, and other observations previously discussed suggest that there may be phenotypic or functional immune profiles that indicate an attempt by the immune system to eliminate infection. The challenge is to identify and manipulate the immune mechanisms involved.

CONCLUSION

Current knowledge of the pathogenesis of immune deficiency due to infection with HIV-1 provides for consistent interconnections between molecular, cellular, and clinical observations. The virus has evolved an affinity for the human CD4 molecule and a replication cycle that is cytopathic for host cells: HIV-1 binds, penetrates, replicates in, and destroys CD4$^+$ T cells. The result is numerical/functional depletion of CD4$^+$ T cells occurring over time. Decline of CD4$^+$ T cells results in progressive paralysis of immune responses, rendering the infected person susceptible to opportunistic infections and malignancies. Within this framework, much remains to be learned about factors that govern the control, extent, and effects of infection. Hopefully, immunologic or other factors that control infection can be identified and therapeutically manipulated in favor of the host in this devastating infection.

REFERENCES

Abrams DI, Lewis BJ, Beckstead JH, Casavant CA, Drew WL (1984): Ann Intern Med 100:801.

Alocer-Varela, J, Alarcon-Segovia, D, and Abud-Mendoza, C (1985): Clin Exp Immunol 60:31.

Ammann AJ, Abrams D, Conant M, Chudwin D, Cowan M, Volberding P, Lewis B, Casavant C (1983): Clin Immunol Immunopathol 27:315.

Ammann AJ, Schiffman G, Abrams D, Volberding P, Ziegler J, Conant M (1984): JAMA 251:1447.

Armstrong JA, Horne R (1985): Lancet 2:370.

Arya SK, Gallo RC (1985): Proc Natl Acad Sci USA 82:8691–8695.

Asjo B, Morfeldt-Manson L, Albert J, Biberfeld G, Karlsson A, Lidman K (1986): Lancet 2:660.

Barin F, McLane MF, Allan JS, Lee TH, Groopman JE, Essex M (1985): Science 228:1094.

Barre-Sinoussi F, Chermann JC, Rey F, Nugeyre MT, Charmarat S, Gruest J, Dauguet C, Axler-Blin C, Brun-Vezinet F, Rouzioux C, Rosenbaum W, Montagnier L (1983): Science 220:868.

Bender BS, Quinn TC, Lawley TJ, Smith W, Brickman C, Frank MM (1984): Clin Res 32:511A.

Benveniste E, Schroff R, Stevens RH, Gottlieb MS (1983): J Clin Immunol 4:359.

Bernstein LJ, Ochs HD, Wedgwood RJ, Rubenstein A (1985): J Pediatr 107:352.

Biddison WE, Rao PE, Talle MA, Goldstein G, Shaw S (1984): J Exp Med 159:783.

Biggar, RJ, Taylor PH, Goldstein AL, Melbye M, Ebbesen P, Mann DL, Strong DM (1983): N Engl J Med 309:49.

Biggar RJ, Melbye M, Ebbesen P, Alexander S, Nielsen JO, Sarin P, Faber V (1985): Br Med J 291:997.

Birx DL, Redfield RR, Tosato G (1986): N Engl J Med 314:874.

Boumpas D, Harris C, Hooks J, Popovic M, Mann D (1984): Clin Res 32:343A.

Centers for Disease Control (1986): MMWR 35:595.

Chan WC, Brynes RK, Spira TJ, Banks PM, Thurmond CC, Ewing EP, Chandler FW (1985): Arch Pathol Lab Med 107:133.

Ciobanu N, Welte K, Kruger G, Venuta S, Gold J, Feldman SP, Wang CY, Koziner B, Moore MAS, Safai B, Mertelsmann R (1983): J Clin Immunol 3:332.

Clement LT, Dagg MK, Landay A (1984a): J Clin Immunol 4:395.

Clement LT, Grossi CE, Gartland LJ (1984b): J Immunol 133:2461.

Cooper DA, Gold J, Maclean P, Donovan B, Finlayson R, Barns TG, Michelmore HM, Brooke P, Penny R (1985): Lancet 1:537.

Crawford DH, Weller I, Iliescu V (1984): N Engl J Med 311:536.

Creemers PC, Stark DF, Boyko WJ (1985): Clin Immunol Immunopathol 36:141.

Cunningham-Rundles S, Michelis MA, Masur H (1983): N Engl J Med 310:1279.

Dalgleish AG, Beverely PCL, Clapham PR, Crawford DH, Greaves MF, Weiss RA (1985): Nature 312:763.

Dalgleish AG, Clapham P (1985): Immunol Today 6:71.

DeRossi A, Franchinin G, Aldorini A, Del Mistro A, Chieco-Bianchi L, Gallo RC, Wong-Staal F (1986): Proc Natl Acad Sci USA 83:4297.

Elie R, Laroche AC, Arnous E, Guerin J-M, Pierre G, Malebranche, R (1983), N Engl J Med 308:841.

Eyster ME, Goedert JJ, Poon M-C, Preble OT (1983): N Engl J Med 309:583.

Eyster ME, Goedert JJ, Sarngadharan MG, Weiss SH, Gallo RC, Blattner WA (1985): JAMA 253:2219.

Fahey JL (1986): Clin Aspects Autoimmun 1:24.

Fahey JL, Prince H, Weaver MM, Groopman J, Visscher B, Schwartz K, Detels R (1983): Am J Med 76:95.

Fauci AS (1984): Clin Res 32:491.

Fauci AS, Macher H, Longo DL, Lane HC, Masur H, Gelmann EP (1984): Ann Intern Med 100:92.

Fauci AS, Masur H, Gelmann EP, Markham PD, Hahn BH, Lane HC (1985): Ann Intern Med 102:800.

Fishbein DB, Kaplan JE, Spira TJ, Miller B, Schonberger LB, Pinsky PF, Getchell JP, Kalyanaraman VS, Braude JS (1985): JAMA 254:930.

Fisher AG, Collalti E, Ratner L, Gallo RC, Wong-Staal F (1985): Nature 316:262.

Fisher AG, Ratner L, Mitsuya H, Marselle LM, Harper ME, Broder S, Gallo RC, Wong-Staal, F (1986): Science 233:655.

Fitzgerald PA, Von Wussow P, Lopez C (1982): J Immunol 129:819.

Folks TM, Benn S, Rabson A, Theodore T, Hoggan MD, Martin M, Lightefoote M, Sell K (1985): Proc Natl Acad Sci USA 82:4539.

Folks TM, Powell DM, Lightefoote MM, Benn S, Martin MA, Fauci AS (1986a): Science 231:600.

Folks TM, Powell D, Lightefoote M, Koenig S, Fauci AS, Benn S, Rabson A, Daugherty D, Gendelman HE, Hoggan MD, Venkatesan S, Martin M (1986b): J Exp Med 164:280.

Fouchard M, Desportes I, Reveil B, Leonard R, Gallo R, Zagury D (1986): International Conference on AIDS, Paris, June 23–25.

Friedman SR, Des Jarlais DC, Marmor D, Yancovitz S, Zolla-Pazner S, El-Sadr W, Cohen H, Garber J, Spira TJ, Beatrice S (1986): Submitted.

Gallo RC, Salahuddin SZ, Popovic M, Shearer AM, Kaplan M, Haynes BF, Palker TJ, Redfield R, Oleske J, Safai B, White G, Foster P, Markham PD (1984): Science 224:500.

Gartner S, Markovits P, Markovitz DM, Betts RF, Popovic M (1986a): JAMA 256:2365.

Gartner S, Markovitz P, Markovitz DM, Kaplan MH, Gallo RC, Popovic M (1986b): Science 233:215.

Gerstoft J, Dickmeiss E, Mathiesen L (1985): Scand J Immunol 22:463.

Gerstoft J, Pallesen G, Mathiesen L, Dickmeiss E, Lundhert BO, Hoffman B, Nielsen CM, Petersen CS, Kroon S (1987): Scand J Immunol 25:93.

Gidlund M, Orn A, Wigzell H, Senik A, Gresser I (1978): Nature 273:759.

Gluckman J-C, Kaltzmann D, Cavaille-Coll M, Brisson E, Messiah A, Lachiver D, Rozenbaum W (1985): Clin Exp Immunol 60:8.

Goedert JJ, Sarngadharan MG, Biggar RJ, Weiss SH, Winn D, Grossman RJ, Greene MH, Bodner A, Mann DL, Strong DM, Gallo RC, Blattner WA (1984): Lancet 2:711.

Goedert JJ, Biggar RJ, Weiss SH, Eyster ME, Melbye M, Wilson S, Ginzberg HM, Grossman RJ, DiGiola RA, Sanchez WC, Giron JA, Ebbesen P, Gallo RC, Blattner WA (1986): Science 231:992.

Gottlieb MS, Schroff R, Schanker HM, Weissman DO, Fan, PT, Wolf, RA, Saxon A (1981): N Engl J Med 305:1425.

Gottlieb MS, Groopman JE, Weinsten WM, Fahey JL, Detels R (1983): Ann Intern med 99:208.

Greene WC, Fleisher TA, Nelson DL, Waldman TA (1982): J Immunol 129:1986.

Grieco MH, Reddy MM, Kothari HB, Lange M, Buimovici-Klein E, William D (1984): Clin Immunol Immunopathol 32:174.

Gupta S, Licorish K (1984): N Engl J Med 311:1530.

Gupta S, Safai B (1983): J Clin Invest 71:296.

Gyorkey F, Melnick JL, Sinkovics JG, Gyorkey P (1985): Lancet 1:106.

Hauser GJ, Bino T, Rosenberg H, Zakuth V, Geller E, Spirer Z (1984): Clin Exp Immunol 56:14.

Heagy W, Kelley VE, Strom TB, Mayer K, Shapiro HM, Mandel R, Finberg R (1984): J Clin Invest 74:2089.

Hersch EM, Reuben JM, Rios, A, Mansell WA, Newell GR, McClure JE, Goldstein AL (1983): N Engl J Med 308:45.

Ho DD, Hartshorn KL, Rota TR, Andrews CA, Kaplan JC, Schooley RT, Hirsch MS (1985a): Lancet 1:602.

Ho DD, Rota TR, Schooley RT, Kaplan JC, Allan JD, Groopman JE, Resnich L, Felsenstein D, Andrews CA, Hirsch MS (1985b): N Engl J Med 313:1493.

Ho DD, Rota TR, Hirsch MS (1986): J Clin Invest 77:1712–1715.

Hoxie JA, Haggarty BS, Rackowski JL, Pillsbury N, Levy JA (1985): Science 229:1400.

Hoxie JA, Alpers JD, Rackowski JL, Huebner K, Haggarty BS, Cedarbaum AJ, Reed JC (1986): Science 234:1123.

Huang K, Ruben FL, Rinaldo CR, Kingsley L, Lyter DW, Ho M (1987): JAMA 257:2047.

Incefy GS, Dardenne M, Pahwa S, Grimmes E, Pahwa RN, Smithwich E, O'Reilly R, Good RA (1977): Proc Natl Acad Sci USA 74:1250.

Jaffe HW, Feorino PM, Darrow WW, O'Malley PM, Getchell JP, Warfield DT, Jones BM, Echenberg DF, Francis DP, Curran JW (1985): Ann Intern Med 102:627.

Joshi VV, Oleske JM (1985): Arch Pathol Lab Med 109:142.

Jothy S, Gilmore N, El'Gabalaway H, Purchal J (1985): Can Med Assoc J 132:141.

Kaminsky LS, McHugh T, Stites D, Volberding P, Henle G, Henle W, Levy JA (1985): J Natl Acad Sci USA 82:5535.

Kitchen L, Malone G, Orgad S, Barin F, Zaizov R, Ramot B, Gazit E, Kreiss J, Leal M, Wichmann I, Martinowitz U, Essex M (1986): J Infect Dis 153:788.

Klatzman D, Barre-Sinoussi F, Nugeyre MT, Dauguet C, Vilmer E, Griscelli C, Brun-Vezinet F, Rouzioux C, Gluckman JC, Chermann J-C, Montagnier L (1984): Science 225:59.

Klatzmann D, Champagne E, Charmarat S, Gruest J, Guetard D, Hercend T, Gluckman J-C, Montagnier L (1985): Nature 312:767.

Koenig S, Gendelman HE, Orenstein JM, Dal Canto MC, Pezeshkpour GH, Yungbluth M, Janotta F, Aksamit A, Martin M, Fauci A (1986): Science 233:1989.

Kolata G (1986): Science 232:1197.

Krasinski K, Borkowsky W, Krugman S (1986): International Conference on AIDS, Paris, June 23–25.

Landesman SH, Ginzberg HM, Weiss SH (1985): N Engl J Med 312:521.

Lane HC, Fauci AS (1985): Annu Rev Immunol 3:477.

Lane HC, Fauci AS (1986) International Conference on AIDS, Paris, June 23–25.

Lane HC, Masur H, Edgar LC, Whalen G, Rook AH, Fauci AS (1983): N Engl J Med 309:453.

Lane HC, Depper JM, Greene WC, Whalen G, Waldmann TA, Fauci AS (1985a): N Engl J Med 313:79.

Lane HC, Masur H, Gelmann EP, Longo DL, Steis RG, Chused T, Whalen G, Edgar L, Fauci AS (1985b): Am J Med 78:417.

Lanier LL, Loken MR (1984): J Immunol 132:151.

Laurence J, Gottlieb AB, Kunkel HG (1983): J Clin Invest 72:2072.

Laurence J, Mayer L (1984): Science 225:66.

Laurence J, Saunders A, Kulkosky J (1987): Science 235:1501.

Levy JA, Hoffman AD, Kramer SM, Landis JA, Shimabukuro JM, Oschiro LS (1984): Science 225:840.

Levy JA, Kaminsky LS, Morrow JW, Steimer K, Luciw P, Dina D, Hoxie J, Oshiro L (1985a): Ann Intern med 103:694.

Levy JA, Shimabukuro J, Hollander H, Millis J, Kaminsky L (1985b): Lancet 2:586.

Levy JA, Shimabukuro J, McHugh T, Casavant C, Stites DP, Oshiro LS (1985c): Virology 147:441.

Levy JA, Cheng-Meyer C, Dina D, Luciw PA (1986): Science 232:998.

Lewis DE, Puck JM, Babcock GF, Rich RR (1985): J Infect Dis 151:555.

Lifson JD, Mark DF, Benike CJ, Koths K, Engleman EG (1984): Lancet 1:698.

Lifson JD, Reyes GR, McGrath MS, Stein BS, Engleman EG (1986): Science 232:1123.

Lightefoote MM, Folks TM, Sell KW (1984): Fed Proc 43:1921.

Lopez C, Fitzgerald PA, Siegal FP (1983): J Infect Dis 148:962.

Maddon PJ, Dalgleish AG, McDougal JS, Clapham PR, Weiss RA, Axel R (1986):Cell 47:333.

Martin LS, McDougal JS, Spira TJ, Loskoski SL (1986): Diagn Immunol 4:117.

Masur H, Michelis MA, Greene J, Onorato I, Vande Stouwe RA, Holtzman RS, Wormser G, Brettman L, Lange M, Murray HW, Cunningham-Rundles S (1981): N Engl J Med 305:1431.

Mawle AC, Scheppler-Campbell JA, McDougal JS (1985): Ann Intern Med 103:777.

Mawle AC, Scheppler-Campbell J, Nicholson, JKA, Hicks D, Cross GD, McDougal JS (1986): International Conference on AIDS, Paris, June 23–25.

McDougal JS, Cort SP, Kennedy MS, Cabradilla CD, Feorino PM, Francis DP, Hicks D, Kalyanaraman VS, Martin LS (1985a): J Immunol Methods 76:171.

McDougal JS, Hubbard M, Nicholson JKA, Jones BM, Holman RC, Roberts J, Fishbein DB, Jaffe HW, Kaplan JE, Spira TJ, Evatt BL (1985b): J Clin Immunol 5:130.

McDougal JS, Mawle A, Cort SP, Nicholson JKA, Cross GD, Scheppler-Campbell JA, Hicks D, Sligh J (1985c): J Immunol 135:3151.

McDougal JS, Kennedy MS, Sligh JM, Cort SP, Mawle A, Nicholson JKA (1986a): Science 231:382.

McDougal JS, Nicholson JKA, Cross GD, Cort SP, Kennedy MS, Mawle AC (1986b): J Immunol 137:2937.

McDougal JS, Kennedy MS, Nicholson JKA, Spira TJ, Jaffe HW, Kaplan JE, Fishbein DB, O'Malley P, Aloisio, CH, Black CM, Hubbard M, Reimer CB (1987): J Clin Invest 80:316.

Melbye M, Biggar RJ, Ebbesen P, Sarngadharan MG, Weiss SH, Gallo RC Blattner WA (1984): Br Med J 289:573.

Melbye M, Biggar RJ, Ebbesen P, Neuland C, Goedert JJ, Faber V, Lorenzen I, Skinhoj P, Gallow RC, Blattner WA (1986): Ann Intern med 104:496.

Metroka CE, Cunningham-Rundles S, Pollack MS, Sonnabend JA, Davis JM, Gordon B, Fernandez RD, Mouradian J (1983): Ann Intern med 99:585.

Mildvan D, Mathur U, Enlow RW, Roman PL, Winchester RJ, Colp C, Singman H, Adelsberg BR, Spingland I (1982): Ann Intern Med 96:700.

Modlin RL, Meyer PR, Hofman FM, Mehlmauer M, Levy NB, Lukes RJ, Parker JW, Ammann AJ, Conant MA, Rea TH, Taylor CR (1983): JAMA 250:1302.

Montagnier L, Gruest J, Charmaret S, Dauguet C, Axler C, Guetard D, Nugeyre MT, Barre-Sinoussi F, Chermann JC, Brunet JB, Klatzmann D, Gluckman JC (1984): Science 225:63.

Montagnier L, Clavel F, Krust B, Charmaret S, Rey F, Barre-Sinoussi, F, Chermann JC (1985): Virology 141:283.

Morris L, Distenfeld A, Amorosi E, Karpatkin S (1982): Ann Intern med 96:714.

Murray HW, Rubin BY, Masur H, Roberts RB (1984): N Engl J Med 310:883.

Murray HW, Welte K, Jacobs JL, Rubin BY, Mertelsmann R, and Roberts RB (1985): J Clin Invest 76:1959.

Nicholson JKA, McDougal JS, Spira TJ, Cross GD, Jones BM, Reinherz EL (1984): J Clin Invest 73:191.

Nicholson JKA, McDougal JS, Jaffe HW, Spira TJ, Kennedy MS, Jones BM, Darrow WW, Morgan M, Hubbard M (1985a): Ann Intern Med 103:37.

Nicholson JKA, McDougal JS, Spira TJ (1985b): Clin Immunol 5:269.

Nicholson JKA, Cross GD, Callaway CS, McDougal JS (1986a): J Immunol 137:323.

Nicholson JKA, Echenberg DF, Jones BM, Jaffe HW, Feorino PM, McDougal JS (1986b): Clin Immunol Immunopathol 40:505.

Nicholson JKA, Jones BM, Echenberg DF, Spira TJ, McDougal JS (1987): Clin Immunol Immunopathol 43:82–87.

Pahwa SG, Quilop MTJ, Lange M, Pahwa RN, Grieco MH (1984): Ann Intern Med 101:757.

Pahwa SG, Pahwa R, Saxinger C, Gallo RC Good RA (1985): Proc Natl Acad Sci USA 82:8198.

Pahwa SG, Pahwa R, Kaplan M, Saxinger C (1986): International Conference on AIDS, Paris, June 23–25.

Pinching AJ, McManus TJ, Jeffries DJ, Moshtael O, Donaghy M, Parkin JM, Munday PE, Harris JRW (1983): Lancet 2:126.

Plata F, Autran B, Martins LP, Wain-Hobson S, Raphael M, Mayaud C, Denis M, Guillon J-M, Debre P (1987): Nature 328:348.

Poli G, Bottazzi B, Acero R, Bersani L, Ross V, Introna M, Lazzarin A, Galli M, Mantavani A (1985a): Clin Exp Immunol 62:136.

Poli G, Introna M, Zanaboni F, Peri G, Carbonari M, Aiuti F, Lazzarin A, Moroni M, Mantovani A (1985b): Clin Exp Immunol 62:128.

Polk BF, Fox R, Brookmeyer R, Kanchanaraksa S, Kaslow R, Visscher B, Rinaldo C, Phair J (1987): N Engl J Med 316:61.

Popovic M, Gallo RC, Mann DL (1984a): Clin Res 33:560A.

Popovic M, Read-Connole E, Gallo RC (1984b): Lancet 2:1472.

Prince HE, Kermani-Arab V, Fahey JL (1984): J Immunol 133:1313.

Prince HE, Kressi JK, Kasper CK, Kleinman S, Saunders AM, Waldbeser L, Manding OO, Kaplan HS (1985a): Blood 66:64.

Prince HE, Moody DJ, Shubin BI, Fahey JL (1985b): J Clin Immunol 5:21.

Quinnan GV, Masur H, Rook AH, Armstrong G, Fredrick WR, Epstein I, Manischewitz JF, Macher AM, Jackson L, Ames J, Smith HA, Parker M, Pearson, GR, Parillo J, Mitchell C, Strauss SE (1984): JAMA 252:72.

Rabson AB, Daugherty DF, Venkatesan S, Boulukos KE, Benn S, Folks TM, Feorino PM, Martin MA (1985): Science 229:1388.

Rao TKS, Filippone EJ, Nicastri AD, Landesman SH, Frank E, Chen CK, Friedman EA (1984): N Engl J Med 310:669.

Reddy MM, Pinyavat N, Greico MH (1984): Infect Immun 44:339.

Robert-Guroff M, Brown M, Gallo RC (1985): Nature 316:72.

Rogers MF, Morens DM, Stewart JA, Kaminski RM, Spira TJ, Feorino PM, Larsen SA, Francis DP, Wilson M, Kaufman L (1983): Ann Intern Med 99:151.

Rook AH, Masur H, Lane HC, Frederick W, Kasahara T, Macher AM, Djeu JY, Manischewitz JF, Jackson L, Fauci AS, Quinnan GV (1983): J Clin Invest 72:398.

Rook AH, Hooks, JJ, Quinnan GV, Lane HC, Manichewitz JF, Macher AM, Fauci AS, Djeu JY (1985a): J Immunol 134:1503.

Rook AH, Manischewitz JF, Frederick WR, Epstein JS, Jackson L, Gelmann E, Steis R, Masur H, Quinnan GV (1985b): J Infect Dis 152:627.

Rook AH, Lane HC, Folks T, McCoy S, Alter H, Fauci AS (1987): J Immunol 138:1064.

Rosen CA, Sodroski JG, Haseltine WA (1985): Cell 41:813.

Ruscetti FW, Mikouits JA, Kalyanarama VS, Overton R, Stevenson H, Stromberg K, Herberman RB, Farrar WL, Ortaldo JR (1986): J Immunol 136:3619.

Safai B, Sarngadharan MG, Groopman JE, Arnett K, Popovic M, Slinski A, Schupbach J, Gallo RC (1984): Lancet 1:1438.

Salahuddin SZ, Markham PD, Lindner SG, Gootenberg J, Popovic M (1984): Science 223:703.

Salazar-Gonzales JF, Moody DJ, Giorgi JV, Martinez-Maza O, Mitsuyasu RT, Fahey JL (1985): J Immunol 135:1778.

Sarin PS, Sun DK, Thornton AH, Naylor PH, Goldstein AL (1986): Science 232:1135.

Sarngadharan MG, Popovic M, Bruch L, Schupbach J, Gallo RC (1984): Science 224:506.

Schnittman SM, Lane HC, Higgens SE, Folks T, Fauci AS (1986): Science 233:1084.

Schroff RW, Gottlieb MS, Prince HE, Chai LL, Fahey JL (1983): Clin Immunol Immunopathol 27:300.

Schupbach J, Haller O, Vogt M, Lathy R, Joller H, Oelz O, Popovic M, Sarngadharan MG, Gallo RC (1985): N Engl J Med 312:265.

Schawartz K, Visscher BR, Detels R, Taylor J, Nisharian P, Fahey JL (1985): Lancet 2:831.

Sharma B, Gupta S (1985): Clin Exp Immunol 62:296.

Shaw GM, Harper ME, Hahn BH, Epstein LG, Gajdusek DC, Prince RW, Navia BA, Petito CK, O'Hara CJ, Groopman JE, Cho E-S, Oleske JM, Wong-Staal F, Gallo RC (1985): Science 227:177.

Shearer GM, Salahuddin SZ, Markham PD, Joseph LJ, Payne SM, Driebel P, Bernstein DC, Biddison WE, Sarngadharan MG, Gallo RC (1985): J Clin Invest 76:1699.

Siegal FP, Lopez C, Hammer GS, Brown AE, Kornfeld SJ, Gold J, Hassett J, Hirshman SZ, Cunningham-Rundles C, Adelsberg BR, Parkham DM, Siegal M, Cunningham-Rundles S, Armstrong D (1981): N Engl J Med 305:1439.

Siegal FP, Lopez C, Fitzgerald PA, Shah K, Baron P, Leiderman IZ, Imperato D, Landesman S (1986): J Clin Invest 78:115.

Siegel JP, Djeu JY, Stocks NI, Masur H, Fauci AS, Lane HC, Gelmann EP, Quinnan GP (1984): Clin Res 32:358A.

Smith PD, Ohura K, Masur H, Lane HC, Fauci AS, Wahl SM (1984): J Clin Invest 74:2121.

Smolen JS, Bettelheim P, Koller U, McDougal S, Graninger W, Luger TA, Knapp W, Lechner K (1985): J Clin Invest 75:1828.

Sodroski J, Patarca R, Rosen C, Wong-Staal F, Haseltine W (1985): Science, 229:74.

Sodroski J, Goh WC, Rosen C, Campbell K, Haseltine WA (1986a): Nature 322:470.

Sodroski J, Goh WC, Rosen C, Dayton A, Terwilliger E, Haseltine W, (1986b): Nature 321:412.

Sodroski J, Goh WC, Rosen C, Tartar A, Portetelle D, Burny A, Haseltine W (1986c): Science 231:1549.

Stahl RE, Friedman-Kein AE, Dubin R, Marmor M, Zolla-Pazner S (1982): Am J Med 73:171.

Stites DP, Casavant CH, McHugh TM, Moss, AR, Beal SL, Ziegler JL, Saunders AM, Warner NL (1986): Clin Immunol Immunopathol 38:161.

Stoler MH, Eskin TA, Benn S, Angever RC, Angever LM (1986): JAMA 256:2360.

Tomar RH, John PA, Hennig AK, Kloster B (1985): Clin Immunol Immunopathol 37:37.

Tsoukas C, Gervais F, Shuster J, Gold P, O'Shaughnessy M, Robert-Guroff M (1984): N Engl J Med 311:1514.

Wachter H, Fuchs D, Hausen A, Huber C, Kuosp O, Reibnegger G, Spira TJ (1983): Hoppe-Seyler's Z Psysiol Chem 364:1345

Walker BD, Chakrabarti S, Moss B, Paradis TJ, Flynn T, Durno AG, Blumberg k? Kaplan JC, Hirsch MS, Schooley RT (1987): Nature 328:345.

Walker CM, Moody DJ, Stites DP, Levy JA (1986): Science 234:1563.

Washburn RG, Tuazon CU, Bennett JE (1984): J Infect Dis 151:565.

Weiss RA, Clapman PR, Cheinsong-Popov R, Dalgleish AG, Carne CA, Weller IVD, Tedder RS (1985): Nature 316:69.

Williams RC, Masur H, Spira TJ (1984): J Clin Immunol 4:118.

Wong-Staal, F, Gallo RC (1985): Nature 317:395.

Wood GS, Warner NL, Warnke RA (1983): J Immunol 131:212.

Wood GS, Burnes BF, Dorfman RD, Warnke RA (1986): Blood 67:596.

Zagury D, Bernard J, Leonard R, Cheynier R, Feldman M, Sarin PS, Gallo RC (1986): Science 231:850.

Zarling JM, Eichberg JW, Moran PA, McClure J, Sridhar P, Shiu-Lok H (1987): J Immunol 139:988.

3

The Immune System: Serology and Applications

MICHAEL S. ASCHER AND RICHARD A. KASLOW

This chapter addresses the application of serologic tests for HIV-1 as used both in clinical or other settings where the risk is variable and in low-risk settings, for which serologic testing was originally developed. Discussion of the early successes of gene amplification at demonstrating the presence of HIV-1 in the absence of serologic evidence (Farzadegan et al., 1988; Wolinsky et al., 1988) and the promising applications of this new technology is beyond the scope of this chapter.

As described in Chapters 2 and 6, HIV-1 infection and AIDS are atypical of most infectious diseases since the presence of antibodies to HIV-1 signifies active infection and infectiousness with few if any exceptions (Barin et al., 1985; Fauci, 1987, 1988). In other infections, antibodies confer immunity and resistance to further challenge. This serologic phenomenon is at once advantageous and devastating: advantageous to public health practice in that a straightforward blood test can nearly always detect infected individuals, and devastating to the infected individual in that it implies the absence of protective immunity.

HIV-1 ANTIBODY TESTS

Antibodies to HIV-1 can be detected by a number of different techniques. Each test configuration will have its own performance characteristics (i.e., sensitivity, specificity, and predictive value), and each of these features will have significantly different behavior depending on the population under investigation (Jackson and Balfour, 1988). In low-risk populations such as blood donors, small changes in sensitivity will cause little or no concern, whereas nonspecificity in such settings can have adverse impact (e.g., loss of units from the blood supply). In a high-risk environment, any loss in sensitivity would lead to improper reassurance of individuals about their seronegative status. Specificity in that setting is of less concern, since secondary tests are available (see later). These competing goals of testing in the disparate settings of blood bank and public health clinic have forced an uneasy compromise in the configuration and use of these tests.

The most commonly used test, automated for screening large numbers of samples, is the enzyme-linked immunoassay (EIA) test. The test is a standard indirect antiantibody procedure using antigen in the form of viral lysate coupled to a solid phase (e.g., plastic). Seven manufacturers have been licensed in the United States to produce kits for screening of blood and diagnosis. The tests entered the market at different times and have shown slight differences in performance. Performance characteristics of the different tests have recently converged (Handsfield et al., 1987; Saah et al., 1987; Burkhardt et al. 1987; Van De Perre et al., 1988). Because the impact of a false-negative test can be devastating to the sexual partner of or the recipient of blood from an infected individual, the EIA test was intentionally designed to emphasize sensitivity over specificity in the establishment of the threshhold between a positive and a negative result (Oldham et al., 1987; Ward et al., 1988). The currently licensed formulations of the EIA kits have, by any historical standards, extremely high sensitivity, but they will falsely indicate the presence of antibody in approximately two per 1,000 uninfected individuals, producing so-called false-positive tests (Ameglio et al., 1987). If the prevalence of antibody in a population being screened is also around two per 1,000 persons, the predictive value of a positive test would be 50 percent at best. With the large numbers of false-positive tests generated by EIA alone in populations with prevalence on this order of magnitude, the need for additional testing is evident (Meyer and Pauker, 1987).

SUPPLEMENTAL TESTS

It has become standard laboratory practice to perform a supplemental assay on specimens that show repeated reactivity by the EIA test (Polesky, 1988). An EIA test is initially performed once and, if positive, is repeated, usually in duplicate. A nonrepeatable positive result is considered negative, although a donated unit of blood with such a positive result is nevertheless discarded. Antibodies to protein products of HIV-1 can also be detected individually with considerable accuracy through use of the immunoblot (Western blot) method. This method yields a series of bands in a pattern distinctive for HIV-1 and can differentiate responses to separate viral components from responses to cellular contaminants in the crude viral lysate used in the EIA (Burke et al., 1987a; Schmidt et al., 1987; Franchini et al., 1987; Blomberg and Klasse, 1988). Thus, the immunoblot test has become an important adjunct in identifying persons who are truly seropositive. False positive tests probably occur in no more than 0.001 percent of sera routinely screened using EIA and immunoblot methods in sequence (Burke et al., 1988). Moreover, band patterns of truly positive individuals can also have epidemiologic and clinical prognostic significance.

Because of the nature of the procedure, however, a significant proportion (up to 15 percent) of individuals without antibody, including EIA negatives, will have antibody to one or more nonmajor viral protein bands on Western blot, or a so-called indeterminate pattern. For this reason alone, the Western blot test should generally not be performed on EIA-negative samples. Conversely, one version of the immunoblot test has recently been licensed for determining whether previously excluded EIA-positive blood donors whose blot is completely negative (i.e., without any visible bands) can be considered unifected and resume donating. However, great care must be exercised in the use and interpretation of the Western blot in evaluating EIA positives. Based on current, extremely stringent criteria, a high proportion of early positive samples are categorized as indeterminate. In screening low-risk groups without notification, as in blood banks, where most positives are actually false-positives, the impact of this problem is slight. But in screening of high-risk groups, where as many as 96 percent of indeterminate blots by current criteria may actually represent positive specimens, the impact of the uncertainty in classifying such specimens is more significant. For the purposes of notification of healthy individuals who meet blood donation criteria, the requirement for anti-bodies to all three gene products—*gag, pol,* and *env*—is appropriate, whereas in sick or late-stage individuals, such criteria are clearly inappropriate, and other approaches are required.

The public health community has responded to these problems in two ways. First, most laboratories engaged in HIV-1 serodiagnosis perform more than one test of a supplemental nature to establish the status of problem specimens. A test commonly used in public health laboratories to confirm positive EIA results and indeterminate Western blot findings is the indirect immunofluorescent antibody test (IFA) performed on infected cell spots on glass slides evaluated microscopically (Gallo et al., 1986; Sandstrome et al., 1985; Lennette et al., 1987; Van der Groen et al., 1987; Levy, 1987). In practice the IFA is usually performed first and the Western blot reserved for nonspecific IFA patterns, but an indeterminate Western blot result can be confirmed with an IFA test in a reverse testing sequence. In some instances, the radioimmunoprecipitation assay (RIPA) can give further valuable information. Many laboratories operating in the reference mode will perform a EIA test of a different manufacturer on referred specimens. As a general principle, the more information of a concordant nature that one can accumulate toward a given interpretation, the greater the confidence in the reliability of that result.

In addition to supplemental testing, criteria have been developed for inter-preting the Western blot in situations other than blood bank screening. In the clin-ical setting, such specifically devised criteria can result in a lower frequency of inde-terminate results. The Western blot may actually establish a positive diagnosis in the absence of bands denoting antibodies to all three major viral proteins. A Con-sensus Conference of Public Health Laboratory Directors has prepared a new set of guidelines for this purpose (Hausler, 1988). These criteria supplement the strin-gent official package insert instructions by relaxing the requirement for anti-*gag* and anti-*pol* antibodies, which frequently decline late in the course of disease (Ped-ersen et al., 1987).

ROLE OF SECOND SPECIMEN

Even with the best combination of tests as described earlier in populations with low seroprevalence, the error rate in testing due to factors external to the test itself—e.g., errors in specimen handling and clerical processing—may introduce false-positive results at a rate approaching the true seroprevalence. A low-risk indi-vidual would have a great likelihood of being falsely labeled positive by such an error. Further testing of the original specimen may be to no avail, but a second specimen can provide definitive results in such situations. Therefore all individuals whose risk, after epidemiologic and clinical evaluation, is not compatible with a positive result should have another blood specimen tested. The military entrance screening program has extensive experience that validates this principle (Burke et al., 1987b). In addition to simple specimen substitution or numerical transposition, an additional feature of HIV-1 testing can produce false-positive results. The tests are so sensitive that they will react with a serum dilution of 1,000 or more in an EIA and as high as 100,000 in the Western blot. A minuscule amout of protein carried over from one specimen to another by splashing or failure to change pipettes between blood tubes can therefore result in a positive test. Every effort should be made to obviate this problem by adherence to meticulous laboratory practice, but repeating the test on a second specimen may provide the greatest reassurance.

HIV-1 ANTIGEN TESTING

Occasionally, early after exposure to HIV-1, infected individuals will have no antibody detectable by any procedure. This situation may persist for several weeks but quite uncommonly for longer than 3 months with currently licensed screening methods. In such circumstances circulating antigen in the form of the p24 protein may be demonstrable in the serum of patients until antibody develops and presumably removes the free antigen from circulation (Allain et al., 1987; Paul et al., 1987; Bowen et al., 1988; Rollag et al., 1987). However, antigenemia probably occurs for only a short period, and antigen testing is therefore relatively insensitive. The exceptional positive result might accelerate the diagnostic process, but a negative result could in no way be taken as reassuring and would still need to be confirmed with standard antibody testing on a follow-up specimen (Cao et al., 1987; Bocker et al., 1987).

There are two situations in which antigen testing will probably assume an increasing role. In the late stages of HIV-1 infection, when intervention with antiviral drugs or prophylactic antimicrobials is indicated, free antigen may appear in the circulation and herald clinical deterioration. At that point there is also an associated decline in the level of specific anti-p24 antibody. Measurements of both antigen and band-specific antibody titers have prospects for use in staging and monitoring infected individuals. Secondly, the status of the infant of an infected mother may sometimes be established earlier with antigen testing than through detection of antibody, the appearance of which may be delayed in some of those children (Borkowsky et al., 1987).

NEW TECHNOLOGY

For the detection of antibody, several new approaches should lead to improved test performance in the future. Major advances are likely to occur in the use of (bio)synthetic antigens for screening and supplemental assays. Several developmental variations of this method based on recombinant DNA technology have been reported (Burke et al., 1987c; Thorn et al., 1987; Dawson et al., 1988), and small synthetic peptides with as few as 10 to 20 amino acids have been shown to perform as well as assays based on whole-virus lysate in the detection of infected individuals (Wang et al., 1986; Smith et al., 1987; Gnann et al., 1987). In theory, with appropriate manufacturing controls, such tests can have improved specificity over lysate-based assays for primary screening, but at this point it is likely that their major role will be in supplemental testing. Although there are exceptions, from the data available, it is clear that epitopes from the HIV-1 envelope glycoprotein alone are sufficient to detect antibody in most cases. Further improvements may combine several virus protein epitopes, either as a mixture in a single test well, as individual proteins in separate wells, or on a strip similar to that used for the immunoblot. The full potential of such assays is under investigation.

Rapid, low-technology tests for use in the physician's office or in the less-developed parts of the world are on the horizon. With sufficient evaluation, such tests could soon be available for antibody detection in various easily applicable formats ranging from latex agglutination to dot-blot techniques (Quinn et al., 1988). The prospects for such tests in improving the efficiency of screening for public health pruposes are good. It is also possible to test eluates from filter paper blood spots with EIA kits and confirmatory procedures. Such methods may have application in low-technology settings or as a method of screening maternal bloods (Farzadegan et al., 1987; Lindhardt et al., 1987; Hoff et al., 1988; Quinn et al., 1988).

Interest in home testing has already been stimulated by premature attempts to market antibody test kits for such purpose. Difficulties with quality control and interpretation are obvious technical barriers to an acceptable commercial product. However, it seems fair to predict that the legal and ethical controversies surrounding the introduction of testing at home and self-testing will most likely eclipse the technical obstacles.

SUMMARY

HIV-1 antibody testing is probably the most accurate blood test ever used. Developed on short notice, the kits have virtually eliminated the risk of transfusion-associated AIDS in the developed world. Supplemental tests have also developed and improved rapidly. Further refinements in those tests, criteria for their interpretation, and application of new technology will push these techniques toward their full potential for public health applications.

REFERENCES

Allain J-P, Laurin Y, Paul DA, et al. (1987): N Engl J Med 317:1114.
Ameglio F, Dolei A, Benedetto A, Sorrentino R, Tanigaki N, Tosi R (1987): J Infect Dis 156:1035.
Barin F, Goudeau A, Romet-Lennone JL, Choutet P, Chassaigne M (1985): Lancet 1:98.
Blomberg J, Klasse PJ (1988): J Clin Microbiol 26:106.
Blocker U, Weinauer F, Gathof G, Eberle J (1987): Lancet 2:1213.
Borkowsky W, Paul D, Bebenroth D, Krasinski K, Moore T, Chandwani S (1987): Lancet 1:1168.
Bowen PA, Lobel SA, Caruana RJ, et al. (1988): Ann Intern Med 108:46.
Burke DS, Brundage JF, Herbold JR, et al., (1987a): N Engl J Med 317:131.
Burke DS, Redfield RR, Putman P, Alexander SS (1987b): J Clin Microbiol 25:81.
Burke DS, Brandt BL, Redfield RR, Lee TH, Thorn RM, Beltz GA, Hung CH (1987c): Ann Intern Med 106:671.

Burke DS, Brundage JF, Redfield RR, Damato JJ, Schable CA, Putman P, Visintine R, Kim HI (1988): N Engl J Med 319:961.

Burkhardt U, Mertens T, Eggers HJ (1987): J Med Virol 23:217.

Cao Y, Valentine F, Hojvat S, et al. (1987): Blood 70:575.

Dawson GJ, Heller JS, Wood CA, et al. (1988): J Infect Dis 157:149.

Farzadegan H, Polis MA, Wolinsky SM, et al. (1988): Ann Intern Med 108:785.

Farzadegan H, Quinn T, Polk BF (1987): J Infect Dis 155:1073.

Fauci AS (1987): Clin Res 35:503.

Fauci AS (1988): Science 239:617.

Franchini G, Robert-Guroff M, Aldovini A, Kan NC, Wong-Staal F (1987): Blood 69:437.

Gallo D, Diggs JL, Shell GR, Dailey PJ, Hoffman MN, Riggers JL (1986): J Clin Microsc 23(6):1049.

Gnann JW, McCormick JB, Mitchell S, Nelson JA, Olstone MBA (1987): Science 237:1346.

Handsfield HH, Wandell M, Goldstein L, Shriver, K (1987): J Clin Microsc 25:879.

Hausler WJ (1988): Infect Control 9:345.

Hoff R, Berardi VP, Weiblen BJ, Mahoney-Trout L, Mitchell ML, Grady GF (1988): N Engl J Med 318:525.

Jackson JB, Balfour HH (1988): Clin Microbiol Rev 1:124.

Lennette ET, Karpatkin S, Levy JA (1987): J Clin Microsc 25:199.

Levy J (1987): JAMA 257:1176.

Lindhardt B, Bygbjerg IC, Ulrich K, Petersen HD, Lausen I, Frederiksen B (1987): J Virol Methods 18:73.

Meyer KB, Pauker SG (1987): N Engl J Med 317:238.

Oldham LJ, Moulsdale HJ, Mortimer PP, RS Tedder, Morgan-Capner P (1987): J Med Virol 21:75.

Paul DA, Falk LA, Kessler HA, et al., (1987): J Med Virol 22:357.

Pederson C, Nielsen CM, Vestergaard BF, Gerstoft J, Krogsgaard K, Neilsen JO (1987): Br Med J 295:567.

Polesky HF (1988): MMWR 36:833.

Quinn TC, Riggin CH, Kline RL, Francis H, Mulanga K, Sension MG, Fauci AS, (1988): Am Med Assoc 260:510.

Rollag H, Eversen SA, Froland SS, Glomstein A (1987): Eur J Haematol 39:353.

Saah AJ, Farzadegan H, Fox R, et al. (1987): J Clin Microbiol 25:1605.

Sandstrom EG, Schooley RT, Ho DD, et al. (1985): Transfusion 20:308.

Schmidt G, Amiraian K, Frey H, Stevens RW, Berns DS (1987): J Clin Microbiol 25:1993.

Smith RS, Naso RB, Rosen J, et al. (1987): J Clin Microsc 25:1498.

Thorn RM, Beltz GA, Hung CH, et al. (1987): J Infect Dis 156:1207.

Van de Perre P, Nzaramba D, Allen S, Riggin CH, Sprecher-Goldberger S, Butzler J-P (1988): J Clin Microsc 26:552.

Van der Groen G, Vercauteren G, Piot P (1987): J Virol Metholds 17:35.

Wang JJG, Steel S, Wisniewolski R, Wang CY (1986): Proc Natl Acad Sci USA 83:6159.

Ward JW, Holmberg SD, Allen JR, et al. (1988): N Engl J Med 318:473.

Wolinsky S, Rinaldo C, Farzadegan H, et al. (1988): Fourth International Conference on Aids, Stockholm, Sweden June 12–16, Abst. 1099.

4

The Immune System: Clinical Manifestations

PAUL ROGERS AND HENRY MASUR

Since the isolation of the human immunodeficiency virus (HIV-1) and the development of accurate serologic tests, clinical studies have demonstrated that HIV-1 infection is associated with a much broader spectrum of clinical manifestations than those included in the Centers for Disease Control's original definition of AIDS (CDC, 1986a, 1987). At the time of infection with HIV-1, individuals may be completely asymptomatic or they may develop transient signs and symptoms that resolve spontaneously, leaving the individual asymptomatic for months to years. Patients may eventually develop a wide variety of non-life-threatening manifestations such as lymphadenopathy, oral candidiasis, or herpes zoster. Ultimately, these individuals develop the opportunistic infections or neoplasms that define the acquired immunodeficiency syndrome. It is not currently understood why the latency period from infection to onset of AIDS varies so greatly from patient to patient or why various clinical manifestations develop in certain patients but not in others.

As further studies are completed over the next several years, our understanding of this spectrum will undoubtedly enlarge. The current CDC classification of HIV-1 infected patients, summarized in Table 4.1, is intended to be used for reporting and surveillance, epidemiologic studies, and public health policy (CDC 1986a; 1987). Each category does not clearly correlate with a predictable and uniform prognosis for all included patients.

ACUTE RETROVIRAL INFECTION

Following the report of an acute febrile illness and seroconversion in a health care worker who sustained a needle-stick injury, an acute mononucleosislike illness with seroconversion was described in 11 previously healthy HIV-1-negative individuals (Cooper et al., 1985). Patients complained of fever, sweats, lethargy, muscle ache, headache and sore throat. Physical examination often revealed a macular erythematous truncal rash, urticaria, adenopathy, and splenomegaly. Patients were noted to have significant lymphopenia and normal $CD4^+$ cell counts. With resolution of the illness, the number of $CD8^+$ cells were noted to increase. Ho et al. (1985)

Table 4.1. Summary of Classification of Clinical Conditions Due to HIV-1

Group	Clinical Condition
I	Acute infection—mononucleosislike syndrome (see Table 4.2)
II	Asymptomatic infection
III	Persistent generalized lymphadenopathy—presence of enlarged (≥ 1 cm) lymph node in each of two or more noncontiguous sites outside the inguinal region for at least 3 months
IV	Other disease (AIDS)—secondary infectious diseases, cancers, and other conditions

1. Without laboratory evidence regarding HIV-1 infection and in the absence of immunosuppressive chemotherapy, certain lymphoreticular neoplasms, or congenital immunodeficiency

   a. Candidiasis in esophagus or respiratory tract
   b. Cryptococcosis, extrapulmonary
   c. Cryptosporidiosis with diarrhea
   d. Cytomegalovirus outside the lymphoreticular system
   e. Herpes simplex virus, mucocutaneous or in esophagus or respiratory tract
   f. Kaposi's sarcoma in person < 60 years of age
   g. Primary lymphoma of the brain in person < 60 years of age
   h. Lymphoid interstitial pneumonia in a child
   i. Disseminated, *Mycobacterium avium* or *M. kansasii* infection
   j. *Pneumocystis carinii* pneumonia
   k. Progressive multifocal leukoencephalopathy
   l. Toxoplasmosis of the brain after infancy

2. With laboratory evidence of HIV-1 infection

   a. Multiple or recurrent systemic or deep tissue pyogenic bacterial infections in a child
   b. Disseminated coccidiodomycosis
   c. CNS manifestations suggesting encephalopathy or dementia
   d. Disseminated histoplasmosis
   e. Isosporiasis
   f. Kaposi's sarcoma at any age
   g. Primary lymphoma of the brain at any age
   h. Other specific non-Hodgkin's lymphoma
   i. Disseminated nontuberculous mycobacterial infection
   j. Extrapulmonary disease with *M. tuberculosis*
   k. Nontyphoid *Salmonella* septicemia
   l. Wasting syndrome (unexplained weight loss plus either chronic diarrhea or chronic weakness and fever)

Source: CDC, 1986a, 1987.

reported three similar patients with an acute febrile illness occurring approximately 6 weeks after an exposure. In addition to the febrile illness, two patients developed a lymphocytic meningitis with CSF showing a lymphocytosis (20 and 28 cells per milliliter), slight increase in protein, and normal glucose. CSF cultures were negative for bacteria, mycobacteria, and fungi. One of the patient's CSF viral cultures were positive for HIV-1, and all three had positive HIV-1 blood cultures. Symptoms usually lasted 2 to 3 weeks and resolved with supportive care. The time of seroconversion was documented to be 8 to 12 weeks following the presumed exposure. How many patients fail to convert their antibody titers during the initial 8 to 12 weeks using the current EIA technique is not known, nor is it clear how many EIA-negative individuals might be positive by other techniques such as the antigen capture assay, Western blot, or polymerase chain reaction. These techniques and further clinical observations (Table 4.2) (Tindall, et al., 1988) are continuing to broaden the understanding of the syndrome of acute HIV-1 infection.

Table 4.2. Symptoms of Acute Illness Associated with
Active HIV-1 Infection[a]

Symptom	No. Reporting	Percent
Fever	30	77
Lethargy/malaise	26	67
Sore throat	22	56
Loss of appetite	22	56
Muscle ache	22	56
Headache	19	49
Joint ache/pain	19	49
Weight loss	18	46
Swollen lymph nodes	17	44
Other	6–15	15–39

[a]Symptoms occurred in the frequencies shown in 39 homosexual men who seroconverted during a 2-year period.
Source: Tindall et al., (1988).

In addition to those patients described above who became symptomatic, a
large number of antibody-positive individuals never manifested any recognized
signs or symptoms of an acute febrile illness. These individuals were clearly often
unaware of their antibody status and their potential infectivity and are thus a public
health concern in terms of possible transmissibility during sexual contacts or when
donating biologic products such as blood or sperm.

Prospective studies of asymptomatic homosexual males have helped to define
the clinical course of healthy seropositive patients. Of 170 individuals studied in
one investigation, 33 were seropositive on admission. From 1982 to 1985, 13 (40
percent) remained asymptomatic, 16 (48 percent) progressed to persistent generalized lymphadenopathy, and 4 (12 percent) developed AIDS (Weber et al., 1986).
Data from one prospective cohort study in San Francisco support these observations: 9% of their recently infected patients followed for 4 years and 38% followed
for 8 years developed AIDS (Hessol et al., 1988). A second, multicenter cohort
study has estimated that approximately 8% of seroconverters developed AIDS at
the end of 3 years of follow-up (Phair et al., 1988). Although their value has not
been defined precisely, a low absolute CD4[+] lymphocyte count or rapid change in
count may predict those patients who will ultimately develop AIDS (Lane et al.,
1985; Goedert et al., 1987; Polk et al., 1987; Kaslow et al., 1987; Murray et al., 1985;
Melbye et al., 1986). Other laboratory and clinical features such as elevated CD8[+]
lymphocyte count, decreased hemoglobin, oral candidiasis, herpes zoster, weight
loss, and chronic fever are also relatively helpful for predicting groups of patients
likely to develop AIDS. Decreased ability to generate gamma interferon in vitro
also correlates with likelihood of progressing to AIDS (Murray et al., 1985).

HIV-1-RELATED SYNDROMES

Months to years after exposure to the HIV-1, some patients will develop clinical
manifestations that appear to be epidemiologically related to the virus but that do

not meet the original or the revised CDC definition of AIDS. These manifestations are strongly linked to HIV-1 infection. Some of these manifestations appear to be a direct consequence of HIV-1 infection, some are consequences of immunologically mediated processes such as antigen–antibody complex deposition, and some are a result of HIV-1-induced immunosuppression. The occurrence of some of these syndromes is predictive of the relatively rapid development of AIDS; the prognostic importance of other syndromes is less well defined (Goedert et al., 1987; Polk et al., 1987; Kaslow et al., 1987; Murray et al., 1985; Melbye et al., 1986; Klein et al., 1984; Greenspan et al., 1985).

A common HIV-1-related condition whose presence appears to be particularly predicitive of the development of AIDS is oral candidiasis. Thrush in a nondiabetic individual without a history of recent antibiotic or corticosteroid therapy should suggest underlying immunosuppression. In one series of 18 patients presenting for evaluation of unexplained candida stomatitis, 50 percent developed AIDS within 3 months of follow-up (Klein et al., 1984).

Hairy leukoplakia on the tongue is also associated with rapid development of AIDS. The slightly raised, poorly demarcated lesion has a corrugated or "hairy" surface. The lesion is usually asymptomatic, and, unlike oral candida, it is not able to be rubbed off the mucosal surface. Papilloma and Epstein-Barr viruses have been found within the lesion and are presumed to be related to its occurrence (Greenspan et al., 1985). This entity causes no direct morbidity for the patient, but it has clear prognostic implications.

Dermatomal and disseminated herpes zoster have been recognized with increased frequency in patients who have ultimately developed an opportunistic infection or neoplasm. The association between herpes zoster and the prompt development of AIDS is not as strong as the association between oral candidiasis or hairy leukoplakia and AIDS. Herpes zoster is usually associated with localized dermatomal disease in HIV-1-infected patients. Visceral dissemination is very unusual. Although intravenous acyclovir appears to produce earlier crusting of lesions and cessation of viral shedding, controlled trials with antiviral therapy have not been carried out on patients with AIDS. Thus, the necessity for using acyclovir to promote earlier healing or to prevent dissemination or postherpetic neuralgia is unclear (Kovacs and Masur, 1985).

A number of constitutional signs and symptoms including weight loss, fever, and diarrhea are commonly seen at some point during the course of HIV-1 infection. Despite a thorough evaluation, infectious etiologies for these complaints may not be found. Alternatively, cytomegalovirus, Epstein-Barr virus, and/or *Mycobacterium avium-intracellulare* (MAI) may be cultured from the patient, but their causative relationship to the fever and weight loss is unclear. Although many of these patients progress to AIDS, a number expire before fulfilling the criteria for AIDS (Murray et al., 1985). This emphasizes the observation that arbitrary categorization of HIV-1-infected patients into AIDS or the so-called AIDS-related complex may not be as clinically helpful as assessing a patient's prognosis based on immunologic status and specific clinical manifestations.

Lymphadenopathy is a common finding on physical examination of HIV-1-positive, asymptomatic patients. As mentioned previously, adenopathy can be observed during acute HIV-1 infection; however, these enlarged nodes may resolve, then reappear later in the course of HIV-1 infection, or they may persist for months or years. To fulfill the CDC criteria for persistent generalized lymphadenopathy (PGL), lymph nodes 1.0 cm in diameter or greater must be present in at least two extrainguinal sites for at least 3 months (CDC, 1986a). Patients at all stages of HIV-1 infection frequently have lymphadenopathy that may or may not fit this surveillance definition. Other etiologic agents including toxoplasmosis, CMV, EBV, TB, MAI, and syphilis as well as neoplasms including Kaposi's sarcoma and lymphoma should be excluded (CDC, 1982; Abrams, 1986; Metroka et al., 1983; Mathur-Wagh et al., 1984; Fishbein et al., 1985). Needle or surgical biopsy of nodes in asymptomatic patients is not clinically indicated in most cases unless there is a large single node or a rapidly enlarging node (Abrams, 1986). Biopsy characteristically shows marked follicular hyperplasia, although follicular involution or a mixed pattern may occasionally be seen (Abrams, 1986; Metroka et al., 1983; Mathur-Wagh et al., 1984; Fishbein et al., 1985).

The prognosis for PGL remains unclear, although it is probably no different from that for seropositive patients without PGL. In a large cross-sectional investigation, seropositive homosexual men with and without PGL had similar $CD4^+$ cell counts, and unpublished data on those two groups show no difference in prognosis (R. Kaslow, personal communication). Prospective studies have found that up to 30 percent of unselected patients develop signs and symptoms fulfilling the CDC criteria for AIDS in the follow-up time elapsed (Mathur-Wagh et al., 1984). The exact figure averages 3 to 5 percent per year for most cases and depends on the length of follow-up and the precise entry criteria of the study (i.e., symptomatic or asymptomatic, stable for many months or recently diagnosed, etc.). Recent data suggest that, as appears to be true of seropositive individuals in general, a low number of $CD4^+$ cells and a depressed response to pokeweed mitogen may help to identify those PGL patients at highest risk for symptoms or progression (Kaslow et al., 1987; Fishbein et al., 1985). Of 78 homosexual males with PGL in one study, 75 (96 percent) were antibody-positive. All five patients who developed AIDS in the 5- to 25-month follow-up period had lower numbers of $CD4^+$ cells and depressed response to pokeweed mitogen on admission to the study.

Some neurologic diseases (e.g. dementia, myelopathy, and polyneuropathy) may occur in the absence of a concurrent opportunistic infection or neoplasm and are presumed to be due to infection with HIV-1 (CDC, 1987) (see Chapter 5).

Pulmonary or extrapulmonary *Mycobacterium tuberculosis* occurs in HIV-1-infected individuals, especially IV drug abusers and patients from developing countries (Sunderam et al., 1986; Louie et al., 1986; Barnes and Arvalo, 1987; CDC 1986b; Pitchenik and Rubinson, 1985). Fourteen patients in one series who presented primarily with extrapulmonary or disseminated disease developed AIDS within 4 to 21 months. As opposed to MAI, this bacillus is usually sensitive to standard antituberculosis medications (CDC, 1986b).

Abnormal hematologic studies are common, and many HIV-1-infected patients present with lymphopenia, anemia, or thrombocytopenia. Unexplained thrombocytopenia has been presumed to have an autoimmune basis with peripheral destruction. Bone marrow exam has revealed increased stores of megakaryocytes. The majority of patients respond to systemic corticosteroids (a therapy associated with considerable risk in HIV-1-infected patients), although a few have required splenectomy, and some remain thrombocytopenic despite all therapeutic efforts (Morris et al., 1982).

Finally, there have been reports of proteinuria, up to 10 g/day, and rapidly progressive azotemia among HIV-1-positive patients (Sreepada Rao et al., 1984). The majority of these patients are intravenous drug abusers. Some of these patients ultimately require dialysis. Biopsy specimens reveal focal and segmental glomerulosclerosis with intraglomerular deposition of IgM and C3. The etiology of this lesion and the rapid deterioration in renal function is unknown.

THE ACQUIRED IMMUNODEFICIENCY SYNDROME

A Spectrum of Illness

As a syndrome, AIDS is characterized by a number of opportunistic infections and neoplasms whose development appears to represent the more severe end of the spectrum of HIV-1-related disease. Although neoplasms are a common manifestation of AIDS, they cause less than 7 percent of deaths in most series. Opportunistic infections, on the other hand, are responsible for 88 percent of patient mortality according to several autopsy series (Table 4.3) (Moskowitz et al., 1985; Niedt and Schinella, 1985; Welch et al., 1984). The specific opportunistic infections are a function of the patient's degree of immunosuppression and his history of exposures. Thus patients from Africa or southern California may develop somewhat different infectious processes from patients in New York City. The respiratory tract and the central nervous system are most often involved in life-threatening illnesses (Moskowitz et al., 1985; Niedt and Schinella, 1985; Welch et al., 1984; Murray et al., 1984; Hopewell and Luce, 1985).

Table 4.3. Immediate Cause of Death in 118 Autopsied AIDS Patients

Cause of Death	No.	Percent
Infections		
CMV infection	34	31%
Pneumocystis carinii pneumonia	26	24
Toxoplasmosis	17	15
Cryptococcosis	7	6
Bacterial Infections	5	5
Mycobacterium avium-intracellulare	1	1
Multiple and other infections	7	6
Total	97	88
Malignancies		
Kaposi's sarcoma	6	5
Lymphoma	2	2
Total	8	7
Other	5	5

Source: Moskowitz et al., and Niedt and Schinella (1985).

Respiratory Tract Disease

While a number of authors suggest that the incidence of pulmonary involvement in persons with AIDS is between 41 and 50 percent (Murray et al., 1984; Hopewell and Luce, 1985; Stover et al., 1985), the CDC estimates that approximately 65 percent of patients present with *Pneumocystis carinii* pneumonia. Undoubtedly, a higher fraction of patients (probably 85 to 90 percent) ultimately develop *Pneumocystis carinii* pneumonia or pulmonary dysfunction due to other infectious or neoplastic processes. The most common causes of pneumonitis among AIDS patients at the National Institutes of Health and the frequency of their occurrence are listed in Table 4.4 (unpublished data).

Pneumocystis carinii is the most common identified cause of serious pulmonary dysfunction in AIDS patients, accounting for 40 percent of the pneumonias seen at the NIH. An interesting aspect of the illness is the way in which it differs epidemiologically and clinically from PCP in patients with malignant neoplasms or organ transplants (Table 4.5) (Kovacs et al., 1984). The CDC estimated an annual attack rate for *Pneumocystis carinii* pneumonia (1968–1970) of 0.01 to 1.1 percent for non-AIDS patients, as compared with the observed attack rate of at least 35 percent per year in patients with AIDS. Both patient groups present with a nonproductive cough and dyspnea. Non-AIDS patients, however, characteristically have an acute onset of symptoms which promptly bring them to medical attention, usually within 5 days. Patients usually have moderate to severe hypoxemia and abnormal chest X-ray. AIDS patients, in comparison, often have an insidious onset with a mean of 28 days to diagnosis. Subjectively, they are usually not as ill and have less tachypnea, milder hypoxemia, and less impressive chest X-rays at the time of diagnosis despite their longer symptomatic history (Kovacs et al., 1984).

Diagnosis of *Pneumocystis carinii* pneumonia requires demonstration of the organism in secretions or tissue specimens. In a number of HIV-1-infected patients, this can be accomplished by Giemsa stain of expectorated sputum (Pitchenik et al.,

Table 4.4. Etiology of 232 Episodes of Pneumonitis in 174 AIDS Patients at National Institutes of Health 1982–1987, Determined by Bronchoscopy or Open Lung Biopsy

Etiology	Percent of Episodes
Pneumocystis ($N = 94$)	40.5
Nonspecific Pneumonitis ($N = 75$)	32.3
CMV ($N = 7$)	3.0
Mycobacterium avium–intracellulare ($N = 4$)	1.7
Kaposi's sarcoma ($N = 12$)	5.2
Bacteria ($N = 6$)	2.6
Cryptococcus ($N = 3$)	1.3
Legionella ($N = 1$)	<1.0
Lymphoma ($N = 1$)	<1.0
No diagnosis ($N = 24$) (negative lavage only or normal lung)	10.3

Table 4.5. *Pneumocystis carinii* Pneumonia: Comparison of Features in Patients with AIDS and Patients with Other Immunodeficiency Diseases

	AIDS	Non-AIDS
Incidence	35 + %	0.01–1.1%
Specific symptoms	Same	Same
Duration of symptoms	28 days	5 days
Initial respiratory rate	23/min	30/min
Initial P_aO_2 room air	69 mm Hg	52 mm Hg
Initial chest radiograph	Frequently normal or minimally abnormal	Usually abnormal
Survival per episode	57%	50%
Adverse reactions to trimethoprim-sulfamethoxazole	65%	12%
Adverse reactions to pentamidine	47%	57%
Relapse/reinfection	20%	0% (adults) 11% (children)

Source: Kovacs et al. (1984).

1986; Kovacs et al., 1988). Others will require bronchoalveolar lavage and transbronchial biopsy. When performed in patients with normal renal function, platelet counts greater than 50,000/mm³, prothrombin time less than 15 sec, and a pO₂ of at least 100 torr on 100 percent FI0₂, the morbidity and mortality of biopsy are very low. If a contraindication to biopsy exists, lavage is safe and has been shown to have a sensitivity of at least 89 percent (Ognibene et al., 1984). If an initial bronchoscopy is nondiagnostic, the procedure should usually be repeated prior to open lung biopsy (Murray et al., 1984). An open biopsy is almost never necessary to document *Pneumocystis carinii* pneumonia if bronchoscopy can be adequately performed. Open lung biopsy may be necessary, however, to document other entities such as Kaposi's sarcoma of the lung and perhaps CMV or fungal pneumonitis.

Symptomatic patients with a normal chest X-ray should undergo evaluation of induced sputum. If this is negative, bronchoalveolar lavage and transbronchial biopsy should be performed. A positive gallium scan has proved to be an insensitive and nonspecific indicator of the presence of *Pneumocystis* (Hopewell and Luce, 1985). Gallium scan and pulmonary function testing are rarely helpful owing to their incomplete sensitivity, incomplete specificity, and cost.

Therapy for *Pneumocystis carinii* pneumonia has conventionally been intravenous trimethoprim-sulfamethoxazole (TMP/S) or pentamidine isethionate. At standard doses, AIDS patients have been noted to have a much higher frequency of adverse side effects, 65 percent, as opposed to 12 percent in non-AIDS patients (Kovacs et al., 1984). Lower doses of TMP/S may be equally effective but less toxic. A pruritic, erythematous, maculopapular rash is the commonest of these reactions, characteristically occurring 8 to 10 days after institution of therapy. Other complications include fever, neutropenia, thrombocytopenia, and a two- to threefold increase in transaminases. Pentamidine, which should be given by IV rather than IM route, is associated with substantial toxicity as well, including neutropenia, renal dysfunction, pancreatitis, and hypoglycemia (Small et al., 1985; Gordin et al., 1984; Wharton et al., 1986).

Aerosolized pentamidine (Montgomery et al., 1987), dapsone alone or in combination with trimethorprim (Leoung et al., 1986), difluoromethylornithine (Allegra et al.,1987a,b), and trimetrexate (Shelhamer et al., 1984) offer the prospect of more effective or better-tolerated regimens in the near future. The efficacy and toxicity of these agents have not been compared to conventional agents in published controlled studies.

Response to TMP/S or pentamidine is approximately 55 to 80 percent in both AIDS and non-AIDS patients, although resolution of fever, improvement in arterial blood gases, and clearing of infiltrates on chest X-ray occur much slower in AIDS patients (Kovacs et al., 1984). Prognosis improves when therapy is instituted early in the course of the pneumonia, before symptoms and signs are far advanced (Brenner et al., 1987). Survival for AIDS patients whose initial episode of *Pneumocystis carinii* pneumonia is recognized and treated early is probably 90 percent. *Pneumocystitis* organisms are more likely to be present in lavage or biopsy specimens after 14 to 21 days of therapy in AIDS patients than in non-AIDS patients. The clinical significance of these cysts is unclear.

However, as the underlying immunodeficiency persists and as there is a 20 percent recurrence rate of *Pneumocystis* pneumonia (Shelhamer et al., 1984), a number of investigators are suggesting prophylactic therapy. TMP/S has been shown to be effective prophylaxis (Fischl et al., 1988). Recent reports of small trials with pyrimethamine-sulfadoxine (Fansidar) suggest this drug is better-tolerated and quite effective. Twenty-eight (84 percent) of 33 patients were able to tolerate the drug, and none of the 28 patients developed an episode of PCP when followed for 5 to 68 weeks (Madoff et al., 1986). Other approaches using monthly systemic pentamidine (Karoffa et al., 1986), aerosolized pentamidine, or trimetrexate are under consideration (Montgomery et al., 1987). Aerosolized pentamidine is a popular approach for therapy and prophylaxis of *Pneumocystis* pneumonia; its use will likely become widespread if and when controlled studies prove its efficacy and safety using a well-defined delivery system.

Several recent reports have described a group of AIDS patients with clinical and radiographic features of pulmonary dysfunction similar to *Pneumocystis carinii* pneumonia. Histologic examination of lung tissue reveals varying degrees of edema, increased numbers of macrophages and lymphocytes, and the absence of identifiable pathogens or tumor on stain or culture. This disease, known as idiopathic interstitial pneumonitis, tends to stabilize or resolve without specific therapy. The pathogenesis of this syndrome is unclear. It is important to recognize this syndrome, because it is usually self-limited, and empiric TMP/S therapy in this setting produces adverse effects without likelihood of benefit (Suffredini et al., 1987).

Other, less common causes of pneumonitis in patients with AIDS include cytomegalovirus, fungi including cryptococci, and MAI and Kaposi's sarcoma. While CMV and MAI have been cultured from 17 percent of patients with pneumonia, it is not clear that either was the etiologic agent. At NIH, diagnosis of CMV pneumonitis is based on the identification of inclusion bodies on histologic examination. The significance of a positive culture alone for CMV or the presence of antigen in a cytospin of lavage fluid without histologic evidence of inclusion bodies is unclear. When this criterion is adhered to, the incidence of CMV pneumonitis has been approximately 3 percent (unpublished data). Pathology varies from minimal inflammatory response to large areas of necrosis, alveolar septal thickening, and hemorrhage. Recent trials with gancyclovir have yielded promising results, and further trials are warranted (Masur et al., 1986, Laskin et al., 1987).

MAI is also commonly cultured, not only from the lung, but from the blood, bone marrow, liver, spleen, and lymph nodes (Hawkins et al., 1986; O'Brien et al., 1985). The organism is characteristically resistant to conventional antituberculous drugs (O'Brien et al., 1985; Masur et al., 1987). Patients who have acid-fast bacteria on histologic specimen (approximately 3 percent of patients evaluated for pneumonia at the NIH) (unpublished data) should be started on therapy for *Mycobacterium tuberculosis* until the identity of the mycobacterium is established. Drug therapy for MAI has not been shown to be effective; two experimental drugs, ansamycin and clofazamine, have been tried, with disappointing initial results (Masur et al., 1987).

In addition to the numerous opportunistic infections that may develop in AIDS patients, it is important to remember that patients may present with common community-acquired pneumonias (Polsky et al., 1986). In adults, common bacterial pathogens such as *Streptococcus pneumoniae* and *Hemophilus influenzae* also occur with increased frequency, although not to the degree recognized in pediatric AIDS (Polsky et al., 1986).

When an AIDS patient initially presents with pneumonitis, if the individual is felt to be rapidly deteriorating, empiric TMP/S is recommended. Early sputum assessment or bronchoscopy to guide therapy in AIDS patients is necessary and prudent considering that many patients will not have *Pneumocystis,* that there are a number of other opportunistic infections responsive to other drugs, that many patients have a nonspecific pneumonitis that requires no therapy, and that the drug usually given empirically, TMP/S, is associated with a number of toxicities.

Central Nervous System

Neurologic manifestations of HIV-1 infection are discussed in detail in Chapter 5, but certain secondary manifestations deserve particular mention in the context of the major clinical expressions of immunodeficiency. *Cryptococcus neoformans* accounts for approximately 2 to 6 percent of opportunistic infections in AIDS patients. It is the fourth most commonly recognized life-threatening infection in AIDS patients (Kovacs et al., 1985a; Zuger et al., 1986). Although extraneural disease occurs, the central nervous system is the most frequently involved organ system (Kovacs et al., 1985a; Zuger et al., 1986; Rico and Penneys, 1985; Borton and Wintroub, 1984; Gal et al., 1986; Ricciardi et al., 1986). Patients usually present with meningitis or meningoencephalitis with complaints of headache, nausea, vomiting, and photophobia. Occasional patients may be asymptomatic. Rarely, patients present with focal neurologic deficits, seizures, or obtundation, in which case a cranial CAT scan is required to rule out mass lesions prior to performing a lumbar puncture. Serum cryptococcal antigen is almost always positive in patients with CNS involvement, though seronegative patients have been reported (Kovacs et al., 1985a; Zuger et al., 1986; Rico and Penneys, 1985; Borton and Wintraub, 1984; Gal et al., 1986; Ricciardi et al., 1986).

Although cerebrospinal fluid is characteristically associated with increased protein, decreased glucose concentration, leukocytosis, and a positive India ink preparation, these parameters may on occasion be normal. The most sensitive means of diagnosis are CSF cryptococcal antigen and culture of the fluid (Kovacs et al., 1985a; Zuger et al., 1986). Treatment has included amphotericin B and flucytosine. Adverse reactions to amphotericin B include fever, chills, and renal dysfunction, which rarely necessitates discontinuation. Flucytosine, however, is associated with marrow suppression and may need to be withheld until leukocyte counts return to baseline or are discontinued. Patients need to be maintained on a chronic suppressive regimen for life to avoid relapses. Fluconazole, a new imidazole drug, shows considerable promise for acute therapy or chronic maintenance. Further trials are needed to define its efficacy and safety compared to conventional agents.

Cerebral toxoplasmosis is the commonest cause of focal brain lesions, being present in 13 percent of all AIDS cases in one series of postmortem examinations. Other focal lesions in the differential diagnosis include primary CNS lymphoma which occurred in 6 percent, progressive multifocal leukoencephalopathy in 2 percent, fungal abscesses (due to candida, aspergillus, and cryptococcus) in 3 percent, and occasional cases of tuberculomas (Navia et al., 1986; Wanke et al., 1987; Wong et al., 1984; Luft et al., 1983, 1984).

Toxoplasma gondii infection usually presents as CNS disease rather than as dissemination in patients with AIDS. The vast majority of patients (90 percent) present with focal neurologic signs including seizures, hemiparesis, and aphasia. On occasion, subtle focal findings are overshadowed by encephalopathy, in which case patients present with cognitive impairment, generalized confusion, and obtundation that progresses to coma (Navia et al., 1986; Wanke et al., 1987; Wong et al., 1984; Luft et al., 1983, 1984).

The diagnosis of *T. gondii* requires the demonstration of organisms (preferably trophozoites) within brain tissue. Other tests are less sensitive and not as specific. In particular, the serologic diagnosis is unreliable, since a diagnostic increase in IgM and IgG is rarely seen (Naot and Remington, 1980). A computerized tomographic (CT) scan that shows characteristic single or multiple peripheral ring-enhancing lesions after double dose contrast is very suggestive of toxoplasmosis but is not completely specific. Solid enhancing or nonenhancing lesions have also been reported (Wanke et al., 1987; Wong et al., 1984). Some patients with early symptomatic disease have had normal CT scan on initial examination. If the lesion is characteristic or if it is not easily accessible to biopsy, an empiric trial of pyrimethamine and sulfadiazine is appropriate.

Those patients who fail to improve clinically or radiographically in 14 to 21 days or those patients presenting with atypical lesions that are easily accessible should undergo biopsy. Biopsy specimens typically reveal acute and chronic inflammation. Free clusters of trophozoites may be seen at the periphery of the lesion. For patients unable to tolerate pyrimethamine and sulfadiazine, there are no clearly effective options. Clindamycin alone, pyrimethamine alone, and clindamycin plus pyrimethamine have infrequently been effective (Navia et al., 1986;

Wanke et al., 1987; Wong et al., 1984; Luft et al., 1983, 1984; Naot and Remington, 1980; Haverkos, 1987, Allegra et al., 1987a,b; Araujo and Remington, 1974; Leport et al., 1986; Norrby et al., 1975). Trimetrexate is a new agent that has shown promise in vitro, but responses have not been sustained (Allegra et al., 1987a).

Primary CNS lymphoma occurs so rarely in non-HIV-1-infected patients (0.3 to 2.0 percent of all newly diagnosed lymphomas) that diagnosis of such a tumor strongly suggests AIDS. Presenting symptoms include behavior and personality changes, headache, lethargy, and a change in cognitive ability. The CT scan shows single or multiple low-density lesions that usually enhance uniformly with contrast. Edema and shift in midline structures may also be apparent. Pathologic evaluation reveals the majority of tumors to be immunoblastic sarcomas and, less frequently, plasmacytoid lymphocytic lymphomas. Despite resection, radiation, and chemotherapy, survival is usually quite short (Gill et al., 1985).

The papovavirus, specifically JC or SV40, is responsible for progressive multifocal leukoencephalopathy (PML). Patients present with mental status changes, blindness, aphasia, hemiparesis, and ataxia which progress slowly until death. CT scan characteristically shows multiple hypodense areas in the cerebral white matter without enhancement or evidence of mass effect. In addition, radiographic findings are usually less remarkable than clinical findings. If the CT scan is characteristic or if empiric therapy for toxoplasmosis fails, PML should be considered. Histologic specimens show focal areas of demyelinization, enlarged oligodendrocytes with intranuclear inclusions, and minimal surrounding inflammatory cells. Special immunofluorescent stains for JC or SV40 are diagnostic. Although initial reports suggested some efficacy of cytosine arabinoside, it now appears there is no effective therapy for PML (Krupp et al., 1985).

Three percent of all CNS lesions are due to fungal abscesses. These patients present with complaints, physical findings, and CT scans that are similar to those of other patients with focal CNS disease. Diagnosis via biopsy is necessary, as specific therapy is required for these potentially treatable lesions.

Retinochoroiditis

Ocular lesions are very common in HIV-1-infected patients; 60 percent of patients in one series had one or more abnormalities. The commonest finding is cotton wool spots, occurring in 50 percent of patients. These spots have no known clinical implications (Holland et al., 1983). Cytomegalovirus retinitis usually presents as a reduction in visual acuity or visual fields or as floaters. Grossly, the retina shows yellow-white hemorrhagic lesions with irregular borders; microscopically, intranuclear inclusion bodies are evident within the necrotic area (Holland et al., 1983, Bachman et al., 1982). Lesions can progress quite rapidly. Vidarabine, acyclovir, and interferon have proved ineffective as chemotherapy. Recent trials with gancyclovir have been encouraging (Masur et al., 1986; Collaborative DHPG Treatment Study Group, 1986) and that drug may soon be in wider use.

Toxoplasma gondii has also been shown to be a rare cause of necrotizing retinochoroiditis in AIDS patients (Parke and Font, 1986). Vitreous cultures and retinal biopsy may be necessary to establish the diagnosis. Treatment with pyrimethamine and sulfadiazine has led to rapid improvement in several cases.

Table 4.6. Intestinal Infections Seen in Patients with AIDS and Patients at High Risk for AIDS

Esophagitis	Proctocolitis
Candida albicans	*Campylobacter* spp.
Herpes simplex virus	*Shigella* spp.
Cytomegalovirus	*Salmonella* spp.
	Entamoeba histolytica
	Clostridium difficile
Enteritis	*Chlamydia trachomatis* (LGV serovars)
Giardia lamblia	Cytomegalovirus
Cryptosporidium spp.	Proctitis
Microsporidia spp.	*Neisseria gonorrheae*
Isospora belli	Herpes simplex virus
Stronglyloides stercoralis	*Chlamydia trachomatis* (non-LGV serovars)
Myobacterium avium-intracellulare	*Treponema pallidum*
Cytomegalovirus	Cytomegalovirus

Gastrointestinal Disease

Gastrointestinal manifestations are common among AIDS patients and can be severely disabling and debilitating (Table 4.6) (Quinn, 1985; Smith et al., 1988). As mentioned earlier, oral candidiasis is a very common occurrence in HIV-1-infected patients (Klein et al., 1984), but *Candida* may affect other regions of the gastrointestinal tract as well. Hairy leukoplakia, associated with EBV and papilloma virus infection, also occurs in HIV-1-infected patients, sometimes as the initial clinical manifestation. It must be distinguished from oral candidiasis by appropriate smears (Greenspan et al., 1985).

Opportunistic infections and neoplasms involving the esophagus usually present as dysphagia or odynophagia. Endoscopy with biopsy and culture is necessary for specific diagnosis. Esophageal candidiasis may produce a flat superficial exudate or a heaped-up "cottage cheese" lesion with deep ulcerations. Biopsy may reveal hyphal invasion of the mucosa and submucosa. Esophagitis can be treated with topical nystatin or miconazole, but ketoconazole is probably preferable. In more severe cases, treatment with low-dose amphotericin B is necessary. Relapses after cessation of therapy are common, and chronic suppressive therapy may thus be necessary.

Intranuclear inclusion bodies and positive cultures are needed for diagnosis of CMV esophagitis (Quinn, 1985). Gancyclovir has been used in several cases of CMV esophagitis with good preliminary results (Smith et al., 1988). The diagnosis of herpes simplex virus esophagitis is based on histopathologic specimens with multinucleate grant cells, intranuclear inclusions, and a positive culture. Excellent results have been obtained by treating with intravenous acyclovir.

Enteric organisms presenting as diarrhea is common among AIDS patients. Pathogenic organisms can often be identified. Treatment of these pathogens can sometimes result in symptomatic improvement (Smith et al., 1988). Potential causes are listed in Table 4.6. Therapy must often be for symptoms if drugs directed at specific pathogens do not cure the disease.

Cryptosporidium spp. are often isolated from the stool of AIDS patients with moderate to severe diarrhea. This protozoan is found in close association with the microvillus border of intestinal epithelia. There is minimal injury to the mucosa. In immunocompetent hosts, the organism is responsible for a self-limited episode of watery diarrhea, nausea, and abdominal pain. In AIDS patients, cryptosporidiosis often causes a chronic, voluminous diarrhea, with up to 15 L of fluid diarrhea per day. Weight loss at presentation may exceed 9 kg (Soave et al., 1984). Diagnosis is based on detection of the organism by Giemsa stain or modified acid-fast stain of the stool (Ma and Soave, 1983). There is no specific therapy available, although some investigators have reported favorable results with spiramycin.

Isospora belli is also capable of causing chronic watery diarrhea, abdominal pain, and weight loss, especially in AIDS patients in Haiti (DeHovitz et al., 1986). Diagnosis is made by acid-fast stain of a stool specimen. Unlike cryptosporidiosis, isosporiasis is treatable. Patients usually have a dramatic response to TMP/S within 2 days. Diarrhea recurs after discontinuation of therapy. Indefinite prophylaxis appears to be necessary (DeHovitz et al., 1986).

MAI has been found in the small-bowel wall of patients with malabsorption and steatorrhea; however, whether MAI accounts for the diarrhea is unclear (Kovacs et al., 1985b).

Other infectious causes of enteritis may be diagnosed by routine culture and examination for ova and parasites. Often no specific etiology is found for the diarrhea, however, in which case patients are presumed to have idiopathic diarrhea, perhaps due to HIV-1 infection of the bowel wall. During the workup, patients are often found to have neoplastic involvement of the bowel with Kaposi's sarcoma or lymphoma. Although these tumors may occasionally ulcerate or cause obstruction or pain, the majority are not unequivocally responsible for identifiable symptoms.

CMV colitis presents as diarrhea, abdominal pain, and hematochezia; fulminant progression to gangrene of the bowel has been reported (Meiselman et al., 1985; Chachoua et al., 1987). Colonoscopy reveals diffuse patchy ulcerations and submucosal hemorrhage which is frequently mistaken for Kaposi's sarcoma. Characteristic intranuclear inclusions are present on biopsy (Meiselman et al., 1985). Gancyclovir has been effective in a small number of cases. Which patients are most likely to benefit from gancyclovir therapy has not been fully clarified, and more extensive trials are warranted (Collaborative DHPG Treatment Study Group, 1986; Smith et al., 1988; Chachoua et al., 1987).

The anorectal and perianal region is frequently involved with severe ulcerations due to herpes simplex virus. Aggressive evaluation of lesions with culture is warranted, since the herpetic lesions are responsive to acyclovir.

Bacteremia and Fungemia

One of the commonest pathogens isolated from the bloodstream of AIDS patients is MAI (Whimbey et al., 1986). Although blood cultures may be positive for extended periods, it is not clear to what extent if any MAI bacteremia may be responsible for chronic fever or weight loss. Therapy for bacteremia does not appear to be effective in terms of regimens tried to date (Masur et al., 1987; Whimbey et al., 1986). Other organisms influenced by T cells that are occasionally isolated from blood cultures include *Salmonella* spp., *Cryptococcus neoformans,* and *Histoplasma capsulatum* (Whimbey et al., 1986).

The B-cell deficit related to HIV-1 infection may be clinically important when considering the apparent increased incidence of bacteremias due to *Streptococcus pneumoniae* and *Hemophilus influenzae* (Lane et al., 1983). Other pathogens, such as gram-negative rods and *Candida,* are not frequent; when they are seen, they are probably due to more prolonged hospitalization, use of broad-spectrum antibiotics, and long-term central venous access rather than cellular immunodeficiency.

In summary, opportunistic infections are frequent occurrences in AIDS patients and cause most of the morbidity and mortality associated with AIDS. Opportunistic pathogens can be divided into two groups in terms of therapeutic options: those pathogens such as *Pneumocystis, Cryptococcus, Toxoplasma,* CMV, and *Candida,* which can be successfully treated in the majority of cases but which have a high likelihood of recurring when therapy is stopped, and those pathogens such as *Cryptosporidium* and MAI for which no effective therapy is currently available. Clearly, if the prognosis for AIDS patients is to improve, more effective therapeutic and preventive strategies for these infections need to be developed.

Neoplasms

Before 1981, Kaposi's sarcoma was a rare neoplasm, occurring primarily among three groups of individuals—elderly males, Africans, and patients with exogenous immune depression, especially renal allograft recipients (Voldberding, 1986). Kaposi's is now a frequently recognized manifestation of AIDS, occurring alone or in combination with opportunistic infections in 30 percent of patients (Voldberding, 1986; Muggia and Lonberg, 1986). Neither the greater incidence among homosexual male as opposed to heterosexual AIDS patients nor the decreasing frequency of KS during the past several years has been explained.

Patients with Kaposi's sarcoma usually present with palpable red to violaceous macules on the head, neck, trunk, and extremities. Mucosal disease of the oropharynx and rectum is common. Lesions are initially discrete but may coalesce with advanced disease. Typically, the tumors are painless, but with progression they may become painful, especially if they are over joints or weight-bearing areas (Friedman-Kien et al., 1982).

Although visceral Kaposi's sarcoma is common, it usually remains clinically silent. Manifestations depend not only on the organ involved but on the extent of involvement. Tumor has been reported to involve the oral cavity, gastrointestinal tract, liver, spleen, lung, adrenal glands, pericardium, and testes. GI involvement occasionally produces blood loss and may be associated with diarrhea, but otherwise the submucosal lesions are usually asymptomatic. Abdominal pain occurs in AIDS patients with Kaposi's sarcoma but has not been clearly linked with Kaposi's lesions. Lesions involving the upper airway may produce obstruction, and emergency treatment with radiation is required. Pulmonary involvement, when extensive, is often confused with *Pneumocystis carinii* pneumonia. Bronchoalveolar lavage and transbronchial biopsy are unable to give adequate tissue for diagnosis because of the size of the specimen obtained and the inevitable crush artifact. Open lung biopsy is required.

Kaposi's sarcoma lesions show a characteristic combination of spindle cells and vascular structures in reticular and collagen fibers. The natural history of Kaposi's sarcoma is extremely variable. Some patients have prolonged periods during which all lesions are stable; others have rapidly progressive disease with involvement of major organs. Therapy for patients with KS must be individualized. Therapy usually depends on the size and extent of involvement. Small papulonodular lesions producing pain, obstruction, or lymphedema often respond to palliative radiation therapy. Chemotherapy with single agents (vinblastine or VP-16) often results in good response rates, although there is concern about further drug-mediated suppression of the immune system (Voldberding, 1986). Recombinant alpha-interferon has been reported to induce complete remission in 25 percent of patients, and partial remission in 15 percent. Fever, chills, and fatigue are the commonest side effects of therapy.

Patients with KS generally manifest deteriorating immunologic function over time and ultimately die of infection rather than tumor. About 20 percent of patients may survive longer than 5 years. The ultimate outcome for this subpopulation is unknown, although the likelihood is that their immune competence will continue to decline, with resulting opportunistic infection, progressive tumor, and death.

Other malignant neoplasms that have been reported with increased frequency among patients with AIDS include extranodal non-Hodgkin's lymphoma. The majority of these tumors are B-cell immunoblastic sarcomas and small, non-cleaved, non-Burkitt lymphomas and are found in the bone marrow, central nervous system (as noted earlier and in Chapter 5), and retroperitoneum. Characteristically, these neoplasms respond very poorly to standard chemotherapy. Prognosis for long-term survival is poor (Levine et al., 1984; Ziegler et al., 1984).

CONCLUSION

The ability to detect HIV-1 infection has expanded the understanding of the clinical spectrum of HIV-1-related disorders. The acquisition of HIV-1 infection can be associated with mild and self-limiting symptoms and signs. A large fraction of HIV-1-infected patients are asymptomatic and have no abnormal physical findings. It is not yet certain what factors determine how likely or how rapidly an individual patient ultimately is to develop significant or life-threatening disease. Once a life-threatening infection does develop, death due to an infectious or neoplastic process seems inevitable. Median survival after an episode of *Pneumocystis carinii* pneumonia is 318 days. With KS, most patients ultimately die (median survival is 750 days) owing to infection, though some patients may survive for longer than 5 years (Rothenberg et al., 1987).

The care of HIV-1-infected individuals is often frustrating and depressing for the patient and health care professional, given the multiple complications and the inevitability of shortened life expectancy. Excellent care can increase the duration and quality of AIDS patients' survival, however, just as it can for other incurable, ultimately fatal illnesses such as coronary artery disease, diabetes, and cancer. While medical science works on developing effective antiviral or biologic response-modifying therapy to alter the underlying virally induced immunodeficiency that is central to HIV-1-induced disease, clinicians need to provide the diagnostic, therapeutic, and psychologic support for this patient population.

REFERENCES

Abrams DI (1986): J Clin Oncol 4:126.

Allegra CJ, Chabner BA, Tuazon CU, Ogata-Arakaki D, Baird B, Drake JC, Simmons JT, Lack EE, et al. (1987a): N Engl J Med 317:978.

Allegra CJ, Kovacs JA, Drake JC, et al. (1987b): J Clin Invest 79:478.

Araujo FG, Remington JS (1974): Antimicrob Agents Chemother 5:647.

Bachman DM, Rodrigues MM, Chu F, Straus SE, Cogan DG, Macher AM (1982): Ophthalmol 89:797.

Barnes PF, Arvalo C (1987): J Infect Dis 156:377.

Borton LK, Wintroub BU (1984): J Am Acad Dermatol 10:387.

Brenner M, Ognibene FP, Lack EE, Simmons JT, Suffredini AF, Lane HC, Fauci AS, Parillo JE, Shelhamer JH, Masur H (1987): Am Rev Respir Dis 136:1199.

CDC (1986a): MMWR 35:334.

CDC (1986b): Ann Intern Med 106:254.

CDC (1987): MMWR 36:1S.

Chachoua A, Deterich D, Krasinski K, Green J, Laubenstein L, Wernz J, Buhles W, Koretz S (1987): Ann Intern Med 197:133.

Collaborative DHPG Treatment Study Group (1986): N Engl J Med 314:801.

Cooper DA, Gold J, MacLean P, Finlayson R, Donovan B, Finlayson R, Barnes TG, Michelmore HM, Brooke P, Penny R (1985): Lancet 1:537.

DeHovitz JA, Pape JW, Boncy M, Johnson WD Jr (1986): N Engl J Med 315:87.

Fauci AS, Masur H, Gelmann EP, Markham PG, Hahn BH, Lane HC (1985): Ann Intern Med 102:800.

Fischl M, Dickinson GM, LaVoie L (1988): JAMA 259:185.

Fishbein DB, Kaplan JE, Spira TJ, Miller B, Schonberger LB, Pinsky PF, Getchell JP, Kalyanaraman VS, Braude JS (1985): JAMA 254:930.

Friedman-Kien AE, Laubenstein LJ, Rubinstein P, et al. (1982): Ann Intern Med 96:693.

Gal AA, Koss MN, Hawkins J, Evans S, Einstein H (1986): Arch Pathol Lab Med 110:502.

Gill PS, Levine AM, Meyer PR, Boswell WD, Burkes RL, Parker JW, Hofman FM, Dworsky RL, Lukes RJ (1985): Am J Med 78:742.

Goedert JJ, Biggar RJ, Melbye M, Mann DL, Wilson S, Gail MH, Grossman RJ, DiGioia RA, Sanchez WC, Weiss SH (1987): JAMA 257:331.

Gordin FM, Simon GL, Wofsy CB, Mills J (1984): Ann Intern Med 100:495.

Greenspan JS, Greenspan D, Lennette ET, Abrams DI, Conant MA, Petersen V, Freese UK (1985): N Engl J Med 3123:1564.

Haverkos W (1987): Am J Med 82:907.

Hawkins CC, Gold JW, Whimbey E, Kiehn TE, Brannon P, Cammarata R, Brown AE, Armstrong D (1986): Ann Intern Med 105:184.

Hessol NA, Rutherford GW, Lifson AR, O'Malley PM, Doll LS, Darrow WW, Jaffe HW, Werdegar D (1988): Fourth International Conference on AIDS June 12–16, Abst. 4096.

Ho D, Sarngadharan MG, Resnick L, Dimarzoveroness F, Rota TR, Hirsch MS (1985): Ann Intern Med 103:880.

Holland GN, Pepose JS, Pettit TH, Gottlieb MS, Yee RD, Foos RY (1983): Ophthalmology 90:859.

Hopewell PC, Luce JM (1985): Chest 87:104.

Karoffa C, Rehm S, Calabrese L, et al. (1986): Abstract of the Twenty-Sixth Conference on Antimicrobial Agents and Chemotherapy, New Orleans. Washington, DC: American Society for Microbiology, p 224.

Kaslow RA, Phair JP, Friedman HB, Lyter D, Solomon RE, Dudley J, Polk BF, Blackwelder W (1987): Ann Intern Med 107:474.

Klein RS, Harris CA, Small CB, Moll B, Lesser M, Friedland GH (1984): N Engl J Med 311:354.

Kovacs JA, Masur H (1985): In Gallin JI, Fauci AS, eds: Advances in Host Defense Mechanisms, Acquired Immunodeficiency Syndrome, Vol 5. New York: Raven Press, p 35.

Kovacs JA, Hiemenz JW, Macher AM, Stover D, Murray HW, Shelhamer J, Lane HC, Urmacher C, Honig C, Longo DL, et al. (1984): Ann Intern Med 100:663.

Kovacs JA, Kovacs AA, Polis M, Wright WC, Gill VJ, Tuazon CU, Gelmann EP, Lane HC, Longfield R, Overturf G, et al. (1985): Ann Intern Med 103:533.

Kovacs JA, Ng VL, Masur H, et al. (1988): N Engl J Med 318:589.

Krupp LB, Lipton RB, Swerdlow ML, Leeds NE, Llena JL (1985): Ann Neurol 17:344.

Krown SE, Rial FX, Cunningham-Rundles S, et al. (1983): N Engl J Med 308:1071.

Lane HC, Masur H, Edgar LC, Whalen G, Rook AH, Fauci AS (1983): N Engl J Med 309:453.

Lane HC, Masur H, Gelmann EP, Longo DL, Steis RG, Chused T, Whalen G, Edgar LC, Fauci AS (1985): Am J Med 78:417.

Laskin OL, Cederberg DM, Mills J, Eron LJ, Mildvan D, Spector SA (1987): Am J Med 83:201.

Leoung GS, Mills J, Hopewell PC, Hughes W, Wofsy C (1986): Ann Intern Med 105:45.

Leport C, Vilde JL, Katlama C, Regnier B, Matheron S, Saimot AB (1986): JAMA 255:2290.

Levine AM, Meyer PR, Byandy MK, Parker JW, Taylor CR, Irwin L, Lukes RJ (1984): Ann Intern Med 100:7.

Louie E, Rice LB, Holaman RS (1986): Chest 90:542.

Luft BJ, Conley F, Remington JS, et al. (1983): Lancet 1:781.

Luft BJ, Brooks RG, Conley FK, McCabe RE, Remington JS (1984): JAMA 252:913.

Ma P, Soave RS (1983): J Infect Dis 147:824.

Madoff LC, Scairizzo D, Roberts RB (1986): Clin Res 34:524A.

Masur H, Lane HC, Palestine A, Smith PD, Manischewitz J, Stevens G, Fujikawa L, Macher AM, Nussenblatt R, Baird B, et al. (1986): Ann Intern Med 104:41.

Masur H, Tuazon C, Gill V, Grimes G, Baird B, Fauci AS, Lane HC (1987): J Infect Dis 155:224.

Mathur-Wagh U, Enlow RW, Spigand I, Winchester RJ, Sachs HS, Rorat E, Uancovitz SR, Klein MJ, William DC, Mildvan D (1984): Lancet 1:1033.

Meiselman MS, Cello JP, Margaretten W (1985): Gastroenterology 88:171.

Melbye M, Biggar RJ, Ebbesen P, Neuland C, Goedert JJ, Faber V, Lorenzen I, Skinhj P, Gallo RC, Blattner WA (1986): Ann Intern Med 104:496.

Metroka CE, Cunningham-Rundles S, Pollack MS, et al. (1983): Ann Intern Med 99:585.

Montgomery AB, Debs RJ, Luce JM, Corkery KJ, Turner J, Brunette EN, Lin, ET, Hopewell PC (1987): Lancet 2:480.

Morris L, Distenfeld A, Amorosi E, Karpatkin S (1982): Ann Intern Med 96:714.

Moskowitz L, Hensley GT, Chan JC, Adams K (1985): Arch Pathol Lab Med 109:735

Muggia FM, Lonberg M (1986): In Cooney TG, Ward TT, eds: AIDS and Other Medical Problems in the Male Homosexual. Philadelphia: Saunders, p 139.

Murray HW, Hillman JK, Rubin BY, Kelly CD, Jacobs JL, Tyler LW, Donelly DM, Carriero SM, Godbold JH, Roberts RB (1985): N Engl J Med 313:1504.

Murray JF, Felton CP, Garay SM, Gottlieb MS, Hopewell PC, Stover DE, Teirstein AS (1984): N Engl J Med 310:1682.

Naot Y, Remington JS (1980): J Infect Dis 142:757.

Navia BA, Petito CK, Gold JW, Cho ES, Jordan BD, Price RW (1986): Ann Neurol 19:224.

Niedt GW, Schinella RA (1985): Arch Pathol Lab Med 109:735.

Norrby R, Eilard T, Svedhem A, Lycke E (1975): Scand J Infect Dis 7:72.

O'Brien RJ, Lyle MA, Snider DE (1985): Am Rev Respir Dis 131:A223.

Ognibene FP, Shelhamer J, Gill V, Macher AM, Loew D, Parker MM, Gelmann E, Fauci AS, Parrillo JE, Masur H (1984): Am Rev Respir Dis 129:929.

Parke DW, Font RL (1986): Arch Ophthalmol 104:571.

Phair J, Munoz A, Kingsley L, Fox R, Kaslow R, Visscher B, Jacobson L (1988): Fourth International Conference on AIDS June 12–16, Abst. 4093.

Pitchenik AE, Rubinson HA (1985): Am Rev Respir Dis 131:393.

Pitchenik AE, Ganjei P, Torres A, Evans DA, Rubin E, Baier H (1986): Am Rev Respir Dis 133:226.

Polk BF, Fox R, Brookmeyer R, Kanchanaraksa S, Kaslow R, Visscher B, Rinaldo C, Phair J (1987): N Engl J Med 316:61.

Polsky B, Gold JW, Whimbey E, Dryjanski J, Brown AE, Schiffman G, Armstrong D (1986): Ann Intern Med 104:38.

Quinn TC (1985): Pract Gastroenterol 9:23.

Ricciardi DD, Sepkowitz DV, Berkowitz LB, Bienenstock H, Maslow M (1986): J Rheumatol 13:455.

Rico MJ, Penneys NS (1985): Arch Dermatol 121:901.

Rothenberg R, Woelfel M, Stoneburner R, Milberg J, Parker R, Truman B (1987): N Engl J Med 317:1297.

Shelhamer JH, Ognibene FP, Macher AM, Tuazon C, Steiss R, Longo D, Kovacs JA, Parker MM, Natanson C, Lane HC, et al. (1984): Am Rev Respir Dis 130:1161.

Small CB, Harris CA, Friedland GH, Klein RS (1985): Arch Intern Med 145:837.

Smith PD, Lane HC, Gill VJ, Manischewitz JF, Quinnan GV, Fauci AS, Masur H (1988): Ann Intern Med 108:328.

Soave RS, Danner RS, Honig CL, Ma P, Hart CC, Nash T, Roberts RB (1984): Ann Intern Med 100:504.

Sreepada Rao TK, Filippone EJ, Nicastri AD, Landesman SH, Frank E, Chen CK, Friedman EA (1984): N Engl J Med 310:669.

Stover DE, White DA, Romano PA, Gellene RA, Robeson WA (1985): Am J Med 78:429.

Suffredini AS, Ognibene FP, Lack EE, Simmons JT, Brenner M, Gill VJ, Lane HC, Fauci AS, Parrillo JE, Masur H, et al. (1987): Ann Intern Med 107:7.

Sunderam G, McDonald RJ, Maniatis T, Olesde J, Kapila R, Reichman LB (1986): JAMA 256:362.

Tindall B, Barker S, Donovan B, Barnes T, Roberts J, Kronenberg C, Gold J, Penney R, Cooper D, and the Sydney AIDS Study Group (1988): Arch Intern Med 148:945.

Voldberding PA (1986): In Cooney TG, Ward TT, eds: AIDS and Other Medical Problems in the Male Homosexual. Philadelphia: Saunders, p 665.

Wanke C, Tuazon CU, Kovacs A, Dina T, Davis DO, Barton N, Katz D, Lunde M, Levy C, Conley FK, et al. (1987): Am J Trop Med Hyg 36:509.

Weber JN, Wadsworth J, Rogers LA, Moshtael O, Scott K, McManus T, Berrie E, Jeffries DJ, Harris JR, Pinching AJ (1986): Lancet 1:1179.

Welch K, Finkbeiner W, Alpers C, Blumenfeld W, Davis RL, Smuckler EA, Beckstead JH (1984): JAMA 252:1152.

Wharton MJ, Coleman DL, Wolfsy CB, Luce JM, Blumenfeld W, Hadley WK, Ingram-Drake L, Volberding PA, Hopewell PC (1986): Ann Intern Med 105:37.

Whimbey E, Gold JW, Polsky B, Dryjanski J, Hawkins C, Blevins A, Brannon P, Kiehn TE, Brown AE, Armstrong D (1986): Ann Intern Med 104:511.

Wong B, Gold JW, Brown AE, Lange M, Fried R, Grieco M, Mildvan D, Giron J, Tapper ML, Lerner CW, et al. (1984): Ann Intern Med 100:36.

Ziegler JL, Beckstead JA, Volberding PA, Abrams DI, Levine AM, Lukes RJ, Gill PS, Burkes RL, Meyer PR, Metroka CE, et al. (1984): N Engl J Med 311:565.

Zuger A, Louie E, Holzman RS, Simberkoff MS, Rahal JJ (1986): Ann Intern Med 104:234.

5

The Nervous System: Pathophysiology and Clinical Manifestations

BRUCE BREW, JOHN J. SIDTIS, AND RICHARD PRICE

The course of infection by human immunodeficiency virus type 1 (HIV-1) is commonly complicated by both central nervous system (CNS) and peripheral nervous system (PNS) disorders that contribute importantly to its morbidity (Table 5.1) (for reviews, see Brew et al., 1988; Britton et al., 1984; Levy et al., 1985b; McArthur et al., 1987a; Navia et al., 1986d; Price and Brew, 1988b; Rosenblum et al., 1988; Snider et al., 1983). As with systemic AIDS, nervous system afflictions include opportunistic infections and opportunistic neoplasms. They also include direct infection of the nervous system by HIV-1 and perhaps immunopathological processes as well. This chapter focuses on the commonest and clinically most important of these disorders, dealing in turn with those known or suspected to relate to direct HIV-1 infection, opportunistic infections, and neoplasms of the CNS and then with PNS disorders. It also indicates some important areas where knowledge of epidemiology, natural history, and pathogenesis is incomplete.

CNS DISORDERS KNOWN OR SUSPECTED TO RELATE TO DIRECT CNS HIV-1 INFECTION

Systemic HIV-1 infection can be complicated by direct infection of the CNS from the time of initial exposure to the virus. This infection may be symptomatic but is probably more often clinically silent. Recognition of early nervous system involvement has importance for diagnosis as well as more general implications regarding the biology of HIV-1 and its interaction with the human host. Late symptomatic involvement of the CNS results in the commonest of the major neurological complications of HIV-1 infection and AIDS, the AIDS dementia complex.

Early Symptomatic Infection of the CNS

The variety of neurological complications occurring early in the course of HIV-1 infection have been described primarily in the form of individual case reports or collections of a few cases with diverse manifestations (Brew et al., 1987; Carne et al., 1985; Denning et al., 1987; Ho et al., 1985b). Either in the context of or follow-

Table 5.1. Major CNS Complications of HIV-1 Infection

Direct HIV-1 infection of the CNS (established or suspected)
  Acute syndromes—acute encephalitis and meningitis
  Aseptic meningitis
  AIDS dementia complex (includes vacuolar myelopathy)
Opportunistic infections
  Cerebral toxoplasmosis
  Cryptococcal meningitis
  Progressive multifocal leukoencephalopathy (PML)
  Cytomegalovirus encephalitis
  Varicella-zoster virus and herpes simplex virus infections
  Tuberculosis
Opportunistic neoplasms
  Primary CNS lymphoma
  Metastatic lymphoma

ing the seroconversion-related illness of initial HIV-1 infection, acutely or sub-acutely evolving neurological disease may take the form of focal or diffuse encephalitis, meningitis, ataxia, or myelopathy, either alone or together with PNS abnormalities. These disorders are monophasic, with most patients recovering within a number of weeks, although cognitive deficit may persist in some (Brew et al., 1987). The cerebrospinal fluid (CSF) usually shows a minor lymphocyte-predominant pleocytosis with a modest rise in protein. These early syndromes are apparently uncommon, but their incidence may be underappreciated, since they are clinically indistinguishable from other acute viral or postinfectious encephalitides, most of which never achieve specific diagnosis. Thus, there is an important need for additional studies of the neurological manifestations of acute HIV-1 infection in order to define more clearly their clinical presentations and incidence as well as to determine their outcome and prognosis for the development of CNS abnormalities later in the course of infection.

Asymptomatic Infection

In contrast to the apparent rarity of these early CNS syndromes, it now appears that early asymptomatic HIV-1 infection of the CNS, or at least infection of the leptomeninges, is common and may, in fact, be the rule. Evidence for this comes from studies of CSF in asymptomatic seropositives that have shown (1) abnormalities of "routine" measures including concentrations of cells, protein, and immunoglobulin; (2) local, "intra-blood-brain barrier" synthesis of anti-HIV-1 antibody; and (3) presence of virus (Appelman et al., 1987; Clotet et al., 1987; Collier et al., 1987; Elovaara et al., 1987; Goudsmit et al., 1986a,b; McArthur et al., 1988; Resnick et al., 1985, 1988). Such early or chronic asymptomatic HIV-1 infection and the accompanying host reactions must be taken into account when interpreting CSF results obtained for other diagnostic purposes, since they may result in later "incidental" abnormalities in CSF protein, immunoglobulin, oligoclonal bands, or even HIV-1 recovery. Early infection of the CNS indicates that involvement of the nervous system is an intrinsic aspect of the ecology of the virus in the human host.

Aseptic Meningitis

Aseptic meningitis occurs not only in the setting of initial seroconversion but, even more commonly, later in the course of HIV-1 infection, usually as asymptomatic seropositivity gives way to various HIV-1-induced symptoms and signs or AIDS (Hollander et al., 1987b; Snider et al., 1983). Both acute and chronic forms of the disorder present with headache as the most prominent feature, and cranial nerve palsies may complicate the course. HIV-1 can be isolated from CSF, which shows a mononuclear pleocytosis, usually with normal glucose and mildly elevated protein. This syndrome itself is benign, although it carries an overall poor prognosis vis-à-vis other AIDS complications. Whether these patients have a higher incidence of the AIDS dementia complex or pursue a different course is uncertain.

AIDS Dementia Complex

This is the commonest and most important of the CNS complications of HIV-1 infection. On the basis of its clinical features, neuropsychological test profile, neuropathology, and virology, this syndrome can be classified among the "subcortical dementias" (Brew et al., 1988; Navia et al., 1986b).

Clinical Features

The AIDS dementia complex is characterized by disturbances in cognition, motor performance, and behavior (Navia et al., 1986b; Price et al., 1988b). Early in the course of the disease, patients characteristically complain of difficulties with concentration and memory. They may lose their train of thought and experience "slowness" in their thinking. Difficulty in reading and following a plot is common. Impairment of memory or concentration leads to missed appointments and the need to keep lists to aid even the most routine aspects of daily living. If a high level of concentration or organization is required for a patient's occupation or activities at home, the effect of the AIDS dementia complex may be evident to the patient quite early in the illness, whereas a friend or family member may note subtle personality or cognitive changes in patients with less demanding activities or less insight. Behavioral abnormalities most frequently manifest as social withdrawal and apathy, and they are not infrequently misconstrued as depression. Although concomitant depression may be present, it is surprisingly infrequent, and typically patients neither complain of nor exhibit true dysphoria. In a minority of patients, a more agitated organic psychosis may be the presenting or predominant aspect of the illness. These patients are often irritable and hyperactive, or they may appear anxious without appropriate cause and, in more severe cases, may exhibit frank mania or delirium.

Early motor dysfunction most often results in complaints of poor balance and clumsiness. Gait incoordination may result in frequent tripping or falling or a perceived need to exercise new care in walking. Patients may drop things more frequently or find hand activities, including writing and eating, slower or less precise than usual.

Early in the illness simple mental status testing often reveals remarkable slowing of patients' responses, even when the content is correct. Patients not infrequently score within the normal range of the "Mini Mental Status" test (Folstein et al., 1975) or similar screens. As the disease progresses, performance declines on tasks requiring concentration and attention such as word or digit reversals, serial 7's, or delayed recall, and a larger array of mental status tests become abnormal.

With careful examination, motor abnormalities can usually be detected early in the disease. Perhaps the earliest to appear are abnormal reflexes, including a snout response and hyperactive deep tendon reflexes. Disturbed ocular motility also occurs early, and this is followed or accompanied by slowing of rapid successive and alternating movements of the fingers, wrists, or feet. Ataxia, at first seen only on rapid turns or tandem gait, may become disabling. More commonly, leg weakness increases, and paraparesis becomes the chief impediment to walking. Bladder and bowel incontinence supervene later.

The course of the disease is highly variable. Usually, the onset is insidious and the course progressive, although some patients exhibit little or no progression over several months. Others may have an abrupt onset or deterioration, commonly in the setting of another systemic or CNS complication of AIDS such as *Pneumocystis carinii* pneumonia or cryptococcal meningitis. Manifestations may reverse with treatment of a complication, reach a plateau of neurological impairment, or follow a relentlessly progressive course.

In the end, patients become nearly vegetative, with only rudimentary intellectual and social function. They lie with a vacant stare, unable to ambulate, and incontinent. Their level of consciousness is usually preserved, except for occasional hypersomnolence, unless affected by intercurrent illness.

Routine examination of the CSF in these patients reveals a mildly elevated protein in approximately two-thirds and a mild mononuclear pleocytosis in nearly a quarter (Navia et al., 1986b). Additionally, HIV-1 can be directly isolated from the CSF of many (Ho et al., 1985b; Hollander et al., 1987b; Levy et al., 1985b). However, as noted above, HIV-1 can also be isolated from the CSF in a variety of infected patients, including those who are asymptomatic or suffering aseptic meningitis. Thus, the diagnostic and prognostic significance of these abnormalities have yet to be defined. Detection of HIV-1 antigens, principally p24, in CSF may offer an accurate and convenient method of quantitating infection for future therapeutic trials (Goudsmit et al., 1986a). Local synthesis of anti-HIV-1 antibody has also been detected in the CSF (Goudsmit et al., 1986b; Resnick et al., 1985, 1988), but its diagnostic and prognostic role remains to be established, since "intra-blood-brain barrier" synthesis of antibodies may occur early in asymptomatic infection (see earlier). Similarly, oligoclonal immunoglobulin bands detected in certain circumstances may represent nonspecific reactions rather than responses to HIV-1 itself.

The most prominent neuroradiological finding in the AIDS dementia complex is cerebral atrophy (Navia et al., 1986b). Its presence in nearly all patients at the time of neurological presentation suggests a chronic process requiring some time to reach a clinical threshold. Widened cortical sulci and, less commonly, enlarged ventricles are readily appreciated by either computerized tomographic (CT) scanning or magnetic resonance imaging (MRI). Additionally, some patients have abnormalities on MRI in the hemispheric white matter and, less commonly, in the basal ganglia and thalamus (Grant et al., 1987; Jarvik et al., 1987; Navia et al.,

1986b). These consist of patchy or diffusely increased signal on the T2-weighted image, consistent with increased water content.

The *childhood form* of the disease parallels that of the adult, although because of less frequent opportunistic infections and perhaps greater vulnerability of the developing system, it may assume a more dominant role (Belman et al., 1985; Epstein et al., 1985b; 1988). Development characteristically begins normally, then fails. There are regression of developmental milestones, gradual loss of previously acquired motor skills, and evolution of motor abnormalities ranging from spastic paraparesis to quadriplegia with pseudobulbar palsy and rigidity. Acquired microcephaly is almost universal, and the CT scan or MRI may detect basal ganglia calcification (Belman et al., 1986).

Neuropsychological Test Profile
Neuropsychological studies of adults quantitatively support the findings on neurological history and examination enumerated above and may be useful in evaluating patients with AIDS dementia complex (Sidtis et al., 1987; Tross et al., 1988). Characteristic abnormalities include difficulty with complex sequencing, impairment of fine and rapid motor movement, and slowed verbal fluency. On all of these tests cognitive and motor slowing is prominent, but errors and inaccuracies are also present. In contrast, verbal abilities tend to be maintained, with naming and vocabulary skills largely preserved even in the most advanced disease group. In general, cognitive problems appear to reflect difficulty with attention and concentration, reduced spontaneity, and a decreased ability to deal with more than one idea or simple task at a time.

Neuropathology
Histopathological abnormalities in these patients are most prominent in subcortical brain structures, with relative sparing of the cortex (Budka 1986; Budka et al., 1987; De la Monte et al., 1987; Navia et al., 1986a; Petito et al., 1986; Price et al., 1988c). The commonest finding is white matter pallor, which tends to more severely involve the central and periventricular white matter and to a less extent the subcortical fibers. Reactive astrocytosis accompanies the white matter change and may extend into subcortical gray structures. In the milder cases, inflammatory changes are characteristically scant, consisting of a few perivascular lymphocytes and brown-pigmented macrophages.

In more severe cases, reactive infiltrates are more prominent and consist of perivascular and parenchymal foamy macrophages, along with characteristic multinucleated cells, principally of macrophage origin. Such infiltrates are most often concentrated in the white matter and deep gray structures, especially the basal ganglia and thalamus. The brainstem and the cerebellum are less frequently involved. In pediatric cases cortical involvement may be more prominent than in adults (Sharer et al., 1986).

Vacuolar myelopathy, occurring in about a quarter of AIDS patients at autopsy in the Memorial Sloan-Kettering/New York Hospital experience, is the commonest spinal abnormality (Navia et al., 1986a; Petito et al., 1985). This disorder pathologically resembles subacute combined degeneration resulting from B_{12}

deficiency, but serum B_{12} levels are normal. The vacuolation principally involves the posterior and lateral columns, without predilection for particular anatomical tracts. By electron microscopy, the vacuolar changes appear to result from intra-myelin swelling, with scattered lipid-laden macrophages infiltrating within the layers of the myelin sheaths. No pediatric examples of vacuolar myelopathy have been published.

Viral Etiology

Accumulating evidence supports the hypothesis that the AIDS dementia complex, at least in part, is due to direct brain infection by HIV-1. Initially suspected on the basis of clinical and pathological observations and precedent in animal models, infection of the brain by HIV-1 has now been demonstrated by a variety of techniques in a number of laboratories. Southern blot analysis has demonstrated pro-viral DNA, and in situ nucleic acid studies have detected both viral DNA and RNA in the brains of some patients with the AIDS dementia complex (Koenig et al., 1986; Shaw et al., 1985; Stoler et al., 1986; Wiley et al., 1986). HIV-1 has also been cultured directly from both brain and CSF of demented patients (Gartner et al., 1986; Ho et al., 1985a; Hollander et al., 1987a; Levy et al., 1985a), and viral antigens have been observed in brains using immunohistochemical techniques (Gabuzda et al., 1986; Michaels et al., 1988; Pumarola-Sune et al., 1987; Vazeux et al., 1987; Wiley et al., 1986). HIV-1 virions have also been found by electron microscopy (Epstein et al., 1985a; Gyorkey et al., 1987). Although these studies clearly show that HIV-1 is present in the brains of some demented patients, a number of fundamental questions remain (Price et al., 1988c; Price and Brew, 1988a). Productive HIV-1 brain infection can only be demonstrated by these various techniques in approximately one-quarter of demented patients, principally those with relatively severe symptomatology. There is also not a uniform relationship between the extent of this productive infection and the severity of the dementia. Yet to be established are the cellular and regional identity of productively and nonproductively infected brain cells, the reason why those cells are selectively targeted by the virus, and the mechanisms involved in brain injury.

Epidemiology

The epidemiology and course of the AIDS dementia complex are imprecisely defined. Since estimates have been derived principally from clinical and pathological series rather than more representative populations, the frequency of this syndrome at each stage of systemic HIV-1 infection remains uncertain. However, if the early monophasic encephalitides are excluded, the AIDS dementia complex appears to be confined to the later phases of systemic infection. Most cases occur in the setting of systemic AIDS as defined by Centers for Disease Control (CDC) criteria relating to life-threatening opportunistic infections (Centers for Disease Control, 1986). In the rather selective Memorial Sloan-Kettering clinical experience (unpublished observations), at the time of AIDS diagnosis, perhaps one-third of patients exhibit overt and one-quarter subclinical AIDS dementia complex; at the preterminal stage, perhaps two-thirds of AIDS patients show clinically significant, and one-quarter show subclinical forms of the disorder (Navia et al., 1986b; Price et al., 1988b).

The disorder may also develop before criteria for AIDS are met, and a substantial number of patients with more "minor" manifestations of immunodeficiency develop the syndrome (Grant et al., 1987; Navia et al., 1987; Janssen et al., 1988). The neuropsychological abnormalities reported in small series should not be extrapolated to the large existing population of seropositives. However, the neuropsychological impairment described in asymptomatic HIV-1 seropositives occurred primarily in immunologically abnormal individuals who were likely on the threshold of the late stages of HIV-1 infection. Additionally, the definition and functional significance of "impairment" in the testing procedures have not been firmly established. Importantly, these findings do not now justify excluding seropositives from employment.

Overall, however, when it occurs, the AIDS dementia complex is one of the most significant complications associated with HIV-1 infection. Whether appearing early or late, whether dominating the course or compounding systemic disease, this neurological condition gradually impairs function in work, in daily life, and eventually in self care. The progressive disability has broad societal implications in lost productivity in addition to the costs of long-term assistance and institutional care.

Whether there was a lag in its recognition or the disorder is now more frequent has not been directly examined. Previous and ongoing experience indicates that when the disorder is mild, a history of intellectual difficulty is often not sought, and the patient is not appropriately questioned. Patient complaints of forgetfulness and poor concentration are simply attributed to fatigue or depression. In the case of more severe affliction, neurological dysfunction may be attributed to the debilitating effects of chronic illness. However, even in chronic illness, an explanation is needed for the marked loss of intellectual capacity, withdrawal, psychomotor retardation, inability to walk, and incontinence characteristic of the AIDS dementia complex. Numerous patients whose AIDS dementia syndrome has been missed are still being referred from prospective studies or for evaluation of other disorders.

Additional, more accurate epidemiological and natural history information is clearly needed. Neurological abnormality should be examined within the context of systemic disease staging and the severity of immunosuppression. Background data regarding approximate date of seroconversion (if available), previous systemic diseases, $CD4^+$ lymphocyte counts or other estimates of immune function, and the presence and degree of viremia should be sought. Careful neurological diagnosis is important so that the many other disorders to which these patients are susceptible are not confused with the AIDS dementia complex.

A staging nomenclature such as that provided in Table 5.2 could provide a helpful framweork. It would provide a common vocabulary for studies attempting to deal with epidemiology, natural history, and therapy. Staging individual patients requires that their neurological incapacity be clinically attributable to the AIDS dementia complex. The abnormalities should not be attributable to simple fatigability or reactive depression and must not be obscured by other CNS disease. Stage 0.5 includes patients with what is now uncertain disease; future studies need to develop methods to deal with thresholds of abnormality so that equivocal cases can be allocated to either stage 0 or stage 1.

Table 5.2. Memorial Sloan-Kettering Cancer Center Neuro-AIDS Study Group Staging of the AIDS Dementia Complex

Stage 0 (normal:	Normal mental and motor function.
Stage 0.5 (equivocal/subclinical):	Absent, minimal, or equivocal symptoms *without impairment of work or capacity to perform activities of daily living (ADL)*. Mild signs (snout response, slowed ocular or extremity movements) may be present. Gait and strength are normal.
Stage 1 (mild):	Able to perform *all but the more demanding aspects of work or ADL* but with unequivocal evidence (symptoms or signs, including performance on neuropsychological testing) of intellectual or motor impairment. Can walk without assistance.
Stage 2 (moderate):	Able to perform *basic activities of self care* but cannot work or maintain more demanding aspects of daily life. Ambulatory, but may require single prop.
Stage 3 (severe):	*Major intellectual incapacity* (cannot follow news or personal events, cannot sustain complex conversation, considerable slowing of all output) or *motor disability* (cannot walk unassisted, requiring walker or personal support, usually with slowing and clumsiness of arms as well).
Stage 4 (end stage):	*Nearly vegetative.* Intellectual and social comprehension and output are at a rudimentary level. Nearly or absolutely mute. Paraparetic or paraplegic with double incontinence.

Therapy

The evolving evidence indicates that the AIDS dementia complex is caused, either partially or wholly, by direct HIV-1 brain infection, in concert with the frequency of CNS infection early in the course of systemic HIV-1 infection. Antiviral drugs capable of penetrating the blood-brain and blood-CSF barriers must therefore be sought for treating the AIDS dementia complex and perhaps for treating HIV-1 infection in general. An uncontrolled pilot study of the nucleoside analog zidovudine (AZT, azidothymidine) has reported improvement in symptomatology and neuropsychological test performance in AIDS dementia complex patients (Yarchoan et al., 1988). Ongoing studies should yield more definitive results.

OPPORTUNISTIC INFECTIONS

The hallmark of AIDS is the development of opportunistic infections, and the CNS shares importantly in this susceptibility. This results in a characteristic spectrum of CNS infections. By virtue of their frequency and potential response to therapy, cerebral toxoplasmosis and cryptococcal meningitis are perhaps the most important of these. Progressive multifocal leukoencephalopathy (PML) is less common but is important in differential diagnosis of focal disease, and infections by the herpesvirus group, including cytomegalovirus (CMV), varicella-zoster virus (VZV), and herpes simplex virus (HSV), may also cause significant CNS disease. Tuberculosis of the CNS is less common, but as the incidence of AIDS increases in drug abusers from a lower socioeconomic population or in patients from the Third World, its importance may well increase.

Toxoplasmosis

Cerebral toxoplasmosis is one of the most frequent treatable CNS disorders complicating AIDS, developing in about 5 to 15 percent of AIDS patients depending on the population at risk (Navia et al., 1986c). The disorder is almost exclusively a reactivation of dormant infection. It may be the presenting manifestation of AIDS or it may complicate the course of patients with other AIDS-defining afflictions. Characteristically, it presents as a subacute illness in which focal cerebral dysfunction predominates, often combined with a nonfocal "encephalitic" component. Focal manifestations usually relate to hemispheric lesions, but, less commonly, cerebellar or even brainstem signs may appear. The nonfocal aspects include general confusion and altered consciousness with lethargy or, at times, coma. Headache and fever are also common.

In approaching AIDS patients with suspected toxoplasmosis or other focal disorders, neuroimaging techniques, particularly computerized tomographic (CT) scanning and more recent magnetic resonance imaging (MRI), are critical both to confirm the presence of macroscopic focal disease and to determine the nature of the lesions. To establish the diagnosis of cerebral toxoplasmosis, clinicians at Memorial Sloan-Kettering now rely principally on therapeutic trial of pyrimethamine and sulfadiazine and reserve brain biopsy for treatment failures or clinically atypical patients, including those who are seronegative (Navia et al., 1986c). When treated promptly, these patients characteristically respond with clear clinical and CT improvement within 1 to 2 weeks, with many, in fact, clinically improved within 24 to 48 hours.

Cryptococcal Meningitis

Cryptococcal meningitis is the commonest CNS fungal infection in AIDS patients (Kovacs et al., 1985; Zugler et al., 1986). It most frequently presents as a subacute meningitis or meningoencephalitis with headache, nausea, vomiting, confusion, and lethargy, but in some AIDS patients the symptomatology may be very mild. Similarly, the CSF formula may be bland, with few or no cells and little or no perturbation in glucose or protein levels. For this reason it is important to routinely obtain CSF for India ink stain, cryptococcal antigen titers, and fungal cultures on all AIDS patients at lumbar puncture. Although therapy with amphotericin B and flucytosine may relieve symptoms and induce an initial response in laboratory findings, patients frequently relapse. Therefore, maintenance treatment is essential.

Progressive Multifocal Leukoencephalopathy

PML is an opportunistic infection caused by a papovavirus, JC virus, and is characterized by selective white matter destruction (Richardson, 1978; Walker, 1978). It complicates the course in perhaps 1 to 5 percent of AIDS patients (Berger et al., 1987; Petito et al., 1986). Patients characteristically present with focal neurological symptoms and signs such as hemiparesis, homonymous visual field deficit, or other evidence of hemispheric disease. Diagnosis is made only by brain biopsy or autopsy, but suspicion is aroused by the clinical history, an examination suggesting more than one cerebral focus, and a CT scan or MRI demonstrating white matter lesions, characteristically without mass effect or contrast enhancement (Krupp et al., 1985). There is no proven effective therapy for the disease. The course is usually inexorably progressive, although a recent report documents arrest of the disease in two AIDS patients (Berger et al., 1987).

Cytomegalovirus Encephalitis

Systemic CMV infection is common in AIDS patients, and evidence of minor brain CMV infection in the form of isolated inclusion-bearing cells within microglial nodules can be found in approximately one-third of such patients at autopsy (Morgello et al., 1987; Navia et al., 1986a; Petito et al., 1986). Although there remains some uncertainty regarding the contribution of this type of CMV infection to neurological symptoms and signs, its effect is likely overshadowed by the AIDS dementia complex, and only occasionally does severe CMV brain infection more clearly cause symptoms. Such patients may present with subacute brain dysfunction, clouded consciousness, or seizures; these patients may also present with CMV-related radiculomyelitis. Ventricular ependymitis with local contrast enhancement may be detected on CT scan, and CMV can be isolated from the CSF of some. The frequency of vision loss due to CMV retinitis and its relationship to CMV infection of the brain are not yet clear.

Other Herpesvirus Infections

Although unusual, varicella-zoster virus (VZV) and, to a lesser extent, HSV types 1 and 2 have been reported to cause CNS disease in AIDS patients. VZV infections are of three types: (1) multifocal direct brain infection affecting principally the white matter and partially mimicking PML (Morgello et al., 1988; Ryder et al., 1986); (2) cerebral vasculitis which characteristically occurs in the setting of ophthalmic herpes zoster and causes contralateral hemiplegia (Eidelberg et al., 1986a; Hilt et al., 1983); and (3) myelopathy complicating herpes zoster (Devinsky et al., 1987). Both HSV-1 and HSV-2 have been identified in brains of some AIDS patients (Levy et al., 1985b). Herpetic encephalitis relating to both serotypes has been described, with the clinical picture either resembling herpes encephalitis in the nonimmunosuppressed or pursuing a more protracted and atypical course. Both serotypes of HSV can also infect the spinal cord, either alone or together with CMV (Tucker et al., 1985).

Mycobacterial Infections

Although infection by atypical mycobacteria, particularly *M. avium–intracellulare,* is one of the common systemic opoprtunistic infections complicating AIDS, there is no evidence that they directly cause CNS or PNS dysfunction. On the other hand, *M. tuberculosis* infection of the CNS may sometimes complicate the course of AIDS, particularly in those patients with a lower socioeconomic background and intravenous drug abuse as a risk factor. This CNS infection resembles that in non-AIDS patients, although it may be more aggressive in the context of AIDS. Three patients were recently reported who developed tuberculous brain abscesses or tuberculomas while they were receiving "adequate" treatment (Sunderam et al., 1986).

OPPORTUNISTIC NEOPLASMS

The CNS of AIDS patients is vulnerable to the development of lymphomas, which may either originate in the nervous system or spread secondarily to the nervous system from a systemic focus. Although there is overlap in clinical presentation of the primary and secondary lymphomas, there are general differences with respect to their time of appearance in the evolution of systemic disease and in their clinical features.

Primary CNS Lymphoma

Primary CNS lymphomas are opportunistic neoplasms which, including those found incidentally at autopsy, develop in about 5 percent of AIDS patients (Petito et al., 1986; So et al., 1986). Clinically these tumors manifest with progressive focal neurological deficit. Their presentation is similar to that of toxoplasmosis, except that their onset and progression are often more indolent. In some cases with bilateral involvement of deep white matter and the basal ganglion region, clinical distinction from the AIDS dementia complex may be difficult. Pathologically, they are multicentric in origin, but clinically and radiographically, frequently only one or two foci may be identified. Anatomically, they most often involve the brain adjacent to the lateral ventricles. Diagnosis involves CT or MRI scanning, CSF evaluation, and, definitively, brain biopsy.

Metastatic Lymphoma

HIV-1-infected patients develop B-cell lymphomas, some of the Burkitt type. These appear to develop earlier in the course of HIV-1 infection than do the opportunistic infections that define AIDS. They may be complicated by secondary spread to the CNS, most commonly manifesting as leptomeningeal metastases with cranial nerve palsies or segmental polyradiculopathies (Levy et al., 1985; Snider et al., 1983; Ziegler et al., 1984). Diagnosis is usually established with CT scanning and CSF examination, although at times cytology may be negative despite meningeal lymphomatosis. Less commonly, but at times in fulminant fashion, parenchymal brain metastases may occur with multifocal or widespread diffuse infiltration of the brain.

PERIPHERAL NEUROPATHIES AND MYOPATHIES COMPLICATING HIV-1 INFECTION

A variety of peripheral neuropathies may complicate HIV-1 infection. The particular susceptibilities vary with the stage of systemic infection and immunosuppression (Table 5.3). Several neuropathies have been described at or near the time of seroconversion, although their incidence appears to be very low (Parry, 1988) and their prognosis favorable.

Table 5.3 Peripheral Neuropathies and Radiculopathies Complicating HIV-1 Infection Classified According to the Stage of Systemic Disease in Which They Characteristically Occur

Early (associated with acute infection and seroconversion)
    Mononeuritides, brachial plexopathy
    Acute demyelinating polyneuropathy

Latent period (asymptomatic seropositive)
    Acute demyelinating polyneuropathy (Guillain-Barré)
    Chronic idiopathic demyelinating polyneuropathy (IDPN)

Late (AIDS and other HIV-1-induced manifestations)
    Mononeuritis multiplex
    Sensorimotor polyneuropathy
    CMV polyradiculopathy
    Herpes zoster
    Mononeuropathies associated with aseptic meningitis
    Mononeuropathies secondary to lymphomatous meningitis

More common is the development of demyelinating neuropathies during the asymptomatic or latent phase of HIV-1 infection (Cornblath et al. 1986). These resemble either the Guillain-Barré syndrome or chronic inflammatory demyelinating polyneuropathy seen in other contexts, with the exception that the CSF often exhibits a mild pleocytosis. The pathophysiology of this neuropathy likely parallels that of the disorder in other settings and has an autoimmune basis, explaining the favorable response to plasmapheresis or cortiocosteroids.

In milder states of immunodeficiency, and more commonly with AIDS, several other neuropathies have been described. These include the infectious radiculoneuropathies caused by VZV (i. e., herpes zoster) and an ascending polyradiculopathy caused by CMV (Eidelberg et al., 1986b). Cranial mononeuropathies may also complicate both the aseptic meningitis related to HIV-1 infection and the metastatic systemic lymphoma discussed earlier. Mononeuritis multiplex has also been described in both early and later stages of immunodeficiency (Lipkin et al., 1985). However, the commonest neuropathy is a distal, predominantly sensory, mainly axonal neuropathy occasionally beginning before AIDS but most often encountered in patients with AIDS (Cornblath, 1988). Characteristically, the sensory symptoms far exceed either sensory or motor dysfunction. Some afflicted patients experience such severe "burning feet" that walking is avoided. The pathogenesis is uncertain but may relate to direct HIV-1 infection of nerve or dorsal root ganglion. Autonomic neuropathy, ranging from severe positional hypotension to cardiovascular collapse in the setting of invasive procedures such as lung biopsy, has also been reported in AIDS patients (Craddock et al., 1987; Lin-Greenberg and Taneja-Uppal, 1987).

Myopathies may also occur at several stages of HIV-1 infection, but they are less common and less well characterized (Bailey et al., 1987; Dalakas et al., 1986; Simpson et al., 1987). Accumulating data suggest that there may be a wide range of presentations, extending from asymptomatic with creatine kinase elevation to progressive proximal weakness with either noninflammatory or inflammatory pathology.

CONCLUSIONS

From its acute onset to its terminal phase, AIDS, HIV-1 infection is complicated by a variety of neurological disorders. Although several of these were recognized and characterized early in the epidemic and are now reasonably well understood, others remain to be precisely defined with respect to their etiology, pathogenesis, epidemiology, natural history, and therapy. These aspects are especially pertinent to those conditions known or suspected to relate to direct HIV-1 infection of the CNS or PNS. These disorders warrant rigorous investigation to include (1) collection of background information (degree of immunosuppression, concomitant systemic diseases, and perhaps cofactors), (2) careful neurological diagnosis (involving diagnostic neurological examinations, neuroimaging, and CSF analysis), (3) standardized quantitative neurological and neuropsychological evaluations, and (4) virological analysis (of CSF and blood in life and tissue at autopsy). Tissue culture and animal models need to be developed and exploited for complementary laboratory studies. The AIDS dementia complex and other manifestations of HIV-1 nervous system infection are clinically and biologically important. Additionally, their understanding has implications not only for AIDS but also for neurological and psychiatric disorders of unknown etiology.

ACKNOWLEDGMENTS

Our studies of the neurological complications of AIDS were supported by research grant AR074 from the New York State AIDS Institute, Public Health Service grant NS-21703 from the National Institutes of Health, the Life and Health Insurance Medical Research Fund, and the Rudin Foundation. We thank Ms. Francine Kaskel for preparation of this manuscript.

REFERENCES

Appelman ME, Brey RL, Marshall DW, Boswell RN, Houk RW, Winn RW (1987): Third International Conference on AIDS, Washington, DC, June 1–5.
Bailey RO, Turok DI, Jaufmann BP, Singh JK (1987): Hum Pathol 18:749.
Belman AL, Ultmann MH, Horoupian D, Novick B, Spiro AJ, Rubinstein A, Kurtzberg D, Cone-Wesson B (1985): Ann Neurol 18:560.
Belman AL, Lantos G, Horoupian D, Novick BE, Ultmann MH, Dickson DW, Rubinstein A (1986): Neurology 36:1192.
Berger JR, Kaszovitz B, Post JD, Dickinson G (1987): Ann Intern Med 107:78.
Brew BJ, Cooper DA, Perdices MJ, White B, Darveniza P (1987): Third International Conference on AIDS, Washington, DC, June 1–5.
Brew B, Sidtis J, Petito CK, Price RW (1988): In Plum F, ed: Advances in Contemporary Neurology. Philadelphia: F. A. Davis 29:1.
Britton CB, Miller JR (1984): Neurol Clin 2:315.
Budka H (1986): Acta Neuropathol (Berl) 69:253.
Budka H, Costanzi G, Cristina S, Lechi A, Parravicini C, Trabattoni R, Vago L (1987): Acta Neuropathol (Berl) 75:195.
Carne CA. Smith A, Elkington SG, Preston FE, Tedder RS, Sutherland S, Daly HM, Craske J (1985): Lancet 2:1206.
Centers for Disease Control (1986): MMWR 35:334.

Centers for Disease Control (1987): MMWR 36:1S.

Clotet B, Barrera JM, Ercilla G, Grifol M, Tor J, Cano J, Argelagues E (1987): Third International Conference on AIDS, Washington, DC, June 1–5.

Collier AC, Coombs RW, Nikora B, Handsfield HH (1987): Third International Conference on AIDS, Washington, DC, June 1–5.

Cornblath DR (1988): Ann Neurol 23:S88.

Cornblath DR, McArthur JC, Kennedy PGE, Witte AS, Griffin JW (1986): Ann Neurol 21:32.

Craddock C, Pasvol G, Bull R, Protheroe A, Hopkin J (1987): Lancet 2:16.

Dalakas MC, Pezeshkpour GH, Gravell M, Sever JL (1986): JAMA 256:2381.

De la Monte SM, Ho DD, Schooley RT, Hirsch MS, Richardson EP (1987): Neurology 37:562.

Denning DA, Anderson J, Rudge P, Smith H (1987): Br Med J 294:143.

Devinsky O, Cho ES, Petito CK, Price RW (1987): Neurology 37 (Suppl 1):319.

Eidelberg D, Sotrel A, Horoupian DS, Neumann PE, Pumarola-Sune T, Price RW (1986a): Ann Neurol 19:7.

Eidelberg D, Sotrel A, Vogel H, Walker P, Kleefield J, Crumpacker CS (1986b): Neurology 36:912.

Elovaara I, Iivanainen M, Valle S-L, Suni J, Tervo T, Lahdevirta J (1987): J Neurol Sci 78:331.

Epstein LG, Sharer LR, Cho ES, Meyenhofer M, Navia BA, Price RW (1985a): AIDS Res 1:447.

Epstein LG, Sharer LR, Joshi V, Fojas MM, Koenigsberger MR, Oleske JM (1985b): Ann Neurol 17:488.

Epstein LG, Sharer LR, Goudsmit J (1988): Ann Neurol 23:S19.

Folstein MF, Folstein SE, McHugh PR (1975): J Psychol Res 12:189.

Gabuzda DH, Ho DD, De la Monte SM, Hirsch MS, Rota TR, Sobel RA (1986): Ann Neurol 20:289.

Gartner S, Markovits P, Markovits DM, Betts RF, Popvic M (1986): JAMA 256:2365.

Goudsmit J, deWolf F, Paul DA, Epstein LG, Lange JMA, Krone WJA Speelman H, Wolters EC Van der Noordaa J, Oleske JM, Van der Helm HJ, Coutinho RA (1986a): Lancet 2:177.

Goudsmit J, Wolters EC, Bakker M, Smit L, Van der Noordaa J, Hische EAH, Tutuarima JA, Van der Helm HJ (1986b): Br Med J 292:1231.

Grant I, Atkinson JH, Hesselink JR, Kennedy CJ, Richman DD, Spector SA, McCutchan JA (1987): Ann Intern Med 107:828.

Gyorkey F, Melnick JL, Gyorkey P (1987): J Infect Dis 155:870.

Hilt DC, Bucholz D, Krumholz A, Weiss H, Wolinsky JS (1983): Ann Neurol 14:543.

Ho DD, Rota TR, Schooley RT, Kaplan JC, Allan JD, Groopman JE, Resnick L, Felsenstein D, Andrews CA, Hirsch, MS (1985a): N Engl J Med 313:1493.

Ho DD, Sarngadharan MG, Resnick L, Dimaro-Veronese F, Rota TR, and Hirsch MS (1985b): Ann Intern Med 103:880.

Hollander H, Levy JA (1987): Ann Intern Med 106:692.

Hollander H, Stringari S (1987): Am J Med 83:81.

Janssen RS, Saykin AJ, Kaplan JE, Spira TJ, Pinsky PF, Sprehn GC, Hoffman JC, Mayer WB, Schonberger LB (1988): Ann Neurol 23:S17.

Jarvik J, Hesselink J, Kennedy C, Teschke R, Wiley C, McCutchan JA (1987): Third International Conference on AIDS, Washington, DC, June 1–5.

Koenig S, Gendelman HE, Orenstein JM, Dal Canto MC, Pezeshkpour GH, Yungbluth M, Janotta F, Aksamit A, Martin MA, Fauci AS (1986): Science 233:1089.

Kovacs JA, Kovacs AA, Polis M, Wright WC, Gill VJ, Tuazon CU, Gelmann EP, Lane HC, Longfield R, Overturf G, Macher AM, Fauci AS, Parrillo JE, Bennett JE, Masur H (1985): Ann Intern Med 103:533.

Krupp LB, Lipton RB, Swerdlow ML, Leeds NE, Llena J (1985): Ann Neurol 17:344.

Levy JA, Shimabukuro J, Hollander H, Mills J, Kaminsky L (1985a): Lancet 2:586.

Levy RL, Bredesen DE, Rosenblum ML (1985b): J Neurosurg 62:475.

Lin-Greenberg A, Taneja-Uppal N (1987): Ann Intern Med 106:167.

Lipkin WI, Parry G, Kiprov D, Abrams D (1985): Neurology 35:1479.

McArthur JC (1987): Medicine 66:407.

McArthur JC, Cohen BA, Farzadegan H, Cornblath DR, Selnes OA, Ostrow D, Johnson RT, Phair J, Polk BF (1988): Ann Neurol 23:S34.

Michaels J, Price RW, Rosenblum MK: (1988) Acta Neuropath 76:373.

Morgello S, Cho ES, Nielsen S, Devinsky O, Petito CK (1987): Hum Pathol 18:289.

Morgello S, Block GA, Price RW, Petito CK: (1988) Arch Pathol Lab Med 112:173.

Navia BA, Price RW (1986): In Pinching AJ, ed: Clinics in Immunology and Allergy, Vol 6. London: WB Saunders, p 543.

Navia BA, Price RW (1987): Arch Neurol 44:65.

Navia BA, Cho ES, Petito CK, Price RW (1986a): Ann Neurol 19:525.

Navia BA, Jordan BD, Price RW (1986b): Ann Neurol 19:517.

Navia BA, Petito CK, Gold JWM, Cho ES, Jordan BD, Price RW (1986c): Ann Neurol 19:224.

Parry GJ (1988): Ann Neurol 23:S49.

Petito CK, Navia BA, Cho ES, Jordan BD, George DC, Price RW (1985): N Engl J Med 312:874.

Petito CK, Cho ES, Lemann W, Navia BA, Price RW (1986): J Neuropathol Exp Neurol 45:635.

Price RW, Brew B (1988a): Ann NY Acad Sci 2:359.

Price RW, Brew B (1988b): In Sande MA, Volberding P, eds: Infectious Disease Clinics of North America. Philadelphia: WB Saunders (in press).

Price RW, Brew B, Sidtis J, Rosenblum M, Scheck AC, Cleary P (1988a): Science 239:586.

Price RW, Sidtis JJ, Navia BA, Pumarola-Sune T, Ornitz DB (1988b): In Rosenblum ML, Levy RM, Bredesen DE, eds: New York: Raven Press, pp 203–219.

Price RW, Sidtis JJ, Rosenblum M (1988c): Ann Neurol 23 (Suppl):27.

Pumarola-Sune, T, Navia BA, Cordon-Cardo C, Cho ES, Price RW (1987): Ann Neurol 21:490.

Resnick L, DiMarzo-Veronese F, Schupbach J, Tourtellotte WW, Ho DD, Muller F, Shapshak P, Vogt M, Groopman JE, Markham PD, Gallo RC (1985): N Engl J Med 313:1498.

Resnick L, Berger JR, Shapshak P, Tourtellotte WW (1988): Neurology 38:9.

Richardson EP (1978): In Vinken PJ, Bruyn GW, eds: Handbook of Clinical Neurology, Vol 34. Amsterdam: Elsevier, p 307.

Rosenblum ML, Levy RM, Bredesen D, eds (1988): AIDS and the Nervous System. New York: Raven Press.

Ryder JW, Croen K, Kleinschmidt-de-Masters BK, Ostrove JM, Straus SR, Cohn DL (1986): Ann Neurol 19:182.

Sharer LR, Epstein LG, Cho ES, Joshi VV, Meyenhofer MF, Rankin LF, Petito CK (1986): Hum Pathol 17:271.

Shaw GM, Harper ME, Hahn BH, Epstein LG, Gajdusek DC, Price RW, Navia BA, Petito CK, O'Hara CJ, Groopman JE, Cho ES, Oleske JM, Wong-Stall F, Gallo RC (1985): Science 277:177.

Sidtis JJ, Amitai H, Ornitz D, Price RW (1987): Third International Conference on AIDS, Washington, DC, June 1–5.

Simpson DM, Bender AN (1988): Ann Neurology 24:79.

Snider WD, Simpson DM, Nielsen S, Gold JWM, Metroka C, Posner JB (1983): Ann Neurol 14:403.

So YT, Beckstead JH, Davis RL (1986): Ann Neurol 20:566.

Stoler MH, Eskin TA, Benn S, Angerer RC, Angerer LM (1986): JAMA 256:2360.

Sunderam G, McDonald RJ, Maniatis T, Oleske J, Kapila R, Reichman LB (1986): JAMA 256:362.

Tross S, Price RW, Navia BA, Thaler HT, Gold J, Hirsch DA, Sidtis JJ: (1988): AIDS 2:81.

Tucker T, Dix RD, Katzen C, David RL, Schmidley JW (1985): Ann Neurol 18:74.

Vazeux R, Brousse N, Jarry A, Henin D, Marche C, Vedrenne C, Mikol J, Wolfe M, Michon C, Rozenbaum W, Bureau JF, Montagnier L, Brahic M (1987): Am J Pathol 126:403.

Walker DL (1978): In Vinken PJ, Bruyn GW, eds: Handbook of Clinical Neurology, part II, Vol 34. Amsterdam: North Holland, p 307.

Wiley CA, Schrier RD, Nelson JA, Lampert PW, Oldstone MBA (1986): Proc Natl Acad Sci USA 83:7089.

Yarchoan R, Thomas RV, Grafman J, Wichman A, Dalakas M, McAtee N, Berg G, Fischl M, Perno FC, Klecker RW, Buchbinder A, Tay S, Larson SM, Myers CE, Broder S (1988): Ann Neurol 23 (Suppl):S82.

Ziegler JL, Beckstead JA, Volberding PA, Abrams DI, Levine AM, Lukes RJ, Gill PS, Burkes RL, Meyer PR, Metroka CE, Mouradian J, Moore A, Riggs SA, Butler JJ, Cabanillas FC, Hersh E, Newell GR, Laubenstein LJ, Knowles D, Odajnyk C, Raphael B, Koziner B, Urmacher C, Clarkson BD (1984): N Engl J Med 311:565.

Zuger A, Louie E, Holzman RS, Simberkoff MS, Rahal JJ (1986): Ann Intern Med 104:234.

II
OCCURRENCE IN POPULATIONS

6

Epidemiology: General Considerations

RICHARD A. KASLOW AND DONALD P. FRANCIS

Many epidemiologic features of HIV-1 infection and AIDS are pertinent to the epidemic as a whole rather than peculiar to one or another group of persons at risk. This chapter addresses the general issues of the origin of the infection, occurrence and surveillance, transmission, cofactors or risk modifiers, natural history, and epidemic models. It is also intended to provide some perspective on the information presented in subsequent chapters.

ORIGINS OF HIV-1 INFECTION

From the moment AIDS was recognized as a strange and frightening phenomenon, speculation about its origin was irresistible. Growing just beneath the fear and speculation was the xenophobia that has often accompanied transcontinental propagation of epidemics. For decades after the great pandemic of syphilis began to sweep through Europe and across the Atlantic in the late 15th century, citizens of nearly every country exchanged recriminations about who was to "blame" for it. With AIDS, as with other epidemics in the past, it has been difficult to separate the scientific and social motives—to encourage observations on the roots of a natural phenomenon but resist tendencies toward self-serving explanations for that phenomenon.

It is easy to suppose that the infection was first acquired by a traveler in a land with primitive and remote areas. Acquisition might have been especially likely in a place where an initially harmless simian retrovirus could have been transmitted to humans—e.g., a country in Africa. There are data to support the notion that the virus first struck Africans some years ago. Recent discovery of antibodies to HIV-1 in serum taken in 1976 from residents of small villages and Kinshasa, Zaire (Nzilambi et al., 1988), supports earlier observations (Nahmias et al., 1986; Nemeth et al., 1986) and heightens the suspicion that the virus has existed in Africa for years.

Precisely where the first case arose seems less significant than how the virus originated. The two most plausible theories have been (1) that HIV-1 is derived from a simian or other animal agent (Lewin, 1985) recently transferred to humans, for whom it is especially lethal, or (2) that copies of the sequence of genetic material closely resembling HIV-1 have existed for ages unobtrusively in some remote, sequestered human population until someone from outside that population acquired it from someone within (Desmyter et al., 1986). It seems far less likely that the agent arose de novo by mutation or other simple genetic rearrangements.

It is doubtful that the origins of the virus will ever be fully known. Regardless of how the primordial AIDS retrovirus first entered humans, once it appeared in an urban area—it could have been in almost any city in the world—it became a matter of when, not whether, the combination of multiple sexual partnerships and exchange of contaminated blood would lead to the earliest cases of AIDS.

OCCURRENCE AND SURVEILLANCE

AIDS and Related Disease

Soon after the first cases of AIDS were reported to the Centers for Disease Control (CDC, 1981a,b), that agency began formal surveillance for opportunistic infections and Kaposi's sarcoma in the presence of unexplained immune deficiency. The earliest clinical–epidemiologic surveillance definition of AIDS was simply "a disease, at least moderately indicative of a defect in cell-mediated immunity, occurring in a person with no known cause for diminished resistance to that disease" (CDC, 1982). It served well until the advent of specific diagnostic techniques for HIV-1 infection and the elucidation of the broad clinical spectrum of HIV-1 infection. The original criteria for AIDS and, more recently, the revised criteria for AIDS and for other manifestations of HIV-1 infection (CDC, 1987a) have been widely accepted for disease surveillance, at least in adults in the developed world. These criteria do not and are not intended to categorize all persons with HIV-1 infection diagnostically or prognostically. Using these surveillance criteria, the CDC, along with state and local health authorities in the United States and their counterparts in many other countries, have compiled increasingly thorough statistics on the occurrence and distribution of AIDS cases. Current summary figures have been readily available for the United States in weekly surveillance reports (CDC, 1988). The patterns of occurrence in the United States as seen in Table 6.1 are drawn from statistics compiled through August 29, 1988. Figure 6.1 represents projections based on earlier data.

The impact of AIDS in the United States may be more fully appreciated when the numerical projections of future cases are considered. As predicted from an empirically based model similar to the one used for the projections published in the Coolfont Report (1986), it is expected that approximately 365,000 cases will have occurred by the end of 1992—more than four times the number reported through mid-1988. In 1992 alone, the expected number of new cases (80,000) will approximate the number seen during the first 7 years of the epidemic (CDC, 1988c).

Most public health authorities have been confident that published data for AIDS in the United States have been relatively accurate and complete. However, certain social disincentives to diagnosing and reporting AIDS have been superimposed on the usual inaccuracies of disease surveillance due to suboptimal diagnostic effort, occurrence of atypical cases, and inadequate updating of initial reports

Table 6.1. United States Cases Reported to Centers for Disease Control as of August 29, 1988

Transmission Categories[a,b]	Males		Females		Total	
	Since Jan. 1 Number (%)	Cumulative Number (%)	Since Jan. 1 Number (%)	Cumulative Number (%)	Since Jan. 1 Number (%)	Cumulative Number (%)
Adults/Adolescents						
Homosexual/Bisexual Male	12,108 (63)	44,402 (68)			12,108 (57)	44,402 (63)
Intravenous (IV) Drug Abuser	3,856 (20)	10,579 (16)	1,157 (54)	3,029 (52)	5,013 (24)	13,608 (19)
Homosexual Male and IV Drug Abuser	1,382 (7)	5,168 (8)			1,382 (7)	5,168 (7)
Hemophilia/Coagulation Disorder	201 (1)	659 (1)	6 (0)	21 (0)	207 (1)	680 (1)
Heterosexual Cases[c]	364 (2)	1,281 (2)	588 (27)	1,700 (29)	952 (4)	2,981 (4)
Transfusion, Blood/Components	375 (2)	1,147 (2)	234 (11)	642 (11)	609 (3)	1,789 (3)
Undetermined[d]	789 (4)	1,806 (3)	175 (8)	448 (8)	964 (5)	2,254 (3)
Subtotal (% of all cases)	19,075 (90)	65,042 (92)	2,160 (10)	5,840 (8)	21,235 (100)	70,882 (100)
Children[e]						
Hemophilia/Coagulation Disorder	23 (11)	64 (10)	1 (1)	3 (1)	24 (6)	67 (6)
Parent with/at risk of AIDS[f]	146 (70)	444 (72)	145 (85)	442 (85)	291 (76)	886 (78)
Transfusion, Blood/Components	33 (16)	94 (15)	16 (9)	56 (11)	49 (13)	150 (13)
Undetermined[c]	8 (4)	18 (3)	9 (5)	21 (4)	17 (4)	39 (3)
Subtotal (% of all cases)	210 (55)	620 (54)	171 (45)	522 (46)	381 (100)	1,142 (100)
Total (% of all cases)	19,285 (89)	65,662 (91)	2,331 (11)	6,362 (9)	21,616 (100)	72,024[g] (100)

[a]Provisional data as of August 29, 1988.

[b]Cases with more than one risk factor other than the combinations listed in the tables or footnotes are tabulated only in the category listed first.

[c]Includes 1,858 persons (418 men, 1,440 women) who have had heterosexual contact with a person with AIDS or at risk for AIDS and 1,123 persons (863 men, 260 women) without other identified risks who were born in countries in which heterosexual transmission is believed to play a major role although precise means of transmission have not yet been fully defined.

[d]Includes patients on whom risk information is incomplete (due to death, refusal to be interviewed or loss to follow-up), patients still under investigation, men reported only to have had heterosexual contact with a prostitute, and interviewed patients for whom no specific risk was identified.

[e]Includes all patients under 13 years of age at time of diagnosis.

[f]Epidemiologic data suggest transmission from an infected mother to her fetus or infant during the perinatal period.

[g]Includes 9,296 patients who meet only the 1987 revised surveillance definition for AIDS.

Source: CDC AIDS Weekly Surveillance Report, August 29, 1988.

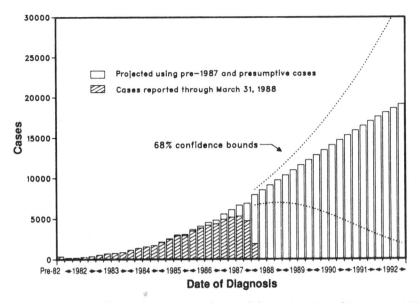

Figure 6.1. Incidence of AIDS, by quarter and year of diagnosis—United States, pre-1982–
1992 (Projected from cases diagnosed as of June 30, 1987, and reported as of March 31,
1988). *Source: MMWR 37(36):552.*

among other shortcomings. In a study of reporting to health departments before
1985, about 20 percent of AIDS cases were escaping local surveillance. In areas like
New York City, where a concerted effort to validate surveillance data has been
supported, the combination of information from active and passive hospital reporting, selected laboratory test results, and autopsy findings (Chamberland et al., 1985)
testified reassuringly to the high quality of AIDS surveillance data. More recent
attempts to corroborate the validity of these data in several US cities suggest even
more complete reporting.

Subsequent chapters in this volume suggest that individuals with HIV-1 infection in different transmission categories, geographic locations, or ethnic groups
have demonstrated distinctive patterns of occurrence and manifestations of AIDS.
These variations generally reflect the distributions of the etiologic agent(s) responsible for the opportunistic conditions. One of the most intriguing variations has
been in the frequency of Kaposi's sarcoma (KS). From early in the epidemic, KS
has occurred preponderantly in homosexual men (DesJarlais et al., 1984; also see
later), with few cases seen in certain other groups. More recently, the proportion of
new cases of AIDS in homosexual men with the diagnosis of KS has been declining
steadily and sharply (Polk et al., 1988). In nonhomosexual risk groups, KS has
accounted for a much smaller proportion of all AIDS cases; comparable declines
in KS have not been verified in these groups. Alternative hypotheses about the
etiology and "disappearance" of KS among homosexual men are discussed below.

Worldwide statistics on AIDS have been quite variable in quality and comprehensiveness. Other developed nations—e.g., in Europe (Glauser et al., 1984)
and Canada (AIDS Surveillance, 1985)—have adopted surveillance procedures as

effective as the U.S. approach. Figures from the developing world are undoubtedly less reliable, since they have been based on less uniform and rigorous reporting practices than those implemented in the United States. In all, 175 countries had reported AIDS cases to the World Health Organization by late July 1988 (WHO, 1988), yet there were still countries where the mere admission or notification of AIDS represented a sensitive political issue. By mid-1988 about 100,000 cases of AIDS had been reported by all countries other than the United States in the face of what most experts believe is a considerably greater burden of illness—perhaps twice the number of AIDS cases and a much larger reservoir of milder immunodeficiency. Ten countries have contributed more than 80% of the reported cases (Table 6.2). Despite an increasingly organized worldwide effort to combat the disease, the combination of diagnostic inadequacies, inaccessibility to medical care, and inconsistent reporting have seriously compromised estimates of the magnitude and patterns of occurrence in many places.

In contrast to the surveillance statistics and the fatality ratios for AIDS, knowledge about the frequency and patterns of other HIV-1-induced conditions is far less systematic. Reports from large cohorts of homosexuals (Jaffe et al., 1985; Lang et al., 1987; Kaslow et al., 1987a,b) and heterosexuals (Melbye et al., 1986; Mann et al., 1986) suggest that a variety of symptoms, signs, and hematologic manifesta-

Table 6.2. Acquired Immunodeficiency Syndrome by World Health Organization Region and Country, February 1988

Area[a]	Date	Number
Americas	2/88	60,409
United States	2/88	53,069
Brazil	6/87	2,325
Canada	6/87	1,695
Haiti	9/87	912
Mexico	10/87	713
Africa	2/88	9.760
Uganda	10/87	2,369
Tanzania	10/87	1,608
Congo	12/87	1,250
Kenya	11/87	964
Rwanda	11/86	705
Burundi	10/87	569
Zambia	12/87	536
Eastern Mediterranean	2/88	82
Europe	2/88	10,245
France	12/87	3,073
Federal Republic of Germany	1/88	1,760
Italy	12/87	1,411
United Kingdom	12/87	1,227
Spain	12/87	718
Southeast Asia	2/88	24
Western Pacific	2/88	913
Australia	2/88	758

[a]Includes individual countries with more then 500 reported cases.

tions of immunodeficiency appear in a significant proportion of infected persons who have not developed AIDS. A disturbing proportion of persons who are infected but who initially have no overt features of immunodeficiency develop significant clinical involvement as time passes (Mann et al. 1986; Kaslow et al., 1988). Although some effort has been made to classify these conditions (e.g., as an AIDS-related complex), no criteria for them have been widely or uniformly adopted. Nor has any conventional surveillance of these conditions been instituted. Although extensive clinical studies of neuropsychological manifestations have been conducted (see Chapter 5), epidemiologic inquiry into this aspect of HIV-1 infection has just begun to yield useful information.

Table 6.3. Estimated Prevalence of HIV Infection in Selected Groups in the United States, 1986–1988

Group	Source	No. Initially under Study	Average % Positive	Comments
High-risk groups				
Homosexuals	STD and other medical clinics	1,700	25	13 states[a]
	Selected cohorts	12,400	45	6 urban areas[b]
Prostitutes	STD clinics/other communities	800	5	Prevalence varies from 0% to 40% by location
IV drug users	Hospitals and detoxification/ methadone clinics			
	New York City	700	55	
	Other East Coast	2,000	25	5 states[c]
	Elsewhere	4,700	5	13 states[d]
Hemophiliacs	Treatment centers	1,500	60	
Low-risk groups				
Blood donors	American Red Cross	3 million	0.01	Jan. to June 1987
Military Recruits	Department of Defense	600,000/yr	0.14	Oct. 1985 to Sept. 1987
Active duty	Department of Defense	1.7 million	0.13	Jan. 1986 to Apr. 1988
Hospital patients	CDC sentinels	9,000	0.32	4 midwestern hospitals
Heterosexuals	Prenatal/family planning clinics	11,000	0.84	Women from 10 states[e]
Newborns	All live births			
	Massachusetts	31,000	0.20	Dec. 1986 to Jan. 1987
	New York			
	New York City	27,000	1.5	Oct. 1987 to Jan. 1988
	Upstate	24,000	0.18	Same

[a]Arkansas, California, Colorado, Georgia, Illinois, Kentucky, Massachusetts, Maryland, Missouri, New Mexico, New York, Pennsylvania, Washington.

[b]Baltimore, Chicago, Los Angeles, Pittsburgh, San Francisco, Washington, D.C.

[c]Massachusetts, Connecticut, New Jersey, Delaware, Maryland.

[d]Florida, Georgia, Illinois, Michigan, Minnesota, Missouri, New Mexico, Ohio, Pennsylvania, Puerto Rico, Texas, Washington, Wisconsin.

[e]Alabama, California, Florida, Illinois, Maryland, North Carolina, New York, Pennsylvania, Puerto Rico, Wisconsin.

Sources: CDC (1987b; 1988a), Novick (1988), Hoff, et al. (1988).

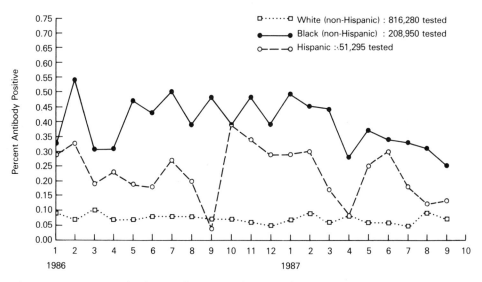

Figure 6.2. HIV-1 antibody prevalence in military applicants (*n* = 1,253,768) by race or ethnicity, United States, Jan. 1986 to Sept. 1987. *Source:* CDC, 1987b.

Prevalence of Infection

Figures compiled by the U.S. Public Health Service (CDC, 1987b) on seroprevalence in the United States have been distilled (Table 6.3) to reflect average estimates for 1986–1987. The estimates for each of the high-risk groups are probably inflated, since the sources of that information (i.e., sexually transmitted disease clinics, drug treatment centers, and selected cohort studies) may have attracted men and women at somewhat higher risk. In other groups prevalence has been highly variable, depending on location and intensity of involvement in high-risk activities.

In mid-1988 it was estimated that 1.5–2 million Americans had been infected. The socially sensitive nature of the information obtained from direct serologic screening has often made it inordinately difficult to conduct broad serosurveys of persons with no apparent risk. Data on antibody prevalence and risk factors have been collected from active duty military personnel and at centers where civilian candidates are recruited for induction into the U.S. Army (Fig. 6.2). However, those data reflect a combination of strong incentives for recruits to deny membership in a risk group and, especially more recently, for the less committed to forego enlistment. Important unbiased information on prevalence in childbearing women has been collected in Massachusetts (Hoff et al., 1988) and New York (Novick, 1988) by testing of blood drawn for other purposes from every newborn delivered during the study interval. Prevalence throughout New York averaged 0.8 percent but reached beyond 2 percent in certain boroughs of New York City, where infants of sexually active parenteral drug users or their partners were heavily represented among those tested.

The diversity of these sources of prevalence information has not quelled con-

a

0–49	
50–100	
100–200	
200–400	
400 +	

137
11 9
89 56
15 7 33 43
16 24 21 43 693
125 49 149 38 66 103 38 45 92 160 MA
372 89 51 51 26 21 88 101 RI
176 32 28 49 160 CT
23 48 159 52 346 NJ
134 278 93 DE
174 MD
1427 DC

64

165

PR 123

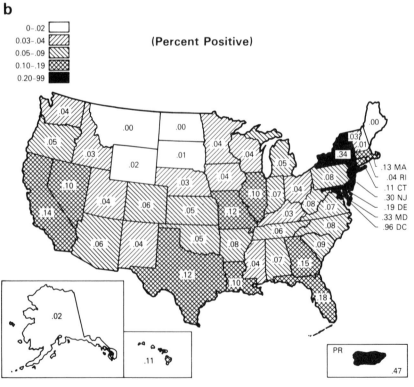

b

0–.02	
0.03–.04	
0.05–.09	
0.10–.19	
0.20–99	

(Percent Positive)

.04
.00 .00
.05 .04
.03 .01 .04 .00
.02 .04 .05 .03 .34
.10 .04 .06 .05 .12 .10 .07 .04 .08 .13 MA
.14 .06 .04 .05 .08 .03 .08 .07 .04 RI
.12 .10 .04 .07 .06 .08 .11 CT
.09 .15 .30 NJ
.18 .19 DE
.33 MD
.96 DC

.02

.11

PR .47

94

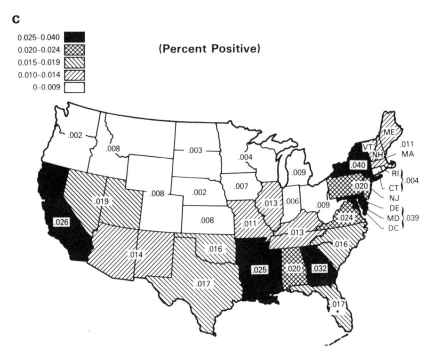

Figure 6.3. Geographic distribution of AIDS and HIV-1 infection in the United States. (a) Incidence of AIDS cases (n = 44,745), by state, per million population, Nov. 2, 1987. *Source:* CDC, 1987b. (b) Sex-adjusted HIV-1 antibody prevalence (percent positive) in military applicants (n = 1,253,768), by state, Oct. 1985 to Sept. 1987. *Source:* CDC, 1987b. (c) HIV-1 antibody prevalence (percent positive) in blood donors, combined data from adjacent centers, by state, July 1986 to June 1987. *Source:* CDC, 1987b.

cern over their incompleteness and selectivity. However, military recruit prevalence figures and similar data on blood donors are consistent with cumulative frequencies of AIDS cases (Fig. 6.3), probably broadly reflecting the relative frequencies of infection by geographic and perhaps other demographic characteristics. Studies aimed at establishing prevalence in more unselected groups throughout the United States are under way. However, a nationwide survey, although contemplated, has not been conducted among randomly or systematically sampled individuals.

Surveys in relatively representative populations of developed areas outside of the United States (e.g., Canada, Europe and Australia) suggest that the prevalence of HIV-1 infection in those groups has remained low, usually far less than 1% as of mid-1988. By that time prevalence estimates had reached measurable levels in a number of areas of the developing world, upwards of 15 percent in certain general urban populations of central Africa (see Chapter 11) and as high as 10 percent in urban areas of Haiti (see Chapter 12). Between 5 and 10 million persons were estimated by the World Health Organization to have been infected worldwide.

Incidence of Infection

Accurate estimates of incidence of HIV-1 infection have been difficult to obtain within the developed world, except in established cohorts of homosexual men. Serial measurements of prevalence can be used to estimate incidence, but they have certain drawbacks. For example, the constant or slightly declining prevalence of antibodies in the pool of military recruits from January 1986 through September 1987 (Fig. 6.2) suggests no rapid rise in incidence of the infection. However, a modest rise in the incidence among all eligibles could have been offset by progressively greater self-exclusion among those actually applying. In fact, in 1986 and early 1987, rising prevalence in recruits examined according to birth year cohort suggested an annual incidence of 0.05 percent. Furthermore, 0.077 percent of active-duty personnel tested on two or more occasions seroconverted (CDC, 1987b). When expected seasonal changes were taken into account, persons donating blood for the first time showed rather constant HIV-1 antibody prevalence during the 2 years prior to July 1987, but the incidence of new infection in donors tested more than once was about 0.003 percent (CDC, 1987b). Regardless of how incidence is assessed, rapid changes in short time intervals have limited the accuracy of the estimates.

During the first 5 to 7 years of the epidemic in urban areas, the average annual incidence must have exceeded 5 percent (Stevens et al., 1986a) in the high-risk groups for prevalence to have reached the levels measured in 1984 and subsequently. More recently, large cohort studies of homosexual men in North America have demonstrated significant reductions in the annual incidence of HIV infection (Table 6.4).

Table 6.4. Estimated Incidence of HIV-1 Infection in Large Cohorts of Homosexual Men in North America Between 1985 and 1987

Location	Dates	No. Studied	New Infection (%)
Albany	85–86	220	2.3
Boston	84–86	334	3.0 (2-year rate)
Vancouver	2/85–10/85	345(1982)	4.3
	11/85–7/86		1.7
MACS	4/84–10/84	2,985	4.3
(Baltimore, Chicago,	11/84–4/86		1.8
Los Angeles,	5/86–10/86		1.8
Pittsburgh)	11/86–4/87		0.9
New York	84–85	446	6.8
	85–86		2.0
	86–87		2.8
San Francisco			
Winkelstein	84–85	615	5.4
	85–86		4.2
Health Department	84	283	2.1
	85		2.1
	86		0.8

Sources: CDC (1987b), Schecter et al. (1987), Detels et al. (1989), Winkelstein et al. (1987b), Stevens (unpublished).

Data from some longitudinal studies (McCusick et al., 1985; Fox et al., 1987; Martin, 1987a; Ekstrand and Coates, 1988) have suggested that homosexual men have made rather profound changes in their sexual behavior during past 3 or 4 years (see also Chapter 16). These trends are encouraging, but the outlook should be cautious. Seronegative men have not invariably responded appropriately (Willoughby et al. 1987). Moreover, since cohorts under study longitudinally have generally been sampled without replacement, the men who have remained seronegative for several years may be less likely to become infected than are currently seronegative homosexual men in general. Of equal concern is that while the probability of infection in these cohorts may have diminished as high-risk behavior was curtailed, in homosexual men in general, the relative effects of safer sexual behavior may not have offset the increased risk due to rising prevalence of infection. Similar changes in intravenous drug addicts and prostitutes will probably be harder to achieve and to document (Hart et al., 1988). A preliminary report has described reluctance in spouses of hemophiliacs to make certain important behavioral changes (Goedert et al., 1987).

Outside the developed world, serial cross-sectional surveys have demonstrated rapid rises in prevalence (see Chapter 11), but systematic follow-up has rarely been available. Early data on hospital personnel in Kinshasa (Ngaly et al., 1987) showed that 41 seroconversions occurred in the 2 years prior to November 1986, for a rate of 1.0/100 person-years of observation. By early 1988, however, reports from Kinshasa were optimistic about substantial declines in both incidence of HIV-1 infection and frequency of clinic visits for other sexually transmitted diseases.

Lacking direct surveillance data on infection rates for whole populations and the mechanisms for gathering them, public health officials in some geographic areas have concentrated on the frequencies of gonorrhea (Judson et al., 1983; Eschenbach, unpublished data), hepatitis B (Alter et al., 1987), and, more recently, syphilis (CDC, 1988b). Although the declines in reported cases of syphilis in homosexual and bisexual men have paralleled their reported reductions in risk-conferring behaviors (see earlier), absence of such a decline in hepatitis B in one area (Osterholm et al., 1987) and striking increases in syphilis in a number of heterosexual populations (CDC, 1988) have raised some doubt that publicity and counseling have been broadly effective in reducing the incidence of HIV-1 infection.

TRANSMISSION

Transmissibility

Very little information is available on the factors that determine when and how easily the virus may be transmitted by infected individuals. There has been a preliminary suggestion that transmissibility may increase during the latter stages of immunodeficiency (Goedert et al, 1987). Recently, a comparison of seropositive and seronegative wives of seropositive men revealed that the seropositive women had actually had fewer sexual contacts than seronegatives and that the range of contact was quite wide (Peterman et al., 1988). The implication of the analysis is that unknown factors must play a significant role in determining transmissibility or susceptibility.

Modes of Transmission

Modes of transmission of the virus have been systematically reviewed recently (Friedland et al., 1987) and are addressed repeatedly in subsequent chapters. Certain aspects of transmission merit further discussion.

Sexual

There is ample epidemiologic evidence that during homosexual intercourse, the virus is transmitted from the penis of the insertive partner into the anus and rectum of the receptive partner. Data from the earliest case–control investigations of prevalent cases and infection and from more recent prospective studies of incident infection have been quite consistent in demonstrating the greatest relative risks for receptive anal intercourse (Jaffe et al., 1983; Goedert et al., 1984; Chmiel et al., 1987; Kingsley et al., 1987; Winkelstein et al., 1987a,b; Schecter et al., 1986a). Insertive anal intercourse may confer some risk, but it has been more difficult to establish the magnitude of that risk (Detels et al., 1988; Goedert et al., 1984). On the other hand, in most of the investigations of homosexual practices where a full range of sex practices was carefully considered, the risk from either insertive or receptive orogenital contact was uncertain but quite low (Jeffries et al., 1985; Lyman et al., 1986; Detels et al., 1988). Among infected heterosexual females and prostitutes (Kreiss et al., 1986), partners of hemophiliacs (Goedert et al., 1987), and other women, modes of transmission other than the penile-vaginal route could be excluded in many cases. This body of evidence has convinced most investigators that receptive anal intercourse in homosexual partners and vaginal intercourse in heterosexual partners are by far the most important routes of sexual spread.

Although these routes have certainly accounted for most of the infection that has occurred, the interpretation of the studies on which that view is based should not be oversimplified. It could be very difficult even in the largest and most meticulously designed study to identify an exposure of very low risk in the presence of a competing very high-risk exposure. For example, from the size of most studies of homosexual men published, it is doubtful that enough of them engaged in oral receptive intercourse with sufficient numbers of partners to the exclusion of other practices to permit detection of a risk only slightly greater than zero. In the Multicenter AIDS Cohort Study (Detels et al., 1988), the finding of a single seroconverter among 234 men who practiced no anal–genital but frequent oral–genital intercourse probably demonstrates the relatively low risk of the orogenital route about as clearly as any epidemiologic investigation could in a cohort where unprotected anal or vaginal intercourse has been common.

Greater controversy has surrounded the issue of female-to-male transmission—controversy that at times has seemed somewhat misdirected. Simply posed, the question has been how much more efficiently HIV-1 is transmitted from woman to man than from man to woman during vaginal intercourse. The premise is not entirely unreasonable, considering the histologic differences between the epithelium of the penis and that of the vagina: the vaginal/cervical mucosal surface would appear to be far more exposed to penetration by virus from infected secretions. If differences do exist, it may be helpful epidemiologically to quantify them.

Very low relative efficiency of female-to-male transmission might focus attention, for example, on urethral or external penile trauma as a major determinant of infection in men or on factors in vaginal secretions that retard transfer of virus. However, from a public health perspective, a well-documented relative efficiency of female-to-male transmission at 1:5, or even 1:20, would make little difference in the approach to prevention. Practically speaking, the "relative risk" to a male versus a female would have to be shown to be unrealistically small for the difference to alter overall preventive strategies substantially.

Salivary/Oral
Although HIV-1 has been isolated from saliva (Groopman et al., 1984) and is probably detectable there at low frequency (Ho et al., 1986), there is indirect but strong and consistent epidemiologic evidence against transmission by saliva through kissing or contact with other oral epithelial surfaces. Sex partners almost invariably report a better-established mode of transmission (see Chapters 7, 8, and 11), and contacts of infected persons do not acquire the infection through intimate nonsexual relationships (see Chapter 14).

Breast Feeding
There have been few but relatively convincing cases of transmission from mother to infant by breast feeding (Ziegler et al., 1988).

Selected Parenteral
Epidemiologic evidence from Africa (Mann et al., 1986) indicates that nonsterile needles used for injection of medications have been the source of HIV-1 infection. On the other hand, there is no evidence that any licensed hepatitis B vaccine or immunoglobulin product transmits the virus: the process of producing the immunizing agent destroys the virus.

Inadvertent transplantation or transfer of an infected organ, tissue, or fluid has caused infection in the recipient on a few occasions. Semen donated for artificial insemination (Stewart et al., 1985; Morgan et al., 1986) and transplanted kidneys (L'age-Stehr et al., 1985) have been the source of HIV-1 infection. Whether the virus is transmitted by mononuclear cells, primary tissue cells, or extracellular fluid is not certain. As for blood products, as discussed in Chapter 10, intensive donor screening can virtually eliminate these possible sources of infection, although their application outside the industrialized world will be costly and difficult.

The possibility that HIV-1 might be spread by arthropod vectors has been raised by two kinds of studies. Genetic material resembling that of HIV-1 has been recovered from mosquitoes (Chermann et al., 1987), and mosquitoes and bedbugs fed with infected blood through a membrane were shown to harbor live virus (as measured by HIV-1 reverse-transcriptase activity in cultures of insect extract) up to 4 hours after feeding (Jupp and Lyons, 1987). However, there is considerable theoretical and empirical evidence against the transmission of HIV-1 by insects. First, considering the low concentrations of virus in the blood of infected individuals and the small quantities of blood usually exchanged with a mosquito bite, transmission is exceedingly unlikely. Second, the intervals between feedings of mosquitoes are longer than HIV-1 has been known to be recoverable from them. Third, in one small study, transmission could not be demonstrated when mosquitoes feeding on infected blood were interrupted, transferred, and allowed to continue feeding on uninfected blood. Human studies also fail to support mosquito-borne spread. In Zaire, HIV-1 infection was found no more frequently among 540 children infected with *P. falciparum* malaria (2.8 percent HIV-1-seropositive) than among 506 uninfected children (4.9 percent HIV-1-seropositive) (Phuc et al., 1987), and the relationship between the prevalence of HIV-1 and malaria parasite antibodies was easily explained by the frequency of prior blood transfusions (Greenberg et al., 1988). Finally, antibodies to five common arthropod-borne viruses were not correlated with the presence of HIV-1 infection in residents of Belle Glade, Florida (Castro et al., 1988). The remotest possibility of vector-borne infection should not be allowed to distract attention from the other well-established and far more important risks (see also Chapter 11).

COFACTORS/RISK MODIFIERS

There is intense interest in host and environmental factors that may promote the acquisition of HIV-1 or alter the pace or ultimate outcome of the immunopathologic process following infection. Although the potential modifiers of the risk of infection and disease are treated separately here, it should be recognized that certain factors could theoretically modify the risk of either or both.

Cofactors for HIV Infection

Mechanical Trauma
A growing body of epidemiologic evidence indicates that mechanical effects of mucosal disruption may facilitate penetration by HIV-1. Paralleling earlier work on hepatitis B (Schreeder et al., 1982), several similar studies in cohorts of homosexual men (Chmiel et al., 1987; Kingsley et al., 1987; Winkelstein et al., 1987a) have provided strong support for the notion that the use of douches or enemas prior to anal intercourse promotes HIV-1 infection by traumatizing the anorectal mucous membranes. Suggestions that menstruation may be associated with HIV-1 infection are consistent with previous observations that other sexually transmissible infections are more readily acquired during menses than at other times in the cycle. On the other hand, study of a single chimpanzee demonstrated that neither gross genital trauma nor menstruation was required to produce vaginal infection (Fultz et al., 1986). Although the association between various types of trauma and HIV-1 infection remains to be confirmed, trauma could well facilitate infection by enhancing contact between virus and target cells in the intestinal or genital tract or merely by stimulating T-helper cell activation.

Coinfection
As a class, the most obvious candidates for the role of cofactor are other infectious agents. There are at least two very plausible mechanisms by which coinfections could promote infection with HIV-1—one traumatic, the other immunologic. The

ulcerative or inflammatory injury by agents like *Hemophilus ducreyi* and herpes simplex virus may resemble the damage caused by a mechanical device to the lining of the rectum or by menstrual degeneration of the endometrial lining (see previous section). Alternatively, the inflammatory response to infectious agents may be accompanied by effects on the immune system critical to the initiation of HIV-1 infection.

Persons at risk of AIDS have often experienced a variety of sexually or parenterally transmissible infections. There are also specific epidemiologic data suggesting a higher risk of AIDS and HIV-1 infection (Piot et al., 1987) in persons with ulcerative genital lesions than in those without them. Recent studies (Handsfield et al., 1987; Quinn et al., 1988) comparing rates of HIV-1 infection among individuals with and without ulcerative perineal infections have been more compelling. Although the ulcers due to the type 2 herpesvirus may be the ones people most often report, and there is some evidence that the presence of HSV-2 antibodies are related to occurrence of HIV-1 infection (Holmberg et al., 1988), the specific etiology of the epithelial disruption may not matter (Greenblatt et al., 1987; Quinn et al., 1988). A study from Zimbabwe (Katzenstein et al., 1987) has also suggested that history of any genital ulcer in males was associated with a higher risk of HIV-1 infection in their female partners. None of these studies has totally accounted for particular practices that could have coincidentally predisposed the patients to both genital ulcers and HIV-1 infection. However, the consistency of the findings in a variety of settings justifies specific warnings about the risk to and from persons with such infections.

Genital ulcers may be accompanied by specific recruitment or stimulation of mononuclear cells targeted for infection by HIV-1. Published data support the general concept of immune stimulation by a variety of genital infections, but there is little epidemiologic or laboratory evidence of T helper cell activation by ulcerogenic agents such as herpesviruses, *Chlamydia trachomatis,* or *Hemophilus ducreyi.* Data on infections that alter T helper cell number or function but do not cause ulcerative lesions could help sort out any immunologic disruption from the purely anatomical one. Thus far, studies of nonulcerogenic agents like cytomegalovirus have not demonstrated a direct influence on acquisition of HIV-1 infection; and there are only very weak epidemiologic data supporting a relationship between hepatitis B virus infection and subsequent HIV-1 seroconversion (Solomon et al., unpublished MACS data).

Chemicals/Drugs

Major classes of psychoactive substances have been studied in large cohorts of homosexual men (Ostrow et al., 1987; Greenblatt et al., 1987; Chmiel et al., 1987; Stevens et al., 1987). Use of these substances, especially during sexual activity, was strongly associated with increased frequency of HIV-1 infection, most likely because users of these drugs engaged in high-risk sexual practices more often. Whether use of those drugs promotes risk-taking behavior or more sexually active men have simply been more inclined to use them is not clear, but considering the strength and consistency of the associations, there can be no hesitation about recommending that their use be curtailed.

Cofactors for Immunodeficiency

Coinfection

Successful propagation of HIV-1 depends on rapid and reliable growth following stimulation of target T lymphocytes. Theoretically, any agent that can activate target cells of HIV-1 may thereby transform a latent HIV-1 infection into a productive one and accelerate the development of immunodeficiency. An obvious major source of stimulation would be an infectious agent, although a great variety of antigens impinge on the immune system almost continually.

Attempts in experimental systems to superinfect cell lines already infected with HIV-1 have yielded discrepant results. In the chimpanzee, coinfection has been established (Fultz et al., 1986), whereas efforts to identify more than one strain of virus in humans have been more suggestive. There is also in vitro evidence of concurrent HIV-1 and HIV-2 infection (Kanki et al., 1987). A number of investigators (Schochetman et al., 1987; Harzic et al., 1987) have identified persons with antibody to both HIV-1 and HIV-2 (see Chapter 1). In some populations, up to about 20 percent of individuals with antibodies to HIV-1 will also show reactivity to HIV-2, but in only a handful of such cases has there been stronger evidence for true dual infection. In any event, it is not clear biologically how infection with a second HIV variant may change the course of events following infection with the first.

Another human retrovirus, HTLV-I, is endemic in several populations, most notably in southern Japan and in blacks living near the Caribbean. More recently, it has been found by itself and in conjunction with HIV-1 in drug abusers and homosexual men in the United States (Robert-Guroff, 1986; Chang et al., 1987; Weiss et al., 1987) and in Trinidad (Bartholomew et al., 1987). True coinfection with HIV-1 and HTLV-I in those groups seems all but certain and raises concern about pathogenic potentiation of retroviruses by each other.

Prior to the discovery of HIV-1, high prevalence of CMV infection in the groups at risk of AIDS and its well-known immunosuppressive properties generated intense interest in CMV as a candidate etiologic agent. Before and since then, several lines of inquiry have suggested a role for CMV in the etiology of KS (Boldogh et al., 1981; Drew et al., 1982; Giraldo et al., 1986). Although CMV-induced immunosuppression is not currently seen as central to the pathogenesis of AIDS, a possible role of herpesviruses in enhancing replication of HIV-1 has been discovered in coinfection experiments (Gendelman et al., 1987; Skolnik et al., 1988). It is unclear whether enhancement is mediated by a regulatory protein gene *(tat)* of the herpesvirus in cells infected with HIV-1, and the clinical/epidemiologic relevance of interaction between HIV-1 and the herpesviruses remains to be seen.

There does not appear to be any important influence of hepatitis B virus infection on progression to AIDS among HIV-1-infected individuals. The slightly slower progression of HIV-1 infection among HBsAg carriers in one study (Osmond et al., 1987) could have been due to their shorter duration of HIV-1 infection. By all accounts to date, vaccination against hepatitis B appears neither to protect against nor promote the development of AIDS. However, there are both observational and experimental suggestions that homosexual men and probably others who are already infected with HIV-1 have an increased risk of becoming HBsAg carriers

(Hadler et al., 1987; Stevens et al., 1987) and mount a suboptimal antibody response to hepatitis B vaccine (Odaka et al., 1988). There is also a growing body of evidence that at least some HIV-1-infected individuals fail to respond appropriately to other vaccines (Ragni et al., 1987; Rhoads et al., 1987; Nelson et al., 1987).

Finally, certain manifestations of HIV-1-induced immunodeficiency may simply be expressions of other known or unknown infectious agents to which persons with HIV-1 infection have been exposed. According to recent data (Greenspan et al., 1986), Epstein-Barr virus and papilloma virus infections appear to be closely related to the occurrence of hairy leukoplakia (see Chapter 4). It seems equally likely that some agent accounts for much of the KS seen in the context of the AIDS epidemic. That could explain not only the concentration of KS in homosexual men but also the recent decline in its occurrence among them (CDC, 1986; Polk et al., 1988). If certain groups of homosexual men were more heavily exposed to an infectious etiologic agent (e.g., a gastrointestinal agent) briefly and early in the course of the epidemic, rapid reduction in their transmissive behavior could have reduced the risk of developing the condition subsequently. A plausible explanation would involve a putative KS agent with a relatively short latency period from infection to onset of disease (Weiss et al., 1986).

As suggested elsewhere, individuals who are already infected with HIV-1 have sufficiently compelling reasons to avoid unnecessary exposure to potentially lymphocyte-activating infectious agents.

Genetics/Race
There are several lines of evidence for a genetic or racial influence on the expression of HIV-1 infection. At the simplest level there is the dramatic explosion of AIDS among black East and central Africans (see Chapter 11). There race must be inextricably connected with socioeconomic, cultural, behavioral, and medical conditions, any of which could largely explain the excessive force of the epidemic. Data from a number of cities and risk groups (see above and Chapters 8 and 9) (Chmiel et al., 1987) in the United States suggest that both prevalence of infection and case rates of AIDS are higher in some nonwhites than in some whites. Here, too, concomitant socioeconomic and behavioral differences as well as differential duration of infection between different racial groups make it difficult to separate the effects on occurrence of disease from effects on acquisition of infection. There has been a suggestion from a large prospective study of seroconverters among ethnically distinct subgroups of homosexual men (VanRaden et al., 1988) that black men had significantly higher and Eastern European Jewish men significantly lower seroconversion rates not directly attributable to high-risk sexual behaviors or local variation in prevalence of infection. Again, it is difficult to exclude confounding factors, and more convincing evidence for effects of race awaits further analysis of prospective studies.

Somewhat more alluring data on possible ethnic/genetic determinants of disease expression have come from several case control studies on the distribution of histocompatibility (HLA) antigens. Populations, methods, and results have differed. The early finding that the occurrence of Kaposi's sarcoma in both AIDS and the classic nonepidemic setting was associated with an increased frequency of the HLA-DR5 antigen (Rubenstein et al., 1984) has been reproduced by some (DePaoli et al., 1986; Scorza-Smeraldi et al., 1986) but not all (Mann et al., 1987a) investigators. In other small studies, DR5 or B35 was found more frequently among certain patients with persistent generalized lymphadenopathy than among health volunteers. A more carefully controlled comparison (Mann et al., 1987a) has demonstrated an association between AIDS of any type and the presence of DR1, but the involvement of HLA in the progression of immunodeficiency remains unconfirmed. A connection between the presence of specific lymphocyte surface markers and expression of a lymphotropic viral infection is extremely attractive, and some experimental data support the concept of an interaction between the gp120 viral protein, the CD4 receptor, and an HLA antigen (Mann et al., 1987b). However, none of the findings to date can be considered definitive. Confirmation of these genetic associations through more convincing segregation studies in families will be difficult.

Finally, a number of investigators (Daiger et al., 1987; Gilles et al., 1987; Thymann et al., 1987) have failed to confirm the initial report (Eales et al., 1987) of an association between progressive infection and carriage of a genetically determined serum protein variant called group-specific component (Gc).

Chemicals/Drugs

Among the first hypotheses about the origin of AIDS was that some chemical agent selectively altered or destroyed the T lymphocytes. Early studies demonstrated a higher frequency of use of nitrites, amphetamines, and other drugs in AIDS cases than in controls. Once the retroviral etiology of AIDS was established, interest shifted to the possibility that drugs might promote infection or modify the disease process. Of course, directly immunosuppressive agents like corticosteroids might be expected to alter the susceptibility to HIV-1 infection or the course of the disease; however, no systematic study has been published on the effects of such drugs in individuals susceptible to or infected with HIV-1.

Two case control studies (Marmor et al., 1984; Haverkos et al., 1985) have, but a third (Polk et al., 1987) has not, suggested that some form or component of nitrite inhalants predisposes homosexual men to KS. The hypothesis has not been confirmed by any prospective studies (Polk et al., 1988).

Except for the data supporting the role of nitrite use in the occurrence of KS, investigators have been unable to discern a relationship between the use of psychoactive substances and any of the major manifestations of HIV-1-induced immunodeficiency (Stevens et al., 1987; Roland et al., 1987). In the Multicenter AIDS Cohort Study, exposure to common nonparenteral psychoactive agents (e.g., marijuana, cocaine, nitrites, amphetamines) was not associated with a lower number or percentage of CD4$^+$ lymphocytes in either seronegative or seropositive men at their entry into the study or with an increase in the risk of developing AIDS in seropositive men during the 18 months after documented drug use (R. Kaslow, unpublished data). An early hint (DesJarlais et al., 1987) of more rapid immunologic deterioration in HIV-1-positive persons who persist in intravenous heroin abuse compared to those who abstain has not been corroborated in other studies.

Age

The progression of HIV-1 infection of uncertain duration has appeared to progress faster in infants and children (see Chapter 10) and to accelerate with increasing age in several studies of adults (see later). In both case control (Polk et al., 1987) and cohort (Wiley et al., 1987) investigations, age was a significant independent correlate of early AIDS. If confirmed, more rapid progression in older adults may relate to the broader decline in immunity at the extremes of age, or it could reflect accumulating exposure to factors specifically involved in activating infected T helper lymphocytes.

Sex

In one small series (Scott et al., 1985), pregnant women showed rather rapid progression of HIV-1 infection. Although this finding has not been studied systematically in a large unselected population, profound physiologic alterations in immune response are well known to occur with natural and experimental changes in sex hormones.

INCUBATION PERIOD/LATENCY

Two fundamental gaps in our current understanding of HIV-1 infection present challenges in biologic and public health terms: (1) the uncertainty about the outer limit of the time interval from exposure to either the earliest symptoms and signs or serologically detectable infection (incubation period), and (2) the unexplained variability measured in years from infection to clinically severe immunodeficiency as signified by AIDS (latency period).

Infection (See Chapter 3)

As with other infections, the time between effective exposure to HIV-1 and the first biologic manifestation of infection depends heavily on the sensitivity of the test system used to detect that manifestation. The remarkably accurate techniques available for detecting antibody to the major core and envelope proteins have provided tools for identifying nearly all individuals with HIV-1 infection within months of its acquisition and the vast majority within a few weeks. For HIV-1, the incubation period (i.e., time from exposure to antibody production) is not dissimilar to that of other infections such as hepatitis B and syphilis, where this period is measured in weeks to months. What has become an increasing concern is that there may be a small but important proportion of individuals in whom the infection can be found by more sensitive culture, antigen, and viral gene detection techniques but who do not begin producing the usual antibodies for months or years or stop producing them after some unknown interval (Groopman et al., 1985; Ranki et al., 1987; Farzadegan et al., 1988; Wolinsky et al., 1988).

Since such findings are highly dependent on the relative sensitivities of the assays employed, great care must be taken to avoid methodologic artifacts. To the extent that such prolonged occult infection does occur, it seems unlikely that these seronegative individuals follow the same clinical course as those who make antibodies. Also, it will be very difficult to assess the ability of these virus-positive but seronegative individuals to spread the infection. That concern has already been raised around the issue of permitting previously rejected EIA-positive blood donors to reenter the pool of donors if subsequent immunoblots are negative. The addition of HIV-1 antigen testing to the battery of screening tests already applied to donated blood may eliminate some of the few remaining infectious units, but only at enormous cost. Clearly, the implications of a long incubation period are profound.

Disease

Many diseases exhibit substantial variations in the latency period between effective exposure to the necessary etiologic agent and clinical onset. Variation in latency has most frequently been attributed to age and intensity of exposure. For acute infectious diseases, that has often meant the size of the inoculum or virulence of the specific isolate of an infectious agent. Host factors have also been implicated, although they have been less well studied.

One of the most fundamental questions is why one individual progresses from initial infection to AIDS in less than 2 years while another may remain well for 6 to 9 years or longer. The full spectrum of the natural history of HIV-1 infection has not yet been displayed, since the features of immunodeficiency with the longest possible latency periods (from infection to disease) have yet to be observed. Among transfusion-associated cases, those with the most clearly documented date of infection, the observed mean latency period has lengthened from about 2.5 years early in the epidemic to 7.8 years more recently (Lui et al., 1986, 1988) simply because of accumulation of cases with increasingly longer latency periods (see Chapter 10). Moreover, comparisons of latency periods among adults in different risk groups (Medley et al., 1987) and between adults and children (Scott et al., 1985) suggest that these groups may differ substantially according to some host factors. Those factors determining (1) how long it will take for an infected individual to develop AIDS or, in the extreme, (2) whether an individual will ever develop it will remain the subject of intensive investigation.

Unfortunately, there are few other directly applicable human models to draw on to gauge the effect of a latency period measured in years on either the population morbidity or the investigation of codeterminants. Experience with the determinants of latency in other chronic human diseases that have infectious etiologies (e.g., syphilis, tuberculosis, schistosomiasis, Burkitt's lymphoma, primary hepatocellular carcinoma) is quite sparse. Even under the simplest assumption that latency periods for AIDS follow a log-normal distribution skewed toward the longer intervals (Rees, 1987), the precise shape of the distribution is critical to any projection of the impact of the disease. Perhaps more important, the shape of the distribution of latency periods may continue to change with time, or the latency period itself may change because of changes in as yet undiscovered host or environmental factors or the introduction of successful early intervention. Since a large proportion of AIDS cases that have already occurred probably had relatively shorter latency periods, studies of early cases exploring a particular codeterminant may have been subject to a type of length bias (Brookmeyer et al., 1987) if cases with shorter latency differ from the remainder of cases with respect to that codeterminant.

MODELS OF INFECTION AND DISEASE

In light of the variable and uncertain latency period and other critical gaps in our knowledge, it seems unlikely that a theoretical model could predict the course of the epidemic in the United States or elsewhere more accurately than a published empirical approach based on occurrence of cases to date (Morgan et al., 1986). Indeed, the actual numbers of cases that have occurred in the 2 years since those fitted-curve projections were first made have shown relatively good agreement with each other. Nevertheless, much effort has been invested in developing models for estimating the current prevalence of infection, describing the magnitude of transmission and the resulting new infections, and projecting the number of AIDS cases.

In one analysis of possible models for estimating prevalence (CDC, 1987b), three major functions have been considered: logistic, log-logistic, and damped exponential. Each appears to be dependent on the number of new infected persons and the number of infected persons who developed AIDS in the previous year. However, they differ in their underlying assumptions—e.g., whether the population is considered closed to new entrants or whether the risk of transmission is uniform by person, place, and time. Not surprisingly, therefore, eacy yielded a substantially different estimate of the number of persons infected at the end of 1987. Yet, when examined in conjunction with the data on progression to AIDS from the San Francisco cohort (Hessol et al., 1987), the midpoint estimates from the models approximated the 0.5 million to 1.5 million persons estimated by the CDC in 1986 (Coolfont Report, 1986).

One controversial model of transmission (May et al., 1987) assumes that the propagatory force of the epidemic depends on (1) the average rate of acquiring new partners, (2) the average probability that infection will be transmitted by a given sexual contact, and (3) the average duration of infectivity. The model emphasizes the dynamic nature of the epidemic: the exponential growth occurs relatively early, while most sexually active individuals are passing the agent to a large proportion of their many new and as yet uninfected partners. At that stage, because a substantial portion of the infectious men or women are in the most highly sexually active groups, early in the epidemic the rate of increase of infected individuals (i.e., the growth rate) can be disproportionally influenced by the removal of those highly active men or women. Thereafter, growth slows and the profile of individuals transmitting infection changes. This model implies that different approaches to prevention would be appropriate depending on the stage of the epidemic.

The proposed models have proliferated, but more often than not their applications lead to inconclusive or speculative results (Pickering and Van de Laar, 1988; Cardell et al., 1988) Artzrouni and Wykoff, 1988; Blythe and Anderson, 1988).

Another approach has addressed both the AIDS epidemic and the dynamics of propagation of the infection (Gonzalez et al., 1987). The emphasis was on the concept of transients—i.e., how changes in infection rates can alter the apparent latency period of disease and the pattern of the epidemic, especially in different times or risk groups. Still other kinds of statistical approaches to the number of AIDS cases have ranged from predictions based on available data (Lemp GF et al., 1988) or standard functions (Whyte et al., 1987) to elaborate multivariate models (Cardell et al., 1987).

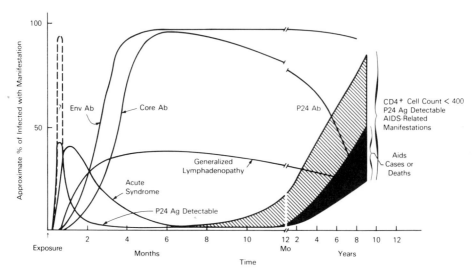

Figure 6.4. Schematic view of the natural history of HIV-1 infection in adults, 1988.

Entire symposia have been held to explore alternative statistical approaches. However, crucial but complex questions remain: What is the range of transmissibility to and from persons passing through different stages of infection and engaging in different practices with different numbers of partners? What factors determine the speed at which T helper cells (or other immune mechanisms involved in the defense against HIV-1) are destroyed once infection is established? Proposed models often assume or imply that there are answers to those questions. However, until such answers emerge, models seem unlikely to govern practical and timely preventive programs or the planning for health care of increasing numbers of affected individuals.

NATURAL HISTORY*

Immunologic

Knowledge of immunologic and clinical events leading to AIDS has unfolded rapidly. Much of the picture summarized below and in Figure 6.4 has been assembled from studies of homosexual men in developed countries. Although the basic features of the infection probably do not vary greatly by person, place, or time, other chapters suggest how those determinants may modulate its precise expression and course.

Within about 2 or 3 months of effective exposure, the appearance of antibodies to the viral envelope and core proteins usually signifies that infection is established. In an unknown percentage of those infected, core (p24 or p55) antigen may be

*See Chapters 1, 2, 3, 4, 7, 11, and 13.

detectable in the blood from days to a few weeks before antibodies appear, and culture and other techniques may reveal the presence of virus.

Several groups of investigators have described individuals carrying cultivable virus, viral antigen, or antibodies to virus protein in questionably low titers for more extended periods (months) in the absence of antibodies detectable with commercially available EIA methods. More frequent or prolonged antibody-negative infection than previously recognized would have important implications for the interpretation and uses of the screening tests currently marketed.

In the vast majority of infected individuals, circulating antibodies produce a characteristic profile as detected by standard immunoblot techniques and persist in substantial amounts while the infected person remains relatively healthy. Then, often months or years after initial infection, as the process becomes more active, the major core antigen (p24) reappears in the blood in increasing amounts. More or less reciprocally, the titers of antibodies to that and other (p17) core antigens begin to fall, often reaching nearly undetectable levels, as clinical and immunologic deterioration progresses (Phair et al., 1987; Lange et al., 1987; Forster et al., 1987; Simmonds et al., 1988).

Clinical

Manifestations of Early or Acute HIV-1 Infection

During the early phases of HIV-1 infection, the immunologic features are often paralleled by clinical findings resembling the syndrome of acute infectious mononucleosis (see Chapter 4). Generalized lymphadenopathy is the most consistent clinical feature of the early infection; it may even be seen before antibodies appear on standard tests (Polis et al., 1988). Certain neurologic abnormalities may be found simultaneously with or soon after this early syndrome of infection (see Chapter 5).

Clinically, in the few months after infection is initiated and the transient symptoms and signs of that process have subsided, the individual may be aware of persistent or increasing enlargement of lymph nodes or remain entirely asymptomatic. Probably half or more of homosexual men and perhaps as many other infected persons develop generalized lymphadenopathy within about 1 year of seroconversion. Lymph node enlargement fluctuates considerably during the early stages of infection, with a proportion of those who are seropositive but initially free of generalized lymphadenopathy continuing to acquire it in subsequent months. This finding appears to be a common, early response to the virus itself and independent of the quantitative changes in lymphocytes that signal progression of immunodeficiency (Kaslow et al., 1987). In direct, carefully controlled comparisons of men with prevalent infection of unknown duration, the proportion of seropositive men who subsequently develop AIDS has been the same in those with and without PGL.

In an extremely variable time course that has now ranged from a few months in infants and certain transfused patients to a decade in the small number of individuals whose infection can be documented that far in the past, CD4$^+$ lymphocytes disappear, and symptoms and signs of immunodeficiency begin to occur. Upwards of 90 percent of seropositive individuals in one small cohort developed one of several immunologic defects within five years of observation (Melbye et al., 1986).

Other cross-sectional studies of seropositives (Boyko et al., 1986; Kaslow et al., 1987) have documented similar or higher frequencies of symptoms, signs, and hematologic abnormalities. In the Multicenter AIDS Cohort Study, some clinical manifestations appeared in a small proportion of homosexual men whose $CD4^+$ cell counts were only minimally depressed (Kaslow et al., 1987). Whether this represents the earliest clinical expression of quantitative T helper cell loss or of abnormalities in lymphocyte function (see Chapter 2) is not known. Conversely, an important minority of infected persons have shown severe depletion of $CD4^+$ lymphocytes and developed AIDS without ever experiencing any of the other AIDS-related manifestations.

As time goes on, longitudinal studies may depict more accurately the pace at which these abnormalities accumulate in seropositive persons who appear initially healthy. Significant, readily detectable clinical features other than depressed $CD4^+$ cell counts occur in an increasing proportion of healthy homosexual men followed over months, but the probability of such clinical expression during the interval is highly dependent on the $CD4^+$ cell count at the beginning of the interval.

At any point after the infection is acquired and acute manifestations have subsided, but probably not very early, neuropsychological manifestations may appear. At their earliest stages they are often subtle. The importance of neurologic manifestations in infected but otherwise healthy persons is controversial and will hopefully be resolved by natural history studies now in progress (see Chapter 5).

Neither the precise sequence nor the determinants of these intermediate HIV-1-induced clinical manifestations are fully established. Their significance has nevertheless grown increasingly clear. Although relatively benign, in aggregate, such clinical features as thrush, zoster, genital herpes, or hairy leukoplakia represent a significant additional burden of illness on the populations infected with HIV-1. More than being troublesome in their own right, AIDS-related clinical features identify those who will develop AIDS sooner (Kaslow et al., 1988). Although prognostic indicators like declining $CD4^+$ cell counts; HIV-1 core antigenemia, and other serologic tests have great predictive value for AIDS, in the absence of those immunologic markers, the clinical features have considerable predictive value. Consequently, in settings where those immunologic markers are unavailable, the clinical ones may be quite helpful in evaluating patients.

Early attempts (Goedert et al., 1986) to estimate the incidence of AIDS in small cohorts of infected persons were limited in several respects. Some smaller cohorts were often unrepresentative of the risk groups from which they were drawn. Estimates from those cohorts were based on occurrence of AIDS in individuals who were already seropositive when they came under observation. In a much larger cohort of homosexual men in San Francisco, who were drawn from a large group originally enrolled in a hepatitis B vaccine trial, dates of infection in many men could be relatively accurately assigned. The incidence of AIDS has been based on a sample of men who had been enrolled for several years and had not had uniform follow-up. Nevertheless, from this large cohort and others in which incidence of AIDS has been based on participants with prevalent infection, reliable estimates suggest that about 35 to 45 percent of previously infected persons might be expected to develop AIDS in 8 years and presumably higher proportions as further time elapses (Fig. 6.4). Whether the shape of the incidence curve will differ by person, place, or time—either for individuals with prevalent infection or for those followed from the time infection first occurred—has yet to be determined. At least the bleakest view on the ultimate outcome of infection can be tempered by the knowledge that, even without effective therapy, the majority of infected people may remain free of AIDS for nearly a decade after they first acquire HIV-1 infection.

REFERENCES

AIDS Surveillance (1985): Can Med Assoc J 133:890.
Alter MJ, Francis D, et al., (1987): Third International Conference on AIDS, Washington, D.C., June 1–5, Th. 5.3.
Artzrouni M, Wykoff R (1988) Fourth International Conference on AIDS, Stockholm, Sweden, June 12–16, Abst. 4691.
Bartholomew C, Saxinger WC, Clark JW, Gail M, Dudgeon A, Mahabir B, Hull-Drysdale B, Cleghorn F, Gallo RC, Blattner WC (1987): JAMA 257:2604.
Biggar RJ, Melbye M, Ebbeson P, Alexander S, Nielsen JO, Sarin P, Faber V (1985): Br Med J 291:997.
Blythe SP, Anderson RM (1988) Fourth International Conference on AIDS, Stockholm, Sweden, June 12–16, Abst. 4704.
Boldogh I, Beth E, Huang ES, Kyalwazi SK, Giraldo G (1981): Int J Cancer 28:469.
Boyko WJ, Schechter MT, Craib KJP, Constance P, Nitz R, Fay S, McLeod A, O'Shaughnessy M (1986): Can Med Assoc J 135:881.
Brookmeyer R, Gail MH, Polk BF (1987): Am J Epidemiol 123:14.
Cardell NS, Kanouse DE, Gorman EM, Serrato C, Reuter PH, Williams AP (1987): Third International Conference on AIDS, Washington, D.C., June 1–5, TP.59.
Cardell NS, Gorman EM, Kanouse DE (1988) Fourth International Conference on AIDS, Stockholm, Sweden, June 12–16, Abst. 4699.
Castro KG, Lieb S, Jaffe HW, Narkunas JP, Calisher CH, Bush TJ, Witte JJ, the Belle Glade Field-Study Group (1988): Science 239:193.
Centers for Disease Control (CDC) (1981a): MMWR 30:250.
CDC (1981b): 30:305.
CDC (1982): MMWR 31:507–508, 513.
CDC (1986): MMWR 35:17.
CDC (1987a): MMWR 36 (Suppl) 1S:1.
CDC (1987b): MMWR 36 (Suppl) S6:1.
CDC (1988b): MMWR 37:35.
CDC (1988a): MMWR 37:461.
CDC (1988c): MMWR 37:551.
CDC (1988): AIDS Weekly Surveillance Report, August 29.
CDC Task Force on Kaposi's Sarcoma and Opportunistic Infections (1982): N Engl J Med 306:248.
Chamberland ME, Allen JR, Monroe JM, Garcia N, Morgan C, Reiss R, Stephens H, Walker J, Friedman SM (1985): JAMA 254:383.
Chang KS, Wang L-C, Alexander S, Log T, Kuo AF, Strickland P (1987): Third International Conference on AIDS, Washington, D.C., June 1–5, MP.95.
Chermann JC, Becker JL, Hazan V, et al. (1987): Third International Conference on AIDS, Washington, D.C., June 1–5, MP.37.
Chmiel JS, Detels R, Kaslow RA, VanRaden M, Kingsley LA, Brookmeyer R, the Multicenter AIDS Cohort Study Group (1987): Am J Epidemiol 126:568.
Coolfont Report (1986): Pub Health Rep 101:341.

Daiger SP, Brewton GW, Rios AA, Mansell PWA, Reuben JM (1987): N Engl J Med 317:631.

DePaoli P, Reitano M, Martelli P, Battistin S, Vallalta D, Carbone A, Tirelli U, Santini G (1986): Tissue Antigen 27:116.

DesJarlais DC, Marmor M, Thomas P, Chamberland M, Zolla-Pazner S, Senger DJ (1984): N Engl J Med 310:1119.

DesJarlais DC, Friedman SR, Marmor M, Mildvan D, Yankovitz S, El-Sadr W, et al. (1987): AIDS 1:105.

DesJarlais DC, Stoneburner R, Thomas P, Friedman SR (1987): Lancet 2:1024.

Desmyter J, Surmont I, Goubau P, Vandepitte J (1986): Br Med J 293:1308.

Detels R, English P, Visscher BR, Kingsley LA, Chmiel JS, Dudley JP, Eldred LJ, Kaslow RA: J AIDS (in press).

Drew WL, Conant MA, Miner RC, et al. (1982): Lancet 2:125.

Eales, L-J, Nye K, Pinching AJ (1987): Lancet 1:999.

Ekstrand ML, Coabes TJ (1988) Fourth International Conference on AIDS, Stockholm, Sweden, Abst. 8072.

Eyster EM, Gail MH, Ballard JO, Al-Mondhiry J, Goedert JJ (1987): Ann Intern Med 107:1.

Farzadegan H, Polis MA, Wolinsky SM, Rinaldo CR Jr, Sninsky JJ, Kwok S, Griffith RL, Kaslow RA, Phair JP, Polk BF, Saah AJ (1988): Ann Intern Med 108:785.

Forster SM, Osborne LM, Cheinsong-Popov R, Kenny C, Burnell R, Jeffries DJ, Pinching AJ, Harris JRW, Weber JN (1987): AIDS 1:235.

Fox R, Odaka N, Brookmeyer R, Polk BF (1987): AIDS 1:199.

Friedland GH, Klein RS (1987): N Eng J Med 317:1125.

Friedman-Kein AE, Laubenstein LJ, Rubenstein P, Buimovici-Klein E, Marmor M, Stahl R, Spigland I, Kim KS, Zolla-Pazner S (1982): Ann Intern Med 96:693.

Fultz PN (1986): J Virol 58:116.

Fultz PN, McClure HM, Daugherty H, Brodie A, McGrath CR, Swenson B, Farris DP (1986): J Infect Dis 154:896.

Gendelman HE, Leonard J, Weck K, Rabson AB, Capon D, Martin MA, Ostrove JM (1987): Third International Conference on AIDS, Washington, D.C., June 1–5, MP.19.

Gilles K, Louie L, Newman B, Crandall J, King M-C (1987): N Engl J Med 317:630.

Giraldo G, Beth E (1986): Prog Allergy 37:319.

Glauser MP, Francioli P (1984): Eur J Clin Microbiol 3:55.

Goedert J J, Sarngadharan M G, Biggar RJ, Weiss SH, Winn D, Grossman RJ, Greene MH, Bodner A, Mann DL, Strong DM, Gallo RC, Blattner WA (1984): Lancet 2:711.

Goedert, JJ, Biggar RJ, Weiss SH, Eyster ME, Melbye M, Wilson S, Ginzburg HM, Grossman RJ, DiGioia RA, Sanchez WC, Giron JA, Ebbeson P, Gallo RC, Blattner WA (1986): Science 23:992.

Goedert JJ, Eyster ME, Biggar RJ, Blattner WA (1987): AIDS Res Hum Retroviruses 3:355.

Gonzalez JJ, Koch MG (1987): Am J Epidemiol 126:985.

Greenberg AC, Phuc N-D, Mann JM, Kabote N, Colebunders RL, Francis H, Quinn TC, Baudoux P, Lyamba B, Davachi F, Roberts JM, Kabeya N, Curran JW, Campbell CC (1988): JAMA 259:545.

Greenblatt RM, Samuel M, Osmond D, Winkelstein W, Levy J, Moss A (1987): Third International Conference on AIDS, Washington, D.C., June 1–5, ThP.47.

Greenspan JS, Greenspan D, Lennette ET, Abrams DI, Conant MA, Peterson V, Freese UK (1986): N Engl J Med 313:1564.

Groopman JE, Salahuddin SZ, Sarngadharan MG, Markham PD, Gonda M, Sliski A, Gallo RC (1984): Science 226:447.

Groopman JE, Hartzband PI, Shulman L, Salahuddin SZ, Sarngadharan MG, McLane MF, Essex M, Gallo R (1985): Blood 66:742.

Hadler S, Judson F, Echenberg D, O'Malley P, Penley K, Darrow B, Schable C (1986): J Med Virol 21:87A.

Handsfield HH, Ashley RL, Rompalo AM, Stamm WE, Wood RW, Corey L (1987): Third International Conference on AIDS, Washington, D.C., June 1–5, F.1.6.

Hart GT, Sonnex C, Petherick A, Johnson AM, Feinmann C, Adler MW (1988) Fourth International Conference on AIDS. Stockholm, Sweden, Abst. 8059

Harzic M, Brun-Vezinet F, Saimot AG, Courtois F, Domart Y, Wain-Hobson S (1987): Third International Conference on AIDS, Washington, D.C., June 1–5, F2.4.

Haverkos HW, Pinsky PF, Drotman DP, Bregman D J (1985): Sex Transm Dis 12:203–208.

Hessol NA, Rutherford GW, O'Malley PM, Doll LS, Darrow WW, Jaffe HW, et al. (1987): Third International Conference on AIDS, Washington, D.C., June 1–5, M.3.1.

Ho DD, Byington RE, Schooley RT, Flynn T, Rota TR, Hirsch MS (1985): N Engl J Med 313:1606.

Hoff R, Berardi VP, Weiblen BJ, Mahoney-Trout L, Mitchell ML, Grady GF (1988): N Engl J Med 313:525.

Holmberg SD, Stewart JA, Gerber AR, Byers RH, Lee FK, O'Malley PM, Nahmias AJ (1988): JAMA 259:1048.

Jaffe HW, Choi K-W, Thomas PA, et al. (1983): Ann Intern Med 99:145.

Jaffe HW, Darrow WW, Echenberg DF, O'Malley PM, Getchell JP, Kalyanaraman VS, Byers RH, Drennan DP, Braff EH, Curran JW, Francis DP (1985): Ann Intern Med 103:210.

Jeffries E, Willoughby B, Boyko WJ, Schecter MT (1985): Can Med Assoc J 132:1373.

Judson FN (1983): Lancet 2:159.

Jupp PG, Lyons SF (1987): AIDS 1:171.

Kanki PJ, M'Boup S, Ricand D, Barin F, Denis F, Boye C, Sangare L, Travers K, Albaum M, Marlink R, Romet-Lemoine JL, Essex M (1987): Science 236:827.

Kaslow RA, Blackwelder WC, Phair JP, Lyter D, Fox R, Visscher B, et al. (1987a): Third International Conference on AIDS, Washington, DC., June 1–5, WP.67.

Kaslow RA, Phair JP, Friedman HB, Lyter D, Solomon RE, Dudley J, Polk BF, Blackwelder W (1987b): Ann Intern Med 107:474.

Kaslow RA, Blackwelder W, Friedman H, Saah A, Lyter D, Murphy R, Visscher B, Wang M (1988): Fourth International Conference on AIDS, June 12–16.

Katzenstein DA, Latif A, Bassett MT, Emmanuel JC (1987): Third International Conference on AIDS, Washington, D.C, June 1–5, M.8.3.

Kingsley L, Detels R, Kaslow R, Polk BF, Rinaldo CR Jr, Chmiel J, Detre K, Kelsey SF, Odaka N, Ostrow D, VanRaden M, Visscher B (1987): Lancet 1:345.

Kreiss JK, Koech D, Plummer FA, Holmes KK, Lightfoote M, Piot P, Ronald AR, Ndinya-Achola, JO, D'Costa LJ, Roberts P, Ngugi EN, Quinn TC (1986): N Engl J Med 314:414.

L'age-Stehr J, Schwarz A, Offerman G, Langmaack H, Bennhold I, Niedrig M, Koch MA (1985): Lancet 2:1361.

Lang W, Anderson RE, Perkins H, Grant RM, Lyman D, Winkelstein W Jr, Royce R, Levy JA (1987): JAMA 257:326.

Lange JMA, De Wolf F, Krone WJA, Danner SA, Coutinho RA, Goudsmit J (1987): AIDS 1:155.

Lewin PK (1985): Can Med Assoc J 132:1110.

Lui K-J, Lawrence DN, Morgan WM, Peterman TA, Haverkos HW, Bregman DJ (1986): Proc Natl Acad Sci USA 83:3051.

Lui K-J, Darrow WW, Rutherford GW III (1988): Science 240:1333.

Lyman D, Winkelstein W, Ascher M, Levy JA (1986): JAMA 255:1763.

Lyons SF (1986): Lancet 2:45.

Mann JM, Francis H, Davachi F, Baudoux P, Quinn TC, Nzilambi N, Ngaly B, Colebunders RL, Piot P, Kabote N, Asila PK, Malonga M, Curran JW (1986): Lancet 2:654.

Mann DL, Lesane F, Blattner WA, Popovic M (1987a): Third International Conference on AIDS, Washington, D.C., June 1–5, F.4.3.

Mann DL, Murray C, Goedert JJ, Blattner NA, Robert-Guroff M (1987b): Third International Conference on AIDS, Washington, D.C., June 1–5, F.1.2.

Marmor M, Friedman-Kien AE, Zolla-Pazner S, Stahl RE, Rubenstein P, Laubenstein L, William DC, Klein RJ, Spigland I (1984): Ann Intern Med 100:809.

Martin JL (1987a): Third International Conference on AIDS, Washington, DC., June 1–5, WP.177.

Martin JL (1987b): Third International Conference on AIDS, Washington, D.C., June 1–5, TP.65.

May RM, Anderson PM (1987): Nature 326:137.

McKusick L, Wiley JA, Coates TJ, Stall R, Saika G, Morin S, Charles K, Horstman W, Conant MA (1985): Public Health Rep 100:622.

Medley GF, Anderson PM, Cox DR, Billard L (1987): Nature 328:719.

Melbye M, Njelesani EK, Bayley A, Mukelabai K, Manuwele JK, Bowa FJ, Clayden SA, Levin A, Blattner WA, Weiss RA, Tedder R, Biggar RW (1986): Lancet 2:1113.

Morgan J (1986): N Engl J Med 314:386.

Morgan WM, Curran JW (1986): Public Health Rep 101:459.

Nahmias AJ, Weiss J, Yao X, Lee F, Kodsi R, Schanfield M, Matthews T, Bolognesi D, Durack D, Motulsky A, Kanki P, Essex M (1986): Lancet 1:1279.

Nelson KE, Clements ML, Miotti P, Colin S, Odaka N, Polk, BF (1987): Third International Conference on AIDS, Washington, D.C., June 1–5, WP.116.

Nemeth A, Bygdeman S, Sandstrom E, Biberfeld G (1986): Sex Transm Dis 13:111.

Ngaly B, Ryder RW, Kapita B, Francis H, Quinn T, Mann JM (1987): Third International Conference on AIDS, Washington, D.C., June 1–5, M3.6.

Novick L (1988): AIDS Epidemiology Program. New York State Department of Health, March 15.

Nzilambi N, De Cock KM, Forthal DN, Francis H, Ryder RW, Malebe I, Getchell J, Laga M, Piot P, McCormick JB (1988): N Engl J Med 318:276.

Odaka N, Solomon R, Kaslow R, Polk BF (1988): JAMA (in press).

Osmond D, Chaisson R, Beasley P, Bacchetti P, Moss A (1987): Third International Conference on AIDS, Washington, D.C., June 1–5, F.1.5.

Osterholm MT, McDonald KL, Schletty SJ, Nielson MD, Danila RN (1987): Third International Conference on AIDS, Washington, D.C., June 1–5, T.7.5.

Ostrow, DG, VanRaden M, Kingsley L, Fox R, Dudley J, Kaslow RA (1987): Third International Conference on AIDS, Washington, D.C., June 1–5, Th.5.6.

Peterman T, Stoneburner RL, Allen JR, Jaffe HW, Curran J W (1988): JAMA 259:55.

Phair JP, Chmiel J, Wallemark C-B, Wu W, Huprikar J (1987): Third International Conference on AIDS, Washington, D.C., June 1–5, T.3.6.

Phuc N-D, Greenberg AE, Ryder RW, Mann JM, Kabote N, Francis H, et al. (1987): Third International Conference on AIDS, Washington, D.C., June 1–5, MP.73.

Pickering J, Van de Laar MJW (1988): Fourth International Conference on AIDS, Stockholm, Sweden, June 12–16, Abst. 4683.

Piot P, Kreiss JK, Ndinya-Achola JO, Ngugi EN, Swonsen JN, Cameron DW, Taalman H, Plumner FA (1987): AIDS 1:199.

Polis, MA, Kaslow R, Fox R, Deloria M, Dudley J, MacDonell K, Lyter D, Su S (1988): Fourth International Conference on AIDS, Stockholm, June 12–16.

Polk BF, Munoz A, Fox R, Phair J, Dudley J, Obrams I, D'Amario R, Kingsley L (1988): Fourth International Conference on AIDS, Stockholm, June 12–16.

Quinn TC, Glasser D, Cannon RO, Matuszak DL, Dunning RW, Kline RL, Campbell CH, Israel E, Fauci AS, Hook EW III (1988): N Engl J Med 318:197.

Ragni MF, Ruben FL, Winkelstein A, Spero JA, Bontempo FA, Lewis JH (1987): J Lab Clin Med 109:545.

Ranki A, Valle S-L, Krohn K, et al. (1987): Lancet 2:589.

Rees M (1987): Nature 326:343.

Robert-Guroff M, Weiss SH, Giron JA, Jennings AM, Ginzburg HM, Margolis IB, Blattner WA, Gallo RC (1986): JAMA 255:3133.

Robertson JR, Skidmore CA, Steel M, Beaton D (1987): Third International Conference on AIDS, Washington, D.C., June 1–5, MP.59.

Roland A, Feigal DW, Abrams D, Volberding PA, Hollander H, Ziegler J, Conant MA (1987): Third International Conference on AIDS, Washington, D.C., June 1–5, ThP.57.

Rhoads JL, Birx DL, Wright DC, Brundage J, Redfield RR, Burke DS (1987): Third International Conference on AIDS, Washington, D.C., June 1–5, WP.110.

Rubenstein P, Rothman WM, Friedman-Kien A (1984): Antibiot Chemother 32:87.

Schecter MT, Boyko WJ, Douglas B, Willoughby B, McLeod A, Maynard M, Craib KJP, O'Shaughnessy M (1986a): Can Med Assoc J 135:1355.

Schecter MT, Boyko, WJ, Douglas WJ, Maynard M, Willoughby B, McLeod A, Craib K J (1986b): Lancet 1:379.

Schechter MT, Boyko WJ, Weaver MS, Douglas B, Willoughby B, McLeod WA, et al. (1987): Third International Conference on AIDS, Washington, D.C., June 1–5, M.3.3.

Schochetman G, Schable CA, Goldstein LC, Epstein J, Zuck TF (1987): Third International Conference on AIDS, Washington, D.C., June 1–5, ThP.52.

Schreeder MT, Thompson SE, Hadler SC (1982): J Infect Dis 146:7.

Scorza-Smeraldi R, Fabio G, Lazzarin A, Eisera NB, Moroni M, Zanussi C (1986): Lancet 2:1187.

Scott GB, Fischl MA, Klimas N, Fletcher MA, Dickenson GM, Levine RS, Parks WP (1985): JAMA 253:363.

Simmonds P, Lainson FAL, Cuthbert R, Steel CM, Peutherer JF, Ludlam CA (1988): Brit Med J 296:593.

Skolnik PR, Kosloff BR, Hirsch MS (1988): J Infect Dis 157:508–514.

Stevens CE, Taylor PE, Zang EA, Morrison JM, Harley EJ, Rodriguez de Cordoba S, Bacino C, Ting RCY, Bodner AJ, Sarngadharan MG, Gallo RC, Rubenstein P (1986a): JAMA 255:2167.

Stevens CE, Taylor PE, Rodriguez de Cordoba S, Rubenstein P (1986b): J Med Virol 21:87A–88A.

Stevens CE, Taylor PE, Rodriguez S, Rubenstein P (1987): Third International Conference on AIDS, Washington, DC., June 1–5, ThP.98.

Stewart GT, Tyler JPP, Cunningham AL, Barr JA, Driscoll GL, Gold J, Lamont B J (1985): Lancet 2:581.

Thymann M, Dickmeiss E, Svejgaard A, Pedersen G, Bygbjerg I, Faber V (1987): Lancet 1:1377.

VanRaden M, Kaslow R, Kingsley L, Dekels R, Jacobson L, Phair J, Polk BF (1988): Fourth International Conference on AIDS, Stockholm, Sweden, June 12–16, Abst. 4553.

Weiss SH, Biggar RJ (1986): Mt Sinai J Med 53:579.

Weiss SH, Ginzburg HM, Saxinger WC, Cantor KP, Mundon FK, Zimmerman DH, Blattner WA (1987): Third International Conference on AIDS, Washington, D.C., June 1–5, F6.5.

Whyte BM, Dobson AJ, Gold J, Cooper DA (1987): Third International Conference on AIDS, Washington, D.C., June 1–5, MP.64.

Wiley JA, Rutherford GW, Moss AR, Winkelstein W Jr (1987): Third International Conference on AIDS, Washington, D.C., June 1–5, F.1.4.

Willoughby B, Schechter MT, Boyko WJ, Craib KJP, Weaver MS, Douglas B, et al. (1987): Third International Conference on AIDS, Washington, D.C., June 1–5, M.6.3.

Winkelstein, WW Jr, Lyman D, Padian N, Grant R, Samuel M, Wiley JA, Anderson RE, Lang W, Riggs J, Levy JA (1987a): JAMA 257:321.

Winkelstein WW Jr, Samuel M, Padian NS, Wiley JA, Lang W, Anderson RE, Levy J (1987b): Am J Public Health 76:685.

Wolinsky S, Rinaldo C, Farzadegan H, Gupta P, Kaslow R, Imagawa D, Chmiel J, Phair J, Kwok S, Sninsky J (1988): Fourth International Conference on AIDS, Stockholm, Sweden, June 12–16, Abst. 1099.

World Health Organization (1988): Update: Acquired Immunodeficiency Syndrome, August.

Ziegler JB, Stewart GJ, Penny R, Stuckey M, Good S (1988): Fourth International Conference on AIDS, Stockholm, Sweden, June 12–16, Abst 5100.

7

Homosexual Men

WARREN WINKELSTEIN JR., NANCY S. PADIAN,
GEORGE RUTHERFORD, AND HAROLD W. JAFFE

Since AIDS was discovered earliest in homosexual men and as a group they have so far been the most heavily affected, much of what we know about the syndrome and its etiologic agent has been learned from the study of these men. Many of the other chapters in this book therefore draw heavily on the experience in this high-risk group. This chapter primarily addresses the basic epidemiologic features of the phenomenon in homosexual men; issues specific to the disease expression and control are discussed separately in appropriate chapters.

HISTORICAL BACKGROUND

After World War II, profound social and cultural changes occurred in the United States and other developed countries. Among the most important was the emergence of identifiable subpopulations of homosexual men and women. In a number of major cities such as New York, Los Angeles, and San Francisco, large geographic concentrations of homosexual men developed. By the late 1960s and early 1970s, sexual promiscuity became a prominent feature of these communities. Along with those changes in life-style, sexually transmitted diseases such as syphilis, gonorrhea, and hepatitis B became hyperendemic. Parasitic infections of the colon, known collectively as the "gay bowel syndrome," were widespread. These communities were clearly vulnerable to the introduction of other sexually transmitted diseases (Shilts, 1987).

In June 1981, the Centers for Disease Control (CDC) reported a cluster of five previously healthy homosexual men from Los Angeles with *Pneumocystis carinii* pneumonia (PCP) and candidiasis (CDC, 1981a), three of whom had abnormalities of cell-mediated immunity. The report postulated "a cellular immune dysfunction related to a common exposure that predisposes individuals to opportunistic infections such as pneumocystosis and candidiasis." One month later, the CDC reported 26 cases of Kaposi's sarcoma (KS), an uncommonly reported malignancy in the United States, among homosexual men in New York City and California ranging in age from 26 to 51 years (CDC, 1981b). By August 1981, an unusual incidence of diseases associated with immunosuppression was apparent, and the CDC reported that "clustering of both PCP and KS among homosexual men suggests a common underlying factor. Both diseases have been associated with host immunosuppression and studies in progress are showing immunosuppression in some of these cases. The extent or cause of immune suppression is not known . . . " (CDC, 1981c).

At a workshop on KS in homosexual men convened at the National Cancer Institute on September 15, 1981 (DeWys et al., 1982), the number of cases available for critical study was limited (<20), but important information about the pathophysiology and epidemiology of these cases was revealed. In a comparison of their physiological characteristics with those of blood donors at the New York Veterans Administration Medical Center, the most striking finding was that the KS cases had significantly elevated OKT8 (CD8$^+$ suppressor/cytotoxic) and significantly lower OKT4 (CD4$^+$ helper/inducer) T lymphocytes and lower ratios of OKT4/OKT8 cells in peripheral blood (Friedman-Kien et al., 1982). Preliminary epidemiological observations indicated that the cases of KS were correlated with a history of sexually transmitted diseases, increased numbers of sexual partners, and use of nitrite inhalants.

Thus, within 3 months after the first cases of PCP were reported in homosexual men, the basic pathophysiological defect (abnormal T-lymphocyte response) and the probable mode of transmission through sexual contact had been identified. Subsequently, primarily for surveillance purposes, the illnesses associated with this epidemic were defined, and the syndrome was given the name acquired immunodeficiency syndrome (AIDS) (CDC, 1982).

By February 1983, the first 1,000 cases of AIDS had been reported, and the epidemiology of the outbreak had become clearer (Jaffe et al., 1983a). By that time, cases had been reported from 37 states and the District of Columbia, with more than half from New York City (465), San Francisco (121), and Los Angeles (69). Homosexual men, who here, as in most references, include bisexual men, made up 73 percent of the first 1,000 cases.

EPIDEMIOLOGY OF AIDS AND HIV-1 INFECTION

Occurrence

Between the first reports of PCP and KS in June 1981 and August 1988, a total of 44,402 cases and 24,880 deaths in homosexual men were reported to the CDC (CDC, 1988). These represented approximately 62 percent of all cases and deaths due to AIDS in the United States during that period. The epidemic for homosexual cases, by calendar quarter, through 1987, is represented in Figure 7-1. In each quarter, cases have increased. However, the rate of increase in case reports has decreased as the epidemic has progressed. The doubling time for incident cases increased from approximately 6 months in 1983 to more than a year by 1987 (CDC, 1988).

It has been projected that by the end of 1992 a cumulative total of more than 365,000 cases of AIDS, of whom the majority will still be homosexual men, will have occurred in the United States (CDC, 1988a). At least 50,000 homosexual cases will probably occur in 1992 alone. By that time, the estimated cumulative total of deaths in homosexual men may reach 100,000.

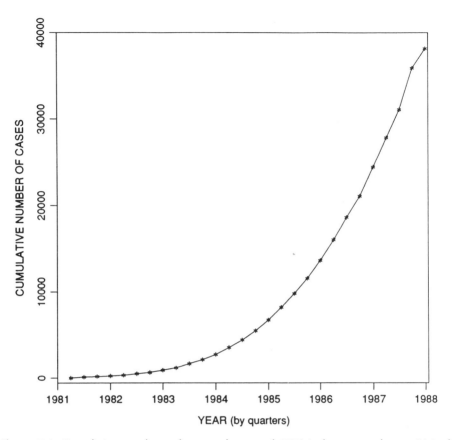

Figure 7.1. Cumulative numbers of reported cases of AIDS in homosexual men, United States, 1981–1987, by calendar quarter.

Geographic Distribution of AIDS Cases

At the time that the first 1,000 cases of AIDS had been recorded by the CDC (of whom 730 were homosexual men), 65 percent had occurred in New York City, San Francisco, and Los Angeles. Thirteen states had not reported any cases. By August 1988, New York City, San Francisco, and Los Angeles reported 38 percent of the total of 72,024 cases reported in that year. By then all 50 states and the District of Columbia had reported cases. Five states—New York, California, Florida, Texas, and New Jersey—reported more than 2,000 cases each and contributed a total of 67 percent of the total reported cases (CDC, 1988). However, 20 states reported fewer than 100 cases. As of August 29, 1988, nearly 80 percent of all reported cases of AIDS had occurred in nine states and the District of Columbia. Table 7.1 shows the distribution of homosexual AIDS cases in these nine areas for the 7 years from 1981 through 1987. The proportion of the total cases in homosexual men reported from each geographic area varied greatly, from 38 percent in New Jersey to 95 percent in the District of Columbia. New York, with the largest number of cases,

Table 7.1. Reported U.S. AIDS Cases by State of
Residence, 1981–1987

| | | Homosexual Men | |
State	Total Cases	No.[a]	%
New York	12,929	8,034	62.1
California	11,084	9,669	87.2
Florida	3,538	1,976	55.8
Texas	3,435	2,901	84.4
New Jersey	3,141	1,187	37.8
Illinois	1,329	1,090	82.0
Pennsylvania	1,279	1,101	86.1
Georgia	1,064	646	60.7
Massachusetts	1,020	846	82.9
District of Columbia	970	918	94.6
Rest of U.S.	9,236	7,496	81.2
Total	49,025	35,864	73.1

[a]Estimated from data supplied by CDC.

reported 62 percent of its cases among homosexual men and California, with the
second largest number of cases, reported 87 percent of its cases among homosexual
men.

Age and Racial/Ethnic Characteristics of AIDS Cases

Table 7.2 shows the age distribution of reported AIDS cases among homosexual
men in the United States. Approximately two-thirds of the cases occurred in men
between the ages of 20 and 40. Almost half were reported from the age group 30 to
39. In the absence of information on the total number of homosexual men in the
population or their age distribution, it is not possible to calculate attack rates for
them. However, if homosexual men represent a constant proportion of the male
population in each age group, the cumulative case rate among homosexual men 30
to 39 years of age has been approximately twice the rate among men 20 to 29 years

Table 7.2. Reported U.S. Homosexual AIDS Cases by Age,
1981–1987

Age (Years)	No. Cases	Percent Distribution
20–29	7,589	21.2
30–39	16,949	47.3
40–49	7,624	21.1
>49	3,702	10.3
Total	35,864	100.0

Source: AIDS Weekly Surveillance Report, Jan. 4, 1988.

Table 7.3. Reported U.S. Homosexual AIDS Cases by
Race/Ethnicity, 1981–1987

Race/Ethnicity	No. Cases	Percent Distribution
White, not Hispanic	26,169	73.0
Black, not Hispanic	5,681	15.8
Hispanic	3,670	10.2
Other/unknown	344	1.0
Total	35,864	100.0

Source: AIDS Weekly Surveillance Report, Jan. 4, 1988.

old (4.4 per 1,000 vs. 2.2 per 1,000). Because of the long latency period between infection and the development of AIDS (see later), the high case rate in the 30 to 39 age group does not necessarily represent an increased risk of acquiring AIDS but may reflect infection by HIV-1 during the previous decade.

Table 7.3 shows the racial/ethnic distribution of AIDS cases in adult homosexual men in the United States. At the end of 1987, 73 percent of AIDS cases occurred in white non-Hispanic homosexual men, 16 percent in non-Hispanic blacks, 10 percent in Hispanics, and the remainder in other or unknown ethnic groups. Again, the racial/ethnic composition of the homosexual population is unknown. Based on the assumption that the racial/ethnic distribution of the homosexual population is the same as for the total population, and using 1980 census data for males 20 to 49 years of age, attack rates for non-Hispanic whites, non-Hispanic blacks, and Hispanics have been estimated to be approximately 64 per 100,000 113 per 100,000, and 117 per 100,000, respectively (rates based on total estimated populations 20–49 years). The population rates for non-Hispanic blacks and for Hispanics may be overestimated owing to underenumeration of these groups in the 1980 census (Passel et al., 1982).

Prevalence of HIV-1 Infection

The overall prevalence of HIV-1 infection among homosexual men is not known. Prevalence estimates based on nonrandom samples in the United States have varied greatly from place to place and time to time (CDC, 1987b). The most reliable U.S. estimates based on nonrandom samples come from the Multicenter AIDS Cohort Study (MACS) (Kaslow et al., 1987) (Table 7.4). This study, which enrolled approximately 5,000 homosexual/bisexual men between April 1984 and April 1985, provides HIV-1 prevalence estimates for the Baltimore/Washington, D.C. area, Chicago, Los Angeles, and the Pittsburgh/tristate area. The period prevalence for designated time periods ranged from approximately 21 percent in the Pittsburgh/tristate area to 51 percent in Los Angeles.

Very few data are available to trace the changing prevalence of HIV-1 infection among homosexual men over time. However, data from a nonrandom and a random sample in San Francisco provide substantial information for this community (Fig. 7.2) (Winkelstein et al., 1987a). These data also emphasize the difference

Table 7.4. Period Prevalence of HIV-1 Antibody, Homosexual Men, Selected Communities, Multicenter AIDS Cohort Study, April 1984 to April 1985

Community	Time Period	No. Observed	Percent HIV-1-Seropositive
Pittsburgh/tristate	4/84–4/85	1,062	21
Baltimore/Washington, D.C.	4/84–11/84	1,153	31
Chicago	4/84–3/85	1,102	43
Los Angeles	4/84–4/85	1,637	51
Total	—	4,954	38

Source: Kaslow et al. (1987) and personal communication.

Figure 7.2. Prevalence of HIV-1 infection in two cohorts of homosexual men, San Francisco, 1978–1987.

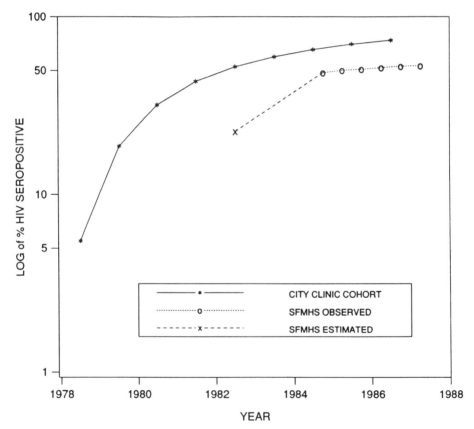

between a prevalence estimate based on samples from a selected, high-risk population and that based on a random samples from a defined geographic area.

The nonrandom City Clinic Cohort was obtained by sampling from 6,875 homosexual men recruited from sexually transmitted disease clinics in San Francisco in 1978 for ongoing studies of hepatitis B virus infections (Jaffe et al., 1985). Serum specimens from this study had been preserved at CDC and were available for testing when HIV-1 was determined to be causally associated with AIDS in 1984. In contrast, the San Francisco Men's Health Study (SFMHS) cohort was recruited in the latter half of 1984 by stratified cluster sampling from 19 census tracts in San Francisco, where the AIDS epidemic had been most intense (Winkelstein et al., 1987a). An estimate of seroprevalence in the latter half of 1982 was possible, because the cohort contained infected men who had no known sexual or blood product exposure to HIV-1 infection during the 2 years prior to the beginning of the study and so must have been infected earlier. This estimate is based on the assumption that these risk-free men who were infected at entry into the study became infected prior to 1984 at the same rate as men infected subsequently (Lyman et al., 1986). The data from the City Clinic Cohort reveal HIV-1 prevalence of slightly less than 5 percent in late 1978 rising to approximately 70 percent in 1984 and remaining essentially constant thereafter. Prevalence in the SFMHS paralleled that in the City Clinic Cohort but was about 30 percent lower, ranging from approximately 23 percent in late 1982 to close to 50 percent in 1984 and remaining essentially the same thereafter.

Data reported from San Francisco for the last 6 months of 1984 indicate that the prevalence of HIV-1 infection among bisexual men in that community, 46 percent, was essentially the same as the prevalence in homosexual men (Winkelstein et al., 1986). In this study, data on the numbers of female partners of infected bisexual men permitted estimates of the potential for transmission of HIV-1 infection from bisexual men in San Francisco to their female sexual partners.

Incidence of HIV-1 Infection

It is possible to estimate annual infection rates in the San Francisco City Clinic Cohort and in the SFMHS. In the City Clinic Cohort, annual incidence rose from approximately 5 to 10 percent between 1978 and 1981 to a peak of approximately 25 percent in 1982–1983 and dropped to a very low rate thereafter (Hessol et al., 1987).

The annual incidence of HIV-1 infection in the SFMHS was estimated to be approximately 18 percent per year between 1982 and 1984, dropping to 5 percent in 1984–1985, and to approximately 2 percent per year (estimated for the period July 1986 to June 1987). A dramatic decline in the incidence of gonorrheal proctitis among homosexual men in San Francisco indicates the marked change in incidence of sexually transmitted diseases among homosexual men in that city after the recognition of the AIDS epidemic (Echenberg et al., 1986). A similar downward trend in the incidence of HIV-1 infection has been observed among homosexual men in New York City in recent years (Marmor et al., 1987; Stevens et al., 1987; Martin, 1987). During the first year of observation of the MACS cohort, April 1984 to April

1985, the annual HIV-1 seroconversion rate was approximately 7.6 percent (Kingsley et al., 1987) and has also declined similarly (Detels et al, in press).

The reasons for the decline in incidence of HIV-1 infection in homosexual men in San Francisco have been examined in the SFMHS (Winkelstein et al., 1987b). The possibility that the observed decline was spurious because of selection bias in the cohort was ruled out. Large declines in sexual behaviors that led to acquisition of infection as well as spread of infection were demonstrated (see later for discussion of modes of transmission). Specifically, numbers of male sexual partners declined from an average of 10.8 in the 6 months during January to June 1984 to 4.2 during January to June 1986. Among HIV-1-seropositive homosexual men in the cohort, the proportion with two or more sexual partners with whom they practiced insertive anal intercourse with ejaculation (the practice by which infection is disseminated) declined from 40 to 13 percent during the same interval. Among HIV-1 seronegative subjects, the proportion with two or more partners with whom they had practiced receptive anal intercourse with ejaculation (the practice by which infection is acquired) declined from 14 to 6 percent.

MODES OF TRANSMISSION

Prior to the identification of HIV-1 as the causal agent for AIDS, a variety of etiologic theories were considered. Such theories included cytomegalovirus infection (Gottlieb et al., 1981), drug use such as amyl nitrites, or an unidentified sexually transmitted agent (Marmor et al., 1982). Once HIV-1 was identified, it quickly became clear that among homosexual men it can be transmitted in two basic ways: sexual transmission and direct contact with infected blood.

Sexual Transmission

Homosexual men usually acquired HIV-1 infection through sexual contact. This mode of transmission was recognized in early case control studies of AIDS which clearly demonstrated the association of sexual activity, as measured by numbers of sexual partners and history of certain sexually transmitted diseases, with the development of AIDS (Jaffe et al., 1983b; Goedert et al., 1984; Marmor et al., 1982, 1984).

The risk of sexually acquiring HIV-1 infection depends on two variables, the probability of exposure to an infected partner and the probability of transmission from an infected partner (Peterman and Curran, 1986). Thus, sexual contact with a known AIDS case has been associated with transmission (Stevens et al., 1986; Polk et al., 1987). As the prevalence of HIV-1 infection has increased, the probability that a randomly chosen sexual partner is infected has increased: all other things being equal, the risk of exposure per contact in 1988 must be substantially higher for a homosexual man than it was in 1980.

Frequent sexual contacts have been considered to be the most important factor in creating the current worldwide epidemic of sexually transmitted diseases (Fleming, 1980). It was not surprising, therefore, that the first major case control study of AIDS should identify multiplicity of sexual partners as the most strongly associated risk factor (Jaffe et al., 1983b). In that study, 50 cases, mostly KS and all occurring among homosexual men, were compared with 120 matched homosexual men. The median number of male sexual partners per year among cases was 61 and among controls 26. Many subsequent studies of risk factors for AIDS or HIV-1 infection have replicated this finding (Chmiel et al., 1987; Winkelstein et al., 1987a). For example, in the SFMHS representative sample of 796 homosexual men recruited from the highest AIDS incidence area of San Francisco during the latter half of 1984, the prevalence of HIV-1 infection was approximately 18 percent in men reporting one or no male sexual partners in the prior 2 years, 32 percent in those reporting six to nine partners, 54 percent in those reporting 10 to 49 partners, and 71 percent in those reporting more than 50 partners in 2 years (Winkelstein et al., 1987a).

The second variable, the risk of effective transfer of infected material, is more difficult to assess. It depends on the probability that cell-associated or cell-free virus in a body fluid from an infected donor will come into contact with an available receptor cell in the uninfected recipient. The sexual acts known to transmit infection include receptive and insertive anal intercourse. Information available on receptive and insertive oral intercourse is sparse and inconclusive, and there are no reliable data on transmission by kissing (see Chapters 6 and 14).

Anal intercourse has been extensively studied, first in case control studies and subsequently in cross-sectional and cohort investigations. Even before HIV-1 was isolated and linked to AIDS, investigators in Los Angeles noted an association between receptive anal intercourse and a low helper–suppressor T-lymphocyte ratio (Detels et al., 1983). Although the first reported case control study of risk factors for AIDS did not implicate receptive anal intercourse as the major mode of transmission (Jaffe et al., 1983b), other early studies did report its strong association with acquisition of AIDS when other putative risk factors were controlled (Marmor et al., 1984; Goedert et al., 1984).

In all of the major cohort studies of prevalent HIV-1 infection, receptive anal intercourse has been the major mode of transmission when other risk factors, including numbers of partners, were controlled (Stevens et al., 1986; Moss et al., 1987; Darrow et al., 1987; Winkelstein et al., 1987a; Chmiel et al., 1987). However, in several studies the statistical power was limited and could not eliminate other modes of transmission such as insertive anal intercourse or receptive or insertive oral intercourse as possible modes of transmission.

Receptive anal intercourse has likewise been shown to be the primary mode of transmission of HIV-1 infection in all cohort studies in which seroconversion has been analyzed during follow-up (Kingsley et al., 1987; Greenblatt et al., 1987). Early in the MACS study, seroconversion rates were 3.8 percent (95/2,507) over 6 months, and by multivariate analysis receptive anal intercourse was the only risk factor associated with seroconversion. Subsequent analysis has confirmed these findings but left open the possibility of occasional transmission by another route (Detels et al., 1988). In two San Francisco cohorts (SFMHS and San Francisco General Hospital), 37 men seroconverted between 1983 and 1988. Seroconversion in these men was strongly associated with number of sexual partners and practice of receptive anal intercourse. Thirty-two percent of the seroconverters reported 10 or more sexual partners during 6 to 12 months prior to seroconversion as compared to 10 percent of seronegative subjects. The corresponding percentages for reported receptive anal intercourse were 78 and 46 percent, respectively.

Infection by Direct Transfer of Infected Blood

Through 1987, less than 2 percent (610) of the reported cases of AIDS in homosexual men in the United States were also associated with blood transfusion (CDC, 1988). Of the 35,864 homosexual reported cases, 3,726 (10.4 percent) were also designated as drug abusers.

Data on the sharing of needles by homosexual men during recreational drug use are available from the SFMHS and the MACS (Winkelstein et al, 1987a; Chmiel et al., 1987). Needle sharing was reported in 8 percent of the SFMHS cohort and 4 percent of the MACS cohort during the previous 5 years. In the SFMHS, 83 percent of those reporting needle sharing were HIV-1-seropositive as compared to 45 percent of those reporting no needle sharing. In the MACS, the proportions were 65 and 37 percent, respectively.

INFECTIVITY OF HIV-1 AMONG HOMOSEXUAL MEN

Infectivity, the proportion of persons who become infected after contact with one or more infected partner (per partner infectivity), or the proportion of actual sexual exposures that result in infection (per contact infectivity), is key to understanding the epidemic spread of the AIDS retrovirus. Per-partner infectivity can be estimated directly by the proportion of partners of infected persons who become infected. Unfortunately, such data are difficult to obtain. Early in the epidemic, investigators attempted to ascertain the incidence of AIDS in the sexual partners of a particularly promiscuous homosexual man suffering from AIDS (Auerbach et al., 1984). Eight (11.1 percent) of this man's 72 named partners had developed AIDS; however, the data were insufficient to exclude sexual encounters with other AIDS cases or infected men. Also, because serological testing for HIV-1 was not available, it is likely that some of the partners were infected even though they did not have AIDS. Because partner tracing of HIV-1-infected men has not proved feasible because of the large numbers of partners, mathematical modeling has been used to estimate the per-partner infectivity of HIV-1 by unprotected receptive anal intercourse among homosexual men (Grant et al., 1987). The data necessary to apply the model were (1) the numbers of partners of a sample of men during a stipulated time period, (2) the prevalence of HIV-1 infection in the sample at the beginning of the time period, and (3) the rate of infection (seroconversions) during the time period. Data from the SFMHS yielded a per-partner rate of 0.102 with a 95 percent confidence interval of 0.043 to 0.160. As for per-contact infectivity, the investigators did not have data for numbers of contacts each partner engaged in and so could only estimate a range of per-contact infectivity values assuming a fixed number of contacts per month. These values ranged from 0.1 to 0.01 per exposure (Wiley and Herschkorn, 1988).

COFACTORS FOR HIV-1 INFECTION*

Two categories of cofactors have been investigated, those that might affect acquisition of HIV-1 infection during or before sexual contact, e.g., ancillary sexual practices (Winkelstein et al., 1987a), and those of a more general nature that might influence susceptibility.

Ancillary Sexual Practices

Four types of ancillary sexual practices among homosexual men have received particular attention. First, there are practices likely to result in disruption (trauma) of the rectal mucosa, thereby facilitating infection (see Chapter 6). Second, certain practices might prevent infection by protecting the rectal mucosa from exposure. Third, there are practices that might alter the physiology of the rectum leaving it more susceptible to infection. Fourth, practices interfering with judgment could render the sexual partners less likely to take precautions against acquiring infection.

The activity that could enhance the permeability of rectal mucosa and has been the most consistently associated with HIV-1 seropositivity has been douching before intercourse (Stevens et al., 1986; Winkelstein et al., 1987a; Moss et al., 1987; Chmiel et al., 1987). This finding duplicated the earlier observation of an association between douching and hepatitis B virus transmission (Schreeder et al., 1982). Other ancillary sexual practices that might produce rectal trauma, such as dildo use and receptive fisting, have shown inconsistent associations with HIV-1 infection (Stevens et al., 1986; Darrow et al., 1987; Winkelstein et al., 1987a; Moss et al., 1987; Chmiel et al., 1987).

The use of condoms has been actively promoted as an effective barrier to infection through the rectal mucosa (USPHS, 1986). In vitro studies have demonstrated that latex condoms do not allow passage of HIV-1 (Conant et al., 1986; Van de Perre et al., 1987). However, whereas logic and clinical experience strongly support the value of condoms, to date only one epidemiological study has documented the usefulness of condoms in preventing the spread of infection among sexually active homosexual men who continued high-risk behavior (Detels et al., 1988). In another study only 20 percent of homosexual men who engaged in sexual activities involving the transfer of "body fluids" used condoms (Martin, 1987), and their effectiveness was not described. The use of contraceptive foam containing nonoxynol-9, which is viricidal, during anal intercourse has also been suggested as being protective (Hicks et al., 1985), but no epidemiological evidence regarding its use or effectiveness has been reported.

Nitrite inhalants (poppers), because of their vasodilator effect, have been considered as possible cofactors for HIV-1 infection (Newell et al., 1985). However, evidence from various epidemiological studies has provided equivocal findings, with two early studies finding an association (Jaffe et al., 1983b; Marmor et al., 1984) but only one of several recent studies replicating this finding (Moss et al., 1987; Chmiel et al., 1987).

---

*See also Chapters 6 and 11.

The association between prevalent HIV-1 infection and the use of other drugs that might impair the participants' judgment, such as amphetamines, cocaine, and marijuana, in proximity to sexual activity or used habitually has been examined in several investigations (Jaffe et al., 1983b; Darrow et al., 1987; Moss et al., 1987; Chmiel et al., 1987). Again, the results were contradictory. One investigator reported weak positive associations with certain drugs after subjecting the data to multiple regression analyses (Chmiel et al., 1987), and two smaller studies reported equivocal or no associations (Darrow et al., 1987; Moss et al., 1987). Careful studies must account not only for differences in sexual practices but also for simultaneous use of multiple psychoactive agents, any of which may promote high-risk behavior or produce physiologic changes that increase risk.

Other Cofactors

From the first report of AIDS in homosexual men, the possibility was considered that concurrent or prior infections might play a role in the etiology of the observed immunosuppression (CDC, 1981a). All five of the originally reported cases had a history of cytomegalovirus (CMV) disease or were shedding this virus during the 5 months prior to their diagnosis of PCP. In the first reported case control study of AIDS, cases were reported to have had a history of syphilis or non-B hepatitis or of treatment for enteric parasites more frequently than controls (Jaffe et al., 1983b). Since then, this issue has been repeatedly examined (see also Chapter 6).

Syphilis and gonorrhea, measured by history, serology, or history of treatment, have been associated with HIV-1 infection, after controlling for confounding, in several studies (Darrow et al., 1987; Moss et al., 1987; Chmiel et al., 1987). In one study, syphilis and HIV-1 infection were associated in bivariate analyses but not in multiple regression analysis (Stevens et al., 1986). Presence of both antibodies to hepatitis B core antigen (HBcAg) and hepatitis B surface antigen (HBsAg) have been associated with HIV-1 in a multiple regression analysis of data from the MACS (Chmiel et al., 1987). In the same study, CMV antibody titer >30 and a history of anal herpes were also strongly associated with HIV-1 infection. Anal genital warts (condylomata acuminata) also have been shown to be associated with HIV-1 infection in homosexual men after controlling for numbers of male sexual partners and the frequency of receptive anal intercourse (Kent et al., 1987). However, this association was shown more likely to be the consequence than an antecedent or cofactor of HIV-1 infection. Enteric parasitic infections, particularly amebiasis and giardiasis, have also been reported as independent contributors to risk of infection by HIV-1 (Moss et al., 1987). However, caution is indicated in interpreting the results of these and other multiple regression analyses because of the possible effects of collinearity.

THE NATURAL HISTORY OF HIV-1 INFECTION IN HOMOSEXUAL MEN

It is not yet clear how much of the experience with the natural history of HIV-1 infection in homosexual men summarized here is generalizable to other groups of persons with HIV-1 infection. Therefore, various aspects of the natural history including experience with the course of the infection in other groups are discussed elsewhere (see Chapters 1, 4, 6, 11, and 13).

The natural history of HIV-1 infection can be divided into three stages, the primary stage extending from the time of infection through seroconversion, the secondary stage from HIV-1 seroconversion until the onset of AIDS, and the tertiary stage from the diagnosis of AIDS until death.

Primary Stage

In several studies investigators have attempted to establish the probable time of exposure to HIV-1 infection and have inferred an incubation period of 1 to 2 weeks for the development of a mild acute syndrome characterized as "infectious-mononucleosis-like" (Cooper et al., 1985; Goldman et al., 1986). The proportion of HIV-1 infections accompanied by this acute syndrome was 55 percent in a preliminary report from the MACS (Fox et al., 1987). In the two other cited studies, duration of symptoms was between 3 and 14 days, although there are cases in which symptoms have persisted for weeks. Where it has been examined, seroconversion was estimated to occur between 6 and 56 days after the presumed exposure, and the great majority of seroconversions probably do occur within 8 to 10 weeks of exposure.

Several recent reports suggest that occasionally the incubation period between infection and seroconversion may be substantially longer than indicated here (Ranki et al., 1987; Loche and Mach, 1988; Ou et al., 1988; Farzadegan et al., 1988; see also Chapters 3 and 6). In one study using the polymerase chain reaction (PCR), a method that detects very small amounts of viral DNA in human cells (Loche and Mach, 1988), five of 16 HIV-1-seronegative sexual partners of HIV-1-seropositive individuals were positive for HIV-1 DNA. Similarly, Ou and colleagues (1988) reported that seven of 11 HIV-1-seropositive but culture-negative homosexual men were PCR positive. In a third study (Farzadegan et al., 1988), four men from the Multicenter AIDS Cohort Study reportedly seroreverted from HIV-1-seropositive to seronegative during 2.5 years. These men lost detectable evidence of HIV-1 infection by standard serologic testing, but all four were PCR positive, possibly indicating a shift from active to latent infection. Although it is doubtful that widespread use of this test will change the current understanding of the epidemiology of HIV-1 infection, this highly sensitive assay has raised important questions about the early natural history of the infection.

Secondary Stage

The time between seroconversion resulting from sexual contact between homosexual men and the onset of AIDS is generally considered to be long and quite variable (Curran et al., 1988). In a study of 63 homosexual men whose dates of HIV-1 seroconversion were known, 20 (30 percent) had developed AIDS over an average follow-up of 76 months (Hessol et al., 1987). Survival analysis demonstrated that between 17 (26 percent) and 30 (46 percent) of these men, and 92 additional men for whom the date of seroconversion could be accurately estimated, developed AIDS within 88 months of seroconversion. The mean latency period between seroconversion and diagnosis of AIDS was 55 months (4.6 years). In homosexual men in general, presumably infected by sexual contact, onset of AIDS has been observed as soon as 12 months (El-Sadr et al., 1987) and as long as 8 years after seroconversion (Jaffe et al., 1985).

Prospective follow-up of cohorts of HIV-1 seroconverters can provide estimates of the latency periods to AIDS only when follow-up has been accomplished for the full range of latency periods. Because this range is longer than the present observation periods of existing cohorts of HIV-1-infected men, mathematical modeling has been used to estimate the "true" latency period. Using data on 84 homosexual men randomly selected from the San Francisco City Clinic Cohort, a maximum likelihood estimate of the latency period has been made (Lui et al., 1988). This estimate is 7.8 years (90 percent confidence interval, 6.9 to 14.4 years).

One of the earliest pathophysiological changes in homosexual men after HIV-1 seroconversion is a drop in the mean CD4$^+$ lymphocyte count and a corresponding drop in the CD4$^+$/CD8$^+$ lymphocyte ratio (El-Sadr et al., 1987). This drop in CD4$^+$ lymphocytes may occur at or soon after seroconversion. However, not all seroconverters experience this immediate decrease in CD4$^+$ lymphocytes. As many as 18 percent of the HIV-1-infected homosexual men in the SFMHS have maintained "normal" CD4$^+$ lymphocyte counts during 30 months of observation (Lang et al., 1987b), although the majority of infected homosexual men experience some decline. In one study, the investigators noted that 71 percent of homosexual men who were HIV-1-seropositive before 1981 and 36 percent who were subsequently HIV-1-seropositive had CD4$^+$/CD8$^+$ cell ratios of less than 1.0 when evaluated in 1984 (Stevens et al., 1986). Figure 7.3 depicts the distributions of CD4$^+$ lympho-

Figure 7.3. Cumulative frequency distributions of homosexual men according to CD4$^+$ T-lymphocyte counts, HIV-1 serostatus, and examination cycle: SFMHS, 1984–1986.

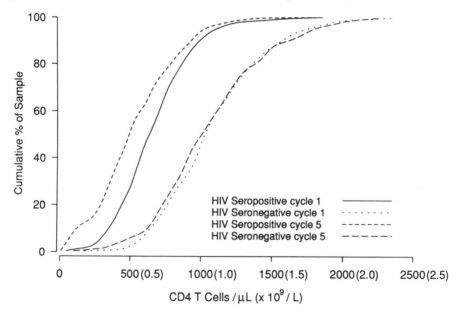

cyte counts in homosexual men observed over a 30-month period in the SFMHS (Lang et al., 1987b). On entry, HIV-1-seronegative homosexual men had a median number of CD4$^+$ helper lymphocytes of approximately 1,000/μl ($\times$ 10^9/L), and HIV-1-seropositive homosexual men approximately 550/μl ($\times$ 10^9/L). After 30 months of observation, CD4$^+$ cell counts in HIV-1-seronegative homosexual men remained approximately the same, whereas men who had remained HIV-1-sero-positive but without AIDS had dropped to approximately 450/μl ($\times$ 10^9/L). Although low CD4$^+$ cell counts are strongly predictive of the development of AIDS in HIV-1-infected homosexual men, they are not included in the criteria for an AIDS diagnosis (Goedert et al., 1987; Polk et al., 1987; CDC, 1987a).

An early but often persistent physical finding in HIV-1-seropositive homosex-ual men is lymphadenopathy (Lang et al., 1987a; Chmiel et al., 1987). In the SFMHS, 57 percent of HIV-1-seropositive homosexual men had generalized lymphadenopathy as compared to 10 percent of HIV-1-seronegative men on entry. The corresponding values for the MACS were 49 percent and 11 percent. Never-theless, neither the occurrence nor the degree of lymphadenopathy has proved to have predictive value for progression to AIDS (Goedert et al., 1987; Polk et al., 1987).

A number of other clinical findings characterize the second stage of HIV-1 infection. Some of these are obvious consequences of disruption of the immune system, some are probably the direct result of cell destruction by the HIV-1, and some are not readily explainable.

Anal warts, oral candidiasis, and skin test anergy are common clinical findings attributable to immunodeficiency in HIV-1-seropositive homosexual men during the latent period (Lang et al., 1987a; Kent et al., 1987). Worsening herpes lesions, including zoster, and bullous impetigo are also rather common (Lang et al., 1987a). Respiratory infections, including the initial bouts of opportunistic infections, char-acterize the latter portion of the second stage of HIV-1 infection.

Besides the cells of the immune system that are infected by the HIV-1 (Fauci, 1988), the retrovirus has been shown to directly infect cells of the central nervous system and the intestinal tract (Shaw et al., 1985; Nelson et al., 1988). The major consequences of HIV-1 infection of the central nervous system are termed AIDS dementia complex and usually do not become manifest until late in the latent period (see Chapter 5). Direct consequences of HIV-1 infection of the gastrointes-tinal tract may contribute importantly to the severe diarrheal syndrome that fre-quently develops late in the secondary stage of infection (Nelson et al., 1988; see also Chapter 4).

Hairy leukoplakia, a recently described oral lesion with a strong positive pre-dictive value for the development of AIDS in HIV-1-infected homosexual men, may be a consequence of immune suppression or direct infection of the oral mucosa (Greenspan et al., 1987). This lesion has been reported to have a preva-lence of 5 to 10 percent in the SFMHS sample of infected men (Lang et al., 1987a). The frequent episodes of fever and night sweats that affect HIV-1-infected men during the symptomatic phase of the second stage of HIV-1 infection may be due to the infections resulting from immune system suppression, to the primary infec-tion, or to soluble mediators of immunity such as IL2 or interferon (see Chapter 2).

The secondary stage of HIV-1 infection in homosexual men often ends with an accelerated decline in immune function, signaled by a sharp decline in $CD4^+$ lymphocyte counts and the onset of clinical findings characteristic of AIDS (El-Sadr et al., 1987).

Tertiary Stage (See Chapter 4)

There have been two revisions of the case definition for AIDS originally proposed (CDC, 1982, 1986, 1987a). The three definitions, however, are quite similar; each revision essentially broadens the criteria, thereby providing for the inclusion of additional cases. The latest revision includes the AIDS dementia complex and a wasting syndrome characterized by diarrhea and severe weight loss. The basis for the definitions is the presence of an opportunistic infection or certain cancers in a person who has an otherwise unexplained suppression of the immune system and who is infected by HIV-1 (provision is made for case designation in the absence of laboratory evidence of infection if no test was performed or if the results were "equivocal"). The indicator infections and cancers that qualify a person for diagnosis are listed in the published diagnostic criteria (CDC, 1987a).

Survival after a diagnosis of AIDS has been comprehensively evaluated from AIDS case surveillance data of San Francisco (Lemp et al., 1987). From these data it has been possible to follow, at 6-month intervals, 3,661 cases of AIDS from diagnosis to death. The maximum follow-up time was 81 months (6.75 years), and the mean follow-up was 17 months. The median survival time, calculated by the Kaplan-Meier product-limit method, for homosexual men was 12.2 months, slightly longer than survival for men who were also IV drug users (10.0 months), and substantially longer than survival for transfusion recipients (2.7 months), who often had serious unrelated conditions. Older men had substantially shorter survival, 8.6 months for men 50 to 59 years of age as compared to 13.1 months for men 20 to 29 years of age. Cases diagnosed on the basis of the presence of KS had longer survival (15.9 months) than cases diagnosed on the basis of PCP (11.4 months). However, survival of PCP cases increased in 1986 to 13.9 months. It is not yet clear whether survival time has continued to increase as newer therapeutic regimens have been introduced.

The tertiary stage of HIV-1 infection is relatively short. The deteriorating clinical status of AIDS patients is characterized by severe wasting, protracted diarrhea, high fevers, respiratory complications, disseminated KS, and, frequently, severe central nervous system complications. To date, no recoveries from the tertiary stage of HIV infection have been reported. However, there are a small number of "long-term survivors" (>3 years) reported nationally; they are all homosexual men with Kaposi's sarcoma.

CONCLUSIONS

By the end of 1987, the AIDS epidemic, first recognized in homosexual men in 1981, had affected more than 35,000 of them in the United States alone, of whom almost 20,000 had died. These cases and deaths accounted for more than 70 percent of the total in the United States since the beginning of the epidemic. Approximately 80 percent of all cases in homosexual men in the United States have occurred in nine states and the District of Columbia. Most of the cases in homosexual men outside of the United States have been reported in the developed countries of Europe and the Americas.

Prevalence of HIV-1 infection in a selected population of homosexual men in San Francisco was 5 percent in 1978 and had reached approximately 70 percent by 1985. In another cohort in San Francisco, HIV-1 seroprevalence was about 50 percent in 1985. Figures in other U.S. cities were occasionally that high but usually lower. Because large numbers of homosexual men have been infected by HIV-1 and because the latency period for AIDS is long, cases will continue to occur for many years to come. By the end of 1992, an estimated 200,000 cases of AIDS will have occurred among homosexual men in the United States; at least 50,000 of these will occur in 1992 alone.

The vast majority of infections are due to sexual contact. Because the infectivity of HIV-1 is relatively low and the major mode of transmission, penile–anal intercourse, has been determined, effective control of the spread of HIV-1 infection has been possible. Homosexual men have substantially reduced their numbers of different sexual partners and their frequency of high-risk practices. Presumably, they have also increased their use of condoms. Whereas annual seroconversion rates in the early 1980s had to have been at least 15 percent, the substantial changes in sexual behavior after 1982 have brought annual HIV-1 seroconversion rates among selected groups of homosexual men to very low levels—1 or 2 percent.

The natural history of HIV-1 infection can be divided into stages. The primary stage, from infection through seroconversion, is characterized by an acute mononucleosislike syndrome and usually lasts for no more than a few weeks. The secondary stage, from seroconversion until the onset of AIDS, has a variable duration of months to years. Clinical manifestations of HIV-1 infection during this stage of the infection vary from trivial to serious. The tertiary stage, from the time AIDS develops, lasts only about 1 year, during which time untreated patients rapidly and almost invariably progress, ultimately, to death. A great variety of therapeutic interventions have begun to offer some hope of reversing that course. As the largest affected group, homosexual men have borne and will continue for some time to bear the major share of the burden in the evaluation of those interventions.

REFERENCES

Auerbach DM, Darrow WW, Jaffe HW, et al. (1984): Am J Med 76:487.
Centers for Disease Control (1981a): MMWR 30:250.
Centers for Disease Control (1981b): MMWR 30:305.
Centers for Disease Control (1981c): MMWR 30:409.
Centers for Disease Control (1982): MMWR 31:507.
Centers for Disease Control (1986): MMWR 35:334.
Centers for Disease Control (1987a): MMWR 36 (Suppl):1S.
Centers for Disease Control (1987b): MMWR 36 (Suppl):S-6.
Centers for Disease Control (1988a): MMWR 37:551.
Centers for Disease Control (1988b): AIDS Weekly Surveillance Report, August 29.
Chmiel JS, Detels R, Kaslow RA, et al., (1987): Am J Epidemiol 126:568.
Conant M, Hardy D, Sernatinger J, et al. (1986): JAMA 225:1706.

Cooper DA, Maclean P, Finlayson R, et al. (1985): Lancet 1:537–540.

Crosby AW Jr (1976): Epidemic and Peace, 1918. Westport, CT: Greenwood Press, pp. 202–226.

Curran JW, Jaffe HW, Hardy AM, et al. (1988): Science 239:610.

Darrow WW, Echenberg DF, Jaffe HW, et al. (1987): Am J Public Health 77:479.

Detels R, Fahey JL, Schwartz K, et al. (1983): Lancet 1:609.

Detels R, English P, Visscher B, et al. (1988): Fourth International Conference on AIDS, June 12–16, Stockholm.

DeWys WD, Curran J, Henle W, et al. (1982): Cancer Treat Rep 66:1387.

Echenberg DF, Rutherford GW, Darrow WW, et al. (1986): Second International Conference on AIDS, Paris, June 23–25.

El-Sadr W, Marmor M, Zolla-Pazner S, et al. (1987): J Infect Dis 155:789.

Farzadegan H, Polis M, Wolinsky SM, et al. (1988): Ann Intern Med 108:785.

Fauci AS (1988): Science 239:617.

Fleming WL (1980): The sexually transmitted diseases. In Last JM (ed.): Public Health and Preventive Medicine, 11th Ed. New York: Appleton-Century-Crofts, 251–273.

Fox R, Eldred LJ, Fuchs EJ, et al. (1987): AIDS 1:35.

Friedman-Kien AE, Laubenstein LJ, Rubinstein P, et al. (1982): Ann Intern Med 96:693.

Goedert JJ, Sarngadharan MG, Biggar RJ, et al. (1984): Lancet 1:711.

Goedert JJ, Biggar RJ, Melbye M, et al. (1987): JAMA 257:331.

Goldman R, Lang W, Lyman D (1986): Am J Med 81:1122.

Gottlieb MS, Schroff R, Schanker HM, et al. (1981): N Engl J Med 305:1425.

Grant R, Wiley JA, Winkelstein W (1987): J Infect Dis 156:189.

Greenblatt RM, Samuel M, Osmond D, et al. (1987): Third International Conference on AIDS, Washington, D.C., June 1–5.

Greenspan D, Greenspan JS, Hearst NG, et al. (1987): J Infect Dis 155(3):475.

Hessol NA, Rutherford GW, O'Malley PM, et al. (1987): Third International Conference on AIDS, Washington, D.C. June 1–5.

Hicks DR, Martin LS, Getchell IP, et al. (1985): Lancet 2:1422.

Jaffe HW, Bregman DJ, Selik RM (1983a): J Infect Dis 148:339.

Jaffe HW, Keewhan C, Thomas PA, et al. (1983b): Ann Intern Med 99(2):145.

Jaffe HW, Darrow WW, Echenberg DF, et al. (1985): Ann Intern Med 103:210.

Kaslow RA, Ostrow DG, Detels R, et al. (1987): Am J Epidemiol 126:310.

Kent C, Samuel M, Winkelstein W Jr (1987): JAMA 258(23):3385.

Kingsley LA, Detels R, Kaslow R, et al. (1987): Lancet 1:345.

Lang W, Anderson RE, Perkins H, et al. (1987a): JAMA 257(3):326.

Lang W, Anderson R, Winkelstein W Jr, et al. (1987b): Third International Conference on AIDS, Washington D.C., June 1–5.

Lemp GF, Barnhart JL, Rutherford GW, et al. (1987): Presented at 115th Annual Meeting, American Public Health Association, New Orleans, October 22.

Loche M, Mach B (1988): Lancet 2:418.

Lui K-J, Darrow WW, Rutherford GW (1988): Science 240:1333.

Lyman D, Winkelstein W, Ascher M, et al. (1986): JAMA 255(13):1703.

Marmor M, Friedman-Kien AE, Laubenstein L, et al. (1982): Lancet 1:1083.

Marmor M, Friedman-Kien AE, Zolla-Pazner S, et al. (1984): Ann Intern Med 100:809.

Marmor M, Zelenrich-Jacquette A, Zolla-Pazner S, et al. (1987): Third International Conference on AIDS, Washington, D.C., June 1–5.

Martin JL (1987): Third International Conference on AIDS, Washington, D.C., June 1–5.

Mayer KH, DeGruttola V (1987): Ann Intern Med 107(3):428.

Moss AR, Osmond D, Bacchetti P, et al. (1987): Am J Epidemiol 125:1035.

Nelson JA, Wiley CA, Reynolds-Kohler C, Margaretten W (1988): Lancet 1:259.

Newell GR, Mansell PW, Spitz MR, et al. (1985): Am J Med 78:811.

Ou C, Kwok S, Mitchell SW, et al. (1988): Science 239:295.

Passel JS, Siegel J, Robinson JG (1982): Current Population Reports, Bureau of the Census, Feb., Series P23, No. 115.

Peterman TA, Curran JW (1986): JAMA 256:2222.

Polk BF, Fox R, Brookmeyer R, et al. (1987): N Engl J med 316:61.

Ranki A, Valle S-L, Krohn K, et al. (1987): Lancet 2:589.

Schreeder MT, Thompson SE, Hadler SC, et al. (1982): J Infect Dis 146:7.

Shaw GM, Harper ME, Hahn BH, et al. (1985): Science 227:177.

Shilts R (1987): And the Band Played On. New York: St. Martin's Press, pp. 11–20.

Stevens CE, Taylor PE, Zang EA, et al. (1986): JAMA 255(16):2167.

Stevens CE, Taylor PE, Zang EA, et al. (1987): Third International Conference on AIDS, Washington D.C., June 1–5.

USPHS (1986): Surgeon General's Report on AIDS.

Van de Perre P, Jacobs D, Sprecher-Goldberger S (1987): AIDS 1:49.

Wiley JA, Herschkorn SJ (1988): J Infect Dis 158:500.

Winkelstein W Jr, Wiley JA, Padian N, Levy JA (1986): JAMA 255(7):901.

Winkelstein W Jr, Lyman D, Padian N, et al. (1987a): JAMA 257:321.

Winkelstein W Jr, Samuel M, Padian N, et al. (1987b): Am J Public Health 77:685.

Winkelstein W Jr, Samuel M, Padian NS, et al. (1987c): Am J Public Health 77:1552.

8

Heterosexuals

HARRY W. HAVERKOS AND ROBERT EDELMAN

Shortly after AIDS was recognized among homosexually active men in New York and California (CDC, 1981a,b), it was found among heterosexual men and women who were intravenous drug abusers. Because blood contact could be implicated in many of the early cases among women and surreptitious use of intravenous drugs could not be excluded in others, sexual transmission from men to women was considered unlikely or, at most, uncommon. However, documentation of sexual transmission of human immunodeficiency virus (HIV-1) from men to women among unmarried women in Africa, spouses of the military, and hemophiliacs rapidly changed this misconception (Clumeck et al., 1984; Redfield et al., 1985a; Pitchenik et al., 1984; Kreiss et al., 1985; Jason et al., 1986; Allain, 1986). Following documentation of male-to-female transmission of HIV-1, many wondered and hoped that exposure to semen through receptive anal intercourse was an exclusive sexual behavior in the spread of HIV-1. However, epidemiologic evidence of increasingly widespread transmission of HIV-1 and AIDS from women to men has dispelled this narrow view (Redfield et al., 1985b; CDC, 1985a; Calabrese and Gopalakrishna, 1986; Steigbigel et al., 1987; Chamberland et al., 1987). Isolation of HIV-1 from cervical secretions of women at risk for AIDS supports this evidence (Vogt et al., 1986; Wofsy et al., 1986).

AIDS IN AFRICA AND HAITI*

In 1983, European investigators reported Kaposi's sarcoma and opportunistic infections consistent with AIDS among healthy African immigrants to Europe and among Europeans working in central Africa (Clumeck et al., 1983, 1984; Brunet et al., 1983; Bygbjerg, 1983). These cases met the CDC definition for AIDS, and the epidemiology suggested a sexual route of transmission. In a study of 18 African-associated AIDS patients hospitalized in Belgium between 1979 and 1983, six were female (Clumeck et al., 1984). The mean ages of male and female patients were 38 and 28 years, respectively. Ten (56 percent) had died by the time of the report. All 18 patients denied homosexuality, intravenous drug use, and blood transfusions.

*See also Chapters 11 and 12.

Heterosexual contact was proposed as the likely means of spread (Clumeck et al., 1984). Shortly thereafter clusters of AIDS among heterosexuals were reported in Zaire (Ellrodt et al., 1984; Piot et al., 1984); they provided still more convincing epidemiological evidence for heterosexual transmission in Africa.

African, American, and European collaborators in parts of Zambia (Melbye et al., 1986) and Rwanda (Clumeck et al., 1985) have assembled similar evidence of heterosexual transmission of HIV-1 infection and AIDS, namely, the nearly equal sex distribution and a lower mean age for female than for male patients in their sexually most active years of life.

Epidemiologic studies of AIDS in Haiti have also suggested heterosexual spread of AIDS. In 1983, Johnson and colleagues could identify a risk factor (e.g., homosexuality, bisexuality, IV drug use, or blood transfusion) in 75 percent of 32 male AIDS cases. But in 1985, any of these risk factors could be identified in only 17 percent of 158 male AIDS cases (Pape et al., 1986). The difference between 1983 and 1985 was ascribed to rising heterosexual transmission rates of HIV-1 from women to men.

AIDS IN THE UNITED STATES

Through national surveillance for AIDS in the United States, between June 1981 and August 29, 1988, 70,882 adolescent/adult cases of AIDS in the United States were reported to CDC (Table 8.1). Most cases have been homosexual or bisexual men, heterosexual intravenous drug abusers, blood transfusion recipients, patients with hemophilia or other coagulation disorders, or infants of those at risk for AIDS. However, 2,981 (4 percent) individuals with AIDS have been reported as heterosexual patients who denied intravenous drug abuse and reported no previous blood transfusions. These cases include 1,858 persons (1,440 women, 418 men) who have had heterosexual contact with a person with AIDS or at risk for AIDS (61 percent

Table 8.1. Adult/Adolescent[a] AIDS Cases by Sex and Transmission Category, Weekly Surveillance Report, Centers for Disease Control, August 29, 1988

Transmission Category	Males (%)	Females (%)
Homosexual or bisexual men	44,402 (68)	—
Intravenous drug abuse	10,579 (16)	3,029 (52)
Homosexual male and IV drug abuser	5,168 (8)	—
Hemophilia/coagulation disorder	659 (1)	21 (0)
Heterosexual contact[b]	1,281 (2)	1,700 (29)
Transfusion, blood/components	1,147 (1)	642 (11)
Undetermined	1,806 (3)	448 (8)
Total	65,042 (100)	5,840 (100)

[a]Excludes 1,142 patients less than 13 years of age.

[b]Includes 1,858 persons (418 men, 1,140 women) who have had heterosexual contact with a person with AIDS or at risk for AIDS and 1,123 (863 men, 260 women) persons without other identified risks who were born in countries in which heterosexual transmission is believed to play a major role although precise means of transmission have not been fully defined.

reported sex with an intravenous drug abuser) and 1,123 persons (260 women, 863 men) without other identified risks who were born in countries (e.g., Haiti) in which heterosexual transmission is believed to play a major role although precise means of transmission have not been fully defined. In total, of the AIDS cases in the United States attributed to heterosexual contact, 1,281 were men and 1,700 were women. Nine hundred fifty-two (32 percent) of all heterosexual AIDS cases reported since 1981 were diagnosed and reported to the CDC in 1988. Similarly, 30 percent of all AIDS cases reported in the United States have been reported during the same time period, suggesting that the proportion of heterosexual cases relative to other risk groups has not changed. However, an analysis of heterosexual cases excluding foreign-born heterosexual cases (Chamberland et al., 1987) reveals that during 1986, the total number of such cases reported increased by 135 percent, from 218 to 513, and reported cases among homosexual/bisexual men and intravenous drug abusers increased by 82 percent and 81 percent, respectively. This reflects a 10-month doubling time for native-born heterosexual cases compared with a doubling time of 14 months for homosexual/bisexual men and intravenous drug abusers. Furthermore, between August 11, 1986, and August 10, 1987, the total number of male heterosexual cases (foreign-born excluded) rose to 174, which represents a 206 percent increase (CDC, 1987a).

In addition, 2,254 (3 percent) adult patients have been listed in an "undetermined" category by the CDC. Although the exact number was not stated, many of the AIDS patients in the "undetermined" category reported sex with prostitutes and/or multiple heterosexual contacts but could not identify any one sexual partner with AIDS or at known risk for AIDS. Thus, it would seem likely that some patients in the "undetermined" category acquired their infection through heterosexual contact.

Many of the heterosexual AIDS cases in the United States can be linked directly to intravenous drug abusers (Moss, 1987). Sixty-one percent of the U.S.-born heterosexual AIDS cases reported sex with an intravenous drug abuser as their source of HIV-1 infection. Twelve percent of cases report a bisexual male as their likely source of infection (M. Chamberland, personal communication, CDC).

Analyzing AIDS patients by race and risk group denotes the relative importance of heterosexual spread and the subsequent spread through childbearing among the major racial groups in the United States (Table 8.2). The proportion of cases attributed to intravenous drug abuse by race parallels the proportion of cases attributed to heterosexual contact and among pediatric patients. Even though blacks account for 26 percent of all cases in the United States, they account for 51 percent of the heterosexual intravenous drug users with AIDS, 67 percent of AIDS cases attributed to heterosexual contact, and 61 percent of pediatric cases whose parent(s) is (are) at risk for AIDS. Similarly, there are more Hispanic AIDS cases among intravenous drug users, heterosexual contacts, and pediatric cases than among whites, even though whites account for 58 percent of all AIDS patients. Looking at the numbers in Table 8.2 another way, 1 percent of AIDS cases among whites are attributed to heterosexual spread of HIV-1, 11 percent of blacks, and 4 percent of Hispanics.

At present, heterosexual spread of HIV-1 infection and AIDS appears to be much more of a problem among blacks and Hispanics than among whites in the

Table 8.2. AIDS Cases by Race[a] and Transmission Category, Centers for Disease Control, August 29, 1988

Transmission Category	White (%)	Black (%)	Hispanic (%)	Total[a] (%)
Homosexual or bisexual men	32,546 (74)	6,910 (16)	4,506 (10)	43,962 (100)
Intravenous drug abuser	2,669 (20)	6,937 (51)	3,940 (29)	13,546 (100)
Homosexual male and IV user	3,129 (61)	1,289 (25)	725 (14)	5,143 (100)
Hemophilia/coagulation disorder	621 (85)	48 (7)	62 (8)	731 (100)
Heterosexual contact	558 (19)	1,976 (67)	429 (14)	2,963 (100)
Transfusion recipient	1,402 (74)	311 (16)	180 (10)	1,893 (100)
Parent with/at risk for AIDS	129 (15)	540 (61)	210 (24)	879 (100)
Undetermined	867 (38)	893 (40)	493 (22)	2,253 (100)
Total	41,921 (58)	18,904 (26)	10,545 (15)	71,370 (100)

[a]Excludes 654 patients listed as "other" or "unknown" race.

United States. This may reflect a larger proportion of bisexual men among black and Hispanic homosexual/bisexual men or a greater overlap of homosexual/bisexual men and intravenous drug abusers in the black and Hispanic communities than among whites. It may also represent an earlier introduction of HIV-1 into the black heterosexual population of the United States or some yet undefined host or cultural factor among blacks and Hispanics that enhances transmission by heterosexual intercourse (see Chapter 9).

National surveillance provides limited information about AIDS patients in the United States. More detailed information and evidence for heterosexual spread of HIV-1 infection and AIDS in the United States have come from several sources. In Miami, interviews of immigrant Haitian men with AIDS indicated that they have tended to have sex with female prostitutes (Fischl and Scott, 1985). However, whether the prostitutes were in Haiti or the United States was not ascertained. A case–control study comparing 45 Haitian men with AIDS with controls in Miami and New York City confirmed the higher frequency of exposure to female prostitutes (Collaborative Study Group, 1987). Additional risk factors for Haitian men included a history of gonorrhea, a positive syphilis serologic reaction, and entry into the United States after 1977 (Collaborative Study Group, 1987). The sum of these data strongly supports the hypothesis that heterosexual contact is a major mode of HIV-1 transmission among Haitians residing in the United States.

In a report by Redfield and colleagues (1985b), 15 of 41 patients (37 percent) with AIDS or other features of immunodeficiency among military personnel and their dependents evaluated at Walter Reed Army Medical Center were attributed to heterosexual contact. Heterosexual contact with partners who had previously developed AIDS or who were at risk for AIDS was reported in six (five female, one male) of the 15 patients with disease. The other nine male patients did not report sex with an AIDS patient or a risk group member but reported more than 50 heterosexual partners over the previous 5 years and/or sexual contact with prostitutes

(Redfield et al., 1985b) and are listed in the "undetermined" category by CDC. Although these results favor heterosexual transmission of HIV-1, they must be tempered by recent evidence suggesting that some soldiers may lie to their military interviewers by underreporting homosexual behavior and use of intravenous drugs and by overreporting heterosexual contact, usually with prostitutes (Potterat et al., 1987).

Recently, CDC intensively studied the occurrence of AIDS and HIV-1 infection in Belle Glade, Florida (Castro et al., 1987), because of the high cumulative incidence of AIDS (3.75 per 1,000). Twenty-nine of 844 (3 percent) adults tested had antibody to HIV-1. The highest age-specific rate was among persons aged 18 to 29 years. No persons over age 60 or under age 11 had antibody to HIV-1. Seropositive persons were associated with infected sexual partners or with adults having serologic evidence of other sexually transmitted diseases, such as hepatitis B or syphilis. The high attack rate of AIDS in Belle Glade appears to be the result of HIV-1 infection among intravenous drug abusers and their sexual partners (Castro et al., 1987).

PREVALENT HIV INFECTION AMONG PROSTITUTES

Female prostitutes have emerged as an important reservoir of HIV in central Africa (Clumeck et al., 1985; Mann et al., 1985a,b; Kreiss et al., 1986; Van de Perre et al., 1985). Only 4 percent of prostitutes tested in Nairobi, Kenya, in 1980–1981 were HIV-1-positive, but 59 percent tested in 1985–1986 were seropositive (Quinn et al., 1986; Piot et al., 1987). The seroprevalence among prostitutes increased with the number of sexual contacts. Prostitutes of lower socioeconomic status who reported an average of 963 partners per year had approximately double the rate of HIV-1 seropositivity as prostitutes of higher socioeconomic status who averaged 124 partners per year (Kreiss et al., 1986; Quinn et al., 1986).

An association between HIV-1 seropositivity and increased educational level and income of the male consorts of prostitutes has been found in urban areas of Rwanda, Zaire, and Zambia (Clumeck et al., 1984; Melbye et al., 1986; Van de Perre et al., 1984). Although this association could reflect differences in access to medical care, it is more likely due to greater opportunity for travel, social contact in urban centers, and the ability to afford the price of urban prostitutes. However, the introduction of the virus into the higher socioeconomic strata of urban centers has laid the foundation for spread into all levels of African society (Biggar, 1986). In contrast to the high rates in urban areas, in one rural area of equatorial Zaire, HIV-1 infection rates have not changed from 1976 to 1986 (De Cock et al., 1987). These findings suggest that social factors associated with urbanization are important in the rapid spread of HIV-1 infection and AIDS in Africa. More studies in rural areas of Africa will be needed to assess the rate of spread into those areas.

In Haiti as in Africa, female prostitutes appear to be a major reservoir of HIV-1 infection. Forty-nine percent of 110 female prostitutes studied in Port-au-Prince were HIV-1-positive (Pape et al., 1987).

Female prostitutes have been studied for evidence of HIV-1 infection in several parts of the world (Table 8.3). Although it is difficult to rule out intravenous

Table 8.3. Seroprevalence of HIV-1 Infection Among Female Prostitutes

City and Country	Number Tested	Number Seropositive	Reference
Africa			
Accra, Ghana	98	1 (1)	Neequaye et al., 1986
Two cities, Ivory Coast	232	29 (13)	Denis et al., 1987
Kinshasa, Zaire	373	100 (27)	Mann et al., 1987
Nairobi, Kenya	90	50 (55)	Kreiss et al., 1986
Butare, Rwanda	80	67 (80)	Clumeck et al., 1985
Ngoma, Rwanda	33	29 (88)	Van de Perre et al., 1985
Europe			
London, England	50	0 (0)	Barton et al., 1985
			Brenky-Faudeux and
Paris, France	56	0 (0)	Fribourg-Blanc, 1985
Nuremburg, W.			
Germany	399	0 (0)	Smith and Smith, 1986
Six cities, W. Germany	2,000 (app.)	17 (1)	Schultz et al., 1986
Israel	27	1 (4)	Dan et al., 1987
Athens, Greece	200	12 (4)	Dan et al., 1987
Athens, Greece	200	12 (6)	Papaevangelou et al., 1985
Pordenone, Italy	24	10 (41)	Tirelli et al., 1985
Zurich, Switzerland	18	14 (78)	Luthy et al., 1987
Caribbean			
Three cities, Dominican			
Republic	255	3 (1)	Koenig et al., 1987
Haiti	110	54 (49)	Pape et al., 1987
United States			
Las Vegas	34	0 (0)	CDC, 1987c
Atlanta	92	1 (1)	CDC, 1987c
Colorado Springs	71	1 (1)	CDC, 1987c
Los Angeles	184	8 (4)	CDC, 1987c
Seattle	92	5 (5)	CDC, 1985b
San Francisco	146	9 (6)	CDC, 1987c
Miami	252	47 (19)	CDC, 1987c
Three cities, New Jersey	56	32 (57)	CDC, 1987c

drug abuse as a confounding variable in some studies (Dan et al., 1987; Papaevangelou et al., 1985; Tirelli et al., 1985), the results from a variety of sources suggest significant spread of HIV-1 infection in some areas on several continents of the world.

HIV INFECTION IN OTHER HETEROSEXUAL GROUPS

In the absence of national surveys for HIV-1 infection, investigators have assessed the spread of HIV-1 infection among heterosexual adults by serosurveys of select population groups from which homosexual behavior and intravenous drug abuse tend to be excluded. Such populations include spouses of AIDS patients or other HIV-1-infected individuals, blood donors, and military recruit applicants. Another strategy has been to survey individuals attending sexually transmitted disease clinics or premarital testing sties with the aim of assessing HIV-1 infection in heterosexuals who are presumed to face the greatest risk of transmission.

Spouses of AIDS Patients

In spouses of AIDS patients in several parts of the world, studies suggest heterosexual spread as a vehicle of HIV-1 transmission. In Kinshasa, Zaire, 11 of 18 spouses (61 percent) of AIDS patients were HIV-1-seropositive (Mann et al., 1986a). In Haiti, Pape et al. (1985a) reported that 60 percent of female spouses of men with AIDS and that 63 percent of male spouses of women with AIDS were seropositive, suggesting that female-to-male and male-to-female transmission were approximately equal. No differences in the types of sexual activities could be found between seropositive and seronegative spouses (Pape et al., 1985b). Haitian men and women with AIDS were more likely than persons without AIDS to report having a large number of heterosexual partners (Pape et al., 1985a).

Evidence supporting heterosexual spread of HIV-1 infection to spouses of AIDS patients in the United States has been reported in Miami (Fischl et al., 1987). Forty-five spouses were followed prospectively from the time of diagnosis in the index spouse. The AIDS patients included 28 men and 17 women of various risk group categories (bisexual men, IV drug abusers, blood transfusion recipients, Haitian natives, heterosexual contacts). Nine of 17 male spouses and four of 28 female spouses were seropositive on entry. In addition, three of eight male spouses seronegative at entry, and 10 of 24 seronegative female spouses seroconverted during the follow-up period of 11 to 36 months. Couples who used condoms (frequency of use was not reported) were less likely to seroconvert (one of 10) than those who did not use condoms (12 of 14). Eight couples abstained from sex after the diagnosis of AIDS in one partner; none of the spouses seroconverted during the study (Fischl et al., 1987).

Steigbigel and colleagues (1987) interviewed and tested spouses of intravenous drug abusers with AIDS. Spouses were excluded from the study if they reported any intravenous drug use, and urine was screened for drugs during the study. Seven of the 12 male spouses of female AIDS patients and 41 of the 88 female spouses of male AIDS patients were HIV-1-seropositive by EIA and immunoblot analysis (Steigbigel et al., 1987).

Heterosexual transmission of HIV-1 from 24 infected male hemophiliacs to four of 24 of their female sexual partners was reported by Goedert et al. (1987). Although based on very small numbers, Goedert et al. suggest that the risk of infection for female partners was indirectly related to the $CD4^+$ lymphocyte counts of the infected male. HIV-1 infection was not inevitable in that five of five women remained seronegative after more than 5 years of sex with a seropositive hemophiliac. All four seropositive women reported vaginal intercourse without condoms (Goedert et al., 1987).

The CDC has tested spouses of AIDS patients who apparently acquired the virus from contaminated blood transfusions (Peterman et al., 1988). Twenty-five male and 55 female spouses of transfusion-acquired AIDS patients have been identified, interviewed, and bled. The average age of spouses was 55 years. Two of 25 male spouses (8 percent) and 10 of 55 female spouses (18 percent) were HIV-1-positive (difference not significant). The rates of seroconversion observed in this study were lower than in other studies and may be due to less sexual activity of transfusion-associated AIDS patients, who were older and possibly sicker (before and after HIV-1 inoculation) than the individuals in the other studies (Peterman et al., 1988).

In San Francisco, 97 female sexual partners of 93 men infected with HIV-1 were studied. Twenty-two (23 percent) of the female partners were HIV-1-seropositive. A greater number of exposures to the index case and the practice of anal intercourse were associated with transmission (Padian et al., 1987).

Military Recruit Applicants

The U.S. Armed Forces have instituted screening of all recruit applicants and active-duty personnel for antibodies to HIV-1 (Burke et al., 1987). The mean prevalence of confirmed positive tests for HIV-1 antibody nationally was 1.5 per 1,000 recruit applicants from October 1985 through 1987. Seroprevalence increased with age from 18 to 27 years, after which age-specific rates plateaued or declined. The seroprevalence was 0.9 per 1,000 for whites, 3.9 per 1,000 for blacks, 1.1 per 1,000 for Hispanics, and 2.6 per 1,000 for other or unknown racial groups. The mean crude male-to-female prevalence ratio was 2.7:1. In the areas in the United States (New York–Newark, San Francisco, Washington, D.C.) with the highest seroprevalence rates (> 10 per 1,000), the combined male-to-female seroprevalence ratio was 1.2:1 (Burke et al., 1987).

Although the infection rate among military recruits has remained constant and has been used as evidence that HIV-1 infection is not spreading into the general heterosexual population, several confounding variables may diminish the ability to extrapolate these data to other groups. For example, this study would exclude previously identified seropositive persons from the applicant pool. The awareness of HIV-1 testing in this setting and the availability of HIV-1 testing to potential recruits through alternate test sites may bias the study sample toward lower rates because at-risk recruits might seek anonymous testing and not volunteer for military service if seropositive.

Blood Donors

Since 1985 blood banks have been screening all blood donors in the United States (see also Chapter 6). Because all men who have had sex with a man since 1977 are asked to refrain from donating, the studies should accurately reflect HIV-1 antibody prevalence among heterosexuals who donate blood. However, blood donors in the United States tend to be older than military recruits and more likely to be in a more stable sexual relationship and to have had fewer sex partners in the recent past. The HIV-1-seropositive rate among blood donors has declined from 35 per 100,000 donors in 1985 to 12 per 100,000 in 1987 (CDC, 1987b). This decline is attributed to the removal of previously identified seropositives from the donor pool (see Chapter 10).

Sexually Transmitted Diseases Clinics

Several studies have assessed the risk of HIV-1 transmission in adults attending sexually transmitted diseases clinics. Among 89 persons enrolled in a sexually transmitted disease clinic in New York City (Queens), antibody to HIV-1 was present in two of four homosexual men, five of 11 bisexual men, and six of nine heterosexual intravenous drug abusers. However, none of 65 heterosexuals who reported no intravenous drug abuse were seropositive, including 10 persons (five men and five women) who had had sexual contact with an intravenous drug abuser (Lifson et al., 1987). The remaining 55 heterosexuals had a median of 15 different partners since 1978; 75 percent had a history of at least one sexually transmitted disease, 29 percent had engaged in rectal intercourse, 65 percent rarely or never used condoms, and 39 percent of men reported sexual contact with a prostitute (Lifson et al., 1987).

In Alameda County, California, blood samples were collected anonymously from women attending sexually transmitted disease clinics and premarital testing sites between November 1985 and August 1986. Two of 377 premarital specimens and two of 299 from sexually transmitted disease clinics tested positive for HIV-1 antibody (Tempelis et al., 1987).

In a large study in Baltimore (Quinn et al., 1988), 4,028 sexually transmitted disease clinic attendees with a 5.2 percent prevalence included a substantial proportion of high-risk individuals. Among those who reported previous high-risk behavior, 2.7 percent of males and 1.8 percent of females were seropositive. Although clearly dependent on factors that determine clinic attendance and on the success in eliciting a history of high-risk behavior, these prevalence figures have raised concern about the need for more extensive assessment and education of such clinic patients.

Surveillance should probably focus on sexually active men and women in areas where heterosexual spread is most likely to occur. In addition to sexually transmitted disease clinic patients, particular attention will have to be paid to adolescents and young adults, marriage license applicants, and pregnant women and their newborns in neighborhoods where AIDS is common among heterosexual intravenous drug abusers. Heterosexual contact tracing and HIV-1 testing of partners of AIDS cases and HIV-1-positive individuals may be another fruitful research approach to assess the extent of spread.

MODES OF TRANSMISSION

Although many epidemiologists were initially skeptical of men claiming heterosexual contact as their only exposure to HIV-1, the reality of female-to-male transmission of the virus is now almost universally accepted. The issue now is not whether it happens but how efficiently it occurs and how widespread it is likely to become (see Chapter 6).

It would be worth reevaluating how CDC data are presented to fully assess the contribution of heterosexual transmission of HIV-1 among AIDS cases in the United States. For example, nearly one-quarter of the males in the "undetermined" category listed in Table 8.1 reported sex with prostitutes, but because the patients could not be sure whether their prostitute contacts used intravenous drugs, their cases are not counted in the "heterosexual contact" category (CDC, 1984). Other male patients in the "undetermined" category reported extramarital heterosexual contacts. In addition, an unknown number of women in the intravenous drug abuser group are prostitutes, some of whom may have acquired AIDS through heterosexual contact rather than by intravenous drug abuse. The categorization of an AIDS case as an "intravenous drug abuser" does not require admission of sharing of needles with a person at risk for AIDS but only an admission of intravenous drug use since 1977. Fully 19 percent of AIDS cases in the United States are reported to be heterosexual intravenous drug abusers who may not have been at risk from drug use unless they shared needles. Most importantly, even though they are listed as "intravenous drug abusers" and not "heterosexual" cases by the CDC, they constitute the largest group of heterosexuals in the United States with AIDS and form a link to other heterosexuals and infants.

Alternatives to the hierarchal system might allow for a more accurate count of AIDS cases attributed to heterosexual transmission. One approach would be to divide heterosexual cases into those attributed to a "first wave" (spread from high-risk groups to sexual partners), "second wave" (spread from first-wave partners to others), and all others (spread from partners that cannot be linked to high-risk groups—e.g., sex with prostitutes not known to be intravenous drug abusers or known to have had sex with high-risk group members or their sexual partners). Epidemiologic studies among intravenous drug users and their sexual partners should help determine the relative importance of sexual versus blood-borne transmission.

Even considering the miscategorized AIDS cases that in reality resulted from heterosexual contact to the total reported by the CDC, there have still been far fewer heterosexual men with AIDS in the United States than homosexual or bisexual men. Several possible explanations exist for this difference. First, the average number of sexual partners reported by homosexual men with AIDS is much greater than the number reported by heterosexual men with AIDS (Jaffe et al., 1983; Chamberland et al., 1984; Guinan et al., 1984). In early studies conducted by the CDC, homosexual men with AIDS reported a median of 1,160 lifetime sexual partners compared with 81 for Haitian men and 40 for male heterosexual intravenous drug users with AIDS (Guinan et al., 1984). Having a greater number of different partners increases the chance of exposure to any sexually transmitted agent, including HIV-1. Second, the cumulative incidence of AIDS has been greater in the homosexual male population than in the heterosexual female population, particularly in epicenters of the disease on the coasts of the United States. Available data also indicate that the prevalence of HIV-1 infection has remained much greater in the homosexual male population than in the heterosexual female population. Therefore, for each random, anonymous sexual encounter, a homosexual male is more likely to contact an infected male partner than is a heterosexual male to encounter an infected female partner.

Third, the sex acts practiced by homosexual men, specifically receptive anal intercourse, may be somewhat more efficient in transmitting HIV-1 than vaginal intercourse practiced by heterosexual men (Nicholson et al., 1985). The columnar epithelium of the rectum may be easier to tear or penetrate than the squamous epithelium of the vagina and penis. In other epidemiologic studies, receptive anal intercourse has also been incriminated as behavior posing the greatest risk to homosexual men with cytomegalovirus and hepatitis B virus infection and is probably not specific for HIV-1 transmission (Mintz et al., 1983; Szmuness et al., 1975).

Although reports of increased receptive anal activity among homosexuals carrying HIV-1 antibody may in part reflect merely increased sexual activity and increased likelihood of exposure to HIV-1 by any of several routes, receptive anal intercourse did account for nearly all new HIV-1 infections in a prospective study of 2,507 homosexual men who were seronegative at enrollment and followed for 6 months (Kingsley et al., 1987) and in subsequent analyses of that cohort (Detels et al., in press).

Finally, it is possible that there are cofactors that may preferentially enhance the development of AIDS in homosexual men compared to heterosexual men once infection with HIV-1 has occurred. A number of sexually transmitted organisms and recreational drugs have been considered as hypothetical cofactors (Melbye et al., 1986; Drew et al., 1986; Holmberg et al., 1988; Haverkos et al., 1985), although the evidence for any such influence is inconclusive (Polk et al., 1987). As a group, homosexual men with AIDS report more sexually transmitted diseases and more frequent recreational drug use than heterosexual men with AIDS (Guinan et al., 1984).

To date, evidence for an oral route of HIV-1 transmission is unconvincing. There is no evidence that kissing of the kind practiced by relatives and household contacts has transmitted the AIDS virus (see Chapter 14). However, it is difficult to exonerate entirely "intimate kissing" with extensive exchange of saliva and perhaps some blood as a rare mode of transmission.

HIV-1 has been isolated from saliva from several asymptomatic homosexual men, but successful isolation has been infrequent compared with the many successful attempts to culture virus from blood (Groopman et al., 1984; Ho et al., 1985). Moreover, Fultz and colleagues (1986) were unable to establish an HIV-1 infection in a chimpanzee orally exposed to cell-free HIV-1 although they were able to infect a chimpanzee by swabbing the vagina with the virus. Epidemiologically, it will be difficult to evaluate partners of infected persons who have practiced only "intimate" kissing that allows for oral exchange of infected saliva with a single partner. Girlfriends of infected adolescent hemophiliacs who report only "intimate" kissing might be a group in which a such a study could be done.

The data concerning heterosexual spread by oral sex are also limited. In one study of spouses of AIDS patients, HIV-1 seropositivity among spouses was increased among couples who practiced oral sex in addition to penile–vaginal sex compared with those couples who practiced only penile–vaginal sex (Fischl et al., 1987).

One of the most important questions for epidemiologists studying AIDS among heterosexuals is the relative rates of transmission of HIV-1 from men to women and from women to men. Theoretically, male-to-female transmission should be more hazardous because of direct inoculation of infected semen into the vaginal vault and because gonorrhea transmission from male to female is estimated to occur more frequently per sexual act than from female to male (Holmes et al., 1970; Hooper et al., 1978; Platt et al., 1983). However, the direct evidence for increased risk of male-to-female transmission of HIV-1 is not convincing. Although the seroconversion rates for spouses of transfusion-associated AIDS cases were slightly higher for female (18 percent) than male (8 percent) spouses, the differences were not statistically significant (Peterman et al., 1988). In addition, studies of spouses of AIDS patients in Africa, Haiti, and Miami suggest that female-to-male and male-to-female transmission rates are approximately equal (Steigbigel et al., 1987; Melbye et al., 1986; Pape et al., 1985; Fischl et al., 1987).

CODETERMINANTS OF INFECTION AND DISEASE*

Epidemiologic studies in Africa provide further evidence that HIV-1 transmission occurs through heterosexual intercourse. Among 86 Zairian prostitutes reporting condom use by their sexual partners during the previous year, use of condoms by 50 percent or more of their partners was associated with a significantly reduced risk of being HIV-1-seropositive (0/8 for condom users versus 26/77 for nonusers) (Mann et al., 1986b). Moreover, vaginal intercourse seems to have been adequate as a means of HIV-1 transmission, because seropositivity was not associated with reported participation in fellatio or anal intercourse, nor did it show any quantitative relationships to kissing behavior (Mann et al., 1986b). In keeping with the finding that unprotected vaginal intercourse is a means of HIV-1 transmission in Africa, heterosexual anal intercourse has been reported uncommonly in Rwanda (Van de Perre et al., 1985). Sexually transmitted diseases affecting the anal region are practically never seen among men or women in the sexually transmitted diseases clinic at the University Teaching Hospital in Lusaka, Zambia (Personal communication, Hira, reported in Melbye et al., 1986). However, one cannot exclude the possibility that important differences in sexual practices, such as frequency of anal intercourse, may exist between African cultures and socioeconomic groups. Although patients in Zambia with sexually transmitted diseases were significantly more likely to be HIV-1-seropositive than control populations (Melbye et al., 1986), the mechanism remains to be elucidated. For example, other sexually transmitted infections may facilitate HIV-1 infection by damaging genital mucous membranes that normally serve as a barrier to HIV-1. Also, individuals with genital infections may practice more frequent sexual intercourse than persons without them, and the frequency of mucous membrane contact may help HIV-1 breach damaged or intact genital surfaces.

Other sexual habits may modulate sexual transmission of HIV-1 from women to men (Hrdy, 1987). Penile contact with infected menstrual blood may increase a male partner's risk of infection, and circumcision may decrease the risk (Fink, 1986). Since circumcision is practiced more widely in North America and Europe than in Africa or Haiti, theoretically this factor could contribute to the high rate of heterosexual transmission in Africa and Haiti. However, to date no data exist to support or refute this hypothesis (Swadley et al., 1987).

High seroprevalence among certain sexually transmitted disease clinic patients could reflect exposure to HIV-1 through frequent parenteral antibiotic treatment with reused needles. However, in one Zambian clinic, needles were not commonly reused, and the seroprevalence was equally high for patients who required parenteral treatment and for those who did not—e.g., those with herpes genitalis (Melbye et al., 1986). The evidence for parenteral transmission by injection was also unconvincing in Kenya, where male clinic patients had lower seropositivity rates than

*See also Chapter 6.

female prostitutes despite equal exposures to injections (Kreiss et al., 1986). The role, if any, of HIV-1 transmission by needles reused in the therapeutic setting needs to be clarified for other African countries.

The presence of host factors in Africa may facilitate HIV-1 transmission and disease. The immune systems of African heterosexuals, similar to those of American homosexual men, are in a chronically activated state associated with chronic viral and parasitic antigenic exposure, which may render them particularly susceptible to HIV-1 infection or disease progression (Quinn et al., 1987).

PREVENTION

Sexual contact tracing has been standard practice in public health to combat sexually transmitted diseases such as gonorrhea and syphilis. Contact tracing provides research information about the extent of spread into a community and provides access to infected individuals and persons at risk for infection. However, contact tracing of HIV-1-infected persons has been avoided by most practicing physicians and public health department personnel because of the possible discrimination against persons with HIV-1 infection and because there has been no effective therapy widely available for the infection or its consequences.

Wide advertisement and use of condoms and antiviral spermicides have been advocated as a public health response (see Chapter 15). Condoms should decrease exposure to semen and vaginal secretions (Conant et al., 1986). Although a spermicide, nonoxynol 9, inhibits HIV-1 in vitro, its efficacy has not been evaluated in clinical trials (Hicks et al., 1985). Even where contraceptives are available, religious beliefs and traditional cultural practices (in Africa) (Omu and Unuigbe, 1986) may discourage their use.

It appears that once HIV-1 is introduced into a population, it can spread to male and female sexual partners of infected individuals. Counting some of the "undetermined" cases as heterosexual ones, the U.S. Public Health Service has predicted that heterosexual spread of AIDS in the United States will rise from 7 percent to 9 percent of the total cases between 1986 and 1991 and the total number of AIDS cases will reach 196,000 at the start of 1991 (USPHS, 1986). All sexually active individuals should be made aware of the potential for acquiring HIV-1 infection and AIDS from sexual activity.

The USPHS has made the following recommendations (CDC, 1986):

1. Persons with negative test (HIV-1 antibody) results should be counseled to reduce their risk of becoming infected by:
   a. Reducing the number of sex partners. A stable, mutually monogamous relationship with an uninfected person eliminates any new risk of sexually transmitted HIV-1 infection.
   b. Protecting themselves during sexual activity with any possibly infected person by taking appropriate precautions to prevent contact with the person's blood, semen, urine, feces, saliva, or vaginal secretions. Although the efficacy of condoms in preventing infections with HIV-1 is still under study, consistent use of condoms should reduce transmission of HIV-1 by preventing exposure to semen and infected lymphocytes. [Since these ini-

tial recommendations were published, information about infected vaginal secretions has been published and should be included in this guideline (Vogt et al., 1986; Wofsy et al., 1986)].

2. Infected persons should be counseled to prevent the further transmission of HIV-1 by:
   a. Informing prospective sex partners of their infection with HIV-1, so they can take appropriate precuations. Clearly, abstention from sexual activity with another person is one option that would eliminate any risk of sexually transmitted HIV-1 infection.
   b. Protecting a partner during any sexual activity by taking precautions as suggested in 2.a cited above.
   c. Informing previous sex partners of their potential exposure to HIV-1 and encouraging them to seek counseling and/or testing.

If a potential sexual partner is known to be at risk of HIV-1 infection owing to previous contact with prostitutes, homosexual contact, intravenous drug use, hemophilia, or heterosexual contact with another person at risk, or if the likelihood of such previous exposure of the potential partner is unknown, it is prudent to assume that that potential partner could be infectious.

If both sexual partners are known to be infected with HIV-1, it can be argued that they should take precautions with each other as if only one were infected. This recommendation is based on the fact that it is not known whether reinoculation with the same or a closely related virus causes more rapid progression of immunodeficiency.

CONCLUSION

It is not clear how far or how fast HIV-1 infection will spread into the heterosexual population of the United States and other parts of the world. AIDS is predominantly a sexually transmitted disease: HIV-1 infection can be transmitted between men and women. Questions can be raised about assessing the likelihood of heterosexual spread by extrapolating from specific regions of the developing world to whole populations in Europe and North America; however, there can be no doubt that female-to-male transmission occurs and can be an important factor in the dissemination of AIDS.

The most difficult social consequences of HIV-1 infection may result from its apparent length of infectivity or "contagiousness." Once infected, the majority of individuals likely remain viremic for years, possibly for their lifetime (Feorino et al., 1985). Because of the morbidity and mortality of AIDS and its apparent foothold in the heterosexual community, societies have already begun to wrestle with such difficult issues as official notification of contacts about exposure and counseling of infected individuals about marriage and natural parenthood.

REFERENCES

Allain JP (1986): N Engl J Med 315:517.
Barton SE, Underhill GS, Gilchrist C, et al. (1985): Lancet, 2:1424.

Biggar RJ (1986): Lancet 1:79.

Brenky-Faudeux D, Fribourg-Blanc A (1985): Lancet 2:1424.

Brunet JB, Bouvet E, Liebowitch J, et al. (1983): Lancet 1:700.

Burke DS, Brundage JF, Heibald JR, et al. (1987): N Engl J Med 317:131.

Bygbjerg IC (1983): Lancet 1:925.

Calabrese LH, Gopalakrishna KV (1986): N Engl J Med 314:987.

Castro KG, Lieb S, Calisher C, et al. (1987): Third International Conference on AIDS, Washington, D.C., June, WP.43:117.

Centers for Disease Control (1984): MMWR 33:661.

Centers for Disease Control (1986): MMWR 35:152.

Centers for Disease Control (1987c): MMWR 36:157.

Centers for Disease Control (1985): MMWR 34:561.

Centers for Disease Control (1987b): Human immunodeficiency virus infections in the United States: a review of current knowledge and plans for expansion of HIV surveillance activities. A Report to the Domestic Policy Council, December 2.

Centers for Disease Control (1981a): MMWR 30:305.

Centers for Disease Control (1981b): MMWR 30:250.

Centers for Disease Control (1987a): MMWR 36:522.

Chamberland ME, Castro KG, Haverkos HW, et al. (1984): Ann Intern Med 101:617.

Chamberland M, White C, Lifson A, Dondero TJ (1987): Third International Conference on AIDS, Washington, D.C., June, W2.6:106.

Clumeck N, Macart-Lemone F, De Maubeuge F, et al. (1983): Lancet 1:642.

Clumeck N, Robert-Guroff M, Van De Perre P, et al. (1985): JAMA 254:2599–2602.

Clumeck N, Sonnet J, Taelman H, et al. (1984): N Engl J Med 310:492–497.

The Collaborative Study Group of AIDS in Haitian-Americans (1987): JAMA 257:635.

Conant M, Hardy D, Sernatinger J, Spicer D, Levy JA (1986): JAMA 255:1706.

Dan M, Rock M, Bar-Shani S (1987): JAMA 257:1047.

De Cock KM, Nzilambi N, Forthal D, et al. (1987): Third International Conference on AIDS, Washington, D.C., June, WP.43:117.

Denis F, Barin F, Gershy-Damet G, et al. (1987): Lancet 1:408.

Detels R, English P, Visscher BR, et al. J AIDS (in press).

Drew WL, Mills J, Hauer L, Miner RC (1986): Program and Abstracts of the 26th Interscience Conference on Antimicrobial Agents and Chemotherapy, New Orleans. Washington D.C.: American Society for Microbiology.

Eales LJ, Nye KE, Parkin JM, et al. (1987): Lancet 1:999.

Ellrodt A, Barre-Sinoussi F, Le Bras P, et al. (1984): Lancet 2:1383.

Feorino P, Jaffe HW, Palmer E, et al. (1985): N Engl J Med 312:1293.

Fink AJ (1986): N Engl J Med 315:1167.

Fischl MA, Dickinson GM, Scott GB, et al. (1987): JAMA 257:640.

Fischl MA, Scott GB (1985): Adv Host Defense Mechanisms 5:109.

Fultz PN, McClure HM, Daugharty H, et al. (1986): J Infect Dis 154:896.

Goedert JJ, Eyster ME, Biggar RJ (1987): Heterosexual transmission of HIV: Third International Conference on AIDS, Washington, D.C., June, W2.6:106.

Groopman JE, Salahuddin SZ, Sarngadharan MG, et al. (1984): Science 226:447.

Guinan ME, Thomas PA, Pinsky PF, et al. (1984): Ann Intern Med 100:213.

Haverkos HW, Pinsky PF, Drotman DP, Bregman DJ (1985): Sex Transm Dis 12:203.

Hicks DR, Martin LS, Getchell JP, et al. (1985): Lancet 2:1422.

Ho DM, Byington RE, Schooley RT, et al. (1985): N Engl J Med 313:1606.

Holmberg SD, Stewart JA, Gerber ARs, et al. (1988): 259:1048.

Holmes KK, Johnson DW, Trostle HJ (1970): Am J Epidemiol 91:170.

Hooper RR, Reynolds GH, Jones OG, et al. (1978): Am J Epidemiol 108:136.

Hrdy DB (1987): Rev Infect Dis 9:1109.

Jaffe HW, Choi K, Thomas PA, et al. (1983): Ann Intern Med 99:145.

Jason JM, McDougal JS, Dixon G, et al. (1986): JAMA 255:212.

Kingsley LA, Detels R, Kaslow R, et al. (1987): Lancet 1:345.

Koenig RE, Pittahiga J, Bogart M, Et al. (1987): JAMA 257:631.

Kreiss JK, Kitchen LW, Prince HE, et al. (1985): Ann Intern Med 102:623.

Kreiss JK, Koech D, Plummer FA, et al. (1986): N Engl J Med 314:414.

Lifson AR, Stoneburner RL, Chaisson MA, Hildebrandt, DS, Schultz S, Jaffe HW (1987): Third International Conference on AIDS, Washington, D.C., June, MP.83:24.

Luthy R, Ledergerber B, Tauber M, et al. (1987): Klinishe Wochenschrift (in press). Cited by MMWR 36:157.

Mann JM, Quinn TC, Francis H, et al. (1986): JAMA 256:721.

Mann JM, Quinn T, Francis H, et al. (1986): Second International Conference on Acquired Immunodeficiency Syndrome (AIDS). Paris, France, June 23–25.

Mann J, Quinn TC, Piot P, et al. (1987): N Engl J Med 316:345.

Melbye M, Njelesani EK, Bayley A, et al. (1986): Lancet 2:1113.

Mintz LM, Drew WL, Miner RC, Braff EH (1983): Ann Intern Med 99:326.

Moss AR (1987): Br Med J 389.

Neequaye AR, Neequaye J, Mingle JA, et al. (1986): Lancet 2:978.

Nicholson JKA, McDougal JS, Jaffe HW, et al. (1985): Ann Intern Med 103:37.

Omu AE, Unuigbe JA (1986): Int J Gynaecol Obstet 24:145.

Padian N, Marquis L, Francis DP, et al. (1987): JAMA 258:788.

Papaevangelou G, Roumeliotou-Karayannis A, Kallinkos G, et al. (1985): Lancet 2:1018.

Pape JW, Liautaud B, Thomas F, et al. (1985): Ann Intern Med 103:674.

Pape JW, Liautaud B, Thomas F, et al. (1986): Clin Res 34:528A.

Pape JW, Liautaud B, Thomas F, et al. (1985): Clin Res 33:414A.

Pape JW, Stanbach M, Pamphile M, et al. (1987): Clin Res 35:486A.

Peterman TA, Stoneburner RL, Allen JR, Jaffe HW, Curran JW (1988): JAMA 259:55.

Piot P, Plummer FA, Rey M, et al. (1987): J Infect Dis 155:1108.

Piot P, Quinn TC, Taelman H, et al. (1984): Lancet 2:65–69.

Pitchenik AE, Shafron RD, Glasser RM, Spira TJ (1984): Ann Intern Med 100:62.

Platt R, Rice PA, McCormack WM (1983): JAMA 250:3205.

Polk BF, Fox R, Brookmeyer R, et al. (1987): N Engl J Med 36:61.

Potterat JJ, Phillips L, Muth JB (1987): JAMA 257:1727.

Quinn TC, Mann JM, Curran JW, Piot P (1986): Science 234:955.

Quinn TC, Piot P, McCormick JB, et al. (1987): JAMA 257:2617.

Redfield RR, Markham PD, Salahuddin SZ, et al. (1985): JAMA 253:1571.

Redfield RR, Markham PD, Salahuddin SZ, et al. (1985): JAMA 254:2094.

Salahuddin SZ, Groopman JE, Markham P, et al. (1984): Lancet 2:1418.

Schultz S, Milberg JA, Kristal AR, et al. (1986): JAMA 255:1703.

Smith GL, Smith KF (1986): Lancet 2:1392.

Steigbigel NH, Maude DW, Feiner CJ, et al. (1987): Third International Conference on AIDS, Washington, D.C., June, W2.5:106.

Swadley JG, Enzenauer RW, Oates JK, Fink AJ (1987): N Engl J Med 316:1545.

Szmuness W, Much MI, Prince AM, et al. (1975): Ann Intern Med 83:489.

Tempelis CD, Shell G, Hoffman M, Benjamin RA, Chandler A, Francis DP (1987): JAMA 258:474.

Thymann M, Dickmeiss E, Svejgaard A, Pedersen C, Bygbjerg I, Faber V (1987): Lancet 1:1378.

Tirelli U, Vaccher E, Carbone A, et al. (1985): Lancet 2:1424.
U.S. Public Health Service (1986): Public Health Rep 101:341–348.
Van de Perre P, Rouvroy D, Lepage P, et al. (1984): Lancet 2:62.
Van de Perre P, Clumeck N, Careal M, et al. (1985): Lancet 2:524.
Vogt WM, Witt DJ, Craven DE, et al. (1986): Lancet 1:525.
Wofsy CB, Cohen JB, Haver LB, et al. (1986): Lancet 1:527.

9

Parenteral Drug Users

GERALD FRIEDLAND

HISTORICAL BACKGROUND OF DRUG ABUSE

Three features of illicit drug use during the past century have provided a fertile field for the amplification of HIV transmission: (1) an epidemic of drug use; (2) a change to the intravenous method administration; (3) an increase in needle sharing behavior.

Although widespread abuse of opiates has existed in the United States since the middle of the 19th century, during the mid-1960's there was a major change in the scope of heroin addiction here (Greene et al., 1975). Virtually every major American city witnessed an explosive increase in the number of new heroin users. In addition, a more pronounced association of heroin use was noted among young men who were of minority backgrounds, unmarried, unemployed, poorly educated, and residing in inner-city areas (Kozel and Adams, 1986). During this period, a system of drug treatment programs and surveillance for recording and tracking of drug trends was developed. However, most data have come from drug users with significant personal, medical, social, criminal, or legal problems (Ginzburg, 1984), and most estimates of the size of the drug abusing population must be considered minimal ones.

The total number of active heroin users in the United States probably peaked at about 626,000 in 1971 (Greene et al., 1975). Heroin use declined during the mid-1970's. Medical problems associated with illicit drug use, including endocarditis, pneumonia, and hepatitis (Louria et al., 1967; Garibaldi et al., 1972), as well as associated immunologic abnormalities (Brown et al., 1974; Cusman and Grieco, 1973; Heathcote and Taylor, 1981) began to be documented. Heroin activity increased again in the late 1970s as drugs became widely available from Mexican and Southeast Asian rather than European sources (Greene et al., 1975).

During the 1970s there was also a marked increase in the use of cocaine (Kozel and Adams, 1986). By the end of the decade, an estimated 10 million people reported having used cocaine during the preceding year (CDC, 1982b). The rate of cocaine-related emergency room visits and cocaine-related deaths increased more than threefold between 1976 and 1981, and the percentage of cocaine-related drug treatment program admissions increased more than sixfold. Medical complications of cocaine abuse appeared to be more prevalent among nonwhites than among whites.

The relationship of these patterns of illicit drug use to the AIDS epidemic becomes clearer because of coincident changes in the route and practice of drug administration. Formerly, opiates had been administered almost exclusively by oral or inhalation routes. By 1935, however, intravenous use was seen in 42 percent, and by 1940 in over 80 percent of men admitted to the Addiction Research Center in Lexington, Kentucky (O'Donnell and Jones, 1968). By the 1940s northern black males had the highest rates of intravenous use. The increase in cocaine use in the 1970s was accompanied by an important change in its route of administration as well (CDC, 1982b). Data from the Treatment Outcome Prospective Study (TOPS), a large longitudinal study of clients admitted to more than 40 drug treatment programs nationwide (Ginzburg, 1984), indicated that a majority of enrollees used drugs intravenously during the year preceding admission. The National Institute of Drug Abuse has estimated that in 1980 there were at least 350,000 to 400,000 active intravenous heroin users in the United States (Ginzburg, 1984). No estimates of the numbers of regular intravenous cocaine or amphetamine users are available, nor are there precise estimates of the numbers of occasional or "recreational" users of heroin, cocaine, or other drugs. However, individuals currently using illicit drugs intravenously and thereby susceptible to HIV-1 infection by this route may number from 750,000 to several million in the United States alone.

The sharing of needles and other drug use paraphernalia among intravenous drug abusers has been assumed to be a common practice responsible for many infections and other medical complications of drug abuse (Louria et al., 1967). Until the 1970s, needle sharing was thought to take place predominantly among friends and in small groups and was associated with socialization and a communal feeling (Des Jarlais et al., 1985). Then in New York City and elsewhere, needle-sharing patterns became more formalized. The "shooting gallery," a semipermanent site such as an apartment, storefront, basement, or burned-out building, became a more common site for drug use. Within shooting galleries, drug users rent needles and syringes, administer drugs, and then return the used apparatus to the proprietor. The apparatus is rented repeatedly with, at most, a rinse with tap water between users. Thus, anonymous, sequential sharing of contaminated needles and syringes among a large number of individuals became a predominant mode of drug administration during the time in which HIV-1 entered this population. The number of shooting galleries in the New York metropolitan area may have been close to 1,000 in the early 1980s (D. Des Jarlais, personal communication). This type of behavior is present in other large metropolitan areas of the United States (Wendt et al., 1987; Chaisson et al., 1987; Black et al., 1986) as well as in Europe (Robertson et al., 1986; Marino et al., 1986). It would be difficult to design a system better suited to promote the transmission of a blood-borne infection among a large number of susceptible individuals.

AIDS AMONG INTRAVENOUS DRUG ABUSERS

Soon after the initial reports of AIDS in 1981 in homosexual men (CDC 1981a,b, 1982c), the identical clinical syndrome was seen in intravenous drug users (Moll et al., 1982; Masur et al., 1981; Small et al., 1983). By mid-1982 the occurrence of the syndrome in heterosexual men and women who used intravenous drugs was recorded in national statistics (CDC 1982c). Among intravenous drug users, AIDS was recognized retrospectively in 1980 (Selik et al., 1984). Since then cases among persons who use intravenous drugs have increased steadily. By August 29, 1988, 13,608 cases among drug users had been reported (CDC, 1988).

From the outset, intravenous drug users have represented the second largest group at risk for AIDS according to the CDC hierarchical risk classification system. Seventeen percent of all cases of AIDS within the United States reported to the CDC have occurred among individuals in whom intravenous drug use was the only risk behavior. However, this proportion represents a systematic underestimate of the importance of intravenous drug use. The hierarchical surveillance system is intentionally mutually exclusive: men who are both homosexual or bisexual and intravenous drug users have been recorded only within the former category. The classification assumes hierarchical risk of transmission. However, there is neither biological nor epidemiologic information to indicate whether sexual or drug use behavior carries a greater risk. Since 1986, the CDC has published surveillance data displaying a separate category of men who are both intravenous drug users and homosexual or bisexual. As of August 1988, among 70,882 cases of AIDS in adults, 5,168 (8 percent) of the total AIDS cases had occurred in men who share both risk behaviors (CDC, 1988). Thus, 26 percent, rather than 19 percent, of total reported AIDS cases have occurred in individuals who have used intravenous drugs. Annual surveillance reporting indicates that the proportion of AIDS in the United States attributable to intravenous drug use has not changed significantly since 1982.

Although intravenous drug use is believed to be rare in Africa (Quinn et al., 1986) and other countries of the developing world, in Europe AIDS in intravenous drug users has been extensively documented. Up to 1984 only five of 421 cases (1.5 percent) reported from 10 European countries had been attributed to intravenous drug use (CDC, 1985; Brunet, 1985). However, more recently intravenous drug use has become the major risk factor in reported cases of AIDS in some European countries, notably Italy and Spain, and substantial and rapidly growing numbers of HIV infected intravenous drug users have been identified in many other countries (Brunet and Ancelle, 1986; Brunet et al., 1987; Des Jarlais et al., 1987b).

Based on a conservative estimate of 750,000 intravenous drug users in the United States in 1983 and the 1,381 reported cases of AIDS within this group from June 1983 to May 1984, the nationwide incidence rate of AIDS in intravenous drug users during this period was estimated to be 113.3 per 100,000 (Hardy et al., 1985). Assuming a relatively stable number of intravenous drug users at risk, this incidence rate might be expected to rise in subsequent years. Indeed, recalculation for the 12-month period ending February 1987 reveals a crude national yearly incidence of 296.7 per 100,000.

Projections based on an empirical model indicate that the proportion of cases in the United States attributable to intravenous drug use alone will remain constant in 1991 at an anticipated 16.4 percent (14.5 and 18.5 lower and upper confidence bounds in that year). This proportion would represent 12,000 of the total 73,000 cases anticipated in that year (Kristal, 1986). A calculation based on nonhierarchical classification involving all intravenous drug users yields an anticipated 18,250 cases of AIDS in 1991 alone in individuals who have used intravenous drugs. This number is likely a conservative estimate, because the proportion of intravenous drug use-related cases in certain geographic areas such as New York has been increasing over time, and other areas with large numbers of HIV-1-infected intravenous drug users have not yet experienced the full force of the epidemic.

The effect of AIDS-specific mortality among intravenous drug users, a group with an already exaggerated mortality rate compared to that of the general population, has been substantial and is increasing dramatically (Kristal, 1986). Between 1980 and 1984, the number of deaths classified as narcotics-related in New York City increased 124 percent, from 544 to 1,240 per year. Most of the increase can be attributed to two categories, AIDS and pneumonia. In comparison, among never-married males aged 15 to 64 years living in areas with large homosexual male populations, there was a 34 percent increase in total mortality during the same time period. In 1984, AIDS accounted for 27 percent and pneumonia for 10 percent of all narcotics-related mortality in New York City. These two categories are not independent; the latter is likely linked to HIV-1 infection (see later). In addition to AIDS-specific excess mortality, another 50 percent excess mortality in intravenous drug users may be produced by HIV-1-induced disease not meeting the AIDS surveillance definition (Alderman et al., 1988).

DEMOGRAPHIC FEATURES OF AIDS AMONG INTRAVENOUS DRUG ABUSERS

The demographic characteristics of intravenous drug users with AIDS differ from other populations at increased risk, most notably in the distribution of disease by the interrelated variables of geography, socioeconomic status, and race and ethnic group.

From the outset of the epidemic to the present, there has been a distinctive national and local geographic distribution of reported cases of AIDS among intravenous drug users. The initial cases in intravenous drug users were recognized in New York City in 1980 (Selik et al., 1984). A disproportionate number of AIDS cases among intravenous drug users have occurred in the New York metropolitan area. By 1984, among 640 reported heterosexual intravenous drug using AIDS cases, 351 (55 percent) lived in New York City, 76 additional cases resided in the remainder of the New York State (most of whom were in correctional institutions and whose original residence and place of infection was New York City), and 99 were from neighboring New Jersey. Thus 82 percent of all intravenous drug-associated AIDS cases in the United States were reported from this localized geographic area (Koplan et al., 1986). In New York City itself, 29 percent of AIDS cases were attributed to intravenous drug use by 1984 (NYC Department of Health, 1986). In contrast, although an estimated 10,000 to 12,000 drug users live in San Francisco, as late as April 1986, only 1 percent of AIDS cases in that city were among heterosexual intravenous drug users (Chaisson et al., 1987). During the past 5 years, although the proportion of U.S. AIDS cases diagnosed in New York City has declined to below 30 percent, the proportion of U.S. intravenous drug user cases reported from New York City has remained constant. Thus, diffusion of AIDS into different geographic areas has been significantly slower for intravenous drug users than for other populations at risk.

Of additional interest is the distribution of cases by risk behavior in New York City itself over time. From 1981 to 1984, the proportion of cases among intravenous drug users increased from 13 to 29 percent while the proportion among homosexual and bisexual men decreased from 63 to 56 percent (NYC Department of Health, 1986). This trend has continued to the present. Of the first 2,000 AIDS cases diagnosed in New York City, 32.3 percent were among intravenous drug users. Of the second 2,000 cases, 38.5 percent have been among intravenous drug users (New York City Department of Health, unpublished data, 1987). As of January 1987, 35 percent of all cases of AIDS reported in New York City occurred among intravenous drug users (NYC Department of Health, 1987). By mid-1988 an estimated 55 percent of AIDS cases in New York City were occurring among intravenous drug users (New York City Department of Health, 1988). The calculated cumulative incidence rate of AIDS for this population in New York City is 1,548 per 100,000 to January 1987 with an annual incidence of greater than 500 per 100,000 for 1986 alone compared to less than 330 per 100,000 for the United States.

There is also a striking geographic difference among risk groups within New York City itself. Analysis by zip code indicates that homosexual and bisexual men with AIDS have been concentrated in midtown Manhattan and intravenous drug users have been largely reported from other areas in the city, including the Lower East Side, Harlem, the South Bronx, and the Bedford-Stuyvesant area of Brooklyn (NYC Department of Health, 1986).

This geographic clustering of intravenous drug use cases is deeply entwined with socioeconomic status. In New York City 50 percent of intravenous drug users are on public assistance and Medicaid, whereas among homosexual men in San Francisco, 44 percent have tax earnings of over $25,000 and 57 percent have college degrees (Drucker, 1986). In the Bronx, 65 percent of intravenous drug users and their families have incomes under $10,000 per year, and in 80 percent of households, this income supports three or more people (Friedland et al., 1986). It is understandable, then, that among inner-city poor populations, the proportion of cases of AIDS attributable to intravenous drug use would be substantial. For example, at Montefiore Medical Center in the Bronx, of 526 cases of AIDS diagnosed by September 1987, 59 percent were intravenous drug users (Saltzman et al, 1988). At Metropolitan Hospital in East Harlem, 70 percent of AIDS patients have been intravenous drug users (Maayan et al., 1985).

The distribution of AIDS by gender among intravenous drug users has not been sufficiently emphasized. Nationally, through 1984, among heterosexual intravenous drug users with AIDS, 21 percent were female. In New York City, through June 1988, 23 percent intravenous drug users with AIDS have been female and 60 percent of females with AIDS have been drug users (NYC Department of Health, 1988). Nationally the majority of women with AIDS have been intravenous drug users (Guinan and Hardy, 1987). Through August 1988, of all men with AIDS, 24 percent (15,747 of 65,042) have used intravenous drugs. However, among women with AIDS, 52 percent (3,029 of 5,840) have been intravenous drug users. An additional 29 percent (1,700 of 5,840) have acquired AIDS through heterosexual sex with a man with AIDS or at increased risk, the majority of whom are intravenous drug users (CDC, 1988). Thus, both directly and indirectly via heterosexual transmission, intravenous drug use is of greater significance proportionately among women with AIDS than among men.

The racial and ethnic characteristics of intravenous drug users with AIDS are strikingly different from those of the general U.S. population and of homosexual men with AIDS (CDC, 1986d). Of the 175 million persons more than 15 years of age in the United States as of October 1986, 81.4 percent were white, 10.6 percent black, and 5.7 percent Hispanic. Among AIDS cases, in contrast, 60.4 percent have been white, 24.8 percent black, and 14.2 percent Hispanic. The overall cumulative incidences for black and Hispanic adults have been 3.1 and 3.4 times higher, respectively, than for whites. Among heterosexual intravenous drug users with AIDS, 18.5 percent have been white, 51.4 percent black, and 29.8 percent Hispanic. The calculated incidence rates of AIDS related to intravenous drug use, adjusted for population size, are 20 and 30 times higher for blacks and Hispanics, respectively, than for whites. These striking differences were noted early in the AIDS epidemic (CDC, 1982c) and have persisted to the present. In New York City over 85 percent of cases in intravenous drug users have been among minorities. Conversely, through 1986, 14 percent of whites but 43 percent of blacks with AIDS were users of intravenous drugs (Bakeman et al., 1986). As with men, the racial distribution of intravenous drug-using women with AIDS is strongly weighted toward blacks and Hispanics. Among 525 drug-using women with AIDS in New York City, 83 (16 percent) were white, 262 (50 percent) black and 180 (34 percent) Hispanic (NYC Department of Health, 1987). The interaction of race, gender, and intravenous drug use is exemplified by the national cumulative incidences of AIDS for black and Hispanic women of 13.3 and 11.1 times, respectively, the incidence for white women (CDC, 1986d).

The racial differences among AIDS patients who are intravenous drug users are most likely a reflection of the phenomenon of illicit intravenous drug use in urban minority populations. Unfortunately, there are no precise population-based estimates of the distribution of intravenous drug users by race and ethnicity. The best information comes from a survey of drug abuse treatment facilities in the United States in 1982 by the National Institute on Drug Abuse (1982). Of the clients using the treatment facilities, 32 percent were white, 40 percent black, and 28 percent Hispanic for the New York City Standard Metropolitan Statistical Area (SMSA); and 41 percent were white, 50 percent black, and 9 percent Hispanic in the neighboring Newark, New Jersey, SMSA.

Over two-thirds of all intravenous drug users with AIDS nationally have resided in these SMSAs, and it is therefore of interest that blacks and Hispanics in these areas are disproportionately represented among those attending drug abuse treatment facilities. The TOPS survey of treatment programs in 1979, 1980, and 1981 shows a similar overrepresentation of minority enrollees (Ginzburg, 1984). These data suggest that the demography of intravenous drug use itself largely explains the ethnic composition of AIDS cases among intravenous drug users. Additional explanations include possible racial and ethnic behavioral differences in drug administration practices, confounding local geographic differences in racial and ethnic composition, choice of needle-sharing partners by racial and ethnic background, and historical differences in the entry of HIV-1 into racial and ethnic population subsets (Weiss et al., 1986). Finally, there may be genetic differences in susceptibility to infection or disease progression. However, these have yet to be convincingly demonstrated.

In the study by Weiss et al. (1986) of New Jersey drug users, although blacks were more likely to be seropositive than other racial groups, there was a strong relationship between race and geography. Proximity to New York City was associated with both the highest rates of seropositivity and the highest proportion of minority populations. Thus, race and geography appeared linked in their relation to prevalence of infection in the New York City area. The observation among black intravenous drug users in Queens of an increased prevalence of antibodies to other human retroviruses, HTLV-I and HTLV-II, is intriguing (Robert-Guroff et al., 1986) and also may be related to geography and needle-sharing patterns.

Since active intravenous drug users are often incarcerated, it is not surprising that AIDS has appeared among prison inmate populations. The majority of cases of AIDS among inmates have been reported from correctional facilities in New York and New Jersey, the two states reporting the largest number of AIDS cases associated with intravenous drug use. In the New York State correctional system, 95 percent of cases of AIDS occurred among inmates with a history of drug use (CDC 1986b). Inmates investigated in New York State correctional facilities were believed to have contracted HIV-1 infection prior to incarceration (Hanrahan et al., 1984). Most had decreased leukocyte counts at the time of imprisonment, and drug use and sexual exposure during confinement was believed to be minimal or nonexistent.

SEROPREVALENCE OF HIV-1 INFECTION AMONG INTRAVENOUS DRUG USERS

Definitive seroprevalence measurements serially performed in multiple settings among large numbers of drug users are not available. Seroprevalence surveys conducted at multiple locations throughout the United States and Europe (Table 9.1) have not been entirely comparable in time, serologic technique, or subject selection. Nevertheless, they provide insights into the distribution of infection by time and place and suggest future trends in AIDS among intravenous drug users in the United States and Europe.

Although one study, using questionable methods, suggested that antibodies to HIV-1 may have been present among intravenous drug users since the early 1970s (Moore et al., 1986), the earliest firm evidence of HIV-1 antibodies among intravenous drug users comes from serum taken in 1978 in New York City (Novick et al., 1986). Of 70 methadone clinic enrollees from whom serum was available in that year, 10 percent were found in retrospect to be seropositive. No positives were found in sera taken in preceding years.

A comparison of seroprevalence figures among intravenous drug users in different geographic areas reveals a wide discrepancy of HIV-1 infection not unlike that seen among AIDS cases (Lange, 1988). Not surprisingly, the highest prevalences have been reported from New York City. A reasonable estimate of HIV-1 seroprevalence among active using intravenous drug users in New York City in 1987 is probably in the range of 50 to 60 percent (Des Jarlais et al 1987; CDC, 1987

Table 9.1. Prevalence Rate of HIV-1 Antibodies Among IV Drug Abusers

Geographic Area	Date of Sample	Source of Subjects	Test[a]	Rate (%)
New York Metropolitan Area				
Robert-Guroff	1981–82	Inpatients	EIA/WB	41
Maayan	1983–84	Outpatients	EIA/WB	33
		Inpatients		70
Spira	1984	Detoxification Program	EIA RIPA	58–87
Marmor	1984	Methadone Detoxification	EIA/WB	51
Schoenbaum	1986	Methadone	EIA/WB	35
Lange	1986	Methadone	EIA/WB	61
Weiss (New Jersey)	1985	Methadone	EIA	1.8–56
Connecticut				
D'Aquila (New Haven)	1982–83	Drug Treatment	EIA/WB	10
Maryland				
Lange (Baltimore)	1986	Drug Treatment	EIA/WB	29
California				
Levy (Statewide)	1985	Statewide Drug Treatment	EIA/WB	1.7
Chaisson (San Francisco)	1984–85	San Francisco Drug Treatment	EIA/WB	10
North Carolina				
Hoffman	1985–86	Drug Treatment	EIA/WB	4
Michigan				
Wendt (Detroit)	1985–86	Inpatients	EIA/WB	8.9–17.5
Colorado				
Lange (Denver)	1987	Drug Treatment	EIA/WB	5
Europe				
United Kingdom (London)	1983–84	Hepatitis Screen	IFA/RIA	1.5
United Kingdom (Edinburgh)	1983–85	General Practice	EIA/WB	51
Switzerland (Zurich)	1984–85	Vaccine Recipients	EIA/RIA	36
Spain (Vizcaya)	1984–85	Drug Treatment	EIA/WB	42
Italy (Milan)	1985	Drug Treatment	EIA/IFA	53
France (Paris)	1986	Prison Inmates	EIA/WB	64

[a]EIA, enzyme-linked immunoabsorbent assay; RIPA, radioimmunoprecipitin assay; RIA, radioimmunoassay; IFA, immunofluorescent assay; WB, Western blot assay.

Suppl 5–6). Of interest is the observation that the frequency of infection falls sharply as the distance from New York City increases. In 1985 in New Jersey, prevalence declined from 56 percent among 204 intravenous drug users living less than 5 miles away from Times Square to 42.7 percent at 5 to 10 miles away, to 21.8 percent at 10 to 50 miles away, to 1.8 percent at 100 miles away or farther (Weiss et al., 1986). In 1982–1983, seroprevalence surveys among drug treatment enrollees in New Haven, Connecticut, 100 miles from New York City, demonstrated 10 percent seropositivity among 283 program enrollees at a time when the prevalence among New York City treatment enrollees was 50 percent (D'Aguila et al., 1986).

In more striking contrast are the results of recent seroprevalence surveys in other parts of the United States. Rates of 5 percent and 2 percent have recently been described in Denver, Colorado, and San Antonio, Texas, respectively (Lange, 1988). Only six of 345 (1.7 percent) of intravenous drug users enrolled in statewide drug treatment programs in California in 1985 had antibodies for HIV-1 (Levy et al., 1986). However, in a study confined to San Francisco treatment program enrollees, 10 percent (28 of 291) of those tested during approximately the same period were positive (Chaisson et al., 1987). Seroprevalence was quite low (4 percent) among drug treatment program enrollees in North Carolina in 1985–1986 (Hoffman and Chorba, 1987) but higher among intravenous drug users in southern Florida (M. Fischl, personal communication) and Detroit (Wendt et al., 1987). Thus, the frequency of seropositivity varies substantially by geographic area, with the highest documented prevalence in New York.

The wide geographic disparity in rates of HIV-1 infection among intravenous drug users is puzzling but may be explained by two observations. First, interviews among intravenous drug users in the Bronx, New York (Friedland et al., 1985), indicate that travel outside New York City is distinctly unusual for this population. Limited by lack of funds or motivation, intravenous drug users tend not to travel beyond their own communities. Although drugs travel widely throughout the country, drug users generally do not, and therefore neither does the opportunity to introduce infection directly by person to person spread into other communities. Infrequent travel among most intravenous drug users has been observed in Europe as well (Robertson et al., 1986), as has clustering of HIV-1 infection in defined geographic localities. Second, there appears to be limited social interaction between intravenous drug users and homosexual men in many U.S. communities. It is logical to speculate that men who are both intravenous drug users and homosexuals form the bridge between the two separate populations and that wherever both populations exist in the same geographic area, this bridge will be crossed. However, the demographic and drug use characteristics of these men vary by geographic area and suggest local differences in their degree of interaction.

National surveillance data show that the geographic distribution of homosexual drug users resembles that of non-drug-using homosexual men more than that of heterosexual drug users. For example, a large proportion of homosexual men in California used intravenous drugs, and 87 percent of California drug users who developed AIDS were homosexual (Koplan et al., 1986). Among these homosexual intravenous drug users, the type of drugs used were not heroin and cocaine; only 2 percent had used heroin (Chaisson et al., 1987). Most using intravenous drugs had used amphetamines and other mood-altering drugs not commonly used by heterosexual intravenous drug users. In addition, the racial composition was similar to that of non-drug-using homosexual men. In New York, in contrast, homosexual intravenous drug users have a racial and ethnic composition midway between that of heterosexual intravenous drug users and homosexual men who do not use intravenous drugs. Further, in one study many heterosexual intravenous drug users in New York City gave a history of sharing needles with homosexual men, and the type of drugs and drug use practices were identical among heterosexual and homosexual intravenous drug users (Friedland et al., 1985). Thus, there appears to be substantial overlap in demography and behavior between the homosexual and heterosexual drug-using populations in New York but not in San Francisco. Intravenous drug users in areas outside of New York may have only recently been exposed to HIV-1, because the opportunities for introduction of the virus have been limited. Finally, disparate seroprevalences among different communities may also be a function of geographic differences in drug use practices such as the frequency of needle sharing (Ginzburg et al., 1985).

In many European countries HIV-1 infection has become well established among intravenous drug users, although, as in the United States, local geographic differences remain. The first documentation of HIV-1 seropositivity among European intravenous drug users was in Italy in 1979 (Lazzarin et al., 1986). Antibodies were first detected in Geneva in 1981 (Hirschel et al., 1986) and in Amsterdam in 1983 (Van den Hoek et al., 1986). The distribution of infection has been widespread, but prevalence has varied markedly from city to city (see Table 9.1).

Seroprevalence surveys also demonstrate the rapidity with which infection may be amplified within this population in defined geographic areas. For example, antibodies to HIV-1 first appeared among intravenous drug users in New York in 1978 (Novick et al., 1986). This was followed by a rapid amplification of infection during the next 2 years to 27 percent, with further increases by 1980, to 50 percent, and 1984 to 58 percent. In a similar situation, in Edinburgh, Robertson reports rapid escalation of seropositivity beginning with a prevalence of 1 percent in 1983 rising to 51 percent in 1985 among a geographically defined population of intravenous heroin users (Robertson et al., 1986). In Spain, Italy, and Switzerland, similar rapid increases in seroprevalence over the period of 1 to 4 years have been observed (Lazzarin et al., 1986; Rodrigo et al., 1985; Hirschel et al., 1986). The major determinant of geographic differences in seroprevalence of HIV-1 infection may be the time of introduction of HIV-1 into the local intravenous drug user community (Brunet et al., 1987).

Differences in results of seroprevalence surveys may depend on selection bias. The type of setting in which intravenous drug users are located and studied within a given geographic area may strongly influence the rate of seropositivity. For example, prevalence estimated at the same time differed widely among "healthy" intravenous drug users within treatment programs and those admitted to hospitals for non-AIDS-related diagnoses.

In two studies in New York City performed in 1983–1984, marked differences in seropositivity were observed between intravenous drug users in inpatient and outpatient settings. At Metropolitan Hospital, antibodies to HIV-1 were found in 33 percent of outpatients and 70 percent of inpatients admitted during the same time period with non-AIDS infection (Maayan et al., 1985). At Montefiore Medical Center and North Central Bronx Hospital in 1984, prevalence varied from 20 percent to 75 percent between outpatients and inpatients, respectively (Shine et al., 1987). These observations have two possible explanations: that HIV-1 and other conditions requiring hospitalization are the result of similar behavior and drug use practices but are otherwise unrelated, or that HIV-1 infection predisposes to other non-AIDS medical complications. Either or both could partially explain the wide discrepancy in seroprevalence by setting.

Finally, as with AIDS, seroprevalence surveys demonstrate more infection among black and Hispanic than among white intravenous drug users. This has been shown in San Francisco (Chaisson et al., 1987) as well as New York (Schoenbaum et al., 1986; Des Jarlais et al., 1987; Lange, 1988), New Jersey (Weiss et al., 1986), Baltimore and Denver (Lange, 1988). In San Francisco, 6 percent of 143 white intravenous drug users tested had antibodies compared to 14 percent of 143 blacks and Hispanics (odds ratio = 2.9). In New York, seropositivity among blacks and Hispanics was two to 4.5 times more common than among whites.

These findings may, in part, result from behavioral differences in drug use by race. In San Francisco (Chaisson et al., 1988), more frequent cocaine injection is present among blacks and associated seropositivity. In New York, shooting gallery use is associated with seropositivity among blacks and Hispanics (Schoenbaum, 1988).

The results of seroprevalence surveys in defined populations of intravenous drug users may be used to construct estimates of the total population both infected and at risk in specific geographic areas of high intravenous drug use prevalence. For example, in the Bronx, New York, it is estimated that there are between 31,300 and 46,200 intravenous drug users in the total population of 1.6 million, a rate of three to four per 1,000 (Vermund and Drucker, 1987). Using available seroprevalence data suggesting HIV-1 seropositivity rates of 30 to 60 percent among intravenous drug users and correcting for the age, racial, and ethnic distribution of most intravenous drug users, it can be estimated that in the age group of 25 to 44, 5 to 12 percent of all Bronx men and 1 to 3 percent of women of black and Hispanic background may be seropositive on the basis of this risk behavior alone. This calculated prevalence is of enormous consequence in terms of subsequent disease burden among intravenous durg users themselves and potential transmission to other populations via heterosexual sex and perinatal events. These levels of infection approach those of young adult populations in central Africa (Quinn et al., 1986).

Diffusion of HIV-1 infection into intravenous drug users outside the epicenter in New York City has been occurring slowly. A substantial uninfected, but at risk, population still exists, and with it a window of opportunity to interrupt transmission in this population. That window will likely close within the next several years as geographic diffusion and saturation of the population of intravenous drug users throughout the United States and other parts of the world take place.

FACTORS ASSOCIATED WITH INFECTION

The AIDS virus has not been cultured from contaminated needles and syringes; however, epidemiologic studies strongly support the association of both needle sharing and nonsexual factors and HIV-1 transmission (Table 9.2). The ubiquity of needle sharing among intravenous drug users in the Bronx, New York, was first described early in the AIDS epidemic (Friedland et al., 1985). In this study, 35 of 40 (88 percent) intravenous drug users with AIDS and AIDS-related conditions shared needles, as did 14 of 14 "healthy" intravenous drug user "controls." Seventy-five and 71 percent, respectively, of these groups attended shooting galleries. Of further interest, 20 of 35 (57 percent) of patients and four of 13 (31 percent) controls were aware of sharing needles with male homosexual intravenous drug users, providing a logical bridge between the two populations at greatest risk for AIDS in New York City, where, as previously described, a demographic overlap between heterosexual and homosexual intravenous drug users exists.

Table 9.2. Variables Associated with HIV-1 Infection Among Intravenous Drug Abusers

---

Drug use variables
  Number of injections of drugs
  Number of episodes of sharing of needles and syringes
  Proportion of injections in "shooting galleries"
  Duration of methadone treatment (negative association)

Non-drug use variables
  Sex with intravenous drug users
  Prostitution
  Nonwhite race
  Geographic proximity to New York City

Sources: Marmor et al. (1987), Schoenbaum et al. (1986), Weiss et al. (1986), Chaisson et al. (1987), Lange et al. (1988).

More comprehensive studies have recently attempted to define the role of needle sharing more fully with comparisons of HIV-1-seropositive and -seronegative intravenous drug users in several settings (Chaisson et al., 1987; Schoenbaum et al., 1986; Marmor et al., 1987; Weiss et al., 1986; Robertson et al., 1986). Among 291 heterosexual long-term intravenous drug users enrolled in opiate addiction treatment programs in San Francisco in 1985, 28 (10 percent) had antibodies to HIV-1. Seropositivity was not significantly associated with the duration of drug use but was related to "regular needle sharing" and to the number of persons with whom needles were shared. Of a subset of 209 subjects for whom needle-sharing data were available, the seroprevalence was 3 percent (two of 65) for those who did not "regularly" share needles, 9 percent (seven of 76) for those who shared "regularly" with only one other person, and 15 percent (10 of 68) for those who shared "regularly" with two or more persons ($p = .02$). The odds ratio was 5.43 (95% confidence interval 1.1 to 52.5) for subjects sharing with two or more persons compared to subjects not regularly sharing. These data are consistent with other studies in both the United States and Europe demonstrating an increased risk of seropositivity among drug users who "regularly" share needles. Among New Jersey intravenous drug users, HIV-1 seropositivity correlated with frequency of parenteral drug use and needle sharing after adjustment for other related variables (Weiss et al., 1986), and the work of other investigators (Robertson et al., 1986) further supports the relationship.

These semiquantitative associations do not establish the frequency or total number of needle-sharing episodes between seropositives and seronegatives so as to permit more precise evaluation of risk and relationships to other drug use variables. Analysis of a seroprevalence and case-control study among close to 500 methadone recipients in the Bronx (Schoenbaum et al., 1988) indicates that seropositivity is significantly associated not only with the practice of needle sharing but with quantitative measures of needle-sharing behavior and social setting of needle use (shooting gallery). Although a minimum level of exposure resulting in infection cannot be determined, these data strongly suggest that the likelihood of infection increases with repetitive exposures to contaminated blood over substantial periods of time.

In Marmor's study among methadone enrollees and inpatients in drug detoxification units (Marmor et al., 1987), significant and independent risks for HIV-1 infection were associated with the average monthly frequency of injection and with the proportion of injections that took place in shooting galleries. The relative risk for HIV-1 seropositivity varied from 1.6 among those injecting > 0.5 times versus 0 times a month to 4.5 among those injecting > 45 times versus 0 times a month. The relative risk associated with the proportion of injections in shooting galleries of 0 to 33 versus 0 percent and > 33 versus 0 percent were 1.7 and 2.8, respectively.

Preliminary information suggests that the drug administration practice rather than type of drug used is more strongly associated with seropositivity. Of great potential importance for interrupting transmission is the observation in several studies of an inverse relationship between seropositivity and duration of participation in drug treatment programs (Schoenbaum et al., 1986; Weiss et al., 1986). However, biases associated with participation in drug treatment are not known.

As for non-drug use variables, age and gender do not appear to be independently associated with seropositivity, whereas prostitution, frequent sexual contact with other intravenous drug users, and exposure to large numbers of sexual partners do appear to be related (Wendt et al., 1987; Schoenbaum et al, 1988; Des Jarlais et al., 1987a). The association with sexual practices has not been found in all studies (Chaisson et al., 1987), and the relative contribution of transmission by the intravenous and sexual routes among sexually active intravenous drug users is unknown, although it is logical to expect an additive risk.

CLINICAL AND IMMUNOLOGIC MANIFESTATIONS OF HIV-1 INFECTION AMONG IV DRUG USERS

Users of intravenous drugs have long been known to display clinical abnormalities resembling those now associated with HIV-1 infection: fever, weight loss, other constitutional symptoms, chronic lymphadenopathy at areas draining sites of intravenous injection, pneumonia, hepatitis, and endocarditis (Louria et al., 1987). Reported immunologic abnormalities antedating the introduction of HIV-1 included perturbations in both humoral and cellular immune functions. These included marked elevation in immunoglobulins (Brown et al., 1974; Cushman and Grieco, 1973; Cherubin and Millian, 1968), false-positive serologic reactions to certain infectious agents including those causing syphilis and lymphogranuloma venereum (Brown et al., 1974, Cherubin and Millian, 1968; Millian and Cherubin, 1971) and depressions in the absolute number of total T lymphocytes as a measured by the formation of rosettes with sheep red blood cells. Quantitative lymphocyte depression attributed to street opiates has been observed in vitro (McDonough et al., 1980), raising the possibility that opiate use may have a direct effect upon T-cell numbers and function. However, a clear influence of specific drugs on disease progression has not been borne out in epidemiologic studies (RA Kaslow, personal communication).

The immunologic and clinical abnormalities described as part of intravenous drug use itself may result in diagnostic confusion in individual patients, especially early in the course of HIV-1 infection. Although some authors have related quantitative alterations in CD4$^+$ cells to nonopportunistic infection in drug users (Hewlett et al., 1985), these alterations have been clearly associated with AIDS or HIV-1 infection when control seronegative intravenous drug users subjects are compared. In Des Jarlais' series (Des Jarlais et al., 1985), among 160 intravenous drug users with antibodies to HIV-1, the mean $CD4^+$ cell number was 790 $\pm$ 455/mm^3 compared to 1,099 $\pm$ 406/mm^3 among 110 intravenous drug users without antibodies ($p < .05$). In addition, decreased total lymphocytes and elevated immunoglobulins, although present among seronegatives, have been shown to be significantly altered in seropositives (Des Jarlais et al., 1987b). Confusion in the interpretation of serologic markers for CMV, HSV, and EBV, a characteristic of HIV-1 infection in all risk groups, may be compounded by the immunopathology associated with intravenous drug use, but the occurrence of unusual opportunistic infections indicative of underlying cellular immunodeficiency is a feature of HIV-1 infection and not drug use per se.

The absence of systematic surveillance for specific clinical entities related to HIV-1 infection apart from AIDS makes it impossible to determine their relative rates of occurrence among intravenous drug users. Clinical experience indicates that HIV-1-related dementia, wasting syndrome, and recurrent bacterial infections occur commonly in seropositive intravenous drug users. The acute retroviral syndrome has not been definitively documented in this population, although many intravenous drug users can recall such a syndrome.

The clinical spectrum of AIDS among intravenous drug users is similar to that of other groups at risk. However, several striking differences in the relative frequency of specific entities have been shown when compared to homosexual men. Intravenous drug users have a decreased risk of developing Kaposi's sarcoma. This difference has been consistently noted in both national (Jaffe et al., 1983; Haverkos, 1985; Guinan et al., 1984) and local reporting (Saltzman et al., 1986b; Des Jarlais et al., 1984) and was apparent early in the AIDS epidemic. Among the first 1,000 cases of AIDS reported in the United States, Kaposi's sarcoma alone was the initial single diagnosis in 36 percent of 727 homosexual or bisexual men and occurred with *Pneumocystis carinii* pneumonia in another 11 percent. Thus, 47 percent of homosexual and bisexual men presented with this diagnosis. In contrast, among 155 heterosexual intravenous drug users, only 2.6 percent presented with Kaposi's sarcoma alone, and another 1.3 percent presented with both Kaposi's sarcoma and *Pneumocystis carinii* pneumonia, for a total of 3.9 percent. This striking and significant difference in disease pattern has persisted to the present. Interestingly, homosexual intravenous drug users had an incidence of Kaposi's sarcoma (29 percent) approaching that among non-drug-using homosexual men, further suggesting some factor linked to male homosexuality as causal. Other malignancies associated with AIDS, such as non-Hodgkin's lymphoma, appear to be equally frequent among intravenous users and homosexual men, but oral hairy leukoplakia has rarely been seen in heterosexual intravenous users with AIDS (see also Chapter 3).

Differences in occurrence of the opportunistic infections of AIDS among intravenous drug users and other risk groups have also been noted. The higher frequency of *Pneumocystis carinii* pnemonia among intravenous drug users compared to homosexual nonusers both nationally (71 percent vs. 45 percent) (Kopian et al., 1986) and in New York City (68 percent vs. 44 percent) may be due, in part, to the difference in frequency of Kaposi's sarcoma as the initial presenting AIDS diagnosis (NYC Department of Health, 1986). Rates of toxoplasmosis, cryptococcosis, and candida esophagitis are higher among heterosexual male and female intrave-

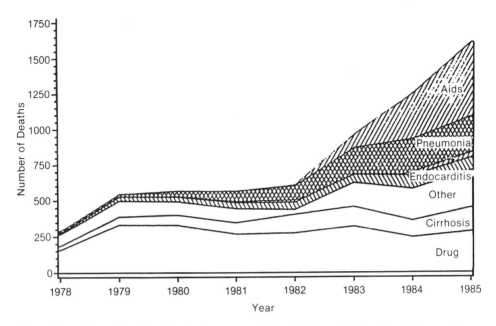

Figure 9.1. "Increasing Mortality in Intravenous Narcotic Users in New York City and its Relationship to the AIDS Epidemic. Is There an Unrecognized Spectrum of HTLV-III-Related Disease?," Rand L. Stoneburner, P. Guigli, A. Kristal, New York City Department of Health, AIDS Unit. Presented at the International Conference on AIDS, Paris, France, June, 1986.

nous drug users than among non-drug-using homosexual men and tend to be intermediate among intravenous drug-using homosexual men.

These differences in diagnoses among the risk groups may be a consequence of differences in previous exposure to infectious or other environmental agents, perhaps due, in turn, to demographic factors such as geography or socioeconomic status. Alternatively, the differences may reflect varying modes of acquisition of infectious agents: sexual versus parenteral.

The importance of non-AIDS indicator infections among HIV-1-infected intravenous drug users is becoming increasingly apparent. In New York City, dramatically increasing mortality has been observed among intravenous drug users coincident with and likely linked to the AIDS epidemic (NYC Department of Health, 1986; Stoneburner and Kristal, 1986) (Fig. 9.1). Between 1981 and 1985, mortality among intravenous drug users increased an average of 30 percent each year, while the total numbers of deaths due to the direct effect of drugs remained constant during this time period. A review of death certificates indicated that AIDS deaths increased from 0 to 529, pneumonia deaths from 15 to 193, endocarditis from 4 to 64, and tuberculosis from 3 to 35. Of note is the absence of documentation of similar trends in other AIDS risk groups, although an apparent increase risk of bacterial infection among homosexual men with AIDS has been reported (Polsky et al., 1986). Further, a review of autopsy material from selected pneumonia deaths among intravenous drug users revealed only seven cases of CDC-defined AIDS. Other record reviews on a subset of intravenous drug users with pneumonia, tuberculosis, and endocarditis deaths indicated that 40 to 50 percent had clinical evidence for HIV-1 infection prior to death and that in a substantial proportion bacterial pneumonia was the probable cause of death. Finally, a sample of pneumonia deaths were reviewed for evidence of mycobacterial disease. Among 24 cases in which specimens for mycobacterial cultures were sent, eight (33 percent) grew *M. tuberculosis*. It therefore appears that a substantial portion of the excess mortality observed among intravenous drug users is the result of tuberculosis and other acute bacterial infections which, although not meeting the CDC AIDS case definition, are likely related to HIV-1-induced immune dysfunction.

Further support for this hypothesis comes from a number of sources. The temporal and geographic relationship of tuberculosis and AIDS in New York City among intravenous drug users is mirrored in a detailed study of tuberculosis and AIDS in New Jersey (Sunderm et al., 1986). Tuberculosis was diagnosed in 48 of 136 adult patients with AIDS between 1981 and 1985. Tuberculosis was strikingly more common among intravenous drug users (24 of 102) and Haitians (4 of 8) than among homosexual men who did not abuse drugs (0 of 22; $p < .05$). All 24 intravenous drug users with tuberculosis were either black or Hispanic. The diagnosis of tuberculosis coincided with the diagnosis of AIDS in this population, and the disease was characterized clinically by frequent extrapulmonary manifestations (72 percent) and unusual clinical features similar to those described among Haitians with AIDS in Florida (Pitchenik et al., 1984). Disturbingly, in eight patients, the diagnosis of tuberculosis was made at postmortem examination. In a population-based study in the Bronx, NY, among intravenous drug users with known positive PPDs, the rate of development of active tuberculosis among HIV-1-seropositives exceeded that among HIV-1 seronegatives by a factor of 25 (Selwyn, 1988b).

This relationship between AIDS, HIV-1 infection, and increasing rates of tuberculosis most likely explains the observation that no decline in the annual morbidity due to tuberculosis in the United States occurred during 1985 (CDC, 1986c). The increase in tuberculosis is likely due to the reactivation of dormant infection in populations in which the prevalence of previous mycobacterial infection is high. Over the past three decades, rates of tuberculosis have been higher among racial minorities than among whites. The proportion of cases occurring among nonwhites has actually doubled during this time period (CDC, 1987a). Since a high proportion of intravenous drug users are of minority ethnic background, the demography of AIDS alone may explain the observed increase in tuberculosis. In another thorough investigation of AIDS and tuberculosis in Atlanta, Georgia (Guanner et al., 1986), disseminated *M. tuberculosis* infection was frequently seen in AIDS patients who were American-born, black homosexual men of lower socioeconomic status but who did not use intravenous drugs. Nevertheless, there is some evidence that intravenous drug use itself may incrase the risk of tuberculosis reactivation (Reichman et al., 1979). In practical terms, health professionals should be mindful of *M. tuberculosis* disease in intravenous drug users infected with HIV-1 and be aware of the increased rate of occult extrapulmonary disease. Aggressive, invasive diagnostic procedures should be used to detect acid-fast bacilli. When found in this population they cannot be assumed to be nontuberculous mycobacteria such as *M. avium–intracellulare*, and institution of therapy effective for *M. tuberculosis* is recommended until definitive identification is accomplished (CDC, 1986c; Saltzman et al., 1986b).

An increased incidence of pneumonia and other bacterial infections among HIV-1-infected drug users has been described elsewhere. Shine et al. (1987) observed that among a small number of intravenous drug users hospitalized for conditions other than AIDS such as endocarditis, pneumonia, and skin infections, the prevalence of antibodies to HIV-1 by EIA was 75 percent, whereas among a sample of healthy drug users in a treatment program, 25 percent were seropositive. In addition, there was a correlation between the presence of one of the bacterial infections, low T helper/suppressor cell ratio, HIV-1 seropositivity, and progression to AIDS within 4 months. The different rates of progression to AIDS in these two populations raised the possibility of an association between common bacterial infections and AIDS.

There are three hypothetical explanations for this association: (1) specific B-cell abnormalities associated with HIV infection; (2) acceleration of HIV-1 infection by bacterial infections; or (3) predisposition to both bacterial infection and HIV-1 infection by certain demographic factors or drug use practices. Findings among HIV-1-seropositive and seronegative drug program enrollees in the Bronx may help to resolve this issue. Among enrollees followed prospectively in a 12-month period, the rate of development of bacterial pneumonia was significantly higher in HIV-1-seropositive than in seronegative individuals (odds ratio = 4.5), even when the data were adjusted for recent drug use (Selwyn et al., 1988a). HIV-1 infection itself appears to be associated with a significantly increased risk for bacterial pneumonia among intravenous drug users. In this study, as in others, the most important bacterial pathogens appeared to be *S. pneumoniae* and *H. influenza,* both encapsulated organisms for which opsonizing antibodies and intact B-cell function are essential host defenses.

Part of the importance of defining more precisely the risk of tuberculosis and serious bacterial infections with HIV-1 infection among intravenous drug users is that strategies exist for their prevention through tuberculin testing and isoniazid prophylaxis, immunization with polysaccharide vaccine, and/or antimicrobial prophylaxis. Whether these interventions will be effective in this population also needs further study.

Although the reasons for the varied distribution of diseases by AIDS risk behaviors remain uncertain, these differences in the distribution of disease influence the apparent prognosis of HIV-1 infection among intravenous drug users. The decreased frequency of Kaposi's sarcoma, increased burden of opportunistic infections, and differences in demography are the most likely explanations for the observed shorter median survival after the diagnosis of AIDS among intravenous drug users compared to homosexual men (Rothenberg et al., 1987). The uncorrected median survival among intravenous drug users is 8 months (it is closer to 12 months for homosexual men). However, when homosexual men with Kaposi's sarcoma as the initial AIDS diagnosis are excluded from analysis, the median survival for both male and female intravenous drug users is similar to that of homosexual men without Kaposi's sarcoma (NYC Department of Health, 1986; Saltzman 1988).

The rate of progression of HIV-1 infection to fully expressed AIDS among intravenous drug users is not available from ongoing prospective natural history studies. Initial impressions indicate that HIV-1-infected intravenous drug users progress to clinical disease and AIDS at a rate that may be similar to that of other risk groups (Selwyn et al., 1988c), Des Jarlais et al., 1987). Continuation of drug use behavior may be associated with worsening of immunologic function and may even be predictive of disease progression (Des Jarlais et al., 1987).

Throughout the course of their HIV-1 infection, intravenous drug users present special difficulties in clinical management. Delay in diagnosis of HIV-1 infection among intravenous drug users is common. This population usually first receives health care related to HIV-1 infection in emergency settings when severe clinical manifestations occur. In the early years of the AIDS epidemic this was partly because intravenous drug users perceive illness as related to intravenous drug use itself rather than to HIV-1 infection. However, the more likely continuing reason is the episodic relationship to the health care system and lack of access to ongoing personal health care. Lack of compliance, inadequate intravenous site access, health care workers' disapproval of intravenous drug users' life-style, and other economic and psychosocial problems compromise care. Finally, home care and hospice care are often complicated by lack of adequate housing and frequent family disarray (Bulkin et al., 1988). Female intravenous drug users with AIDS present special problems such as issues of childbearing, child care, and custody (Callan et al., 1986). For many, however, intact family support systems do allow continuity and comprehensiveness of care if supportive services are provided. Institutions caring for intravenous drug-using AIDS patients have attempted to organize services around teams of providers with expertise in technical medical, social service, and drug dependency issues, and successful volunteer support programs have been developed (Tenneriello et al., 1987).

INTRAVENOUS DRUG ABUSE AND OTHER POPULATIONS

Intravenous drug users infected with HIV-1 occupy a pivotal position in the AIDS epidemic, because they represent the major bridge to other adult populations through heterosexual transmission and to children via perinatal transmission (Fig. 9.2; see also Chapters 8 and 13). The reasons are obvious. Intravenous drug users comprise the largest group of infected heterosexuals in the United States and Europe. The 90 percent of intravenous drug users who are heterosexual (Drucker, 1986) place large numbers of non-drug-using heterosexual men and women at risk for acquiring HIV-1 infection. The earliest instances of heterosexual transmission of HIV-1 were reported among the steady female sexual partners of AIDS male index cases, six of seven of whom were intravenous drug users (Harris et al., 1983). In studies of long-term relationships, approximately 50 percent of partners have acquired infection through heterosexual sex with an intravenous drug user (Steigbiegel et al., 1988, Redfield, et al., 1985, Fischl et al., 1987). Interviews among AIDS patients who are heterosexual intravenous drug users indicate that more than 50 percent of intravenous drug users have had regular heterosexual sexual partners who were not themselves drug users (Des Jarlais et al., 1987a; Friedland, unpublished data). In New York City alone, an estimated 50 percent of the 200,000 active intravenous drug users are HIV-1-infected. Therefore, a minimum of 50,000 non-drug-using sexual partners either have or are at risk for acquisition of HIV-1 infec-

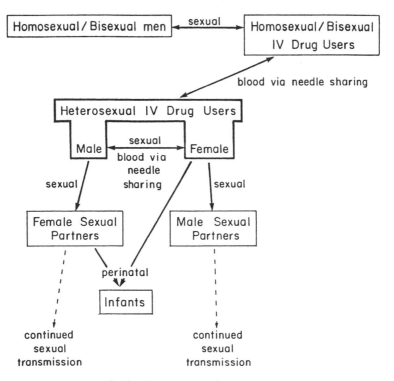

Figure 9.2. Central role of intravenous drug use in HIV-1 transmission.

tion by this route. In addition, countless additional more casual heterosexual contacts may be at risk.

It is important to realize that 30 percent of intravenous drug users in the United States are women, and 30 to 50 percent of these have engaged in prostitution to support their drug use (Ginzburg, 1984; Drucker, 1986; Ginzburg, et al., 1985). Studies of female prostitutes in the United States (Wallace et al., 1986; Fischl et al., 1986; CDC, 1987b) and Europe (Vaccher et al., 1986; Kohler et al., 1986) have indicated that HIV-1 seropositivity was associated with intravenous drug use. The male customers of female intravenous drug-using prostitutes are therefore at risk of acquiring HIV-1 infection as well.

Precise measures of current heterosexual transmission related to intravenous drug use are unavailable in the absence of large-scale seroprevalence surveys. Review of heterosexual AIDS cases acquired in the United States, reflecting transmission of HIV-1 3 to 8 years previously, indicate that the majority of patients acquiring AIDS in this manner have been sexual partners of intravenous drug users. As of August 29, 1988, this category included 1,858 persons, 80 percent of whom were sex partners of intravenous drug users (CDC, 1988). In New York City, among 204 heterosexual acquired cases of AIDS, the majority were sex partners of intravenous drug users (R. Stoneburner, NYC Department of Health, personal communication). At Montefiore Medical Center, of 132 women with AIDS, half were themselves intravenous drug users, and an additional third were the sexual partners of intravenous drug users (Saltzman et al., 1988). Nationally, among AIDS cases acquired by heterosexual transmission, the ratio of sex partners of intravenous drug users to sex partners of bisexual men is 5:1 (CDC, 1986d).

The clear linkage of intravenous drug use to heterosexual transmission is further seen by comparing different geographic areas in the United States by proportions in AIDS patients in various risk groups. As the proportion of intravenous drug users in different populations of AIDS patients increases, so does the proportion of cases attributable to heterosexual transmission (Saltzman et al., 1986).

In the United States and Europe, pediatric AIDS is largely a direct or indirect consequence of intravenous drug use. A clear linkage of intravenous drug use to perinatal transmission can be demonstrated. The initial descriptions of pediatric AIDS in the United States in 1983 were among infants born to mothers who were intravenous drug users or sexual partners of intravenous drug users (Oleske et al., 1983; Rubinstein et al., 1983). The geographic distribution of pediatric cases overlaps that of intravenous drug-related cases. Through August 1988, among 886 of 1,142 (78 percent) children with AIDS, one or both parents were at risk via intravenous drug use (CDC, 1988). In New York City, 199 pediatric AIDS cases reported to January 1987 were probably acquired by maternal transmission rather than by transfusion. Of these, 139 (80 percent) occurred in families in which one or both parents were drug users or the mother was the former sex partner of an intravenous drug user (NYC Department of Health, 1987). Based on the estimated numbers of female intravenous drug users and steady sexual partners of male intravenous drug users, the known birth rate in this population, and a presumed rate of perinatal transmission of 30 to 70 percent, the numbers of HIV-1-infected infants born per year in New York City alone may range between 566 and 1,297 (P. Selwyn, personal communication).

For the clinician caring for infants with AIDS, it is not uncommon that the issue of drug use in the parents is uncovered only after the appearance of an infected and clinically ill infant. Clinical and social care for infected infants in this milieu is complicated by the preexisting family disruption or illness secondary to drug use and AIDS. As a consequence, many infected infants remain the responsibility of health care institutions. Clearly, reduction in intravenous drug-related transmission is central to the reduction of pediatric AIDS. Programs to detect HIV-1 infection in women of childbearing age at risk combined with comprehensive family planning services may reduce the numbers of infected infants in the future.

REDUCTION OF RISK AMONG INTRAVENOUS DRUG USERS

Reduction of transmission of HIV-1 infection among intravenous drug users must take into account three factors: (1) the powerful physiologic, psychologic, social, and economic motivation toward drug use; (2) the demography and illicit nature of intravenous drug users, "hidden" and becoming "visible" only when they seek treatment or are arrested; and (3) the central role of needle sharing in disease transmission. (see also Chapters 5, 15, and 16). Widespread illicit drug distribution and injection have eluded all attempts at prevention and law enforcement, both in the United States and worldwide. The current estimate of 200,000 active intravenous drug users in New York City has shown no appreciable decline over the past decade. No major new forms of treatment or prevention of intravenous drug use are envisioned. Realistic measures directed at reduction of illicit drug use and practices resulting in HIV-1 transmission should be developed in the context of the AIDS epidemic. Foremost among these is education, specifically and appropriately directed toward intravenous drug users within treatment programs and correctional facilities, "on the street," and through the news media. Informal surveys among drug users indicated increasing awareness and concern about AIDS as early as 1983 (Des Jarlais and Hopkins, 1985; Institute of Medicine, 1986; Des Jarlais et al., 1987b). More formal recent surveys among both incarcerated and treatment program drug users have shown a generally high level of knowledge about AIDS and associated risk factors, particularly needle sharing (Ginzburg, 1986; Selwyn et al., 1987, Schoenbaum et al., 1987). In one study, there was a 40 percent decrease in self-reported needle sharing when compared to behavior in the previous year. Virtually all participants knew of and worried about AIDS and recognized its relationship to needle-sharing behavior. Others have made similar observations both in the United States and Europe (Des Jarlais et al., 1987b). These data contradict the commonly held view that intravenous drug users are uninterested in or unconcerned about their health and incapable of modifying their behavior.

Educational programs must creatively and explicitly stress the risk of sharing contaminated needles and syringes. Programs must be geared to the educational level and cultural context of intravenous drug users. Because the majority of drug users are not reachable through a defined community or existing institutions, such an effort must reach out into the users' environment. Employment of former drug users themselves in this educational effort should be encouraged (Marmor et al., 1985; Des Jarlais et al., 1987b). Beyond addressing persons already using drugs, educational programs about AIDS and intravenous drug use must be targeted at reducing new intravenous drug users, particularly young men and women in geographic areas where drug use is prevalent.

Reduction in drug use and needle sharing may be achievable by the provision of adequate drug treatment. Available evidence suggests but does not prove that participation in drug treatment programs is associated with less drug use or elimination of needle sharing (Hartel D, 1988; Blix, 1988). However, participation in drug treatment programs is associated with a lower rate of seropositivity (Schoenbaum, 1986). In most major cities with large intravenous drug user populations, the current demand for drug abuse treatment far exceeds the treatment capacity. Drug-addicted persons commonly apply for and then must wait for weeks to months before being able to enter treatment, continuing to use intravenous drugs during this period. Education about reduction of intravenous drug use may prove futile without the ability to link it to immediately available treatment and counseling. Successful educational efforts and growing fear of AIDS could well drive significant numbers of intravenous drug users to seek treatment for their drug use, further compounding the inadequacy of the drug abuse treatment system. Indeed, a recent survey indicates that approximately half of the intravenous drug users now entering treatment programs give fear of AIDS as one of their reasons for seeking treatment (Des Jarlais et al., 1987). Treatment programs themselves offer unique and continuing opportunities for direct one-on-one education of intravenous drug users and opportunities for prevention and early identification of pregnancy. However, even if adequate funding is made available, a massive expansion of the drug abuse treatment system would require considerable time invested in public debate, creation of treatment facilities, and staff recruitment and training.

Additional creative and emergency strategies must be employed for reducing the spread of HIV-1 among intravenous drug users. Strategies focusing directly on needle sharing itself among persons likely to continue using drugs are essential and logical (Ginzburg, 1986). For many intravenous drug users, the irresistible urge to inject drugs leads to the use of any available needle or syringe, sterile or contaminated. Studies among intravenous drug users indicate that the unavailability of a sterile needle at the time of drug injection is the commonest reason for continued sharing (Lewis and Galea, 1986). AIDS has had sufficient impact on drug users to stimulate the increased illicit sale of sterile disposable needles and syringes; an increasing demand for sterile needles has been observed among New York City drug users (Des Jarlais et al., 1985). Novel marketing devices including provision of "free" needles with large sales of heroin and "two for one" sales of needles and syringes have been observed by street workers. Programs instructing intravenous drug users in the sterilization of drug paraphernalia have been advocated and adopted in San Francisco and areas of New Jersey and New York. These programs promote the use of a 1:10 solution of household bleach, which inactivates HIV-1, and provide "bleach bottles" to active intravenous drug users.

The greatest interest has focused on the legally sanctioned provision of sterile needles and syringes. The actual effects of making sterile needles and syringes available to intravenous drug users are unknown. Exploration of this strategy has been advocated by the New York City Department of Health (Joseph, 1987), the Public Health Service (Coolfont Report, 1986), the Institute of Medicine (Institute of Medicine, 1986) and the Committee on Medicine and Law of the New York Bar Association (1986). Although controversial and politically unpopular, test programs began in New York City in 1988. To put the issue in perspective, only 12 states in the United States require prescriptions for the purchase of needles and syringes, and programs of needle exchange have been instituted in other countries in Europe including Holland and England (Des Jarlais et al., 1987b, Buning, 1988, Alldritt, 1988, Ljungberg, 1988). The needle exchange program was first established in Holland in the early 1980s after a perceived failure of repressive criminalization policies in response to the risk of hepatitis B, not HIV-1 transmission. Approximately 300,000 needles were distributed in an exchange program in Amsterdam in 1986 (two syringes per week for the estimated 3,000 intravenous drug users). Concurrent with awareness of AIDS, there has been an increase in the use of needle exchanges during this period. This program has not resulted in any measurable increase in drug use, and the effectiveness in reducing the spread of HIV-1 has not yet been demonstrated. This and other potential needle exchange programs have the additional merit of providing a basis for contact with intravenous drug users to engage in education related to risk reduction.

Programs directed at the reduction, if not elimination, of needle sharing among intravenous drug users must be introduced into our society as emergency measures to reduce HIV-1 transmission. The appearance of a new lethal virus transmitted by the blood-borne route in the midst of large populations of illicit intravenous drug users represents an especially inadequately addressed danger of the AIDS epidemic. Until efficacious measures for treatment and prevention of HIV-1 infection are available, any measure that promises to reduce illicit intravenous drug use and consequent HIV-1 transmission, no matter how bold or radical, should be carefully considered.

REFERENCES

Alderman MH, Drucker E, Rosenfield A, Healton C (1988): Bull. NY Acad Med 64:175.

Aldritt L, Dolan K, Donoshoe M, Stimson GV (1988): IV International Conference on AIDS, Stockholm Sweden.

Bakeman R, Lumb JR, Jackson Smith DW (1986): N Engl J Med 315:191.

Black, JL, Dowlen MP, Ford HA, Rubinstein JA (1986): N Engl J Med 314:446.

Blix O, Gronbladh BA (1988): Fourth International Conference on AIDS, Stockholm, Sweden.

Bouchard I, Espinoza P, Buffeti C, Courouce AM, Girard M, Etienne JP (1986): Second International Conference on AIDS, Paris.

Brown SM, Stimel B, Taub RN, Koshwa S, Rosenfeld RE (1974): Arch Intern Med 134:1001.

Brunet JB, Ancelle RA (1986): Ann Intern Med 103:670.

Brunet JB, DesJarlais DC, Koch MA (1987): AIDS 1:59.

Bulkin W, McNally L, McGuire G, Brown L, Friedland GH (1988): J. AIDS (1988), in press.

Buning EC, Van Brusse GHA, Van Santen GW (1988): NIDA Research Monograph 80.

Callan M, Gordon L, Friedland GH, Kahl PA, Vileno JL, Klein RS (1986): Second International Conference on AIDS, Paris.

Centers for Disease Control (CDC) (1981a): MMWR 30:250.

CDC (1981b): MMWR 30:305.

CDC (1982a): MMWR 31:249.

CDC (1982b): MMWR 31:265.

CDC (1982c): MMWR 31:294.

CDC (1985): MMWR 33:607.

CDC (1986a): MMWR 35:17.

CDC (1986b): MMWR 35:195.

CDC (1986c): MMWR 35:448.

CDC (1986d): MMWR 35:655.

CDC (1987a): MMWR 36:77.

CDC (1987b): MMWR 36:157.

CDC (1987): MMWR 36, Suppl. no. S-6.1.

CDC (1988): AIDS Weekly Surveillance Report, August 29.

Chaisson RE, Moss AR, Onishi R, Osmund D, Carlson J (1987): Am J Pub Health 77:169.

Chaisson RE, Osmond D, Bacchetti P, Brodie MA, Sande M, Moss AR (1988): IV International Conference on AIDS, Stockholm, Sweden.

Cherubin CE, Millian SJ (1968): Ann Intern Med 69:739.

Coolfont Report (1986): Public Health Rep 101:341.

Committee on Medicine and Law (1986): Legalization of Non-Prescription Sale of Hypodermic Needles: A Response to the AIDS Crisis.

Costigliola P, Ricchi E, Verani P, McRe THF, Chiodi F (1986): Second International Conference on AIDS, Paris.

Cushman P, Grieco MH (1973): Am J Med 54:320.

D'Aquila R, Williams AE, Kleber HD (1986): N Engl J Med 314:117.

Des Jarlais DC, Friedman S (1987): AIDS 2:67.

Des Jarlais DC, Hopkins W (1985): N Engl J Med 313:1476.

Des Jarlais DC, Marmor M, Thomas P, Chamberland M, Zolla-Pazner S, Sencer D (1984): N Engl J Med 310:1119.

Des Jarlais DC, Friedman SR, Hopkins W (1985): Ann Intern Med 103:755.

Des Jarlais DC, Wish E, Friedman SR, Stoneburner R, Yankovitz S, Mildvan D, El-Sadr W, Brady E, Cuadrado M (1987a): NY State J Med 87:283.

Des Jarlais DC, Friedman S, Marmor M, Cohen H, Mildvan D, Yancovitz S, Mathur U, El-Sadr, W, Spira T, Garber J, Beatrice S, Abdul-Quader A, Sotheran J (1987b): AIDS 2:105.

Drucker E (1986): Am J Drug Alc Abuse 12:165.

Ferroni P, Gerold D, Galli C, Zanbetti AR, Cargnil A (1985): Lancet 2:52.

Fischl MA, Dickenson G, Flanagan S, Fletcher MA (1986): Second International Conference on AIDS, Paris.

Fischl MA, Scott GB, Klimas N, Fletcher MA, Parks W (1987): JAMA 257:640.

Friedland GH, Harris C, Butkus-Small C, Shine D, Moll B, Darrow W, Klein RS (1985): Arch Intern Med 145:1413.

Friedland GH, Saltzman B, Rogers MF, Kahl PA, Lesser ML, Mayers MM, Klein RS (1986): N Engl J Med 314:344.

Garibaldi RA, Hanson B, Gregg MB (1972): J Infect Dis 126:288.

Ginzburg HM (1984): Public Health Rep 99:206.

Ginzburg HM, Weiss SH, Hubbard RL, French J, Hartsock PI, Blattner WA (1985): Second International Conference on AIDS, Paris.

Ginzburg HM (1986): Law Med Health Care 14:268.

Goedert JJ, Wallen WC, Mann DC, Strong DM, Newland CY, Greene MH, Murray C, Fraumeni JF, Blattner WA (1982): Lancet 412.

Greene MH, Nightingale SL, DuPont R (1975): Ann Intern Med 83:402.

Guanner J, Del Rio C, Slade B (1986): JAMA 256:3092.

Guinan ME, Thomas PA, Pinsky PF (1984): Ann Intern Med 100:213.

Guinan ME, Hardy AM (1987): JAMA 257:2039.

Hanrahan JP, Wormser GP, Reilly AA, McGuire G, Morse DL (1984): J Infect Dis 150:264.

Hardy AM, Allen JR, Morgan WM, Curran JW (1985): JAMA 253:215.

Harris C, Small CB, Klein RS, Friedland GH, Steigbigel NS (1983): N Engl J Med 308:1181.

Hartel D, Selwyn P, Schoenbaum EE, Klein RS, Friedland GH (1988): Fourth International Conference on AIDS, Stockholm, Sweden. Abst. 8546.

Heathcote J, Taylor KB (1981): Drug Alc Dependence 8:245.

Hewlett D, Maayan S, Miller SN, Rodrigues A, Perla E, Lenox T, Lue Y, Duncanson FP, Wormser GP (1985): J Infect Dis 151:748.

Hirschel B, Carpenter N, Gale PJ, Bourquin M, Bouchardy L, Jeannet M (1986): Second International Conference on AIDS, Paris.

Hoffman I, Chorba T (1987): JAMA 257:783.

Institute of Medicine, National Academy of Sciences (1986): Confronting AIDS, Directions for Public Health, Health Care and Research. Washington, D.C.: National Academy Press.

Jaffe H, Bregman DJ, Selik RM (1983): J Infect Dis 148:339.

Joseph SC (1987): Testimony to the New York State Assembly Standing Committee on Health, New York City Health Department.

Kohler H, Lange W, Rex W, Koch MA, Clage-Stehr JL (1986): Second International Conference on AIDS, Paris.

Koplan JP, Hardy AM, Allen JR (1986): Controversies Alc Substance Abuse 13:23.

Kozel KJ, Adams EH (1986): Science 234:970.

Kristal AR (1986): JAMA 255:2306.

Landrigo JM, Sera MA, Aguilar E, Delaolmo JA, Gimeno V, Aparece L (1985): Lancet 2:156.

Lange WR, Snyder FR, Lozovsky D, Kaistha V, Kaczaniuk MA, Jaffe JH and the ARC Epidemiology Collaborating Group (1988): Am J Public Health 78:443.

Lazzarin A, Crocchiolo P, Gall M, Uberti FT, Re M (1986): Second International Conference on AIDS, Paris.

Levy N, Carlson JR, Hinrichs S, Lerchen et al. (1986): N Engl J Med 314:446 (letter).

Lewis BF, Galea RP (1986): Health Matrix 4:14.

Ljungberg B, Andersson B, Christensson B, Hugo-Persson M, Tunving K, Ursing B (1988): IV International Conference on AIDS, Stockholm, Sweden. Abst. 8514.

Louria DB, Hensle T, Rose J (1967): Ann Intern Med 67:1.

Maayan S, Backenroth R, Ribert E, Jainchill N, Yaeger A, DeLeon G, Getchell J, Miller S, Pollack CC, Wormser G, Francis D (1985): J Infect Dis 152:843.

Maayan S, Wormser JP, Hewlett D, Miller SN, Duncanson FP, Rodriguez A, Perla EN, Koppel B, Rieber EE (1985): Arch Intern Med 145:1607.

Marino F, Esperanza B, Aizpiri J, Fernandez J, DeMaselvae L, Arrieta A, Velasquez D, Volsky J, San Cristobal E, De Izaquirre A, Santa Maria JM, Martinez M, Curral J (1986): AIDS Res 2:133.

Marmor M, Des Jarlais DC, Friedman SR, Lyden M, El-Sadr W (1985): J Subs Abuse Treat 1:237.

Marmor M, Friedman-Kien AE, Zolla-Pazner S, Stahl RE, Rubinstein P, Lauberstein L, William DC, Klein RS, Spigland I (1986): Ann Intern Med 100:809.

Marmor M, Des Jarlais DC, Cohen H, Friedman SR, Beatrice ST, Dubin N, El-Sadr W, Mildvan D, Yancovitz S, Mathur U, Holtzman R (1987): AIDS 1:39.

Masur H, Michelis MA, Green JB, et al. (1981): N Engl J Med 305:1431.

McDonough RJ, Madden JJ, Falek A, Shafer DA, Pline D, Bokos P, Kuehnle JC, Mendelson J (1980): J Immunol 125:2539.

Millian SJ, Cherubin CE (1971): Am J Path 56:693.

Moll B, Emeson EE, Small CB, Friedland GH, Klein RS, Spigland I (1982): Clin Immunol Immunopathol 25:417.

Moore JD, Cone EJ, Alexander SS (1986): N Engl J Med 314:1387.

National Institute on Drug Abuse (1982): National Drug Abuse Treatment Utilization Survey, U.S. Public Health Service, Rockville, MD.

New York City Department of Health AIDS Surveillance (1986): Am J Epidemiol 123:1013.

New York City Department of Health (1987): AIDS Surveillance Update. City Health Information (1986). Prevalence and Mortality, 5, 1.

New York City Department of Health (1988): AIDS Surveillance Update, June 1.

Novick D, Kreek MJ, Des Jarlais DC, Spira T, Khuri ET (1986): In Harris L (ed): Proceedings of 47th Annual Scientific Meeting National Institute on Drug Abuse, Bethesda, MD.

O'Donnell JA, Jones JP (1968): J Health Soc Behav 9:120.

Oleske J, Minnefor A, Cooper R, Thomas K, Dela Cruz A, Ahdieh H, Guerro I, Joshi R, Desposito F (1983): JAMA 249:2345.

Pitchenik AE, Cole C, Russell BW, Fischl MA, Spira TJ, Snider DE (1984): Ann Intern Med 101:641.

Polsky B, Gold JWM, Whimby E, Dryjanski J, Brown A, Schiffman G, Armstrong D (1986): Ann Intern Med 104:38.

Quinn T, Mann JM, Curran JW, Piot P (1986): Science 234:955.

Redfield RR, Markham PD, Salahuddin SZ (1985): JAMA 253:1511.

Reichman LB, Felton CP, Edsall JR (1979): Arch Intern Med 139:337.

Robert-Guroff RM, Weiss SH, Giron JA, Jennings AN (1986): JAMA 253:215.

Robertson JR, Bucknall AV, Wells TD, Roberts JJK (1986): Br Med J 292:527.

Rodrigo JM, Serra MA, Aguilar E, Del Olmo JA, Gimenov A (1985): Lancet 2:156.

Rothenberg R, Woelfel M, Stoneburner R, Milberg J, Parker R, Truman B (1987): N Engl J Med 317:1297.

Rubinstein A, Sicklick M, Gupta A, Bernstein L, Klein N, Rubinstein E, Spigland I, Fruchter L, Litman N, Hollander M (1983): JAMA 249:2350.

Saltzman BR, Friedland GH, Klein RS, Freeman K, Gutelle P, Schrager LK, Vileno JL (1988): Fourth International Conference on AIDS, Stockholm, Sweden.

Saltzman BR, Motyl MR, Friedland GH, McKitrick JC, Klein RS (1986): JAMA 256:390.

Schoenbaum EE, Selwyn PA, Feiner CA, Hartel D, Freeman KH, Ciccarelli R, DeCroce R, Klein RS, Friedland GH (1986): Second International Conference on AIDS, Paris.

Schoenbaum EE, Selwyn PA, Hartel D, Klein RS, Davenny K, Friedland GH (1987): Third International Conference on AIDS, Washington, D.C.

Schoenbaum EE, Selwyn PA, Hartel D, Friedland GH (1988): Fourth International Conference on AIDS, Stockholm, Sweden.

Selik RM, Haverkos HW, Curran JW (1984): Amer J Med 76:493.

Selwyn PA, Cox CP, Feiner CA, Lipsher C, Cohn RL (1987a): AIDS 1:247.

Selwyn PA, Feingold AR, Hartel D, Schoenbaum EE, Friedland GH, Alderman MH (1987b): Third International Conference on AIDS, Washington, D.C.

Selwyn PA, Schoenbaum EE, Hartel D, Peterman T, Klein RS, Friedland GH (1988a): AIDS, 2:267.

Selwyn PA, Lewis VA, Schoenbaum EE, Hartel D, Klein RS, Friedland GH (1988b): Fourth International Conference on AIDS, Stockholm, Sweden.

Selwyn PA, Schoenbaum EE, Hartel D, Davenny K, Klein RS, Friedland GH (1988c): Fourth International Conference on AIDS, Stockholm, Sweden.

Shine D, Moll B, Friedland GH, Emeson E, Spigland II, Weiss S, Bodner A, Harris C, Small C, Gallo R (1987): Am J Drug Alc Abuse 13:4.

Shupack J, Haller O, Vogt M, Luthy R, Joller H, Delz O, Popovic M, Sarngadharran MG (1985): N Engl J Med 312:265.

Small CB, Klein RS, Friedland GH, Moll B, Emeson E, Spigland I (1983): Am J Med 74:433.

Spira T, Des Jarlais DC, Marmor M (1984): N Engl J Med 311:467 (letter).

Steigbigel MS, Maude DW, Feiner CJ, Harris CA, Saltzman BR, Klein RS (1988): Fourth International Conference on AIDS, Stockholm Sweden, Abst. 4057.

Stoneburner RL, Kristal A (1986): Second International Conference on AIDS, Paris.

Sunderm G, McDonald RJ, Maniatis T, Oleske J, Kapila R, Reichman LB (1986): JAMA 256:362.

Tenneriello L, Callan M, Gordon L, Levine J, Poust B, Drucker E (1987): Third International Conference on AIDS, Washington, D.C.

Van den Hoek JAR, Van Zadelhof AW, Goudsmit J, Coutinho RA (1986): Second International Conference on AIDS, Paris.

Vaccher E, Tirell U, Bosio R, Diodato S, Tamburlini S (1986): Second International Conference on AIDS, Paris.

Vermund SH, Drucker E (1987): Third International Conference on AIDS, Washington, D.C.

Wallace J, Christonikos N, Marlink R, Robert-Guroff M, Weiss S (1986): Second International Conference on AIDS, Paris.

Weiss SH, Ginzburg HM, Altman R, Taylor F, Durako S, Blattner WA (1986): Second International Conference on AIDS, Paris.

Wendt D, Sadowski L, Markowitz N, Saravolatz L (1987): J Infect Dis 155:151.

10

Recipients of Blood and Blood Products

THOMAS PETERMAN AND JAMES ALLEN

In the United States and other developed countries, recipients of blood transfusions and clotting-factor concentrates are exposed to blood products carefully collected from healthy donors. The discovery of AIDS in both groups of recipients suggested a viral etiology for AIDS and supported the analogy to the epidemiology of hepatitis B. Efforts to prevent human immunodeficiency virus (HIV-1) infection in these two groups are unique in that they initially relied on changing the behavior of the donors rather than the behavior of the persons at risk (the recipients). With the development of an HIV-1 antibody screening test, the recipients have become the only AIDS risk groups for whom the risk of acquiring infection has been nearly eliminated.

There are many important differences between the two blood product recipient groups. First, blood transfusion recipients usually receive a single transfusion of blood from a few donors, whereas hemophiliacs* often receive multiple transfusions of clotting factor concentrated from thousands of donors. Second, blood transfusion recipients can often determine the date they became infected, but hemophiliacs cannot. Third, transfusion recipients are exposed to only a few donors, and they have the lowest risk of HIV-1 infection seen among the major AIDS risk groups, whereas hemophiliacs have extensive donor exposure and have a seroprevalence nearly 1,000 times that of transfusion recipients, the highest of all AIDS risk groups.

This chapter reviews the risk of infection for hemophiliacs and transfusion recipients, the natural history of infection in persons infected by these routes, and the prevention programs that have nearly eliminated the risk of HIV transmission to these groups. The emphasis is on the role of transfusions in the developed world; for consideration of their role in Africa, see Chapter 11.

CLOTTING-FACTOR CONCENTRATES

The first report linking hemophilia and AIDS was published in July 1982 (Centers for Disease Control, 1982a). Three men with hemophilia and no history of intra-

---

*Clotting-factor recipients will be referred to as "hemophiliacs," although not all clotting-factor concentrate recipients have hemophilia.

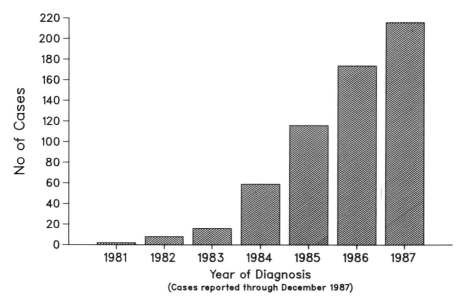

Figure 10.1. Cases of factor concentrate-associated AIDS by year of diagnosis. Cases reported through Dec. 1987.

venous drug abuse or homosexuality had developed *Pneumocystis carinii* pneumonia (Davis et al., 1983; Poon et al., 1983; Elliott et al., 1983). The association with clotting-factor concentrates was striking, because two of the three men lived in areas with a particularly low incidence of AIDS. By the end of 1987, 592 cases associated with clotting-factor concentrates had been reported in the United States (Figure 10.1), over 4 percent of the estimated 14,000 hemophiliacs in the country had developed AIDS (Hardy et al., 1985), and AIDS was the leading cause of death for hemophiliacs. These patients lived in 42 different states, a distribution that reflects the wide distribution of factor concentrates. Factor concentrates are made by pooling plasma from 2,000 to 20,000 donors and are distributed throughout the United States and exported around the world. In some countries, the first cases of AIDS were related to factor concentrates imported from the United States.

The risk of HIV-1 transmission during injection of a single lot of contaminated factor concentrate is not known, but it is clearly less than 100 percent. One study found no difference in HIV-1 seroprevalence for recipients of known contaminated lots of factor VIII (38 of 51; 75 percent) and controls matched for clotting factor requirements (44 of 51; 86 percent) (Jason et al., 1986). Similarly, recipients of specific lots of contaminated factor IX were no more likely to be seropositive (9 of 30; 30 percent) than recipients not exposed to the traced lots (12 of 30; 40 percent). In Edinburgh, 33 hemophiliacs received contaminated factor concentrate in April 1984. Variable follow-up schedules make it difficult to categorize the time to seroconversion, but 13 (39 percent) developed antibody within 15 weeks, 1 (3 percent) in 11 to 36 weeks, 4 (12 percent) after more than 20 weeks, and 15 (45 percent) remain seronegative (Ludlam et al., 1987).

The likelihood of HIV-1 infection in a person with hemophilia depends on the amount of clotting-factor concentrate exposure (Ramsey et al., 1984; Evatt et al., 1985, Lederman et al., 1985; Ragni et al., 1986). Persons with a factor VIII deficiency are more likely to be seropositive for HIV-1 than persons with a factor IX deficiency, partly because of a higher factor requirement and perhaps also because of differences in the efficiency of transmission with these two products. After the hemophilia–AIDS link was described, factor VIII use became more conservative, and demand increased for cryoprecipitated clotting-factor concentrate, which is made from plasma from fewer donors (Sandler et al., 1984).

Studies using stored serum found evidence of HIV-1 infection in hemophiliacs in the United States as early as 1979. By the time of the first reported association of AIDS and hemophilia, in 1982, as many as 20 percent of all U.S. hemophiliacs may have been infected with HIV-1. The largest increase in prevalence apparently occurred in 1982 and 1983 (Table 10.1) (Evatt et al., 1985; Lederman et al., 1985; Ragni et al., 1986). In the United States, hemophiliacs have the highest prevalence of HIV-1 antibody of any AIDS risk group (over 70 percent).

Since the prevalence of infection is fairly uniform among U.S. hemophiliacs and the prevalence can be estimated from different studies, the proportion of HIV-1-infected hemophiliacs who have developed AIDS can be estimated: 592 cases reported/(14,000 hemophiliacs × 70 percent prevalence of infection) = 6.0 percent of infected hemophiliacs have developed AIDS. This proportion is lower for hemophiliacs than for homosexual men in specific cohorts (Goedert et al., 1984; Jaffe et al., 1985a), leading to speculation that some seropositive hemophiliacs may not be infected with HIV-1. However, the likelihood of developing AIDS is directly proportional to the duration of infection (Darrow et al., 1986), so this difference in the rate of progression to AIDS may simply reflect differences in the duration of infection. Also, there may be a longer latency period for persons infected via factor concentrates, resulting in a delay (but not a reduction) in the progression to AIDS. Older age has been suggested as a cofactor for progression in hemophiliacs (Eyster et al., 1987), but it may simply be a marker for earlier infection (Johnson et al., 1985). Persons with a high factor requirement have had a higher incidence of AIDS, suggesting that repeated exposure to HIV-1 may increase the rate of progression; however, higher factor requirement probably also resulted in earlier infection.

Many cohort studies of hemophiliacs are in progress. In one, 10 (12 percent) of 84 seropositive hemophiliacs developed AIDS 24 to 95 months after the estimated day of seoconversion (Eyster et al., 1987). Another cohort of 34 adults with severe hemophilia has been followed for 5 years. The seroprevalence in this cohort

Table 10.1. Percentage of Hemophiliacs Seropositive for HIV-1 1979 to 1984

Reference	Year Serum Was Collected					
	1979	1980	1981	1982	1983	1984
Ragni et al. (1986)	—	—	8% (26)[a]	20% (40)	46% (44)	63% (80)
Evatt et al. (1985)	0% (18)	25% (8)	50% (8)	33% (9)	61% (18)	78% (23)
Lederman et al. (1985)	5% (21)	10% (10)	33% (3)	—	87% (15)	—

[a]Numbers in parentheses indicate number tested.

was 60 percent in 1982 and 97 percent in 1984. All subjects were asymptomatic at the beginning of the study, but by 5 years 38 percent had developed AIDS or related clinical features (Tsoukas et al., 1987).

SINGLE-DONOR PRODUCTS

The first case of AIDS associated with a blood transfusion was reported in 1982 (CDC, 1982b; Amman et al., 1983). A child in San Francisco developed *Pneumocystis carinii* pneumonia after receiving blood from a donor who later developed AIDS. Patients were considered to have transfusion-associated AIDS if they had no risk factors for AIDS other than a blood transfusion between 1978 and the onset of symptoms of AIDS. By the end of 1987, 1,401 such cases had been reported (Fig. 10.2), a small fraction of the several million transfusion recipients. Since blood has usually been collected and used locally, the risk of transfusion-associated infection has been roughly correlated with the number of AIDS cases in the region served by a blood bank. Although cases have been reported by 43 states, 36 percent of the first 752 cases were reported by New York or California.

Unlike hemophiliacs, transfusion recipients receive blood from a relatively small number of donors, so donors could be investigated to see whether they had AIDS or were at risk for AIDS (had risk factors for infection, a low T-helper-to-T-suppressor lymphocyte ratio, or unexplained generalized lymphadenopathy). The first seven completed investigations identified eight high-risk donors—at least one for each recipient (Curran et al., 1984). Subsequent investigations identified at least one high-risk donor for each case when all donors were investigated (Peterman et

Figure 10.2. Cases of transfusion-associated AIDS by year of diagnosis. Cases reported through Dec. 1987.

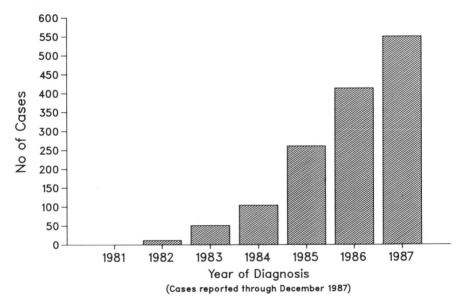

Year of Diagnosis
(Cases reported through December 1987)

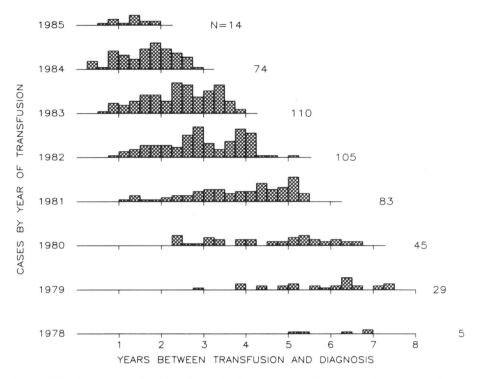

Figure 10.3. Time from blood transfusion to diagnosis of AIDS, by year of transfusion. Cases reported as of April 25, 1987.

al., 1985). After HIV-1 was identified as the cause of AIDS in 1984, serologic testing detected HIV-1 antibody in donors considered high risk by the above criteria (Jaffe et al., 1985b; Peterman et al., 1985). Virus has been isolated from several donor–recipient pairs (Feorino et al., 1984), and genetic mapping has found that isolates from these pairs were slightly different from each other but much more alike than would be expected by chance (Douglas et al., 1986). Virus was isolated from 22 of 24 seropositive donors 12 to 58 months after the donation associated with transmission; most of these donors were apparently asymptomatic chronic carriers (Feorino et al., 1985).

Cases of transfusion-associated AIDS are unique in that the date the recipients acquired infection is often known. This allows calculation of the latency period—that is, the time between infection and the diagnosis of AIDS (Peterman et al., 1985; Lui et al., 1986). For the first 752 cases, the average latency period was 36 months for adults and 24 months for children under age 13 years. However, these averages are misleadingly short, because the limited duration of observation has precluded detection of cases with very long latency periods. This bias was particularly important early in the AIDS epidemic, when the incidence of infection was increasing (Fig. 10.3). One mathematical model had suggested the mean latency for adults would be about 5 years (Lui et al., 1986); however, two more recent estimates suggest a mean closer to 8 years (Medley et al., 1987; Lui et al., 1988). These mathematical models rest on many assumptions, and the resulting estimates have wide confidence intervals, but they are useful in showing that latency will be longer than initially projected. More accurate estimates may eventually come from cohort studies.

The long latency for AIDS has made it difficult to estimate the risk of HIV-1 transmission by transfusion. Transfusions of platelets, plasma, red cells, and whole blood appear equally able to transmit infection (Peterman et al., 1985; Mosley, 1986; Ward et al., 1987a,d). Although the vast majority of recipients of seropositive units acquire infection (Ward et al., 1987a; Kakaiya et al., 1987), some exceptions have been reported. In one case, a unit of red blood cells was split and given to three infants; only one has developed HIV-1 antibody (Kleinman and Secord, 1987). In another, 10 (11 percent) of 89 recipients of HIV-1 antibody-positive components remained seronegative for more than a year after their contaminated transfusions (Kleinman et al., 1987). there were no significant differences between the seropositive and seronegative recipients in terms of age, underlying disease, or type of component received.

The risk of having received a seropositive unit before HIV-1 antibody screening was established can be estimated by using the seroprevalence when screening began (0.04 percent by Western blot) (Schorr et al., 1985). If all seropositive units transmit infection and each infected unit goes to a different person, the risk of a transfusion-associated infection in 1984 or early 1985 would have been about 40 per 100,000 units. Although the risk is very low, with approximately 18 million units of red cells, platelets, plasma and whole blood transfused per year (N. Holland, personal communication, 1986), a total of 7,200 transmissions may have occurred in the year before donor screening (1984). Projections back to previous years suggest that 28,000 people may have been infected by transfusion (Peterman et al., 1987). If 60 percent of the recipients have died from the underlying condition that necessitated the transfusion (Perkins et al., 1985a), there may be as many as 12,000 living infected blood transfusion recipients.

Transfusion recipients are a diverse group, and this facilitates the search for cofactors for the development of disease after infection. Children who received transfusions soon after birth have a shorter latency period for AIDS (mean currently 24 months) than adults (36 months). In addition, the proportion of transfusion-associated AIDS patients that received blood during infancy is higher than the proportion of recipients that are infants (Peterman et al., 1985). These findings may reflect an increased susceptibility to the development of AIDS in newborns, perhaps due to their immature immune systems. They may also reflect an inoculum effect, since a large transfusion to a newborn would come from a single donor, whereas a large transfusion to an adult could come from multiple donors. Another possible cofactor is suggested by the high proportion of adults with transfusion-associated AIDS who have had cardiac surgery (Peterman et al., 1985). However, this finding may represent a difference in survival after transfusion rather than a difference in the risk of progression to AIDS.

Cohort studies of transfusion recipients are in progress to elucidate the natural history of infection in transfusion recipients (Ward et al., 1987b; Mosley, 1986). One study has investigated 457 (59 percent) of 777 recipients of blood from 131 donors who were later found to be seropositive for HIV-1 antibody (Ward et al.,

1987b). Of these, 155 (34 percent) survived less than 4 months, 249 (54 percent) survived more than 4 months, and 53 (12 percent) were lost to follow-up. Of those surviving, 18 (7 percent) developed AIDS. Of 54 HIV-1 seropositives followed for an average of 46 months after their transfusion, 28 (52 percent) were asymptomatic, 12 (22 percent) had generalized lymphadenopathy, 9 (17 percent) had other clinical findings, and 5 (9 percent) had AIDS. There was no significant difference between the recipients who developed AIDS and those who remained asymptomatic, except that the AIDS patients were more likely to have received immunosuppressive therapy.

PRODUCTS THAT HAVE NOT TRANSMITTED INFECTION

Several products derived from human plasma have not been associated with transmission of HIV-1. Albumin is heat-treated sufficiently to kill most infectious agents, including retroviruses. The processing of immunoglobulin for injection causes an estimated 15-log reduction in titers of retrovirus, making transmission extremely unlikely (CDC, 1986a; Wells et al., 1986). Hepatitis B immune globulin, a pooled product taken from persons with high titers of antibody to hepatitis B surface antigen (HBsAg), has been associated with the passive transfer of HIV-1 antibody (Tedder et al., 1985) but has not been associated with the transmission of infection. Antibody might also be passively transfused with other immune globulins such as Rh_o (D) immune globulin (Rho GAM), but this has not been reported, perhaps because donors of this product (multiparous women) are not very likely to be infected with HIV-1. The first widely available hepatitis B vaccine was manufactured using virus from hepatitis B carriers, some of whom were at risk for HIV-1 infection. Each of the three steps in the purification process for the hepatitis B vaccine has been shown to kill retroviruses, and epidemiologic studies have found no association between vaccination for hepatitis B and HIV-1 infection (CDC, 1984; Stevens et al., 1985; Francis et al., 1986; and Solomon R. unpublished MACS data).

PREVENTION

Donor Deferral

Soon after the first cases of AIDS in hemophiliacs and transfusion recipients were recognized, the Public Health Service and blood collection agencies began asking donors at risk for AIDS (homosexual men with multiple sex partners, intravenous drug abusers, hemophiliacs, immigrants from Haiti) to stop donating blood or plasma (CDC, 1983). Studies have shown that this intervention resulted in significant changes in the blood donor population. In New York City, the number of male donors 21 to 35 years old decreased by 12 percent (Pindyck et al., 1985). In Atlanta, there were decreases in the number of units with serologic evidence of syphilis (from 0.47 percent to 0.29 percent) and HBsAg (from 0.09 percent to 0.07 percent) (Grindon, 1984). In Philadelphia, the number of units with HBsAg decreased by 57 percent (Dahlke, 1984).

Donor deferral has been an evolving process. Many blood banks have developed additional procedures for deferral after donation so that blood from donors who feel peer pressure to donate but have a risk factor for HIV-1 infection will not be transfused. Some centers give donors a card with AIDS information and a telephone number to call if they think that their blood should not be transfused. The New York Blood Center has asked all donors to indicate confidentially, at the end of the blood donation process, whether their blood should be used "for transfusion" or "for studies" (Pindyck et al., 1985). Only blood designated "for transfusion" (98 percent) is used. The prevalence of antibodies to HIV-1 by Western blot was 0.09% for the blood designated "for transfusion" and 2.1 percent for the blood designated "for studies" (Pindyck et al., 1987). It is not known how much of the difference was due to donations "for studies" by persons with risk factors who went to the blood bank for free HIV-1 testing and would not have donated at all if this option had not been available. This mechanism of confidential deferral after blood donation has been recommended to all blood banks by the Food and Drug Administration (FDA).

There have also been changes in criteria for deferral. In September 1985, the Public Health Service recommended that men who had even a single homosexual sex partner since 1977 should not donate (CDC, 1985). This new donor deferral statement was accompanied by a drop in the proportion of Western blot-positive donors from 0.034 percent to 0.008 percent in Connecticut (Kalish et al., 1986). In October 1986, The FDA recommended indefinite deferral of all prostitutes and deferral of their customers for 6 months after their encounter. The number of donors deferring for this reason and their HIV-1 seroprevalence rates are not known.

Some patients like to choose their own blood donors. Designated donation has been resisted by most blood banks because of difficulties in coordinating designated donations and the fear that a person at risk for HIV-1 infection or other infections might feel more pressure to donate if asked by a friend or family member. Irwin Memorial Blood Bank, in San Francisco, has accepted designated donations since June 1984 (Cordell et al., 1986). In the ensuing 18 months, nearly 12,000 units of blood and components was collected from designated donors. Serologic testing has shown that the designated donors were as safe as, but not demonstrably safer than, volunteer donors.

Serologic Screening

Screening donated blood is a second line of defense against transfusion-associated AIDS. Even before HIV-1 was identified, some investigators suggested tests using surrogate markers for AIDS. For example, screening for antibody to hepatitis B core antigen (HBcAg) was used at some centers. The specificity of the test was estimated at only 95 percent (5 percent of uninfected blood would have been discarded), and the sensitivity for detecting an AIDS patient was estimated at 88 percent, but neither estimate has been fully documented (Perkins et al., 1985b). Furthermore, hepatitis B tests may be less sensitive for HIV-1 infection than for detecting early cases of AIDS. Another surrogate market, antibody to cytomegalovirus (CMV), was coincidentally introduced in recent years as a serologic screen for blood given to infants in an effort to prevent the severe illnesses associated with CMV infection in premature infants. CMV screening may have fortuitously prevented some HIV-1 transmission to this group.

The first HIV-1 antibody tests were licensed in March 1985. Although early enzyme-linked immunosorbent assay (EIA) kits from different manufacturers vary somewhat, the specificity is similar (Deinhardt et al, 1987). Since 99.7 percent of blood donors had a negative test, the specificity of the EIA was probably at least 99.7 percent (Kuritsky et al., 1986). In Atlanta, 0.25 percent of blood donors tested in early 1985 had a positive EIA. Of these, 30 percent also had a positive Western blot and/or HIV culture (Ward et al., 1986). Donors with highly reactive EIAs were much more likely to have a positive Western blot or culture than were donors with reactivity near the threshold. Many of the specimens with low reactivity show biologic false reactivity due to antibody to antigens on human H9 cells used to propagate HIV-1 for manufacturing the test kits (Hunter et al., 1985; Peterman et al., 1986). Antibodies to H9 cell antigens are more common in multiparous women and transfusion recipients than in other donors and may also be more likely in needle-sharing drug abusers, hemophiliacs, and perhaps homosexual men. Newer versions of the EIA tests try to avoid this cross-reactivity by the use of recombinant technology (Mimms et al., 1987).

The issue of specificity is particularly important when screening in blood banks, because the prevalence of HIV-1 infection is so low. Donors with a positive EIA and a negative Western blot are usually not infected (the EIA is a false positive). Recipients of transfusions from donors who later tested positive by EIA but negative by Western blot have been followed. Of 69 recipients, three (4 percent) had HIV-1 antibody, but two were hemophiliacs, and the other had received many other transfusions (Ward et al., 1987c). The FDA now allows donors with a history of a positive EIA and a negative Western blot to be reinstated as donors if (1) EIA and Western blot tests on two samples drawn at least 6 months apart are negative, (2) the most recent Western blot is performed using a Western blot licensed by FDA, and (3) an EIA produced by using a virus grown in a cell line different from that of the initially positive EIA is also negative on both samples. Rapid developments in serologic testing will undoubtedly lead to further refinement of this policy.

The sensitivity of the HIV-1 antibody EIA is more difficult to assess than the specificity, since there are no definitive criteria for HIV-1 infection. However, the sensitivity of the test appears to be 98 to 100 percent for persons who have been infected for several months or longer (Deinhardt et al., 1987). As with any antibody test, the test results will be negative for the period of weeks or months between acquisition of infection and development of antibodies (Esteban et al., 1985). By Western blot, antibody to the core protein (p24) appears early; therefore, EIAs that are particularly sensitive for this protein tend to yield positive results before those that rely more on antibody to transmembrane glycoprotein (gp41). In some instances the virus has apparently been transmitted before the donor developed antibody (CDC, 1986b; Ward et al., 1988). Moreover, with development of techniques for detecting HIV-1 antigen and nucleic acid, the demonstration that virus may be present in blood for months in the absence of antibody, albeit in a small number of high-risk individuals (Wolinsky et al., 1988), has raised some concern about the sensitivity of antibody testing alone.

Although the HIV-1 antibody testing of millions of blood donors is designed to protect the blood supply, it also provides valuable information on the epidemiology of HIV-1 infection in the general population. When they are carefully evaluated, donors who are seropositive continue to have risk factors for infection. Seropositive donors in Los Angeles, San Francisco, and Baltimore have been primarily men, 396 (88 percent) of 450, of whom 77 percent reported homosexual contact (Ward et al., 1987d). This study and others (Operskalski et al., 1987; Starcher et al., 1987) have found that seropositive blood donors are more often bisexual than homosexual, suggesting that bisexual men do not recognize or acknowledge their risk for HIV-1 infection as readily as homosexual men.

HIV-1 antibody tests are now used to screen all blood and plasma donors in North America, Western Europe, and Australia. Some countries in Asia and South America also screen some donors. HIV-1 seroprevalence in most of these countries is lower than in the United States. In Toronto, Canada, the seropositivity rate fell from 0.03 percent in November 1985 to 0.008 percent in April 1986 (Derrick et al., 1987). In the United Kingdom, 0.002 percent of 2.8 million units tested positive (Gunson et al., 1987). In Victoria, Australia, only 15 (0.007 percent) of the first 214,699 donors screened were positive by Western blot, and most of them were women who appeared to have false-positive test results (Giraldo et al., 1987).

Transfusion practices and economic considerations have made donor screening difficult in central African countries, where the seroprevalence is highest. In Kinshasha, Zaire, 16 (5 percent) of 325 donors were seropositive by Western blot. Simple histories and physical exams were unable to define the seropositive individuals without excluding numerous seronegative donors. When five exclusionary criteria were combined, the seroprevalence was reduced to 1 percent but resulted in the exclusion of 70 percent of the donations (Nzilambi et al., 1987). New serologic testing techniques are being developed, and some are already available in certain areas. In one test, a bright blue color develops for positive specimens (Carlson et al., 1987). Another uses latex agglutination (Quinn et al., 1987). Both tests can be done in 30 minutes or less, and results show good correlations (over 98 percent) with those of Western blot tests.

Heat Treatment of Factor Concentrates

A third intervention, inactivation of HIV-1 in the blood product, has been accomplished by heating clotting-factor concentrates. Lyophilization and heating at 60°C for 2 hours caused a 6-log reduction in in vitro infectious units of virus (Quinnan et al., 1986). Most recipients of heat-treated products have remained seronegative (Allain et al., 1985; Rouzioux et al., 1985; CDC, 1987a). However, there are several reports of apparent transmission by heat-treated factor concentrates manufactured before donor screening began, suggesting that some methods of heat treatment may not have been 100 percent effective (CDC, 1987b). In addition, a cluster of six documented seroconversions among hemophiliacs in British Columbia has shown that transmission could occur even in donor-screened factor concentrates that have been dry-heated at 60°C for 30 hours (Remis, 1988). Manufacturers have since increased the temperature or duration of the dry heating, or used wet heat, which may be more effective.

Changes in Transfusion Practices

A fourth intervention is the more judicious use of blood transfusions. In their early recommendations, the Public Health Service recommended that "physicians should adhere strictly to medical indications for transfusions, and autologous transfusions are encouraged" (CDC, 1983). Total blood use has apparently declined, but this decline is difficult to quantify, since there are no national records of the number of units transfused per year. Anecdotal reports have also indicated that the number of donors used for neonates has been reduced in some areas by using aliquots from the same unit of blood for the multiple transfusions a neonate may require during a week rather than distributing the unit of blood to multiple infants.

Autologous transfusions are an option for patients undergoing elective surgery, where blood is routinely cross-matched. They also reduce the risk of other transfusion-associated infections, which are much more common than HIV-1. The donor requirements are less stringent than for regular blood donation, and most patients can deposit 2 or 3 units in the 3 to 4 weeks preceding their surgery (Surgenor, 1987). The impact of autologous programs has been minimal. An aggressive program at Beth Israel Hospital in Boston recruited 11.6 percent of the eligible patients, who donated an average of 2.2 units of red cells (Kruskall et al., 1986). During subsequent hospitalizations, 29 percent of the autologous donors required no transfusion, 37 percent received only autologous components, and 34 percent required additional homologous components. Overall, the autologous program collected 6 percent of the red cell units used by elective surgery patients and 2 percent of the total red cell units used by the hospital. In another study covering 18 tertiary-care hospitals in 1986, only 590 (12 percent) of 4,996 elective-surgery patients met their criteria for predeposit, and only 32 (0.6 percent of all surgery patients) predeposited blood (Toy et al., 1987).

Preventing Transmission from Infected Recipients

Donor screening and the heat treatment of factor concentrates have nearly eliminated the risk of HIV-1 transmission to hemophiliacs and transfusion recipients. Currently, secondary transmission from the estimated 22,000 recipients who were infected before donor screening began may be more common than primary transmission via blood products. Hemophiliacs and transfusion recipients have transmitted infection to their sexual contacts and, perinatally, to their children (Ragni et al., 1985; Kreiss et al., 1985; Allain et al., 1986; Peterman et al., 1988; CDC, 1987b). Studies have found that 5 to 20 percent of the sex partners of infected hemophiliacs or transfusion recipients have acquired infection (Kreiss et al., 1985; Allain et al., 1986; Peterman et al., 1988).

Blood centers identify some infected recipients by tracing previous recipients of blood from donors who now test positive for HIV-1 antibody. This approach is relatively specific (38 to 70 percent of the recipients are seropositive (Kakaiya et al., 1987; Menitove, 1986)), but it works only if the donor has donated in the same region both before and after screening began. In San Francisco, this approach identified 32 donors to 200 recipients (Samson et al., 1987). Linking the health department's AIDS case list to the donor list identified 139 donors to 950 recipients, and an additional 28 seropositive donors to 322 recipients were identified by investigating the donors to transfusion-associated AIDS cases. This expansion of their recipient tracing led to a sevenfold increase in the number of potentially infected recipients identified. Recipients in all three of these groups had seroprevalence rates of about 50 percent.

Additional transfusion recipients with asymptomatic infections could be identified by comparing state AIDS case lists with blood bank donor records and notifying previous recipients when a match occurs. Testing all transfusion recipients would be an even more sensitive approach; however, since the risk of infection averages less than 0.04 percent per component received, many recipients would have to be tested before an infected person is discovered. Thus, physicians should consider offering the HIV-1 antibody test to some transfusion recipients based on their likelihood of infection and the likelihood of transmission if the recipient is infected (CDC, 1987b). The expected HIV-1 seroprevalence in hemophiliacs is much higher, so they should all be encouraged to be tested to determine whether they need to take precautions during sexual contact.

LEGAL ISSUES

Transfusion recipients in at least eight states have already begun lawsuits against blood suppliers, hospitals, physicians, and municipalities (Matthews and Neslund, 1987). Under traditional product liability law, a product carries an implied warranty; that is, the blood that is sold would be deemed fit for transfusion. If blood is considered a product, producers could be held liable if the product was faulty even if their actions were not. However, transfused blood is generally regarded as a service rather than a product (Miller et al., 1985; Matthews and Neslund, 1987). If transfusions are a service, the plaintiff must demonstrate negligence on the part of the blood bank or physician to establish liability. Since there was no way to test the blood at the time it was given to most infected recipients, it has been difficult to demonstrate negligence.

CONCLUSIONS

Transmission of HIV-1 by blood transfusions and clotting-factor concentrates has been nearly eliminated less than 4 years after it was first described. However, 20,000 to 30,000 hemophiliacs and transfusion recipients have already been infected. Preventing AIDS in their sex partners requires identifying HIV-1-infected recipients and helping them to avoid transmitting infection to their sex partners. Preventing or postponing AIDS in persons already infected with HIV-1 depends on identification of those individuals who are appropriate candidates for chemoprophylaxis with zidovudine (AZT) and other agents now available.

REFERENCES

Allain JP (1986): N Engl J Med 315:517.
Allain JP, Masson PL, Dolkart RE (1985): Lancet 1:814.
Amman AJ, Cowan MJ, Wara DW, et al. (1983): Lancet 1:956.

Carlson JR, Mertens SC, Yee JL, et al. (1987): Lancet 1:361.

Centers for Disease Control (CDC) (1982a): MMWR 31:365.

CDC (1982b): MMWR 31:652.

CDC (1983): MMWR 32:101.

CDC (1984): MMWR 33:685.

CDC (1985): MMWR 34:547.

CDC (1986a): MMWR 35:231.

CDC (1986b): MMWR 35:389.

CDC (1987a): MMWR 36:121.

CDC (1987b): MMWR 36:137.

Cordell RR, Yalon VA, Cigahn-Haskell C, et al. (1986): Transfusion 26:484.

Curran JW, Lawrence DN, Jaffe H, et al. (1984): N Engl J Med 310:69.

Dahlke MB (1984): N Engl J Med 310:1195.

Darrow WW, Byers RH, Jaffe HW, et al. (1986): Second International Conference on AIDS, Paris, June 23, 40:S4c.

Davis KC, Horsburgh CR, Hasiba U, et al. (1983): Ann Intern Med 98:284.

Deinhardt F, Eberle J, Gurtler L (1987): Lancet 1:40.

Derrick JB, Buchner BK, Humphreys P, Davey MG (1987): Third International Conference on AIDS, Washington, D.C., June 1–5, TP.243.

Douglas D, Harper M, Ness PM, et al. (1986): Transfusion 26:576.

Elliott JL, Hoppes WL, Platt MS, et al. (1983): Ann Intern Med 98:290.

Esteban JI, Shih JW-K, Tai C-C, et al. (1985): Lancet 2:1083.

Evatt BL, Gomperts ED, McDougal JS, et al. (1985): N Engl J MEd 312:483.

Eyster ME, Gail MH, Ballard JO, et al. (1987): Ann Intern Med 107:1.

Feorino PM, Kalyanaraman VS, Haverkos HV, et al. (1984): Science 225:69.

Feorino PM, Jaffe HW, Palmer E, et al. (1985): N Engl J Med 312:1293.

Francis DP, Feorino PM, McDougal S, et al. (1986): JAMA 256:869.

Giraldo G, Beth-Giraldo E, De Basi R, et al. (1987): Third International Conference on AIDS, Washington, D.C., June 1–5, TP.244.

Goedert JJ, Sarngadharan MG, Biggar RJ, et al. (1984): Lancet 2:711.

Grindon A (1984): Transfusion 24:434.

Gunson HH, Rawlinson VI (1987): Third International Conference on AIDS, Washington, D.C., June 1–5, MP.233.

Hardy AM, Allen JR, Morgan WM, Curran JW (1985): JAMA 253:215.

Hunter JB, Menitove JE (1985): Lancet 2:397.

Jaffe HW, Darrow WW, Echenberg DF, et al. (1985a): Ann Intern Med 103:210.

Jaffe HW, Sarngadharan MG, DeVico AL, et al. (1985b): JAMA 254:770.

Jason J, Holman RC, Dixon G, et al. (1986): JAMA 256:1758.

Johnson RE, Lawrence DN, Evatt BL, et al. (1985): Am J Epidemiol 121:797.

Kakaiya RM, Cable RG, Keltonic J (1987): JAMA 257:1176.

Kalish RI, Cable RG, Roberts SC (1986): N Engl J Med 314:1115.

Kleinman S, Secord K (1987a): Third International Conference on AIDS, Washington, D.C., June 1–5, MP.232.

Kleinman S, Transfusion Safety Study Group (1987): Third International Conference on AIDS, Washington, D.C., June 1–5, TP.234.

Kreiss JK, Kitchen LW, Prince HE, et al. (1985): Ann Intern Med 102:623.

Kruskall MS, Glazer EE, Leonard SS, et al. (1986): Transfusion 26:335.

Kuritsky JN, Rastogi SC, Faich GA, et al. (1986): Transfusion 26:205.

Lederman MM, Ratnoff OD, Evatt BL, et al. (1985): Ann Intern Med 102:753.

Ludlam CA, Cuthbert RJG, Beatson D, et al. (1987): Third International Conference on AIDS, Washington, D.C., June 1–5, TP.238.

Lui KJ, Lawrence DN, Morgan WM, et al. (1986): Proc Natl Acad Sci USA 83:3051.

Lui KJ, Darrow WW, Rutherford GW (1988): Science 240:1333.

Matthews GW, Neslund VS (1987): JAMA 257:344.

Medley GF, Anderson RM, Cox DR, Billard L (1987): Nature 328:719.

Menitove JE (1986): N Engl J Med 315:1095.

Miller PJ, O'Connell J, Leipold A, Wenzel RP (1985): JAMA 253:3419.

Mimms L, Braun B, Worobec S, et al. (1987): Third International Conference on AIDS, Washington, D.C., June 1–5, TP.235.

Mosley JW (1986): Transfusion-transmitted HTLV-III. National Institutes of Health Consensus Development Conference: Impact of Routine HTLV-III Antibody Testing on Public Health, July 7.

Nzilambi N, Colebunders RL, Mann JM, et al. (1987): Third International Conference on AIDS, Washington, D.C., June 1–5, W.4.6.

Operskalski EA, Transfusion Safety Study Group (1987): Third International Conference on AIDS, Washington, D.C., June 1–5, TP.60.

Peterman TA, Jaffe HW, Feorino PM, et al. (1985): JAMA 254:2913.

Peterman TA, Lang GR, Mikos NJ, et al. (1986): JAMA 255:2324.

Peterman TA, Lui K-J, Lawrence DN, et al. (1987): Transfusion 27:371.

Peterman TA, Stoneburner RL, Allen JR, et al. (1988): JAMA 259:55.

Perkins HA, Samson S, Rosenschein S, et al. (1985a): International AIDS Conference, Atlanta, April 16, S13/2:30.

Perkins HA, Samson S, Rosenschein S, et al. (1985b): Am J Hematol 19:307.

Poon MC, Landay A, Prasthofer EF, et al. (1983): Ann Intern Med 98:287.

Pindyck J, Waldman A, Zang E, et al. (1985): Transfusion 25:3.

Pindyck J, Hosein B, Waldman A, et al. (1987): Third International Conference on AIDS, Washington, D.C., June 1–5, TP.240.

Quinn TC, Francis H, Kline R, et al. (1987): Third International Conference on AIDS, Washington, D.C., June 1–5, THP.19.

Quinnan GV Jr, Wells MA, Wittek AE, et al. (1986): Transfusion 26:481.

Ragni MV, Urbach AH, Kiernan S, et al. (1985): Lancet 1:133.

Ragni MW, Tegtmeier GE, Levy JA, et al. (1986): Blood 67:592.

Ramsey RB, Palmer EL, McDougal JS, et al. (1984): Lancet 2:397.

Rouzioux C, Chamaret S, Montagnier L, et al. (1985): Lancet 1:271.

Samson S, Busch M, Garner J, et al. (1987): Third International Conference on AIDS, Washington, D.C., June 1–5, WP.237.

Sandler SG, Katz AJ (1984): Vox Sang 46:1.

Schorr JB, Berkowitz A, Cumming PD, et al. (1985): N Engl J Med 313:384.

Starcher ET II, Noa MC, Ward JW, et al. (1987): Third International Conference on AIDS, Washington, D.C., June 1–5, WP.190.

Stevens CE, Taylor PE, Rubinstein P, et al. (1985): N Engl J Med 312:375.

Surgenor DM (1987): N Engl J Med 316:542.

Tedder RS, Uttley A, Cheingsong-Popov R (1985): Lancet 1:815.

Toy PTCY, Strauss RG, Stehling LC, et al. (1987): N Engl J Med 316:517.

Tsoukas C, Strawczynski H, Gervais F, et al. (1987): Third International Conference on AIDS, Washington, D.C., June 1–5, TP.89.

Ward JW, Grindon AJ, Feorino PM, et al. (1986): JAMA 256:357.

Ward JW, Deppe DE, Samson S, et al. (1987a): Ann Intern Med 106:61.

Ward JW, Deppe D, Perkins H, et al. (1987b): Third International Conference on AIDS, Washington, D.C., June 1–5, M.3.5.

Ward JW, Grindon A, Critchley S, et al. (1987c): Third International Conference on AIDS, Washington, D.C., June 1–5, MP.241.

Ward JW, Kleinman S, Douglas D, et al. (1987d): Third International Conference on AIDS, Washington, D.C., June 1–5, W.4.1.

Ward JW, Holmberg SD, Allen JR, et al. (1988): N Engl J Med 318:473.

Wells MA, Wittek AE, Epstein JS, et al. (1986): Transfusion 26:210.

Wolinsky S, Rinaldo C, Farzadegan H, et al. (1988): Fourth International Conference on AIDS, Stockholm, Sweden, Abst. 1099.

11

HIV-1 Infection and AIDS in Africa

THOMAS P. QUINN AND JONATHAN MANN

Although the United States has the highest number of officially reported cases of AIDS, the disease has probably had its greatest impact in the countries of central Africa (Quinn et al., 1986; Anonymous, 1987; Institute of Medicine, 1986). As of February 1988, 39 African countries have reported over 10,000 cases of AIDS (Fig. 11.1), but these statistics underestimate the true number of AIDS cases, since the diagnosis of AIDS often requires techniques not widely available in developing countries, and the medical infrastructure for surveillance in most African countries is limited. However, a variety of clinical and serologic studies have provided an insight into the true impact of AIDS in some African countries and have produced important information about the modes of transmission of HIV-1. With seroprevalence rates in some areas ranging from 5 to 15 percent among pregnant women and blood donors and as high as 20 to 80 percent among prostitutes and people attending sexually transmitted disease clinics, it is evident that HIV-1 infection has spread widely throughout sub-Saharan Africa and already imposes a tremendous health burden on many of these developing countries (Quinn et al., 1986).

HISTORY OF HIV-1 INFECTION IN AFRICA

The first confirmed AIDS cases among sub-Saharan Africans were reported from Europe in 1983 (Taelman et al., 1983; Clumeck et al., 1983, 1984; Brunet et al., 1983) (Table 11.1). Among these initial cases were persons who had come to Europe seeking medical care after exposure to HIV-1 while in Africa (Sonnet et al., 1983; WHO, 1986; Brunet and Ancelle, 1985). In late 1983, epidemiologic studies conducted by international teams in Kinshasa, Zaire, and Kigali, Rwanda, confirmed the indigenous occurrence of AIDS in central Africa (Piot et al., 1984; Van de Perre, 1984). This discovery of a major focus of HIV-1 infection in Africa led to seroarchaeological efforts to explore the regional history of HIV-1 and to a substantial number of national and international collaborative studies of HIV-1 epidemiology in Africa. As a result of these investigations, a cohesive picture of HIV-1 infections in Africa is gradually emerging.

Seroarchaeology, the examination of stored sera collected in the past for other purposes, provides intriguing hints regarding the past presence of HIV-1 infection in Africa. Yet it is handicapped by false-positive results due to any of several factors

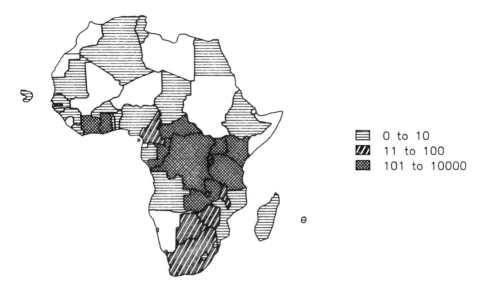

Figure 11.1 Distribution of AIDS cases in Africa as reported to WHO, Dec. 1987.

including (1) repeated cycles of freezing and thawing or other problems during storage, (2) hypergammaglobulinemia due to prior intercurrent infections, and (3) limited specificity of testing methods, especially of initial prelicensure EIA methods (Biggar et al., 1985). The recent reporting of false-positive confirmation tests by Western blot from fresh sera (Kuhnl et al., 1985; Weiss et al., 1985) and the realization that cross-reacting retroviruses may also be circulating in Africa (Clavel et al., 1986a; Kanki et al., 1986) should temper even further any enthusiasm regarding HIV-1 seroarchaeology. Indeed, some of the early reports of high seroprevalence in sera from East and West Africa in the 1960s and early 1970s are now considered uninterpretable (Biggar, 1986; Saxinger et al., 1984).

With these caveats, and using more refined and reliable EIA assays and stringent Western blot criteria, the earliest apparent serologic response to HIV-1 thus

Table 11.1. Approximate History of HIV-1 Infection in Central Africa

1959	Serum from one individual in Kinshasa, Zaire, reported retrospectively to be seropositive for HIV-1
1970	1/500 (0.2%) of surveyed pregnant women in Kinshasa seropositive for HIV-1
1970–74	Possibly 1 or 2 seropositive individuals of 2,574 tested in mine workers in South Africa
1972–75	Danish surgeon living in Zaire diagnosed in 1976 with possible AIDS
1976	HIV-1 recovered from frozen sera from possible AIDS patients in Zaire; 5/659 (0.8%) individuals in same area seropositive for HIV-1
1980	3% of 500 pregnant women in Zaire and 4% of 116 prostitutes in Kenya HIV-1-seropositive
1981–83	Clinical epidemics of "slim disease," cryptococcal meningitis, progressive Kaposi's sarcoma, and esophageal candidiasis recognized in Zaire, Zambia, Uganda, Rwanda, and Tanzania
1983–88	Clinical cases of AIDS reported to WHO from 39 African countries. Seroprevalence studies confirm extent of HIV-1 infection

far detected was in sera collected in Kinshasa, Zaire, in 1959 (Nahmias et al., 1986). In 1970, one of 500 (0.2 percent) pregnant women was found to be HIV-1-seropositive in Kinshasa (Brun-Vezinet et al., 1985). A review of clinical records for suspected AIDS cases among Africans or visitors to Africa include a Danish surgeon who was apparently exposed to HIV-1 in Zaire between 1972 and 1975 and subsequently developed probable AIDS in 1976 (Bygbjerg, 1983). In 1976, sera were collected in the northern Zairian equator region during investigations of Ebola virus. In addition to the finding of HIV-1 seropositivity by EIA and Western blot, in five of 659 (0.8 percent) Zairians tested in this area, an isolate of HIV-1 was recovered from the serum of one antibody-positive person who subsequently died of an AIDS-like illness in 1978 (DeCock et al., 1987).

AIDS cases, however, appear to have been uncommon in Africa prior to the 1970s. Hospital chart reviews in Europe identified only a few cases clinically compatible with AIDS among Africans or others associated with Africa prior to 1978 (Biggar et al., 1984; Clumeck et al., 1984). The absence of atypical Kaposi's sarcoma or changes in Kaposi's sarcoma epidemiology in Uganda (1951–1976), northeastern Zaire (1971–1983), Zambia (pre-1973), and Kinshasa (pre-1980) provide further indirect evidence against widespread HIV-1-associated disease during this period (Safai and Good, 1980; Hutt, 1981; Taylor et al., 1971). More importantly, evidence of dramatic increases in AIDS-associated pathology starting in the late 1970s and early 1980s corroborates the impressions of practitioners in Africa that AIDS was rare or uncommon prior to this period.

By the early 1980s, epidemics of atypical, aggressive Kaposi's sarcoma associated with HIV-1 seropositivity were noted in Zaire, Zambia, and Uganda. Epidemic increases in chronic, life-threatening enteropathic illnesses referred to as "slim disease" were identified during this period in Zaire, Uganda, and Tanzania (Serwadda et al., 1985; Marquart et al., 1985). In Rwanda, an epidemic of esophageal candidiasis was detected in 1983 in a hospital where approximately 300 esophagoscopies had been performed annually since 1979 (Van de Perre et al., 1984). Finally, careful surveillance of cryptococcal meningitis in Kinshasa, Zaire, starting prior to 1960, showed a rapid increase in the annual number of cases starting in 1978 with over a sevenfold increase in 1978–1984 compared with a period in 1959–1977 (Table 11.1) (Piot et al., 1984; Vandepitte et al., 1983).

METHODOLOGIC ISSUES

The geographic scope and intensity of AIDS and HIV-1 infection in Africa are difficult to assess precisely. First, infectious disease surveillance capability is often limited because of weaknesses in the health infrastructure and inadequate financial resources. Second, the widely used CDC/WHO definition of AIDS requires sophisticated laboratory support for diagnosis of opportunistic infections and malignancies and exclusion of other known causes of immunodeficiency, and is therefore not applicable to developing countries. A clinical case definition for AIDS has recently been developed to overcome these obstacles (WHO, 1986a) and will be discussed in detail later. Third, serodiagnosis of HIV-1 infection is generally unavailable and complicated by the need for confirmatory testing. Finally, political sensitivities about AIDS have impeded full exchange of information. This situation has been exacerbated by unfounded or poorly documented speculations in the international press regarding the origins of AIDS and different aspects of African life that might have contributed to the AIDS epidemic. Fortunately, enlightened national and international leadership is overcoming these problems. For example, national AIDS committees have been established in over 40 African countries, expressing a growing willingness to confront AIDS as a public health problem. A clinical case definition for AIDS surveillance in Africa was designed at a WHO workshop in Bangui, Central African Republic, in October 1985 and subsequently refined at a second meeting of the WHO collaborating centers on AIDS in December 1985 (WHO, 1986a). Preliminary evaluation in one African country suggests that the definition may be highly specific (although only moderately sensitive), at least in some areas (Colebunders et al., 1987c). In addition, national laboratory capabilities for serologic diagnosis of HIV-1 are being strengthened throughout Africa, and earlier errors in serologic testing are less likely to be repeated.

From the available information, it appears that central, eastern and parts of southern Africa have been most severely affected by HIV-1, whereas populations thus far studied in western and most of southern Africa have generally had less or little evidence of HIV-1 infection (Quinn et al., 1986). More recently, other human retroviruses have been identified in western Africa either associated with AIDS-like clinical and immunologic manifestations in Cape Verde and Guinea-Bissau, or in apparently healthy and immunologically intact persons, as in Senegal (Kanki et al., 1985a,b, 1986; Clavel et al., 1986a). These viral isolates had been referred to as LAV-2 and HTLV-IV, respectively, but are now collectively called HIV-2. However, little is known about the epidemiology of these newly recognized retroviral infections. Additional studies are in progress to examine the genomic structure and the natural history of HIV-2 infection. In other areas of Africa previously thought to be free of infection, HIV-1 and HIV-2 infection have only recently been detected; however, with few exceptions, the data are inadequate to distinguish recent introduction of the virus from recent recognition or awareness of the problem.

Intensive national or international studies of HIV-1 infection in some areas, such as Kinshasa, Kigali, Lusaka, and Nairobi, may have created a misleading impression that AIDS is concentrated in some areas compared to others less well studied. Although some evidence of HIV-1 infection could be found in many African countries, the laboratory techniques and population selection methods of seroepidemiologic studies can be difficult to compare. Local or regional findings cannot be generalized to the national level, and the extraordinary culture diversity in Africa should temper unwarranted extrapolations from small, more intensively studied groups, to large populations.

AIDS SURVEILLANCE

Systematic AIDS surveillance in Kinshasa, Zaire, was carried out initially between July 1984 and February 1985, when 332 cases were identified for an adjusted annual incidence of approximately 176 cases per million population (Mann et al., 1986a). Incidence in adult Kinshasa residents was approximately 380 cases per million, since nearly all the reported cases occurred among persons 20 years of age or older. Peak age-specific incidence rates of 786/million and 601/million were pres-

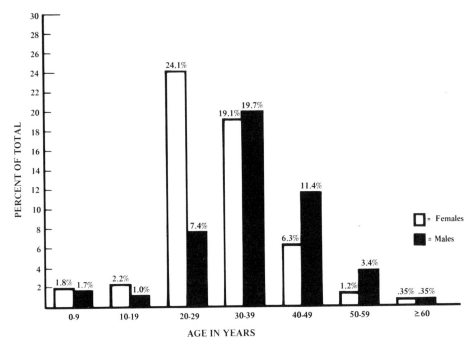

Figure 11.2. Distribution by age and sex of 500 AIDS cases diagnosed in Kinshasa, Zaire, in 1985. Women accounted for the majority of AIDS cases in the age group 20 to 29, whereas men accounted for the majority of cases in the age groups 40 to 49 and 50 to 59. (Reprinted with permission, Quinn et al., 1986.)

ent among 30 to 39-year-old men and women, respectively. By the end of 1985 the annual incidence was updated to approximately 1,000 cases per million adults (Quinn et al., 1986), and data from 1987 suggest that these rates may actually approach 2,000 cases per million adults. As disturbing as these numbers are, they are probably minimal estimates, reflecting only reported cases of AIDS in several hospitals within Kinshasa.

Surveillance data reflect some of the basic epidemiologic trends of AIDS in Africa. In 1986, the male-to-female sex ratio of AIDS cases in Zaire was approximately 1:1.3. As in developed countries, AIDS in Africa primarily affects young and middle-aged persons. The mean age of AIDS patients in Kinshasa was 33.6 (median 32, range 1.5 to 64 years), and men were significantly older than women (mean 37.4 years vs. 30.0 years). The sex and age distributions of these AIDS cases (Fig. 11.2) reflect patterns seen both in developed and developing countries with other sexually transmitted diseases in which the incidence and morbidity rates are higher among younger women and slightly older men (Aral and Holmes, 1984). Women with AIDS were more likely than men to be unmarried (61 percent vs. 36 percent), and nearly one-third of the married AIDS patients had at least one previous marriage or *"union libre"* (persistent cohabitation without formal marriage) (Mann et al., 1986a). One-third of AIDS patients reported having at least one sexually transmitted disease during the 3 years preceding their illness. Twenty-nine percent of patients utilized traditional medical practices, and 80 percent reported receiving medical injections. Nine percent of the patients received a blood transfusion during the 3-year period before onset of illness. Obviously, these data do not allow for direct assessment of the risk associated with AIDS activity, since no information was provided from a control population without HIV-1 infection, but they provided some information comparable to that collected in the United States and Europe.

SEROPREVALENCE STUDIES

Serologic studies indicate the extent of HIV-1 infection through Africa and are useful in identifying high-risk populations (Table 11.2). Published reports of HIV-1 seropositivity using both the screening and the confirmatory test have confirmed

Table 11.2. HIV-1 Seroprevalence Studies Conducted in Selected Populations in Africa[a]

Population and location	Year	Number studied	Percent seropositive	Reference
General population surveys				
Cameroon	1985	1,273	1	Durand et al., 1987
Central African Republic	1985	1,263	4	Merlin et al., 1987
Congo	1985	368	5	Merlin et al., 1987
Ivory Coast	1986	184	2	Kanki et al., 1987
Senegal	1986	166	0	Kanki et al., 1987
Zaire	1986	1,527	8	Ryder, 1987
Zambia	1985	100	19	Melbye et al., 1986
Blood donors				
South Africa	1985	1,740	0.3	Sher et al., 1987
Uganda	1986	370	11	Liskin, 1986
Zaire	1986	1,648	9	Ryder, 1987
Zambia	1985	207	18	Melbye, et al., 1986
Pregnant women				
Gabon	1986	768	0.3	DeLaporte et al., 1987
Ivory Coast	1986	365	0.5	Kanki et al., 1987
Kenya	1985	2,389	3	Braddick et al., 1987
Uganda	1986	1,011	14	Liskin, 1986
Zaire	1986	8,264	6	Ryder, 1987
Zambia	1985	184	9	Melbye et al., 1986
STD clinic population				
Burundi	1985	123	29	Petat, 1986
Kenya	1985	107	18	Piot et al., 1987
Zambia	1985	144	29	Melbye et al., 1986
Tanzania	1986	400	9	Mhalu et al., 1987
Prostitutes				
Cameroon	1985	221	8	Denis et al., 1987
Central African Republic	1985	234	14	Georges et al., 1987
Ivory Coast	1987	232	20	Kanki et al., 1987
Kenya	1985	286	61	Piot et al., 1987
Malawi	1986	265	56	Jayaraman, 1986
Rwanda	1985	84	80	Van de Perre et al., 1985
Tanzania	1986	225	29	Mhalu et al., 1987
Zaire	1986	377	27	Mann et al., 1986

[a]These data should not be generalized; refer to reference for specific details and population selection.

HIV-1 infection in Burundi, Botswana, Camaroon, Central African Republic, Chad, Congo, Equatorial Guinea, Gabon, Gambia, Kenya, Lesotho, Ivory Coast, Malawi, Rwanda, Senegal, South Africa, Tanzania, Uganda, Zaire, Zambia, and Zimbabwe. HIV-1 seroprevalence rates among healthy populations in these areas range from 0.03 percent in Chad to as high as 18 percent in Rwanda and Uganda. Rates among high-risk groups such as female prostitutes have been reported to range from 27 percent to 88 percent, depending on subject selection, socioeconomic status, and geographic location.

Longitudinal studies on HIV-1 seroprevalence are useful in monitoring the spread of HIV-1 infection within a given population. Longitudinal data are available from two studies in Kenya and Zaire. In a Kenyan study, sera were collected from 543 men and 123 women in Nairobi who had genital ulcer disease and who were attending a sexually transmitted disease clinic between 1980 and 1985, as part of studies on the etiology and epidemiology of chancroid in Kenya (Piot et al., 1987). Sera were tested from 535 prostitutes seen between 1981 and 1985 in a special prostitute research clinic in Nairobi. Similarly, sera from 1,100 pregnant women selected on the basis of residence in eastern Nairobi were collected in 1981 and 1985. Demographic variables such as mean age, duration of residence, duration of prostitution, place of birth, and average number of sex partners were comparable for the groups tested within each population studied. The prevalence of antibodies to HIV-1 in the prostitutes rose from 4 percent in 1981 to 61 percent in 1985 ($p < .0001$). In 1981 and 1982, 4 and 8 percent, respectively, of women with STDs were seropositive. Antibodies to HIV-1 in men with genital ulcers was first detected in 1981, and the prevalence of antibodies rose to 15 percent ($p < .001$). Although in 1981 none of 111 pregnant women were seropositive, by 1985, 2 percent of 1,100 pregnant women delivering at Pumwani Maternity Hospital had antibody to HIV-1 ($p = .09$).

In a series of studies in Kinshasa, sera from one of 500 (0.2 percent) healthy mothers in 1970 was seropositive compared with 5 of 100 (5 percent) in 1983 and 36 of 449 (8 percent) women in 1985. Consistent with this apparent rate of increase, all employees of a major hospital in Kinshasa were tested for HIV-1 antibody between October 1984 and November 1986 (Mann et al., 1986d; Ngaly et al., 1987). HIV-1 seroprevalence rate had increased from 6.4 percent in 1984 to 7.8 percent in 1986. Between 1984 and 1986 there were 56 new infections, for a 2-year incidence rate of 3.7 percent. On the basis of these studies, it would appear that HIV-1 was introduced into Kenya later than in Kinshasa, Zaire. The fairly recent introduction of the AIDS virus in Nairobi is further supported by the virtual absence of cases of AIDS in Nairobi until early 1985. By mid-1985, generalized lymphadenopathy and opportunistic infections were found in a substantial number of prostitutes (Kreiss et al., 1986). These results demonstrate that HIV-1 can spread as rapidly in a high-risk population of heterosexuals as in homosexual men in San Francisco, with large numbers of sexual partners as the common risk factor. In contrast, the evolution of infection rate was shown in a non-high-risk group for AIDS such as pregnant women.

Although all the factors responsible for the spread of HIV-1 from one area to another are not known, data from Nairobi suggest that the AIDS virus may have spread in Kenya by migration of prostitutes from neighboring countries, by travelers from other parts of Africa to Nairobi, and by continuous spread from bordering nations (Kreiss et al., 1986). For example, birth in the most western provinces of Kenya was associated with an increased risk of AIDS virus infection in men with STDs and in pregnant women. These men were young and recently migrated to the capital to seek work, often leaving their families and their regions of origin. Both of these provinces are crossed by the overland routes between Uganda, Rwanda, Burundi, and Mombassa, the major ocean port for these countries. Consequently, this road may have functioned as a portal entry of the AIDS virus, with heterosexual men from central Africa serving as vectors of the infection.

Important rural/urban differences have also been suggested, although limited data are available to confirm these impressions (DeLalla et al., 1987; DeCock et al., 1987; Petersen et al., 1987). In Burundi, Rwanda, and Zaire, seroprevalence appears higher in urban areas. For example, whereas seroprevalence rates range between 6 and 8 percent in people in urban Kinshasa, a serosurvey in 1986 in a rural area of northern Zaire, using a cluster sampling technique, showed a prevalence of HIV-1 antibody of 0.8 percent in 389 healthy adult villagers sampled (DeCock et al., 1987). In 136 pregnant women in northern Zaire, the seroprevalence rate was 2 percent, compared to 8 percent in Kinshasa. The seroprevalence rate was 11 percent in 283 prostitutes in the rural region, whereas it was 27 percent in 377 urban prostitutes. The rate of infection in the healthy adult villagers in 1986 was similar to that documented in the retrospective serologic survey, which demonstrated 0.8 percent infection rate of 659 serum samples collected in 1976 following an epidemic of the Ebola hemorrhagic fever. Thus, whereas HIV-1 infection rates may increase rapidly in some selected populations as demonstrated in the prostitutes in Nairobi, they may remain relatively stable in other populations, such as those described in the rural areas. Of interest, risk factors associated with HIV-1 seropositivity in patients residing in the rural area included increased numbers of sexual partners and travel or residence outside the area. These findings suggest that social factors associated with urbanization may play an important role in the spread of AIDS in Africa.

Two major serosurveys have been undertaken examining the age- and sex-specific infection rates in a general population. HIV-1 seroprevalence data from over 5,000 healthy persons in Kinshasa between 1984 and 1985 demonstrated a bimodal distribution with one peak in infants under 1 year of age and another among young adults (16 to 29 years of age) (Quinn et al., 1986). A combination of passive antibody transfer and transmission of virus from mother to infant is probably responsible for the high seroprevalence rates in children under age 1. Seroprevalence declined from nearly 8 percent among those 16 to 29 years old to 6 percent among those 30 to 49 years of age and to 4 percent among persons 50 years of age or older. Similarily, in a study in Lusaka, Zambia, which was primarily a hospital-based survey including outpatient clinics and prenatal clinics, the prevalence of antibodies was low in subjects aged less than 20 or older than 60 years of age (Melbye et al., 1986). In men the peak prevalence (32.9 percent) occurred in those aged 30 to 35 years, and in women the peak (24.4 percent) occurred in 20 to 25-year-olds. There was no significant difference in prevalence by sex after adjusting for age. Similar to the surveillance data on AIDS, these seroprevalence data strongly suggest that HIV-1 infection is most common in sexually active age groups and is transmitted predominantly by the heterosexual mode.

MODES OF TRANSMISSION

The most important epidemiologic conclusion derived from African studies is that HIV-1 is transmitted through the same routes—primarily sexual, parenteral, and perinatally—as it is throughout the rest of the world. Nevertheless, important regional variations exist within each of these transmission categories, which will be discussed below.

Sexual Transmission

The predominant mode of HIV-1 transmission Africa as in other areas is sexual (Quinn, 1987). In Africa, sexual transmission involves primarily heterosexual, bidirectional viral spread. In addition to the 1:1 male-to-female ratio among AIDS cases, and the younger age and single marital status for female cases, serologic studies also confirm an overall equal HIV-1 infection rate among the sexes, but with higher rates among younger women and slightly older men. These age–sex patterns of infection are those commonly seen with other sexually transmissible diseases such as gonorrhea, chlamydia, and syphilis (Aral and Holmes, 1984). In addition, case-control studies have also shown that AIDS patients in Rwanda have a significantly higher number of heterosexual partners than controls (mean of 32 vs. 3), that male patients have had sex significantly more often with female prostitutes (81 percent vs. 34 percent), and that the risk of seropositivity increases significantly with the number of different sexual partners per year and with the history of other sexually transmitted diseases (Clumeck et al., 1985a; Van de Perre et al., 1985b).

Urban prostitutes have had high infection rate (27 percent to 88 percent) and may have played an important role in the dissemination of HIV-1 in Nairobi, since HIV-1 antibody prevalence was initially higher in prostitutes in that city than in men with sexually transmissible diseases whom they served (Kreiss et al., 1986; Piot et al., 1987; Quinn, 1987). HIV-1 infection rates have also been elevated in patients attending STD clinics with rates of 15 to 30 percent in Nairobi and Lusaka (Piot et al., 1987; Melbye et al., 1986). Although high prevalence rates have been documented among male clients of female prostitutes, HIV seropositivity among both men and women was always correlated with the number of sexual partners.

Bidirectional transmission has also been documented in African studies, although the efficiency of female-to-male transmission versus male-to-female transmission is not clear. The precise mechanisms of heterosexual transmission have not been fully elucidated, but HIV-1 can be isolated from the semen of seropositive men and from the cervical-vaginal secretions of seropositive women (Vogt et al., 1986; Wofsy et al., 1986; Zagury et al., 1984; Ho et al., 1984). Genital-tract shedding of HIV-1 in women may occur throughout the menstrual cycle (Vogt et al., 1986). Household studies of AIDS patients have shown that HIV-1 antibody prevalence is significantly higher among spouses of AIDS patients than among spouses of controls. In one such study in Zaire, 11 (three men, eight women) (61 percent) of 18 spouses of three female and 15 male AIDS cases were HIV-1 antibody-positive compared to only one (3.7 percent) of 27 spouses of seronegative control patients (Mann et al., 1986).

In another household study, in Uganda, 71 percent of the sexual partners of 23 patients with AIDS were found to be seropositive (Sewankambo et al., 1987). As in the Zaire study, there were no significant differences in HIV-1 seropositivity rates between male and female sexual partners of the female and male index cases, respectively. In addition to these household studies, several clusters of African AIDS cases have been identified in whom the chronology of events suggested both female-to-male and male-to-female transmission of HIV-1 (Jonckheer et al., 1985). Although these spousal studies have documented high rates of infection among spouses of infected persons, this cross-sectional methodology does not permit assessment of the directionality of HIV-1 transmission. Prospective cohort studies of sexual partners of newly seroconverted HIV-1-infected individuals will be required to establish definitively the efficiency of bidirectional sexual transmission.

Risk factors associated with HIV-1 infection among heterosexuals include the number of sexual partners, sex with prostitutes, being a prostitute, and being a sexual partner of an infected person. No specific sexual activity, including anal intercourse, was associated with HIV-1 infection in surveys in Kenya, Zaire, Rwanda, and Zambia (Kreiss et al., 1986; Mann et al., 1986c; Clumeck et al., 1985b; Melbye et al., 1986). Thus, receptive anal intercourse, which is a major risk factor for HIV-1 infection in male homosexuals, is by no means required for heterosexual transmission.

Several important factors appear to have promoted sexual transmission of HIV-1 in African studies. Among Nairobi prostitutes, HIV-1 seropositivity was significantly associated with a history of sexually transmitted disease such as gonorrhea, genital ulcers, and syphilis (Kreiss et al., 1986). In studies in Zambia and Kenya, seropositivity in men was also correlated with the presence of genital ulcers (Melbye et al., 1986; Greenblatt et al., 1988). In a prospective study of 116 initially seronegative prostitutes followed for 2 years in Nairobi, 54 (76 percent) of 71 women with one or more episodes of genital ulcer disease seroconverted compared to 20 (44 percent) of 45 women lacking such disease (Piot et al., 1987; Plummer et al., 1987). In another prospective study of men with an STD and a history of recent prostitute exposure, 13 (14 percent) of 91 men with genital ulcer disease seroconverted during a 2 to 3-month follow-up period compared to three (3 percent) of 108 men with urethritis (Cameron et al., 1987). In a study of female prostitutes in Zaire, HIV-1 seropositivity, though not associated with a past history of STD, was associated with the placing of products within the vagina for hygienic purposes. All of these studies support the role of genital mucosal disruption, due either to trauma or to other sexually transmitted diseases, in enhancing HIV-1 heterosexual transmission (Piot et al., 1988).

Another cofactor that may be important in facilitating HIV-1 sexual transmission is the use of oral contraceptive pills in exposed women. In a prospective study of Nairobi prostitutes, the incidence of HIV-1 infection was significantly greater in oral contraceptive users (28 [80 percent] of 35) than in nonusers (46 [57 percent] of 81) (Plummer et al., 1987). This association persisted after controlling for such covariates as the number of sexual partners, history of sexually transmissible disease, and condom use. A similar finding was evident in female prostitutes in Zaire in whom HIV-1 seropositivity was significantly correlated with use of oral medications to prevent pregnancy or sexually transmitted diseases (Mann et al., 1986c).

Parenteral Transmission—Blood Transfusions

The importance of blood transfusions and HIV-1 transmission in Africa can be gauged by the finding of a 6 to 18 percent seroprevalence rate in blood donors in Uganda, Tanzania, Rwanda, Zambia, and Zaire (Van de Perre et al., 1985a; Brun-Vezinet, 1985; Mhalu et al., 1987). These figures are not surprising, as they parallel HIV-1 seroprevalence rates documented among healthy adults in those areas. In Kinshasa, 9 percent of 295 AIDS patients interviewed during 1984 and early 1985 reported receiving at least one blood transfusion during the previous 5 years (Mann et al., 1986a). In a large case control study of seropositivity in healthy persons in Kinshasa, 9.3 percent of HIV-1 seropositives compared with 4.8 percent of seronegatives reported receiving blood transfusions (Mann et al., 1986d). Similarly, 31 percent of hospitalized seropositive children aged 2 to 24 months with seronegative mothers reported a blood transfusion prior to the present hospitalization, compared with 7 percent of seronegative control children of the same age (Mann et al., 1986f). Seventeen percent of 50 patients with sickle cell anemia in Zaire had confirmed antibody to HIV-1; the majority of these had also received multiple blood transfusions.

In a study that examined the role of blood transfusions and the transmission of HIV-1 among African children, 147 (14.1 percent) of 1,046 pediatric patients at Mama Yemo Hospital in Kinshasa, Zaire, had a history of previous blood transfusion (Greenberg et al., 1987). Forty (3.8 percent) of these 1,046 pediatric patients were HIV-1-seropositive, and there was a strong dose-response association between history of blood transfusion and HIV-1 seropositivity (Nguyen-Dinh et al., 1987). The odds ratio of being HIV-1-seropositive increased to 43 in those that received three or more blood transfusions. In a follow-up study of 167 children hospitalized with acute malaria, 21 (12.6 percent) were HIV-1-seropositive, and 10 of 11 patients had received blood transfusions during the hospitalization. Follow-up of four children who were documented to have been seronegative prior to the transfusion demonstrated the development of IgM antibodies and persistence of IgG antibodies to HIV-1 6 months after receiving these transfusions. Thus, the impact of this mode of HIV-1 transmission may be substantial. In 1986, approximately 8,900 blood transfusions (69.2 percent of 12,858) were given to children with malaria at Mama Yemo Hospital. Since the HIV-1 seropositivity rate among the blood donors was recently shown to be 6.3 percent, we can estimate that 561 HIV-1-seropositive blood donations were given to children with malaria in this hospital setting alone.

Blood bank screening has been a difficult problem, since adequate facilities for blood banking and the financial support for routine HIV-1 screening by conventional methods are not available. In Kinshasa, the introduction of a rapid latex agglutination slide test for routine HIV-1 will hopefully help eliminate a large number of infected units (Quinn et al., 1988; Carlson et al., 1987).

Parenteral Transmission—Injections and Scarifications

While intravenous drug use is exceedingly rare in sub-Saharan Africa, injections administered for medical purposes appear to play an analogous role as a route of exposure to HIV-1. Among nearly 2,400 hospital workers in Kinshasa, significantly more HIV-1 seropositives than seronegatives reported receiving medical injections during the previous 3 years (Mann et al., 1986d). In addition, among those reporting injections, seroprevalence was nearly twice as high in the groups reporting five or more injections as in the group reporting fewer than five injections. In studies of hospitalized children in Kinshasa, including 368 children 2 to 14 years of age and 258 children 2 to 24 months old, a history of receiving medical injections prior to the current hospitalization was significantly associated with HIV-1 seropositivity (Mann et al., 1986e,f). Among the younger children, seropositive infants and children of HIV-1-seronegative mothers had a mean of 44 lifetime injections (vaccinations excluded) compared with 23 injections for hospitalized seronegative children of seronegative mothers ($p < .01$).

Exposure to unsterilized needles for the treatment of sexually transmitted diseases has frequently been suggested as the possible means of infection among high-risk groups, and some have postulated an even more important role for this kind of parenteral transmission than for sexual transmission. However, in two studies of female prostitutes in Nairobi and Kinshasa, as well as in a study of males with genital ulcers, HIV-1 seropositivity was directly associated with the number of sexual exposures and history of genital ulcerations, independent of the frequency of needle exposures, which was not associated with HIV-1 seropositivity (Kreiss et al., 1986; Plummer et al., 1987; Mann et al., 1986c). Thus, while some studies show a relationship between HIV-1 infection and injections, others do not, particularly when compared with sexual activity. A major limitation and interpretation of these studies is the difficulty in distinguishing injection as a mode of exposure to HIV-1 from injections as treatment for early symptoms of HIV-1-associated disease or from injections for treatment of conditions that are themselves associated with exposure to HIV-1 such as sexually transmitted diseases.

However, the potential for HIV-1 transmission by unsterilized needles should not be underestimated. For example, whereas the entire group of hospitalized seropositive children 2 to 24 months old in Kinshasa had similar medical problems, seropositive children of seronegative mothers had received significantly more injections than seropositive children of seropositive mothers, who would presumably have infected their infants perinatally (Mann et al., 1986f). Second, among tuberculosis sanitorium patients from Kinshasa, HIV-1 seropositives reported significantly more injections during the 5 years prior to hospitalization but reported an equal number of injections since hospitalization. Among married men in Rwanda, HIV-1 seropositivity was linked to injections from malaria treatment (Clumeck et al., 1985b). Finally, the plausibility of transmission by injection is supported by well-documented instances of nosocomial needle-stick transmission in the United States and Europe (CDC, 1987) (see Chapter 14).

In the above-mentioned studies of hospitalized and healthy children in Zaire, no association was observed between HIV-1 seropositivity and receipt of childhood vaccinations. This finding probably reflects wider use of properly sterilized injection equipment in childhood immunization programs, the relatively small number of vaccinations per child, the nonparticipation of traditional healers and vaccination programs, and the generally low seroprevalence rates among healthy young children in Kinshasa. However, the use of other skin-piercing instruments, as for medical or other ritual purposes, has theoretical potential for HIV-1 transmission (Desmyter, 1984).

Perinatal Transmission

Studies in Kinshasa have documented an equal HIV-1 seroprevalence of approximately 8 percent among women attending prenatal clinics, mothers of 1- to 24-month-old children, and over 1,500 women 16 to 34 years old (Mann et al., 1986f; Quinn et al., 1986; Nzila et al., 1987). Peak age and sex HIV-1 seroprevalence has been found among 15 to 19-year-old males and females. That pattern is consistent with the dominant role of heterosexual HIV-1 transmission in Africa. Not unexpectedly, a seroprevalence of 8.1 percent was present in 132 children less than 1 year of age, which represents, at a minimum, maternal passive IgG antibody to HIV-1 which subsequently declines with age if the child is uninfected (Quinn et al., 1986). In areas other than Zaire, HIV-1 seropositivity was confirmed in 0.3 percent of 768 pregnant women and new mothers in Gabon, 2.6 percent of 2,389 pregnant women in Nairobi, 2 percent of 200 women attending a prenatal clinic in Malawi, 14 percent of 1,011 women attending a prenatal clinic in Kampala, Uganda, and 8.7 percent of 184 women delivering in Lusaka, Zambia (Melbye et al., 1986; Braddick et al., 1987). The efficiency and risk factors associated with perinatal HIV-1 transmission are unknown, and prospective perinatal studies are now under way in several African countries.

Perinatal transmission of HIV-1 may occur in utero through transplacental passage of HIV-1, at time of delivery through maternal–fetal blood exchange or mucous membrane exposure to infected blood and/or body fluids, or postnatally through breast feeding or other possible routes (Rogers, 1985; Lapointe et al., 1985; Ziegler et al., 1985). Preliminary data from Kinshasa and Nairobi suggest that approximately 40 to 50 percent of children born to HIV-1 antibody-positive mothers either have IgM antibody to HIV-1 in cord blood or in 3-month follow-up positive blood specimens or have positive HIV-1 cultures from cord blood (Nzila et al., 1987; Braddick et al., 1987). In Kinshasa, 39 (11 percent) of 351 children born to HIV-1-positive mothers died within 3 months after birth compared to only 2 (0.6 percent) of 351 control children born to seronegative mothers ($p < .001$). Five percent of these children died within the first week of life, and the remaining 6 percent died after the first week. The mean birth weight of children dying within the first week of life was 1,651 g compared to 2,509 g in those dying after the first week of life. Immunologic studies performed in concert with IgM antibody studies of cord blood demonstrated a marked association between low number of CD4$^+$ cells in the mother and probability of an infected child. The number of CD4$^+$ cells per cubic millimeter in mothers of IgM-positive children was 278/mm^3 compared to 510/mm^3 in seropositive mothers of seronegative children and to 703/mm^3 in seronegative mothers with seronegative children ($p < .001$) (Francis et al., 1987).

Prospective studies already under way will hopefully define the consequences of HIV-1 infection in pregnant African women, to determine the incidence of congenital HIV-1 infection in children born to HIV-1-infected African women, identify the risk factors for congenital or perinatally HIV-1 infection, describe the natural history of congenital or perinatal HIV-1 infection, and examine the effectiveness and consequences of immunization in HIV-1-infected children. Factors such as breast feeding are critical in promoting and protecting the health of children in Africa, especially where there are borderline nutritional resources and a high frequency of diarrheal diseases. Intensive studies are urgently needed to determine the consequences of postnatal infection by other agents during HIV-1 infection.

With increased evidence of perinatal and parenteral HIV-1 transmission to children in Africa, a major concern has been raised regarding the safety and immunogenicity of childhood immunizations likely to be given to HIV-1-infected children (LaForce, 1987; CDC, 1986; Redfield et al., 1987; Halsey and Henderson, 1987). The possible adverse effects of immunizations in children infected with HIV-1 are under study. The relationship of measles, measles vaccine, and HIV-1 infection was recently examined in Kinshasa (Sension et al., 1987). Sixteen (5.1 percent) of 314 children admitted to Mama Yemo Hospital with acute measles were HIV-1-seropositive. Seventy-three (23.2 percent of the children with measles had a history of measles vaccination, including three (18.8 percent) of HIV-1-seropositive and 70 (23.5 percent) of HIV-1-seronegative children. Overall, there was no difference in case fatality ratios; five (31.3 percent) of 16 HIV-1-seropositive, compared to 82 (28.1 percent) of 292 HIV-1-seronegative, children died. However, among HIV-1-seropositive children more than 9 months of age, there was a trend toward higher case fatality ratios. Among unvaccinated children more than 9 months of age, four (80 percent) of five seropositive children died compared to 45 (32.1 percent) of 140 HIV-1-seronegative ($p = .04$). These data suggest that measles vaccination, even among HIV-1-seropositive children, decreases morbidity and mortality. A WHO meeting on childhood immunizations and HIV-1 concluded that measles, poliomyelitis, diphtheria, tetanus, and pertussis vaccination should not be witheld from any HIV-1-seropositive children; however, Bacille-Calmette-Guerin (BCG) vaccine should be given to asymptomatic children but withheld from symptomatic HIV-1-infected children (Von Reyn et al., 1987).

Transmission Through Other Routes

As in Europe and the United States, no evidence exists to support casual or household transmission of HIV-1 in Africa. For example, the rate of HIV-1 seropositivity did not differ significantly between 186 nonspousal household contacts of 46 AIDS cases and 128 nonspousal household contacts of 43 seronegative controls in a study in Kinshasa (Mann et al., 1986b). In Uganda, 10 (71 percent) of the sexual partners of 14 index AIDS cases were found to be seropositive, whereas only two (2 percent) of 100 nonsexual household contacts had evidence of infection (Sewankambo et al., 1986). These seropositive nonsexual household contacts had their own independent risk factors for acquisition of HIV-1 (including perinatal transmission), and evidence of household transmission other than through sexual exposure was not present. No association has been observed in hospital workers between the measure of patient or blood contact and HIV-1 seroprevalence (Mann et al., 1986d). In addition, the absence of HIV-1 infection among expatriates who lack recognized risk factors for HIV-1 infection despite living in close proximity to possibly infected individuals reaffirm the apparent lack of casual transmission of HIV-1 in Africa.

Epidemiologic data from Africa and the United States (Belle Glade, Florida) argue against insect transmission (see Chapter 6). In Africa, the sex- and age-specific AIDS incidence and HIV-1 seroprevalence data are not consistent with the vector-borne disease (Quinn et al., 1986). The low seroprevalence among children 1 to 14 years old and among persons over 50 years old and the significantly higher seroprevalence rate among women compared with men in the 20 to 39-year-old group argues against the vector-borne route of transmission as a major one. Virtually all seropositive children 1 to 24 months old in Kinshasa had identifiable risk factors for HIV-1 infection such as maternal infection, history of blood transfusions, or multiple injections (Mann et al., 1986f). The lack of evidence for household clustering of HIV-1, except as explained by heterosexual or perinatal routes, also argues against vector transmission over short distances as might occur with bedbugs or mosquitoes following interrupted feeding (Mann et al., 1986b). As mentioned earlier, the absence of unexplained HIV-1 infection in expatriates is also relevant. In Burundi and Kinshasa, the geographic distribution of HIV-1 infections and malaria appear discordant (Greenberg et al., 1987). The low titer of HIV-1 in the blood of infected persons and the small amount of blood on insect mouthparts reinforce the improbability of mechanical transmission of HIV-1 by insect vectors. Finally, hepatitis B virus, which is more readily parenterally transmitted, has not been found to be transmitted by arthropods (Zuckerman, 1986). In summary, the epidemiologic evidence to date suggests that if insects have played a role in HIV-1 transmission, this role has been negligible.

CLINICAL FEATURES

In tropical areas, such as central Africa and Haiti, gastrointestinal and dermatologic manifestations are commonly observed (Malebranche et al., 1983; Pape et al., 1985; Serwadda et al., 1985; Mann et al., 1986a; DeHovitz et al., 1986; Sonnet and Taelman, 1986), whereas generalized lymphadenopathy and pulmonary symptoms are frequently seen in AIDS patients in the United States and Europe (Fauci et al., 1985; Biggar et al., 1984). In a review of 196 AIDS patients in Kinshasa (Mann et al., 1986a), the mean duration of symptoms prior to diagnosis was 11.8 months (range 1 to 78 months; median 8 months). Symptoms consisted of profound weight loss (99 percent of patients), fever (81 percent), diarrhea (68 percent), cough (37 percent), dysphagia (35 percent), pruritis (30 percent), and dyspnea (23 percent). On physical examination, oral candidiasis was present in 47 of the patients, of whom 61 percent had dysphagia. A generalized pruritic macular eruption frequently referred to as "prurigo" was seen in 22 percent (Mann et al., 1986a; Colebunders et al., 1987d), and generalized lymphadenopathy was seen in 11 percent of patients. The most commonly observed opportunistic infections in African patients diagnosed in Europe included oral esophageal candidiasis, central nervous system cryptococcosis, toxoplasmosis, tuberculosis, and cryptosporidiosis in approximately equal frequency (Clumeck et al., 1984).

Other opportunistic infections include disseminated histoplasmosis, salmonellosis, disseminated strongyloidiasis, and mycobacterial disease (Colebunders et al., 1986). In Zaire, 53 (33 percent) of 159 confirmed pulmonary patients hospitalized at a tuberculosis sanitorium were HIV-1-positive, including 10 (67 percent) of 15 patients with extrapulmonary tuberculosis (Mann et al., 1986h). Seropositivity was significantly associated with anergy to intradermally injected tuberculin and history of blood transfusion during the previous 5 years. Among patients with tuberculosis there was no significant association between HIV-1 infection and extent of radiographic lesions, duration of disease, or initial response to treatment. Thus, HIV-1 inections may substantially complicate both the management of individual patients with tuberculosis and the strategies for tuberculosis control in countries where HIV-1 infection occurs. It is possible that patients who live in tropical areas and who are immunosuppressed as a result of HIV-1 will manifest other infections endemic in these areas such as leishmaniasis, leprosy, malaria, filariasis, and other parasitic and bacterial infections.

Perhaps most impressive of the clinical presentations of HIV-1 infection in Africa is the appearance of enteropathic AIDS, frequently referred to as "slim disease" (Serwadda et al., 1985). In most clinical studies in central Africa, profound weight loss and unexplained diarrhea occur in 99 percent and 80 percent of cases, respectively (Mann et al., 1986a; Colebunders et al., 1987a). Seroprevalence studies among these patients demonstrated HIV-1 antibody in all the patients who present with clinical diarrhea and a weight loss of 10 kg or more. Microbiologic evaluations detect pathogens in approximately 50 percent of the patients, including *Cryptosporidium, Isospora, Entamoeba histolytica, Strongyloides, Giardia lamblia,* and *Salmonella* (Colebunders et al., 1986; Henry et al., 1986). Approximately 40 to 50 percent of these patients have no identifiable gastrointestinal pathogen and suffer from chronic malabsorption and a debilitating idiopathic diarrheal illness. In Zaire, the positive predictive value of chronic diarrhea, weight loss, and oral candidiasis for HIV-1 infection in hospitalized patients was 97 percent (Colebunders et al., 1986). Consequently, the World Health Organization has developed a provisional clinical case definition for AIDS in Africa, where sophisticated diagnostic equipment may not be available (Table 11.3) (WHO, 1986a). The definition consists of having at least two major signs in association with at least one minor sign consistent with systemic immunosuppression.

In an attempt to validate this case definition, 174 inpatients at Mama Yemo Hospital in Kinshasa were examined, of whom 34 percent had antibody to HIV-1 (Colebunders et al., 1987c). Using HIV-1 seropositivity as the ultimate standard, the WHO clinical case definition had a sensitivity of 59 percent, specificity of 90 percent, and positive predictive value of 74 percent. Sensitivity of the definition could be improved to 75 percent by including moderate to severe asthenia as a major clinical sign. The sensitivity for the diagnosis of outright AIDS is most probably higher, since all patients with HIV-1 antibody were considered when evaluating the validity of the case definition, including patients with coincidental HIV-1 seropositivity, early clinical features, and AIDS. A major problem in the differential diagnosis of AIDS has been tuberculosis, which has many of the signs

Table 11.3. Provisional WHO Clinical Case Definition for AIDS Where Diagnostic Resources Are Limited (Definition developed at WHO Workshop on AIDS in Bangui, Central African Republic).

Adults

AIDS in an adult is defined by the existence of at least two of the major signs associated with at least one minor sign, in the absence of known causes of immunosuppression such as cancer or severe malnutrition or other recognized etiologies.

Major signs
  (a) Weight loss > 10% of body weight
  (b) Chronic diarrhea > 1 month
  (c) Prolonged fever > 1 month (intermittent or constant)

Minor signs
  (a) Persistent cough for > 1 month
  (b) Generalized pruritic dermatitis
  (c) Recurrent herpes zoster
  (d) Oropharyngeal candidiasis
  (e) Chronic progressive and disseminated herpex simplex infection
  (f) Generalized lymphadenopathy

The presence of generalized Kaposi's sarcoma or cryptococcal meningitis is sufficient in itself for the diagnosis of AIDS.

Children

Pediatric AIDS is suspected in an infant or child presenting with at least two major signs associated with at least two minor signs in the absence of known cases of immunosuppression.

Major signs
  (a) Weight loss or abnormally slow growth
  (b) Chronic diarrhea > 1 month
  (c) Prolonged fever > 1 month

Minor signs
  (a) Generalized lymphadenopathy
  (b) Oropharyngeal candidiasis
  (c) Repeated common infections (otitis, pharyngitis, etc.)
  (d) Persistent cough > 1 month
  (e) Generalized dermatitis
  (f) Confirmed maternal HIV-1 (LAV/HTLV-III) infection

and symptoms commonly seen in HIV-1 infection, and it is also frequently associated with HIV-1. Thus in Kinshasa, nine (75 percent) of 12 HIV-1-seronegative patients who met the clinical criteria for AIDS had tuberculosis.

A simplified clinical case definition for pediatric AIDS has also been proposed by WHO. In a survey to examine this case definition, of 159 hospitalized children in Kinshasa, 21 (13 percent) were found to be seropositive for HIV-1 (Colebunders et al., 1987b). The provisional WHO clinical case definition for pediatric AIDS was found to be fairly specific (87 percent) for HIV-1 infection, but it lacked sensitivity (35 percent). The low predictive value (25 percent) of the case definition for pediatric AIDS is most likely due to the frequent occurrence of malnutrition, diarrhea, and respiratory diseases that are highly endemic within this population and which mimic the symptoms of HIV-1 infection. As more clinical data become available development of clinical definitions that best discriminate between HIV-1 disease and other conditions should be encouraged for surveillance and epidemiologic purposes.

NATURAL HISTORY OF HIV-1 INFECTION

In comparison to HIV-1 infection in developed countries, little is known about the natural course of HIV-1 infection in tropical areas. However, a 2-year natural history study in Kinshasa, Zaire, has provided some information in this area (Mann et al., 1987g; Ngaly et al., 1987). Between October 1984 and November 1986, virtually all employees at Mama Yemo Hospital were tested for HIV-1 antibody. The HIV-1 seroprevalence rate increased from 6.4 percent in 1984 to 7.8 percent in 1986. During that time, 41 persons in the original cohort were known to have died, of whom 11 were known to have died from AIDS. Information was not available on the remaining 30 persons. Between 1984 and 1986, there were 56 additional new infections, for a 2-year incidence of 3.7 percent. Incidence figures did not vary significantly by employment category within the hospital.

Of the asymptomatic seroprevalent cases in 1984, 16.3 percent developed HIV-1-induced clinical manifestations, 3.3 percent developed AIDS, and 12 percent presumably died from AIDS during the 2-year period. Except for the higher mortality rate, these progression rates are similar to those documented in cohort studies within the United States (Jaffe et al., 1985; Curran et al., 1985). Additional studies are clearly needed for a better understanding of the natural history of HIV-1 infection in Africa and of the role of cofactors that might influence disease progression. For example, it has been postulated that endemic infectious agents widely prevalent throughout Africa may serve as cofactors in increasing HIV susceptibility and/or disease progression. In one study comparing the serologic evidence of exposure to infectious agents between heterosexual Americans, homosexual Americans, and heterosexual Africans, it was evident that African heterosexuals were similar to American homosexual men in their rates of infection by infectious agents including cytomegalovirus, herpes simplex virus, hepatitis B virus, hepatitis A virus, Epstein-Barr virus, syphilis, and toxoplasmosis, and showed a significantly greater rate than that observed in American heterosexual men (Quinn et al., 1987b).

Immunologic studies also demonstrated a significant elevation of activated (HLA-DR$^+$ and CD3$^+$) lymphocytes and immune complexes in both African heterosexual and U.S. homosexual populations, compared with the U.S. heterosexual population. The immune systems of both African heterosexuals and U.S. homosexual men may be in a chronically activated state as a result of repeated viral and parasitic antigenic exposure and thus be particularly susceptible to HIV-1 infection or disease progression. Prospective studies in different populations should examine the specific impact of these viral, bacterial, and parasitic infections and other antigenic stimuli on the susceptibility to and development of HIV-1 disease.

OTHER HIV INFECTION IN WEST AFRICA*

In 1985, Kanki and colleagues found anti-HIV-1 antibody in prostitutes in Dakar, Senegal, an area in West Africa where AIDS had not been previously reported (Barin et al., 1985; Kanki et al., 1985a). By radioimmunoprecipitation, these Senegalese sera reacted more strongly with a retrovirus from an African green monkey

*See also Chapter 1.

referred to as SIV_{agm} than with HIV-1 (Letvin et al., 1983; Hunt et al., 1983; Daniel et al., 1985). These observations led to the search for a new human lentivirus from West Africa. Kanki et al. (1986) isolated a virus provisionally named HTLV-IV from a Senegalese prostitute, and this virus is clearly much more closely related serologically and genetically to SIV_{agm} than to HIV-1.

Clavel et al. (1986a) also isolated a virus initially named LAV-2 (renamed HIV-2) from patients with AIDS-like symptoms in Guinea-Bissau and Cape Verde Island in West Africa. HIV-2 is also more closely related to SIV_{agm} than to HIV-1. Genomic analysis has indicated that HIV-1 and HIV-2 have a similar genomic organization, indicating a common evolutionary origin, but differ significantly in their nucleotide and amino acid sequences (Guyader et al., 1987). The more conserved *gag* and *pol* genes, respectively, displayed a 56 and 66 percent nucleotide sequence homology and less than 60 percent amino acid identity. The calculation of the nucleotide sequence homology for the other viral genes gives even lower values, making HIV-1 and HIV-2 42 percent homologous overall (Clavel et al., 1986b). This confirms that these two viruses are distinct members of the HIV family and cannot be considered strains of the same virus, according to the recommendations of the International Taxonomy Committee.

HIV-2, although serologically cross-reactive with SIV_{agm}, has been shown to have distinct differences. Clavel et al. (1987) recently reported on the clinical, immunologic, virologic data on 30 patients with HIV-2 infection, of whom 17 had AIDS, four had related clinical findings, one had diffuse lymphadenopathy, two had other clinical problems, and six were asymptomatic. The most frequent clinical presentations of HIV-2 were chronic diarrhea (14 patients) and severe weight loss (13 patients). Common infections diagnosed in HIV-2 patients were similar to opportunistic infections seen in HIV-1 patients, including *Isospora belli, Cryptosporidium, M. tuberculosis,* aspergillosis, and *Pneumocystis carinii* pneumonia. Four HIV-2-infected patients had Kaposi's sarcoma, four had diffuse lymphadenopathy, one had cerebral lymphoma, and one had acute encephalitis. Thus the clinical spectrum of HIV-1 and HIV-2 infections appear to be quite similar.

Unfortunately, very little is known about the epidemiology of these related human retroviruses (Marlink and Essex, 1987). The serological diagnosis of HIV-2 is difficult, since antibodies to HIV-2 occasionally cross-react with HIV-1. Natural-history studies on HIV-2 infection have been limited by the lack of effective serologic assays and confusion regarding the classification of these retroviruses. With the development of better serologic assays, the spread of the virus into other areas, including other parts of Africa, Europe, and the United States, will need to be assessed by large-scale prospective seroepidemiologic studies (Gurtler et al., 1987). However, it is apparent that HIV-2, a virus related to yet distinct from HIV-1, is the cause of AIDS in some West Africans.

PREVENTION AND CONTROL OF HIV-1 IN AFRICA

With estimates of several million HIV-1-infected people in Africa, it is evident that the AIDS virus has created a major health problem in that continent. Nearly 25 percent of adult and 10 percent of pediatric inpatients in several hospitals in central Africa are HIV-1-seropositive (Quinn et al., 1986), and other infectious diseases endemic in Africa may potentiate expression of the virus through T-cell activation, resulting in exacerbation of HIV-1 disease (Quinn et al., 1987; Marlink and Essex, 1987). In addition, the morbidity and mortality caused by other infectious diseases may increase as a result of underlying immunosuppression induced by HIV-1 infection.

Control of HIV-1 infection has become a public health priority in many countries of the world. With the lack of an effective vaccine, or curative treatment within the near future, prevention is the only effective means to control HIV-1 infection in AIDS. Major routes of spread are heterosexual transmission, blood transfusions, contaminated needles, and perinatal transmission, and each of these modes must be dealt with effectively in any control program. However, prevention of HIV-1 infection in Africa will be exceedingly complex, given the general social, political, and economic context of modern Africa and for reasons related to many of the factors that may have facilitated HIV-1 transmission (Quinn et al., 1986). The rapid urbanization in many parts of Africa has resulted in economic and sociologic change that has influenced behavior and affected the health infrastructure. Consequently, public health officials cannot immediately upgrade blood transfusion services to prevent HIV-1 infection, if the proposed intervention is likely to cost, per person, approximately 10 to 30 times the annual per-capita public health budget. Similarily, reuse of disposable injection equipment cannot be prevented when many hospital budgets are insufficient for the purchase of antibiotics.

To meet this challenge and in respose to recent data on the AIDS epidemic, the World Health Organization's Special Program on AIDS, along with representatives from 45 African countries, has developed a plan of action for the prevention and control of AIDS (WHO, 1986c). This plan has recommended that member nations first create a national AIDS committee or task force to bring together representatives from health, social services, education, and other relevant sectors. The committee would develop and implement details of the national strategies. Member states, with WHO technical and financial support, would undertake (1) initial assessments of prevalence of HIV-1 infection through seroepidemiologic studies along with the evaluation of existing resources; (2) strengthening of the health infrastructure in order to support AIDS-related epidemiological, laboratory, clinical, and prevention activities; (3) programs of education and information on AIDS and its prevention directed to the general public, high-risk groups in the population, and health care workers at all levels; and (4) exchange of information including the reporting of AIDS cases.

These national AIDS programs will emphasize prevention of HIV-1 transmission. Based on epidemiologic information about modes of transmission, prevention of sexual transmission must translate to reduced number of sexual partners and increased use of condoms. Motivating such changes in behavior will require creative approaches. Similarly, changes in medical practices, including traditional practices, may be required to reduce transmission risks associated with injections, scarifications, and blood transfusions. Interruption of perinatal transmission may require screening of women of childbearing age and counseling regarding contraception for HIV-1-seropositive women. These fundamental issues of social psychological concerns such as sexual behavior, illness behavior, and procreation are complex and vary from one subculture to another. On this level, the challenges for

AIDS prevention in Africa and in the developed world are similar. The major difference is economic. No individual nation in Africa has the resources required to build and sustain the epidemiologic, laboratory, clinical, and prevention activities outlined above. Therefore, WHO, which has the mandate to coordinate and direct international health, has offered to coordinate an international effort to control AIDS, providing financial, scientific, educational, and technical support to African countries.

Control of HIV-1 by Sexual Transmission

It is estimated that in 1987, 75 to 80 percent of all new HIV-1 infections in Africa were acquired through sexual activities. Even if partially effective education leading to changes in sexual behavior should have a significant impact on the further spread of HIV-1, it could also contribute to control of other sexually transmitted diseases, which may enhance the transmissibility of HIV-1. Thus, an effective program to prevent the transmission of sexually transmitted diseases would have multiple beneficial effects.

The most important target groups for modification of sexual behavior are individuals exhibiting high-risk behavior and their sexual partners. Depending on the area, this may in practice mean all sexually active men and women, but particularly persons with sexually transmitted diseases, prostitutes, barmaids, and adolescents. A community-based approach to STD control for prostitutes and promiscuous individuals with establishment of area health committees selected by target group members is usually an effective and acceptable method to the group at risk (Ngugi et al., 1987). A monogamous relationship between seronegative individuals, or the use of condoms between partners of unknown serologic status, should help prevent the further sexual transmission of HIV-1. Women must persuade men to use condoms, and men must take the responsibility of using condoms to protect themselves and their partners.

Control of HIV-1 Transmission by Blood Transfusions

In Africa, blood transfusions are probably the second most important route of HIV-1 transmission, accounting for up to 10 percent of infection in adults and up to 30 percent in children. An HIV-1-free blood supply is feasible with available technology and has an immediate impact on the spread of AIDS. Major drawbacks have been cost and the logistic problems involved in setting up blood bank screening infrastructures. In addition, patient expectations and the medical overuse of blood transfusions contribute unnecessarily to the potential spread of HIV-1 through transfusions. In a recent review of transfusion practices in a large public hospital in central Africa, over 90 percent of transfusions to adult patients involved only a single unit of blood. In an analysis of indications for blood transfusions in children, over 70 percent of transfusions in one large hospital were for anemia associated with malaria. Indications for transfusion for malaria are a particularly difficult problem in areas of Africa where that disease is highly endemic. However, an intensive program to educate physicians about the risk of HIV-1 transmission through transfusions and the development of stringent criteria for prescribing transfusions should result in a dramatic decrease in the number of blood transfusions. Thus, educational programs linked with the increased availability of rapid diagnostic assays (Carlson et al., 1987; Quinn et al., 1988) should be effective in preventing HIV-1 transmission through blood transfusions.

Control of HIV-1 Transmission by Injections

HIV-1 infection is not easily transmitted via subdermal or intramuscular needle sticks, as documented from studies on needle-stick exposure in North America and Europe, but considering the extent of exposure to injections in some populations in Africa, the frequent exposure to contamined needles and syringes may result in a substantial number of HIV-1 infections. The potential importance of HIV-1 transmission by needles reflects several cultural factors that merit emphasis. Patients often express a strong preference for parenteral rather than oral therapy. For example, in a survey of 50 mothers in Kinshasa, 84 percent expressed the belief that parenteral medication is more effective than oral medication. Injections as well as scarifications may be administered in clinics or nonmedical sites by personnel inadequately trained in aseptic technique. Financial and other practical constraints also lead to reuse of disposable equipment and to insufficient sterilization of needles and instruments. In contrast, the lack of association between HIV-1 seropositivity and childhood vaccination probably reflects the wider use of properly sterilized injection equipment and immunization programs, relatively small numbers of vaccinations received per child, and the general absence of traditional healers in vaccination programs.

Prevention of HIV-1 transmission through injections is theoretically feasible by using disposable needles and syringes. However, this may be too costly in many countries and even result in further dissemination of improper injection practices. Health workers should be intensively trained to minimize the number of injections and to sterilize reusable needles and syringes properly. Health education programs should carefully inform the population about the risk of HIV-1 transmission through contaminated needles and other skin-piercing instruments without eroding confidence in the immunization and medical programs.

Control of HIV-1 Perinatal Transmission

Preventing perinatal transmission of HIV-1 infection requires prevention of HIV-1 infection in women of childbearing age and counseling on contraception for HIV-1 seropositive women. This delicate problem calls for multidisciplinary counseling and education involving physicians, nurses, midwives, other health workers, and social workers. Prevention may further depend on repeated campaigns to recruit men and women who are considering becoming parents into voluntary testing and counseling programs.

THE FUTURE

The AIDS problem in Africa is already severe. In areas where more than 10 percent of the population appear to be infected, the toll of disease and death in the next decade or so will be enormous if the infection manifests a natural history similar to that seen in the United States. The impact on maternally acquired infection on child mortality rates may be profound. In West Africa, where HIV-1 is less common, it is less clear whether the more prevalent second AIDS virus, HIV-2, will have the same force of morbidity.

AIDS threatens the economic and social development and even the political stability of Africa, because it affects primarily young people between 20 and 40 years old, the age group that contributes most to national development. Perinatally transmitted AIDS may also potentiate the many health problems that already affect the survival of Africa's children.

Thus the most urgent priority is to implement comprehensive national AIDS programs to prevent the further spread of infection; virtually all countries are already collaborating with WHO's Special Program on AIDS and also receiving support from bilateral assistance agencies.

There are still many gaps in our general understanding of AIDS in Africa, and careful, systematic research must fill those gaps. There is a need to define the size of the problem in different geographical areas through serosurveys of representative samples of the population. Research is needed to clarify the dynamics of transmission and the possible role of intercurrent infections or other cofactors in increasing the risk of infection or of disease. However, the most pressing need is for research directed toward development of effective control measures. Such research must include studies of patterns of sexual behavior and evaluation of the efficacy of health education interventions. Ultimately the modification of African political, social, and cultural commitment and resources will be the decisive factor in the struggle against HIV-1 infection and its consequences.

REFERENCES

Anonymous (1987): Lancet, 1:192
Aral SO, Holmes KK (1984): Sexually Transmitted Diseases. New York: McGraw-Hill, p 127.
Barin F, M'Boup S, Denis F, Kanki P, Allan JS, Lee TH, Essex M (1985): Lancet 2:1387.
Bayley AC (1983): Lancet 1:1318.
Bayley AC, Downing RG, Cheingsong-Popov R, et al. (1985): Lancet 1:359.
Biggar RJ (1986): Lancet 1:79.
Biggar RJ, Bouvet E, Ebbesen P, et al. (1984): Eur J Cancer Clin Oncol 20:165.
Biggar RJ, Gigase PL, Melbye M (1985): Lancet 2:520.
Braddick M, Kreiss JK, Quinn TC, Ndinya-Achola JO, Vercauteren G, Plummer FA (1987): Third International Conference on AIDS, Washington, D.C., TH7.5, p 158.
Brun-Vezinet F (1985): International Symposium on African AIDS, Brussels, Belgium.
Brun-Vezinet F, Rouzioux C, Montagnier L, Chamaret S, Gruest J, Mitchell S, Piot P, Quinn TC (1985): Science 226:453.
Brunet JB, Ancelle RA (1985): Ann Intern Med 103:670.
Brunet JB, Bouvet E, Leibowitch J (1983): Lancet 1:700.
Bygbjerg IC (1983): Lancet 1:925.
Cameron DW, Plummer FA, Simonsen JN, Ndinya-Achola JO, D'Costa LJ, Piot P (1987): Third International Conference on AIDS, Washington, D.C., MP91, p 25.

Carlson JR, Mertens SC, Yee JL, Gardner MB, Watson-Williams EJ, Ghrayeb J, Jennings MB, Biggar RJ (1987): Lancet 1:361.

Centers for Disease Control (1986): MMWR 34:227.

Centers for Disease Control (1987): MMWR 36:285.

Clavel F, Guetard D, Brun-Vezinet F, Chamaret S, Rey MA, Santos-Ferreira MO, Laurent AG, Dauguet C, Katlama C, Rouzioux C (1986a): Science 233:343.

Clavel F, Guyader M, Guetard D, Salle M, Montagnier L, Alizon M (1986b): Nature 324:691.

Clavel F, Mansinho K, Chamaret S, Guetard D, Favier V, Nina J, Santos-Ferreria MO, Champalimaud JL, Montagnier L (1987): N Engl J Med 316:1180.

Clumeck N, Mascart-Lemone F, De Maulbeuge J, Brenez D, Marcelis L (1983): Lancet 1:642.

Clumeck N, Sonnet J, Taelman H, Mascart-Lemone F, De-Bruyers M, Van de Perre P, Dasnoy J, Marcelis L, Lamy M, Jonas C, Robert-Guroff M (1984): N Engl J Med 310:492.

Clumeck N, Van de Perre P, Carael M (1985a): N Engl J Med 311:182.

Clumeck N, Robert-Guroff M, Van de Perre P, Jennings A, Sibomana J, Demol P, Cran S, Gallo RC (1985b): JAMA 254:2599.

Colebunders R, Mann J, Francis H, Kapita B, Ndangi K, Lusadumunu K, Lebughe I, Piot P (1986): Med Mal Infect 15:350.

Colebunders R, Francis H, Mann JM, Bila KM, Izaley L, Kimputu L, Behets F, Vander-Groen G, Quinn TC, Curran JW (1987a): Am J Gastroenterol 82:859.

Colebunders R, Greenberg A, Nguyen-Dinh P, Francis H, Kaboti N, Izaley L, Davichi F, Baudoux P, Embonge B, Quinn TC, Piot P (1987b): Third International Conference on AIDS, Washington, D.C., TP139, p 85.

Colebunders R, Mann JM, Francis H, Kapita B, Lebughe I, Ndangi K, Kanyinda K, Limbaka I, Nzila N, Quinn TC, Van der Groen G, Curran JW, Vercauteren G, Piot P (1987c): Lancet 1:492.

Colebunders R, Mann JM, Francis H, Kapita B, Lebughe I, Ndange K, Hood AF, Quinn TC, Ngandu K, Gigase P, Van Marck E, Vercauteren G, Curran JW, Piot P (1987d): AIDS 1:117.

Curran JW, Morgan, WM, Hardy, AM, Jaffe HW, Darrow WW, Dowdle WR (1985): Science 229:1352.

Daniel MD, Letvin NL, King NW, Kannagi M, Sehgal PK, Hunt RD, Kanki PJ, Essex M, Desrosiers RC (1985): Science 228:1201.

DeCock KM, Nzilambi N, Fortnah D, Ryder R, Piot P, McCormick JB (1987): Third International Conference on AIDS, Washington, D.C., WP43, p 117.

DeHovitz JA, Pape JW, Boncy M, Johnson WD (1986): N Engl J Med 315:87.

DeLalla F, Galli M, Ciantia F, Zeli PL, Rizzardi NI, Saracco A (1987): Third International Conference on AIDS, Washington D.C., THP84, p 177.

DeLaporte E, Dazza MC, Wain-Hobson S, Brun-Vezinet F, Larouze B, Saimot AG (1987): Third International Conference on AIDS, Washington, D.C., WP32, p 115.

Denis F, Barin F, Gershy-Damet G, Rey, J-L, Lhuillier M, Mounier M, Leonard G, Sangare A, Goudeau A, M'Boup S, Essex M, Kanki P (1987): Lancet 1:408.

Desmyter J (1984): Lancet 2:336.

Downing RG, Eglin RP, Bayley AC (1984): Lancet 1:475.

Durand JP, Merlin M, Josse R, Garrigue G, Kaptue Noche L (1987): Third International Conference on AIDS, Washington, D.C., WP78, p 123.

Fauci AS, Masur H, Gelman EP, Markham PD, Hahn BH, Lane HC (1985): Ann Intern Med 102:800.

Francis H, Lubaki N, Duma MP, Ryder RW, Mann J, Quinn TC (1987): Third International Conference on AIDS, Washington, D.C., F9.6, p 214.

Georges AJ, Salaun D, Merlin M, Gonzalez JP, Barre-Sinoussi F, Courbot MC (1987): Third International Conference on AIDS, Washington, D.C., WP77, p 123.

Greenberg AE, Sulzer AJ, Schable CA, Collins WE, Nguyen-Dinh P (1986): Lancet 1:247.

Greenberg AE, Nguyen-Dinh P, Mann JM, Kabote N, Colebunders RL, Francis H, Quinn T, Baudoux P, Lyamba B, Davachi F, Roberts JM, Kabeya N, Curran JW, Campbell CC (1988): JAMA 259:545.

Greenblatt RM, Lukehart SL, Plummer FA, Quinn TC, Critchlow CW, D'Costa LJ (1988): AIDS 2:47.

Gurtler LG, Zoulek G, Frosner G, Deinhardt F (1987): Third International Conference on AIDS, Washington, D.C., THP93, p 179.

Guyader M, Emerman M, Sonigo P, Clavel F, Montagnier L, Alizon M (1987): Nature 326:662.

Halsey NA, Henderson DA (1987): N Engl J Med 316:683.

Henry MC, DeClerq D, Lokombe B, Kayembe K, Kapita K, Mamba N, Mbendi N, Mazebo P (1986): Trans R Soc Trop Med Hyg 80:309.

Ho DD, Schooley RT, Rota TR, Kaplan JC, Flynn T, Salahuddin SZ, Gonda MA, Hirsch MS (1984): Science 226:449.

Hunt RD, Blake BJ, Chalifoux LV, Sehgal PK, King NW, Letvin NL (1983): Proc Natl Acad Sci USA 80:5085.

Hutt MS (1981): Antibiot Chemother 29:3.

Institute of Medicine, National Academy of Sciences (1986): Confronting AIDS, Directions for Public Health, Health Care and Research. Washington, D.C.: National Academy Press.

Jaffe HW, Darrow WW, Echenberg DF, O'Malley PM, Getchell JP, Kalyanaraman VS, Byers RH, Drennan DP, Braff EH, Curran JW (1985): Ann Intern Med 103:210.

Jonckheer T, Dab I, Van de Perre P, Lepage P, Dasnoy J, Taelman H (1985): Lancet 1:400.

Kanki PJ, McLane MF, King NW, Letvin NL, Hunter RD, Sehgal P, Daniel MD, Sesrosiers RC, Essex M (1985a): Science 228:1199.

Kanki PJ, Alroy J, Essex M (1985b): Science 230:952.

Kanki PJ, Barin F, M'Boup S, Allan JS, Romet-Lemonne JL, Marlink R, McLane MF, Lee TH, Arbeille B, Denis F (1986): Science 232:238.

Kanki PJ, M'Boup S, Ricard D, Barin F, Denis F, Boye C, Sangare L, Travers K, Albaum M, Marlink R, Romet-Lemonne JL, Essex M (1987): Science 236:827.

Kornfeld H, Riedel N, Viglianti GA, Hirsch V, Mullins JI (1987): Nature 326:610.

Kreiss JK, Koech D, Plummer FA, Holmes KK, Lightfoote M, Piot R, Ronald AR, Ndinya-Achola JO, D'Costa LJ, Roberts P, Ngugi EN, Quinn TC (1986): N Engl J Med 314:414.

Kuhnl P, Seidl S, Holzberger G (1985): Lancet 1:1222.

LaForce FM (1987): Eur J Clin Microbiol 6:613.

Lapointe N, Michaud J, Pekovic D, Chausseau JP, Dupuy JM (1985): N Engl J Med 312:1325.

Letvin NL, Eaton KA, Aldrich WR, Sehgal PK, Blake BJ, Schlossman SF, King NW, Hunt RD (1983): Proc Natl Acad Sci 80:27718.

Lesbordes JL, Chassignol S, Ray E, Manaud F, Siopathis MR, Salaun D, Georges MC, Bouquetz JC, Georges AJ (1986): Lancet 2:337.

Liskin L (1986): Population Rep 14:L193.

Malebranche R, Arnoux E, Grerin JM, Pierre GD, Karoche AC, Pean-Guichard C, Elie R, Morisett PH, Spira T, Manderike R (1983): Lancet 2:873.

Mann JM, Francis H, Quinn TC, Pangu KA, Ngaly B, Nzila N, Kapita B, Muymbe T, Kalisa R, Piot P, McCormick J, Curran JW (1986a): JAMA 255:3255.

Mann JM, Quinn TC, Francis H, Nzilambi N, Bosenge N, Bila K, McCormick JB, Ruti K, Asila PK, Curran JW (1986b): JAMA 256:721.

Mann JM, Quinn TC, Francis H, Miatudila M, Piot P, Curran J (1986c): Second International Conference on AIDS, Paris, S17e, p 105.

Mann JM, Francis H, Quinn TC, Bila K, Asila PK, Bosenge N, Nzilambi N, Jansegers L, Piot P, Ruti K, Curran JW (1986d): JAMA 256:3099.

Mann JM, Francis H, Davachi F, Baudoux P, Quinn TC, Nzilambi N, Colebunders RL, Curran JW (1986e): Pediatrics 78:673.

Mann JM, Francis H, Davachi F, Baudoux P, Quinn TC, Nzila N, Ngaly B, Colebunders RL, Piot P, Ndoko K, Pangu KA, Miatudila M, Curran JW (1986f): Lancet 2:654.

Mann JM, Kapita B, Colebunders RL, Kapela K, Nolangi K, Ngali B, Nzila N, Miatudila M, Jansegers L, Francis H, McCormick JB, Piot P, Quinn TC, Curran JW (1986g): Lancet 2:707.

Mann JM, Snider DE, Francis H, Quinn TC, Colebunders RL, Piot P, Curran JW, Nzilambi N, Bagala N (1986h): JAMA 256:346.

Mann JM, Quinn TC, Piot P, Ngaly B, Nzilambi N, KaLala M (1987): N Engl J Med 316:345 (Correspondence).

Marlink R, Essex M (1987): JAMA 257:2632.

Marquart K-H, Muller HAG, Sailer J, Moser R (1985): Lancet 2:186.

Melbye M, Njelesani EK, Bayley A, Mukelabai K, Manuwele JK, Bowa FJ, Clayden SA, Levin A, Blattner WA, Weiss RA, Tedder R, Biggar RJ (1986): Lancet 2:1113.

Merlin M, Josse R, Delaporte E, Durand JP, Hengy C, Georges AJ (1987): Third International Conference on AIDS, Washington, D.C. M8.1, p 5.

Mhalu F, Mbena E, Bredberg-Raden U, Kiango J, Nuamuryekunge K, Biberfeld G (1987): Third International Conference on AIDS, Washington, D.C., M3.6, p 2.

Nahmias AJ, Weiss J, Yao X, Lee F, Kodsi R, Schanfield M, Matthews T, Bolognesi D, Durack D, Motulsky A (1986): Lancet 1:1279.

Ngaly B, Ryder RW, Kapita B, Francis H, Quinn T, Mann JM (1987): Third International Conference on AIDS, Washington, D.C., M3.6, p 2.

Ngugi EN, Plummer FA, Cameron DW, Bosire M, Ndinya-Achola JO (1987): Third International Conference on AIDS, Washington, D.C., TH5.5, p 157.

Nguyen-Dinh P, Greenberg AE, Mann JE, Kabote N, Francis H, Colebunders RL, Huong AY, Quinn T, Davachi F, Lyamba B, Kalemba K, Embonga B (1987): Bull WHO 65:607.

Nzila N, Ryder RW, Behets F, Francis H, Bayende E, Nelson A, Mann JB (1987): Third International Conference on AIDS, Washington, D.C., TH7.6, p 158.

Pape JW, Liautaud B, Thoms F, Mathurin JR, St. Amand MM, Boncy M, Pean V, Pamphile M, Laroche AC, Dehovitz J, Johnson W (1985): Ann Intern Med 103:674.

Petersen HD, Lindhurst BO, Nyarango PM, Bowry T, Chemtai A, Krogsgaad K (1987): Third International Conference on AIDS, Washington, D.C., TP41, p 69.

Piot P, Mann JM (1986): Second International Conference on AIDS, Paris.

Piot P, Quinn TC, Taelman H, Feinsod FM, Minlangu KB, Wobin O, Mbendi N, Mazebo P, Ndangi K, Stevens W, Kayembe K, Mitchell S, Bridts C, McCormick JB (1984): Lancet 2:65.

Piot P, Plummer FA, Rey MA, Ngugi EN, Rouzioux C, Ndinya-Achola JO, Vercauteren G, D'Costa LJ, Laga M, Nsanze H, Fransen L, Haase D, van der Groen G, Ronald AR, Brun-Vezinet F (1987): J Infect Dis 155:1108.

Piot P, Kreiss JK, Ndinya-Achola JO, Ngugi E, Simonsen JN, Cameron DW, Taelman H, Plummer FA (1987): AIDS 1:199.

Plummer FA, Simonsen JN, Ngugi EN, Cameron DW, Piot P, Ndinya-Achola JO (1987): Third International Conference on AIDS, Washington, D.C., M8.4, p 6.

Quinn TC (1987): NY State J Med 87:286.

Quinn TC, Mann JM, Curran JW, Piot P (1986): Science 234:955.

Quinn TC, Piot P, McCormick JB, Feinsod FM, Taelman H, Kupita B, Fauci AS (1987): JAMA 257:2617.

Quinn TC, Riggin CH, Kline RL, Francis H, Mulanga K, Sension MG, Fauci AS (1988): JAMA 260:510.

Redfield RR, Wright DC, James WD, Jones TS, Brown C, Burke DS (1987): N Engl J Med 326:673.

Rogers MF (1985): Pediatr Infect Dis 4:230.

Safai B, Good RA (1980): Clin Bull 10:52.

Saxinger WC, Levine PH, Dean AG (1984): Science 225:1473.

Sension MG, Nzila N, Duma M, Ryder R, Quinn TC, Linnan M (1987): Third International Conference on AIDS, Washington, D.C., THP159, p 190.

Serwadda D, Mugerwa RD, Sewankambo NK, Lwegaba A, Carswell JW, Kirya GB, Bayley AC, Downing RG, Tedder RS, Clayden SA, Weiss RA, Dalgleish AG (1985): Lancet 2:849.

Sewankambo N, Mugerwa RD, Goodgame R, Carswell JW, Moody A, Lloyd G, Luca SB (1986): AIDS 1:9.

Sher R, Antunes E, Reid B, Falcke H (1987): Third International Conference on AIDS, Washington, D.C., MP42, p 17.

Sonnet J, DeBruyere M (1983): Louvain Med 102:297.

Sonnet J, Taelman H (1986): Clinical Aspects of AIDS and AIDS-Related Complex. Oxford, U.K.: Oxford University Press.

Taelman H, Dasnoy J, Van Marck E, Eyckmans L (1983): Ann Soc Belge Med Trop 63:73.

Taylor JF, Templeton AC, Vogel CC (1971): Int J Cancer 8:122.

U.S. Public Health Service (1986): Public Health Rep 101:341.

Van de Perre P, Rouvroy D, Lepage P, Bogaerts J, Kestelyn P, Kayihigi J, Hekker AC, Butzler JP, Clumeck N (1984): Lancet 2:62.

Van de Perre P, Munyambuga D, Zissis G, Butlzer JP, Nzaramba D, Clumeck N (1985a): Lancet 1:336.

Van de Perre P, Clumeck N, Carael M, Nzabihimana E, Robert-Guroff M, DeMol P, Freyens P, Butzler JP, Gallo RC, Kanyamupira JB (1985b): Lancet 2:524.

Vandepitte J, Verwilghen R, Zachee P (1983): Lancet 1:925.

Vogt MW, Witt DJ, Craven DE, Hirsch MS (1986): Lancet 1:525.

Von Reyn CF, Clements CJ, Mann JM (1987): Lancet 2:669.

Weiss SH, Mann DL, Murray C, Popovic M (1985): Lancet 2:157.

WHO Collaborating Center on AIDS, AIDS Surveillance in Europe (1986): Paris: WHO, Report 9.

Wofsy CB, Cohen JB, Hauer LB, Padian NS, Michaelis BA, Evans LA, Levy JA (1986): Lancet 1:527.

World Health Organization (1986a): Weekly Epidemiol Rec 61:69.

World Health Organization (1986b): Weekly Epidemiol Rec 61:72.

World Health Organization (1986c): Weekly Epidemiol Rec 61:93.

World Health Organization (1986d): Weekly Epidemiol Rec 61:125.

Zagury D, Bernard J, Leibowitch J (1984): Science 226:449.

Ziegler JB, Cooper DA, Johnson RO, Gold J (1985): Lancet 1:896.

Zuckerman AJ (1986): Br Med J 292:1094.

12

HIV-1 Infection and AIDS in Haiti

JEAN W. PAPE AND WARREN D. JOHNSON, Jr.

EARLY EXPERIENCE

Since the first recognition of cases of AIDS in Haiti in the late 1970s (Pape et al., 1983; Malebranche et al., 1983), the number of cases has continued to increase (Table 12.1). The first patient with Kaposi's sarcoma (KS) was diagnosed in June 1979, and the first patient with an opportunistic infection was seen in February 1980. In 1983, 21 practicing dermatologists and pathologists in Haiti were surveyed about their past experience with Kaposi's sarcoma. The only patient recognized by these physicians was a 54-year-old man with Kaposi's sarcoma documented by biopsy in 1972, but the course of his illness is not known. Two early reviews of cancer biopsies gave negative results. The first, a review of records of cancer biopsies from three private hospitals in Port-au-Prince with a combined total of 180 beds, revealed no recorded cases of KS during the period from 1968 to 1983. The second, a review of the records of over 1,000 cancer biopsies at the Albert Schweitzer Hospital in Deschapelles, a hospital that serves a rural population of 115,000 persons (Berggren et al., 1981), likewise revealed no recorded cases of KS during the same period. A review of autopsy records in that hospital from 1978 to July 1982 failed to uncover any cases of KS, but a review of hospital records disclosed a previously healthy 20-year-old man who had generalized seizures in July 1978 and died 2 weeks later. At autopsy he was found to have central nervous system toxoplasmosis without evidence of underlying cancer or history of immunosuppressive therapy. He is the earliest known patient with possible AIDS in Haiti (Pape et al., 1983).

In a search for antibodies to HIV-1 in one set of stored sera, none of 191 adults bled in Haiti during a 1977–1979 outbreak of dengue (Pape et al., 1987a,b) were positive by EIA (whole virus) or by a radioimmunoprecipitation assay (RIPA) for antibody to the p24 and gp 120 HIV-1 antigens. These findings and the aforementioned epidemiological data have led to the conclusion that AIDS probably did not exist in Haiti before 1978. Appearance at that time coincides with the earliest reports of AIDS in the United States and is over 20 years after an HIV-1-seropositive person was identified in Africa (Nahmias et al., 1986). In addition, no Haitian with AIDS and a history of previous travel to Africa has been identified. In contrast, 10 to 15 percent of Haitian AIDS patients seen in the major AIDS clinic had

Table 12.1. AIDS Cases Diagnosed by the
Haitian Study Group on Kaposi's Sarcoma
and Opportunistic Infection

Year	Kaposi's sarcoma	Opportunistic infection	Total
1979	2	0	2
1980	2	5	7
1981	7	9	16
1982	5	35	40
1983	8	53	61
1984	11	103	114
1985	8	136	144
1986	10	160	170
Total	53	501	554

traveled to either the United States or Europe during the 5 years prior to the onset of their illness. Haiti also has been popular among French- and English-speaking tourists, including homosexual men. These data and studies from Africa (Quinn et al., 1986) are consistent with the hypothesis that HIV-1 originated in that continent, came to the United States and Europe, and was subsequently introduced into Haiti by either tourists or returning Haitians.

There is in Haiti neither a national reporting system nor a data base similar to that collated by the U.S. Centers for Disease Control, and the incidence of AIDS in Haiti is not known. Table 12.1 indicates the number of AIDS cases annually diagnosed by the Haitian Study Group on Kaposi's Sarcoma and Opportunistic Infection (GHESKIO) (Pape et al., 1987b) in Port-au-Prince since 1979. It is of note that 57 percent of the 554 cases were diagnosed in 1985–1986. These data cannot be used to estimate the rate of increase in AIDS cases in the country as a whole, since patients were primarily from Port-au-Prince, and increased numbers of patients may have sought care or been referred as GHESKIO's interest in AIDS became known.

AIDS AND PREVALENCE OF HIV-1 INFECTION

As part of a case control study to determine risk factors for transmission of HIV-1, 384 AIDS patients, 174 of their heterosexual sex partners, and 244 of their siblings and friends were evaluated in 1984–1985 (Table 12.2). The seroprevalence rate was identical, 96 percent, by EIA (whole virus) and RIPA (p24, gp 120) for the 278 male and 106 female AIDS patients. Among the group of 136 sex-matched siblings, 17 percent were seropositive—19 percent of the males and 14 percent of females. None of the siblings were homosexual, and none had been transfused. The seroprevalence of HIV-1 was 19 percent in the 108 sex-matched friends with no sexual relationship to the patient. Twenty-six percent of the male friends were seropositive, whereas all of the females were seronegative. Homosexual practices were reported by only 5 percent of the male friends, all of whom were seropositive. Two percent of the male and 3 percent of the female friends had received blood trans-fusions during the preceding 5 years, but none were HIV-1-seropositive. Finally, 55 percent of the sera from 174 regular sex partners or spouses of the AIDS patients were positive for HIV-1 antibody. The seroprevalence rates were comparable for male and female sex partners—61 percent and 54 percent, respectively. Only 3 per-cent and 6 percent of male and female spouses, respectively, had received a trans-fusion, and neither homosexual practices nor IV drug abuse was reported by either group.

Sera from a number of Haitian population groups unrelated to the case control study sample have been analyzed for antibody to HIV-1. Sera were obtained from urban and rural groups. In two groups of apparently healthy urban adults—hotel and factory workers (Table 12.3)—seroprevalence rates were 12 percent and 5 per-cent, respectively. Rates were comparable for males and females. In a group of 502 mothers of children hospitalized with diarrhea and in a group of 190 urban adults with comparable socioeconomic backgrounds, the seroprevalence rates were 12 percent and 13 percent, respectively. All of a sample of 57 health workers involved in the care of AIDS patients were seronegative. Overall, 10 percent of 912 healthy urban adults (medical workers, college graduates, factory and hotel workers, moth-ers of sick infants, and other adults) were seropositive to HIV-1. In an area more distant from urban centers, 1 percent of 191 adults present for immunizations were seropositive.

Eight percent of sera obtained from 1,037 adults bled during the first 6 months of 1986 by three commercial laboratories in Port-au-Prince were also positive for HIV-1 antibody (Table 12.3) (Pape et al., 1987b). The sera were not obtained for the purpose of HIV-1 testing but rather were "left over" after other recommended tests were performed. The health status of these persons was not recorded, but since none of the three laboratories perform HIV-1 serologic tests, persons were not being bled for that purpose. These sera represent about 10 percent of the total num-ber of persons bled for serum by the three laboratories during that period. Of 241

Table 12.2. Prevalence of HIV-1 Antibody in AIDS Patients, Family Members, Friends, and Sex Partners/Spouses

| | | Males | | | Females | | Total | |
| | | | | | | | HIV-I antibody | |
Group	n	Mean age (years)	HIV-1 antibody (%)	n	Mean age (years)	HIV-1 antibody (%)	No	%
AIDS patients	278	34	96	106	31	96	369/384	96
Siblings[a]	86	29	19	50	29	14	23/136	17
Friends[b]	82	30	26	26	29	0	21/108	19
Sex partners/ spouses[c]	38	36	61	136	30	54	96/174	55

[a]Same-sex siblings of AIDS patients, matched for age within 5 years.

[b]Same-sex friends of AIDS patients, with no sexual relationship to the patient, matched for age within 5 years.

[c]Heterosexual sex partners of AIDS patients included 38 male sex partners/spouses of female AIDS patients and 136 sex partners/spouses of male AIDS patients.

Table 12.3. HIV-1 Seroprevalence in Haiti

Group[a]	n	Mean age (years)	HIV-1 (%)
Medical workers	57	40	0
College graduates	54	35	0
Blood donors			
Rural	245	32	4
Factory workers	84	30	5
Leprosy patients	157	40	5
Lab specimens			
Lab A	353	38	6
Lab B	188	37	8
Lab C	496	36	9
Total	1,037	37	8
Other adults[b]			
Urban	190	33	13
Rural	191	29	1
Hotel workers	25	45	12
Mothers of sick infants			
Urban	502	29	12
Rural	97	25	3
Tuberculosis pts.			
Urban	129	32	45
Rural	112	34	15
Prostitutes	139	24	53

[a]All persons lived in Port-au-Prince unless identified as "rural." Rural subjects were bled in either hospitals or clinics ≥ 75 miles from Port-au-Prince. "Urban" refers to Port-au-Prince.
[b]Low socioeconomic group.

patients with active tuberculosis, 31 percent were HIV-1-seropositive, with higher rates in the urban (45 percent) than in the rural (15 percent) patients (Table 12.3). The seroprevalence in leprosy patients was lower (5 percent) than that in the normal adult population. The highest rate observed was in the Haitian prostitutes (53 percent). Collectively, these data indicate that HIV-1 infection is widespread and is more prevalent in urban areas and in lower socioeconomic groups.

MODES OF TRANSMISSION

In the United States, over 95 percent of non-Haitian AIDS patients report either homosexuality, transfusion, or IV drug abuse. In contrast, these risk factors have been reported in less than 15 percent of both Haitian-American and African patients. The initial observations in Haiti were largely retrospective and identified these factors in less than 20 percent of AIDS patients seen prior to 1983 (Pape et al., 1983). Prospective studies in 1983 identified potential risk factors in 74 percent of patients (Table 12.4) (Pape et al., 1986). Since then there has been a progressive *decrease* in the percent of patients reporting bisexuality and blood transfusions and an *increase* in those reporting a spouse with antecedent AIDS, a history of prostitution, or none of the aforementioned activities. In 1986, only 11 percent of the

170 male and female AIDS patients reported either bisexuality, blood transfusions, or IV drug abuse. Heterosexual transmission is assumed in the 16 percent of patients who were prostitutes or had a spouse with AIDS and is the most probable source of the infection in the patients reporting none of the aforementioned. Additional evidence for heterosexual transmission of HIV-1 is the finding that 53 percent of 139 Haitian prostitutes in the Port-au-Prince area were seropositive. Prostitute contact among males was common and reported by 61 percent of the AIDS patients and 40 percent of their siblings and friends. One-half of the male sex partners of female AIDS patients also reported contact with prostitutes.

Another potential mode of transmission of HIV-1 is through the use of contaminated needles. It is a common practice in Haiti for persons to obtain intramuscular injections when they are "not feeling well." The injections are frequently given for nonspecific symptoms (fatigue, malaise, and myalgia) without a specific etiologic diagnosis. The injections may be given by either medical personnel or "piqueristes" (injection givers). Disposable needles and syringes are not readily available in Haiti; both may be reused without sterilization. During the 5-year period before the onset of AIDS symptoms, intramuscular medications were received by 83 percent of male and 88 percent of female AIDS patients (Pape et al., 1985); injections were reported by 66 percent of male and 69 percent of female siblings and friends ($p < .001$). Despite the comparable injection rates, the seroprevalence of HIV-1 was much lower in the female sibling and friends (9 percent vs. 22 percent; Table 12.2), suggesting that factors other than intramuscular injections were responsible for HIV-1 transmission. One of these may be the number of opposite-sex partners. The female siblings and friends had a mean of 1 ± 1 sex partners per year during the preceding 5 years and a seroprevalence of 9 percent, while the male siblings and friends had six or seven opposite-sex partners annually and a seroprevalence of 22 percent. These conclusions are tentative, and further assessment of the role of injections in HIV-1 transmission is needed.

Mosquitoes have been suggested as another potential mode of HIV-1 trans-

Table 12.4. Risk Factors in Haitian AIDS Patients[a] (in percent)

	Year of AIDS diagnosis				
	1983	1984	1985	1986	Total
Bisexual[b]	50	27	8	4	16
Transfusion	23	12	8	7	10
IV drug abuser	<1	1	1	0	1
Heterosexual[c]	5	6	14	16	12
Undetermined	21	54	69	73	61

[a]The number of AIDS cases with complete risk factor data available by year: 1983, 53 patients; 1984, 103; 1985, 131; 1986, 170.

[b]Males engaged in homosexual activities uniformly characterize themselves as being bisexual rather than exclusively homosexual.

[c]The category "heterosexual" includes persons who accepted money for sex (prostitutes) and persons whose spouse had a diagnosis of AIDS prior to onset of their illness.

mission (see Chapter 6). *Plasmodium falciparum* infection is endemic in Haiti, with prevalence rates of 5 to 40 percent in some areas. In 154 persons examined for the presence of antibody to HIV-1 and *P. falciparum,* 112 were HIV-1-seropositive and 22 were definitely positive by indirect fluorescent antibody testing for *P. falciparum* (Johnson et al., 1987). There was no correlation between the presence of antibodies to HIV-1 and antibodies to the malaria parasite. Within the families of AIDS patients, children aged 5 to 13 have almost invariably been HIV-1-seronegative despite experiencing frequent transmission of malaria. Serologic data from Haiti, like the recent detailed studies by the CDC in Florida (CDC, 1986), provide no evidence for an arthropod vector of HIV-1.

CLINICAL FEATURES

The physical appearance of an AIDS patient in Haiti is sufficiently characteristic that the term "maladi mor" has been applied—literally translated it means "illness of death." This designation connotes the prognosis as well as the physical appearance, unlike the African description "slim disease."

Most of the patients referred to AIDS clinics for evaluation have little or no prior medical work-up. Nonetheless, the syndrome is so easily recognized that only 16 percent of patients are subsequently found to have illnesses unrelated to AIDS. A classification scheme has been useful in depicting the spectrum of HIV-1 infection in Haiti (Pape et al., 1987c). By that scheme, 339 HIV-1-seropositive patients referred to the AIDS clinic from July 1983 to June 1985 were classified and their condition assessed 1 year later (Table 12.5). AIDS was previously diagnosed or was evident (lesions of Kaposi's sarcoma) in 11 percent of patients at their initial evaluation. All other patients were placed in six groups based on their major symptoms or findings. Patients in group 1 were asymptomatic and referred because of known exposure to HIV-1. Group 2 patients had intensely pruritic skin lesions (prurigo) alone. Group 3 patients had lymphadenopathy in at least two noncontiguous sites.

Table 12.5. Classification of HIV-1 Infection in Haiti

	Number of patients (%)	
Groups	Initial evaluation	One-year evaluation
1. Asymptomatic	7 (2)	3 (1)
2. Prurigo[a]	29 (9)	7 (2)
3. Adenopathy	7 (2)	1 (<1)
4. Oral thrush[b]	48 (14)	36 (11)
5. Weight loss and either fever or diarrhea[c]	209 (62)	27 (8)
6. AIDS	39 (11)	211 (62)
Dead	—	54 (16)

[a]Intensely pruritic skin lesions of $\geq$ 2 months' duration for which neither specific etiologic nor categorical diagnosis can be established.
[b]Alone or with either tuberculosis, salmonellosis, or herpes zoster.
[c]For more than 2 months.

Table 12.6. AIDS: Opportunistic
Pathogens[a] (in percent)

Agents	Haiti	New York[b]
Candida	68	21
Cryptosporidium	48	11
Mycobacterium	31	25
Herpesvirus	16	29
Isospora	16	<1
Cytomegalovirus	8	40
Toxoplasma	7	5
Pneumocystis	7	71
Salmonella	5	5
Cryptococcus	5	8
Aspergillus	2	6

[a]Data from 131 Haitian AIDS patients (1983–84) and
from 80 New York AIDS patients (1981–83).
[b]Roberts et al. (1983).

Group 4 patients had oropharyngeal candidiasis alone (21) or with tuberculosis (18), salmonellosis (5), or herpes zoster (4). Weight loss in excess of 10 percent of body weight was the common finding in group 5 patients and was associated with either fever or diarrhea for $\geq$ 2 months.

The principal difference between this classification and the provisional WHO clinical case definition is the inclusion of prurigo, diffuse lymphadenopathy and, oropharyngeal candidiasis as major signs, which alone suggest AIDS in the absence of other known causes of immunosuppression (CDC, 1987). The validity of the classification is evident in the status of these patients when recategorized 1 year later. At the initial evaluation 11 percent had AIDS, 62 percent of patients were in group 5 (weight loss and either fever or diarrhea), 14 percent were in group 4 (oropharyngeal candidasis alone or with other infections), and 11 percent were in groups 2 or 3 (either prurigo or adenopathy). During the following year 16 percent died, 62 percent had AIDS, and only 21 percent remained in the other groups.

The availability of HIV-1 serologic testing further refines this classification. There were only 66 patients referred during this period (July 1983 to June 1985) who were HIV-1-seronegative and had other diagnoses established—pulmonary tuberculosis (30), extrapulmonary tuberculosis (3), typhoid fever (4), hepatitis (2), giardiasis (2), amoebiasis (2)—and 15 asymptomatic individuals; 25 others were either lost (14) or not followed (11).

The prevalence of the different opportunistic infections in AIDS patients in Haiti differs considerably from that seen in the United States. The frequency of infectious agents in Haitian AIDS patients is contrasted with the experience in New York Hospital–Cornell Medical Center's first 80 AIDS patients (Table 12.6). Oroesophageal candidiasis (68 percent) and cryptosporidiosis (48 percent) were most common in Haiti, whereas *Pneumocystis carinii* pneumonia (71 percent) and cytomegalovirus infection (40 percent) were most common in New York.

Mycobacterial infections were common in both groups, but in New York they were predominantly *M. avium-intracellulare* whereas in Haiti they were almost exclusively due to *M. tuberculosis*. The Haitians had either pulmonary tuberculosis (43 percent), miliary disease (23 percent), or tuberculous lymphadenitis (34 percent). Tuberculosis preceded full-blown AIDS in 25 percent of cases and occurred during the course of AIDS in 72 percent; only 3 percent of patients developed active tuberculosis after the diagnosis of AIDS was established. There was a difference in the type of tuberculosis depending on whether tuberculosis preceded AIDS by more than 2 months or was diagnosed at the same time as (within 2 months of) the diagnosis of AIDS. When tuberculosis preceded AIDS, 52 percent of cases had tuberculous lymphadenitis, 48 percent had pulmonary tuberculosis, and there were no cases of disseminated tuberculosis. In contrast, when tuberculosis occurred at the same time as AIDS, 27 percent of cases had tuberculous lymphadenitis, 42 percent had pulmonary tuberculosis, and 31 percent had disseminated tuberculosis. The high percentage of tuberculous lymphadenitis seen in these patients, particularly when tuberculosis preceded AIDS (52 percent), is in marked contrast to that of HIV-1 antibody-negative adult patients evaluated in a major tuberculosis clinic in Port-au-Prince (5 percent). Hence, Haitian adults with tuberculosis, particularly those with tuberculous lymphadenitis, should be investigated for HIV-1 infection.

Over 95 percent of *M. tuberculosis* strains were sensitive to all antituberculous drugs including isoniazid (INH), and AIDS patients responded to therapy as promptly as did non-AIDS patients. Two drugs (INH and either rifampin or ethambutol) were as effective as all three drugs together. However, relapse following therapy in AIDS patients did occur, and the length of optimal therapy of tuberculosis in AIDS patients is unknown.

Coccidial infections of the gastrointestinal tract occurred in 64 percent of Haitian AIDS patients (DeHovitz et al., 1986). *Cryptosporidium* (48 percent and *Isospora belli* (16 percent) were found only in patients with diarrhea and were not detected in the spouses and siblings of AIDS patients (DeHovitz et al., 1986). The reservoir for these organisms and the modes of transmission are unknown. In all patients with isosporiasis, diarrhea stopped within 2 days of initiating treatment with oral trimethoprim–sulfamethoxazole. Recurrent symptomatic isosporiasis developed in one-half of patients, but it also responded promptly to therapy with trimethoprim–sulfamethoxazole. An initial short course (1 to 2 weeks) of therapy, followed by prophylaxis for an indefinite period with either daily doses of trimethoprim–sulfamethoxazole or weekly doses of pyrimethamine sulfadoxine, may represent optimal management. Unlike isosporiasis, cryptosporidiosis did not respond to any of the therapeutic regimens employed.

Salmonella bacteremia occurred in 5 percent of Haitian AIDS patients. Surprisingly, all patients had *S. enteriditis* (91 percent group D; 9 percent group B); no strains of *S. typhi* were isolated. Salmonellosis was the first infection diagnosed in 61 percent of these cases. *S. enteriditis* was the most common organism isolated from blood (92 percent) in AIDS and other clinically affected patients presenting with fever; the next most common was *Escherichia coli* (8 percent). *S. enteriditis* was isolated six times more frequently during the dry season of the year, when potable water was scarce. All isolates were sensitive to chloramphenicol, ampicillin, and trimethoprim–sulfamethoxasole. All patients had resolution of fever within 48 hours of initiating therapy. There were no recurrences of bacteremia during a mean follow-up period of 6 months in patients who completed a 2-week course of either chloramphenicol, ampicillin, or trimethroprim–sulfomethoxasole.

As indicated above, another clinical manifestation of AIDS in Haiti that differs from those seen in the United States and Europe is the occurrence of intensely pruritic skin lesions (prurigo) for which neither specific etiologic nor categorical diagnoses can be established (Pape et al., 1983; Liautaud et al., 1987). Prurigo occurred in 50 percent of patients and was characterized by multiple erythematous, round, 2- to 8-mm macules or papules usually appearing first on the exterior surface of the arms but subsequently involving the legs, trunk, and face. The scalp, palms, and soles were not involved. These lesions were not present in the family members of AIDS patients unless they were also infected with HIV-1. Prurigo resembled insect bites but was unresponsive to all therapeutic regimens (antihistamines, phenothiazine, topical steroids, lindane) and usually persisted throughout the entire AIDS illness. Histologically, the usual diagnosis was "dermal hypersensitivity reaction." There was no relationship between the occurrence of prurigo and either the degree of eosinophilia or serum IgE level. An association with an unknown environmental factor was suggested by the disappearance of prurigo in three patients within 2 weeks of traveling to the United States. The prevalence of prurigo was also much higher in patients living in tropical regions of Haiti (50 percent) than in residents of temperate mountainous areas (6 percent).

SUMMARY

The first cases of AIDS in Haiti were recognized in 1978–1979, a period that coincides with the earliest reports of AIDS in the United States. Current data are consistent with the hypothesis that AIDS originated in Africa, was subsequently brought to the United States and Europe, and was then introduced into Haiti either by tourists or by returning Haitians. The seroprevalence of HIV-1 among healthy sexually active adults in Port-au-Prince is approximately 10 percent. This rate of HIV-1 infection is three times that observed in rural areas. The highest prevalence rates were observed in female prostitutes (53 percent) and in the male and female spouses of AIDS patients (55 percent).

The types of opportunistic infections and the clinical course in Haitians with AIDS were similar in many respects to those in patients with AIDS in the United States. However, important differences were noted in the prevalence of specific opportunistic pathogens in Haiti and in the occurrence of prurigo.

More recently, there has been a progressive decrease in the percent of patients reporting either bisexuality or previous blood transfusion, and an increase in those reporting either a spouse with antecedent AIDS, prostitution, or none of these activities. In 1986, heterosexual transmission probably accounted for over 70 percent of AIDS cases.

REFERENCES

Berggren WL, Ewbank DC, Berggren GG (1981): N Engl J Med 304:1324.
CDC (1986): MMWR 35:609.
CDC (1987): 36:1s.

DeHovitz JA, Pape JW, Boncy M, Johnson WD Jr (1986): N Engl J Med 315:87.

Johnson WD Jr, Stanback M, Howard R, Quakyi I, Pape JW (1987): 27th Interscience Conference on Antimicrobial Agents and Chemotherapy, New York, Abstracts, 701.

Liautaud B, Pape JW, DeHovitz JA, Verdier RI, Deschamps MM, Johnson WD Jr (1987) Third International Conference on AIDS, Washington, D.C., MP.136.

Malebranche R, Arnoux E, Guerin JM, Pierre GD, Laroche AC, Pean-Guichard C, Elie R, Morisset PH, Spira T, Mandeville R, Drotman P, Seemayer T, Dupuy J-M (1983): Lancet 2:873.

Nahmias AJ, Weiss J, Yao X, Lee F, Kodsi R, Schanfield M, Matthews T, Bolognesi D, Durack D, Motulsky A, Kanki P, Essex M (1986): Lancet 1:1279.

Pape JW, Liautaud B, Thomas F, Mathurin JR, St. Amand MM, Boncy M, Pean V, Pamphile M, Laroche AC, Johnson WD Jr (1983): N Engl J Med 309:945.

Pape JW, Liautaud B, Thomas F, Mathurin JR, St. Amand MM, Boncy M, Pean V, Pamphile M, Laroche AC, DeHovitz J, Johnson WD Jr (1985): Ann Intern Med 103:674.

Pape JW, Liautaud B, Thomas F, DeHovitz J, Deschamps MM, Verdier RI, Stanback ME, Johnson WD Jr (1986): Clin Res 34:528A.

Pape JW, Stanback M, Pamphile M, Boncy M, Deschamps MM, DeHovitz JA, Verdier R, Beaulieu ME, Lasseque A, Blattner W, Johnson WD Jr (1987a): Clin Res 35:486A.

Pape JW, Stanback ME, Pamphile M, Verdier RI, Deschamps MM, Johnson WD Jr (1987b): Third International Conference on AIDS, Washington, D.C., M.8.6.

Pape JW, Deschamps MM, Kellie S, Verdier RI, Johnson WD Jr (1987c): Third International Conference on AIDS, Washington, D.C., MP.68.

Quinn TC, Mann JM, Curran JW, Piot D (1986): Science 234:955.

13

Perinatal Infection

MARTHA ROGERS

AIDS in children was first described in 1982 by physicians in New York City, New Jersey, and Miami (Oleske et al., 1983; Rubinstein et al., 1983; Scott et al., 1984). Since that time, more than 1,000 cases of AIDS in children under 13 years of age have been reported to the Centers for Disease Control (CDC), and an estimated two to three times that number of children have been found to have human immunodeficiency virus (HIV-1) infection but not AIDS, according to the CDC AIDS case definition. Most of these children with AIDS (78 percent) acquired HIV-1 in the perinatal period from their mothers.

To date, just over 6,000 cases of AIDS have been reported in women, 80 percent of whom are of childbearing age. This number is expected to increase to over 20,000 cases by the end of 1991 (Morgan and Curran, 1986). As more women become infected, more children born to these women will be infected. HIV-1 infection in children will become an increasingly common pediatric infection.

This chapter summarizes the epidemiologic characteristics of children with perinatally acquired AIDS, transmission patterns, clinical course, and prevention strategies.

EPIDEMIOLOGIC CHARACTERISTICS OF PERINATALLY ACQUIRED AIDS

As of August 1988, 1,142 children under 13 years of age with AIDS had been reported to the CDC, accounting for about 2 percent of all reported AIDS cases. Most (78 percent) of these children had acquired HIV-1 from their mothers in the perinatal period. The first cases were reported in 1982, and the number has increased steadily over the years since. Eighty-one percent of the cases have been reported since 1985 (Fig. 13.1).

The time of transmission of HIV-1 in these children can be estimated by the year of birth. Children who later developed perinatally acquired AIDS were born as early as 1976, indicating that this mode of transmission was occurring early in the AIDS epidemic.

In most (73 percent) of these cases, the mothers were either IV drug users themselves or sex partners of men who used IV drugs (Table 13.1). Sixty-seven percent of all heterosexual AIDS patients were IV drug users or their sex partners.

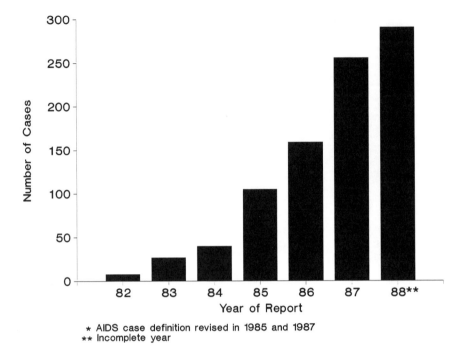

* AIDS case definition revised in 1985 and 1987
** Incomplete year

Figure 13.1. Perinatally acquired AIDS cases by date of report, CDC national surveillance. Includes children under 13 years of age reported as of August 30, 1988, and includes chronic lymphoid interstitial pneumonitis after June 30, 1985.

Table 13.1. Risk Factors of Mothers of Children with Perinatally Acquired AIDS Reported to the Centers for Disease Control[a]

Mother's risk	No.	Percent
IV drug user	479	54
Haitian-born	101	12
Transfusion recipient	22	2
Heterosexual contact	224	25
Sex partner IV drug abuser	169	19
Sex partner bisexual	22	2
Sex partner hemophiliac	6	1
Sex partner's risk unknown	23	3
Sex partner transfusion recipient	1	<1
Unknown	60	7
Total	886	100.0

[a]Includes cases reported as of August 1988.

Twelve percent of these children were born to women from areas where heterosexual transmission is thought to be the major mode of spread (e.g., Haiti, central Africa). A small proportion of the children were born to women who are the sex partners of men at increased risk of infection or to women who have received blood or blood products transfusions.

Most (65 percent) of the children with perinatally acquired AIDS have come from three states—New York, New Jersey, and Florida—reflecting the occurrence of AIDS cases in IV drug users (75 percent of whom come from New York or New Jersey) and in Haitian immigrants (45 percent of whom reside in Florida). The proportion of children reported from these high-prevalence areas, however, has decreased over time from 76 percent in 1982–1984 to 58 percent in 1987–1988. This trend in reporting is expected to continue over the next 5 years as the AIDS epidemic spreads to other areas of the United States. Cities with large IV drug-using populations can expect increases in the number of perinatally acquired AIDS cases as the prevalence of infection increases among drug users.

Since most perinatally acquired AIDS cases are linked to IV drug users, the demographic characteristics of these children are similar to those of IV drug users with AIDS. Most (85 percent) of the children with perinatally acquired AIDS are black or Hispanic. The cumulative incidence of AIDS in black and Hispanic children is 15 and 9 times, respectively, the cumulative incidence of the disease in white, non-Hispanic children.

Over 85 percent of the children with perinatally acquired AIDS were diagnosed (i.e., met the CDC case definition for AIDS) in the first 3 years of life (median age at diagnosis, 10 months). However, a small proportion (5 percent) were not diagnosed until 6 to 9 years of age, indicating that the latent period, although usually less than 3 years, can be quite long.

AIDS, as defined by CDC, represents only the most severe form of HIV-1 infection; the CDC case count does not include children with less severe manifestations. In hospital-based case series, about one-third to one-half of the children with HIV-1 infection meet the CDC case definition (Parks and Scott, 1987; Pahwa et al. 1986). Thus, the number of children with symptomatic HIV-1 infection is estimated at two to three times the number of reported cases. The epidemiologic characteristics of the children with less severe forms of HIV-1 infection who are not reported do not differ from those of children with AIDS. CDC in cooperation with state and local health departments has made recent changes in the AIDS case definition to reflect the use of the HIV-1 diagnostic tests and other, more recently described manifestations of HIV-1 infection such as neurologic disease (CDC, 1987). These changes are expected to produce a greater increase in pediatric AIDS case reporting than in reporting of adult cases.

PREVALENCE

Infection rates for populations of children are unknown, since no seroprevalence studies have been published. The potential for perinatal transmission is reflected in seroprevalence studies of heterosexual populations. Seroprevalence studies of IV drug users show rates from as high as 60 percent in New York City to as low as 10 percent in San Francisco (Robert-Guroff et al., 1986; D'Aquila et al., 1986; Chaisson et al., 1987). The seroprevalence for recent Haitian immigrants in the United States is around 5 percent (Collaborative Study Group, 1987). Transmission rates for the female sex partners of men at increased risk have also varied, from 10 to 15 percent in partners of transfusion recipients and hemophilia patients to around 50 percent in partners of IV drug users and infected Haitian-born men (Saltzman et al., 1986; Fischl et al., 1987; Peterman et al., 1986; Jason et al., 1986).

The infection rate for the general female population is unknown. Seroprevalence rates for female blood donors average around five positives per 100,000 (Schorr et al., 1985), and rates for female military recruit applicants average around 60 positives per 100,000 (CDC, 1986a). These populations may not be representative of the female U.S. population at large, but they provide an estimate range for overall seroprevalence for women who perceive themselves to be at low risk for HIV-1 infection, since both the military recruitment and blood donation centers discourage persons with high-risk behaviors from applying or donating.

Recently developed techniques for testing antibody to HIV-1 using blood collected on filter paper for newborn screening programs have allowed for screening of populations of newborns for HIV-1. This method has been used in two states, Massachusetts and New York, to estimate the seroprevalence of anti-HIV-1 in live-born infants. Anti-HIV-1 in newborns is a measurement of passively acquired maternal antibody and thus reflects the seroprevalence in their mothers. In Massachusetts, an estimated 2.1 per 1,000 women giving birth were positive for anti-HIV-1 (Hoff et al., 1988). Rates of seropositivity were highest in inner-city hospitals (eight per 1,000 women). In New York City, rates were as high as 16 per 1,000 women (Lambert, 1988).

TRANSMISSION OF HIV-1 FROM MOTHER TO INFANT

It has been hypothesized that HIV-1 is transmitted from mothers to their infants in utero through transplacental passage of the virus, during labor and delivery through exposure to infective maternal blood and vaginal secretions, or postnatally through breast feeding. There is evidence that transmission can occur through all of these modes. The occurrence of AIDS in children who had no further contact with their mothers after birth (Lapointe et al., 1985; Cowan et al., 1984) and the identification of HIV-1 in fetal tissue and amniotic fluid (Jovaisas et al., 1985; Sprecher et al., 1986; Mundy et al., 1987) are evidence of prenatal or intrapartum transmission. Three reports of HIV-1 infection in infants born to women who became infected via postpartum blood transfusions and who breast-fed their infants suggest that transmission can occur through this route (Ziegler et al., 1985; LePage et al., 1987). HIV-1 has been isolated from cell-free breast milk (Thiry et al., 1985). Transmission by breast milk is probably rare in the United States, because the vast majority of transmitting mothers, most of whom are IV drug abusers, have not breast-fed their infants.

The proportion of perinatally acquired cases of HIV-1 infection attributable to each of these three mechanisms is unknown. Prevention approaches differ markedly depending on the relative contribution of these three mechanisms. For example, the use of HIV-1 hyperimmune gamma globulin in the infant would have little effect if most transmission occurred in utero.

The frequency of transmission from mothers to their infants has not been accurately determined. In one study of mothers who had already delivered an infected child, 54 percent transmitted to their subsequent children (Scott et al., 1987). This rate may be high, since these mothers may represent a group of women who for unclear reasons readily transmit virus. Prospective studies of HIV-1-infected pregnant women without this bias are ongoing and have reported rates of 30 to 40 percent (Selwyn et al., 1987; New York City Collaborative Study Group, 1987; DeMaria et al., 1987; Blanche et al., 1987; Nzilambi et al., 1987; Mok et al., 1987; Willoughby et al., 1987).

Factors affecting the likelihood of mother-to-infant transmission have not been clearly defined. Preliminary data from one study suggest that immunologic factors in the mother may play a role (Francis et al., 1987). In this study, anti-HIV-1-positive mothers of HIV-1-specific IgM-positive infants had lower $CD4^+/CD8^+$ cell ratios than anti-HIV-1-positive mothers of IgM-negative infants. Other factors such as persistent viremia, stage of HIV-1 disease, percentage of infected cells, presence of neutralizing antibody, continued exposure to HIV-1 during pregnancy, environmental factors, and other intrinsic host factors are to be considered.

Little is known about the effect of pregnancy on the health of HIV-1-infected women. In ongoing prospective studies, none of the women progressed in their stage of HIV-1 disease during pregnancy (Schoenbaum et al., 1986; Goedert et al., 1987; New York City Collaborative Study Group, 1987). However, pregnancy may enhance the progression of HIV-1 disease over the long term (Schoenbaum et al., 1987). Further study is needed to clarify this issue.

CLINICAL COURSE

HIV-1 infection in both children and adults is a chronic, persistent infection characterized by a relatively long latent period (i.e., months to years) from establishment of infection to onset of AIDS. Children with perinatally acquired HIV-1 infection usually do not show signs and symptoms of the infection at birth or in the neonatal period. Possible reasons for the delayed onset of symptoms in the infected infants include the possibility that most infants acquire HIV-1 intrapartum rather than in utero or that infection acquired in utero remains latent until several months after birth.

In the mother, HIV-1 infection in early stages has not been associated with poor pregnancy outcomes, such as premature delivery, low birth weight, or low Apgar scores in excess of what is expected of a low-income, predominantly non-white population with frequent IV drug use. An increased incidence of fetal wastage has been reported in one study from Haiti (Johnson et al., 1986) and in a preliminary report from a study in Boston (Witt et al., 1986) but not in similar studies among female IV drug users in New York (Schoenbaum et al., 1986; New York City Collaborative Study Group, 1987). Prematurity and infant mortality were higher in seropositive mothers with more advanced stage of illness than in seronegative mothers in one study in Zaire (Nzilambi et al., 1987). Two African studies found that HIV-1-seropositive pregnant women were more likely than seronegative women to report having lost a previous child (Nzilambi et al., 1987; Braddick et al., 1987). Poor fetal and neonatal outcomes of pregnancies of seropositive women

are probably related more to maternal health and stage of disease than to fetal/
infant virus infection, whereas infant and child deaths are likely due to HIV-1
infection in the child.

Typical signs and symptoms of HIV-1 infection in children begin occurring
around 4 to 6 months of age and include failure to thrive or weight loss, chronic or
recurrent diarrhea (usually idiopathic), persistent or recurrent fever, generalized
lymphadenopathy, and persistent and severe oral candidiasis (Parks and Scott,
1987; Rubinstein, 1986). Chronic parotitis is found less often.

Recurrent bacterial infections have been reported in over half of the children
with HIV-1 infection (Parks and Scott, 1987; Pahwa et al., 1986). Purulent otitis
media is common, but more severe infections such as multiple episodes of sepsis,
meningitis, or pneumonia also occur. The offending organisms are those commonly
occurring in immune-competent children such as *Haemophilus influenzae, Streptococcus pneumoniae,* and *Salmonella* (Bernstein et al., 1985).

Involvement of many organ systems has been described. Cardiomyopathy
characterized by congestive heart failure, left and biventricular hypertrophy, peri-
cardial effusion, and coronary artery thrombosis has been reported (Parks and
Scott, 1987; Joshi et al., 1988). Hepatitis has been reported in 10 percent of cases
in one study with biopsy showing noncaseating granulomas (Parks and Scott,
1987). Proteinuria and nephrotic syndrome have also occurred. Atopic dermatitis
and other dermatologic manifestations have been described (Tong et al., 1986;
Shannon and Ammann, 1985).

Encephalopathy has been reported in as many as 50 to 60 percent of children
with HIV-1 infection (Epstein et al., 1986; Belman et al., 1985). Neurologic signs
and symptoms are usually progressive and include loss of developmental milestones or intellectual ability; impaired brain growth; symmetrical motor deficiencies manifested by paresis, abnormal tone, pathologic reflexes, ataxia, or gait
disturbance; and seizures. Computerized tomographic scan findings include
cerebral atrophy and calcifications. Cerebrospinal fluid is often normal, or there
may be a mild, predominantly lymphocytic pleocytosis or modest elevation of
protein.

Lymphoid interstitial pneumonitis (LIP) has occurred in 30 to 40 percent of
HIV-1-infected children (Parks and Scott, 1987; Pahwa et al., 1986). The etiology
is unknown, but Epstein-Barr virus (EBV) infection, direct infection of HIV-1, and
immune response to HIV-1 have been hypothesized (Rubinstein et al., 1986; Andiman et al., 1985; Chayt et al., 1986; Parks and Scott, 1987). LIP is often associated
with generalized lymphadenopathy, hepatosplenomegaly, and markedly elevated
serum immunoglobulin levels. Clinically, LIP is characterized by a slow progressive course in comparison with the acute course of PCP. Cough, digital clubbing,
and normal auscultatory examination are characteristic. The chest X-ray shows
persistent bilateral reticulonodular interstitial infiltrates, with or without hilar
lymphadenopathy. Lung biopsies are characterized by a diffuse lymphocytic interstitial infiltration without identification of pathogens, such as cytomegalovirus or
P. carinii.

As the course of HIV-1 infection progresses and immune deficiency worsens,
opportunistic infections and malignancies occur. The most common opportunistic

infection in children is PCP, characterized by acute onset, cough, tachypnea, fever, diminished breath sounds, wheezing, and rhonchi. Ventilatory support is often required. Other opportunistic infections occur, including disseminated cytomegalovirus infection, *Candida* esophagitis, disseminated atypical mycobacteriosis, crytosporidiosis, chronic herpes simplex virus infection, disseminated toxoplasmosis, and progressive multifocal leukoencephalopathy.

Malignancies are unusual in children. Kaposi's sarcoma, seen frequently in homosexual men with AIDS, has been reported in only 5 children. Lymphomas are even rarer.

Common laboratory findings of pediatric HIV-1 infection include defects in both cell-mediated and humoral immunity (Parks and Scott, 1987; Rubinstein, 1986). Decreased $CD4^+$ (helper) lymphocytes, increased $CD8^+$ (suppressor) lymphocytes, reversed $CD4^+/CD8^+$ ratios, poor response to mitogen stimulation of lymphocytes indicating poor function, and increased serum immunoglobulins are common. Lymphopenia and hypogammaglobulinemia are rare. Other hematologic abnormalities, such as anemia and thrombocytopenia, have also been reported.

The prognosis for all children with perinatally acquired AIDS is poor, but survival time varies depending on the type of clinical presentation. Two clinical courses have been described: (1) children whose predominant manifestation is an opportunistic infection, and (2) children whose predominant manifestation is lymphoid interstitial pneumonitis (Parks and Scott, 1987). The first group is characterized by early onset of disease, usually within the first year of life (mean age at diagnosis, 6 months), and rapid demise. The median survival of these children is 5 months. Children in the second group are usually diagnosed at a later age (mean age at diagnosis, 14 months) and have a more indolent course, with a median survival time of 19 months (Parks and Scott, 1987; Rubinstein et al., 1986; Rogers et al., 1987).

Diagnosis of perinatally acquired infection in infants has been difficult for several reasons. Early signs and symptoms of HIV infection, such as failure-to-thrive, generalized lymphadenopathy, and developmental delay, are often nonspecific. Maternal antibody can persist up to at least 15 months of age (Mok et al., 1987). Viral culture can take up to 3–4 weeks to complete. Serum antigen as measured by the p24 capture assay is often negative at birth and may not become positive until the infant has developed advanced disease (Rogers et al., 1988). Recently developed assays such as the polymerase chain reaction (PCR), which detects amplified proviral sequences, and the in vitro production of HIV-specific antibody may prove to be quite useful in newborn and infant diagnosis (Rogers et al., 1988; Laure et al., 1988, De Rossi et al., 1988).

Managing children with HIV-1 infection requires a multidisciplinary approach. Involvement of many organ systems requires coordination of care among many subspeciality pediatricians. Problems with growth and development often require specialized therapy and home health care, including parenteral nutrition. Because many of these children come from poor, inner-city families and many of their mothers are either too sick or otherwise unable to care for their infants, social services are almost always needed.

PREVENTION

Preventing perinatally acquired HIV-1 infection requires preventing infection of women and preventing pregnancy in HIV-1-infected women (CDC, 1985). Since female IV drug users and female sex partners of male IV drug users account for most of the women at increased risk of HIV-1 infection, these populations should have high priority. More drug treatment facilities and education on how to avoid HIV-1 infection acquired through IV drug use need to be provided. Counseling on how to avoid acquiring HIV-1 through sexual contact should be made available to all IV drug users and their sex partners (CDC, 1986b). Other heterosexual groups at increased risk, such as those who have received blood or blood products before March 1985, particularly partners of hemophilia patients, should also be counseled.

Following counseling, women at increased risk should be encouraged to undergo testing for HIV-1 infection. Those who are seropositive should avoid pregnancy both to prevent transmission to infants and to avoid the possible adverse effects to their own health. Programs that link populations of infected women, such as IV drug users, to family planning centers need to be established.

Lack of information regarding the frequency of transmission from mother to infant by the various modes (prepartum, intrapartum, or postpartum) has hindered our ability to prevent transmission from infected women who become pregnant. If most transmission occurs in utero, then early diagnosis to offer the option of pregnancy termination should be the focus. If most of the transmission is intrapartum, then delivery by cesarean section might be protective and should be studied. The use of passive hyperimmune anti-HIV-1 globulin might also be useful if most transmission is intrapartum or postpartum. Avoidance of breast feeding has been recommended for infected women to prevent postpartum transmission. As effective treatments or vaccines become available, early diagnosis will be critical. Further study of the potentially useful techniques such as PCR and in vitro production of HIV-1-specific antibody should receive priority.

Education of the general population, of teenagers, and particularly of inner-city minority teens is especially important. The Surgeon General has recommended that schoolchildren at all grade levels receive age-appropriate education regarding AIDS. Both adults and teens need to understand how to avoid acquiring HIV-1 infection through sexual contact and IV drug use (USPHS, 1987).

PROSPECTS FOR THE FUTURE

Clearly HIV-1 infection in women and children is increasing. CDC predicts a 10-fold increase in the cumulative number of cases of AIDS by 1992 (CDC, 1988). This increase will probably occur even in the face of an all-out prevention drive, since many of these cases will represent the occurrence of disease in persons already infected.

Ongoing prospective studies will better define perinatal transmission patterns, natural history, and treatment of perinatally acquired infection. Seroprevalence studies of women and children are under way and will allow for better direction of efforts to prevent HIV-1 infection. Improved assessment of the social service and health care needs of these children is needed to adequately provide for their care, both now and in the future. Studies of ways to elicit changes in high-risk behaviors in teenagers and adults are needed.

At present, preventing perinatal infection requires education and behavioral modification by women and their sex partners. Pediatricians and family physicians can contribute greatly to this effort, since identifying infection in a child is often the first indication of HIV-1 infection in the parents. Providing or referring for appropriate counseling, testing, and ongoing prevention measures for parents should be an integral part of the management and prevention of HIV-1 infection in children.

REFERENCES

Andiman WA, Eastman R, Martin K, et al. (1985): Lancet 2:1390.

Belman AL, Ultmann MH, Horoupian D, et al. (1985): Ann Neurol 18:560.

Bernstein LJ, Krieger BZ, Novick B, Sicklick MJ, Rubinstein A (1985): Pediatr Infect Dis 4:472.

Blanche S, Rouzioux C, Veber F, Le Deist F, Mayaux MJ, Griscelli C (1987): Prospective study on newborns of HIV seropositive women. Presented at the Third International Conference on AIDS, Washington, D.C.

Braddick M, Kreiss JK, Quinn T, Ndinya-Achola J, Vercauteren G, Plummer FA (1987): Congenital transmission of HIV in Nairobi, Kenya. Presented at the Third International Conference on AIDS, Washington, D.C.

CDC (1985): MMWR 34:721.

CDC (1986a): MMWR 35:421.

CDC (1986b): MMWR 35:152.

CDC (1987): MMWR 36 (Suppl):2S.

CDC (1988): MMWR 37:551.

Chaisson RE, Moss AR, Onishi R, Osmond D, Carlson JR (1987): Am J Public Health 77:169.

Chayt KJ, Harper ME, Marselle LM, et al. (1986): JAMA 256:2356.

Collaborative Study Group of AIDS in Haitian-Americans (1987): JAMA 257:635.

Cowan MJ, Hellman D, Chudwin D, Wara DW, Chang RS, Ammann AJ (1984): Pediatrics 73:382.

D'Aquila R, Williams AB, Kleber HD, Williams AE (1986): N Engl J Med 314:117.

DeMaria A, Varnier DE, Melica G, Pantarotto F, Grovari P, Terragna A (1987): Transmission of HTLV III (HIV) in infants of seropositive mothers. Presented at the Third International Conference on AIDS, Washington, D.C.

De Rossi A, Amadori A, Chieco-Bianchi L, et al. (1988): Lancet 2:278.

Epstein LG, Sharer LR, Oleske JM, et al. (1986): Pediatrics 78:678.

Fischl MA, Dickinson GM, Scott GB, Klimas N, Fletcher MA, Parks W (1987): JAMA 257:640.

Francis H, Lubake N, Duma MP, Ryder RW, Mann J, Quinn TC, et al. (1987): Immunologic profiles of mothers in perinatal transmission of HIV infection. Presented at the Third International Conference on AIDS, Washington, D.C.

Goedert JJ, Landesman SH, Eyster ME, Biggar RJ (1987): AIDS incidence in pregnant women, their babies, homosexual men and hemophiliacs. Presented at the Third International Conference on AIDS, Washington, D.C.

Hoff R, Berardi VP, Weiblen BJ, Mahoney-Trout L, Mitchell ML, Grady GF (1988): N Engl J Med 318:525.

Jason JM, McDougal JS, Lawrence DN, Kennedy MS, Hilgartner M, Evatt BL (1986): JAMA 255:212.

Johnson WD, Standback M, Verdier R, Deschamps MM, Pape JW (1986): Fetal and postnatal mortality associated with HTLV-III infection. Presented at the Twenty-Sixth Interscience Conference on Antimicrobial Agents and Chemotherapy, New Orleans.

Joshi VV, Gadol C, Connor E, Oleske JM, Mendelson J, Marin-Garcia J (1988): Human Pathol 19:69.

Jovaisas E, Koch MA, Schafer A, Stauber M, Lowenthal D (1985): Lancet 2:1129.

Lambert B (1988): One in 61 babies in New York City has AIDS antibodies, study says. New York Times, Jan. 13, p A1.

Lapointe N, Michaud J, Pekovic D, Chausseau JP, Dupuy JM (1985): N Engl J Med 312:1325.

Laure F, Courgnaud V, Rouzioux C, et al. (1988): Lancet 2:538.

Lepage P, Van de Perre P, Carael M, Nsengumuremyi F, Nkurunziza J, Butzler J, Sprecher S (1987): Lancet 2:400.

Mok JQ, Giaquinto C, De Rossi A, Grosch-Wörner I, Ades AE, Peckham CS, (1987): Lancet 1:1164.

Morgan WM, Curran JW (1986): Public Health Rep 101:459.

Mundy DC, Schinazi RF, Gerber AR, Nahmias AJ, Randall HW (1987): Lancet 2:459.

New York City Collaborative Study Group for Vertical Transmission of HIV (1987): Presented at the Third International Conference on AIDS, Washington, D.C.

Nzilambi N, Ryder RW, Behets F, Francis H, Bayende E, Nelson A, Mann J, et al. (1987): Perinatal transmission in two African hospitals. Presented at the Third International Conference on AIDS, Washington, D.C.

Oleske J, Minnefor A, Cooper R, et al. (1983): JAMA 249:2345.

Parks WP, Scott GB (1987): An overview of pediatric AIDS: Approaches to diagnosis and outcome assessment. In Broder S (ed): AIDS—Modern Concepts and Therapeutic Challenges. New York: Marcel Dekker, pp 245–262.

Pahwa S, Kaplan M, Fikrig S, Pahwa R, Sarngadharan MG, Popovic M, Gallo RC (1986): JAMA 255:2299.

Peterman TA, Stoneburner RL, Allen JR, Jaffe HW, Curran JW (1988): JAMA 259:55.

Robert-Guroff M, Weiss SH, Giron JA, et al. (1986): JAMA 255:3133.

Rogers MF, Thomas PA, Starcher ET, Noa MC, Bush TJ, Jaffe HW (1987): Pediatrics 79:1008.

Rogers M, Montefiore Medical Center HIV Perinatal Transmission Study Group, New York City Collaborative Study Group (1988): Presented at Fourth International Conference on AIDS, Stockholm, Sweden.

Rubinstein A (1986): Pediatric AIDS. In Lockhard JD (ed): Current Problems in Pediatrics. Chicago: Year Book, pp 362–409.

Rubinstein A, Sicklick M, Gupta A, et al. (1983): JAMA 249:2350.

Rubinstein A, Morecki R, Silverman B, et al. (1986): J Pediatr 108:498.

Saltzman BR, Friedland GH, Klein RS, Maude DW, Steigbigel NH (1986): Female to male sexual transmission of HTLV-III/LAV. Presented at the Twenty-Sixth Interscience Conference on Antimicrobial Agents and Chemotherapy, New Orleans.

Schoenbaum EE, Selwyn PA, Mayers MM, et al. (1986): HTLV-III/LAV infection and pregnancy outcomes in intravenous drug abusers. Presented at the Twenty-Sixth Interscience Conference on Antimicrobial Agents and Chemotherapy, New Orleans.

Schoenbaum EE, Selwyn PA, Feingold AR, Davenny K, Robertson V, Rogers MF (1987): The effect of pregnancy on progression of HIV related disease. Presented at the Third International Conference on AIDS, Washington, D.C.

Schorr JB, Berkowitz A, Cumming PD, Katz AJ, Sandler SG (1985): N Engl J Med 313:384.

Scott GB, Buck BE, Leterman JG, Bloom FL, Parks WP (1984): N Engl J Med 310:76.

Scott GB, Mastrucci MT, Hutto SC, Parks WP (1987): Mothers of infants with HIV infection: Outcome of subsequent pregnancies. Presented at the Third International Conference on AIDS, Washington, D.C.

Selwyn PA, Schoenbaum EE, Feingold AR, Mayers M, Davenny K, Rogers MF (1987): Perinatal transmission of HIV in intravenous drug abusers (IVDAs). Presented at the Third International Conference on AIDS, Washington, D.C.

Shannon KM, Ammann AJ (1985): J Pediatr 106:332.

Sprecher S, Soumenkoff G, Puissant F, Degueldre M (1986): Lancet 2:288.

Thiry L, Sprecher-Goldberger S, Jonckheer T, et al. (1985): Lancet 2:891.

Tong TK, Andrew LR, Albert A, Mickell JJ (1986): J Pediatr 108:426.

USPHS (1987): DHHS Publication No. HRS-D-MC 87-1.

Willoughby A, Mendez H, Minkoff H, Holman S, Goedert J, Landesman S (1987): Presented at Third International Conference on AIDS, Washington, DC.

Witt DJ, Vogt MW, Hutchinson MS, Hirsch MS, Craven DE (1986): Clinical and virologic evaluation of pregnant women with antibody to human T-lymphotropic virus, type III (HTLV-III). Presented at the Twenty-Sixth Interscience Conference on Antimicrobial Agents and Chemotherapy, New Orleans.

Ziegler JB, Cooper DA, Johnson RO, Gold J (1985): Lancet 1:896.

14

HIV-1 Infection in Low-Risk Populations

ALFRED J. SAAH

Fear of infection by the human immunodeficiency virus (HIV-1) has fueled both hysteria and legitimate concern in diverse groups in the United States. Many institutions such as hospitals, schools, prisons, day care centers, and businesses have confronted this fear and have sought guidance to develop procedures that reduce risk of transmission. Infection with HIV-1 occurs in certain groups whose activities place them at high risk: homosexual men, intravenous drug users, hemophiliacs, recipients of unscreened blood or blood products, and sexual partners of infected individuals in those groups, for instance. The unifying theme that connects these diverse risk groups is that HIV-1 is a blood-borne virus and is transmitted by sexual contact or by exchange of blood.

At the other extreme, there is ample evidence that HIV-1 infection is not transmitted casually and that fear of infection from routine or social contact with an infected individual is unfounded. For example, contact in the classroom or office poses no risk of HIV-1 transmission.

However, there are several types of contact that fall between casual contact and intensive repeated exposure to blood or secretions. Certain occupations or social activities foster close interaction with HIV-1-infected persons. It is this intermediate level of contact that characterizes low-risk groups. Such groups include health care workers, correctional facilities personnel, day care personnel, and, to a lesser extent, household contacts who are not sexual partners. This chapter presents the evidence on transmission to individuals in each low-risk group in some detail. It summarizes data showing the low risk of transmission from needle-stick or parenteral exposures to blood or other body fluids from patients with AIDS or HIV-1 infection. Research in each of the groups is reviewed, with emphasis on conditions surrounding documented episodes of HIV-1 transmission. Finally, the chapter includes current specific guidelines and strategies to prevent transmission of HIV-1 in these groups.

HOUSEHOLD CONTACTS

A household contact is someone who routinely shares kitchen or bathroom facilities with a person who has AIDS and HIV-1 infection but who is not a sexual part-

Table 14.1. Type of Contact with Patients with AIDS Among 101 Household Members

Activity	Percentage of members in activity
Sharing of household items	
Razors	9
Toothbrushes	7
Nail clippers	42
Combs	51
Towels	37
Eating utensils	25
Eating plates	46
Drinking glasses	48
Sharing of household facilities	
Bed	37
Toilet	90
Bath or shower	92
Kitchen	93
Washing items used by patients	
Dishes	65
Toilet	49
Bath	55
Clothes	38
Interacting with patient	
Helping to bathe	10
Helping to dress	16
Helping to eat	13
Shaking hands	21
Hugging	79
Kissing on cheek	83
Kissing on lips	17

Source: Friedland et al. (1986).

ner. Studies of household contacts of patients with AIDS have shown that the major source of risk for infection with HIV-1 is sexual contact. Investigators in New York City (Friedland et al., 1986, 1987) have studied 200 household contacts of 85 AIDS patients. Exposure occurred during the period from 18 months before onset of symptoms to the time of screening and lasted for a median of 31 months. Household exposures included activities such as sharing personal grooming items, kitchen facilities, and personal interactions (Table 14.1). A biologic child of a woman with AIDS was the only one of the 200 contacts who had evidence of HIV-1 infection. This child appeared to have been infected perinatally, because signs and symptoms of HIV-1 infection had been present since infancy.

In another study (Fischl et al., 1987), 138 nonspouse household contacts (109 children, 29 adults) were studied in 45 households for a median of 24 months. Fifteen of the children had AIDS or HIV-1-related disease at enrollment. All were less than 4 years old and had been born to HIV-1-positive mothers. Two older children of Haitian ancestry, who were sexually active and had lived in Zaire for approximately 13 years before entering the United States, had antibody to HIV-1. The remaining adults and children were seronegative and remained negative through the follow-up period despite contact similar to that described in the New York study.

This accumulating evidence against transmission in the household places in perspective the early reports of HIV-1 isolation from saliva (Groopman et al., 1984). A subsequent report (Ho et al., 1985) has emphasized the relative difficulty of culturing HIV-1 from saliva. From the epidemiology of HIV-1 infection thus far, saliva and tears appear to play a very minor, if any, role in transmission. Nonetheless, it seems prudent not to share personal items such as toothbrushes and razors.

HEALTH CARE WORKERS

As used here, the term "health care workers" includes physicians, dentists, nurses, emergency medical technicians, nurses' aides, clinical and research laboratory personnel, phlebotomists, radiology technicians, other technical support staff, autopsy personnel, morticians, housekeeping and laundry personnel in health care facilities, and individuals performing nursing care at home. Between June 1981, when AIDS was first reported, and August 1988, more than 72,000 cases of AIDS were seen in doctors' offices, outpatient departments, dental clinics, and hospitals in the United States. There have been countless thousands of contacts between health care workers and infected patients. But the proportion of cases of AIDS employed in the health care industry (5.4%) is similar to the proportion of the general U.S. population employed in that industry (CDC, 1988). However, because HIV-1 is bloodborne, it is logical to expect some risk to health care workers from needle-stick injuries or certain other types of exposure such as a mucous membrane splash with blood or another body fluid.

Unfortunately, numerous needle-stick and mucous membrane exposures in settings where HIV-1 infection is present have been reported in the past 6 years. A number of studies have documented parenteral exposures in health care workers. Of the 609 exposures (Henderson et al., 1986; Hirsch et al., 1985; Kuhls et al., 1987; McCray, 1986; Shanson et al., 1985) reported from prospective studies, seroconversion occurred in only one. In a nationwise prospective study (CDC, 1988) the risk of HIV-1 infection due to needle-stick or parenteral exposure was estimated to be 0.5% (4/870) with the upper bound of the 95 percent confidence interval at 1.1%. There is also a report of a seroconversion in a nurse from Great Britain (Anonymous, 1984). All of the above seroconversions followed accidental injection with a moderate amount of blood or body fluid. There have also been two reports of needle-stick injuries from patients with AIDS that have resulted in transmission of hepatitis B (Gerberding et al., 1985) or cryptococcus (Glaser and Garden, 1985) without concomitant transmission of HIV-1, thus indicating relatively low transmissibility. Other reports describe a seropositive child whose mother presumably seroconverted as a result of performing unprotected medical procedures involving extensive blood exposure (CDC, 1986a) and three female health care workers who were found to be seropositive following exposure of their broken skin to blood of infected patients (CDC, 1987a). Indirect parenteral HIV-1 transmission via blood-to-broken-skin exposure is not unexpected. It confirms the need for using appropriate precautions when such exposure is anticipated, and it emphasizes the importance of efforts to reduce the frequency of direct contact with blood that occurs in the clinical setting. Systematic approaches to needle-stick injury should contribute to these efforts (Jagger et al., 1988).

A study from New York City (Klein et al., 1987) reported that one of approximately 1,200 dentists was identified as seropositive. This dentist apparently had no other risk factor; the source of his infection is thought to have been through his practice. He used gloves haphazardly, but he denied knowingly treating patients with AIDS. This case underscores the need to employ sound health care practices with every patient who is treated.

As the prevalence of HIV-1 infection has increased in the United States, so has the potential exposure to contaminated blood in the laboratory setting. In addition to the greatly increased exposure in clinical laboratories, there has also been a proliferation of research laboratories performing HIV-1 cultures and other procedures that potentially involve exposure to high concentrations of virus. There have been two apparently laboratory-acquired infections in individuals who worked with highly concentrated solutions of HIV-1. Accounts indicate that these incidents were preventable (Weiss et al., 1988).

In short, the risk to the health care worker is very low, but it is clearly not zero. Given the number of times that blood-to-skin contact or needle punctures involving HIV-1-positive blood must have occurred in the United States since the epidemic began, the data support rather than refute the low risk of infection.

The risk of infection to health care workers and those in allied professions can be minimized if relatively simple precautions are exercised. There has been a series of advisories about these precautions (CDC, 1985c, 1986a,c, 1987b). Specifically, recommendations for preventing transmission of HIV-1 to health care workers and allied professions have been promulgated by the U.S. Public Health Service, published in a Morbidity and Mortality Weekly Report supplement (CDC, 1987b) and summarized in Table 14.2.

These recommendations are similar to those made for the prevention of nosocomial hepatitis B virus infection. The major difference is that now *all* blood must be considered potentially infectious, thus making special labels for patients and specimens redundant. Universal blood precautions have prevented and will continue to prevent transmission of known blood-borne agents and of those yet to be identified.

HIV-1 transmission from health care workers to patients has not been reported. However, current standards of medical and surgical practice should prevent transmission of blood-borne viruses in either direction. Health care workers who are infected with HIV-1 and have weeping lesions should refrain from all direct patient care and from handling patient care equipment until the condition resolves.

INMATES AND PERSONNEL OF CORRECTIONAL FACILITIES

There have been considerable concern and publicity about the risk to prisoners, guards, or support staff in prisons or jails. AIDS and HIV-1 infection in prisons are associated with the same risk factors as those operating in the free-living population. During 1985, the National Institute of Justice of the U.S. Department of Jus-

Table 14.2. Recommendations for Prevention of HIV-1 Transmission in Health Care Settings

Universal precautions for health care workers with patient contact

Appropriate barriers should be used to prevent skin and mucous membrane exposure when contact with blood or other body fluid is anticipated

Gloves for touching contaminated fluids, surfaces or items and for venipuncture
Masks and protective eyewear for droplet-producing procedures
Gowns or aprons for procedures leading to splashes

Hands and skin should be washed if contaminated and after gloves are removed

Injuries by needles and other sharp objects should be avoided

Resuscitation equipment should be available where frequent use is predictable in order to minimize the need for mouth-to-mouth breathing

Personnel with moist or exudative lesions should refrain from contact with patients or patient care equipment

Pregnant personnel should adhere strictly to precautions against HIV-1 transmission

Precautions for invasive procedures (in addition to the above)

Gloves and masks must be worn for all invasive procedures

Gloves and gowns should be worn during obstetrical deliveries when handling the placenta or the newborn infant until fluids are removed and during umbilical cord care

Torn gloves should be removed and replaced with new gloves, and an instrument involved in an injury should be removed from the sterile field

Precautions for dental procedures

Gloves should be worn for all direct contact with oral mucous membranes

Surgical masks and protective eyewear or face shields should be worn when splashing of saliva, blood, or other fluid is expected

Precautions for preventing spread of infection by tears

Hands should be washed after contact with tears; gloves should be worn when there are open lesions on hands; gloves may be worn routinely, if practical

Equipment

Detailed guidelines should be followed for disinfecting surfaces, devices, and equipment likely to be contaminated

Source: Adapted from CDC (1985b,c, 1986c, 1987b).

tice and the American Correctional Association surveyed all 50 of the state correctional departments, the Federal Bureau of Prisons, and 33 of 37 large city and county jail systems (CDC, 1986b). A total of 766 cases of AIDS meeting the CDC surveillance definition were reported during the survey. Respondents also reported eight AIDS cases among current or former correctional staff. Seven of the eight had known risk factors. None of these staff members reported an incident with an inmate wherein transmission of HIV-1 might have occurred, and investigation of the eighth case was not complete.

In the same survey it was found that approximately 75 percent of AIDS cases occurred within correctional systems in four locations: New York State, New York City, New Jersey, and Florida. These four jurisdictions followed the same combinations of policies: (1) segregation of all inmates with confirmed AIDS, but no segregation of inmates with AIDS-related symptoms or asymptomatic HIV-1 infection; (2) clinical evaluation and monitoring (without HIV-1 antibody testing) of inmates in known risk groups; and (3) intensive and continuous education programs for both staff and inmates.

In two other settings, the Maryland Division of Corrections in Baltimore studied (1) prisoners entering the institution and (2) prisoners who had been incarcerated for at least 7 years. In the first study, 1,000 consenting males and 30 consenting females were studied. Approximately 7 percent of the males were found to be EIA and Western blot reactive; approximately 14 percent of the female inmates were found to be seropositive. In the second study, blood samples from two of 137 inmates who participated were seropositive. Both of these inmates had been incarcerated for 9 years. Their period of incarceration would indicate that both individuals became infected while in prison. The testing was done anonymously, so no information is available on these two inmates.

In a study from a military maximum-security prison (Kelly et al., 1986), baseline seroprevalence of 1 percent was found; no seroconversion occurred in 567 initially negative inmates. Brewer et al. (in press) found a 7 percent baseline seroprevalance in another prison system. The rate of transmission was found to be 41 percent per prison-year of follow-up in 393 inmates. Both studies included only inmates who were incarcerated at the time of follow-up testing; nonetheless, the data suggest that the risk of transmission within prison is low.

In summary, the physical activities associated with HIV-1 infection are the same within prisons as they are in the community outside. What differs are the legal and ethical relationships among prisoners and between the institution and its inmates. Clarification of those relationships will help resolve such controversial issues as the value of screening, the uses of HIV-1 serology, and the distribution of sterile needles and/or condoms in the prison environment. Additional data on both seroprevalence and seroconversion in prisons should also aid in proper decision making and hasten the resolution of these controversies (see also Chapter 20).

PERSONNEL IN SCHOOLS, OFFICES, AND SIMILAR INSTITUTIONS

Questions have been raised about the risk from regular social interaction between an HIV-1-positive member of a group and the rest of the individuals in that group (e.g., students, teachers, aides, bus drivers, office and custodial staff). As of August 1988, 1,142 cases of AIDS have been reported to CDC in children under the age of 13 years at the time of diagnosis. Of these, 884 (nearly 80 percent) have occurred in children on whom available epidemiologic data suggest transmission from the mother during the perinatal period. Another 217 children (18 percent) became infected with HIV-1 through blood transfusion or from treatment for hemophilia. Data on the remainder are insufficient to establish a mode of transmission. As noted above, other than in sexual partners of HIV-1-infected persons and infants born to infected mothers, transmission of HIV-1 has not been documented in family members of the more than 72,000 AIDS patients reported to the CDC. Taken together, the studies of children, household contacts, and health care workers exposed to patients with AIDS testify that under normal classroom or office conditions, the risk of HIV-1 transmission is virtually nonexistent. However, in geographic areas with high prevalences of HIV-1 infection, certain precautionary measures may be appropriate for teachers and other institutional personnel to deal with

Table 14.3. Recommendations for Prevention of HIV-1 Transmission in Schools, Offices, and Other Institutions

Disposable gloves should be worn if exposure to blood or other body fluids is expected

Surfaces contaminated with blood or body fluids should be cleaned and disinfected with a 10% solution of household bleach (1 cup of bleach mixed with 9 cups of water) made within the previous 24 hours

Disposable items such as gloves, paper towels, or sanitary napkins should be discarded in sealable plastic bags

Mops and other nondisposable items should be avoided, but if used, should be rinsed in disinfectant

Hands should be washed thoroughly after removal of gloves

injuries from which exposure to blood or secretions is likely. Body fluids that have been documented to transmit HIV-1 include blood, semen, vaginal secretions, and breast milk.

One approach recently adopted in New York City and other jurisdictions is provision of protective gloves and clear guidelines for when such protection should be used. Such school guidelines usually include the types of recommendations summarized in Table 14.3.

VERY YOUNG OR IMPAIRED CHILDREN

Preschool children or those who are mentally or neurologically impaired are a special group. Although research has shown that person-to-person contact in the office or school poses no measurable risk for transmission, very little information on transmission of HIV-1 is available in young or impaired children. From research in other blood-borne virus infections, such as hepatitis B virus, transmission from the young or the mentally and/or physically handicapped should be anticipated (Breuer et al., 1985). This is especially true in HIV-1-positive children who are unable to control their bodily functions or who have weeping or open lesions. Restriction of their environment is the prudent course of action for these children in order to minimize exposure of other children. In this setting, adults who care for impaired children or perform day care for young children should be cognizant of the children's HIV-1 infection and adopt the appropriate precautions during direct care and strict hand washing afterward. Surfaces that have been soiled by blood or bodily fluids should be cleaned with a 10 percent solution of household bleach or with other effective agents (Martin et al., 1987). Further advice can be found in the Morbidity and Mortality Weekly Report (CDC, 1985a).

Day care of older children is similar to school or office contact, where casual contact plays no role in HIV-1 transmission.

REFERENCES

Anonymous (1984): Lancet 2:1376–1377.

Baker JL, Kelen G, Sivertson K, Quinn T (1987): Third International Conference on AIDS, Washington, D.C., June 4.

Breuer B, Friedman SM, Millner ES, Kane MA, Snyder RH, Maynard JE (1985): JAMA 254:3190–3195.

Brewer TF, Vlahov D, Taylor E, Hall D, Munoz A, Polk BF AIDS (in press).

Center for Disease Control (CDC) (1985a): MMWR 34:517.

CDC (1985b): MMWR 34:533.

CDC (1985c): MMWR 34:681.

CDC (1986a): MMWR 35:76.

CDC (1986b): MMWR 35:195.

CDC (1986c): MMWR 35:221.

CDC (1987a): MMWR 36:285.

CDC (1987b): MMWR 36:2S.

CDC (1988): MMWR 37:229.

Fischl MA, Dickinson GM, Scott GB, Klimas N, Fletcher MA, Parks W (1987): JAMA 257:640.

Friedland GH, Saltzman BR, Rogers MF, Kahl PA, Lesser ML, Mayers MM, Klein RS (1986): N Engl J Med 314:344.

Friedland GH, Saltzman BR, Rogers MF, Kahl PA, Feiner C, Mayers MM (1987): Third International Conference on AIDS, Washington, D.C., June 2.

Gerberding JL, Hopewell PC, Kaminsky LS, Sande MA (1985): N Engl J Med 312:56.

Gerberding JL, Bryant CE, Moss A, Levy JA, Carlson J, Sande MA (1986): Second International Conference on AIDS, Paris, June 23.

Glaser JB, Garden A (1985): N Engl J Med 313:266.

Groopman JE, Salahuddin SZ, Sarngadharan MG, Markham PD, Gonda M, Sliski A, Gallo RC (1984): Science 226:447.

Henderson DK, Saah AJ, Zak BJ, Kaslow RA, Lane HC, Folks T, Blackwelder WC, Schmitt J, LaCamera DJ, Masur H, Fauci AS (1986): Ann Intern Med 104:644.

Hirsch MS, Wormser GP, Schooley RT, Ho DD, Felsenstein D, Hopkins CC, Joline C, Duncanson F, Sarngadharan MG, Saxinger C, Gallo RC (1985): N Engl J Med 312:1.

Ho DD, Byington RE, Schooley RT, Flynn T, Rota TR, Hirsch MS (1985): N Engl J Med 313:1606.

Jagger J, Hunt EH, Brand-Elnaggar J, Pearson RD (1988): N Engl J Med 319:284.

Kelly PW, Redfield RR, Ward DL, Burke DS, Miller RN (1986): JAMA 256:2198.

Klein RS, Phelan J, Friedland GH, Freeman K, Schable C, Steigbigel N (1987): Third International Conference on AIDS, Washington, D.C., June 4.

Kuhls TL, Viker S, Parris NB, Garakian BS, Sullivan-Bolyai J, Cherry JD (1987): Am J Public Health 77:1306.

Martin LS, Loskoski SL, Bond WW (1987): Third International Conference on AIDS, Washington, D.C., June 3.

McCray E (1986): N Engl J Med 314:1127.

Shanson DC, Evans R, Lai L (1985): J Hosp Infect 6 (Suppl C):15.

Weiss SH, Goedert JJ, Gartner S, Popovic M, Waters D, Markham P, Di Marzo Veronese F, Gail MH, Barkley WE, Gibbons J, Gill FA, Leuther M, Shaw GM, Gallo RC, Blattner WA (1988): Science 239:68.

III
CONTROL: THE BIOMEDICAL AND SOCIAL RESPONSES

15

Prevention: General Considerations

DONALD P. FRANCIS AND RICHARD A. KASLOW

From the preceding chapters, it is clear that HIV-1 is an extremely virulent virus, which has already been effectively seeded throughout much of the world. It has caused substantial worldwide morbidity and mortality, and much more can be expected. Moreover, HIV-2, a less well understood member of this class of retroviruses, has appeared in individuals traveling or residing in West Africa.

With a pandemic of such magnitude, especially one that has spread unrecognized, grim reports of relentless illness and death have become common. Nonetheless, for as long as the basic epidemiology of HIV-1 has been understood, it has been clear that individuals and societies are not powerless in confronting this disaster. Quite the opposite. Nearly all transmission of HIV-1 around the world could be stopped if people at risk learned how to avoid infection and behaved accordingly. Well-designed public health programs can impart the knowledge, motivation, and skills necessary to prevent individuals from becoming infected. Voluntary programs aimed at changing individual behavior, together with government-mandated programs like screening of blood, are required in all at-risk communities around the world (Francis et al., 1987; Koop, 1987; Institute of Medicine, 1986). This chapter summarizes the essential elements of a community AIDS prevention program.

RESPONSIBILITY AND APPROACH

Each segment of the society, and ultimately each individual, must take some responsibility for preventing AIDS. In the prevention of infectious diseases, government public health authorities historically have played a large part. National, provincial or state, and local governments have had their roles. In the AIDS epidemic, each will have to provide guidance (policy) and resources (people and funds) according to its capabilities. Health care professionals, both individually in their practices and collectively through their organizations, will have to assume leadership roles. Success in preventing AIDS will depend on the effectiveness of the combined endeavors of local public health authorities and physicians who, together, can best reach the members of their communities whose behavior must be changed to interrupt transmission. Ultimately, it is the individual who must take responsibility to protect himself or herself. In short, public health authorities and practicing physicians have the responsibility for assuring that each person is given the opportunity to avoid HIV-1 infection, and the individual bears responsibility to exercise that opportunity. In addition, community groups must help foster concern, amplify prevention programs, and help maintain altered social norms.

The greatest attention of AIDS prevention programs should be paid to the most common transmission routes—those that involve mutually consensual acts, including sexual intercourse (between heterosexual men and women and between homosexual men) and needle and syringe sharing (between intravenous drug users). Reduction of or changes in these behaviors could stop further transmission. But this strategy for behavior change can only succeed in the proper atmosphere. Beyond the need for effective, goals, messages, and delivery programs, successful induction of behavior change will require building a level of trust between the public health workers (and physicians) and the public at risk. A successful strategy will require removal of any perceived threat of retribution or social ostracism attendant upon participation in an AIDS prevention program.

For HIV-1 transmission settings where exposure is not the result of a consenting act, more authoritarian approaches are clearly justified. A straightforward example is infection through blood, where, to prevent inadvertent administration of HIV-1-infected blood, governments and blood transfusion services have, in many areas of the world, promulgated regulations for donor testing. A less straightforward example of nonconsensual infection is that where HIV-1 is transmitted to a partner by someone who conceals his or her risk (or infection) from the partner. In this setting, although the exposed partner may consent to at-risk (sexual) behavior, the mistaken assumption of no HIV-1 risk places the partner at risk without having agreed to take that risk. In this case, physicians and public health practitioners must decide whether and how to intercede and warn the partner (see later).

For public health authorities and practitioners, ongoing prevention of HIV-1 infection will require considerable change in their historical roles. The task of changing behavior is complex, requiring the use of modern behavior modification techniques (see Chapter 16). For health departments and public health workers whose major activities in recent years have been childhood immunization, sexually transmitted disease and tuberculosis treatment, environmental toxin risk reduction, and indigent patient primary health care, AIDS prevention means a considerable program alteration.

Likewise for physicians, the required changes in practice will necessarily be considerable. For example, detailed sexual histories have not generally been obtained as a part of the standard medical history. Now, however, it has become an essential. The knowledge of sexual (and intravenous drug-using) history is important both for diagnostic and preventive clinical decisions. For effective prevention of AIDS, frank exchange of information about a patient's life-style will have to become a routine part of patient care.

Community groups have played and will continue to play a crucial role in AIDS prevention. The substantial changes in standards of homosexual practice, motivated in large part by homosexual communities around the world (see Chapter 16), are a model for other at-risk communities. The involvement of social, religious, and health community leaders is essential to achieving and maintaining changes in community standards.

Businesses, as part of the greater community, can play an increasingly important role in AIDS prevention. Businesses (and other employers) provide unique access points for persons at risk of HIV-1 infection. As a site for education and motivation, a business could become an important nidus of future social change.

PROGRAM COMPONENTS

Built on a commitment to AIDS prevention, on an understanding of the approaches to be used and on the involvement of public health personnel and physicians are the actual components of a well-designed program. The following summary will stress those components of prevention per se without further elaborating upon the patient and community support groups essential for adequate AIDS prevention.

Disease Monitoring and Program Evaluation

Surveillance
Surveillance—the collection, analysis, and dissemination of data—is essential for monitoring disease occurrence and the rates of infection in various segments of the society. These data are essential for making plans for care of patients and for assessing the impact of any prevention efforts.

Surveillance of cases of AIDS depends on physician reporting of diagnosed cases that meet standardized case definitions (CDC, 1987). It is required by law in many areas of the world. But reliance on passive reporting of cases will not suffice. Effective disease monitoring requires constant active surveillance by public health staffs and physicians. Depending on the local situation, a variety of active surveillance approaches have included involvement of infection control nurses and monitoring of pathology laboratory reports and death certificates.

Surveillance of infection (in contrast to disease) is somewhat more complex. It requires the systematic collection of serum and epidemiologic information on population groups. The results are collated and analyzed according to various epidemiologic classifications of risk. Ideally, regular collection of samples from such groups as patients of sexually transmitted disease clinics, drug treatment clinics, family planning clinics, and prenatal clinics and newborn babies should yield information that is valuable for informing the public on their chance of contacting an infected individual.

Evaluation
Ongoing evaluation of AIDS prevention programs is essential for assessing the effects of a given component and changing it if necessary. For many disease control programs, the occurrence of disease is used as the ultimate measure of control effectiveness. With the long latency period for AIDS, case monitoring is not timely enough to help in program evaluation. More useful information can be gleaned from monitoring infection rates, either prevalence or incidence rates.

Yet prevalence surveys have limited usefulness in terms of evaluation of program objectives, since the prevalance may vary considerably depending on patient makeup at the sampling time. More reliable, although more expensive, data can be obtained from the follow-up of cohorts of individuals from the major risk groups (McKusick et al., 1985; Winkelstein et al., 1987; Polk et al., 1987; Hessol et al., 1987) to determine incidence. Still, even fixed cohorts are not perfect, since yesterday's enrollees may not be representative of today's population. In addition to prevalence and incidence data, useful evaluation data can be obtained from close monitoring of cases of sexually transmitted disease or behavior surveys of at-risk populations.

Several means of evaluating various program "process" outputs should be built into program evaluation. Examples of these include measures such as the proportion of STD patients receiving instruction in AIDS prevention, the length of delay for those desiring serologic testing, and the length of delay in hiring staff or funding community programs after resources are identified.

Intervention

Intervention strategies to interrupt HIV-1 transmission can be divided according to the degree of consensuality in the HIV-1 exposure. As mentioned previously, this division is helpful for understanding the very different public health approaches needed to address the risk of transmission through consensual acts versus the risk of transmission through nonconsensual acts. The basic difference is that neither physicians nor public health authorities have an obligation other than to apply the best behavior modification techniques to interdict the behavior of people who choose to expose themselves or knowledgeable partners through mutually consensual acts. In other words, the obligation of health authorities is to attempt to teach the public, through information, motivation, and skill building, what behaviors confer risk and how to minimize that risk. If adequately informed individuals continue to take risks, that is their decision. For example, AIDS-knowledgeable homosexual men in the United States who continue to have unprotected anal intercourse or AIDS-informed heterosexual men in central Africa who continue to have unprotected vaginal intercourse with prostitutes should be subjected to authoritarian intervention only with extreme caution. They should receive the best prevention information available, delivered by the most effective means. Threats to autonomy in this setting may ultimately raise rather than lower resistance to preventive behavior.

It is important to stress that the implementation of such an approach is predicated upon having in place public health programs of the highest quality, including such elements as education, behavior modification, and the provision of condoms or other needs, before people can be assumed to have been given the fullest opportunity to decide what risk they personally are willing to take.

Where, however, there are people who are being exposed without their consent, the obligation to intervene directly is more compelling. The best example is the blood/blood products testing requirements instituted by governments that acknowledge their obligation to protect the blood supply (see Chapters 10 and 20).

In the setting of nonconsensual transmission, the message is, "The Government has taken action, and you can assume, to the extent possible through current technology, that the Government will act to protect, for example, transfused blood from HIV-1 contamination." In the setting of consensual transmission, the message is the opposite: "Individuals with HIV-1 infection exist, and you must assume that any of your sexual or needle-sharing partners may be infected with HIV-1 and take precautions to prevent yourself from becoming infected."

Prevention of Transmission Outside of Consensual Relationships

Blood and Blood Products

In areas where the prevalence of infection is high enough to justify serologic screening of blood and blood products, these products should be tested before being transfused (see Chapter 10).

Medical Injection Equipment

Although accidental injections using blood-contaminated equipment appear to be an inefficient route of HIV-1 transmission, such procedures can transmit infection. It is standard medical practice around the world to use sterilized or disposable injection equipment. However, in some areas, because of costs and habits, unsterilized equipment is commonly used for several different patients. In these areas, some alternative must be found. First, injections should be used only when they are essential; otherwise, alternate routes or different medications should be employed. Second, economical methods of sterilization must be incorporated into medical practices. If this is not possible, a last alternative is the use of disinfectants such as sodium hypochlorite.

Prenatal Screening

It is recommended that HIV-1 infected women postpone pregnancy until more is known about preventing infection of their offspring. An effective system to accomplish this is complex, requiring serologic testing, follow-up, and counseling. Because questions remain regarding the most cost-effective approach, studies are under way to clarify several points. Specifically, should all women be tested prior to marriage, when being seen in family planning clinics, and/or at the time of their prenatal visits? If not all women, then how should programs best be targeted toward persons at highest risk? At what prevalence of infection is universal screening justified? What is the effectiveness of pregnancy prevention among the identified women?

Answering these questions will take time. In the meantime, recommendations can be made regarding targeted screening programs. Clearly, there are already identified geographic areas and groups within those areas where the prevalence of infection is high enough to justify screening. These are areas where sexual activity and intravenous drug use overlap (see Chapters 9 and 13). In addition, special attention needs to be given to women who are known, either through testing or through having given birth to an infected child, to be infected; are known to be intravenous drug users; are known to have had sexual contact with persons known or presumed to be infected; are known to have received transfusions of untested blood in areas where rates of infection were high.

Unknowingly Exposed Sexual or Needle-Sharing Partners

It is unethical and, in many areas, possibly unlawful for a person who suspects or knows that he or she is infected with HIV-1 to engage in sexual intercourse or needle sharing with an uninformed person. For example, a bisexual man in the United States who has unprotected anal intercourse with men or a heterosexual man in central Africa who has unprotected vaginal intercourse with a prostitute should not be having unprotected intercourse with his wife unless the wife is thoroughly informed of the risk and willing to take that risk. This would presumably be true both for persons who have been tested and found positive and for those who have not been tested. The roles of the Government and the physician in preventing exposure in this situation are complex and are outlined later under "Partner Notification."

Prevention of Transmission Occurring Through Consensual Acts

With regard to HIV-1 transmission occurring through consensual acts, the ultimate aim, as stated above, is to empower uninfected individuals, through information, motivation, and skill building, to prevent themselves from becoming infected and to keep infected persons from spreading the virus to others. These individual changes will be most effective if accompanied by change in social norms—that is, by institutionalization of the practices that prevent the transmission of HIV-1 throughout the society. Some of the major goals and psychosocial principles governing personal and social changes in behavior are detailed in Chapter 16.

It is important from the outset in designing and implementing behavior modification programs to realize that people do change their behaviors. The profound attitude changes that have occurred in the United States with regard to smoking and drinking while driving are but two examples. In addition, it is important to realize that the extent of behavior change realized from any given intervention will vary depending on the delivery and content of the message. Some communication and motivation techniques will be more effective than others in empowering those at risk with the skills necessary to protect themselves.

Although individuals and societies do change, the world's populations are extremely varied. Within one country or even one community, individual variation is immense. Some are offended by the actions of others; some want to change the ways of others. Leaders in the struggle against AIDS must accept the variations in individuals as they are and deal with the task at hand under that realization. They must be tolerant of what exists and focus clearly on those behaviors that, if changed, limit the spread of this deadly virus. In other words, the ideal AIDS prevention program would be maximally effective at diminishing HIV-1 transmission but minimally disruptive to society.

Behavior change requires communication with all of those at risk regarding their specific hazardous behaviors. These communications must be explicit, with reference to sexual or needle-sharing acts in language that some individuals and communities may consider offensive. Opponents of AIDS prevention programs frequently claim that AIDS information, because it deals directly with sexual acts or intravenous drug use, condones these behaviors. Offensiveness to anyone should be minimized, but the superficial offense of some should not justify distorting or obscuring reality and, ultimately, jeopardizing the lives of others. No program will completely satisfy everyone. Whole programs cannot be interrupted for extended periods in attempt to mollify a few with extreme views.

Table 15.1. The AIDS Message

---

1. HIV-1 is an extremely dangerous virus. If you get it, it severely threatens your health and many of your life's activities.
2. You can get HIV-1 through sexual relations (both homosexual and heterosexual) and through sharing of drug injection equipment. Infected women can also give it to their babies around the time of birth.
3. By following a few simple rules, you can avoid HIV-1:
    a. Either don't engage in vaginal, anal, or oral sexual intercourse or, if you do, use a condom with spermicide jelly for all such activities.[a]
    b. Don't use intravenous drugs. If you must use intravenous drugs, don't share your "works." If you must share your "works," flush them with bleach between each use.
    c. If you are or want to get pregnant and have possibly been exposed to HIV-1, get tested. If you are infected, postpone or consider terminating your pregnancy.

---

[a]Exceptions would be long-term mutually monogamous relationships or relationships in which both members have tested negative for HIV-1 antibodies.

The message to be transmitted to the public by AIDS prevention programs is quite straightforward (see Table 15.1). In language and pictures tailored to the specific target audience, it should give a clear understanding of ways to prevent HIV-1 transmission. The essential components of the message are these: (1) Infection through sexual contact can be prevented by avoiding insertive sexual intercourse or by using condoms together with a nonoxynol-9-containing spermicide for all insertive penile activities. (2) Infection through use of intravenous drugs can be prevented by not sharing needles and syringes or, if needles are shared, by disinfecting with household bleach equipment that is reused. (3) Transmission of infection from mother to infant can be prevented by screening for antibody before or early in pregnancy and postponing (or terminating) pregnancy in seropositive women.

This message gives each person the minimal information necessary to understand transmission and how to avoid becoming infected. Together with information on the prevalence of infection in the local area, it forms the basis for AIDS prevention programs.

EDUCATION/INTERVENTION

The primary goal of prevention of consensual transmission is to communicate the AIDS prevention message (along with the message on how HIV-1 is *not* transmitted) to all members of the society in a manner that reduces HIV-1 transmission without provoking intensely emotional reactions. Educational messages can be aimed broadly to the general population or targeted to those at highest risk of infection. Both approaches are necessary, but for both general and targeted communication, the messages must be highly tailored to the cultural and educational status of the audience.

General Intervention Programs

Everyone needs to know the facts of AIDS whether or not he or she is actually at risk of infection. AIDS has generated considerable anxiety in many places around the world, unduly so in many cases, because the information was incomplete or inaccurate. It is therefore important that general information on modes of transmission, the nature and extent of individual risk, and the means of prevention be communicated to all. That can be accomplished through the mass media, places of employment (see earlier), schools, and other institutions. Schools have a special role, because they offer access to the next generation of persons at risk. Regardless of how effectively behavior modification programs are currently targeted to higher-risk individuals (see later), new and previously missed members of those groups will require continued attention. Schools offer the best access for future generations of persons at risk, and many schools have begun offering AIDS prevention programs. All students should begin to receive education in advance of beginning at-risk behavior.

Targeted Intervention Programs

As described in detail in previous chapters, HIV-1 infection clusters within groups whose behavior or medical care places them at increased risk of infection. It is therefore far more efficient to concentrate (or "target") active intervention programs toward those at increased risk (Table 15.2). What persons to target and what sites of contact ("access points") to use will depend on the epidemiology of HIV-1 infection and the social structures in the areas where the programs are aimed. The most obvious groups are homosexual men, intravenous drug users, prostitutes, hemophiliacs and other recipients of potentially infectious transfusions, sexual

Table 15.2. Target Groups and Access Points for Intervention Programs

Target Group	Access Point
Homosexual men	Community/street outreach
	Baths/bookstores/bars
	Gay press
	STD clinics
Intravenous drug users	Methadone/detoxification centers
	Needle exchange programs
	Hospitals
	Community/street outreach
	Correctional facilities
	STD clinics
Heterosexually promiscuous	STD clinics
	Family planning clinics
	Community/street outreach
	Correctional facilities
Blood/blood product recipients	Clinics/hospitals
Partners of infected people	Testing centers
	Physicians' offices/clinics
High-risk mothers	Methandone/detoxification centers
	Correctional facilities
	Family planning clinics
	Community/street outreach
	STD clinics

contacts of infected persons, heterosexual persons with multiple partners, and women of childbearing age at risk of infection.

Homosexual Men
The greatest experience has been gained in risk reduction programs of homosexual men. Various approaches have been taken, and the combined effect has been most dramatic (see Chapters 7 and 16), exemplifying the ability to change not only individual behavior but community standards of sexual practice. Continued reinforcement of current, and even improved, standards will be required to further limit transmission.

Intravenous Drug Users
Intravenous drug users have been targeted in intervention programs in several cities around the world (see Chapters 9 and 16). Different approaches have been taken. Educating IV drug users by a variety of programs has shown considerable effect on knowledge but not necessarily on behavior change (Watters, 1987; Chaisson, 1987). Important effects have reportedly resulted from distribution of free bleach and condoms by street outreach workers. Although the deficit of treatment opportunities in methadone programs for heroin addicts has been almost universal, at least in the United States, many areas are attempting to reopen these programs. The availability of this alternative to sharing injection paraphernalia is an obvious and necessary addition to AIDS prevention. The need for greatly expanded facilities for drug addiction treatment programs has been prominently publicized (Presidential Commission, 1988). On the other hand, controversy has surrounded the supply of free injection equipment to addicts. This strategy has obvious appeal, and there is increasing evidence that its benefits outweigh its risks (Ljungberg et al., 1988). Intravenous drug users are a unique challenge because of the varied cultural makeup in various geographical areas. Overall success will depend, no doubt, on using all available options and tailoring programs to the specific cultural groups.

Hemophiliacs
Because of the extremely high rates of infection in recipients of factor VIII, special counseling programs are required to prevent transmission to their sexual contacts.

Transfusion Recipients
Between 1978 and mid-1985, when HIV-1 donor testing began in many parts of the world, infected blood was transfused into susceptible recipients. The rates of infection varied greatly in different geographic regions. Follow-up serologic testing has been recommended for recipients in many high-prevalence areas, and, in the case of infected recipients, specific counseling will be required to prevent transmission to their sexual contacts.

STD Patients
Heterosexually active persons can be attracted into HIV-1 counseling through a variety of efforts. HIV-1 testing centers, prostitute outreach, jails, and community outreach are discussed later. One indicator of HIV-1 risk is the acquisition of other sexually transmitted infections. Patients presenting to private or public facilities for

the diagnosis and treatment of sexually transmitted diseases deserve special targeting for AIDS prevention.

Prostitutes

In areas of the world where prostitution is legal and the practice requires assurances of freedom from sexually transmitted diseases, it may be reasonable to add HIV-1 screening to the ongoing health screening program. In areas where prostitution is illegal, it has been suggested that mandatory testing be instituted in jails and other points where prostitutes are apprehended. However, before initiating such programs in either area, plans for counseling; for providing health care, housing, and subsistence; and for monitoring at-risk behavior of seropositive prostitutes must be fully established. The goal of these components would be to prevent identified infected prostitutes from merely migrating and possibly increasing the frequency of contact with uninfected customers. Furthermore, before launching AIDS prevention campaigns among prostitutes, it is important for public health officials to understand exactly what message may be communicated to the potential clients of prostitutes. Through a highly publicized testing and removal program (and all such programs will become highly publicized), the message may be inappropriately translated: "All infected prostitutes are being removed; therefore, it is safe to have unprotected sex with prostitutes." It may, in fact, be wiser to send the opposite message: "Infected prostitutes are out there; to protect yourself, you had better assume that all prostitutes are infected and take appropriate precautions."

"Hot Spots"

Geographic areas deserving special targeting of HIV-1 prevention can be identified by several indicators. The best, although not always available, is HIV-1 infection itself. Through seroprevalence surveys or through case surveillance, high-rate areas can be identified. In absence of such knowledge, surrogate indicators of elevated AIDS risk, such as the occurrence of other sexually transmitted diseases or IV drug use–related incidents, can be used. These indicators can identify specific geographic areas and specific groups in which aggressive community-based and culturally sensitive intervention programs should be undertaken. Many of these areas will be in inner-city concentrations of poverty compounded by high rates of IV drug use and prostitution. The potential for HIV-1 spread in these areas is considerable. Community-based intervention programs must be launched in these areas as soon as the combination of infection and risk-provoking behavior is discovered.

Health Care Workers

Education of health care workers is essential for a successful AIDS prevention program. Although the risk of nosocomial HIV-1 infection is extremely low for health care workers, it does occur. A safe environment for health care workers to care for HIV-1-infected persons requires clear guidelines together with continuing staff education (see Chapter 14). Serologic testing of all (or selected) patients may be justified for patient care reasons but is not so readily recommended for prevention of nosocomial infection. An exception to this guideline may exist for some invasive procedures carrying a high probability of accidental percutaneous exposure, particularly where there are no safer alternative procedures.

Access to Targeted Persons

There are specific sites where persons at increased risk for HIV-1 infection can be reached. These "access points" can be convenient sites for basing behavioral change programs.

Correctional Facilities

Correctional facilities are, in many areas, important places to access persons at high risk for HIV-1 infection. Since both prostitutes and intravenous drug users have high rates of arrest, jails and other holding facilities offer a unique opportunity to influence these individuals. Although it can be difficult to instill personal responsibility with a sense of mutual cooperation and concern about health in a punitive environment, the use of counselors or prisoner advocates who are unambiguously separate from the correctional staff may help circumvent this problem.

Family Planning and Prenatal Clinics

Clients of family planning and prenatal clinics are, by definition, sexually active and of childbearing age. Thus, these clinics are excellent access points to target the AIDS prevention message. Protection of sexual contacts and future offspring requires serologic testing of some patients. Who should be tested and how to identify these persons are discussed earlier.

HIV Testing Centers

In the United States the Alternate Test Site (ATS) program was established to provide cost-free testing for infection outside of the blood banks. These ATS centers are used by persons who perceive themselves to be or to have been at increased risk for HIV-1 infection. Indeed, the prevalence of infection in persons attending these clinics is far higher than in the general population. Thus, intensive counseling of these persons should employ the most effective techniques of behavior modification.

Prevention/Treatment Centers

An extremely important target group for AIDS prevention messages is persons already carrying the AIDS virus. After all, the next generation of infections will result from risk-taking behavior of these persons and their susceptible partners. The combination of medical and immunological follow-up together with effective behavioral counseling could dramatically affect the rate of future transmission of HIV-1. The link between medical and behavioral interventions will remain essential for the AIDS prevention programs in many parts of the world. The challenge is to integrate the medical personnel and the public health counselors under the great variety of medical systems that exist worldwide.

Other Issues

Serologic Testing

Broad serologic testing for HIV-1 antibodies, although at times controversial, is a key element of AIDS control programs in many parts of the world. A substantial proportion of people who may have been exposed to HIV-1 often want to know whether they have been infected. Important for public health, the motivation behind this desire is often concern about preventing infection of others. In addition, the whole psychologic process surrounding the decision to be tested offers an opportunity for instilling behavior change (see Chapter 16).

But preventive reasons alone are not the sole justification for encouraging serologic testing. With increasing prospects of effective medical intervention, which may be more effective early in the clinical course, increased demand for testing can be expected. Serologic testing is, and will continue to be, performed in both the public and private health care sectors. For public health reasons, it is imperative that the opportunity to change hazardous behavior be taken in such settings. There is an important need to develop programs through which HIV-1-infected persons identified by testing in the private sector are motivated and instructed in the same behavioral changes as are those seen in the public sector.

Partner Nofitication

A group at very high risk of infection in most need of intensive counseling is susceptible sexual partners of HIV-1-infected people. Many contacts of infected persons are not infected at the time of contact (Padian, 1987) yet continue to be exposed. The possibility of breaking the infection chain at this point is real. However, these situations are often difficult, especially when the relationship is an ongoing one, because notification of the susceptible partner involves not only the revelation of infection in the partnership but often disclosure of previously unknown past sexual or intravenous drug-using activities. In general, this notification process can be accomplished smoothly through cooperative interaction of both members of the couple and the physician or public health counselor.

However, occasionally the infected person refuses to notify his or her partner. For a relationship that has ended, the exposed partner can be notified of the possible exposure without revealing the identity of the source. For a relationship in which at-risk behaviors are continuing and the infected person refuses to inform the partner, there is a serious conflict between the infected individual's right to privacy and the exposed individual's right to know of life-threatening exposure. Most practitioners of public health and medicine believe that the rights of the exposed person outweigh the rights of privacy of the infected individual. In some cases statutes have been passed to protect the professional who informs a susceptible individual in such situations (Hughes, 1987) (see Chapter 20).

It should be stressed again that, ideally, partner notification, like most other AIDS prevention activities, should be undertaken in an atmosphere of cooperation. Repeated efforts should be made by the physician to convince the infected person to inform the at-risk partner. With steadfast refusal, however, the physician or the health department must diplomatically intervene. Although this intervention can become authoritarian, all involved should realize that the desired end is behavior change, which ultimately will require mutual trust and cooperation. These situations must obviously be addressed with extreme tact. Finally, since the issue is informed consent to continued exposure, once the partner is informed (and hopefully educated, motivated, and provided the skills to avoid infection), then the government's or physician's responsibility has logically ended.

Confidentiality and Privacy

As time goes on, knowledge spreads, and confidence in the truth about HIV-1 transmission overshadows the unwarranted fears, people infected with HIV-1 may be able to discuss their plight freely with all concerned. Until then, the knowledge of a person's infection status must be kept confidential. The health professionals caring for the infected individual and his or her contacts must protect their privacy as effectively as their health. The results of HIV-1 testing simply cannot be treated like those of other diagnostic tests. At the same time, patient counseling should stress that the relatively infrequent major breaches of confidentiality have often been due not to any fault of the medical/testing system but rather to violations by acquaintances who had actually been informed by the infected individual.

CONCLUSION

AIDS prevention is both simple and complex. The means of prevention are simple. But because this prevention requires changes in human behavior, and because discussion of sexual and intravenous drug-using behaviors are extremely difficult for many people in various places in the world, the process of counseling infected persons and protecting uninfected ones may be delicate and complex. Public health and medical professionals must convince the political leaders that, with institutional guidance and support, individuals, for whom they are all responsible, can stop the further spread of HIV-1.

REFERENCES

Chaisson RE (1987): Lancet 1:1430.

Francis DP, Chin J (1987): JAMA 257:1357–1366.

Hessol NA (1987): Society of Epidemiologic Research, 20th Annual Meeting, Amherst, MA.

Hughes T (1987): Assembly Bill 250, State of California, AIDS Diagnosis Disclosure. Signed Sept. 11, 1987, effective Jan. 1, 1988.

Institute of Medicine, National Academy of Sciences (1986): Confronting AIDS. Directions for Public Health, Health Care and Research. Washington, D.C.: National Academy Press.

Koop CE (1987): Surgeon General's Report on Acquired Immune Deficiency Syndrome. Washington, D.C.: U.S. Department of Health and Human Services.

Ljungberg B, Andersson B, Christensson B, Hugo-Persson M, Tunving K, Ursing B (1988): Fourth International Conference on AIDS, Stockholm, Sweden, June 12–16.

McKusick L, Horstman W, et al. (1985): Am J Public Health 75:493–496.

CDC (1987): MMWR 35:1s.

Padian N (1987): Infect Dis 9:947.

Polk BF, Fox R, et al. (1987): N Engl J Med 316:61.

Presidential Commission on the Human Immunodeficiency Virus Epidemic (1988): Report, Washington, D.C., June 24.

Watters J (1987): Personal communication. Of 600 cross-sectioned IVDU's studied over the last 5 months of 1987 (in treatment and out of treatment), 82% of those studied used bleach.

Winkelstein WW, Lyman DM, et al. (1987): JAMA 257:321.

16

Behavioral Factors and Intervention

RON STALL, THOMAS J. COATES, JEFFREY S. MANDEL,
EDWARD S. MORALES, AND JAMES L. SORENSEN

Since the earliest days of the epidemic, health educators and the lay public have shown strong interest in the psychosocial aspects of AIDS. The focus has been primarily on the responses of the disparate social groups in which the AIDS epidemic was initially concentrated and on the effects of psychosocial factors on the onset of AIDS after HIV-1 infection. Early in the epidemic, prevention and behavioral research efforts stimulated the development of a psychosocial research agenda for AIDS (Coates et al., 1984) that had four major components: (1) strategies for preventing the spread of infection; (2) the impact of psychosocial variables on disease incidence and progression; (3) the impact of the disease process itself on behaviors and psychological functioning of those infected with the AIDS virus; and (4) the efficacy of interventions for modifying the effect of the epidemic on individuals coping with the threat of disease. This chapter highlights empirical findings on the first three components.

PREVENTION OF HIV-1 INFECTION AMONG HOMOSEXUAL MEN

The absence of either a cure or a vaccine for AIDS has lent tremendous importance to efforts aimed at health education and behavior change. The extent and correlates of high-risk behaviors for HIV-1 infection have been increasingly well studied among homosexual men in various cities across the United States. Individual studies have documented behavior changes within the male homosexual community in response to the AIDS epidemic, comparisons of the correlates of high-risk behavior across studies have guided the continuing development of prevention campaigns, and these campaigns may represent points of departure for similar efforts within other populations.

Numerous health education efforts have been undertaken to inform the homosexual male population how to avoid HIV-1 infection. As early as 1984, many homosexual men in San Francisco, for example, could correctly identify the sexual behaviors thought likely to spread the AIDS virus (McKusick et al., 1985a). Since that time they have significantly reduced their participation in these dangerous sexual practices (McKusick et al, 1985b, 1986) although not always with concomitant

Table 16.1. Trends in Selected Sexual Behaviors During the Previous 30 Days in the AIDS Behavioral Research Project

	Nov. 1984 ($N = 728$)	Nov. 1985 ($N = 676$)	Nov. 1986 ($N = 584$)
5+ Sexual partners	16.5%	15.7%	15.8%
Unprotected anal intercourse	54.2%	36.2%	29.5%
Protected anal intercourse	14.1%	23.8%	30.3%

increases in "safe" sexual practices. In other words, the modal response among homosexual men in San Francisco to the AIDS epidemic seems to have included important declines in risky sexual activity and in sexual activity itself. Data from the San Francisco AIDS Behavioral Research Project (Table 16.1) reflect changes in the percentage of men who engage in unprotected anal intercourse, who use condoms, and who have multiple sexual partners. These findings describe trends in sexual behavior from a convenience sample of self-identified homosexual men drawn in San Francisco over a 2-year period. There was apparently little change in the proportion of men in the sample with five or more sexual partners during the previous month. This can be attributed, in part, to the tendency of AIDS education efforts in San Francisco to stress the risk associated with particular sexual acts rather than the absolute number of sexual partners. In contrast, the proportion of men who engaged in unprotected anal intercourse at least once during the previous month decreased by nearly half during the same period. Educating the homosexual male population about the risks associated with unprotected anal intercourse has been the primary focus of AIDS prevention campaigns in San Francisco, and these declines give some evidence of the efficacy of these efforts. These figures include men in monogamous couples, who, if uninfected, may engage in anal intercourse without any risk of exposure to HIV-1. Conversely, the proportion of men who in the previous month engaged in anal intercourse while using a condom approximately doubled during the same time period. Of course, during each measurement period, many of these who were not engaging in protected anal sex were not engaging in anal sex at all. Other studies based on convenience samples of self-identified urban homosexual males have also detected striking changes in high-risk sexual behavior.

As a result of these behavior changes, the incidence of HIV-1 infection and of other sexually transmitted diseases had decreased markedly among homosexual men in San Francisco and elsewhere (see Chapters 6 and 7). There nevertheless remain critical uncertainties about whether these reported changes are real, whether these reported changes can be generalized to behaviorally homosexual men who do not live in large urban cities or who do not identify themselves as homosexuals, and how much effect these changes will have on the further spread of HIV-1 infection among behaviorally homosexual populations.

In fact, behavioral changes made by homosexual men in response to the AIDS epidemic have been uneven (Ostrow et al., 1986; Siegel et al., 1987). In May 1985, approximately 25 percent of a cohort of homosexual men in the San Francisco AIDS Behavioral Research Project were still engaging in at least one high-risk sexual act per month outside of a primary relationship. Such findings suggest that there are certain circumstances (or sets of circumstances) under which homosexual men have failed to change behaviors that were vitally affecting their health.

Continued high-risk sexual behavior appeared to be associated with denial of personal risk for AIDS (Ostrow et al., 1986; Weber et al., unpublished). The latter investigators selected for analysis only those men who frequent gay bars. This group of 199 men was divided into four categories based on reported sexual behavior during the previous month: safe sex only (including monogamy and celibacy), sexual behavior capable of infecting self (receptors), sexual behavior capable of infecting others (transmitters), and those who were both transmitters and receptors. Those who engaged in any kind of transmitter behavior scored higher in denial than any of the other groups.

A strong relationship has been found between drug and alcohol use during sexual activity and noncompliance with safe sex techniques (Stall et al., 1986; Ostrow et al, 1987; Stall and Ostrow, in press). A cross-sectional analysis showed that use of particular drugs (including alcohol), the number of drugs, and the frequency of combining drugs with sexual activity were all strongly associated with measures of risk for HIV-1 infection. Retrospective data from the same analysis showed that men who abstained from combining drug use with sexual activity were relatively unlikely to have practiced high-risk behavior during the previous year, whereas the men who combined drug use with sexual activity were more likely to have engaged in such high-risk sex acts. Ostrow et al. (1987) found in a prospective analysis that as the proportion of acts involving alcohol or drugs increased, so did risk of exposure to HIV-1. Although the causal direction of the relationship between high-risk sex and drug and/or alcohol use during sexual activity has not been firmly established, the consequences of HIV-1 infection are so profound that groups at risk for sexual exposure to HIV-1 should be made aware of the potential dangers of combining these behaviors.

A number of other factors may interact to influence one's ability to modify sexual risk for HIV-1 exposure. For example, in one study, significantly more potentially unsafe sexual activity occurred within primary homosexual relationships than between men who were not as seriously involved with each other (McKusick et al., 1985a). Of course, if the relationship was monogamous and both partners were seronegative, then no risk for HIV-1 infection was involved. However, absolute confidence in either seronegativity or monogamy carries its own risk. Another variable that may be important to successful modification of high-risk behaviors is age. As of 1984, a higher proportion of homosexual men 40 years of age and older in the AIDS Behavioral Research Project sample participated in unsafe sexual behavior than did younger men (McKusick et al., 1986). However, these older men seemed more likely to sustain lower sexual risk than men in their 20s. Furthermore, men who believed that they had been exposed to, but had fought off, the AIDS virus reported significantly greater numbers of sexual partners and more high-risk sexual activity than those who believed that they were incubating the virus or those who believed that they had not been exposed (McKusick et al., 1985b).

In a recent 18-month prospective analysis of 672 men in the San Francisco AIDS Behavioral Research Project (McKusick et al., 1986), a number of measures of psychiatric status, health beliefs, demography, health status, and social support were simultaneously assessed. Five variables were found to be significantly related to sustained high-risk sexual behavior ($R = .47$, $p < .05$). The belief that one is capable of making recommended changes were most powerfully associated with the level of high-risk activity. Men in primary relationships (monogamous and non-monogamous) were also found to have engaged more frequently in behavior that might transmit HIV-1 than men not in such relationships. Increased familiarity with one's partner may have led to relaxation of restrictions on behavior, although other confounding factors (e.g. knowledge of antibody status) may also explain this relationship. Depression, the third most powerful predictor, was greater in those who subsequently reduced risk. Fourth, younger men were more likely than older men to be engaged in high-risk activity during the 18-month period. The fifth significant correlate was level of agreement with AIDS risk reduction guidelines, with those more likely to agree being more likely to sustain low levels of sexual risk activity throughout the period.

These general findings have been replicated by analyses of data from the Multicenter AIDS Cohort Study of homosexual men in four American cities. In that cohort (Emmons et al., 1986), three variables—perceived efficacy of behavioral change, knowledge regarding AIDS risk reduction guidelines, and the perceived personal risk of AIDS—were related retrospectively to measures of behavioral risk reduction. In a subsequent analysis of this cohort, with better control for confounding variables, perceived personal risk for AIDS no longer remained related to risk reduction (Joseph et al., 1987a). Prospective analyses in the Chicago portion of the cohort demonstrated a negative association between sense of personal risk for AIDS and risk-reducing behavior change and psychosocial distress. In contrast, availability of supportive peer norms was associated with sexual risk reduction (Joseph et al., 1987b). These findings suggest why a policy that involves a social or legal risk like automatic testing for HIV-1 antibody should be forged with care, and how mandatory testing could well result in unfortunate public health outcomes. That is, it has been shown that increasing perception of risk for AIDS is not associated with desirable sexual risk reductions, whereas increasing the sense of risk for this disease may result in a wide variety of psychological impairments. Those who wish to prevent further HIV-1 infection among homosexual men should work to find an effective alternative that does not result in demonstrable psychosocial costs to a population already in crisis. [For further detail, see Stall et al., in press; Coates et al., in press (a,b)].

PREVENTION OF HIV-1 INFECTION AMONG INTRAVENOUS DRUG USERS

Although intravenous drug users present special difficulties for AIDS health education and prevention efforts, few studies regarding the behavioral epidemiology of risk for HIV-1 infection within this group have actually been completed. Ginzburg (1984) outlined the scope of the problem for drug abusers and those who treat them. One barrier to implementing effective health intervention for intravenous drug users is the common stereotype that they are not concerned about health and will not change their behavior to avoid exposure to HIV-1 (Des Jarlais et al, 1985c); however, some observations contradict this common misperception (Friedman et al., 1986). Certainly not as much is known about the psychosocial correlates of high-risk behaviors for HIV-1 infection among needle users as is known for homosexual male populations. As late as 1986, there had been only one study of AIDS and addiction compared to 10 concerned with AIDS among homosexual men (Drucker, 1986).

High-risk behaviors have been quite common among intravenous drug abusers (see Chapter 9). From one study in New York, 88 percent of intravenous drug users with AIDS or related illness had shared needles (Friedland et al., 1985). From another study in Dallas, 68 percent of intravenous drug abusers applying to a 30-day inpatient drug treatment program reported that they engaged in needle sharing, and they did so in 40 percent of their drug use episodes (Black et al., 1986). Operating from street-front outposts in New York City, Des Jarlais et al. (1985b) found that needle sharing was endemic in "shooting galleries." HIV-1 seroprevalence among intravenous opiate abusers throughout the United States has shown wide variation: the prevalence was 1 to 2 percent in urban Ohio programs in 1986 (Seligman et al., 1988), less than 2 percent in California in 1985 (Levy et al., 1986), ten percent in New Haven in 1982 (D'Aquilla et al., 1986) 10 percent in San Francisco in 1985 (Chaisson et al., 1987), and up to 58 percent in New York City in 1984 (Spira et al., 1984).

Although drug users are well aware of the dangers of needle sharing (Ginzburg et al., 1986), there are few data to demonstrate how the prevalence of needle sharing has changed as the AIDS epidemic has progressed. Similarly, little is known of changes in sexual practices that may be occurring among needle users and their sexual partners, although many needle users have sexual partners who do not use drugs (Murphy, 1987). Workers in New York City (Des Jarlais et al., 1985a) have suggested that needle users have made attempts to control exposure to HIV-1 by increasing demand for new needles. Participants in this study reported that resealed needles were sold as new, in a market response to the fear of AIDS (Des Jarlais et al., 1985a). Needles have been distributed in "two-for-one" sales or offered "free" with sales of $25 or more of heroin (Des Jarlais and Hopkins, 1985).

Biernacki (1986) reported that among needle users who were aware of the dangers of HIV-1 infection posed by needle sharing, certain factors were important in continuing this behavior. Among these were the risk of arrest if needles were carried, cultural beliefs concerning the meaning of needle sharing, and a general suspicion accorded messages from mainstream society. As has often been noted (see Chapter 9), the transmission of HIV-1 infection through needle sharing and consequent heterosexual contact with those who share needles serves as a conduit to the heterosexual community as a whole. This route of spread of HIV-1 infection presents a particular threat to black and Hispanic urban communities. To be effective, future AIDS prevention and health education programs must reflect strong involvement by the affected communities.

Only a few health professionals have directly assessed interventions aimed at reducing the spread of HIV-1 infection among drug users. One pilot study reported the need for a program to prevent initiation into intravenous drug use (Des Jarlais, Friedman, Cariel, and Kott, 1987). Another approach is small group education, which has promising preliminary results with IV drug abusers in residential treatment (Sorensen et al., 1988a,b) and is being attempted by research groups in San

Francisco, New York, Boston, and Seattle. Individualized education has also met with some success (Gibson et al., 1988). Friedman et al. (1986) have pointed out, in their thoughtful review of issues relevant to intravenous drug users, that AIDS prevention efforts can be attempted from outside the subculture (e.g., health education messages, public billboards, interventions based in detoxification clinics) and from within the subculture (e.g., street intervention workers who were once intravenous drug users). Efficacy of prevention and health education strategies appears more likely to result if both avenues of intervention are followed. Drug users may be accepting of HIV-1 testing, especially in areas where prevalence of infection is low (Carlsen and McLellan, 1987; Weddington and Brown, 1988). Simply conducting HIV-1 testing in a methadone program may lead to decreased needle sharing among those who were seropositive, those who were seronegative, and even those who were recruited for study but not tested for HIV-1 antibody (Des Jarlais et al., 1986). Methadone maintenance is a promising method of diverting both HIV-1-infected and uninfected persons out of the needle-using population, and has appeared to reduce needle use among HIV-1 infected addicts (Batki et al., in press).

An important proportion—perhaps the majority—of those who recreationally inject drugs are not in treatment. For these persons methadone maintenance does not represent an effective means of controlling further HIV-1 infection. Two alternative methods have been proposed for the primary prevention of HIV-1 infection among nonclinical intravenous drug-using populations. The first of these is the community health outreach model, in which health workers go to the settings in which intravenous drug users congregrate and inform them which behaviors risk HIV-1 infection, the consequence of infection, and how to protect themselves and others against infection. Included as part of this training are demonstrations of how to sterilize needles if abstinence from drugs is not an option. In San Francisco thousands of 1-oz bottles of bleach have been distributed to encourage sterilization, and preliminary evaluations have indicated that intravenous drug users readily change needle hygiene as a result of contact with street-level health workers (Watters, 1987). The tendency of intravenous drug users to change the style of using drugs rather than to stop using drugs altogether in order to reduce risk has obvious parallels among smokers who switch to "low-tar" brands.

The second strategy for preventing HIV-1 infection among intravenous drug users not in treatment is that of needle exchange. This approach to prevention involves exchange of sterile needles for used needles. Exchange has recently been initiated in the United States, owing in part to fears that needle exchange programs will encourage intravenous drug use. Indeed, considerable controversy is attached to both of these approaches. There is little agreement as to which of these approaches is most efficacious, and rigorous evaluations have only begun to yield results (Stimson et al., 1988).

It is almost certainly unwise to think of HIV-1 risk reduction among intravenous drug users as being the domain of any single strategy for risk reduction. Because of the diversity among intravenous drug users, no one preventive approach is likely to control risk entirely. Among intravenous drug users, as among other populations at high risk of HIV-1 infection, there is no simple or uniform solution to risk reduction, no one magic bullet. To control the risk of HIV-1 infection among intravenous drug users, continued program development must remain sensitive to the changing correlates of risk as the AIDS epidemic progresses, with rigorous evaluation of demonstration projects.

PREVENTION OF HIV-1 INFECTION AMONG ETHNIC MINORITIES

Because the AIDS epidemic has affected ethnic minorities disproportionately (see Chapters 6, 8, and 9), standard health education and prevention efforts must be modified to meet the special needs of these populations. As of August 1988, over 40 percent of all AIDS cases in the United States were members of minority groups. Cases of AIDS among blacks have been overrepresented by 2.3 times according to their proportion of the general population, and Hispanics are overrepresented by 2.5 times. These overrepresentations are more extreme among the heterosexual cases: approximately 50 percent of all heterosexual male cases are black, and 24 percent are Hispanic. Thus, approximately two-thirds of the heterosexual AIDS cases are members of minority groups. Minority issues are also important in the consideration of the pediatric patients with AIDS. The overrepresentation of ethnic minorities among the heterosexual AIDS cases can be largely attributed to infection related to intravenous drug use. Since heterosexual contact with infected intravenous drug users can result in further infection, AIDS is clearly an issue of paramount importance to the disproportionately affected minority populations.

Although there has been considerable discussion of AIDS and heterosexual ethnic minorities, AIDS is also a problem for men who are both homosexual and members of ethnic minorities. Approximately half of the minority AIDS cases are homosexual, and these men, while gravely ill, must deal with homophobia from within their own ethnic communities as well as ethnocentrism or racism within the homosexual male community. Furthermore, neither the gay male community nor the ethnic minority communities have designed prevention efforts with the needs of ethnic minority homosexuals in mind. Although meeting their needs in the face of the AIDS epidemic will not be easy, it seems reasonable to recommend that minority health care agencies concerned with AIDS recruit and train ethnic minority homosexual professionals who are best able to meet the special needs of ethnic homosexual men.

Given this epidemiological profile, it is clear that effective prevention and health education strategies must be designed for ethnic minority populations. Such strategies will be most effective if they are responsive to the values and behaviors of the particular populations being addressed—that is, it cannot be assumed that generic messages on AIDS prevention regarding drug or sexual transmission will be effective in reaching ethnic minority populations if sexuality and drug use are perceived differently among minority populations than among the general population. Thus, developing successful intervention strategies must begin with reliable group-specific data on community awareness of the AIDS threat, on attitudes toward the disease and the high-risk behaviors, and on the degree of participation in those behaviors. These data do not yet exist. However, even after this information has been assembled and analyzed, prevention and health education strategies should be attempted only with an intimate understanding of the unique language and cultural characteristics of a particular community. Given the dearth of behavioral research in ethnic communities at greatest risk, it is not surprising that few insights are currently available to guide intervention within these communities. However, the threat of AIDS has become so immediate within certain ethnic communities that undertaking rigorous risk-related research and health policy analyses before initiating prevention efforts has almost certainly become an unaffordable luxury.

For these reasons minority researchers can make invaluable contributions to AIDS prevention teams. Without effective minority participation, significant lapses in protocol design or data analysis and failures in the implementation of health prevention or education strategies seem likely. The effectiveness of grass roots minority organizations in conducting AIDS prevention or health education efforts should be assessed. Organizations with strong ties to the local community will most likely be more effective in conducting campaigns consistent with minority perceptions and values than will organizations based outside the community. The effectiveness of grass roots minority organizations should be ever greater if the participation of community leaders is sought. Thus, participation of both minority researchers and minority organizations is a crucial step toward mobilizing ethnic communities at large against AIDS.

PREVENTION OF HIV-1 INFECTION AMONG HETEROSEXUALS

Heterosexual risk reduction programs need to target adolescents, minority groups, known contacts of HIV-1-positive individuals, prostitutes, sexually transmitted disease clinic patients, childbearing women and their partners, men and women in military service, prisoners, sexual partners of persons with hemophilia, and others that received blood products during the period 1978–1985. For all of these groups at risk, health education programs and other prevention efforts must be sensitive to the special characteristics of the target population and encourage indigenous efforts to prevent HIV-1 infection. Expertise gained with these specialized heterosexual populations may well be useful in guiding prevention strategies for other groups of heterosexuals.

In the case of adolescents, it appears that sex education programs can be used to play an effective role in AIDS prevention. Recent evaluations of sex education programs among adolescents have supported the view that (1) sex education is effective in increasing use of contraceptives and decreasing pregnancy rates (Zelnik and Kantor, 1980), and (2) sex education does not increase sexual activity—namely initiation, frequency, or number of multiple partners (Kirby, 1984; Kirby et al., 1979).

However, a number of important issues need to be considered in the development of sex education programs for adolescents (Schinke et al., 1979; Urberg, 1982). Sex education should teach skills and basic information so that the individual can make decisions that can lead to health-enhancing outcomes. In the context of AIDS, sex education must facilitate recognition of risk, enhance personalization of risk, strengthen ability to act on ways to avoid risk, and facilitate recognition of the benefits for avoiding risk. These skills are of obvious utility in diminishing risk of HIV-1 infection as well as the risk of other sexually transmitted diseases. Lastly, the ability to avoid risk for sexually transmitted diseases among adolescents is also dependent on emotions (anxiety), cognitive development (formal-concrete operations, egocentrism), and social support (from peers, friends, and family).

PREVENTION ISSUES: CONCLUSION

Because the only means of interrupting the AIDS epidemic at present is through behavior change, psychosocial factors are of central importance in the prevention of the further spread of HIV-1 infection. Although homosexual men generally demonstrate a high degree of correct identification of AIDS as an epidemic, certain groups of them do not consistently comply with safe sex recommendations. Psychosocial variables associated with engaging in risky sexual behavior for AIDS transmission include relationship status, age, personal efficacy, belief that it is possible to resolve AIDS infection without deleterious effect, and use of drugs or alcohol during sexual encounters.

As indicated earlier, certain cultural and legal factors promote or perpetuate needle sharing. Far less is known about the reasons why heterosexual partners of HIV-1 antibody-positive individuals do not practice safe-sex techniques. More research is needed to identify the circumstances under which certain members of each of the distinct high-risk populations decline to comply with prevention guidelines.

It is important to realize that AIDS prevention strategies have, to date, relied most heavily on health education efforts. This widespread policy has been based on the assumption that informing individuals of the risk associated with certain behaviors will cause a discontinuance of these behaviors. However, as shown above, compliance with risk reduction guidelines has been uneven. Perhaps the most important lesson learned so far from the AIDS prevention efforts is that health education is a necessary but not sufficient cause for risk-related behavioral change. This lesson should surprise no one: it had already been learned from efforts to control smoking and to encourage drivers to wear seat belts.

The real challenge thus lies in the identification and implementation of prevention strategies which, in combination with health education efforts, will serve as sufficient incentives for further AIDS risk reduction. For example, AIDS prevention efforts might go beyond the dissemination of risk reduction information to modify unobtrusively the physical or cultural environment in which risk taking occurs. That is, condoms can be made easily available in "pickup" bars, needle disinfection equipment can be made available to intravenous drug users, and indigenous community attempts to mobilize against AIDS can be encouraged. The probability of success for such prevention/health education strategies will be increased if they respond to the reasons why individuals decline to comply with risk reduction guidelines. Thus, determining the causes of continued high-risk behavior is a necessary first step toward the creation of an effective AIDS prevention policy. Further, the ability to identify the conditions under which risk occurs and the ability to act appropriately on such knowledge should increase if research teams include members of the affected communities.

With societies moving quickly to avert disaster, important health education ideas may be disseminated before their effectiveness is fully documented. Numerous health education and some behavior modification techniques have been developed or proposed to reduce new HIV-1 infection within the nonmonogamous homosexual male, the nonmonogamous heterosexual, and the needle-using populations, yet few of these have received proper scientific evaluation. Clearly, it will not be a simple matter to devise effective and evaluable solutions to the difficult sociomedical problem of AIDS.

CONSEQUENCES OF HIV-1 INFECTION

Knowledge of HIV-1 Infection

Tests for detecting antibodies to HIV-1 were licensed for use in March 1985, the primary objective being the protection of the nation's blood supply from contamination. The availability of the HIV-1 antibody test and of newer methods of detection raises serious public health policy questions. Individuals at risk for AIDS face a serious dilemma over whether to be tested voluntarily. Proponents claim that testing might motivate reductions in high-risk behavior. Opponents claim that the risks of discrimination or psychological distress far outweigh the benefits of this test and that high-risk persons have already been motivated to reduce risk of infection (Handsfield, 1985).

Morin et al. (1986) studied the reasons given by 695 homosexual men for wanting to be tested for antibodies to HIV-1. The primary motivations for being tested were to reduce uncertainty and anxiety and to learn whether one was capable of infecting others. The primary motivations for not being tested were fear of increasing anxiety, perception that the test lacked meaning, and concerns about confidentiality with the associated fears of increasing risks for AIDS-related discrimination (see also Lyter et al., 1987).

Coates et al. (1986) followed 550 of those 695 homosexual and bisexual men from before AIDS antibody testing became available until after the test was widely available to determine the consequences of testing on high-risk sexual behavior, psychological distress, and status of sexual relationships. By November 1986, 40.8 percent of the cohort had been tested; of these, 14.9 percent were antibody-positive, 21.5 percent were negative, and the remainder did not know their test results or declined to answer. Only 9.3 percent of the original cohort still desired to be tested for HIV-1 antibody status but had not yet undergone testing. In November 1984, before antibody testing was available, there were no differences between the groups later tested and not tested in participation in high-risk sexual behavior. By November 1986, significantly greater percentages of those who had been told that they were antibody-positive had reduced their high-risk sexual activity compared with those who were told they were negative or those who had not yet been tested (Fig. 16.1). The finding that reductions in risk have occurred in conjunction with knowledge of a positive antibody test have been duplicated in Europe and Canada (Van Griensven et al., 1987; Willoughby et al., 1987; Farthing et al., 1987). The antibody-positive group also reported significantly greater stress and depression than the

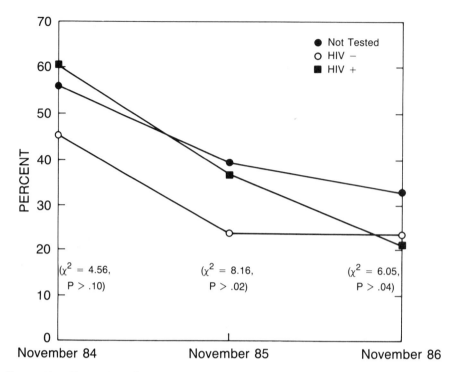

Figure 16.1. Proportion of men reporting unprotected anal intercourse in the past month, in three assessment periods.

other three groups. There was also a significantly greater decline in percentage of men in primary homosexual relationships among the antibody-positive group than among the other groups.

Thus, knowledge of positive antibody status was associated with subsequent reductions in sexual behavior leading to HIV-1 and other infections; it was also associated with increased accuracy of perceptions regarding the consequences of infection. However, testing also seems to have been associated with higher levels of stress and depression and a decreased ability to maintain a primary relationship. For these reasons more intensive study of antibody-positive persons is needed to determine the full significance of knowledge of antibody status, particularly for long-term mental health consequences.

There is a need to identify and address the specific concerns of those who do not want to be tested. For example, participants in the Coates et al. (1986) study had strong feelings about confidentiality of test results. Those who wanted to be tested but had not yet done so were concerned about the confidentiality of the results. At this point in the epidemic, voluntary compliance with safe sex guidelines is the only way to prevent spread of infection. Antibody testing can have an impact on that compliance when done under conditions of confidentiality or anonymity. People will be less resistant to testing if guarantees about confidentiality and against discrimination are assured.

Psychosocial Consequences of HIV-1 Infection and Clinical Immunodeficiency

Seropositivity or the appearance of unmistakable symptoms of immunodeficiency raise the dilemma of whether the affected individual should inform others of health problems. Many infected people choose to disclose their health problems in the attempt to ameliorate stress through support found within their social networks. However, disclosing HIV-1 antibody status or the onset of illness involves, for some people, a revelation about membership in a stigmatized group that may profoundly change important personal relationships in unknown ways. Many individuals with immunodeficiency have chosen not to disclose their status to significant people in their lives for fear of harsh judgment or rejection (Mandel, 1985; Mandel et al., 1986).

Most of the information on the difficulties of disclosure of HIV-1 status has been based on studies of homosexual men. Homosexual men who are better adjusted in integrating or managing their identity as such are more likely to have disclosed their sexual identity to others (McDonald, 1984; De Monteflores and Schultz, 1978). Several researchers have suggested that prior openness about being homosexual assists in a healthy adaptation to the diagnosis of AIDS itself as well as other AIDS-related fears and concerns (Forstein, 1984; Dilley, 1984; Mandel, 1985).

Mandel et al. (1986) found that patients with clinical features of AIDS who choose to reveal their health concerns generally report a positive experience. Further, those who disclose their health problems report less distress than those who withhold this information. Indeed, at all points of AIDS progression, support from social networks was identified as the most useful source of help. Unfortunately, however, not all those who disclose meet with a positive response. The stress of worrying about an AIDS-related health problem may be exacerbated if a friend, family member, or employer declines to be supportive.

A number of barriers exist to greater disclosure of HIV-1 disease status among homosexual men: fear of job problems, fear of being considered a carrier of AIDS, fear of being physically injured by heterosexuals, fear of endangering family relations, and fear of losing health insurance were prominent among these. Some of these fears can also be expected in heterosexual men and women with HIV-1 infection. Further, given the religious proscriptions against homosexual activity, diagnosis of clinical symptoms may usher in feelings of guilt or anxiety about homosexuality.

With the emergence of clinical manifestations of immunodeficiency, patients often search for reasons why their health problems occurred. Moulton et al. (1987) found that among men with AIDS, holding oneself responsible for the onset of disease was associated with significantly greater emotional distress. However, among persons with manifestations less likely to be perceived as irreversible or lethal, a different finding emerged. Self-attribution of possible improvements in health was associated with less distress. Feeling that one can influence the course of illness may be an important factor differentiating those persons who become psychosocially disabled and those who adapt to the challenge of their health condition. The same study also found that changes made after diagnosis and thought to be salubrious (e.g., changes in diet, exercise, or stress reduction techniques) may be part of the coping process to restore psychological and social equilibrium once a health crisis has occurred. That is, men who made many "healthy" life changes were less distressed or felt more hopeful than those who had made few such changes. These results indicate that it may be useful to consider the meaning that clinically affected patients attribute to their diagnosis.

Psychosocial Variables and Disease Progression

As with other infectious diseases, populations infected with HIV-1 show variation in the evolution of their immune system response and expression of clinical illness. Only a minority of those infected with HIV-1 have developed AIDS to date. Levy and Zeigler (1983) proposed that AIDS itself is an opportunistic disease occurring only in those who are already immunocompromised. A number of factors have been proposed: multiple infections, drug and alcohol use, and repeated viral assaults. Other factors such as health habits, nutrition, social support and psychosocial stress have also been considered (Kaplan, 1986), although evidence for their contribution to risk is lacking.

A wide spectrum of disease often follows viral infection, and variation in consequences of infection may be due in part to psychosocial factors. For example, persons infected with Epstein-Barr virus show a wide range of response to the virus, and this response has been associated with psychosocial host factors. Some individuals show no signs of infection, whereas others have a variety of disorders ranging from chronic lymphocytosis, clinical infectious mononucleosis, and malignant B-cell lymphoma (Henle et al., 1986; Kasl et al., 1979). Similarly, outbreaks of herpes lesions are variables among individuals and have been related to, among other things, psychosocial stress (Kemeny et al., 1984).

This and other evidence supports the notion that certain factors acting alone or in combination may alter immune function either directly through qualitative or quantitative derangement of lymphocytes or indirectly through the stimulation of T helper cells with increased virus replication or conversion from latent to productive infection. These considerations have moderated the early strong focus on sexual activity and drug use (Darrow et al., 1983; Jaffe et al., 1983) and prompted examination of other possible factors related to immunocompromise including environmental, psychosocial, and behavioral variables. Although sexual activity and drug use are of primary importance in facilitating exposure to HIV-1, a set of as yet unknown factors (e.g., stress, age, nutritional status, depression, social support) may partly determine host response.

SUMMARY AND CONCLUSIONS

Both the awareness of exposure to HIV-1 and the onset of illness or AIDS have profound psychosocial consequences for an individual. For infection, the consequence of being generally assumed to have participated in stigmatizing behaviors is important. For illness, psychological and behavioral reactions vary widely. Among homosexual men, prior openness concerning sexual identity had been associated with the ability to draw upon social network support, and response to the onset of AIDS-related illness appears to vary with interpretations given to that illness. Considerably less is known of the psychosocial sequelae of the discovery of infection or disease in members of other high-risk groups. Their responses to AIDS have to be studied more carefully in order to provide medically and socially appropriate care.

Much less is known about the role of psychosocial factors in promoting progression of infection. If research on psychoneuroimmunological variables demonstrates meaningful effects, carefully designed intervention efforts, alone or in combination with effective antiviral drugs, may prevent or delay the onset of serious clinical consequences.

The course of the AIDS epidemic has been governed to no small degree by psychosocial factors. Psychosocial research and intervention efforts have already increased our ability to prevent spread of infection and to care humanely for those so tragically stricken. Future research will hopefully further refine prevention strategies, determine whether psychosocial factors alter disease progression, expand our understanding of the needs of those who suffer from HIV-1 disease, and help modify care and prevention programs to meet the needs of affected populations.

ACKNOWLEDGMENTS

Supported in part by NIMH/NIDA grant MH 42459 (The Center for AIDS Prevention Studies (S. Hulley, P.I.); NIMH grant MH 39553 (T. Coates, P.I.); NIDA grant DA 04340 (James L. Sorensen, P.I.); NIHM contract 278860010 (L. Ligans, P.I.); and NIAAA grant AA 05595 (R. Stall, Study Director).

REFERENCES

Batki SL, Sorensen JL, Coates C, Gibson DR: In LS Harris, ed. Problems of drug dependence 1988: Proceedings of the Committee on the Problems of Drug Dependence. Washington, D.C.: U.S. Government Printing Office (in press).

Biernacki P (1986): American Public Health Association Annual Meetings, Las Vegas, Sept., 1986.

Black J, Dolan M, Defort H et al. (1986): N Engl J Med 314:445.

Carlsen GA, McLellan AT (1987): Public Health Rep 102:391.

Centers for Disease Control (1986): MMW 33:54.

Chaisson D, Moss A, Onishi R et al. (1987): Am J Public Health 77:169–172.

Coates TJ, Temoshok L, Mandel J (1984): Am Psychol 39(11):1309.

Coates TJ, Morin S, McKusick L (1987): JAMA 258:1889.

Coates TJ, Morin S, Lo B, Kegeles S, Stall R, McKusick L (a): Amer Psychologist (in press).

Coates TJ, Stall R, Catania S, Kegeles S (b): AIDS (in press).

Darrow W, Jaffe H, Curran J (1983): Lancet 2:160.

D'Aquila R, Williams A, Kleber H, Williams A (1986): N Engl J Med 314:446.

De Monteflores C, Shultz S (1978): J Soc Sci 34(3):59.

Des Jarlais DC, Friedman SR, Casriel C, Kott A (1987): Psychology and Health 1:179.

Des Jarlais D, Hopkins W (1985): N Engl J Med 313:23.

Des Jarlais D, Friedman S, Hopkins W (1985a): Ann Intern Med 103:755.

Des Jarlais D, Friedman S, Strus D (1985b): In Feldman D, Johnson T (eds.): The Social Dimensions of AIDS: Methods and Theory. New York: Praeger, 111–125.

Des Jarlais D, Jainchill N, Friedman S (1985c): In Acampora AP, Nebelkopf E (eds.): Bridging Services: Proceedings of the 9th World Conference of Therapeutic Communities, San Francisco, 1985. Abacus 59–73.

Des Jarlais D, Friedman S, Marmor M, Cohen H (1986): American Psychological Association, Washington, D.C., 1986.

Dilley J (1984): In Nichols S, Ostrow D (eds): Psychiatric Aspects of AIDS. Washington, D.C.: American Psychiatric Press.

Drucker E (1986): Drug Alcohol Abuse 12:165.

Emmons C, Joseph J, Kessler R, et al. (1986): Health Educ Q 13(4):331.

Farthing CF, Jesson W, Taylor HL, Lawrence AG, Gazzard B (1987): Third International Conference on AIDS, Washington, D.C., June 1–5.

Forstein M (1984): Semin Oncol 11:77.

Friedland G, Harris C, Butkus-Small C et al. (1985): Arch Intern Med 145:1413.

Friedman S, Des Jarlais D, Sotheran J (1986): Health Educ Q 13(4):383–393.

Gibson DR, Wermuth Lovelle-Drache J, Ergas B, Sorensen JL (1987): Fourth International Conference on AIDS.

Ginzburg HM (1984): Public Health Reports 99:206.

Ginzburg HM, French J, Jackson J, et al. (1986): Health Educ Q 13:373.

Godfried J, Van Griensven P, Tielman R, Goudsmit J, Van der Noordaa J, De Wolf F, Coutinho R (1987): Third International Conference on AIDS, Washington, D.C., June.

Handsfield H (1985): N Engl J Med 14:888.

Henle W, Henle G, Lennete E (1986) Sci Am 241:48.

Hubbard RL, Marsden ME, Cavanaugh E, Rachal JV, Ginzburg HM (1988): Rev Infect Dis 10:377.

Jaffee H, et al. (1983): Ann Intern Med 99:145.

Joseph J, Montgomery S, Emmons C, et al. (1987a): J Appl Soc Psychol (in press).

Joseph J, Montgomery S, Emmons C, et al. (1987b): Psychol Health (in press).

Kaplan GA (1986): In Criqui M, Kaplan R (eds): Behavioral Epidemiology and Disease Prevention. New York: Plenum.

Kasl S, Evan A, Niederman J (1979): Psychosom Med 41:445.

Kemeny M, Cohen F, Zegans L (1984): American Psychological Association Annual Meetings, Toronto, August.

Kirby D (1984): In Lief H, Hock Z (eds): International Research in Sexology: Selected Papers from the Fifth World Congress. New York: Praeger, pp. 5–11.

Kirby D, Alter J, Scales F (1979): An Analysis of U.S. Sex Education Programs and Evaluation Methods. Washington, D.C.: Department of Health, Education and Welfare, Report No. CD-12-21-76-DK-FR).

Koop C. (1986): Washington, D.C.: U.S. Dept. of Health and Human Services.

Kuritsky J, Rastogi S, Faich G, et al. (1986): Transfusion 26:205.

Levy N, Carlson J, Hinrichs S, et al. (1986): N Engl J Med 314:446.

Levy J, Ziegler J. (1983): Lancet 1:78.

Lyter D, Valdiserri R, Kingsley L, Amoroso W, Rinaldo D (1987): Third International AIDS Conference, Washington, D.C., June.

Mandel JS (1985): Unpublished doctoral dissertation. Wright Institute, Los Angeles.

Mandel JS, Coates TJ, Wiley J, et al. (1986): Second International Conference on AIDS, Paris, June 23–25.

McDonald GJ (1984): Unpublished doctoral dissertation, University of Windsor, Windsor, Ontario, Canada.

McKusick L, Horstman W, Coates TJ (1985a): Am J Public Health 75:493.

McKusick L, Wiley J, Coates TJ, et al. (1985b): Public Health Rep 100:622.

McKusick L, Wiley J, Coates TJ, Morin SF (1986): New Zealand AIDS Foundation Prevention Education Planning Workshop, November.

Morgan W, Curran J. (1986):Public Health Rep 101:459.

Morin S, Coates TJ, Woods W, McKusick L. (1986): (Submitted.)

Moulton J, Sweet D, Temoshok L, Mandel J (1987): J Appl Soc Psychol 17:493.

Murphy DL (1987): Adv Alcohol Substance Abuse 7:89.

Ostrow D, Gayle T (1986): Qual Rev Bull 12(6):284.

Ostrow DG, Joseph J, Monjan A, et al (1986): Psychopharmacol Bull 22(3):678.

Ostrow DG, VanRaden M, Kingsley L, Fox R, Dudley J, Kaslow RA (1987): Third International AIDS Conference, Washington, D.C., June 1–5.

Quinn R, Mann J, Curran J, Piot P (1986): Science 234:955.

Schinke SP, Gilchrist LD, Small RW (1979): Am J Orthopsychiatry 49:81.

Seligman PJ, Campbell RJ, Keeler GP, Halpin TJ (1988): Amer J Public Health 78:20.

Siegel K, Chen JY, Mesagno F, Christ G (1987): Third International Conference on AIDS, Washington, D.C., June 1–5.

Sorensen JL, Gibson D, Heitzmann C, Calvillo A, Dumontet R, Morales E, Acampora A: In LS Harris, ed. Problems of drug dependence 1988: Proceedings of the Committee on the Problems of Drug Dependence. Washington, D.C.: U.S. Government Printing Office (in press).

Sorensen JL, Gibson DR, Heitzmann C, Dumontet R, Acampora A (1988): American Psychological Association, Atlanta, Georgia, August 1988.

Spira T, Des Jarlais D, Marmor M, et al. (1984): N Engl J Med 311:46.

Stall R, Coates TJ, Hoff C: Amer Psychologist (in press).

Stall R, Ostrow D: J Drug Issues (in press).

Stall R, McKusick L, Wiley J, et al. (1986): Health Educ Q 13(4):359.

Stimson GV, Aldrett L, Dolan K, et al. (1988): Brit Med J 296:1217.

Urberg KA (1980): Adolescence 3:527.

Watters J (1987): Third International AIDS Meetings, Washington, D.C., June 1–5.

Watters J, Feldman H, Biernacki P, Newmeyer J (1986): In Community Epidemiology Workgroup: Proceedings, Vol. 2. Rockville, MD: NIDA.

Weddington WW, Brown BS (1988): J Substance Abuse Treatment 5:145.

Wiley J, Winkelstein W, Piazza T, et al. (1986): Survey Research Center Working Paper No. 49. Berkeley: Survey Reserach Center, University of California, August.

Willoughby B, Schechter M, Boyko W, Craib K, Weaver M, Douglas G (1987): Third International AIDS Conference. Washington, D.C., June 1–5.

Woods W (1985): Unpublished doctoral disseration, Ohio State University, Columbus.

Zelnick M, Katner JF (1980): Family Planning Perspect 12:230.

17

Chemotherapy and Chemoprophylaxis

GAIL SKOWRON AND THOMAS C. MERIGAN

Approaches to therapies against human immunodeficiency virus (HIV-1) infections require a thorough understanding of the virus itself and of its effects on the body. It is clear that HIV-1 causes a broad spectrum of clinical disease. Symptomatic infections include the apparent progression from persistent generalized lymphadenopathy (PGL) to the inconsistently defined AIDS-related complex (ARC) to CDC-defined acquired immunodeficiency syndrome (AIDS). Successful therapy may need to be tailored to the stage of disease and to coexisting opportunistic infections or AIDS-related cancers.

HIV-1 is cytopathic in vitro to CD4$^+$ lymphocytes, which may in part explain the marked defects in number and function of these cells in patients with AIDS (Popovic et al., 1984). HIV-1 is also capable of latency, and lytic infection in vitro leaves a small percentage of infected cells that do not actively produce virus (Folks et al., 1986) or that produce virus without causing cell death (Hoxie et al., 1985). In addition, HIV-1 infection is not restricted to CD4$^+$ lymphocytes; the virus can infect B lymphocytes, macrophages, early hematopoietic stem cells, and several types of epithelial cells (Montagnier et al., 1984; Gartner et al., 1986; Markham et al., 1986). Of particular concern is the neutrotropic property of the virus, as evidenced by emergence of a distinct syndrome of central nervous system (CNS) infection (Carne et al., 1985; Snider et al., 1983; Navia et al., 1986) and identification of HIV-1 in brain tissue (Shaw et al., 1985) and cerebrospinal fluid (Ho et al., 1985a). Thus, activity against latent forms of the virus and control or eradication of virus in the "sanctuary" of the CNS become of major concern in choosing an agent.

Several strategies for identifying potential therapeutic agents against HIV-1 are available. First, drugs previously identified to have either broad-spectrum antiviral activity (ribavirin, interferon) or specific antiretroviral activity (suramin, phosphonoformate) can be rapidly tested against HIV-1 infection. Those drugs previously found to be safe in man can be rapidly tested in patients with AIDS. Second, existing agents can be modified to create analogs with greater specific activity against HIV-1 (2'-3'-dideoxycytidine). Third, novel compounds specific for HIV-1 can be identified using in vitro screening techniques: Three such assays in current use monitor reduction in HIV-1-mediated lysis of susceptible cells (Broder 1987), inhibition of virus-induced cytopathic effect (Balzarini et al., 1986), or release of reverse transcriptase into the supernatent (McCormick et al., 1984). Fourth, specific therapeutics previously developed for similar immune deficiency syndromes (bone marrow transplantation, intravenous gamma globulin) can be used alone or in combination with specific antiviral therapy. Fifth, new and novel HIV-1-specific therapies can be devised as more is learned about the virus and its interactions with the host (recombinant soluble CD4).

At present there is no suitable animal model for AIDS; therefore, in vitro data are of utmost importance in predicting both safety and efficacy in vivo. To evaluate a drug's possible efficacy against HIV-1, one must measure its ability to inhibit viral replication and to reverse defects in immune function in vitro. The same virologic methods used in screening of potential agents (reduction of viral antigen expression, cytopathic effect, or release of reverse transcriptase) can be used to determine effective tissue culture concentration of each drug. Agents can also be tested for ability to correct specific defects in lymphokine production, lymphocyte cytotoxicity, and natural killer cell activity.

Potential clinical toxicity may be predicted by calculating a "selectivity index," comparing inhibition of growth of normal, uninfected T-cell clones with inhibition of infected cells (De Clercq, 1986). Animal testing remains an important guide to other properties of potential antiviral agents: bioavailability, pharmacokinetics, metabolism, short-term toxicity, CNS penetration, teratogenicity, effects on fertility, and side effects of combination with other drugs, particularly those used against opportunistic infections, AIDS-related cancers, and other antivirals/immunomodulators. Effective agents may require long-term administration, and consideration must therefore be given to reasonable cost, preferability of oral formulations, and minimal side effects.

Once drug testing has progressed to clinical trials, human pharmacology and safety can be determined, and additional virologic, immunologic, and clinical variables are available for study. Viral isolation from cultures of peripheral blood mononuclear cells remains a qualitative measure of virus activity, and interpretation is limited by incomplete knowledge of fluctuations in virus production over time. Viral load in response to therapy may be more accurately predicted by techniques that use a radiolabeled RNA or DNA probe to measure HIV-1 RNA or DNA, particularly after amplification with the polymerase chain reaction (Crumpacker et al., 1987; Carter et al., 1987; Kwok et al., 1987). Quantitative measurement of the viral p24 antigen in blood is now available on a limited basis, and preliminary data suggest that this is a specific indicator of disease activity and response to therapy in some patients (Goudsmit et al., 1986; Chaisson et al., 1986). Serum beta-2 microglobulin may be another surrogate marker for disease activity in response to antiviral therapy (Jacobson et al., 1988). Immunologic response can be measured by quantitation of total lymphocyte and T helper/inducer numbers, delayed-type hypersensitivity skin testing, and in vitro assessments of cell-mediated immunity. Clinical assessment includes monitoring the frequency of opportunistic infections, mortality, and the status of AIDS-associated cancers, constitutional symptoms, and neurologic symptoms.

Therapeutic agents against HIV-1 can be broadly divided into those that specifically inhibit HIV-1 (antivirals) and those that augment the body's own defenses against HIV-1 infection (immunomodulators), with some agents showing dual activity (Table 17.1).

ANTIVIRALS

Antiviral therapy in HIV-1 infection is based on the assumption that interruption of the viral replicative cycle will result in control of the virus and its effects on the body. Although they may substantially alter the course of clinical disease, it must be remembered that proviral DNA may not be influenced by these agents, and a long-term virologic "cure" may not be achieved. Advances in the molecular biology of viral replication have identified steps in the viral cycle that are potential targets of antiviral therapy (Fig. 17.1).

HIV-1 enters the cell by first binding to or in association with the $CD4^+$ molecule of the T helper/inducer cell. Blocking this receptor with monoclonal antibody or soluble CD4 molecules have been shown in vitro to prevent virus binding and subsequent infection of target cells (Dalgleish et al., 1984; Smith et al., 1987).

After uncoating, transcription of the HIV-1 retroviral RNA genome to a cDNA copy occurs via an RNA-directed DNA polymerase or reverse transcriptase. This is a viral-specific enzyme, and most of the antivirals under study have been directed against it. The single-stranded DNA serves as a template for a complementary DNA strand, and some of this double-stranded proviral DNA is subsequently integrated into the host cell DNA. Proviral DNA is then transcribed into copies of the viral RNA genome and viral messenger RNA.

Translation of viral RNA into proteins for viral packaging occurs next. Transcription and translation are accelerated by the products of two viral genes, *tat*-III and *rev* (*art*/*trs*), and inhibition of viral protein synthesis may be achieved by interfering with the function of these gene products (Sodroski et al., 1985, 1986).

Viral components then undergo processing and assembly. Budding of the newly formed virus from the host cell membrane may be inhibited by interferons and can be neutralized by circulating antibodies.

Since the identification of HIV-1 as the agent responsible for AIDS and AIDS-related syndromes, several antiviral drugs have been investigated in vitro and in vivo.

Suramin

Suramin, an antitrypanasomal agent, was first identified as a reverse transcriptase inhibitor in 1979 (De Clercq, 1979). It is poorly absorbed orally, undergoes little metabolism, and can persist in the bloodstream for up to 6 months (Hawking et al., 1978). In vitro, suramin has a reversible, virustatic effect on HIV-1 infectivity and reverse transcriptase activity, and it blocks expression of p24 antigen (Mitsuya et al., 1984).

Suramin was the first antiviral drug to be studied against HIV-1 in vivo. An initial report in 1985 of five ARC patients was encouraging, with weight gain and improvement in lymphadenopathy, diarrhea, anthralgia, $CD4^+$ cell numbers, and skin test reactivity (Rouvroy et al., 1985). Subsequent reports, however, did not confirm early optimism. Side effects of fever, malaise, and rash occurred in nearly

Table 17.1. Therapeutic Modalities Against HIV-1

Agent	Toxicity	Efficacy	Current Status
Suramin	Fever, malaise, rash, anemia, proteinuria, elevated transaminases, adrenal insufficiency	AIDS: suppression of viremia; worsened clinical status in half	Toxicity outweights benefit at present
AZT (zidovudine)	Anemia, leukopenia, headache myalgia, nausea, insomia	Advanced ARC and AIDS: dec mortality and opportunistic infections, improved Karnofsky scores, CD4$^+$ numbers, skin tests; weight gain	FDA approved for advanced ARC and AIDS; ongoing trials in other patient groups and in combination
ddC	Rash, thrombocytopenia aphthostomatitis, peripheral neuropathy	Advanced ARC and AIDS: dec p24 antigen	Neuropathy at high dose: ongoing trials at low dose and alternating with AZT
Ribavirin	Insomnia, nausea, vomiting, anemia	PGL: improved in vitro lymphocyte responses and CD8 numbers; dec reverse transcriptase activity and ?dec progression to AIDS ARC/AIDS: improved CD4 cell numbers, skin tests, and lymphocyte responses; dec viral RNA, reverse transcriptase; weight gain, dec fevers, inc well-being; ?dec incidence of pneumocystis pneumonia	FDA licensing on hold pending further study of data. Further studies planned in USA
HPA-23	Thrombocytopenia, elevated SGOT	Asymptomatic, ARC, AIDS: dec viremia, no change in CD4$^+$ number	Trials discontinued
Rifabutin	Well tolerated	ARC: no change in p24 antigen, CD4 numbers or skin test positivity	Continued study for *Mycobacterium ovium* complex
Phosphonoformate	Nausea, headache, fatigue, elevated creatinine	PGL, ARC, AIDS: improved clinical status, skin test positivity; clearance of viremia	Undergoing phase 1 trials in USA alone and in combination with AZT
AL-721	Well tolerated	PGL: dec reverse transcriptase in vitro, improved mitogen-induced lymphocyte proliferation	Undergoing phase 1 trials in USA
Peptide T	Hypotension with rapid intravenous infusion	Late-stage AIDS: improved lymphocyte counts; clinically stable for 1 month	Undergoing phase I trials in USA
Interleukin-2	Fever, chills, dermatitis, hypotension	AIDS: improved CD4$^+$ and total lymphocyte numbers; improved spontaneous and antigen-induced lymphocyte proliferation; improved natural killer cell activity, improved skin tests; dec viremia, minor tumor regression	Ongoing clinical trials combined with AZT

Table 17.1. Therapeutic Modalities Against HIV-1 (*Continued*)

Agent	Toxicity	Efficacy	Current Status
		ARC: improved antigen-induced lymphocyte proliferation and skin tests	
Gamma interferon	Chills, fever, fatigue, diarrhea, headache, sweats, nausea, vomiting, anorexia	AIDS: variable CD4$^+$ cell response; improved in vitro macrophage and natural killer cell activity; progression of Kaposi's sarcoma and opportunistic infections	Ongoing clinical trials combined with tumor necrosis factor
Alpha interferon	Fever, chills, fatigue, headache, myalgia, nausea, vomiting, change in taste, leukopenia, thrombocytopenia, elevated transaminases	AIDS/KS: dec incidence of opportunistic infections in patients with response of Kaposi's sarcoma; dec viral shedding; fall in CD4$^+$ number AIDS (no KS): No change in CD4$^+$ number, survival, or opportunistic infections	Ongoing clinical trials combined with AZT
Ampligen	Well tolerated	LAS, ARC, AIDS: improved symptoms, CD4$^+$ number, skin tests; dec lymphadenopathy, HIV-1 mRNA in peripheral blood mononuclear cells, viremia; dec p24 antigen	Further clinical trials planned
Thymic hormones	Burning at injection site	At risk, AIDS: improved mitogen-induced lymphocyte proliferation, cell-mediated lympholysis, PHA-induced IL2 production, virus-induced alpha interferon production, improved CD4$^+$ and total lymphocyte numbers, CD4$^+$/CD8$^+$ ratio; weight gain, dec fever, constitutional symptoms	
Thymic fragment transplantation	Minimal transient local inflammation	AIDS: variable improvement in CD4$^+$ and total lymphocyte number, transient clinical stability	
Isoprinosine	Well tolerated	Prodromal AIDS: symptomatic improvement, improved CD4$^+$ and total lymphocyte number; improved natural killer cell activity; dec CD8$^+$ cell number	
Imuthiol	Antabuselike activity	ARC, AIDS: symptomatic improvement, dec lymphadenopathy; variable CD4$^+$ number; possible dec progression to AIDS	

Table 17.1. Therapeutic Modalities Against HIV-1 (*Continued*)

Agent	Toxicity	Efficacy	Current Status
Cyclosporin A	Nausea, vomiting, anorexia, fatigue	AIDS: inc Kaposi's sarcoma lesions, transient inc CD4$^+$ numbers sero+: inc CD4$^+$ number, regression of lymphadenopathy; ?dec progression to AIDS	
Lymphocyte transfusion	Fever, rash	AIDS: transfer of specific skin test positivity	
Bone marrow transplantation	Well tolerated	AIDS: no clinical or immunologic improvement	Ongoing trials combined with AZT
Intravenous gamma globulin	Well tolerated	ARC, AIDS: dec opportunistic and bacterial infection; dec mortality; dec lymphadenopathy and hepatosplenomegaly	Continuing clinical trials in pediatric patients

all patients, and self-limiting proteinuria, transfusion-requiring anemia, and reversible elevation of aminotransferases were common (Levine et al., 1986). Furthermore, in one study, five of six patients on prolonged therapy (12 to 24 weeks) developed adrenal insufficiency (Fauci and Lane, 1987).

In the most recent trial, only one of 12 AIDS patients studied had clinical improvement, one-third of patients had suppression of viremia, and nearly half had worsening of their clinical status with recurrent opportunistic infection or significant toxicity (Levine et al., 1986). This study did confirm suramin's ability to block viral replication for up to 18 weeks with adequate levels; however, one-third of patients with adequate levels remained viremic. At this point, suramin is considered too toxic to be an effective single agent against HIV, however, whether it

Figure 17.1. HIV-1 replication and establishment of latency: sites of action of antiviral agents. (Adapted from De Clerq, 1986).

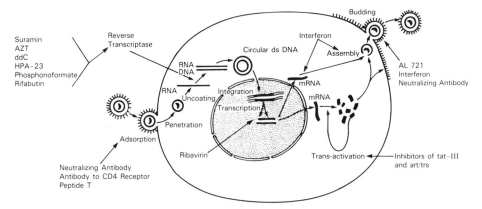

may prove more effective and less toxic in combination with other antivirals remains to be determined.

Azidothymidine

At the present time, the most clinically active antiviral agent against HIV-1 is azidothymidine (AZT). AZT (3'-azido-3'-deoxythymidine, zidovudine, Retrovir) is a synthetic thymidine analog in which a single hydroxyl group at the 3' position on the deoxyribosyl moiety of thymidine is replaced by an azido group. Following uptake into the cell, AZT is converted to the active triphosphate by cellular enzymes. The viral reverse transcriptase incorporates this form into viral DNA which terminates further 5'-3' phosphodiesterase linkage (Yarchoan et al., 1986). AZT is well absorbed orally, penetrates into the CSF, and is cleared rapidly from the blood, being both metabolized by the liver and excreted by the kidneys (Yarchoan et al., 1986). In vitro against HIV-1, AZT acts as a competitive inhibitor of HIV-1 reverse transcriptase and inhibits cytopathic effects and p24 antigen expression (Mitsuya et al., 1985).

The earliest in vivo trials of AZT in 19 ARC and AIDS patients showed promise in reversing clinical and immunologic abnormalities (Yarchoan et al., 1986). Overall, there was some subjective improvement, with weight gain and resolution of minor infections, night sweats, and fevers. Numbers of circulating helper-inducer T cells rose in 15 of 19 patients, and skin tests reactivity improved. At the highest dosages tested (2.5 to 5 mg/kg IV every 4 hours for 2 weeks followed by twice the IV dosage orally for 4 weeks), three patients showed clearance of viremia.

The 1986 placebo-controlled trial of AZT in 282 AIDS and ARC patients demonstrated both the efficacy and toxicity of the drug. AIDS patients were limited to those within 120 days of their first episode of *Pneumocystis carinii* pneumonia, and ARC patients were those displaying symptoms of weight loss, thrush, oral hairy leukoplakia, herpes zoster, and/or unexplained fever, night sweats, or diarrhea. All patients had 500 or fewer $CD4^+$ cells/mm^3. After only 6 months, the trial was halted owing to a significantly lower death rate in patients receiving AZT compared with those receiving placebo: 19 deaths occurred in the placebo group, compared with one death of an AIDS patient on AZT.

A decrease in frequency of opportunistic infection was also noted after 6 weeks of therapy. Twenty-four AZT recipients developed opportunistic infection compared with 45 in the placebo group. Significant improvement in Karnofsky score, $CD4^+$ cell number, skin test reactivity, and weight gain was noted by week 12. After week 20, however, $CD4^+$ cell numbers fell to baseline in many AIDS patients on AZT, whereas ARC patients generally showed continued improvement in $CD4^+$ cell counts. Circulating levels of p24 antigen decreased significantly, and subsequent rises in antigen predicted worsening of clinical disease (Chaisson et al., 1986). No effect was seen on lesions of Kaposi's sarcoma, compared with placebo, and viral isolation, although reduced in those patients on AZT, did not reach statistical significance (Fischl et al., 1987).

This trial also identified the major toxicities of AZT, mainly due to its bone marrow suppressive effect. A dose-related macrocytic anemia was seen in 38 percent of all patients on AZT, and transfusion was necessary for 31 percent of AZT-treated patients compared with 11 percent of placebo controls. Forty-five percent of AZT recipients had grade 3 marrow suppression (hemoglobin < 7.5 g/dl, neutrophils < 750/mm^3, or white blood cells < 1,500/mm^3). Severe granulocytopenia (<500 cells/mm^3) occurred in 16 percent of AZT recipients and was most marked in patients with AIDS and low CD4$^+$ cell counts at entry. Low values for hemoglobin, neutrophil count, CD4$^+$ cell number, and serum vitamin B$_{12}$ at entry were all independent predictors of neutropenia. Acetominophen, but not acyclovir, aspirin, ketoconazole, or trimethoprim/sulfamethoxazole, was associated with an increased frequency of marrow suppression (Richman et al., 1987). Other side effects that were significantly more likely to occur in AZT recipients included severe headache, myalgias, nausea, and insomnia. Similar doses of AZT improved HIV-1 related neurologic disorders (chronic dementia, peripheral neuropathy) in three of four patients studied (Yarchoan et al., 1987).

In a pilot study of 21 pediatric AIDS patients, AZT produced immunologic and clinical improvement, similar to that seen in adults. In addition, all patients showed neurodevelopmental improvement with therapy (Pizzo et al., 1988).

The exact mechanism by which AZT improves survival and allows some immunologic recovery remains unclear. Despite AZT's inhibition of HIV-1 replication in cultured cells, viremia persisted in patients who received AZT in the trial. Questions remain as to whether AZT is able to affect virus that has integrated into host DNA or replicated within other cells in the body (i.e., macrophages) or within the CNS.

AZT is currently licensed by the FDA for AIDS and advanced ARC patients who have a history of *Pneumocystis carinii* pneumonia or an absolute CD4$^+$ lymphocyte count of less than 200/mm^3 in the peripheral blood. Current clinical trials of AZT are focusing on patients who do not qualify for licensed drugs. Placebo-controlled trials are underway in AIDS patients with localized Kaposi's sarcoma, in early ARC, and in asymptomatic, HIV-1-seropositive patients. Studies to optimize dosage in subsets of HIV-1-infected patients are ongoing in patients with ARC, neurologic disease, or AIDS after *Pneumocystis carinii* pneumonia. Further trials in the pediatric population are also planned.

Additional studies are underway using AZT in combination with other agents such as ddC, phosphonoformate, alpha interferon or interleukin-2. One combination, AZT plus acyclovir, has been tested in a European/Australian study in 404 AIDS and ARC patients. Preliminary results from that trial demonstrated serum p24 antigen suppression, CD4$^+$ cell count enhancement and a reduction in herpes infections. Of particular interest is an apparent decrease in mortality of the combination: After 24 weeks, 3 deaths occurred in the AZT/acyclovir group compared to 15 deaths in the AZT alone group (Fiddian et al., 1988). Efforts to confirm these findings are underway in several trials in the United States.

2′,3′-Dideoxycytidine and Other Nucleoside Analogs

2′,3′-Dideoxycytidine (ddC) is a nucleoside analog, with hydrogen substitution at both 2′ and 3′ positions of cytidine. This analog, like AZT, undergoes intracellular phosphorylation and is incorporated into the growing 3′ end of the DNA strand, thereby terminating chain elongation. The drug prevents HIV-1-induced cytopathic effect and p24 antigen expression. Effective concentrations of ddC are non-toxic to uninfected cells, and levels 10-fold higher exert little effect on antigen- or mitogen-induced lymphocyte proliferation (Mitsuya and Broder, 1986).

In a phase I/II trial in 61 patients with AIDS or advanced ARC, ddC significantly reduced serum p24 antigen. Early side effects of ddC included transient fever, rash, and aphthostomatitis, which resolved without drug discontinuation. Therapy was limited by the development of a predominantly sensory peripheral neuropathy in all patients at the three highest dose levels tested (0.06, 0.03, and 0.01 mg/kg every 4 hours) between 4 and 14 weeks of therapy. $CD4^+$ cell numbers, skin test reactivity, and HIV-1 culture positivity were not significantly altered on therapy. At the lowest dose tested (0.005 mg/kg), p24 antigen suppression was more gradual and ddC-related peripheral neuropathy and arthralgia occurred in three of 15 patients treated. Three patients have continued on this dose of ddC for 9–14 months without adverse effects (Merigan et al., 1989).

The dose-limiting neuropathy of ddC precludes its use as a single, continuous agent at high doses. At a dose of 0.03 mg/kg, ddC has been tested in a weekly alternating regimen with standard dose AZT (Yarchoan et al., 1988). Seventeen patients completed 9 weeks or more, with neuropathy occurring in 3 patients and dose limiting anemia in 2 patients. In these patients, $CD4^+$ cell numbers rose and 5 patients had significant p24 antigen suppression. This regimen has been tolerated for up to 70 weeks without development of neuropathy (R. Yarchoan, personal communication).

Two multicenter trials of AZT and ddC are currently underway: One study of 112 antigen-positive ARC and AIDS patients is studying monthly and weekly alternating regimens of AZT and ddC, and week-on/week-off regimens of AZT or ddC in comparison to continuous AZT alone. A parallel study of 96 patients unable to tolerate AZT because of hematologic toxicity will compare all limbs except continuous AZT.

Additional nucleoside analogs under study include dideoxyinosine (ddI) (Mitsuya and Broder, 1986), azidodideoxyuridine (AZDU or CS-87) (Eriksson et al., 1988) phosphonomethlylethyladenine (PMEA) (Balzarini et al., 1988), and dideoxydidehydrothymidine (d4T) (Mansuri et al., 1988).

Ribavirin

Ribavirin is a broad-spectrum antiviral agent with in vitro activity against RNA and DNA viruses including the herpesviruses, influenza, respiratory syncytial virus, and oncornaviruses (Sidwell et al., 1980). It is a synthetic guanosine analog, which acts as a potent inhibitor of the 5′ capping guanylation of viral mRNA (Goswami et al., 1979). In vitro ribavirin suppresses HIV-1 reverse transcriptase activity and viral antigen expression for up to 7 days (McCormick et al., 1984).

An oral regimen of ribavirin has been investigated in patients with advanced ARC or AIDS after *Pneumocystis carinii* pneumonia. With prolonged administration levels were attainable in the CSF at 67 to 100 percent of serum levels (Crumpacker et al., 1986). Of 14 patients completing 8 weeks of therapy, some patients showed return of skin test reactivity, improved mitogen- and antigen-stimulated lymphocyte responses, and transient increase in total T and $CD4^+$ lymphocytes. A decrease in viral load was seen by detection of reverse transcriptase or dot-blot hybridization for cytoplasmic HIV-1 RNA in cocultivated lymphocytes. Most patients also had weight gain, an enhanced feeling of well-being, and absence of fever during treatment. After therapy, AIDS-associated events (CMV retinitis and hepatitis, AIDS encephalopathy, *Pneumocystis carinii* pneumonia, disseminated *Mycobacterium avium-intracellulare,* and Kaposi's sarcoma) continued, and five of 10 AIDS patients died. Of eight patients given ribavirin for a full year, four died, and the remainder had no episodes of primary or recurrent *Pneumocystis carinii* pneumonia (Crumpacker et al., 1987). In this small, uncontrolled trial, ribavirin was well tolerated for up to 1 year, and there was a suggestion of HIV-1 suppression and immunologic and clinical improvement in some patients with AIDS and ARC.

Preliminary data are available from a multicenter, randomized, placebo-controlled trial of ribavirin in 163 patients with HIV-1-associated lymphadenopathy and other symptoms. Patients were those with lymphadenopathy for more than 6 months, positive HIV-1 cultures, and less than 500 $CD4^+$ cells/mm^3. Those patients with diarrhea, fever, thrush, or weight loss were excluded. Over a mean follow-up period of 28 weeks, none of 52 patients receiving 800 mg/day of ribavirin orally progressed to AIDS, compared with six of 55 patients receiving 600 mg/day and 10 of 56 patients given placebo. No change in HIV-1 culture status or immunologic function was seen (Mansell et al., 1987). Side effects of insomnia, nausea, vomiting, and anemia were seen. Controversy surrounds the results of this trial because of the unexpectedly high rate of progression to AIDS among placebo recipients. FDA licensing of ribavirin for use in patients with HIV-1-associated lymphadenopathy has been delayed pending further inspection of the data collected. Preliminary analysis suggests that patients in the placebo arm had lower $CD4^+$ cell counts than did patients in the apparently effective arm.

HPA-23

HPA-23 (heteropolyanion-23) is an inorganic condensed polyanion with in vivo activity against a broad spectrum of RNA and DNA viruses, including murine leukemia and sarcoma viruses, Creutzfeld-Jacob virus, and the scrapie agent (Chermann et al., 1975; Kimberlin and Walker, 1983). HPA-23 has been shown in vitro to inhibit HIV-1 reverse transcriptase activity (Dormont et al., 1985). When assayed for activity against HIV-1-induced CPE, however, the compound was inactive in high concentrations while lower concentrations significantly inhibited uninfected control cells (Balzarini et al., 1986).

The initial reports of in vitro activity prompted preliminary trials of HPA-23 in patients. The earliest report of four patients treated with HPA-23 suggested that viremia was suppressed transiently, and both mortality and opportunistic infection were reduced (Rozenbaum et al., 1985). Nineteen additional patients (12 AIDS, three ARC, four seropositive) were treated. After 2 months of therapy, 18 became virus negative; by 4 to 6 months, one ARC and four AIDS patients were again viremic. No increase in $CD4^+$ cell number was seen in the patients with AIDS or ARC (Dormont et al., 1986). A more recent multicenter trial confirmed a dose-related thrombocytopenia and elevation in SGOT; however, over the 2-month period of therapy, no change in clinical status or $CD4^+$ cell count was seen (Moskovitz et al., 1987). Based on these preliminary results, further trials with this agent are not planned by the sponsoring pharmaceutical company.

Rifabutin (Ansamycin LM427)

Rifabutin, a derivative of rifamycin-S, possesses a broad-spectrum antibacterial and antimycobacterial activity (Della Bruna et al., 1983). Also known as Ansamycin, rifabutin has in vitro effectiveness against *Mycobacterium avium* complex organisms and has been widely used in AIDS patients with disseminated disease due to this organism (Woodley and Kilburn, 1982). In man, rifabutin is well tolerated, penetrates tissues well, and attains concentrations in the cerebrospinal fluid that are 30 to 40 percent of serum levels (Davidson et al., 1987).

In vitro against HIV-1, rifabutin inhibits reverse transcriptase activity in peripheral blood mononuclear cells up to 99.7 percent at low concentrations, but higher concentrations are required to inhibit chronically infected H9 cells (Anand et al., 1986). The mechanism of action of rifabutin against HIV-1 is unknown, but it may be related to binding of the reverse transcriptase (Balzarini et al., 1986).

Pilot studies are now underway to evaluate the safety and efficacy of rifabutin in ARC and AIDS patients. In one study of 15 ARC patients, daily doses of 300–1200 mg for 28 days did not significantly improve $CD4^+$ cell counts or skin test positivity. Serum p24 antigen levels were not suppressed and only four of 15 patients developed negative HIV-1 cultures by the end of therapy (Torseth et al., 1989).

At the present time, rifabutin is being studied primarily as an agent for *Mycobacterium avium–intracellulare* infections in AIDS patients.

Phosphonoformate

Phosphonoformate (phosphonoformic acid, PFA, Foscarnet) is a pyrophosphate derivative with broad activity against polymerases of both influenza and the herpesviruses and the reverse transcriptase of several mammalian retroviruses (Oberg, 1983). Phosphonoformate binds noncompetitively to the pyrophosphate binding site on the polymerase enzyme, effecting a rapid shutoff of reverse transcriptase activity and blocking elongation of the polynucleotide (Oberg, 1983).

In vitro, PFA inhibits cytopathic effect and reduces antigen expression and reverse transcriptase activity of HIV-1 (Sandstrom et al., 1985). At high concentration, it inhibits cytopathic effect and viral antigen expression when added as late as day 5 after infection, with minimal inhibition of uninfected H9 cells.

Preliminary reports on 11 AIDS and five ARC patients receiving intravenous PFA indicate clinical improvement, return of skin test positivity, and clearing of viremia in some (Farthing et al., 1986). An additional eight homosexual men with PGL or ARC were given PFA by continuous infusion. Side effects of nausea, headache, fatigue, and elevations in serum creatinine were reversible and related to plasma PFA levels. Eighty percent of patients reported improvement in HIV-1-related symptoms. The frequency of HIV-1 isolation was reduced in patients with PGL but not in patients with ARC, and suppression was maintained for up to 8 weeks following therapy. No effect was seen on $CD4^+$ cell numbers or lymphocyte stimulation tests (Åsjö et al., 1987; Bergdahl et al., 1987). PFA was also able to suppress serum p24 antigen levels in 14 patients with ARC or AIDS during a 28-day period of treatment (Bergdahl et al., 1988).

Dextran Sulfate

Dextran sulfate is a sulfated polymer of glucose with a molecular weight of 7000–8000. It is active as an anticoagulant, and has been used in Japan as an antilipemic agent (Ueno and Kuno, 1987). In vitro, it inhibits HIV-1 cytopathic effect and antigen expression without reducing reverse transcriptase activity, suggesting that it inhibits the virus by another mechanism (Ito et al., 1987). In addition, dextran sulfate is able to inhibit syncytia formation between uninfected CD4$^+$ cells and HIV-1-infected H9 cells, while AZT or ddA, which act as DNA chain terminators, do not (Mitsuya et al., 1988). It also exerts in vitro synergy with AZT against cytopathic effect of HIV-1 (Ueno and Kuno, 1987).

A phase I trial of dextran sulfate gave 900–5400 mg/day for 8 weeks to 20 patients with AIDS or ARC (Abrams et al., 1988). Side effects of diarrhea and neutropenia were seen. A larger phase II study is now underway in patients with serum p24 antigen to determine whether dextran sulfate is sufficiently absorbed to allow the polymer to reach virus-infected cells.

Dextran sulfate obtained from Japan has been used widely by HIV-1-infected patients. Its popularity has led to increasing patient demand for access to experimental drugs outside of clinical trials.

Recombinant, Soluble CD4

The CD4 antigen is found on the surface of T-helper lymphocytes and is involved in Class II MHC recognition. In HIV-1 infection, CD4 functions as the cellular receptor for HIV-1 and participates with viral gp120 molecules in the formation of syncytia. Recombinant forms of this protein have been produced by several laboratories that contain only the extracellular portion of CD4 (Smith et al., 1987, Hussey et al., 1988). This secreted, soluble antigen binds radiolabeled gp120 and inhibits HIV-1 infection of susceptible cells in vitro as measured by production of HIV-1 antigen or syncytia formation. Addition of recombinant, soluble CD4 (rsCD4) does not interfere with Class II specific cytotoxicity or proliferation of CD4$^+$ T lymphocyte clones (Hussey et al., 1988).

Phase I dose-ranging trials of recombinant, soluble CD4 as a continuous, intravenous infusion or as intermittent intravenous boluses have started in the United States.

AL-721

AL-721 is a lipid proprietary compound consisting of neutral glycerides, phosphatidyl choline, and phosphatidylethanolamine. It extracts cholesterol from cellular membranes and may affect the retroviral envelope in a similar manner, thereby reducing viral infectivity. In vitro AL-721 blocks HIV-1-induced destruction of peripheral blood lymphocytes and inhibits reverse transcriptase activity and viral antigen expression by 50 percent, with little effect on uninfected cells. Higher concentrations are required to decrease HIV-1 antigen expression further (Sarin et al., 1985).

Eight patients with HIV-1-associated lymphadenopathy were enrolled in an open trial of AL-721. No side effects of treatment were seen, and seven of eight patients remained clinically stable over 8 weeks of therapy and 8 weeks of follow-up. Five of seven subjects had a reduction in reverse transcriptase activity in lymphocyte cocultures, and responses to pokeweed mitogen increased in five. No effect was seen on lymphocyte subsets (Grieco et al., 1987). Additional controlled trials of AL-721 are under way. The likelihood that this agent could not reach virus-infected sites intact by intestinal absorption makes a reproducible beneficial effect unlikely. At present, this compound continues to be used extensively in the patient community, with apparently few adverse effects.

Peptide T

Peptide T is a synthetic oligopeptide, with a sequence identical to a portion of the HIV-1 envelope. It was originally reported to inhibit binding of gp120 to CD4 antigen in brain tissue and to reduce reverse transcriptase activity (Pert et al., 1986). However, at least nine laboratories have since been unable to reproduce the finding of viral inhibition (Barnes et al., 1987). One laboratory confirmed the result, but only when narrowly defined concentrations of peptide and virus were used in certain cell types. Peptide T given to four patients in Sweden with late stage AIDS reportedly improved lymphocyte counts and stabilized clinical status (Wetterberg et al., 1987). The activity of peptide T remains to be clarified by laboratory and clinical studies.

IMMUNOMODULATORS

HIV-1 infection and lysis of $CD4^+$ cells results in marked defects in the number and function of T helper/inducer lymphocyte subset, leading to profound deficiencies in cell-mediated immunity (see Chapter 2). Defects are seen in antigen-induced lymphocyte proliferation and cytotoxicity, macrophage and natural killer cell-mediated killing, and B-cell production of specific antibody.

These defects in in vitro measurements of cellular and humoral immunity and abnormal levels of circulating lymphokines have led investigators to attempt to replete or enhance the function of the immune system by the use of immunomodulators (Table 17.2).

Interleukin 2

Interleukin-2 (IL2) is a low-molecular-weight protein produced by T cells in response to antigenic, mitogenic, or alloantigenic stimulation (Ruscetti and Gallo, 1981). In the normal host, IL2 enhances natural killer cell activity, mitogen- or antigen-induced lymphocyte proliferation, and cytotoxic T-cell activity and stimulates gamma interferon generation.

Table 17.2. Immunomodulators and Biological Effects In Vitro

Interleukin-2	Enhances natural killer cell activity, antigen- and mitogen-induced lymphocyte proliferation, cytotoxic T-lymphocyte activity, and gamma interferon production
Gamma interferon	Increases macrophage antimicrobial activity, natural killer cell activity
Alpha interferon	Increases natural killer, antibody-dependent and T-cell cytotoxicity; influences antibody and cellular immunity
Ampligen	Induces interferons and tumor necrosis factor, augments natural killer cell and monocyte activity
Thymic hormones	Promotes T-cell differentiation and lymphokine production
Thymus fragment transplantation	Replacement of abnormal thymic environment and thymic hormones
Isoprinosine	Increases mitogen- and antigen-stimulated lymphocyte proliferation, lymphocyte cytotoxicity; improves IL2 production, mitogen-stimulated B-cell proliferation; increases CD4$^+$ cell numbers
Imuthiol	Increases mitogen-stimulated lymphocyte proliferation, increases CD4$^+$ cell number
Cyclosporin A	Decreases antigen-stimulated lymphocyte proliferation and differentiation
Lymphocyte transfusion	Repopulates mature T lymphocytes
Bone marrow transplantation	Repopulated stem cells
Gamma globulin	Replaces diminished immunoglobulins; ?feedback decreases in B-cell activation

In patients with AIDS, defects in these same in vitro measures of cellular immunity are seen, and production of IL2 is depressed (Ciobanu et al., 1983). Several of these defects can be improved by the addition of exogenous IL2. Natural killer cell activity in patients with AIDS is depressed to 30 to 50 percent of normal and improves up to ninefold when lymphocytes are incubated with IL2 (Rook et al., 1983; Reddy et al., 1984).

Antigen-induced cellular immune responses are particularly impaired: Despite active CMV infection, AIDS patients exhibit low or absent virus-specific cytotoxic lymphocyte activity. In these patients, IL2 dramatically enhances CMV-specific T-lymphocyte cytotoxicity to levels above those of normal controls (Rook et al., 1983). IL2 also improves deficient alloantigen-stimulated proliferation in mixed lymphocyte reactions (Lifson et al., 1984).

Fauci and Lane (1987) have treated over 50 AIDS patients with intravenous IL2 and observed both a rise in total and CD4$^+$ lymphocyte counts and enhanced spontaneous lymphocyte proliferation. Some patients also had clearing of viremia and minor tumor regression (Fauci, 1987). Natural killer cell responses, antigen-stimulated T-cell proliferative responses, and skin test reactivity have also improved in some AIDS and ARC patients given IL2 (Ernst et al., 1986). Fever, chills, dermatitis, and hypotension with IL2 may be dose-limiting in some patients.

Studies are under way to determine whether IL2 will demonstrate better immunoenhancement with concurrent administration of AZT.

Gamma Interferon

Gamma interferon is a major component of the human lymphokines produced by activated T cells. It influences monocytes/macrophages to increase expression of class II MHC antigens, increase IL1 production, and exert enhanced antimicrobial activity against intracellular pathogens (Basham and Merigan, 1983; Nathan et al., 1983). In patients with AIDS, lymphokines produced on exposure to antigen appear generally inactive in stimulating normal macrophages to produce H_2O_2 or to kill or inhibit intracellular replication of *T. gondii* or *C. psittaci* (Murray et al., 1984). Mitogen-induced production of gamma interferon by macrophages from these patients is impaired, and antigen-induced production is absent or barely detectable. Macrophage effector cells, however, appear to have normal function when stimulated by normal lymphokines or purified gamma interferon (Murray et al., 1984).

Gamma interferon also possesses antiviral properties. Under certain conditions it significantly inhibits reverse transcriptase activity and HIV-1 antigen expression (Hammer et al., 1986). In phase I and II trials of gamma interferon in AIDS patients, a small number of patients with Kaposi's sarcoma had transient improvement, CD4+ cell number responded variably, and in vitro macrophage function and natural killer cell activity improved (Lane and Fauci, 1985; Miles et al., 1986; Parkin et al., 1986). Despite improved immune function in vitro, however, opportunistic infections and Kaposi's sarcoma progressed, and considerable dose-limiting toxicity (chills, fever, fatigue, diarrhea, headache, sweats, nausea, vomiting, anorexia) was seen (Miles et al., 1986). In addition, at higher doses there was evidence of immunosuppression (Parkin et al., 1986; Pennington et al., 1986).

Gamma interferon and tumor necrosis factor synergistically inhibit HIV-1 and kill acutely infected cells in vitro (Wong et al. 1987). A search is under way for a similar in vivo effect.

Alpha Interferon

Natural alpha interferon is a mixture of 20 or more soluble proteins produced by buffy-coat cells (leukocyte interferon) and B lymphocytes (lymphoblastoid interferon) in response to a number of different infections, in particular, viral infections. Interferon, though not directly virucidal, inhibits virus production in infected cells and confers resistance to viral infection on uninfected cells. Inhibition of viral replication occurs primarily by interruption of translation, by inducing hydrolysis of messenger RNA and inhibiting peptide chain initiation, or by inhibiting assembly and release of infectious virions. Alpha interferon additionally increases natural killer cell activity, antibody-dependent cellular cytotoxicity, and T-cell cytotoxicity, and it enhances antibody production (Baron et al. 1984).

Alpha interferon production is abnormal in patients infected with HIV-1. In vitro, stimulation of peripheral blood mononuclear cells with microbial antigens reveals a severe deficiency (Lopez et al. 1983). In vivo, however, alpha interferon increases in concentration and exhibits an acid lability previously seen in patients with autoimmune diseases (DeStefano et al., 1982; Eyster et al., 1983). Furthermore, in healthy homosexuals, appearance of elevated serum acid-labile alpha interferon levels correlates with progression to AIDS or related manifestations (Buimovici-Klein et al., 1986). Elevated levels of acid-labile alpha interferon in patients with HIV-1 disease may, therefore, represent a poorly functional or interfering substance.

Recombinant alpha interferon is active in vitro against HIV-1, with more complete inhibition at higher concentrations (Ho et al., 1985b). Moreover, antibody to alpha interferon markedly increases viral production in long-term cultures of HIV-1 (Gallo et al., 1984).

The in vivo use of alpha interferon for its antiviral, antiproliferative, and immunomodulating effect has been extensively studied in patients with AIDS-associated Kaposi's sarcoma. Side effects of fever, chills, fatigue, headache, myalgia, nausea, vomiting, change in taste, leukopenia, thrombycytopenia, and elevated transaminases were seen and were dose-limiting in some patients (Groopman et al., 1984). Clinical response of cutaneous and visceral lesions was correlated with pretherapy immune competence (higher total and CD4$^+$ lymphocyte counts), absence of elevated serum levels of endogenous acid-labile alpha interferon, higher T-cell colony numbers, and absence of a history of opportunistic infections or systemic symptoms (fever, weight loss) (Gelmann et al., 1985; Mitsuyasu et al., 1986; Krown et al., 1986). Significantly, those patients who responded to interferon have subsequently shown a lower incidence of opportunistic infection. In some patients, therapy was associated with a fall in CD4$^+$ cell numbers and a simultaneous decrease in viral shedding (Fauci, 1987).

A recent trial in AIDS patients without Kaposi's sarcoma compared placebo to two regimens of recombinant alpha interferon. No significant difference in CD4$^+$ or CD4$^+$/CD8$^+$ cell ratio was seen, and no difference in survival or rate of opportunistic infection during or after treatment was noted (Friedland et al., 1987).

Combination therapy with AZT is now under way to determine whether alpha interferon might be more effective in conjunction with AZT.

Ampligen

Ampligen is a mismatched double-stranded RNA. Double-stranded RNAs are inducers of tumor necrosis factor and interferons and, in vivo, augment natural killer cell and monocyte activities. Against HIV-1 in vitro, ampligen protects the T-cell line, C3, from HIV-1 infection as measured by p24 antigen expression, reverse transcriptase activity, and cytopathic effect (Montefiore and Mitchell, 1987). In combination with AZT, a moderate in vitro additive effect against HIV-1 is seen (Mitchell et al., 1987).

A trial of intravenous ampligen in patients with AIDS, ARC, or lymphadenopathy detected no side effects or toxicity and demonstrated improved skin test reactivity and reduced lymphadenopathy or symptoms in the majority. This study used a radiolabeled RNA probe of the HIV *pol* gene to quantify viral messenger RNA and HIV-1 activity in peripheral blood mononuclear cells. Of the nine patients with detectable HIV-1 mRNA on entry, all had undetectable levels during therapy. Patients with ARC (but not AIDS), showed a fall in HIV-1 load by lymphocyte coculture methods, and some patients had improvement in CD4$^+$ cell numbers and HIV-1 p24 antigen levels (Carter et al., 1987). The results of this study are of particular interest because a novel technique (i.e., HIV-1 mRNA detection) was used to monitor viral inhibition and virologic response to ampligen was most pronounced by this method. Further study of this technique and of ampligen as an antiviral and immunomodulating therapy will be of interest to confirm these results.

Thymic Hormones and Thymus Fragment Transplantation

Thymic hormones are involved in normal differentiation and maturation of functioning T lymphocytes. Coincident with abnormalities of T-cell function in HIV-1 infection, abnormalities in thymic architecture and levels of various thymic hormones may be seen (Elie et al., 1983; Naylor et al., 1984). Thymosin alpha-1 is one thymic hormone that influences terminal differentiation of T helper cells and stimulates T lymphocytes to produce lymphokines (Hersh et al., 1983). Levels of circulting thymosin alpha-1 are elevated in patients with AIDS or risk factors for AIDS (e.g.,. hemophiliacs, homosexuals) (Naylor, et al., 1984; Hersh et al., 1983; Biggar et al., 1983), possibly owing to end-organ failure with elevation by loss of feedback inhibition, release of hormone with destruction of thymic tissue, or ectopic production (Naylor et al., 1984).

These results led to in vitro and in vivo examination of thymic hormone replacement in an effort to replete abnormal circulating levels. In vitro incubation of lymphocytes from patients at risk, or with frank AIDS, with Thymosin Fraction-5 improved mixed lymphocyte responses and mitogen-induced proliferation (Naylor et al., 1984; Rubinstein et al., 1986). Subcutaneous administration of Thymosin Fraction-5 for 2 to 8 months to at-risk hemophiliacs and homosexuals and adults and children with AIDS improved in vitro mitogen-induced lymphocyte proliferation, cell-mediated lympholysis, virus-induced alpha interferon production, and PHA-induced IL2 production (Naylor et al., 1984; Rubinstein et al., 1976; Mascart-Lemone et al., 1983). Improvement in $CD4^+$ cell numbers, T helper/suppressor ratio, or total lymphocyte count has been seen by some investigators (Rubinstein et al., 1986; Benn et al., 1986); they were accompanied by diminished AIDS-related symptoms in two-thirds of patients in one study (Benn et al., 1986). Transient clinical improvement was also seen in three children with AIDS, with weight gain, defervescence, and absence of new infections for 2 to 3 months. Unfortunately, after cessation of therapy, $CD4^+$ cells fell to below pretreatment levels, accompanied by the return of fevers, with eventual death due to fulminant infection (Rubinstein et al., 1986).

Similarly, attempts have been made to reconstitute absent thymic hormones by transplantation of thymus fragments. Initial responses of AIDS patients receiving thymic fragment transplants were favorable: A variable improvement in number of total and $CD4^+$ lymphocytes was seen, accompanied by a 6-week to 6-month period of improved or stable clinical course (Ciobanu et al., 1985; Danner et al., 1986; Dwyer et al., 1987). Subsequently, however, nearly all patients had progression of Kaposi's sarcoma lesions or development of opportunistic infections.

The failure of transplanted thymic tissue to effect a sustained improvement may be related to several factors. Newly generated $CD4^+$ cells remain targets of

HIV-1 infection and may be destroyed in the absence of additional methods directed toward virus inhibition. Alternatively, the amount of thymic tissue may insufficient, or grafted tissue may be rejected (Danner et al., 1986). Replacement of thymic hormones remains a possible effective method of improving T-lymphocyte function and number if combined with specific antiviral therapy.

Isoprinosine

Isoprinosine (inosine pranobex) is the p-acetamidobenzoate salt of N,N,-diethyl-amino-2-propanol and inosine. Isoprinosine increases proliferative responses of normal human lymphocytes to mitogens and alloantigens, and it increases lymphocyte cytotoxicity to viral-infected target cells (Simon and Clasky, 1978; Grieco et al., 1984). Clinical effectiveness has been reported for several viral infections including subacute sclerosing panencephalitis, cutaneous herpes, aphthous stomatitis, CMV hepatitis, and warts (Grieco et al., 1984).

In vitro, isoprinosine exerts a synergistic effect with phytohemagglutinin on lymphocyte stimulation in patients with AIDS-related features and produces an increase in both absolute CD4$^+$ cell numbers and T helper/suppressor ratios (Pompidou et al., 1985a). The same concentration of isoprinosine improves depressed IL2 production and expression of IL2 receptors to normal or near-normal levels in patients with AIDS (Tsang et al., 1985).

Isoprinosine also exerts moderate in vitro activity directly against HIV-1 in infected peripheral blood lymphocytes, as measured by decreased reverse transcriptase activity and p15 and p24 expression. Slight reduction in antigen expression, but not reverse transcriptase activity, is also demonstrated with chronically infected H9 cells (Pompidou et al., 1985b).

Initially, in vivo isoprinosine demonstrated no increase in T helper/suppressor ratio or proliferation responses to mitogens in patients with AIDS, and only one ARC patient had a significant but transient improvement in response to Con A (Grieco et al., 1984). More recently, in a randomized, double-blind, placebo-controlled trial of isoprinosine in 63 patients with "prodromal AIDS," isoprinosine increased total lymphocyte and T helper cell numbers, decreased T suppressor numbers, and reduced T-cell activation. Natural killer cell activity was markedly improved and persisted for 5 months after cessation of therapy. In addition, clinical improvement was reported by 52 percent of patients receiving 3 g/day, compared with 10 percent of placebo recipients. No side effects were attributable to the treatment (Bekesi et al., 1986).

Diethyldithiocarbamate (Imuthiol)

Diethydithiocarbamate (Imuthiol, DDTC) is a low-molecular-weight sulfur compound that acts, like isoprinosine, as a T-cell inducer and causes an increase in CD4$^+$ cell number. In vitro, it acts synergistically with phytohemagglutinin to increase nuclear activation in lymphocytes from patients with ARC and induces a 78 percent rise in absolute CD4$^+$ numbers (Pompidou et al., 1985a).

Imuthiol has also shown a moderate ability to inhibit HIV-1 in vitro. Peripheral blood lymphocytes infected with HIV-1 and cultured in the presence of Imu-thiol show inhibition of reverse transcriptase activity and decreased expression of p15 and p24 antigens (Pompidou et al., 1985b).

Early, small trials in ARC patients suggested that Imuthiol improved CD4[+] cell numbers and skin test reactivity and induced regression of lymphadenopathy (Pompidou et al., 1985a; Lang et al., 1985). Larger trials have also shown symptom-atic improvement and reduction in lymphadenopathy; however, data concerning immunologic improvement are conflicting. In one trial, 83 ARC patients were ran-domized to receive an oral dose of Imuthiol or placebo. After 4 months of therapy, three of 39 placebo patients had progressed to AIDS compared with none of the Imuthiol-treated patients. Mean CD4[+] cell counts rose significantly in the Imu-thiol-treated group compared to placebo, and in 36 percent of the treated patients, CD4 cell rises of > 200 cells/mm^3 were sustained throughout 16 weeks of therapy (Lang et al., 1988). In contrast, a second trial in 44 symptomatic ARC and AIDS patients randomized to receive either intravenous Imuthiol for 4 months or no therapy showed no significant changes in lymphocyte surface markers, lymphocyte blastogenesis, or skin test reactivity (Brewton et al., 1987).

Cyclosporin A

Activation of lymphocytes increases active HIV-1 expression, and this activation may correlate in vivo with one or more cofactors—e.g., exposures to alloantigens, viruses, or other infectious antigens (Zagury et al., 1986). Cyclosporin A, an inhib-itor of antigen-stimulated T-lymphocyte proliferation and differentiation, might be expected to inhibit spread of HIV-1 and protect newly formed CD4[+] cells from virus infection. Cyclosporin A added to cultures of peripheral blood lymphocytes 2 hours after the virus was able to completely inhibit HIV-1 replication over 21 days (Wainberg et al., 1986). Several small trials of cyclosporin A in AIDS patients showed a transient rise in CD4[+] cell numbers, which returned to baseline during treatment with no effect on virus isolation (Leport et al., 1986; Andrieu et al., 1986). Some patients experienced severe toxic side effects including nausea, vom-iting, anorexia, fatigue, and increase in size and number of Kaposi's sarcoma lesions (Phillips et al., 1987). A more favorable, sustained rise in CD4[+] cells and fall in CD8[+] cells were seen in 15 HIV-1 seropositive, non-AIDS patients with more than 300 CD4[+] cells on entry. Additionally, in these patients, lymphadenop-athy regressed, and there was a suggestion of decreased rate of progression to AIDS (Andrieu et al., 1987). These results suggest that cyclosporin may prevent further spread of the virus to uninfected cells, but in patients who are already CD4[+] cell depleted and immunosuppressed or infected, it should be used with caution if at all.

Lymphocyte Transfusion and Bone Marrow Transplantation

The marked depletion of CD4[+] cells in AIDS and the success of bone marrow transplantation in patients with congenital immunodeficiencies have led some investigators to attempt immunoreconstitution with lymphocyte transfusions or bone marrow transplantation.

HLA-matched lymphocyte transfusion has been attempted in at least two patients. One patient received a single transfusion with no resultant improvement in T helper/suppressor ratio or total lymphocyte count (Davis et al., 1983). A second patient received lymphocyte transfusions every 2 to 4 weeks for approximately 1 year; this resulted in a transient rise in total $CD4^+$ cells and T helper/suppressor ratio but no change in clinical course (Lane et al., 1984). Side effects and graft versus host disease were mild (fever and rash) and decreased with repeated transfusion. Specific skin test immunity was transferred in both patients; however, no antibody response to the antigens or antigen-induced proliferation was documented.

Bone marrow transplantation has been attempted in a small number of patients with AIDS. Bone marrow transplant from an identical twin (Mitsuyasu et al., 1984) or HLA-matched family member (Hassett et al., 1983) to four patients with AIDS and Kaposi's sarcoma, without prior conditioning, resulted in no significant clinical or immunologic improvement. One patient conditioned with vinblastine had significant improvement in Kaposi's sarcoma lesions but subsequently died of opportunistic infection (Mitsuyasu et al., 1984). Another patient, who received both bone marrow transplant and lymphocyte transfer from an identical twin, had transient immunologic improvement but no clinical response (Lane et al., 1984).

Adoptive immunotherapy seems likely to fail in the absence of antiviral therapy aimed at preventing HIV-1 infection of the replacement lymphocytes. Three patients with AIDS and Kaposi's sarcoma have been treated with both suramin and bone marrow transplantation from identical twin siblings. Two patients had progression of Kaposi's sarcoma and clinical decline, one despite a rise to 600 to 800 $CD4^+$ cells/mm^3. The third patient remained clinically stable and regained in vitro blastogenic responses and skin test reactivity (Fauci and Lane, 1987). Four additional patients have received AZT prior to and following bone marrow transplantation from an identical twin sibling; evaluation of these patients is continuing (Lane et al., 1987).

Intravenous Gamma Globulin

Intravenous gamma globulin has been used primarily in the pediatric population, in whom AIDS is accompanied by frequent and severe bacterial infection and sepsis (Scott et al., 1984; Shannon and Ammann, 1985). Most of these children, as well as adults with AIDS, exhibit polyclonal hypergammaglobulinemia and hyperactive spontaneous B-cell responses in vitro (Shannon and Ammann, 1985; Lane et al., 1983). Tests of B-cell function in vitro reveal a poor specific antibody response to both T-cell-dependent and -independent antigens (Bernstein et al., 1985).

In a study of 16 adults and 17 children with AIDS or ARC, marked elevation in serum lactate dehydrogenase (LDH) was noted in those patients with interstitial pneumonia, caused by *Pneumocystis carinii* in adults or characterized as lymphoid interstitial pneumonitis in children (Silverman et al., 1985). Four adults and five children received intravenous gamma globulin at 50 mg/kg, increasing over 3 weeks to 300 mg/kg biweekly as maintenance. All treated adults improved clinically and immunologically and survived longer than 4 months after peak LDH, compared with one of five patients surviving who did not receive gamma globulin.

Children given gamma globulin showed a lack of progression of interstitial pneumonitis, a decrease in frequency and severity of bacterial and viral infection, and a reduction in hepatosplenomegaly and lymphadenopathy. Serum levels of LDH fell to within normal limits in all patients receiving gamma globulin (Silverman et al., 1985). Administration of intravenous gamma globulin to infants with AIDS also increased CD4$^+$ cell percentages, reduced elevated circulating immune complexes, and improved in vitro mitogenic responses to pokeweed mitogen and phytohemagglutinin (Calvelli and Rubinstein, 1986; Rubinstein et al., 1984).

The observed improvement in clinical and immunologic findings may be related to reduced activation of B cells via feedback inhibition by gamma globulin. Since activated B cells produce LDH, the fall in serum LDH may reflect this decreased activation (Silverman et al., 1985). Responses to gamma globulin are encouraging in adults and children with AIDS, and controlled trials using larger patient groups are under way.

FUTURE PROSPECTS

Effective strategies against HIV-1 infection are still in their formative stages. With increasing public and political recognition of AIDS as a major national health problem, clinical and basic research on HIV-1 has accelerated. New strategies will become available as our knowledge of HIV-1 increases.

The success of an antiviral agent rests on its ability to affect the virus to a greater extent than it affects host cells. Retroviruses use both host cell enzymes and replicative machinery, and therapy aimed at these shared functions would cause unacceptable toxicity to the host cells. The ideal target would be an enzyme, nucleic acid, receptor, or protein that is possessed by the virus alone. Much of the work already done in HIV-1 antiviral research has concentrated on one such enzyme exclusive to retroviruses—the reverse transcriptase. Even with such a specific target, many compounds, such as nucleoside analogs, which are active against reverse transcriptase, also inhibit the major DNA polymerase alpha of human cells, thereby causing considerable toxicity. Additionally, although inhibition of reverse transcriptase prevents formation of the DNA copy of the viral genome, it does not prevent formation of new virus from the DNA provirus already formed. Still, early in the course of infection this would be a valuable therapy, and attempts to produce more potent and specific compounds are continuing.

Sequences of nucleotides or amino acids unique to HIV-1 and exhibiting little diversity between isolates are also appropriate targets of rapidly developing techniques in molecular genetics and gene regulation. Oligonucleotides of DNA or RNA can be synthesized in a complementary or "antisense" orientation to critical areas of viral DNA or RNA (mRNA). By penetrating cells and binding to these critical areas, these synthetic products can inhibit replication, transcription, translation, or function of regulatory peptides. The *tat*-III or *rev* (*trs/art*) gene products, which amplify viral protein synthesis, are prime targets of these oligonucleotides. HIV-1 replication has been shown to be inhibited up to 95 percent by a 20-nucleotide antisense DNA which blocks the *tat*-III protein binding site on mRNA (Zamecnik et al., 1986).

Proviral DNA, whether in integrated or unintegrated, circular or linear form, once synthesized, has the potential to produce infectious virus. In the absence of known methods to eliminate these forms of provirus, cells containing them will need to be destroyed by immunotoxins or cytotoxic cells specifically sensitized against infected cells. Autologous $CD8^+$ cells, which suppress HIV-1 replication in vitro, may play a role in suppressing detectable virus in vivo. Expansion of this population in vivo or in vitro stimulation with IL2, followed by adoptive transfer back, may prove effective in reducing further spread of virus (Walker et al., 1986). To what extent inhibition of virus replication will allow a patient's own defenses to kill latently infected cells is unknown. It still needs to be determined which surface marker, perhaps a viral glycoprotein, is found specifically and universally on all infected cells.

Many questions remain, even about therapy known to be active against HIV-1. In the face of devastating symptoms of CNS disease and the demonstration of HIV-1 genome in brain tissue (see Chapter 5), relatively little is known about the CNS penetration or activity of many drugs already tried. Effective therapy and effective prophylaxis before or during early stages of infection may be found in one or more agents able to cross the blood-brain barrier in therapeutic concentrations, or an effective drug may require intrathecal administration. An equally important but untested property of these drugs is the ability to cross the placenta—i.e., to combat intrauterine infection and cause fetal damage.

No therapy yet available offers a complete cure, and it is likely that even an effective, virustatic drug will need to be given for long periods of time, if not for the life of the patient. Consideration must be given to a drug's future harmful side effects, such as infertility, chromosomal damage, or late carcinogenic potential, especially in children.

The potential toxicities of effective therapy might be decreased with the use of combinations, and synergistic or complementary effects could even be achieved. Antiviral combinations can be used to interrupt the viral cycle at more than one site, increasing the efficacy of any single agent. It seems likely that in late stages of HIV-1 infection with significant T helper cell depletion, immunorestorative methods will be needed to replenish the immune system and stimulate the remaining host defenses to control or eliminate residual infection.

Techniques to monitor disease activity and response to therapy are improving rapidly. The measurement of a viral antigen such as p24 in blood is already available. Refinements in viral culture, in detection of viral RNA, and in assessment of HIV-1 specific cell-mediated immunity should provide additional information on disease progression and response to intervention.

CHEMOPROPHYLAXIS

For some time, over 1 million people in the United States alone have been estimated to be infected with HIV-1 (Curran et al., 1985), and it is hoped that the rate of new infection will decline with continued public awareness of at-risk behavior. These infected individuals may progress to AIDS at a rate of 5 percent per year or higher (Goedert et al., 1986). Cofactors, such as antigenic stimuli, may influence whether or not symptomatic disease will occur, and control of these cofactors might possibly decrease the number and severity of AIDS and other manifestations.

Additional means of modifying the natural history of HIV-1 infection may be found in therapies aimed at the halting the spread of the virus at an early stage. This type of chemoprophylaxis, aimed at preventing disease in the infected individual, has been used successfully against tuberculosis. Infected persons at high risk of serious disease are treated early, when the number of bacilli are small and host damage is minimal. A similar goal may be set for control of HIV-1 infection, whereby disease is modified or prevented. In early infection the immune system is relatively intact, and opportunistic infection has not yet occurred. At this point, inhibition of the virus could presumably limit the number of cells affected, decelerate the course of disease, or prevent disease entirely. Indeed, some forms of therapy described earlier appear to be more effective in patients at earlier stages than in those with AIDS (e.g., cyclosporin A, isoprinosine, thymic hormone replacement). With the combined use of antiviral therapy and immunomodulators in a relatively intact host, the outlook for cure may be brighter.

Progression of clinical disease appears to correlate within a decrease in specific antibody responses: antibodies to the p24 *gag* protein, those mediating antibody-dependent cellular cytotoxicity, reverse transcriptase-inhibiting antibody, and neutralizing antibody (Weber et al., 1987; Laurence et al., 1987; Rook et al., 1987). If loss of antibody has a causal role in immunologic deterioration, then immunotherapy using pooled sera or monoclonal antibody may lead to clinical stabilization or improvement (Jackson et al., 1988). In those seropositive patients still able to mount an antibody response, active immunization with a specific vaccine containing those antigenic eptiopes that stimulate the desired protective antibodies may achieve the same end (Salk, 1987).

Prophylaxis can also be applied before the virus has established infection. The prevention of sexually acquired infection may be aided at the portal of entry by the use of surface-active agents like nonoxynol-9 (Hicks et al., 1985), interferon, or another antiviral agent to decrease the likelihood of systemic infection. Alternatively, postexposure prophylaxis, as in hepatitis B or rabies, can be employed to block infection after the virus has gained entry into the bloodstream. Passive immunization with antisera having neutralizing activity against HIV-1 may prevent virus attachment and the establishment of infection (see Chapter 18). As in hepatitis B, the efficacy of this therapy may depend on the promptness with which intervention is instituted. At a later step in initial infection, after the virus has entered the cell but prior to integration, the various reverse transcriptase inhibitors could be used to block production of virus progeny and prevent establishment of latency. Two protocols from Burroughs–Wellcome are currently in place for the prophylactic use of AZT in the setting of accidental needlestick or laboratory exposure to HIV. The eventual prevention of infection may require the use of more than one of these methods concomitantly. Clearly, the most effective prophylaxis, short of abstinence from at-risk behavior, would be a vaccine that stimulates the humoral and cellular immune system prior to contact with the virus, inhibiting it at the earliest possible point.

Much more information needs to be gathered on the natural history of early infection before potentially toxic chemoprophylactic regimens are instituted. In these patients, risk of therapy must be weighed especially carefully against an as yet ,unknown, eventual risk of developing AIDS.

REFERENCES

Abrams D, Kuno S, Wong R, et al. (1988): Fourth International Conference on AIDS, Stockholm, June 12–16.

Anand R, Moore J, Feorino P, et al. (1986): Lancet 1:97.

Andrieu JM, Even P, Venet A, et al. (1986): Second International Conference on AIDS, Paris, June 23–25.

Andrieu JM, Even P, Venet A, et al. (1987): Third International Conference on AIDS, Washington, D.C., June 1–5.

Åsjö B, Morfeldt-Månson L, Bergdahl S, et al. (1978): Third International Conference on AIDS, Washington, D.C., June 1–5.

Balzarini J, Mitsuya H, De Clercq E, Broder S, (1986): Int J Cancer 37:451.

Balzarini J, Naesens L, Pauwels R, et al. (1988): Fourth International Conference on AIDS, Stockholm, June 12–16.

Barnes DM (1987): Science 237:138.

Baron S, Grossberg SE, Klimpel GR, Brunell PA, (1984): Immune and interferon systems. In Galasso GG, Merigan TC, Buchanan RA (eds): Antimicrobial Agents and Viral Diseases of Man. New York: Raven Press, pp. 123–178.

Basham TY, Merigan TC, (1983): J Immunol 130:1492.

Bekesi JG, Wallace JI, Roboz JP, Glasky A (1986): Second International Conference on AIDS, Paris, June 23–25.

Benn VJ, Garber J, Gottlieb MS, et al. (1986): Second International Conference on AIDS, Paris, June 23–25.

Bergdahl S, Biberfeld G, Julander I, et al. (1987): Third International Conference on AIDS, Washington, D.C., June 1–5.

Bergdahl S, Sonnerborg A, Larsson A, Strannegard O: Lancet 1:1052.

Bernstein LJ, Ochs HD, Wedgewood RJ, Rubinstein A (1985) J Pediatr 107:352.

Biggar RJ, Taylor PH, Goldstein AL, et al. (1983): N Engl J Med 309:49.

Brewton GW, Hersh E, Mansell P, et al. (1978): Third International Conference on AIDS, Washington, D.C., June 1–5.

Broder S (1987): Ann Intern Med 106:569.

Buimovici-Klein E, Lange M, Klein RJ, et al. (1986): AIDS Res 2:99.

Calvelli TA, Rubinstein A (1986): Pediatr Infect Dis 5:S07.

Carne CA, Tedder RS, Smith A, et al. (1985): Lancet 2:1206.

Carter WA, Strayer DR, Brodsky I, et al. (1987): Lancet 1:1286.

Chaisson RE, Allain J-P, Volberding PA (1986): N Engl J Med 315:1610.

Chermann JC, Sinoussi FC, Jasmin C (1975): Biochem Biophys Res Commun 65:1229.

Ciobanu N, Welte K, Kruger G, et al. (1983); J Clin Immunol 3:332.

Ciobanu N, Paietta E, Karten M, et al. (1985): Ann Intern Med 103:479.

Crumpacker C, Bubley G, Lucey D, et al. (1986): Lancet 2:45.

Crumpacker C, Heagy W, Bubley G (1987): Ann Intern Med 197:664.

Curran JW, Meade, Morgan W, Hardy AM, et al. (1985): Science 229:1352.

Dalgleish AG, Beverly PCL, Clapham PR, et al. (1984): Nature 312:763.

Danner SA, Schuurman HJ, Lange JMA, et al. (1986): Arch Intern Med 146:1133.

Davidson BP, Siegal FP, Reife RA, et al. (1987): Third International Conference on AIDS, Washington, D.C., June 1–5.

Davis KC, Hayward A, Ozturk G, Kohler PF (1983): Lancet 1:599.

De Clercq E (1979): Cancer Lett 8:9.

De Clercq E (1986): J Med Chem 29:1561.

Della Bruna C, Schioppacassi G, Ungheri D, et al. (1983): J Antibiot 36:1502.

DeStefano E, Friedman RM, Friedman-Kein AE, et al. (1982): J Infect Dis 146:451.

Dormont D, Spire B, Barre-Sinoussi F, et al. (1985): Ann Inst Pasteur/Virol 136E:75.

Dormont D, Maillet T, Di Maria H, et al. (1986): Second International Conference on AIDS, Paris, June 23–25.

Dwyer JM, Wood CC, McNamara J, Kinder B (1987): Arch Intern Med 147:513.

Elie R, Laroche AC, Arnoux E, et al. (1983): N Engl J Med 308:841.

Eriksson BFH, Schinazi RF, Chu CK (1988): Fourth International Conference on AIDS, Stockholm, June 12–16.

Ernst M, Kern P, Flad HD, Ulmer AJ (1986): J Clin Immunol 6:170.

Eyster ME, Goedert JJ, Poon MC, Preble OT (1983): N Engl J Med 309:583.

Farthing CF, Dalgleish AG, Clark AL, et al. (1986): Second International Conference on AIDS, Paris, June 25–25, 1986.

Fauci AS (1987): Ann Intern Med 106:574.

Fauci AS, Lane, HC (1987): Ann Inst Pasteur/Immunol 138:261.

Fiddian AP, and a European/Australian Collaborative Study Group (1988): Program and Abstracts of the Twenty-Eighth Interscience Conference on Antimicrobial Agents and Chemotherapy, October 23–26.

Fischl MA, Richman DD, Grieco MH, et al. (1987): N Engl J Med 317:185.

Folks T, Powell DM, Lightfoote MM, et al. (1986): Science 231:600.

Friedland GH, Landesman SH, Crumpacker CS, et al. (1987): Third International Conference on AIDS, Washington, D.C., June 1–5.

Gallo RC, Salahuddin SZ, Popovic M, et al. (1984): Science 224:500.

Gartner S, Markovits P, Markovitz DM, et al. (1986): Science 233:215.

Gelmann EP, Preble OT, Steis R, et al. (1985): Am J Med 78:737.

Goedert JJ, Biggar RJ, Weiss SH, et al. (1986): Science 231:992.

Goswami BB, Borek E, Sharma OK, (1979): Biochem Biophys Res Cummun 89:830.

Goudsmit J, De Wolf F, Paul DA, et al. (1986): Lancet 2:177.

Grieco MH, Reddy MM, Manvar D, et al. (1984): Ann Intern Med 101:206.

Grieco MH, Lange M, Klein EB, et al. (1987): Third International Conference on AIDS, Washington, D.C., June 1–5.

Groopman JE, Gottlieb MS, Goodman J, et al. (1984): Ann Intern Med 100:671.

Hammer SM, Gillis JM, Groopman JE, et al. (1986): Second International Conference on AIDS, Paris, June 23–25.

Hassett JM, Zaroulis CG, Greenberg ML, Siegal FP (1983): N Engl J Med 309:665.

Hawking F (1978): Adv Pharmacol Chemother 15:289.

Hersh EM, Reuben JM, Rios A, et al. (1983): N Engl J Med 308:45.

Hicks DR, Martin LS, Getchell JP, et al. (1985): Lancet 2:1422.

Ho DD, Rota TR, Schooley RT, et al. (1985a): N Engl J Med 313:1493.

Ho DD, Hartshorn KL, Rota TR, et al. (1985b): Lancet 1:602.

Hoxie JA, Haggarty BS, Pillsbury N, Levy JA (1985): Science 229:1400.

Hussey RE, Richardson NE, Kowalski M, et al. (1988): Nature 331:78.

Ito M, Baba M, Sato A, et al. (1987): Antiviral Res 7:361.

Jackson GG, Perkins JT, Rubenis M, et al. (1988): Lancet 2:647.

Jacobson MA, Abrams D, Wilber J, et al. (1988): Program and Abstracts of the Twenty-Eighth Interscience Conference on Antimicrobial Agents and Chemotherapy, October 23–26.

Kimberlin RH, Walker CA (1983): Arch Virol 78:9.

Krown SE, Real FX, Vadhan-Raj S, et al. (1986): Cancer 57:1662.

Kwok S, Mack DH, Mullis KB, et al. (1987): J Virol 61:1690.

Lane HC, Fauci AS (1985): Ann Intern Med 103:714.

Lane HC Masur H, Edgar LC, et al. (1983): N Engl J Med 309:453.

Lane HC, Masur H, Longo DL, et al. (1984): N Engl J Med 311:1099.

Lane HC, Masur H, Kovacs J, et al. (1987): Third International Conference on AIDS, Washington, D.C., June 1-5.

Lang JM, Oberling F, Aleksijevic A, et al. (1985): Lancet 2:1066.

Lang JM, Touraine JL, Trepo C, et al. (1988): Lancet 2:702.

Laurence J, Saunders A, Kulkosky J (1987): Science 235:1501.

Leport C, Matheron S, Martin S, et al. (1986): Second International Conference on AIDS, Paris, June 23-25.

Levine AM, Gill PS, Cohen J, et al. (1986): Ann Intern Med 105:32.

Lifson JD, Benike CJ, Mark DF, et al. (1984): Lancet 1:698.

Lopez C, Fitzgerald PA, Siegal FP (1983): J Infect Dis 148:962.

Mansell PWA, Heseltine PNR, Roberts RB, et al. (1987): Third International Conference on AIDS, Washington, D.C., June 1-5.

Markham PD, Salahuddin SZ, Nakamura S, et al. (1986): Second International Conference on AIDS, Paris, June 23-25.

Mansuri M, Ghazzouli I, Hitchcock M, et al. (1988): Fourth International Conference on AIDS, Stockholm, June 12-16.

Mascart-Lemone F, Huygen K, Clumeck N, et al. (1983): Lancet 2:735.

McCormick JB, Getchell JP, Mitchell SW, Hicks DR (1984): Lancet 2:1367.

Merigan TC, Skowron G, Bozzette S, et al. (1989): Ann Intern Med (in press).

Miles SA, Martinez O, Sherwin S, et al. (1986): Second International Conference on AIDS, Paris, June 23-25.

Mitchell WM, Montefiore DC, Robinson WE, et al. (1987): Lancet 1:890.

Mitsuya H, Broder S (1986): Proc Natl Acad Sci USA 83;1911.

Mitsuya H, Looney DJ, Kuno S, et al. (1988): Science 240:646.

Mitsuya H, Popovic M, Yarchoan R, et al. (1984): Science 226:172.

Mitsuya H, Weinhold KJ, Furman PA, et al. (1985): Proc Natl Acad Sci USA 82:7096.

Mitsuyasu R, Volberding P, Groopman J, Champlin R (1984): J Cell Biochem (Suppl) 8A:22.

Mitsuyasu RT, Taylor JMG, Glaspy J, Fahey JL (1986): Cancer 57:1657.

Montagnier L, Gruest J, Chamaret S, et al. (1984): Science 225:63.

Montefiore DC, Mitchell WM (1987): Proc Natl Acad Sci USA 84:2985.

Moskovitz BL, et al. (1987): Third International Conference on AIDS, Washington, D.C., June 1-5.

Murray HW, Rubin BY, Masur H, Roberts RB (1984): N Engl J Med 310:883.

Nathan CF, Murray HW, Wiebe ME, Rubin BY (1983): J Exp Med 158:670.

Navia BA, Jordan BD, Price RW (1986): Ann Neurol 19:517.

Naylor PH, Schulof RS, Sztein MB (1984): Ann NY Acad Sci 437:88.

Öberg B (1983): Pharmacol Ther 19:387.

Parkin JM, Eales LJ, Moshtael D, et al. (1986): Second International Conference on AIDS, Paris, June 23-25.

Pennington JE, Groopman JE, Small GJ, et al. (1986): J Infect Dis 153:609.

Pert CB, Hill JM, Ruff MR, et al. (1986): Proc Natl Acad Sci USA 83:9254.

Phillips A, Fanning M, Halloran P, et al. (1987): Third International Conference on AIDS, Washington, D.C., June 1-5.

Pizzo PA, Eddy J, Falloon J, et al. (1988): N Engl J Med 319:889.

Pompidou A, Delsaux MC, Telvi L, et al. (1985a): Cancer Res (Suppl) 45:4671s.

Pompidou A, Zagury D, Gallo RC, et al. (1985b): Lancet 2:1423.

Popovic M, Sarngadharan MG, Read E, Gallo RC (1984): Science 224:497.

Reddy MN, Pinyavat N, Grieco MH (1984): Infect Immun 44:339.

Richman DD, Fischl MA, Grieco MH, et al. (1987): N Engl J Med 317:192.

Rook AH, Masur H, Lane HC, et al. (1983): J Clin Invest 72:398–403.

Rook AH, Lane HC, Folk T, et al. (1987): J Immunol 138:1064.

Rouvroy D, Bogaerts J, Habyarimana J-B, et al. (1985): Lancet 1:878.

Rozenbaum W, Dormont D, Spire B, et al. (1985): Lancet 1:450.

Rubinstein A, Sicklick M, Bernstein L, et al. (1984): Pediatr Res 18:264A.

Rubinstein A, Novick BE, Sicklick MJ, et al. (1986): J Pediatr 109:422.

Ruscetti FW, Gallo RC (1981): Blood 57:379.

Salk J (1987): Nature 327:473.

Sandstrom EG, Kaplan JC, Byington RE, Hirsch MS (1985): Lancet 1:1480.

Sarin PS, Gallo RC, Scheer DI, et al. (1985): N Engl J Med 313:1289.

Scott GB, Buck BE, Leterman JG, et al. (1984): N Engl J Med 310:76.

Shannon KM, Ammann AJ (1985): J Pediatr 106:332.

Shaw GM, Harper ME, Hahn BH, et al. (1985): Science 227:177.

Sidwell RW (1980): Ribavirin: In vitro antiviral activity. In Smith RA, Kirkpatrick W (eds): Ribavirin: A Broad Spectrum Antiviral Agent. New York: Academic Press, pp. 23–42.

Silverman BA, Rubinstein A (1985): Am J Med 78:728.

Simon LN, Glasky AJ (1978): Cancer Treat Rep 62:1963.

Smith DH, Byrn RA, Marsters SA, et al. (1987): Science 238:1704.

Snider WD, Simpson DM, Nielsen S, et al. (1983): Ann Neurol 14:403.

Sodroski J, Rosen C, Wong-Staal F, et al. (1985): Science 227:171.

Sodroski J, Goh WC, Rosen C, et al. (1986): Nature 321:412.

Torseth J, Bhatia G, Harkonen S, et al. J Infect Dis (submitted).

Tsang KY, Fudenberg HH, Galbraith GMP, et al. (1985): J Clin Invest 75:1538.

Ueno R, Kuno S (1987): Lancet 1:1379.

Wainberg MA, Roy S, Blain N, Tsoukas C (1986): Second International Conference on AIDS, Paris, June 23–25.

Walker CM, Moody DJ, Stites DP, Levy JA (1986): Science 234:1536.

Weber JN, Clapham PR, Weiss RA, et al. (1987): Lancet 1:119.

Wetterberg L, Alexius B, Saaf J (1987): Lancet 1:159.

Wong GHW, Krowka J, Stites DP, Goeddel DV (1987): Third International Conference on AIDS, Washington, D.C., June 1–5.

Woodley CL, Kilburn JO (1982): Am Rev Respir Dis 126:586.

Yarchoan R, Berg G, Brouwers P, et al. (1987): Lancet 1:132.

Yarchoan R, Klecker RW, Weinhold KJ, et al. (1986): Lancet 1:575.

Yarchoan R, Perno CF, Thomas RV, et al. (1988): Lancet 1:76.

Zagury D, Bernard J, Leonard R, et al. (1986): Science 231:850.

Zamecnik PC, Goodchild J, Taguchi Y, Sarin PS (1986): Proc Natl Acad Sci USA 83:4143.

18

Immunization

DONALD P. FRANCIS

PREEXPOSURE, ACTIVE IMMUNIZATION

The need for a vaccine to protect against HIV-1 infection is pressing, but our meager understanding of the natural history of HIV-1 infection, especially the immunologic correlates of protection (see Chapter 2), has slowed progress in vaccine development. Nonetheless, research on vaccines for AIDS has been pursued aggressively by both the public and private sectors of the biomedical research community. Using the current understanding of HIV-1 and the experience gained from developing vaccines for other viruses, especially hepatitis B virus, a plan was proposed for the development of an AIDS vaccine (Francis and Petricciani, 1985).

This plan assumed that one of the surface components of the virus within the gp 120 (envelope) and/or the gp 41 (transmembrane) proteins would induce protective immunity, represented by antibody that would kill free virus in vitro. More specifically, surface antigen(s), purified from cultured, inactivated virus, derived from some recombinant method or produced synthetically, would induce protective (neutralizing) antibodies when presented to the host's immune system before infection. The scheme called for testing of the prototype vaccine in inexpensive laboratory animals. Only after successful induction of significant titers of neutralizing antibodies in laboratory animals would chimpanzee experiments be justified. This staging of experiments was designed to conserve the rare and expensive chimpanzee, the only available nonhuman host known to be susceptible to HIV-1 infection (Fultz et al., 1986). Once a given prototype vaccine had induced neutralizing antibodies (or some other presumably protective effect) in the chimpanzee, then the chimpanzee would be challenged with live virus. The protection of a chimpanzee, given a live virus challenge, was felt to be a necessary step before human safety and efficacy studies could begin.

Though much has been learned over the past few years, a vaccine for AIDS does not seem to be at hand. A variety of antigen preparations have been made and tested in laboratory animals, and by early 1988 four antigen preparations had passed through chimpanzee challenge studies. The four prototype vaccines have passed through the entire screening process and have been produced by a variety of techniques including (1) purification from cell culture (Arthur et al., 1987), (2) production by recombinant expression of gp 120 in mammalian cells (Lasky et al.,

Table 18.1. Status of Prototype Vaccine Antigens (U.S.)

Producer	Source[a]	Antigen(s)	Status[b]	
Envelope				
Genentech	R/CHO	GP 120	LA/N, Ch/N(F),	?Hu
Oncogene/BM	R/Vacc	GP 160	LA/N, Ch/C(F),→	Hu
NCI/Duke University	Cell	Gp 120	LA/N, Ch/N(F)	
Southwest Foundation	SP	Gp 41	LA/±N, Ch/±N(F)	
MicroGenSys	R/Baculo	Gp 160	? ? →	Hu
Repligen	R/_E. coli_ + Baculo	Gp 120/160	LA/N, Ch(?)	
Chiron	R/yeast	Gp 120+	LA/N, Ch(?)	
Core				
George Washington University/Alpha	SP	p17	LA/±N	?Hu
Salk/Immune Resp. Corp.	Cell	Whole	LA/? Ch(?)	

[a]R, recombinant; SP, synthetic peptide; CHO, Chinese hamster ovary cells; Vacc, vaccinia virus; Baculo, baculovirus; Cell, cell culture.

[b]LA, laboratory animal; N, neutralizing antibody; C, cell-mediated immunity; Ch, chimpanzee; (F), failed challenge; Hu, human trials.

1986), (3) production by recombinant expression of gp 160 (120 plus 41) in vaccinia virus (Hu et al., 1987; Zagury et al., 1987), and (4) direct synthesis of a peptide segment of gp 41 (Dreesman, 1986). All of these prototype vaccines have induced either neutralizing antibodies in laboratory animals or chimpanzees or, in the case of the vaccinia recombinant, cell-mediated immunity in chimpanzees. Yet all have failed to protect chimpanzees against infection upon subsequent challenge with HIV-1. Other antigen constructs are at earlier stages in the process of screening described above (see Table 18.1). Two additional protototype vaccines have bypassed chimpanzee challenge experiments and have been injected into humans. One is a vaccinia recombinant, which alone or together with autologous cells infected by the vaccinia recombinant has been injected into humans in France and Zaire (Zagury et al., 1987). The other is a baculovirus recombinant-produced antigen, which has been administered to humans in the United States (Ezzell, 1987). Human experiments are planned for the vaccinia recombinant prototype that has failed chimpanzee challenge trial (see Table 18.1).

    The failure of the first-generation vaccine prototypes must be viewed in perspective. Although discouraging in some ways, the attempts were begun without a full understanding of the immunologic correlates of infection with HIV-1. Indeed, although the initial plans specified neutralizing antibody as the major indicator of success, accumulating data leave unanswered questions about the protective effect of neutralizing antibodies. In fact, except for a single study in children, neutralizing antibody has not correlated well with the stage of disease progression (Chapter 2). Specifically, titers of neutralizing antibody have not been significantly different in patients with AIDS, patients with less severe immunodeficiency, or asymptomatic seropositive persons. Other serologic markers (e.g., antibodies to the core [p24]) protein and antibodies that inhibit reverse transcriptase activity) have correlated inversely with disease severity (see Chapter 2). More recent attempts at other vaccine prototypes have broadened the representation of viral proteins.

Much remains to be understood about the chimpanzee model. Chimpanzees and humans show a great deal of similarity in their immune systems. Moreover, although AIDS itself has not been documented in chimpanzees, the response of chimpanzees to HIV-1 infection appears to parallel the response in humans quite well. But there may be important differences yet to be discovered that may affect vaccine-induced immunity. Important comparison data will be available when humans are given antigens that have been tested in chimpanzees.

Other important questions about the chimpanzee model concern the dose and route of virus challenge. Some challenges have involved extremely large doses of intravenous virus. It is possible that the challenge dose overwhelmed an immune response that might be protective in the natural setting with exposure through mucous membranes. Considerable work is necessary to standardize the chimpanzee model in order to conserve precious chimpanzees.

POSTEXPOSURE, ACTIVE IMMUNIZATION

Since the latency period from HIV-1 infection to disease is quite long, immunization of infected people at some time before the expression of disease might prevent, or at least delay, the development of serious disease (Salk, 1987). Studies are under way to determine if virus-specific immune stimulation using whole inactivated HIV-1 will prevent disease.

POSTEXPOSURE, PASSIVE IMMUNIZATION

Prevention of infection using immunoglobulin in postexposure settings (e.g., after contaminated needle injury or perinatal infection) has theoretical appeal for HIV-1 and documented efficacy for other agents. Preliminary results in chimpanzees immunized with high-titer human sera have not shown protection from subsequent challenge (F. Prince, personal communication, 1988).

The use of immunoglobulin for the therapy of AIDS has so far been shown to be effective only in babies and only in the realm of other, predominantly nonviral, agents that opportunistically infect these patients (see also Chapter 17). Whether HIV-1-specific immunoglobulins offer any protection against the primary infection remains to be shown.

SUMMARY

Thus, unless there is some remarkable breakthrough, an AIDS vaccine does not appear to be on the horizon. Although there is no reason to believe that an HIV-1 vaccine is not feasible, the road toward its production appears complex and may take several years to negotiate.

REFERENCES

Arthur LO, Pyle SW, et al. (1987): Proc Natl Acad Sci USA 84(23):8583.

Dreesman GR (1986): Synthetic HIV peptide vaccine candidates and protection studies in chimpanzees. Retroviruses of human AIDS and related animal diseases. "Colloque des Cent Gardes," Oct. 29–30, Paris.

Ezzell C (1987): Nature 330:687.
Francis DP, Petricciani JC (1985): N Engl J Med 313:1586.
Fultz PN, McClure HM, et al. (1986): J Virol April: 116.
Hu SL, Fultz PN, et al. (1987): Nature 328:721.
Lasky LA, Groopman JE, et al. (1986) Science 233:209.
Salk J (1987): Commentary: Nature 327:473.
Zagury D, Leonard R, et al. (1987): Nature 326:249.

19

Responses in the Health Care System

MICHAEL A. POLIS AND ANTHONY PASCAL

The epidemic of HIV-1 infection has begun to affect the delivery of health care to every American. In the United States, the financial burdens imposed by the costs of treating this disease have disproportionately affected public hospitals, Medicaid, and many large urban areas. Paradoxically, although chemotherapy with zidovudine (AZT) promises to prolong the life of some patients with HIV-1 infection, the added life expectancy, together with the cost of the drug itself and the expenses involved in treating its toxic side effects, may increase the demand for health care resources.

The response of the health care system to the epidemic has been uneven, differing remarkably by locale, diagnosis, risk group, and other demographic factors. Nationwide data on the health care of persons with HIV-1 infections have become increasingly available, however, and the patterns will undoubtedly influence the overall distribution and use of health care resources for at least the near future. Moreover, some 450 bills about AIDS were introduced into state legislatures in 1987, reflecting nationwide, but fragmented, concern about the disease (Lewis, 1987). In this chapter we summarize the response of the U.S. health care and health insurance industries to the AIDS epidemic.

PATTERNS OF HOSPITALIZATION

Numbers of Hospitalizations

Data from the National Hospital Discharge Survey indicate that there were approximately 10,000 discharges from short-stay hospitals with the diagnosis of AIDS in 1984 and 23,000 such discharges in 1985 (Graves et al., 1987). Because the Committee for the International Classification of Diseases did not classify AIDS until October 1986 (Centers for Disease Control, 1987b) and because fear of stigmatization has led to underdiagnosis and misclassification, these figures undoubtedly underestimated the true frequency of hospital discharges. In March 1986, a survey by the National Association of Public Hospitals and the Association of American Medical Colleges' Council of Teaching Hospitals (Andrulis et al., 1987) requesting 1985 calendar-year data about provision and financing of care to AIDS patients was sent to 465 metropolitan public and private teaching hospitals. Of the 198 (43

313

percent) of hospitals that responded, 169 (64 public, 74 private, and 31 VA hospitals) reported providing care for an average of 32 patients with AIDS (range, 1 to 330). Although the hospitals did not optimally respond (43 percent replied), the study produced nationwide data from hospitals caring for almost 30 percent of cases of AIDS identified in 1985. The average number of patients with AIDS treated at the responding hospitals ranged from seven in the Midwest and 20 in the South to 36 in the West and 58 in the Northeast. The total number of admissions for AIDS were 11, 36, 61, and 91, respectively. The numbers of admissions per patient-year were similar in each region, ranging from 1.5 to 1.8.

New York City, where approximately one-quarter of the AIDS patients in the United States have been diagnosed, may serve as a sentinel to the future health care needs of AIDS patients. Compared to other cities with large numbers of AIDS patients, New York City has had a disproportionate number of intravenous drug abusers (IVDAs) among its cases. These patients may require more hospitalization than AIDS patients in other risk groups (see later). Other cities may experience a shift toward parenterally transmitted AIDS as well; preliminary results from a study sponsored by the National Institute on Drug Abuse found that the prevalence of HIV-1 infection among IVDAs in San Francisco increased from 10 to 15 percent in 1 year (MacDonald, 1987). Reversing the 10-year trend toward reducing the number of hospital beds in the city to reduce costs, in response to AIDS, New York State health officials increased the overall capacity of hospital beds in New York City by as many as 500 beds in December 1987 (State of New York Department of Health, 1987). Ambulances have been diverted from hospitals where there has been no room, and patients have waited several days in emergency rooms for available hospital beds (Pinckney, 1988). In October 1987, there were 1,335 AIDS patients hospitalized in the city, accounting for 6 percent of all hospitalized patients. That figure was projected to rise to 2,500, or 9 percent by 1989 (Sullivan, 1987b). Including other HIV-1-related illnesses will further increase the need for hospital beds.

Length of Hospitalization

One of the first widely cited studies, using data from New York City, Philadelphia, and San Francisco, estimated that for the first 10,000 patients in the United States diagnosed with AIDS from 1982 to 1984, the average number of hospital inpatient days from diagnosis to death was 168 and the average length of hospital admission was 31 days (Hardy et al., 1986). In 1984, the mean length of stay for all admissions for AIDS at San Francisco General Hospital (SFGH), including 201 patients overall, was approximately 11.7 days (Scitovsky et al., 1986), roughly consistent with the 14-day average length of admission discussed later for the West. At New England Deaconess Hospital, 45 patients with AIDS treated in the 1-year period from 1984 to 1985 had an average hospitalization of 21 days with an annualized number of hospital days per year of 61.9. This estimate did not necessarily cover the period from diagnosis to death and may have been biased by the oversampling of terminally ill patients with especially heavy hospital use (Seage et al., 1986).

The average length of stay in the hospitals surveyed for the nationwide study (Andrulis et al., 1987) was 19 days, and the average number of inpatient days per patient per year was 32, or about 1.7 hospitalizations per patient per year. Homosexual patients accounted for 47 percent of the admissions in the reporting hospitals overall, but 58 percent in private hospitals, 55 percent in VA hospitals, and only 39 percent in public hospitals. Although heterosexual IVDAs accounted for 32 percent of the total number of admissions, they accounted for nearly twice as many public as private hospital admissions (39 percent vs. 21 percent), predominantly on the East Coast (Andrulis et al., 1987). The total proportion of homosexual AIDS patients was probably underestimated because of response bias.

Length of hospitalization differed markedly by the region of country. The West and South averaged only 14 and 15 days per admission, respectively; the Midwest, 19 days; and the Northeast, 24 days. Similarly, for average days per patient per year, the West and South averaged 23 and 27 days, respectively; the Midwest, 31 days; and the Northeast, 37 days. This disparity was largely due to regional differences in the type of patients hospitalized. In the Northeast, 46 percent of the admissions were of heterosexual IVDAs, whose hospitalizations are often extended because of the nature, severity, and therapeutic expense of their illnesses and because of the social barriers to their outpatient care (see Chapter 9). Heterosexual drug abusers accounted for no more than 8 percent of admissions in the West, South, or Midwest. In contrast, homosexuals accounted for only 33 percent of admissions in the Northeast, compared to 64 to 79 percent in the other three regions (Andrulis et al., 1987).

At San Francisco General Hospital (Scitovsky et al., 1986), the mean length of hospitalization varied considerably by diagnosis, with admissions for *Pneumocystis carinii* pneumonia (PCP) having a mean length of 18.1 days, those for Kaposi's sarcoma (KS) 7.6 days, and those for other infectious diseases and other neoplasms having a mean length of 13.6 and 14.3 days, respectively. Since KS has occurred disproportionately in homosexual men (see Chapters 6 and 7), generally shorter and less expensive hospitalizations would have been expected among that risk group. Since 97 percent of patients with AIDS in San Francisco have been homosexual men compared with 50 to 60 percent in New York City (O'Brien, 1987), longer hospitalizations would have been anticipated in New York City. Median survival among AIDS patients presenting with KS ranges from 21 to 25 months, highlighting that AIDS with KS alone is generally a less virulent disease requiring fewer and shorter hospitalizations. In contrast, AIDS patients presenting with PCP, other opportunistic infections, or KS with opportunistic infections had median survival of 9 to 13 months (Moss et al., 1984; Rothenberg et al., 1987). However, KS as the sole presenting diagnosis of AIDS has been decreasing (Des Jarlais et al., 1987; Polk et al., 1988).

Costs of Hospitalization and Health Care

Costs of hospitalization for AIDS have been calculated in a variety of ways and have therefore been difficult to compare at different institutions. Estimates of the costs of medical care for AIDS patients have varied widely by locality of treatment, patient diagnosis, and hospital type. Early estimates of the lifetime medical care costs of a patient with AIDS were from $42,000 to $50,000 (Landesman et al., 1985; Groopman and Detsky, 1983). The first well-documented estimate of the lifetime hospital care costs of persons with AIDS was $147,000 (Hardy et al., 1986). Currently available data from San Francisco and Boston indicate that the lifetime care costs will now average $40,000 to $50,000 per patient (Scitovsky et al., 1986; Seage et al., 1986).

The lifetime direct costs per patient with AIDS approximate corresponding costs for other selected serious impairments. For men in the 35-to-44-year age group, lifetime per-patient direct costs have been estimated at $66,837 for myocardial infarction, $47,542 for cancer of the digestive system, and $28,636 for leukemia. For the total population, the cost per patient for paraplegia from an auto crash has been estimated to be $68,700 (Pascal 1987; Hartunian et al., 1981).

The cost per day in the Andrulis study averaged $635 for a cost per admission of $12,065 and a cost per patient per year of $20,320. Although the daily cost of hospitalization varied little by region (range, $626 to $646), the cost per admission (range, $9044 to $15,192) and cost per patient per year (range, $14,858 to $23,421) showed a wide range due to the variable length of stay in different regions in the country. This study did not take into account medical, psychosocial, or supportive outpatient care (Andrulis et al., 1987).

Scitovsky et al. (1986) found that for the patients with AIDS dying in 1984 who received all of their inpatient hospital care at SFGH, the average lifetime cost from diagnosis to death of hospital and inpatient professional services averaged $27,571. The average time to death of these patients was only 7.5 months, much shorter than estimates in other large studies including those of Hardy et al. (13.1 months) and Rothenberg et al. (12 months). Adjusting the SFGH data to a more probable median survival time of 11.2 months and a national caseload (San Francisco has a disproportionate number of persons with AIDS presenting with KS), the lifetime hospital costs incurred by recent AIDS patients would more likely be $60,000 to $70,000 (Scitovsky and Rice, 1987).

• The New England Deaconess Hospital study, using a mean life expectancy of 13 months, estimates that each patient with AIDS will incur an average of $50,380 of health care expenditure after diagnosis, including inpatient and outpatient care (Seage et al., 1986). The earlier estimate of $147,000 for lifetime hospital care for each AIDS patient (Hardy et al., 1986) was based on a high estimate (168 days) for lifetime inpatient care. A small, early study from the Baltimore metropolitan area estimated the cost per patient in Maryland to be $27,500 (Berger, 1985).

Attempts have been made to quantify the indirect costs of the AIDS epidemic—i.e., the morbidity costs (the value of productivity losses due to illness and disability) and mortality costs (the value of future earnings lost for those who died prematurely). In AIDS, which has affected primarily young males in their most productive years, the indirect costs due to premature mortality may outweigh direct medical costs by as much as 4 times. From several assumptions about prevalance of medical conditions and medical expenditures it has been predicted that only medical expenses of victims of automobile accidents will exceed the medical care costs of AIDS patients by 1991. Although the projected direct medical costs of AIDS may be as high as 2.4 percent of the U.S. personal health care expenditures for 1991, the indirect costs of AIDS may represent close to 12 percent of the estimated total indirect costs of all illnesses in that year (Scitovsky and Rice, 1987).

The problem of pediatric HIV-1 infection warrants further discussion. The total cost of care for all HIV-1 infected children at Harlem Hospital in New York

City from 1981 through 1986 was more than $3 million for 37 children, an average lifetime cost of more than $90 thousand per child, significantly more than the estimated lifetime cost of adult HIV-1 infection (Hegarty et al., 1988).

Projections

By March 1988, 40 percent of the cases of AIDS in the United States came from the cities of New York, San Francisco, and Los Angeles, whose residents accounted for less than 9 percent of the U.S. population according to the 1980 Census. The nine metropolitan areas reporting the most cases of AIDS (the three above plus Houston, Washington, D.C., Miami, Newark, Chicago, and Dallas) contained only 17 percent of the U.S. population in 1980 but reported 56 percent of all cases of AIDS (U.S. Department of Health and Human Services, 1988). It is clear that the major economic, social, and political impact of the epidemic will continue to fall on these locales as well as on other urban areas. The impact will be felt nationwide, however, through higher taxes to pay for federal, state, and local programs; through higher health insurance premiums and HMO membership fees; and through greater competition for the available federal health care dollars.

The U.S. Public Health Service has projected that there will have been more than 365,000 cases and 263,000 deaths from AIDS by 1992, with close to 100,000 cases alive at the beginning of that year and 80,000 new cases diagnosed during that year. The minimum estimated direct health care costs of persons with AIDS in 1992 will be between $5 billion and $13 billion, or up to 2 percent of the expected U.S. personal health care expenditures. Underreporting and underascertainment of cases were incorporated in that estimate, which was still conservative in its failure to account for care of other conditions associated with HIV-1 infection and for nonmedical costs of management of these illnesses (CDC, 1988). In addition, the CDC projections were based on extrapolations of incidence data. They have taken no account of the potential underlying dynamics of the epidemic, i.e., alterations in the natural history of the disease due to medical interventions or changes in human behavior and patterns of virus transmission.

A study prepared for the Health Care Financing Administration by the Rand Corporation has estimated cumulative direct medical care costs for the 1986–1991 period and the costs to Medicaid (Table 19.1). The low caseload projection was

Table 19.1. Estimates of Cumulative Costs for AIDS Treatment, 1986–1991

Factor	Range of Estimates		
	Low	Intermediate	High
Thousands of cases, cumulative	220	400	750
Percent of cases on Medicaid	30	45	60
Lifetime cost per case ($ thousands)	70	94	150
Percent reimbursed by Medicaid	50	60	70
National costs ($ billions)	15.4	37.6	112.5
Medicaid costs ($ billions)	2.3	10.2	47.4

Source: Pascal (1987).

based on CDC projections (adjusted to the 1986–1991 time period), whereas the high estimate was based on CDC seroprevalence estimates and Institute of Medicine (1986) estimates of conversion-to-symptoms rate. Lifetime cost estimates were based on studies cited above. (See Pascal, 1987, for details on Medicaid coverage and reimbursement calculations.)

THE ECONOMICS OF HEALTH CARE FOR PEOPLE WITH AIDS

Sources of Payment

Federal Government

A nonworking individual with CDC-defined AIDS is presumptively disabled and is eligible for disability income. Persons with non-AIDS HIV-1 infections do not automatically qualify. Supplemental Security Income is available as soon as a patient is disabled and in most states automatically qualifies him for Medicaid, a state program with federal matching funds designed to cover medical expenses for the dependent and indigent (Pascal, 1987). State-imposed means tests for eligibility limit the assets that a recipient can possess. Eligibility for Social Security Disability Income (SSDI) insures eligibility for Medicare coverage, but Medicare coverage does not start until 2 years after the first SSDI payment, too late for most AIDS patients.

Data from the National Hospital Discharge Survey on hospitalizations for AIDS were analyzed for 1984 and 1985. Private insurance was found to have paid for 55 percent of the hospitalizations and Medicaid for 21 percent. These figures differed significantly from the distribution for all patients under 65 years of age, where 63 percent of the total discharges indicated private insurance as the principal source of payment and only 13 percent indicated Medicaid (Graves and Moien, 1987). Medicaid was the payment source for 62 percent of public hospital and only 35 percent of private hospital admissions in the national hospital survey (Andrulis et al., 1987). Private insurance payments were made in 7 percent of public and 45 percent of private hospital admissions. The self-insured population differed little by hospital type, accounting for 18 percent of admissions to public hospitals and 13 percent to private institutions.

The expansion of the official definition of AIDS in August 1987 (Centers for Disease Control, 1987a) has increased the number of persons fulfilling the definition of AIDS and qualifying for Medicaid eligibility. Since the parenteral drug-abusing patients with AIDS are disproportionately covered by Medicaid reimbursement, as their numbers grow, so will the number of patients who qualify for Medicaid.

State Governments

There is considerable regional variation in Medicaid coverage for AIDS patients. In the national hospital survey in 1985 (Andrulis et al., 1987), Medicaid reimbursement was claimed by 60 percent of hospitalized AIDS patients in the Northeast, 54 percent of patients from the West, 36 percent from the Midwest, and only 15 percent from the South, partially due to restrictive policies for Medicaid eligibility in the South. However, the study was overweighted by a higher proportion of public hospitals among the responding hospitals than among the nonresponders. There was also a much larger percentage of unreimbursed care rendered in the South than in other regions. If that care is rendered in public hospitals, the states will ultimately absorb the cost. Since states pay roughly half of Medicaid and none of Medicare benefits, states can be expected to put pressure on the federal government to ease Medicare eligibility rules (Pascal, 1987). California had already noted an increasing share of AIDS patients requiring coverage by Medi-Cal, its local version of Medicaid (Kizer et al., 1987).

Local Governments
The largest burden on local governments will occur through social and support services needed by people with AIDS. These include psychosocial counseling, nutrition and housekeeping assistance, personal care, and transportation. Thus far, they have usually been provided through county and municipal social service agencies, but they have sometimes been delivered by nonprofit AIDS support groups. Some people with AIDS qualify for general relief, which is usually a county responsibility.

Private Health Insurance
Expanded coverage under the Consolidated Omnibus Budget Reconciliation Act of 1986 (COBRA) has begun to help people with AIDS. However, it is afforded only to workers employed by businesses with 20 or more employees. Any employee terminated for anything other than gross misconduct can continue his health insurance coverage for 18 months at a premium of no more than 102 percent of what it would have cost his employer to cover him. Workers who have held individual policies or who worked for smaller employers have no such protection and are more likely to require Medicaid assistance (Pascal, 1987). Few data are available on self-payment for the health care costs of AIDS and HIV-1 infection.

Insurance Issues

"Redlining"
In 1987, only the District of Columbia and California restricted both health and life insurers from testing for HIV-1 (Harris, 1987). Michigan and Wisconsin insurance companies have been proscribed from using results of antibody tests as a condition for health insurance. Some insurers have attempted to test applicants for immune-system impairment or ask questions regarding life-style and health history to screen out those who may subsequently make claims for the treatment of AIDS (Pascal, 1987). Whether it is appropriate to treat persons exposed and persons not exposed to HIV-1 identically for insurance purposes is a socioeconomic and ethical dilemma that will not easily be resolved.

Coverage Ceilings
Kaiser Permanente estimated that although it covered 2 percent of the U.S. population with its prepaid health plan in 1987, it handled 5 percent of the AIDS patients. Its reputation for comprehensive care may be a powerful attraction for AIDS patients, and Kaiser has established a national committee for dealing with

the disorder (Kramon, 1987). To limit its exposure to some of the costs of treating AIDS patients, the George Washington University Health Plan, a health maintenance organization in Washington, D.C., announced plans beginning in 1988 to limit reimbursement for prescription drugs to $3,000 per year. Some self-insured companies, which are exempt from most state insurance regulations, have capped or refused reimbursement for AIDS, except under special defined circumstances (Boodman, 1987). The ability of third-party insurers to control expenditures for specific diseases has not been tested in the courts and may be precluded by the laws of some states.

Assigned Risk Pools

If the insurance industry succeeds in limiting its financial exposure to AIDS and self-insured firms further exclude or limit coverage for AIDS-related care, subsidization of health care by the private sector will be reduced, and the costs of indigent care will, by necessity, be borne by Medicaid (state and federal), the cities, counties, and public hospitals. Risk pooling has been offered as one solution to provide insurance for persons with AIDS who are unable to obtain insurance elsewhere. The AMA Council on Medical Service believes that private insurance and existing public programs, coupled with expanded use of state risk pools, may provide the best means of assuring adequate access to health care coverage for HIV-1-infected persons (AMA Council on Medical Service, 1987). At least 10 states had established such pools, and many others were considering them. High premiums and large deductibles have limited accessibility by the general public to state risk pools. Premiums for pool participants have averaged about 150 percent of the median insurance rate (New York State Senate Majority Task Force on AIDS, 1987). Some reforms will be necessary if risk pools are to serve AIDS patients (Arno, 1987). The epidemic of AIDS may ultimately force development of some form of guaranteed payment for medical care at the federal level.

THE SETTING OF HEALTH CARE

Response to the AIDS Epidemic by Locality

San Francisco

AIDS has occurred disproportionately among whites in California, although minority representation has been increasing (Kizer et al., 1987). Next to New York City, San Francisco has the largest known AIDS caseload in the world. The response by nonprofit, community-based services to deal with the epidemic in San Francisco is unprecedented. The AIDS Emergency Fund in San Francisco has provided up to $1,000 a year to anyone with AIDS whose monthly income is less than $700 (Micheli, 1978). The San Francisco AIDS Foundation (SFAF) was founded in 1982 as a direct response to the epidemic. SFAF has formally contracted with the San Francisco Department of Public Health (SFDPH) to provide educational services in San Francisco. The Shanti Project was founded in 1974 as a nonprofit community-based organization to address the problems of death and dying. In 1981 its focus shifted to the AIDS epidemic, and a year later Shanti entered into the first of a series of contracts with the SFDPH to provide counseling services and a housing program for persons with AIDS. Hospice of San Francisco, formed in 1978 as a nonprofit corporation to provide care for terminally ill patients and their families, has also entered into a contract with the SFDPH to augment its existing programs to serve AIDS patients.

The unique aspect of these programs, particularly the SFAF and Shanti Project, has been their heavy reliance on donated labor by unpaid volunteers. The City of San Francisco, recognizing the cost-effectiveness of supporting volunteer efforts of these groups, has provided the required financial support.

The low frequency of hospitalization for AIDS patients in San Francisco has partly been a result of the evolution there of the "case management" model where outpatient care, including in-home care, hospices, and social, psychological, and homemaker services, has been stressed and inpatient care minimized. Not only has this approach reduced the need for hospitalization, it may also enhance the quality of life of AIDS patients. Depending as this model does on the continued participation of unpaid volunteers, it is uncertain whether it is exportable to other cities without well-organized homosexual communities or even sustainable in San Francisco with the increasing burden of AIDS patients and a relatively fixed pool of volunteers.

Several issues regarding the future viability of these programs have been raised. Local government support of community-based programs, tapping the hidden subsidy inherent in a large supply of unpaid community labor, has been a cost-effective means of caring for patients with AIDS. Inpatient and outpatient services may be better coordinated, resulting in shorter and fewer hospital admissions and better home-based and hospice care. Unfortunately, there are limits to the contributions made by local government, private charity, and unpaid labor. Volunteers, for example, may suffer "burnout." Recent efforts to contain health care costs have reduced the cross-subsidies from the public and third-party payers that used to provide care to the poor. Inevitable mounting pressures on the local health care system could evoke a demand for intervention at the state and federal levels (Arno, 1986).

New York City and Vicinity

In contrast to the California experience, the much greater proportion of AIDS patients in New York City with IV drug abuse as a risk factor has had a major bearing on the epidemic there (see Chapter 9). Although 24 percent of the city's population is black and 20 percent Hispanic, 86 percent of male New York drug abusers with AIDS belong to those groups. Hispanics and blacks are even more disproportionately represented among mothers of children with AIDS: 90 percent are black or Hispanic. There are few social or community groups by which drug abusers and their mates and children can be reached through education (Weinberg and Murray, 1987). Pediatric cases of AIDS, predominantly children of HIV-1-infected mothers, have been correspondingly more common in New York City than in areas where HIV-1 has been transmitted largely via homosexual relations. In a study conducted by the New York State Department of Health (1987), the rate of infection of blood samples from newborn infants in New York City was 1.64 percent, or one in every 60 women giving birth. Caring for children with HIV-1 infection, who are often abandoned by infected mothers with few resources, has been a problem peculiar to New York City. Outpatient services provided by voluntary groups have also not been widely available for drug users and their associates.

Near New York City, at Yale-New Haven (Conn) Hospital, of 34 HIV-1 seropositive children admitted through October 1987, 54 percent of their hospital days were judged medically unnecessary (Kemper and Forsyth, 1988). Many of the hospital stays at both institutions were for "boarder babies", children abandoned by families unable or unwilling to care for them, or for children awaiting placement in foster care. Improved soical services, particularly better access to foster care, is required for these disadvantaged and chronically ill children.

Other High-Incidence Communities

Local AIDS organizations in some other communities have offered financial assistance. Los Angeles has been adopting many of the approaches used in San Francisco. Group residences for destitute AIDS victims have opened in Washington, San Francisco, Philadelphia, Detroit, Chicago, and other large cities. In Chicago, Chicago House has depended for its operation on private funds, donations, and volunteers (Scheier, 1987).

Low-Incidence Communities

Though the Midwest accounts for 25 percent of the U.S. population, only about 7 percent of the cases of AIDS diagnosed in the country have come from there, and about half of those have been reported from Chicago. Nevertheless, health care officials there and in other parts of the country have shifted money and staff from non-AIDS programs to deal with the problem. For example, the Oregon Department of Health had reportedly abandoned plans to launch an adult immunization program and to combat chlamydia (Harris, 1987) as a consequence of AIDS program demands.

Outpatient Care of the AIDS Patient

The Robert Wood Johnson Foundation has pledged a $17.2 million effort over 4 years to support projects that emphasize community-based and in-home care (Iglehart, 1987). By early 1988, the foundation had funded nine AIDS service delivery demonstration projects in addition to 13 funded by the U.S. Public Health Service (Presidential Commission, 1988a). Many states have applied to the Health Care Financing Administration for "waivers" that would permit their Medicaid programs to cover home/community-based health services for people with AIDS and to reimburse for them more generously. By the end of 1987 the first waivers had been granted to New Jersey and New Mexico (Presidential Commission, 1987).

Consolidation of Care

Hospitals in cities with large numbers of AIDS patients have established or were considering establishing AIDS wards, similar to oncology wards in many large hospitals. In New York City, the 60-bed Spellman Center for HIV-Related Disease opened in November 1985 in St. Clare's Hospital, a small general hospital near the Manhattan theater district, to augment the number of hospital beds dedicated to comprehensive treatment of AIDS. The increased utilization allowed the hospital to upgrade its deteriorating facilities. Nevertheless, fearing it would destroy its mission as a community hospital, officials denounced New York State's plan to transform the hospital into the state's first all-AIDS treatment center (Pitt, 1987). The Institute for Immunological Disorders in Houston, the nation's first all-AIDS hospital, was forced to close when its indigent patients failed to meet strict Texas eligibility criteria for Medicaid and threatened the Institute's solvency. Johns Hopkins University in Baltimore announced the formation of an AIDS Institute in December 1987 to coordinate efforts to combat the epidemic. The Institute would seek more laboratories for AIDS-related research, double the hospital's 10 AIDS inpatient beds, and establish a hospice and a long-term care facility (Newman, 1988).

The consolidation of care of AIDS patients may improve patient care by coordinating inpatient and outpatient services and improving follow-up. Physicians and nurses dedicated to the care of AIDS patients may strengthen the educational and emotional resources for patients and their families and facilitate the clinical trials of new chemotherapeutic agents. There are drawbacks to consolidation, however. Identification of patients with an AIDS care program may stigmatize them. Recruitment of physicians and nurses to staff these wards may be increasingly difficult and may affect the training of medical students and house staff in the high-incidence, urban locales (Weinberg and Murray, 1987).

Current projections for the caseload of AIDS patients will make the disease increasingly costly. This cost can be substantially reduced with the use of case management and community support services in place in various cities around the country, as has been shown in San Francisco with its well-organized support network (Health and Public Policy Committee, 1988). Although those support services may be possible to duplicate for homosexual patients in other communities, establishing such systems for IVDAs may prove more difficult owing to the lack of stable support systems and home environments.

SOCIETAL ISSUES IN HEALTH CARE OF THE AIDS PATIENT

Federal Leadership

There have been suggestions (Shilts, 1987) that a loosely orchestrated response of the U.S. Government to many issues surrounding the AIDS epidemic may have delayed the organization and delivery of care to those who needed it. It was 5 years from the time the Public Health Service first publicized concern about the disease to the first Presidential address on AIDS at a fund-raising dinner sponsored by the American Foundation for AIDS Research on the eve of the Third International Conference on AIDS held in Washington, D.C. (Iglehart, 1987). Following a period of open controversy over motives and qualifications of its members, culminating in resignations of its chairman, cochairman, and executive director (Booth, 1987), the newly appointed Presidential Commission on the HIV Epidemic issued a preliminary report identifying as one of four critical issues the need for home health and other outpatient care programs for AIDS patients (Presidential Commission, 1987). The Commission's Interim Report (Presidential Commission, 1988a) itemized specific immediate health care needs at a projected budget of $265 million.

The final report of the Presidential Commission on the Immunodeficiency Virus Epidemic (Presidential Commission, 1988b) has attempted to portray a balanced view of the epidemic and has made numerous specific recommendations on health care and other issues. Among the most important were recommendations for: comprehensive federal anti-discrimination legislation which would prohibit discrimination against persons with disabilities, to include HIV infection; stronger federal and state laws to protect the privacy of those with HIV infection; programs to encourage health care professionals to serve in areas of high HIV impact; examination of more equitable and cost-effective financing of care for persons with HIV infection, to include demonstration programs involving federal and state subsidy of private insurance premiums and greater contribution to risk pools; and use of case management as a principal tool to control costs and provide quality care.

The immediate public response to the report was generally favorable. Its implementation will require substantial change in the way recipients, providers, and insurers think about how health care is delivered and financed.

Refusal to Treat

Exaggerated fear of acquiring the infection by casual contact with any infected person has extended into the medical community, especially among those professionals in regular contact with possibly infected secretions. Studies have shown that the risk of transmission of HIV-1 to health care workers is very low, but real (see Chapter 14).

The Arizona Board of Medical Examiners has affirmed the right of Arizona physicians to refuse to continue treatment of AIDS patients, but they must make an effort to help those patients find treatment elsewhere (Arizona Board of Medical Examiners, 1987). A similar policy has been adopted by the Texas Medical Association (Texas Medical Association, 1987). Both the American College of Physicians (ACP) and the American Medical Association (AMA) have established the position that to deny appropriate care to sick and dying patients, specifically including AIDS patients, is clearly unethical (Health and Public Policy Committee, American College of Physicians, 1988a; AMA Council on Ethical and Judicial Affairs, 1987). New York State's 13 medical colleges have established strong penalties for refusal to treat AIDS patients, stating that any faculty member, hospital resident, or medical student who refuses to treat such patients will be dismissed. In a policy statement they affirmed that physicians had a "most fundamental responsibility" to treat AIDS, regardless of risk (Sullivan, 1987a). The New Jersey Board of Medical Examiners (1987) adopted a similarly stringent policy, stating that a New Jersey licensee "may not categorically refuse to treat a patient [with an HIV infection] when he or she possesses the skill and experience to treat the condition presented."

Confidentiality

The issue of confidentiality in the testing, diagnosis, and treatment of AIDS has provoked significant controversy. Advocates of mandatory reporting of all HIV-1-positive persons have contended that such persons need to be identified in order to educate them and prevent the further transmission of the virus. Detractors have countered that the stigma associated with such a diagnosis would place an undue burden on those persons: HIV-1-positive persons have been fired from jobs, refused admission to public schools, denied housing, refused entrance into public swimming pools, refused insurance, and otherwise mistreated. A study of 157 physicians from three cities found physicians harboring harshly prejudicial attitudes toward AIDS patients (Kelly et al., 1987). As noted, opponents have also argued that mandatory reporting will discourage high-risk persons from having themselves tested for HIV-1. A U.S. Justice Department ruling had affirmed the right of employers to fire an HIV-1-positive employee even if the fear that he will transmit the disease is unfounded.* The public health need to prevent transmission is in direct conflict with the right to privacy and tolerance among HIV-1 carriers. Recently, the Justice Department ruling has been replaced by an opinion that federal agencies should not discriminate against HIV-1 positive workers and that adopts a broad interpretation of the anti-discrimination law (Marcus, 1988). This opinion does not, however, prohibit discrimination by private employers.

The AMA Board of Trustees has recommended (1987) that access to patient information should be limited to health care personnel who have a legitimate need to know to assist the patient or to protect the health of others closely associated with the patient. The report also suggested that confidential reporting of HIV-1 infection should be extended to all non-AIDS HIV-1 infections as well as AIDS. Finally, the report suggested that specific statutes be drafted to protect patient confidentiality to the greatest extent possible while providing a method for warning unsuspecting sexual partners and to protect physicians against liability for failure to warn the unsuspecting third party.

The Pharmaceutical Industry

Zidovudine, or AZT, produced by the Burroughs Wellcome Co., was the first drug shown to be effective in prolonging the lives of certain patients with HIV-1 infection (Fischl et al., 1987). The cost of the drug, initially more than $10,000 per year, has been prohibitive to many HIV-1-infected persons. At least 44 states have covered the drug under Medicaid for those persons eligible (Presidential Commission, 1987). Approval for the drug was given a "fast track" through the Food and Drug Administration—it was approved to treat certain patients with AIDS on March 20, 1987, just 4 months after the new drug application was received (U.S. Department of Health and Human Services, 1988a). Partly because of its rapid approval, the availability of the drug was limited in the first few months after approval, and the

---

*[1]Memorandum for Ronald E. Robertson, General Counsel, U.S. Department of Health and Human Services, from Charles J. Cooper, Assistant Attorney General, Office of Legal Counsel, U.S. Department of Justice, June 20, 1986.

producer carefully restricted its use to those patients with AIDS who had had *Pneumocystis carinii* pneumonia (PCP) in the past or other HIV-1-infected persons who had a CD4$^+$ cell count of less than 200/mm^3 (Burroughs Wellcome Co., 1987a).

An issue was the cost of the drug, especially since the federal government had subsidized a large portion of the research involved in bringing AZT to market. Once the drug became readily available, Burroughs no longer restricted distribution of AZT and lowered the cost of the drug 20 percent (Burroughs Wellcome Co., 1987b). The practice of prescribing AZT to patients without symptoms or low CD4$^+$ cell counts became widespread in spite of the official recommendations (Kolata, 1987). The company has been criticized for making excessive profits from the sale of AZT (Pollack, 1988). LyphoMed Inc. has also been alleged to be making excessive profits by quadrupling the price of pentamidine, used for the treatment of PCP, from $25 to $100, coincident with the increase in cases of PCP (Chase, 1988). Further government regulation of the pharmaceutical industry has been suggested to curb abuses.

New Drug Development

Recognizing its responsibility for the rapid development and approval of drugs, the Food and Drug Administration has created a new top-priority category in the process to expedite development, testing, and approval of drugs for the treatment of HIV-1 infection (Presidential Commission, 1987). Effective June 22, 1987, new FDA rules permitted promising investigational new drugs to be used to treat desperately ill patients as early in the drug development phase as possible (U.S. Department of Health and Human Services, 1987). Many private organizations have noted that few drugs have been fully tested and have suggested that experimental drugs be available to critical patients on a compassionate basis. A community-based group, the Community Research Initiative, has been organized to identify and test potentially useful drugs more quickly than can formal university-based trials (Kolata, 1988). In an attempt to speed approval of new treatments, in September 1987, California became the first state to indicate that it will supervise testing of drugs for the treatment of AIDS and potentially approve them without the involvement of the federal government (Bishop, 1987).

It has been suggested that it is unethical to conduct placebo-controlled clinical trials when the placebo arm of the trial could have a mortality approaching 100 percent. The Presidential Commission on the Human Immunodeficiency Virus Epidemic (1988a) has made the recommendations to decrease the need for placebo-controlled trials by developing a "historical control" for AIDS and to use such trials only for patients without immediately life-threatening disease. However, certain drugs used to treat HIV-1 infection may increase the morbidity and mortality associated with HIV-1 infection (Cheson et al., 1987), and controlled clinical trials may be the most efficient or only way to discern the efficacy of a drug definitively.

CONCLUSION

The epidemic of AIDS in the United States is a public health crisis of unprecedented magnitude. An appropriate approach to the provision of care for patients with clinically significant HIV-1 infection demands a concerted, coherent, compassionate, and rational effort by the health, political, and business communities.

REFERENCES

AMA Board of Trustees (1987): JAMA 258;2097.

AMA Council on Ethical and Judicial Affairs (1987): Report A (I-87).

AMA Council on Medical Service (1987): Report B (I-87).

Andrulis DP, Beers VS, Bentley JD, Gage LS (1987): JAMA 258:1343.

Arizona Board of Medical Examiners (1987): Minutes of regular meeting, Oct. 16.

Arno PS (1986): Am J Public Health 76:1325.

Arno PS (1987): JAMA 258:1376.

Berger R (1985): Maryland Med J 34:1173.

Bishop K (1987): New York Times, Sept. 30.

Boodman SG (1987): Washington Post, Dec. 21.

Booth W (1987): Science 238:262.

Burroughs Wellcome Co. (1987a): Retrovir (Zidovudine). The Retrovir Distribution Kit. Research Triangle Park, NC: Burroughs Wellcome Co.

Burroughs Wellcome Co. (1987b): Letter to doctors, Dec. 15. Research Triangle Park, NC: Burroughs Wellcome Co.

Centers for Disease Control (1987a): MMWR 36 (Suppl 1S):1S.

Centers for Disease Control (1987b): MMWR 36:1.

Centers for Disease Control (1988): 37:551.

Chase M (1988): Wall Street Journal, March 1.

Cheson BD, Levine AM, Mildvan D, et al. (1987): JAMA 258:1347.

Des Jarlais DC, Stoneburner R, Thomas P, Friedman SR (1987): Lancet 2:1024.

Farber BF, Kaplan MH (1987): J Infect Dis 155:1097.

Fischl MA, Richman DD, Grieco MH, et al. (1987): N Engl J Med 317:185.

Graves EJ, Moien M (1987): Am J Public Health 77:729.

Groopman JE, Detsky A (1983): Ann Intern Med 99:259.

Hardy A, Rauch K, Echenberg D, Morgan WM, Curran JW (1986): JAMA 255:209.

Harris D (1987): Money, Nov.

Hartunian NS, Smart CN, Thompson MS (1981): The Incidence and Economic Costs of Major Health Impairments. Lexington, MA: Lexington Books.

Health and Public Policy Committee, American College of Physicians (1988a): Ann Intern Med 108:460.

Health and Public Policy Committee, American College of Physicians (1988b): Ann Intern Med 108:470.

Hegarty JD, Abrams EJ, Hutchinson VE, Nicholas SW, Suarez MS, Hegarty MC (1988): JAMA 260:1901.

Iglehart JK (1987): N Engl J Med 317:180.

Institute of Medicine, National Academy of Sciences (1986): Confronting AIDS. Directions for Public Health, Health Care, and Research. Washington, D.C.: National Academy Press.

Kelly JA, St. Lawrence JS, Smith S, Hood HV, Cook DJ (1987): Am J Public Health 77:789.

Kemper K, Forsyth B (1988): JAMA 260:1906.

Kizer KW, Rodriguez J, McHolland GF (1987): An Updated Quantitative Analysis of AIDS in California. Sacramento: California Department of Health Services, April.

Kolata G (1987): New York Times, Dec. 21.

Kolata G (1988): New York Times, March 15.

Kramon G (1987): New York Times, Nov. 17.

Landesman SH, Ginzberg H, Weiss SH (1985): N Engl J Med 312:521.

Lewis HE (1987): JAMA 258:2410.

MacDonald DI (1987): JAMA 258:2642.

Marcus R (1988): Washington Post, Oct. 7.

Micheli R (1987): Money, Nov.

Moss AR, McCallum G, Volberding PA, Bacchetti P, Dritz S (1984): JNCI 73:1281.

New Jersey Board of Medical Examiners (1987): AIDS policy, adopted Nov. 18.

Newman A (1988): Johns Hopkins Mag, Feb.

New York State Department of Health (1987): Newborn HIV seroprevalence study data.

New York State Senate Majority Task Force on AIDS (1987): The AIDS Crisis in New York, June.

O'Brien C (1987): Am Med News, Nov. 13.

Pascal A (1987): The cost of treating AIDS under Medicaid: 1986–1991. Santa Monica, CA: Rand Corporation.

Pinckney DS (1988): Am Med News, Feb. 5.

Pitt DE (1987): New York Times, Nov. 22.

Polk BF, Munoz A, Fox R, et al. (1988): Fourth International Conference on AIDS, Stockholm, Sweden, June 12–16.

Pollack A (1988): New York Times, Feb. 9.

Presidential Commission on the Human Immunodeficiency Virus Epidemic: Preliminary Report (1987): Washington, D.C.: U.S. Government Printing Office, Dec. 2.

Presidential Commission on the Human Immunodeficiency Virus Epidemic: Interim Report (1988a): Washington, D.C.: U.S. Government Printing Office, March 15.

Presidential Commission on the Human Immunodeficiency Virus Epidemic: Report (1988b): Washington, D.C.: U.S. Government Printing Office, June 24.

Rothenberg R, Woelfel M, Stoneburner R, Milberg J, Parker R, Truman B (1987): N Engl J Med 317:1297.

Scheier RL (1987): Am Med News, Oct. 2.

Scitovsky AA, Rice DP (1987): Public Health Rep 102:5.

Scitovsky AA, Cline M, Lee PR (1986): JAMA 256:3103.

Shilts R (1987): And the Band Played On. New York: St. Martin's Press.

Seage GR, Landers S, Barry MA, Groopman J, Lamb GA, Epstein AM (1986): JAMA 256:3107.

State of New York Department of Health (1987): DOH News, Dec. 17.

Sullivan R (1987a): New York Times, Dec. 9.

Sullivan R (1987b): New York Times, Dec. 18.

Texas Medical Association (1987): Second supplemental report of the Board of Councilors, Nov. 20.

U.S. Department of Health and Human Services (1987): Fed Reg, May 22.

U.S. Department of Health and Human Services (1988a): From test tube to patient: New drug development in the United States. Washington, D.C.: HHS Publication No. (FDA) 88–3168, Jan.

U.S. Department of Health and Human Services (1988b): AIDS weekly surveillance report— United States. AIDS program, Center for Infectious Diseases, Centers for Disease Control. Washington, D.C.: U.S. Public Health Service, March 14.

U.S. Public Health Service (1986): Public Health Rep 101:341.

Weinberg DS, Murray HW (1987): N Engl J Med 317:1469.

20

Responses in the Legal System

JOHN MILLS AND MICHAEL MILLS

Because many infectious diseases are communicable to others, patients with these infections and the providers caring for them have been subject to special laws and regulations. Although these laws constrain individual liberty and invade privacy, they help protect the health of the state's citizens and thus on balance are considered beneficial. Patients with communicable diseases have an affirmative obligation to minimize transmission of the infection to others; physicians, in addition to diagnosing and treating the disease correctly, must properly instruct the patients in the behavior necessary to prevent transmission of infection, must notify the public health authorities as required by law, and in certain circumstances may breach the usually confidential doctor–patient relationship to warn other individuals at risk of acquiring the infection from the patient.

The human immunodeficiency viruses are transmitted exclusively from person to person. In most jurisdictions, AIDS is classified as a communicable disease (in some it is subclassified as a venereal or sexually transmitted disease). Some states include all HIV-1-infected subjects in the classification. Thus, the laws and regulations that apply to other communicable diseases should apply to the AIDS and HIV-1 infection as well. However, the emotional and political response to AIDS and HIV-1 infection has been far greater than the response to any other infectious disease in modern history. There are several likely explanations. Much social opprobrium is attached to HIV-1 infection and AIDS because of their association with homosexuality and intravenous drug abuse and the fact of likely sexual transmission even if these risk factors are not present. Although medical scientists perceive the disease as being transmitted inefficiently, the lay public has not had sufficient time or experience to form a reasoned opinion. The high fatality rate and lack of curative therapy magnify public concern. Thus, it would not be surprising if efforts to control the spread of AIDS and HIV-1 infection include attempts to restrict the individual liberties guaranteed by the Constitution and affirmed by numerous court decisions.

This chapter summarizes the existing laws and statutes that apply to communicable diseases in general and to AIDS and HIV-1 infection in particular. The emphasis is on the American legal system; reference is made to unusual statutes in other countries where the authors are aware of them. In addition we have

Table 20.1. Characteristics of HIV-1 Infection Relevant to Public Health Law

1. AIDS and other clinical manifestations are due to infection by one or more of the human immunodeficiency viruses (HIV-1, HIV-2; possibly others); cofactors may be of minor importance or irrelevant to the outcome of infection.
2. Infection with HIV-1 persists for the life of the host; the duration of infectivity is unknown but is at least potentially lifelong as well.
3. Infection is almost invariably accompanied by an antibody response. Antibody to HIV-1 is currently detected by a solid-phase, enzyme-linked immunosorbent assay (EIA). Because false positives with EIA may be frequent in some situations, a positive EIA must be confirmed by another test (currently, immunofluorescence, or detection of antibody to specific viral proteins by Western blotting [immunoblotting]). With these confirmatory procedures, false-negative antibody tests occur less than 0.5% of the time, and false positives less than 0.1% of the time. As used in this chapter, a "positive" antibody test means a confirmed positive.
4. HIV-1-infected patients may be asymptomatic. Individuals with laboratory-documented HIV-1 infection may be totally free of symptoms, signs, or laboratory abnormalities (other than specific evidence of HIV-1 infection, such as the presence of anti-HIV-1 antibody), or they may have a spectrum of diseases ranging from mild, asymptomatic lymphadenopathy to AIDS. The proportion of a cohort of infected individuals developing each of these manifestations, either at any point in time or after a lifetime of HIV-1 infection, is unknown. At present (1988), there appear to be well over 10 times as many asymptomatic or minimally symptomatic HIV-1 infected individuals as there are cases of AIDS.
5. Transmission of HIV-1 is predominantly by sexual contact and through sharing of needles in the context of illicit drug abuse; transmission due to heterosexual contact, blood or blood product transfusion, organ donation, and hospital and laboratory accidents is well documented but is relatively rare in the United States. Perinatal transmission (mother to child) occurs about half the time if the mother is HIV-1-infected. Fewer than 5% of U.S. cases result from other (or unknown) means of transmission. Casual contact (hand shaking, sneezing, etc.) appears to carry a truly zero or negligible risk of infection.

attempted to apply legal principles to future incidents likely to arise from the AIDS epidemic. Our legal reasoning is based on existing statutes and court cases; our medical reasoning is based on current knowledge regarding AIDS and HIV-1 infection (Table 20.1).

In addition to these legal doctrines and the medical facts, proposed measures to control the spread of HIV-1 infection must be guided by a societal perspective. What other hazards do American citizens face at present? How serious are they in comparison to AIDS and HIV-1 infection? Of the hazards that appear to be preventable, how has our society attempted to limit these hazards through legislation? How have these laws restricted liberty or privacy?

The current and proposed response to AIDS can be compared with legal efforts to control other diseases due to hazardous personal behavior. For example, tobacco abuse is estimated to cause 300,000 premature deaths each year in the United States alone (CDC, 1987b); these deaths would not occur if tobacco were not abused. No laws generally prohibit tobacco use, although there are some regulations as to where one can or cannot smoke. This situation persists despite incontrovertible evidence that tobacco is harmful to the user and that vicarious inhalation of tobacco smoke by nonsmokers (so-called passive or involuntary smoking) is also harmful. Other entirely or partially preventable conditions responsible for thousands of illnesses and premature deaths each year include alcohol abuse, motor vehicle accidents, and suicide (Table 20.2).

In a recent Centers for Disease Control tabulation of the causes of years of potential life lost in calendar year 1985, AIDS accounted for 152,595 years, whereas

Table 20.2. Preventable or Potentially Preventable Causes of Premature Deaths in the United States

Cause of Death	Estimated Deaths per Year[a]
Tobacco abuse	350,000
Alcohol abuse	100,000
Motor vehicle accidents	46,250
Suicide	29,300
Homicide	19,800
Drug abuse (other than alcohol or tobacco)	3,550
AIDS	5,500

[a]Estimates for calendar year 1985.

Sources: National Center for Health Statistics, Advance Report of Final Yearly Mortality Statistics, 1984; U.S. Department of Health and Human Services, Office of Smoking and Health; National Institute of Alcohol Abuse and Alcoholism; National Institute on Drug Abuse (CDC, 1987b).

unintentional injuries, the majority of which are attributable to motor vehicle accidents, accounted for nearly 15 times as many—2,235,064 (CDC, 1987a). Many motor vehicle accidents could be prevented by law, through disincentives to driving while intoxicated and mandated seat belt usage and airbag installation. Although laws in some states have recently been strengthened, preventable deaths from such things as motor vehicle accidents and tobacco use have by and large escaped legislative attention. Although the transmissible nature of HIV-1 infection sets it apart in certain respects, many restrictive measures proposed to control HIV-1 infection should be viewed in this context.

LEGAL PRINCIPLES

The general welfare of its citizens is the most important responsibility of the state. Health is crucial to the general welfare, and measures to protect the public health may be taken by the state even though they conflict with or restrict other liberties, such as the rights to privacy and personal freedom. Phrased differently, the state may use its police power to protect the public health. One of the oldest court tests of this principle was Jacobson v. Massachusetts (1905), in which the Supreme Court ruled that the need for public immunization against smallpox health overrode an individual religious objection to immunization. This case illustrates well the three legal tests used to determine whether restriction of personal liberty is justified in pursuit of the public health (Table 20.3).

First, the state must rationally assess the magnitude of the risk posed by a threat to the public health (Lazzo and McElgunn, 1986; Merritt, 1986). In the past, courts have upheld legislation without a clear evaluation of risk or in reliance upon the lay public's estimate of the risk. For example, quarantine for patients with leprosy was approved even though the medical community recognized that communicability of the disease was very low (Parmet, 1985; Kirk v. Wyman, 1909). In more recent years, courts have relied primarily on testimony from medical experts to assess the degree of risk to the population. The courts (and the medical experts) have tended to divide risks into two tiers—significant and negligible. *Significant*

Table 20.3. Issues in Determining the Constitutionality of Laws to Protect the Public Health

---

1. The risk to the population or a group must be significant. The opinions of medical experts are the principal determinant of what risks are significant.
2. There must be a rational relationship between the proposed control measures and the outcome to be avoided. Again, the opinions of medical experts are the principal determinant.
3. The proposed measures must be the least restrictive means of achieving the public health aims. The more fundamental the right being curtailed and the greater the infringement of the right, the stricter the scrutiny to which the measures will be subjected. If the regulation affects a classification by race, sex, national origin, or alienage—a constitutionally "suspect" classification—strict scrutiny will also be given.

---

risks are substantially likely to cause harm to a group of citizens (e.g., transmission of measles to a nonimmune population). *Negligible* or remote risks are highly unlikely to cause harm.

In many instances, hazards deemed to have negligible risk of harming others in fact have *no* such risk. But medical scientists prefer to avoid saying "no risk" or "zero risk" because of the logical inability to prove a negative; instead, they describe the risk as "vanishingly small" or some similar phrase. However, there are negligible hazards from which the risk of harm is *not* zero—for example, the negligible (but not zero) risk of being killed by a lightning strike in downtown Manhattan. The best subjective description of a negligible risk is that it is a risk encountered in everyday life with equanimity (by all except the extremely neurotic); examples include the risk of being struck by lightning or being killed by a meteorite, or even the chance of being killed in a plane crash. In the case of HIV-1 infection, the risk of transmission by casual contact, by insect bite, or by using a telephone previously used by an infected patient is clearly negligible by that test. The risk of acquiring the infection as a health care worker or a laboratory worker is somewhere in between negligible and significant, whereas the risk of intravenous drug abusers and homosexually active men is clearly significant.

Second, there must be a rational relationship between the proposed means of control and the desired outcome (Lazzo and McElgunn, 1986; Merritt, 1986). In the past, courts have accepted opinions of the lay public as to this connection; for example, the Supreme Court stated in 1905 that "the legislature has the right to pass laws which, according to the common belief of the people, are adapted to prevent the spread of contagious diseases" (Jacobson v. Massachusetts, 1905). In recent years, testimony of medical experts has been the primary basis for this determination. For example, in two recent cases involving the risk of transmission of hepatitis B and tuberculosis to children, the courts relied almost exclusively on medical testimony to determine whether the proposed restrictions were rational (New York State Association for Retarded Children v. Carey, 1979; Arline v. School Board of Nassau County, 1985).

Third, when the proposed control measures infringe upon fundamental rights or classify groups on a basis the courts call "suspect" then the measure must be subjected to "strict scrutiny." Strict scrutiny will require that a measure be narrowly drawn to serve a compelling state interest and be the least restrictive available means of achieving the desired end (Lazzo and McElgunn, 1986; Merritt,

1986). More subtly, the courts will apply proportionally stricter standards as the interests affected increase—more fundamental rights, more deeply invaded (Mills et al., 1986).

Fundamental rights include those guaranteed by the Constitution and the Bill of Rights, such as the rights of free speech, travel, and privacy. The right of privacy has been defined by the Supreme Court to include a general "individual interest in avoiding disclosure of personal matters" and an "interest in independence in making certain kinds of important decisions" (Whalen v. Roe, 1977). The right to privacy may thus be very broad, and virtually all measures to control the public health would infringe upon it. Nevertheless, the Supreme Court ruled in 1986 that the right to privacy does *not* protect homosexuals against criminal prosecution for their sexual conduct (Bowers v. Hardwick, 1986).

Strict scrutiny is also required if the proposed control measure affects members of a "suspect" class. Determination of membership in a suspect class is a function of their treatment by other citizens and the ability of the class members to participate in society. As stated by one review, "political powerlessness, [societal] stigmatization, a history of unequal treatment, and the inability of individuals to control their membership in the class" are identifying features of suspect classes (Harvard Law Review, 1986). Homosexual men, intravenous drug abusers, carriers of HIV-1 infection, and the other minority groups most at risk for HIV-1 infection acquired from heterosexual intercourse, all share many of these characteristics, but only race, national origin, sex, and alienage have been firmly accepted as suspect classifications by the courts.

Since avoiding the spread of AIDS is clearly a compelling state interest, the key questions will be whether there is a "close fit" between means and ends and whether other, less restrictive means would achieve the same ends (Lazzo and McElgunn, 1986; Merritt, 1986). At the beginning of the century, as a particularly clear example, a federal Court of Appeals struck down a quarantine ordered by the City of San Francisco in which 15,000 people in 12 city blocks were confined to prevent the spread of bubonic plague (Jew Ho v. Williamson, 1900). The court held that the proposed quarantine was unreasonable and oppressive when measured against the threat—nine cases of plague.

SPECIFIC LEGAL ISSUES RELATING TO HIV-1 INFECTION AND AIDS

Reporting of Cases

The legal issues relating to reporting of cases of AIDS or other manifestations of HIV-1 infection have been summarized elsewhere (Gostin and Curran, 1987a; Mills et al., 1986). Reporting of specified communicable and "venereal" diseases is required by law in every country and by the World Health Organization (Mills et al, 1986; Gostin and Curran, 1987a; WHO, 1987). Reporting of AIDS as defined by the Centers for Disease Control (1988) is required in every state in the Union. We are not aware that the legality of reporting communicable diseases in general, or AIDS in particular has been tested in the courts, and the state has rational reasons for requiring such reporting in its efforts to maintain the health of its citizens. The nature and breadth of the public health response to an epidemic depends, in part, on the magnitude of the problem; reporting is a direct method for assessing the size of the epidemic and its rate of growth or decline. In addition, the need for health care for the patients and counseling for the risk groups must be planned in advance, and such planning requires data on the rate at which the epidemic is expanding or slowing. Although reporting may be used to control spread of communicable diseases by treating reported cases, this practice is not possible with HIV-1 infection at present. Tracing of contacts is another legitimate use of reporting and is discussed below.

The epidemiologic information derived from the reporting of communicable diseases like AIDS is maintained confidentially (although AIDS as a cause of death, if inserted on the death certificate by the attending physician or by the coroner, becomes public information), and thus the right of privacy is not materially infringed. As the Supreme Court stated, although not in relation to a communicable disease, "limited reporting requirements in the medical field are familiar and generally are not regarded as an invasion of privacy" (Whalen v. Roe, 1977). The confidentiality of epidemiologic records maintained by health departments has been upheld (California Morbidity, 1978). However, enforcing the confidentiality of these records may be difficult, and the liability if the records are inadvertently released (e.g., a list of HIV-1-infected individuals stolen from a health department) is unclear (Mills et al., 1986). Despite the remaining uncertainties regarding the effect of reporting on personal privacy, there is little question that a statutory reporting requirement for cases of AIDS would be upheld if challenged in court (Gostin and Curran, 1987a).

State laws set penalties for failure to report cases of communicable disease, with fines varying from $5 to $1,000 and some states even prescribing jail sentences up to 90 days (Mills et al., 1986). Although we are unaware of anyone who has been fined or imprisoned for failure to report cases of communicable disease, a physician's license to practice may be suspended or revoked for especially egregious failure to report communicable diseases (California Morbidity, 1978). In addition, physicians or other health care providers may be liable to damages if injuries result from failure to report communicable diseases such as AIDS. In 1974, for example, the neighbor of a patient with staphylococcal infection sued health care providers for failing to report the disease, claiming that it prevented public health officers from implementing necessary preventive measures (Derrick v. Ontario Community Hospital, 1985). The California appeals court accepted the plaintiff's legal reasoning and permitted a trial to determine the failure to report and the risk posed by the neighbor's illness.

In the case of AIDS, however, a causal link between failure to report and secondary infection would be difficult to prove. Transmission generally occurs in private, during activities unlikely to be witnessed. Participation in these activities is usually consensual, and the defendant would likely claim that the patient with the secondary infection has assumed the risk of infection or had in fact contributed to its acquisition.

Should the reporting requirements be broadened from AIDS itself to all cases of HIV-1 infection, as has been done in Colorado and a few other states? The relationship between this reporting requirement and control of disease is not clear. Sufficient information about the changing magnitude of the epidemic may be just as easily obtained, as has been done successfully in San Francisco, by monitoring the prevalence of HIV-1 infection within specific populations by using sequential, anonymous serologic testing at varying intervals (Moss et al., 1988; Mills, 1987). Most current testing programs cover only quite restricted population groups, which are either self-selected populations or otherwise biased samples; testing of these groups may provide a less accurate estimate of the prevalence of HIV-1 infection than that obtained through reporting of cases of AIDS. Since these samples may be drawn heavily from constitutionally suspect population groups, the reporting may be held discriminatory. Finally, little can be done with the information gathered to control the spread of HIV-1 infection until drugs are available that suppress or cure the infection or markedly reduce infectivity. Thus, the "rational relationship" legal test may be difficult to meet.

Reporting for purposes of providing the counseling needed to prevent transmission also fails the least-restrictive-means test, because such counseling can just as easily be provided in the setting of anonymous testing. In fact, as of mid-1988, Colorado had not yet initiated any specific actions with the confidential register of HIV-1-infected patients that it maintains.

The Right to Confidentiality and the Duty to Warn

The patient's right to a confidential relationship with his physician, except for the physician's duty in specific instances, has been upheld in many court decisions (Mills et al., 1986). Improper disclosure of patient information may have serious adverse consequences for those infected with HIV-1, such as loss of a job, stigmatization, or even eviction from a dwelling. The patient may, in turn, be able to claim damages from the person making the wrongful disclosure (Horne v. Patton, 1973; Doe v. Roe, 1977).

However, confidentiality may be breached in specific instances where an unequivocal threat of transmission exists to a clearly defined set of individuals. In California, for example, such warnings are specified by law: "It shall be the duty of the physician in attendance on a case considered to be an infectious or communicable disease, to give detailed instructions to members of the household in regard to precautionary measures to be taken for preventing the spread of disease (California Admiralty Code, Title 17, Section 2514). Although there are several cases relating to infectious diseases that affirm the health care provider's duty to warn in specific instances (Skillings v. Allen 1919; Perkins and Jonsen, 1981; Gill v. Hartford Accident and Indemnity Co., 1978), the most important case, Tarasoff v. Regents of the University of California (1976), related to psychiatric illness. In this case, a patient of a psychiatrist employed by the University of California repeatedly indicated his intent to harm a former girlfriend, who was not warned of these statements. After the patient assaulted and killed the girl, the family successfully sued the university for damages; the award was upheld by the California Supreme Court.

These rules regarding confidentiality would apply to patients with AIDS, patients with other manifestations of HIV-1 infection and asymptomatic HIV-1-infected persons. California's Assembly Bill 403 (1987) forbidding disclosure of the results of testing for antibody to HIV-1 is in direct conflict with the legal principle that the nature of the patient's illness (or the fact of infection) may be disclosed to specific individuals clearly at risk of infection; in California the principle is incorporated in an earlier statute (California Admiralty Code Title 17, Section 2514) and has been upheld by the California Supreme Court in the Tarasoff case. This conflict in the law was recently partially resolved by permitting notification of spouses directly at risk of acquiring HIV-1 infection (California Assembly Bill 250, 1987). In nonspousal cases, California physicians can seek the assistance of public health authorities.

The issue of confidentiality also bears directly on clinical and epidemiologic research involving persons with HIV-1 infection or persons in risk groups for infection. The reasons for maintaining confidentiality are obvious—public knowledge of the individual's participation in a study related to HIV-1 infection could lead to the assumption (whether correct or not) that the subject *was* HIV-1-infected and attendant discrimination. Clinical and epidemiologic research records are considered confidential, and this concept has withstood court challenge (California Morbidity, 1978). Groups which for ethical reasons cannot otherwise be used for medical research, like prisoners, should not be used for clinical studies such as antiviral therapy trials, but they may be suitable subjects for anonymous epidemiologic research where no substitute is possible. For example, only studies of prisoners will provide information about the prevalence of HIV-1 infection in prisoners.

Contact Tracing

Contact tracing consists of reporting index cases of communicable disease to public health authorities, interviewing the index cases to determine the identity of other persons—contacts—from whom the index case might have acquired infection or to whom he might have transmitted it, and then using that information to control spread of the disease. Contact tracing requires the cooperation of the index case, as current laws in most states do not compel them to provide this information. With AIDS and HIV-1 infection, the index case could be disclosing the commission of a criminal offense, since homosexual intercourse remains a crime in many states and parenteral drug abuse is a crime everywhere. Thus, it is doubtful that much information would be volunteered by index cases without legal protection.

Nor is it likely that laws forcing patients with AIDS or HIV-1 infection to reveal their contacts will be passed or, if passed, will be found constitutional. Contact tracing is a deep invasion of personal privacy and thus would be subject to close scrutiny to determine whether the method was rational and whether less restrictive or invasive means would suffice for control. At present, public health authorities do not have definitive treatment to offer infected patients or to prevent further spread of infection and must rely on education and counseling. This information can be provided without contact tracing.

Requirement for Education of Patients

By law in many regions, and morally and ethically in any case, patients with communicable diseases must be provided with full information about the currently accepted means of preventing transmission (Mills, 1983). These laws and principles apply to patients with AIDS as well as all those infected with HIV-1. If instructions are not given, the health care provider may risk liability for damages to another person who becomes infected as the result (Arline v. School Board of Nassau County, 1985; Davis v. Rodman, 1921). Recommended instructions for preventing transmission of HIV-1 infection have been adopted by the U.S. Public Health Service, and they represent a reasonable approach to this issue (U.S. DHHS, 1985). As there may be some controversy about what sort of instruction was provided to patients if the issue of liability arises at a later time, providers for whom patient instruction is a major activity (e.g., a health center providing testing for HIV-1 antibody and counseling services) should give the instructions in a standardized fashion such as a slide show or a videotape cassette.

The Patient's Responsibility for Preventing Transmission

Failure to adhere to the prescribed measures to prevent infecting others can subject patients to criminal or civil liability for damages (Mills et al., 1986). For example, in California, "any person afflicted with any contagious, infectious, or communicable diseases who willfully exposes" another person to the disease is guilty of a misdemeanor (California Health and Safety Code, Section 3353). Penalties are modest and consist of fines of $25 to $50, up to 90 days in jail, or both. We are unaware of instances in which these penalties have been imposed.

Although no cases of civil liability for transmission of HIV-1 infection are known to us, such cases would be accepted by the courts if transmission were proven. In the recent case of Kathleen K. v. Robert B. (1984), a woman claimed that she had acquired genital herpes during sexual intercourse with a man at a time when he knew (or should have known) that he had the infection but did not disclose it to her. Guided by earlier similar cases, the court held that Kathleen K.'s legal theories were sound and that she could go forward at trial to prove that the facts were as she claimed. Recently the U.S. Army accused a soldier of assault because he had sexual intercourse with three people after being told that he was infected with HIV-1 (New York Times, 1987c). The judge held that the results of the man's test for HIV-1 antibody were confidential and could not be used as evidence; this decision was recently overturned, however (New York Times, 1987a,b). Other difficulties will confront prosecutors attempting to prove blame for transmission of HIV-1 infection, as discussed earlier in the section on reporting. The activities that result in transmission are generally consensual and occur unwitnessed and in private; the defense of coresponsibility may be raised. Proving that the infection came from the defendant and not from another person, perhaps by restriction endonuclease fingerprinting, is almost impossible without full cooperation of the defendant and access to a research laboratory, as in the recent case of laboratory-acquired infection (Weiss et al., 1988).

Quarantine

Isolation and quarantine have been employed by public health authorities for over a century to control the spread of communicable diseases, and the courts have upheld the laws that permit such confinement (Westfall, 1986). In the famous case of Mary Mallon, or Typhoid Mary, the prolonged quarantine of this uncooperative typhoid carrier withstood two court challenges (Mills, 1983). Quarantine has been widely proposed as one solution to the control of HIV-1 infection; Connecticut has already passed a law permitting quarantine of AIDS patients in select cases (Connecticut General Laws Section 19a-221). But quarantine has generally been used only for individual cases and for narrow purposes: to enforce treatment of a noncompliant patient, to segregate a patient with a self-limited but highly communicable disease, or to control the spread of a severe and highly communicable disease (Gostin and Curran, 1987a; Harvard Law Review, 1986; Lazzo and McElgunn, 1986; Mills, 1983). Widespread quarantine for AIDS patients is likely to be held unconstitutional, because the facts of HIV-1 infection will make the circumstances of quarantine so Draconian. HIV-1 infection may persist for life; hence, quarantine may have to be lifelong. Quarantine is generally employed for diseases acquired nonconsensually, yet the actions resulting in transmission of HIV-1 are usually consensual and private, and thus the conditions of quarantine would have to be very intrusive.

Any quarantine drastically restricts fundamental individual rights, including liberty, association, privacy, and travel. A quarantine to prevent HIV-1 transmission may affect a suspect class. Quarantine would thus be subject to strict scrutiny by the courts. A rational relationship between means and end would be difficult to support, as there is no evidence that quarantine, short of permanent, enforced isolation, is effective for preventing spread of HIV-1 infection. The courts would also require that less restrictive means be attempted first. And, based on several recent cases, the courts are likely to require exhaustive procedures to guarantee due process to those about to be quarantined (Greene v. Edwards, 1980; Balderas v. Pitchess, 1980). These would include the right to counsel and the right to a jury trial to determine the necessity for quarantine. It is highly unlikely that large-scale quarantine could be implemented under these constraints.

For the reasons articulated above, broadly conceived quarantine proposals—for example, isolation of all risk group members, or all HIV-1 carriers—would probably not withstand even minimal court scrutiny. Quarantine of groups presumed to be irresponsible in their behavior—for example, intravenous drug users—would also fail, because they would be difficult to identify with certainty, and the predictions of future behavior would be uncertain enough that the legal tests of close fit and least restrictive means would not be met. Groups of citizens cannot be confined for life simply on the basis of assumptions about what they might do in the future.

Nevertheless, a narrowly conceived quarantine of a specific person, based on documented past irresponsible behavior and reasonable projection of such behavior in the future, has been suggested as a means of controlling spread of HIV-1 infection (Francis and Chin, 1987) and would likely be upheld even if for an indefinite period of time. Such a quarantine would be more likely to be implemented, and more likely to be upheld by the courts, if the behavior resulting in transmission was nonconsensual. But there are many reasons why such a quarantine, even if constitutional, might be ineffective, or even detrimental, as a means of controlling the spread of HIV-1 infection. Those actually quarantined would be a minuscule fraction of the population of HIV-1-infected persons and a small fraction of those whose behavior would justify quarantine; quarantining them would have a trivial impact on the course of the epidemic. Quarantine would be highly visible in the press, and such coercive measures might dramatically discourage other risk-group members from cooperating with public health authorities. The public might also gain a false sense of security, assuming that all HIV-1-infected patients had been removed by the quarantine. Thus, except in the case of the truly malicious individual, quarantine has virtually no role in the control of the spread of HIV-1 infection.

Segregation of HIV-1-infected prisoners is a special problem (Gostin and Curran, 1987b; Parmet, 1985; Jarrett v. Faulkner, 1987). Similar proposals have been made for members of other institutionalized populations (Gostin and Curran, 1987b). The case for mandatory HIV-1 antibody testing of prisoners (considered later) and segregation of those who are infected is based on the risk of involuntary transmission through homosexual rape or intravenous drug use as well as on the risk to the infected prisoner from assault by other prisoners with homophobia, bacteriophobia, or other severe neuroses. The first argument is specious, as studies have shown that transmission of HIV-1 within prisons has been negligible (Kelley et al., 1986). However, prisoners thought to be homosexual have a real danger of assault, and suspicion of HIV-1 infection would increase that danger. HIV-1 testing programs and mandatory segregation have been implemented in many prisons in the United States and overseas, and these practices have been upheld in lower courts (Gostin and Curran, 1987b). But these programs admit a major defect in the prison system—that they are unable to control the prisoners sufficiently to prevent rape and assault. A more humane approach would be to structure the prison environment so that these incidents occurred much less frequently or not at all. Until such measures are in place, however, segregation of HIV-1-infected prisoners may be the best means of protecting them.

Mandatory Serologic Testing and Other Screening Programs

Mandatory serologic testing for HIV-1 has been widely proposed as a means of controlling the spread of this infection and has been implemented to some extent in a number of foreign countries (WHO, 1987; Frosner, 1987). Large-scale, mandatory serologic testing programs would most likely be held unconstitutional in the United States. Although drawing blood and testing it for antibodies to HIV-1 are not in themselves a major infringement of personal liberty or privacy, the procedures used to determine who gets tested, and the results of the test, may be considered invasive. For this reason, and because the individuals targeted for screening (if screening is not universal) are likely to be members of suspect classes, the statutes will be closely scrutinized by the rational-relationship, close-fit, and least-restrictive criteria articulated previously.

The rationale for screening is obscure to most public health authorities, because it is not clear what would be done with the information collected. With no treatment known to reduce infectivity, no curative drug for those who are infected, and no vaccine for the uninfected, only counseling, education, and behavior modification could be offered to the participants of the screening programs. These measures must be applied equally to infected and uninfected subjects: it is just as important, perhaps more important, to keep uninfected persons uninfected as it is to reduce transmissive behavior by HIV-1-infected subjects. Enormous numbers of

Table 20.4. Populations for Whom Mandatory Testing for HIV-1 Infection Has Been Implemented or Proposed in the United States

1. Armed forces personnel (Herbold, 1986)
2. Foreign service workers (Local 1812, 1987)
3. Prisoners (Jarrett v. Faulkner, 1987)
4. Applicants for marriage licenses (Lewis, 1987)
5. Immigrants (Miller, 1987)
6. Convicted rapists
7. Hospitalized patients; candidates for elective surgical procedures; candidates for organ transplantation
8. Blood, blood product, and organ donors.

individuals would be screened, at great economic and social cost, to find small numbers of HIV-1-infected subjects. Additional social disruption would be induced by the inevitable false positives. Lastly, in the opinion of most authorities, less restrictive measures, such as widespread *anonymous* testing, would be just as effective (Gostin and Curran, 1987b). The economic cost of such mandatory screening programs would drain valuable resources away from more effective measures such as education. Thus, without a public health rationale, and with sound legal arguments against it, implementation of widespread mandatory screening programs seems unlikely.

In special populations, however, mandatory screening has been implemented, or implementation has been proposed, and in some instances this testing has withstood court challenge (Gostin and Curran, 1987b) (Table 20.4).

In the armed forces, one of the major justifications for the testing program (HIV-1 antibody testing of all active-duty personnel and all new recruits) was to preserve the "walking blood supply" in the military in time of war. This argument is logically incontrovertible, although the prevalence of HIV-1 infection in the military (about 1/1,000) makes the risk of HIV-1 transmission through transfusion appear inconsequential compared with the hazards of weaponry. Military employment decisions also have been subjected to different standards of judicial review from civilian employment (Rostker v. Goldberg, 1981).

Serologic testing of Foreign Service personnel was proposed, challenged, and upheld (Local 1812, 1987). The stated purposes here were to prevent emergency illness in isolated locations (which might be triggered by the exotic infections found there), to protect the "walking blood supply," and to assuage the foreign governments where the employees were stationed.

Mandatory serologic testing of prisoners has been implemented in many states and foreign countries with the express purpose of segregating infected prisoners (Gostin and Curran, 1987b). The arguments for and against this procedure are discussed earlier. Mandatory serologic testing of immigrants has been ordered by the U.S. Immigration and Naturalization Service but has not yet been subjected to court challenge (Miller, 1987).

Mandatory premarital testing for HIV-1 infection has been proposed (Gostin and Curran, 1987b) and would probably be found constitutional, although it is unlikely to contribute materially to the control of HIV-1 infection. The goal of testing is rational—to prevent transmission to the uninfected spouse and potentially to any children that might result—and there is precedent for other obligatory serologic tests prior to marriage, such as the tests for syphilis and rubella required by many states (and once required by all). However, few of the individuals likely to spread infection get married before sexual contact, and many do not get married at all. Illinois has recently passed an innovative law providing protection of privacy in premarital testing (New York Times, 1987c).

Mandatory serologic testing has been proposed for patients in various categories: all patients being hospitalized; patients undergoing elective surgery; and patients being considered for organ transplantation (CDC, 1987c). There is little public health rationale for testing all hospitalized patients to prevent HIV-1 transmission to health care personnel. The results are not available immediately, and the likelihood of transmission, albeit quite low (see Chapter 14), is highest early in the hospital course, when patients are sickest and invasive procedures are more likely. Such a testing program might also fail constitutionality tests as being overly inclusive: only a very small proportion of all hospitalized patients are infected, and many of them are known to be risk-group members. HIV-1 antibody testing of potential recipients of organ transplants has a sound medical basis, as the immunosuppression and graft versus host reactions accompanying the transplantation are likely to reactivate latent HIV-1 infection or accelerate the course of the disease.

Although mandatory serologic testing of convicted rapists appears logical (providing needed information to the victim) and would likely withstand court challenge, it would serve little or no useful purpose. While there may be rare exceptions, a negative serologic test at 6 months after exposure to HIV-1 is considered absolute evidence against infection from that exposure. Information obtained more than 6 months after the event regarding the serologic status of the rapist thus would be virtually useless. A more useful approach would be to obtain early, voluntary consent from accused rapists, to permit early serologic testing.

Serologic testing of blood donors and candidates for organ donation is medically justified, because transfusion and transplantation of infected tissue represent nonconsensual transmission of infection that is almost completely preventable. Testing is legally justifiable, because blood donation (and the accompanying tests for HIV-1, hepatitis B virus, and *Treponema pallidum*) is a voluntary procedure, and those donating are notified in advance that serologic testing will be performed.

Restrictions on Free Association to Control HIV-1 Transmission

At present, AIDS is transmitted primarily by homosexual intercourse and intravenous drug abuse. There is perforce some logic in attempting to control the spread of HIV-1 infection by eliminating the locations where homosexual intercourse and intravenous drug abuse occur. Some elements of such an approach would probably withstand judicial scrutiny.

Association of citizens is expressly permitted by the Bill of Rights, but not for all purposes. Association for the express or implied purpose of conducting otherwise illegal activities is not condoned. Sexual intercourse in public or quasipublic places has also not achieved protection from the courts. Public bathhouses have been a major target in the efforts of public health authorities to control the spread of HIV-1 (Gostin and Curran, 1987a; New York v. St. Mark's Baths, 1986; Mills et al., 1986; Collier, 1985). These bathhouses are nominally for people to relax in saunas or steam rooms; however, in fact many of them have been notorious as sites for multiple, anonymous sexual contacts—ideal circumstances for the transmission of HIV-1. A court order closing bathhouses in San Francisco was not upheld and was replaced by a requirement for specific measures (lights, removal of curtains, monitors) to ensure that unsafe sexual practices did not occur in the baths. At the time, courts probably could have upheld a health department order closing bathhouses that were demonstrated to have ignored or defied less restrictive regulations (Mills et al., 1986). Closing bathhouses closely fit the desired end since they were major sites of the type of sexual activity (multiple unprotected contacts with multiple partners) most likely to transmit HIV-1. The ban would not have been unduly restrictive, because it did not prohibit any other type of association between homosexual men. These principles were subsequently invoked by an appeals court in New York County that upheld the closing of a bathhouse and a homosexual bar in New York City frequented by homosexual men and known as sites for multiple anonymous sexual contacts (New York v. St. Mark's Baths, 1986). However, closure or restriction of institutions frequented by homosexual men, but at which high-risk activities were not occurring, would likely be held unconstitutional.

These considerations aside, there remains much controversy among public health experts about the role of such closures in controlling the spread of HIV-1. As Gostin and Curran (1987a) state, "The major concern of health authorities is human behavior, not where it takes place." Closing bathhouses could simply result in shifting the activity to another location—perhaps leaving it less concentrated or less obvious. Maintaining institutions such as the baths may concentrate individuals practicing high-risk behavior so that they are more accessible to education efforts (Gostin and Curran, 1987a).

The legality of homosexual intercourse in private, between consenting adults, remains in doubt, but generally it has failed to achieve protection by the Supreme Court (Bowers v. Hardwick, 1986). In Doe v. Virginia (1976), the Court summarily affirmed a lower-court decision condoning Virginia's statutes against consensual sodomy. Summary affirmances have little precedential value, however, and several lower courts have ruled that the right of privacy does extend to homosexual intercourse (Gostin and Curran, 1987a). However, in Bowers v. Hardwick (1983), the Supreme Court expressly rejected that view. Because of these rulings, some people fear additional legislative attempts to strengthen regulations against homosexual intercourse in the hopes that this will stem transmission of HIV-1 infection (Nichols, 1984).

Heterosexual intercourse is more clearly protected by the Supreme Court. The Court has firmly supported the right to marry; thus, if the results of mandatory premarital testing were used to forbid marriage, such testing would probably be struck down by the courts. The protection accorded to heterosexual intercourse between couples who are not married is less clear from recent Supreme Court decisions, although many states have given unmarried heterosexuals the same rights of privacy afforded married couples, and many believe that the Supreme Court would likely rule in this fashion as well (Gostin and Curran, 1986). Thus, laws attempting to prevent sexual contact between antibody-discordant couples probably would also be found unconstitutional. Existing statutes against "knowingly exposing" individuals to a communicable disease might apply, however.

Blood Bank Liability for Transfusion-Associated HIV-1 Infection

As the result of litigation surrounding transfusion-related hepatitis cases in the 1960s, blood transfusions were deemed, by statute, to be services rather than products and thus exempt from the strict liability imposed upon products (Greif, 1986). However, there is still an affirmative obligation on the part of the blood bank to make the "service" as safe as possible. Numerous cases relating to transfusion-induced HIV-1 infection and AIDS are now in the courts, and the main points of contention will be whether the blood banks did all that could be done (prior to March 1985, when the EIA test for HIV-1 antibody became available) to prevent collection and distribution of blood from individuals potentially infected with HIV-1. These issues, which do not relate directly to public health, are dealt with extensively elsewhere (Hermann and Gorman, 1987; Hermann, 1987; Whalen v. Roe, 1977; Westfall, 1986).

Employment Discrimination

AIDS patients (and to some extent, probably patients with less severe illness and even asymptomatic seropositives) are protected from employment discrimination through a number of avenues. In some jurisdictions, statutes specifically forbid discrimination against AIDS patients in housing or employment (Lazzo and McElgunn, 1986; WHO, 1987). The first of these was passed by Los Angeles in August 1985 (Lazzo and McElgunn, 1986).

The broadest protection for AIDS patients comes from statutory coverage for the handicapped, as there is substantial legal and medical basis for believing that AIDS would be classified as a handicap. The federal government and 48 of the 50 states have passed legislation prohibiting discrimination against the handicapped for employment, provided the individual is otherwise able to perform the work. The employer cannot use an indirect route to avoid hiring the handicapped (e.g., screening applicants with tests for HIV-1 antibody) and cannot discriminate against groups likely to have a handicap (e.g., homosexual men). Infectious diseases, specifically the epidemiologically analogous hepatitis B virus infection, have been held to be handicaps by the courts (New York State Association for Retarded Children v. Carey, 1979; Arline v. School Board of Nassau County, 1985). In an early Florida employment case, a homosexual man with AIDS was reinstated after being fired from his county job on the basis that AIDS was a handicap (Shuttleworth v. Broward County Office of Budget and Management Policy, 1985). However, Florida uses a broader definition of "handicap" than the more restrictive definitions employed in many other states (Lazzo and McElgunn, 1986).

The affirmative obligation of employers to employ handicapped individuals with AIDS may create serious conflicts with another statutory obligation, the duty to maintain a safe workplace. Federal workplace legislation (the Occupational Safety and Health Act, the National Labor Relations Act, and the Labor Management Relations Act) has given employees a broad right to refuse to work in places that they believe are unsafe. The employees need only believe that the workplace is unsafe, regardless of whether any evidence supports their belief or whether other employees have similar opinions. The walkout need not be preceded by any advance notice (Union Boiler Co., 1974). Thus, the employer is faced with the situation, no longer theoretical, of being forced to hire patients with AIDS and then having the other employees walk off the job because they believe that the workplace is unsafe (Lazzo and McElgunn, 1986).

Hospitals and other health care providers pose difficult issues (New York Times, 1987e). Caring for AIDS patients represents some risk to the health care worker; the duties of the employer and the rights of the worker in this situation have been only partially defined. The employer in the health care business has the same obligation as any other employer to make the workplace as safe as possible, and the federal government has recently proposed regulations that relate specifically to preventing transmission of HIV-1 (New York Times, 1987e). Does the employee have the right to leave the job or to institute exaggerated infection control precautions, simply because he is fearful of infection? The issue is undecided.

There is a wide consensus that health care providers cannot avoid caring for AIDS patients because of fear (justified or not) of acquiring HIV-1 infection. In part, this is because health care workers have always been subjected to some risk of acquiring disease from their patients, and these diseases are sometimes fatal or untreatable (e.g., tuberculosis in the prechemotherapy era; hepatitis B in the present) (New York Times, 1987e; Mills et al., 1986). In a recent case heard by the California Labor Commissioner, several nurses at San Francisco General Hospital claimed they had been unlawfully transferred to other jobs in the hospital because of their insistence on wearing protective clothing that the hospital had deemed unnecessary (Kadzielski, 1986). Although the complaint was dismissed, the hearing officer noted that the nurses' concern was "understandable" and that their conduct was protected under California law. A California court upheld a state statute that forbids disciplining employees for complaining about health hazards even if there is no actual danger. Thus, health care employers are advised to deal with employee dissatisfactions relating to caring for AIDS patients by education and counseling, and perhaps transfer to other duties, rather than by confrontation.

Whether health care providers infected with HIV-1 or AIDS can continue to care for patients is the subject of current controversy (Dalton and Burris, 1987). The medical facts are that no case of HIV-1 infection has been attributed to transmission from health care worker to patient (although the reverse has occurred). Continuing the analogy with hepatitis B, where provider-to-patient transmission is hundreds of times less common than from patient to provider, it is reasonable to predict that provider-to-patient transmission of HIV-1 will occur extraordinarily infrequently. The precedent set with health care workers who are carriers of hepatitis B virus has been that their practice is not restricted unless they are shown to infect their patients (Wenzel and Townsend, 1983; Lettau et al., 1986). Thus, there appears to be no reason to deny patient care employment to persons with AIDS or HIV-1 infection who are otherwise able to work. Although some of the opportunistic pathogens that infect AIDS patients may be communicable to others, this is also true for other immunosuppressed individuals who are not denied employment as health care providers. A recent decision by the New Jersey Supreme Court hints that patients cared for under circumstances that they feel might be unsafe, even if no injury occurs, can still sue for damages for mental anguish (Perna v. Pirozzi, 1983). This result would appear to create a statutory imperative to inform patients about all possible hazards associated with their care—perhaps including the presence of HIV-1 infection. Pending further development of the law, however, it is widely accepted that health care providers with HIV-1 infection or even AIDS should be permitted to care for patients.

SUMMARY

Efforts to control the spread of HIV-1 infection are likely to result in major challenges to the liberty and privacy guaranteed by the Constitution and Bill of Rights. The interpretation of existing laws may be exaggerated or distorted; new laws of dubious constitutionality may be proposed, passed, or implemented; and existing court decisions may be overturned or reinterpreted. Because AIDS occurs most commonly among groups subject to societal disapproval or ostracism, the pressure to restrict the liberty and privacy of these groups in the pursuit of the public health will doubtless be intense, and it will test the commitment of American society to the freedom of minority groups.

REFERENCES

Arline v. School Board of Nassau County (1985): Federal Reporter (2d Ser) 772:759).
Balderas v. Pitchess (1980): California Superior Court, Los Angeles County (No. CA 000617).
Bowers v. Hardwick (1986): United States Reporter 480:1.
California Morbidity (1978): Disciplinary action by Board of Medical Quality Assurance for
    failure to report a reportable infectious disease. California Morbidity Aug. 11.
CDC (1987a): MMWR 36:311.
CDC (1987b): MMWR 36:693.
CDC (1987c): MMWR 36:509.
CDC (1988): MMWR 36:50.
Collier S (1985): Golden Gate L Rev 301.
Dalton HL, Burris S (1987): AIDS and the Law. New Haven, CT: Yale University Press.
Davis v. Rodman (1921): Southwestern Reporter 227:612 (Arkansas).
Derrick v. Ontario Community Hospital (1985): California Reporter 120:566–572.
Doe v. Roe (1977): New York Supplement (2d Ser) 400:668 (Supreme Court, New York
    County).
Doe v. Virginia (1976): Federal Supplement 1975:403:1199 (District Court for the Eastern
    District of Virginia). Affirmed memorandum opinion. United States Reporter
    1976:425:901.
Farnsworth v. Procter and Gamble Company (1985): 758 F. 2d 1545.
Francis DP, Chin J (1987): JAMA 257:357.
Frosner GG (1987): Infection 15:1.
Gill v. Hartford Accident and Indemnity Co. (1978): Southern Reporter (2nd Ser) 337:420.
    (Florida Second District Court of Appeal).
Gostin L, Curran WJ (1986): Hasting Center Report Special Supplement 1986.
Gostin L, Curran WJ (1987a): Am J Public Health 77:214.
Gostin L, Curran WJ (1987b): Am J Public Health 77:361.

Greene v. Edwards (1980): Southeastern Reporter (2d Ser) 263:661.

Greif, RC (1986): San Diego L Rev 23:875.

Harvard Law Review (1986): Harvard L Rev 6:1274–1292.

Herbold JR (1986): Milit Med 151:623.

Hermann DHJ (1987): Univ Colorado L Rev 58:63.

Hermann DHJ, Gorman RD (1987): Univ Calif Davis L Rev 20:441.

Horne v. Patton (1973): Southern Reporter (2d Ser) 287:824. (Alabama Supreme Court).

Jacobson v. Massachusetts (1950): United States Reporter 198:11.

Jarrett v. Faulkner (1987): Federal Supplement 662:928 (District Court for the Southern District of Indiana).

Jew Ho v. Williamson (1900): Federal Reporter 103:10.

Kadzielski MA (1986): Health Prog, May, p. 48.

Kathleen K v. Robert B (1984): California Reporter 198:273 (Court of Appeal, Second District).

Kelley PW, Redfield RR, Ward DL, Burke DS, Miller RN (1986): JAMA 256:2198.

Kirk v. Wyman (1909): South Carolina Reporter 83:372.

Lettau LA, Smith JD, Williams D, Lundquist WD, Cruz F, Sikes K, Hadler SC (1986): JAMA 255:934.

Lazzo MJ, McElgunn, CA (1986): Washburn LJ 25:505.

Lewis HE (1987): JAMA 358:2410.

Local 1812, American Federation of Government Employees v. United States Department of State (1987): Federal Supplement 662:50.

Merritt DJ (1986): New York Univ L Rev 61:739.

Miller RM (1987): Memorandum to designated civil surgeons. Subject: Additional requirements, medical examination of aliens in the United States. Immigration and Naturalization Service Memo, Aug. 31.

Mills J (1987): Infection 15:160.

Mills M (1983): Med Times 111(8):83.

Mills M, Wofsy, CB, Mills J (1986): N Engl J Med 314:931.

Moss AR, Bacchetti P, Osmond D, et al. (1988): Br Med J 296:745.

New York v. St. Mark's Baths (1986): New York Misc. Reports (2d Ser) 130:911.

New York State Association for Retarded Children v. Carey (1979): Federal Reporter (2d Ser) 612:644.

New York Times (1987a): New York Times, Aug. 6, p. 8, col. 1.

New York Times (1987b): New York Times, Oct. 18, p. 5, col. 3.

New York Times (1987c): New York Times, July 1, p. A22, col. 1.

New York Times (1987d): New York Times, April 4, p. 7, col. 1.

New York Times (1987e): New York Times, July 22, p. 1, col. 1.

Nichols CD (1984): J Contemp L 11:315.

Parmet WE (1985): Hofstra L Rev 14:53.

Perkins HS, Jonsen AR (1981): Ann Intern Med 94:523.

Perna v. Pirozzi (1983): New Jersey Reports (2d Ser) 92:431.

Rostker v. Goldberg (1981): United States Reports 453:57.

Shuttleworth v. Broward County Office of Budget and Management Policy (1985): Daily Labor Reporter (BNA) Dec. 17, at e-1.

Skillings v. Allen (1919): Northwestern Reporter 173:663 (Minnesota Supreme Court).

Tarasoff v. Regents of the University of California (1976): California Reporter 131:14 (California Supreme Court).

Union Boiler Co. (1974): National Labor Relations Board Decisions 213:818.

U.S. Department of Health and Human Services, Public Health Service (1985): AIDS Information Bulletin: The Public Health Service Response to AIDS. Washington, D.C.: U.S. DHHS.

Weiss SM, Goedert JJ, Gartner S, et al. (1988): Science 239:68.

Wenzel RP, Townsend TR (1983): When can the infected hospital employee return to work? In Remington JS, Swartz, MN (eds): Current Clinical Topics in Infectious Diseases, McGraw-Hill, New York Vol. 4, pp.75–95.

Westfall PT (1986): Hastings L J 37:1101.

Whalen v. Roe (1977): United States Reporter 429:589.

World Health Organization (1987): WHO SPA/HLE/87.1.

Index